WYOMING
HANDBOOK

WYOMING
HANDBOOK

DON PITCHER

MOON
PUBLICATIONS INC.

WYOMING HANDBOOK

Please send all comments,
corrections, additions,
amendments, and critiques to:

DON PITCHER
C/o MOON PUBLICATIONS
722 WALL STREET
CHICO, CA 95928, USA

Published by
Moon Publications, Inc.
722 Wall Street
Chico, California 95928, USA

Printed by
Colorcraft Ltd.

Printing History
1st edition—July 1991

© Text Copyright Don Pitcher 1991. All rights reserved.
© Maps Copyright Moon Publications 1991. All rights reserved.
Some photos and illustrations are used by permission
and are the property of the original copyright owners.

Library of Congress Cataloging in Publications Data
Pitcher, Don, 1953–
Wyoming Handbook / by Don Pitcher
p.   cm.
Includes bibliographical references (p.413) and index.
ISBN 0-918373-54-9
1. Wyoming—Description and travel—1981- —Guide-books.
I. Title.
F759.3.P58   1991
917.8704'33—dc20
91-9388
CIP

ISBN 0-918373-54-9

Printed in Hong Kong

Front cover photo of Mormon Row by Don Pitcher. Illustrations on pages 1, 5, and 7 by Bob Race.

Wyoming seems to be the doing of a mad architect—tumbled and twisted, ribboned with faded, deathbed colors, thrust up and pulled down as if the place had been startled out of a deep sleep and thrown into a pure light.
—Gretel Ehrlich in *The Solace of Open Spaces*

God bless Wyoming and keep it wild.
—*last entry in the diary of a girl who died in the Tetons*

ACKNOWLEDGMENTS

When I mentioned to a cousin that this guide to Wyoming—the nation's smallest state in population—would exceed 500 pages, he accused me of using the James Michener approach to writing. In reality, I found it difficult to trim the text to even the current size. Wyoming is an utterly fascinating and intriguing place, and anyone who does a bit of exploring is bound to discover far more than I have touched on in these pages.

For those of us who string words together, the acknowledgements section provides a chance to repay a few of the generous contributions of others. Kudos first to the staff at Moon who herded this through, from initial proposal, to gut-wrenching delays (OK, so I was eight months beyond my deadline), to the book's final layout and production. Thanks especially to editor Beth Rhudy, who spent many months poring over the manuscript in an attempt to make sense of my ramblings and to Bob Race who turned my map scribbles into works of art. Brian Bardwell, Cathy Carlson, Todd Clark, and Bob Race all contributed excellent illustrations, while Dave Hurst did a fine job in designing the cover and interior layout. Thanks also to others connected with Moon for their help, including Bill Dalton, Magnus Bartlett, and Mark Morris. Kit Duane provided valuable assistance by editing parts of two chapters.

In Wyoming, there are countless people who assisted in one form or another. Charlie Otto kindly put me up in his back cabin in Wilson, right next to the state's only brewery. A number of individuals deserve special commendation for taking the time to read through earlier drafts and make suggestions: Joan Anzelmo (Yellowstone National Park), Scott Binning (Cheyenne Chamber of Commerce), Sharlene Milligan (Grand Teton National Park), Maureen Murphy (Laramie Chamber of Commerce), Shari Pullar (Buffalo Bill Historical Center), Claudia Rowdabaugh (Cody Chamber of Commerce), and Carol Waller (Jackson Hole Chamber of Commerce). This book represents my own perceptions of Wyoming, views that are not always in congruence with these reviewers or their agencies.

Many other people deserve credit for their help along the way. The following individuals—covering the spectrum from brand inspectors to archaelologists—provided particularly useful information: Cynthia Andrus, Debbie Bancroft, Phil Bobrow, Bob and Joyce Boyer, Eric Boyer, Dan Brict, Bob Budd, Jim Carlson, Shanna Driscoll, Julie Francis, Mary Garman, Keith Hardisty, John Jakubowski, Thomas Lindmier, Jim Maher, Ron Mamot, Ron Marrs, Michael Randall, Elmer "Sonny" Reisch, Cecil Sanderson, Jim Schellenger, Jack Shea, Howard Smith, Rick Steenberg, Carmella Vavold, Kay Weber, and Don West. The following chamber of commerce people also provided especially helpful information: Linda Alley, Kay Bennington, Marlyn Black, Joyce Bloom, Sue Bromley, Phyllis "PJ" Crerar, Andrea DeBolt, Alice Eddy, Jim Ficterman, Kay Gore, Jeremy Hayek, Ann Hotaling, Alan Huston, Martha Jolley, Donna Madson, Claudine Murdock, Vicki Schoeber, Carol Sherrod, Joan Smith, Linda Standifer, Georgia Stiles, and Debbie Stoetzel. Thanks also go to my parents for "test-driving" portions of the manuscript.

Seeing this book completed reminds me of a quote by Struthers Burt in *Powder River Let 'er Buck:* "An old stagecoach driver of my acquaintance died recently. His last words—he was delirious—were, 'Turn 'em loose! It's all downhill and a shady road!'"

CONTENTS

MAPS

MAP SYMBOLS

FREEWAY
MAIN HIGHWAY
SECONDARY ROAD
UNPAVED ROAD
FOOT PATH, TRAIL
STATE BORDER
OTHER BORDER
TUNNEL
PASS
RAILROAD
BRIDGE

INTERSTATE HIGHWAY

U.S. HIGHWAY

STATE HIGHWAY

O   LARGE CITY
o   SMALL CITIES & TOWNS
▲   MOUNTAIN
▲   CAMPGROUND
■   POINT OF INTEREST

 WATERFALL
 WATER
PICNIC AREA
SKI AREA

N.W.R. NATIONAL WILDLIFE REFUGE
N.P. NATIONAL PARK
S.P. STATE PARK
CG. CAMPGROUND

ALL MAPS ARE ORIENTED WITH NORTH
AT TOP UNLESS OTHERWISE NOTED

CHARTS

ABBREVIATIONS

a/c—air conditioned
B&B—bed and breakfast
d—double occupancy
I—interstate highway

mph—miles per hour
OW—one way
PP—per person
RT—roundtrip
RV—recreational vehicle

s—single occupancy
t—triple occupancy
WW I—World War I
WW II—World War II

IS THIS BOOK OUT OF DATE?

This is the first edition of the *Wyoming Handbook,* and like a new ship, its initial voyage is bound to reveal glitches. As with other Moon guides, this one will be completely updated every two years. Wyoming is not a static place; prices change, places go out of business, new ones show up, and others change hands. If you find any glaring omissions, take offense at what is said, discover a place worthy of mention, find inaccurate maps, or have any other comments or complaints concerning this book, I would be happy to hear from you. All contributions will be acknowledged. Send your comments to:

Don Pitcher
c/o Moon Publications
722 Wall Street
Chico, CA 95928

STOP PRESS

As this book was going to press, **AMTRAK** reinstated passenger train service across southern Wyoming following an eight-year hiatus. The Pioneer Line now connects Seattle and Denver with Wyoming stops in Evanston, Green River, Rock Springs, Rawlins, Laramie, and Cheyenne. A variety of special fares are available for passengers traveling within or between regions, with daily service east and west. For price and scheduling information, call AMTRAK at (800) 872-7245.

INTRODUCTION

"It's kind of funny how you get used to the country. When I go to town, the noises keep me awake. The coal trains, the sirens going down the road, even if they are a long ways away. People get used to that. We've had people come out here who couldn't sleep because it was so quiet. No noise to lull them to sleep or whatever. My nearest neighbor is five miles away. It takes all kinds of people to make the world go around. If everybody in the world wanted to be a rancher, I probably wouldn't, because there wouldn't be any-place to live."

—*Ed Swartz, quoted in Steve Gardiner's* **Rumblings From Razor City**

The expansively rugged land called Wyoming resonates with the spirit of the American West. For anyone who has spent time in Wyoming, the state evokes vivid images: cattle standing in the lee of snow fences; children riding horses along dusty dirt roads; weather-beaten ranches lit by the slanting light of late afternoon; oil-covered roustabouts struggling with the furious machinery of a drilling rig; the sounds of drumming and singing at a powwow; and cow towns where the area code is larger than the population. Here is the original "Wild West," the real-life inspiration for countless Western novels, movies, and songs.

A frontier spirit pervades both Wyoming's landscape and its people, mixing the past and present so completely that it sometimes seems as though around the next bend you might see Chief Washakie's braves circling a massive herd of bison, or Butch Cassidy and the Sundance Kid shooting it out with lawmen, or a party of fur trappers setting out for the mountains. Officially known as "The Equality State" because it was the first to allow women to vote, Wyoming actually revels in another title, "The Cowboy State." License plates carry the state emblem: a cowboy, hat in hand, atop a furiously bucking bronco. A cowboy hat and boots are acceptable dress anywhere, and the unpolished individuality embodied in the cowboy remains the state's heritage, even for those whose only connection is country-western music.

The earliest Anglo explorers described Wyoming in less than flattering terms. The image that stuck was the "Great American Desert," a

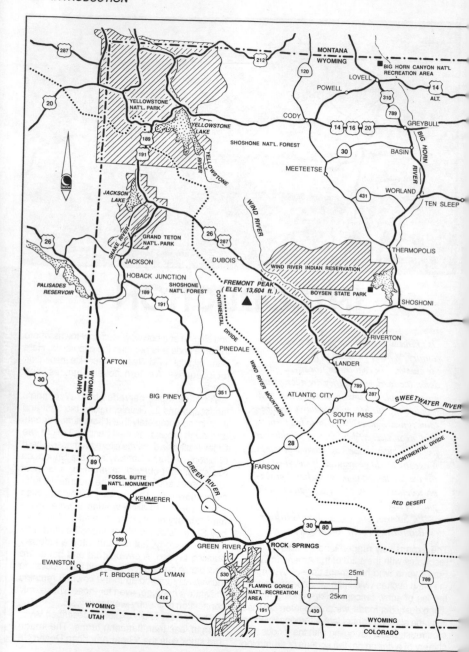

WYOMING
ROADS AND
HIGHWAYS

© MOON PUBLICATIONS, INC.

place where buffalo, antelope, jackrabbits, rattlesnakes, and the native peoples flourished, but where homesteaders and ranchers struggled to survive. Hundreds of thousands of travelers pushed across Wyoming's basins and mountain ranges in the 19th century, bound for greener pastures and gold. Very few considered staying in such an unforgiving environment. Even today, the vast majority of those who enter Wyoming are en route to someplace else.

Seeing Wyoming

Although Wyoming is divided by three major interstate highways, the best way to see the state is from the smaller asphalt and gravel roads where the pace slows and tumbleweeds pile against fences. From the freeways, the landscape is just a blur, but along the back roads this same land becomes transformed into a thing of raw-edged, surreal beauty. Old ranches hunker in the valleys, herds of deer and antelope glance up warily at passing cars, oddly colored rock pinnacles crown the crest of hills, and winding streams become glowing silver ribbons of light. The sense of stillness is broken only by the wind, the singing of birds, and the buzz of insects. Writer Gretel Ehrlich in *The Solace of Open Spaces* describes it best:

"To live and work in this kind of open country, with its hundred-mile views, is to lose the distinction between background and foreground. When I asked an older ranch hand to describe Wyoming's openness, he said, 'It's all a bunch of nothing—wind and rattlesnakes—and so much of it you can't tell where you're going or where you've been and it don't make much difference.'"

On the back roads you'll find folks lifting a hand to wave as you pass. Small-town cafes serve downhome food, friendly motel owners greet tired travelers, and the pace of living slows measurably. You can almost feel the stress of city life dissipating. People leave their homes, cars, and bikes unlocked; they load up clothes in the laundromat and come back later to move them to the drier. They pull in at the drive-up liquor store for a six-pack. Unlike big cities where waiting in lines becomes a way of life, the bank, grocery store, and post office queues are short or nonexistent. Try on a cowboy hat and boots, take a look around the local museum, or stop in for a beer at a country bar and joke with the locals. In a short while you'll gain an appreciation for Wyoming and the down-to-earth people who live here.

The Sky

In the vast open spaces of Wyoming, the sky takes on its own importance, sometimes making the land seem like an afterthought. The land changes slowly with the seasons—first a carpet of winter white, then the mud and first luminescent green buds of spring growth, followed by the verdant summer flowers, and finally the brilliance of fall cottonwood trees along a dry creekbed. But the sky follows the beat of another drummer, changing moment by moment throughout each day. Cottonball clouds float overhead, sending moving shadows across the landscape and coloring the sun's light. Storm clouds build on a summer afternoon, and in the distance a lightning bolt leaps to earth. Perhaps the most memorable times are the lingering sunsets, when colors seem to bounce back and forth across the sky, finally exiting as a fringe of color on the western horizon. At night, coyotes howl the same way they have for millennia, and an enormous panorama of stars arches above, undimmed by discordant city lights.

THE LAND

Covering nearly 98,000 square miles, Wyoming is the ninth-largest state. The states of Connecticut, Delaware, Hawaii, Maryland, Massachusetts, New Hampshire, New Jersey, Rhode Island, Vermont, and West Virginia would all fit within Wyoming's borders with room to spare. With just 456,000 inhabitants—the smallest population of any state—Wyoming remains a remarkably undeveloped and unsettled place. Cattle outnumber people by nearly three to one. The population density averages fewer than five people per square mile, and in some counties there is nearly a square mile of land for each person. With an average elevation of 6,700 feet (range 3,125 feet to 13,804 feet), Wyoming is the third-highest state in the nation. Only Alaska and Colorado are higher.

GEOGRAPHY

On the map, Wyoming is simply a gigantic trapezoidal chunk of earth. It's straight line borders (375 miles from east to west and 276 miles north to south) are an arbitrary human creation that encompass a surprising diversity of country. The Continental Divide wanders diagonally across the state from the northwest corner to south-central Wyoming. Two-thirds of Wyoming's lakes, rivers, and streams drain into trib-

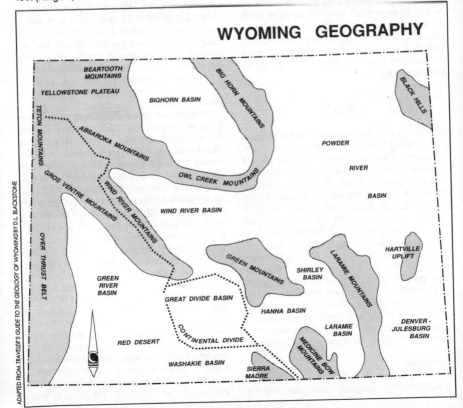

WYOMING GEOGRAPHY

ADAPTED FROM TRAVELER'S GUIDE TO THE GEOLOGY OF WYOMING BY D.L. BLACKSTONE

utaries of the Missouri River, eventually reaching the Atlantic Ocean; most of the rest flow into tributaries of the Colorado and Columbia rivers and hence to the Pacific Ocean. Small portions drop into the Great Basin (Salt Lake) or the Great Divide Basin (between Rock Springs and Rawlins) where the water evaporates or percolates into the ground.

Wyoming's mountains generally trend in a northwest to southeast direction, but this gross overall pattern is broken up by smaller ranges. Northwest Wyoming is dominated by a complex melange of mountains: the Absaroka, Teton, Gros Ventre, Wyoming, and Wind River ranges. North-central Wyoming is divided by the Big Horn Mountains, while the Laramie Range and the Medicine Bow Mountains dominate south-central Wyoming. The far northeast corner holds the Black Hills. In between these ranges, the land spreads out in broad basins, including Bighorn Basin and Powder River Basin in northern Wyoming, Wind River Basin in west-central Wyoming, and the Green River, Red Desert, and Washakie basins in the southwest. The eastern portion of Wyoming drops gently into the Great Plains.

CLIMATE

Wyoming's climate mirrors its diverse geography, ranging from arid deserts to cool mountain forests. The mountain ranges act as barriers to eastward-moving weather systems. Moist air is forced upward by the mountains, releasing rain or snow along the western slopes. By the time the clouds reach the east side, much of the water has been wrung out, creating a "rain shadow." Because of this, midwinter finds Togwotee Pass smothered under many feet of snow while Dubois, in the lee of the Absaroka Range, may have only a dusting on the ground. Wyoming weather is typical of the West's high plains and mountains: hot, dry summers punctuated by fierce thunderstorms, and cold winters with a fair amount of snow. Conditions vary greatly throughout the state, however, with cooler summers and heavy winter snows in the mountains.

Extremes

Wyoming has a reputation for extreme conditions. Wintertime blizzards periodically lash the land, and strong winds pile the snow into huge drifts. Summertime thunderstorms—particularly in the mountains—can be an almost daily occurrence. Southeast Wyoming—with an average of nine hailstorms a year—is the hail capital of North America. Temperatures have been recorded from -66° F (Yellowstone National Park) to 114° F (the town of Basin). Precipitation shows a similar variation. In the high mountain ranges of northwest Wyoming, as much as 60 inches (mostly snow) lands on the ground, while parched desert areas in Bighorn Basin and Great Divide Basin receive only six inches a year.

Wyoming is well known for its wind. Through much of the state, the wind never seems to stop blowing, averaging more than 16 miles an hour along the eastern border. Buffalo Bill Cody, a man who symbolizes the West in the American conscience, once defended Wyoming when a friend complained of the wind: "You know where those winds come from? Well, this country up here is so close to paradise you can feel the breezes from heaven. That wind comes from the angels' wings. When they flap their wings the wind comes right down this valley."

Basin Weather

In the expansive basins that cover much of Wyoming, typical midsummer daytime temperatures are in the 80s and 90s, with nights dropping into the 50s and 60s. Low relative humidity makes the heat easier to take. The wettest months are April and May, with lots of sun in the summer. Afternoon thunderheads often build up, temporarily blocking the sun, but generally dropping more lightning than rain. Fall can be a most pleasant time of year, with shirt-sleeve weather in the day and cool evenings.

When winter arrives in November and December, it can do so with a vengeance, pushing the mercury well below zero. Snowfall is not great, totalling from 15 to 60 inches over the winter months, but when combined with winds pushing 50 mph, it can look like a lot more. In places, snow fences extend for many miles beside the highways, attempting to blunt the blowing snow. Ground blizzards sometimes halt traffic along I-80 for days at a time. Locals joke that it only snows a couple of inches in December and then blows back and forth across the state the rest of the winter until the snow is finally

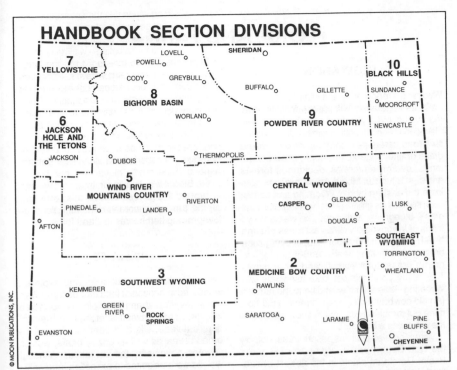

HANDBOOK SECTION DIVISIONS

7 YELLOWSTONE

POWELL LOVELL SHERIDAN

CODY GREYBULL

8 BIGHORN BASIN

BUFFALO GILLETTE

WORLAND

10 BLACK HILLS

SUNDANCE

MOORCROFT

NEWCASTLE

6 JACKSON HOLE AND THE TETONS

JACKSON DUBOIS THERMOPOLIS

9 POWDER RIVER COUNTRY

5 WIND RIVER MOUNTAINS COUNTRY

PINEDALE LANDER RIVERTON

AFTON

4 CENTRAL WYOMING

CASPER GLENROCK LUSK

DOUGLAS

1 SOUTHEAST WYOMING

TORRINGTON

WHEATLAND

3 SOUTHWEST WYOMING

KEMMERER

GREEN RIVER ROCK SPRINGS

EVANSTON

2 MEDICINE BOW COUNTRY

RAWLINS

SARATOGA LARAMIE

PINE BLUFFS

CHEYENNE

© MOON PUBLICATIONS, INC.

worn out. Actually, winters are not all so bleak, and temperatures occasionally rise into the 50s. You can expect sun 60% of the time. Chinooks —warm downslope winds—are common in the winters along the eastern slopes of the mountains, particularly around Sheridan, Dubois, and Cody.

Mountain Weather

Many of the favorite sites in Wyoming—including Yellowstone and Grand Teton national parks—lie primarily above 7,000 feet. Here, the weather is considerably cooler than the basins. Summertime temperatures rarely top 80° F, while nights often dip into the 40s. Snow is possible at any time of the year. April and May are generally the wettest months. Spring comes late in the mountains, and high passes are often blocked by drifts until mid-July. Summer thunderstorms are common, especially in the northwest mountains, where they gather over the high peaks most afternoons. Mid-September brings fall conditions as mountain temperatures often drop 20-30 degrees below summer readings, quickly turning the aspen leaves into a brilliant orange and sending most folks scurrying for warmer climes.

High-country winters are often severely cold and snowy, with temperatures below zero for days at a time. Snow depths often exceed six feet in the higher mountains. Grand Targhee Ski Resort receives some 42 feet of snow over a typical winter! Fortunately, the relative humidity is quite low, making the temperatures easier to tolerate and creating fluffy powder snow conditions. One surprising winter feature is the presence of temperature inversions in intermountain valleys such as Big Piney and Jackson Hole. These often occur on cold, clear nights when the cold air sinks into the valley floors. Skiers who leave the lodge bundled in down parkas and polypro are often surprised to find temperatures 30 degrees warmer on the mountaintop.

FLORA AND FAUNA

VEGETATION

Wyoming's topography and climate are reflected in its vegetation, with dense forests in the mountains and dry grasses and shrubs at lower elevations. The vegetation can be classified into six broad categories (see map, below): mixed-grass prairie, sagebrush steppe, desert shrublands, evergreen forests, deciduous forests, and alpine tundra. **Mixed-grass prairies** dominate the eastern third of Wyoming and contain such species as grama grass, wheatgrass, junegrass, bluegrass, and sage. The western two-thirds of Wyoming contains vast areas of **sagebrush steppe**, a threadbare carpet of big sagebrush, wheatgrass, needle-and-thread grass, grama grass, tumbleweed, and other plants. This is the country most folks associate with Wyoming—sagebrush extending to the horizon. (An old cowboy saying goes, "I reckon the Lord done put tumbleweeds here to show which way the wind was a blowin'.")

Wyoming also contains desert areas, notably the Red Desert and a large part of Bighorn Basin. Dominant plants in the **desert shrublands** include greasewood, saltbush, shadscale, and various kinds of sagebrush. At higher elevations where more moisture falls, the land is covered with **evergreen forests**. Ponderosa pines dominate forested parts of eastern Wyoming, while lodgepole pine, Douglas fir, Engelmann spruce, and subalpine fir exist in mountains to the west. A few areas also have pinyon pine and juniper trees. **Deciduous forests** are scattered in small patches around Wyoming, consisting of cottonwoods along river bottoms, aspens in the middle elevations, and bur oak in the Black Hills. Treeline in much of Wyoming is around 9,500 feet. Above this, one finds **alpine tundra**, where the dominant plants are low-growing herbs, grasses, and forbs.

WILDLIFE

When the first mountain men and explorers wandered into the vast land that became Wyoming, they found an incredible abundance of wildlife: herds of bison stretching to the horizon; antelope, elk, and deer grazing on the broad plains; as well as grizzly bears, wolves, coyotes, cottontails, and jackrabbits. Although wolves were poisoned to extinction, and only a few hundred bison and grizzlies remain, other animals fared better. Today, the two most common large mammals are mule deer and pronghorn antelope, both of which are found across much of Wyoming. The sagebrush lands also provide cover for sage grouse, a large chicken-like bird. The males perform an elaborate X-rated mating display. In the mountains, one often hears the early-summer drumming of ruffed grouse. Rarest of Wyoming's animals is the endangered black-footed ferret (see "Southwest Wyoming," p. 68). Everyone's least favorite reptile is the prairie rattlesnake, found at low elevations throughout Wyoming. Watch your step!

Viewing Wildlife
Because Wyoming remains essentially undeveloped, it is a mecca for those who enjoy seeing wild animals. Yellowstone National Park is a favorite place to look for bison and elk, along with coyotes, moose, mule deer, bighorn sheep, river otters, and trumpeter swans. Both black

WYOMING VEGETATION

YELLOWSTONE
SHERIDAN
CODY
WORLAND
GILLETTE
JACKSON   DUBOIS
PINEDALE
RIVERTON
CASPER
ROCK SPRINGS
RAWLINS
WHEATLAND
EVANSTON
LARAMIE
CHEYENNE

EVERGREEN FORESTS	DECIDUOUS FORESTS
SAGEBRUSH STEPPE	ALPINE TUNDRA
MIXED GRASS PRAIRIE	DESERT SHRUBLAND

0   100mi
0   100km

ADAPTED FROM WYOMING GEOMAPS BY SHEILA ROBERTS /GEOLOGICAL SURVEY OF WYOMING

and grizzly bears are also found here, but less commonly seen. Another popular place is the National Elk Refuge in Jackson Hole, the winter home for a herd of more than 7,500 elk. A good place to see bighorn sheep is Bighorn National Recreation Area. Also watch for wild horses here or in the Red Desert. (Wyoming has around 3,500 wild horses.) Mountain goats live in the Beartooth Mountains along Wyoming's border with Montana. The high mountains of the Tetons and Wind River Range have such animals as pikas and yellow-bellied marmots, while the sagebrush country abounds with deer, antelope, coyotes, jackrabbits, cottontails, and prairie dogs.

Pronghorn Antelope

With more than 360,000 antelope—Wyoming contains over half the world's population— they are common sights. Antelope are able to survive on plants that other animals avoid, notably sagebrush, perhaps Wyoming's most abundant plant. Antelope are built for speed. Their oversized lungs and windpipe give them the ability to run for miles at a 30 mph pace, and accelerate to twice that for short bursts. To watch for predators, they have the largest eyes by body weight of any mammal. Despite this speed, pronghorn have an innate inquisitiveness that sometimes makes them relatively easy to hunt, an attribute that nearly drove them to extinction by market hunting early in this century. Strict laws and careful management have brought antelope populations back.

Deer

Wyoming has more deer than people. Actually, two species can be seen along the state's roads: white-tailed deer (common in the Black Hills), and the larger mule deer (found across the state). Be especially careful when driving after dusk during the fall breeding season since the hormone-crazed bucks tend to leap out in front of cars. Nearly everyone who has lived in Wyoming has hit a deer under these circumstances. Slow down at night, especially in areas posted with deer-crossing signs.

Elk

A majestic member of the deer family, elk (many biologists prefer the term wapiti) are a favorite, both with tourists and hunters. Elk inhabit much of Wyoming, with the largest herds along the western mountains. More than 30,000 elk graze in Yellowstone National Park alone. With bulls weighing up to 900 pounds and cows up to 600 pounds, they are some of the largest antlered animals in the Americas.

Elk spend summers high in the mountains, feeding in alpine meadows and along forest edges. Mature bulls graze alone, but the cows and calves group into large herds for protection. When the fall rutting season arrives, bulls attempt to herd the cows and calves around, mating with cows when they come into estrus, and defending their harem from other bulls. During this time of year the bugling of bull elk is a common sound in the mountains, a challenge to any bull within earshot. When a competitor appears, a dominance display often follows—complete with bugling, stomping, and thrashing of the ground—to show who is the baddest bull around. In a fight, the bulls lock their massive antlers and try to push and twist until one finally gives in and retreats. These battles help ensure that the healthiest bulls produce the most offspring. Ironically, other bulls often wait in the wings for battles over the harem and rush in to mate with the cows while the larger bulls are sparing. (When the cat's away . . . .) The snows of late fall push elk to lower-elevation winter ranges, notably at the National Elk Refuge in Jackson Hole. When spring comes, the bulls drop their antlers and immediately begin to grow new ones. The elk head back into the high country, following the melting snowline.

Bison

Bison are the definitive frontier animal and Wyoming's state mammal. An outline of one graces the Wyoming state flag. Weighing up to 3,000 pounds, they are also the largest land mammal in the New World. Bison live 45 years or more, with females bearing calves until they are in their 40s. The calves weigh 30 to 40 pounds at birth, and within minutes are standing and able to graze. Two races of bison exist, the plains bison primarily east of the Rockies, and the mountain bison (sometimes called wood bison) in the higher elevations. (Technically these huge, hairy beasts are bison—the only true buffalo are the water buffalo of Southeast Asia—but the name buffalo is commonly used.)

With their massive heads, huge shoulder humps, heavy coats of fur, and small posteriors, buffalo are one of the strangest animals in North America. They look so front-heavy as to seem unstable, ready to topple forward onto their snout at any time. Despite this impression, buffalo are remarkably well adapted to life on the plains. They use their strong sense of smell to find grass buried in deep snowdrifts and then sweep it away with a sideways motion of their head. They are also surprisingly fleet of foot, as careless Yellowstone photographers have discovered. In addition, they are one very tough critter. In 1907, a buffalo was pitted against four of the meanest Mexican bulls at a Juarez, Mexico bullring. After knocking heads several times with the buffalo, the bulls fled and were saved only when bullfighters opened the chute gates to let them escape.

Blackening the Plains: When Europeans first reached the New World, they found massive herds of buffalo in the Appalachians and even more as they headed west. Daniel Boone hunted them in North Carolina in the 1750s; Pennsylvanians shot hundreds of buffalo that were invading their winter stores of hay. By 1820, settlers had nearly driven the buffalo to extinction in the East. But there were far more living to the west. As explorers, mountain men, and the first tentative settlers reached the "Great American Desert," they were awestruck by the numbers. Travelers told of slowly moving masses of buffalo blackening the plains, and watched in astonishment as the herds stopped at a river and literally drank it dry. A fair estimate of the original population of buffalo in North America is 75 million. Even in the middle 1860s, travelers through Wyoming's Wind River Valley reported seeing ten thousand bison at one time.

Indians and Buffalo: The Plains Indians depended heavily upon the buffalo for food, and—like the proverbial hot dog containing everything but the moo—they used every part of the animal. Hooves were carved into spoons, skins became buffalo robes and covers for boats and tepees, rawhide was used for drumheads, calf skins became storage sacks, hair was turned into earrings, and horns were formed into cups and arrow points. Everything that remained—including the muzzle, penis, eyes, and cartilage—was boiled down to use as glue for arrowheads.

The ubiquitous buffalo chips became a cooking fuel on the treeless prairies.

Hunting techniques varied depending upon the terrain. When possible, Indians drove herds of bison into arroyos with no exit, over cliffs, or into deep sand or snow, making them easier to kill. When Spanish horses began arriving in the 16th century, they made it far easier to hunt bison. In the surround, mounted hunters attacked from at least two sides, creating chaos in the herd, and allowing buffalo to be shot with arrows or guns.

When whites first spread across the Plains, they found the bison a plentiful food source, but also viewed the massive herds as a hindrance to agriculture and cattle raising. These were not the only reasons whites wanted to destroy the buffalo; killing off the buffalo would starve the Indians into submission and force them to take a more "civilized" way of life. Gen. Philip Sheridan, commenting in support of white buffalo hunters, said:

"Instead of stopping the [white] hunters they ought to give them a hearty, unanimous vote of thanks, and appropriate a sufficient sum of money to strike and present to each one a medal of bronze, with a dead buffalo on one side and a discouraged Indian on the other. They are destroying the Indian's commissary, and it is a well-known fact that an army losing its base of supplies is placed at a great disadvantage. Send them powder and lead, if you will; for the sake of a lasting peace, let them kill, skin and sell until the buffaloes are exterminated."

This reckless slaughter did indeed endanger the Indians, but it also had an unwanted side effect, they went on the war path. The loss of their primary food source helped convince many Indians that their own extinction was next. The warriors who massacred Custer and his men at Little Big Horn had watched their people pushed to the brink of starvation by the destruction of the buffalo.

The Slaughter: Two factors propelled the slaughter to new heights in the 1870s: new railroads across the Plains, and a sudden international demand for buffalo robes and hides. Buffalo meat proved to be a readily available food source for railway construction workers, and hunters such as "Buffalo Bill" Cody provided a steady supply, generally taking just the hind quarters and hump while leaving the rest on the plains. Many thousands were killed. Once the railroads were complete, a new "sport" appeared, shooting buffalo from the moving railcars and leaving them to rot on the prairie. Wealthy gentry from the East Coast and Europe also discovered the joys of killing. One Irish nobleman had an entourage of 40 servants, with an entire wagon just for firearms; he killed 2,000 buffalo in a three-year carnage.

In 1872, thousands of hide hunters spread through Kansas, Nebraska, and Colorado in search of buffalo. Over the next three years, they brought in more than three million buffalo hides, with Indians killing another 400,000 bison for meat and robes. Good hide hunters could bring down 25-100 buffalo in a typical day, keeping five skinners busy from sunup to sundown. One hunter, Jim White, killed at least 16,000 buffalo in his career. Only the hides, cured hams, and buffalo tongues (which could be salted and shipped in barrels), were saved. When Gen. Grenville M. Dodge toured Kansas in the fall of 1873, he noted that, "The air was foul with a sickening stench, and the vast plain, which only a short twelvemonth before teemed with animal life, was a dead, solitary, putrid desert." Buffalo carcasses dotted the plains in such numbers that in later years bone pickers would collect massive piles of bones for knife handles, combs, and buttons, or to be ground up for sugar refining, fertilizer, or glue.

When the buffalo of the central states approached extinction, hunters turned their attention elsewhere, reaching Wyoming, Montana, and the Dakotas in 1880. In 1882, more than 200,000 hides were taken, and another 40,000 the following year. By 1884, only 300 hides were shipped. The slaughter was nearly over; only a few private herds and scattered individual bison

remained. The Indians who had once depended so heavily on buffalo for all the necessities of life were reduced to eating muskrats, gophers, and even grass. Some killed their horses, others stole settler's cattle, and the rest had to beg the government for food. In only a couple of years, an entire culture had been decimated. But it was not just the buffalo that died or the Indians whose lives had been destroyed. Hide hunters often spiked buffalo carcasses with strychnine, returning later to skin the wolves that had come to feed on the meat. Coyotes, kit foxes, badgers, vultures, eagles, ravens, and anything else that ate the meat were also killed. With both the buffalo and the "vermin" out of the way, Wyoming and the West were safe for domestic sheep and cattle.

Protection: The first federal legislation protecting buffalo (only in Yellowstone National Park, however) did not pass until 1894. The following year, only 800 buffalo remained in all of North America, one-thousandth of one percent of their original numbers. Despite this dismal picture, the population has rebounded dramatically, and today an estimated 65,000 bison roam across America. In Wyoming, small populations can be seen in Hot Springs State Park and Grand Teton National Park, while one of the few large wild populations remains in Yellowstone National Park.

In recent years, a strong demand for buffalo meat has led some Wyoming ranchers to raise bison. It's a highly specialized ranching endeavor since they can flatten most fences, and standard roundup techniques don't work. Durham Buffalo Ranch near Wright has one of the largest private buffalo herds in the country: 2,500 head. Ranchers have discovered that bison are more efficient grazers than cattle, making it possible to produce more meat per acre, and they are less susceptible to disease. Perhaps some day the vast herds of bison may return to Wyoming's rangelands in the form of bison ranches.

HISTORY

Although Wyoming is a young state—only reaching the century mark in 1990—it seems to have more history per square inch than just about any other place in America. The Wyoming of the 19th and early 20th centuries captured America's imagination and sparked countless books, songs, and movies. This history is a mixture of Indians and cowboys, settlers and outlaws, schemers and dreamers, railroad magnates and cattle barons, and plain folks clinging to a plot of marginal farmland despite unbelievable odds. This rich treasure trove from the past is stored not just in the little-changed landscape where the ruts from wagon trains are still visible and emigrant names remain carved in rocky buttes, but also in the cattle drives and rodeos, and the weather-etched faces of sheepherders and cowboys working the range. It is hard to imagine a place with a richer past.

NATIVE AMERICANS

Humans have been in Wyoming for a very long time, perhaps 25,000 years. A mammoth kill site near Worland dates back more than 11,000 years. The Plains Indians—made up of 27 different tribes—were found from the Mississippi River to the Rockies, and from Texas to central Canada. The lives of these people revolved around the buffalo as they followed the vast herds, migrating where the buffalo led. Because of this nomadic lifestyle, everything they had was pared to the minimum. Pottery, so common in the southwestern deserts, was replaced by woven baskets on the Plains. The tipi, an easily portable lodge, offered protection from the elements, and clothing was warm, yet not burdensome.

Days Of Glory

Although many people view the Plains Indians as being in a state of balance with their environment, there is ample evidence that things were changing even before whites first pushed their way onto the Plains. The arrival of horses and guns in the 17th and 18th centuries created a time of plenty that has rarely been known among nomadic hunting tribes. Horses made it easier to follow and hunt the huge bison herds, and tribes that had been at least partially farmers, turned entirely to hunting. Native populations grew rapidly with the abundance of food. The warrior also gained in importance with the changing culture, as raiding parties stole horses and attacked other tribes. Villages grew larger as families gathered for mutual protection from their enemies.

The turmoil that resulted led to a constantly changing situation in Wyoming during the 19th century as the tribes strove for control. It was this turbulent society that greeted the first Euro-American explorers. Whites were accustomed to well-defined land ownership, with definite boundaries within which one lived; here the territories were in a state of flux, with each tribe claiming overlapping areas.

During the 1700s, Indians from the Great Lakes and Canadian Plains had moved into what would become Wyoming. By the 1850s, the Sioux were in Powder River Basin, the Crow in Bighorn Basin, and the Cheyenne and Arapaho south of the North Platte River. The Shoshones and Bannocks—originally from the Great Basin—had moved into the Green River and Wind River valleys, while their relatives, the Utes, held the Sierra Madre and desert land to the west. Communication between these diverse tribes was possible by a well-developed sign language.

Treaties

During the first half of the 19th century, American explorers, fur trappers, traders, and settlers began to push across Wyoming. As emigration westward increased in the 1840s, so did conflicts with Indians. Whites complained of random attacks and stolen horses. Indians complained of trampled grass, polluted water, and wasteful killing of bison. To deal with these problems, a great council was called at Fort Laramie in 1851, attracting 10,000 Indians from many different tribes. Indian agent Thomas Fitzpatrick was anxious to gain permission for settlers to use the Oregon Trail across Indian lands in Wyoming. In exchange for gifts from the federal government in the form of annuities, the tribes agreed to stay within specified boundaries, and to punish those who violated the accord or attacked white emigrants.

Father Pierre DeSmet drew up the boundaries, with allowances for hunting outside the "home" regions. The unstated long-term goal of the treaty was to transform the Indians into farmers rather than hunters. By developing a paternalistic system of dependency on the government combined with educational programs and settlement, the Indians would, in theory, become like the whites. Violence erupted almost immediately among the tribes and with Anglo emigrants. Soon, whites would be more concerned over how to dispossess the Indians of their land than how to get through it safely.

The Battle Begins

Colorado's Sand Creek Massacre of 1865 proved a turning point in the history of Indian-white relations. A small band of Arapahos attacked a family farm, brutally murdering the family. When the mutilated bodies were put on display in Denver, public outrage pushed Col. John M. Chivington—formerly a Methodist minister—to lead one of the most vicious and unwarranted attacks ever perpetrated by the Army. Two hundred Cheyennes and Arapahos died in the daybreak attack on Chief Black Kettle's peaceful village.

The Indians—not just the Cheyenne and Arapaho, but also the Sioux—quickly retaliated by striking throughout Colorado and Wyoming, killing some 75 settlers around the Rock Creek Station (northwest of present-day Laramie) and destroying stage stations all along the Oregon Trail. Over the next several years, hundreds died on both sides. The main focus of Indian attacks was the Bozeman Trail through the lush Powder River country of the Sioux. The Army responded with an alternating series of military campaigns and peace overtures as the national mood flip-flopped between war and accommodation.

A major cause of these conflicts was the hysteria that gold created. Each new gold rush—California in 1849, Colorado in 1859, Montana in 1864, and finally the Black Hills in 1874—led to new incursions onto Indian lands. When whites found Indians standing in the way of development, they attempted to renegotiate the

The Sioux warrior Red Cloud proved a formidable military leader during the Plains Indian wars.

treaties, or failing that, to find some excuse to set them aside. Once gold had been found, the end of Indian culture was almost a given. Senator John Sherman noted, "If the whole Army of the United States stood in the way, the wave of emigration would pass over it to seek the valley where gold was to be found."

Other factors also played critical roles in the destruction of the Indian way of life on the Plains. Many tribes were devastated by diseases brought by contact with Europeans, especially smallpox, cholera, whooping cough, and venereal diseases. But perhaps the most crucial factor was the loss of their primary food source, the buffalo (see p.19).

Cultural Mistrust

Many whites viewed the Indians with deep distrust. Writer James Chisholm provides a typical frontier attitude, calling them "useless, strutting, ridiculous, pompous humbugs—lying, faithless, stealing, begging, cruel, hungry, howling vagabonds—cowardly, treacherous red devils."

AMERICAN HERITAGE CENTER, LARAMIE, WY

In 1869, Gen. Philip Sheridan took matters even further by claiming, "The only good Indian is a dead Indian."

The Indians themselves were not entirely innocent. Attacks on wagon trains were frequent, and many of the trappers, stagecoach drivers, and ranchers who settled in Wyoming were murdered and their bodies mutilated by the Sioux, Cheyenne, or Arapaho. Scalping—a practice introduced by white traders—became commonplace. Whites complained that the federal government was arming and feeding the Indians at the same time it was leading military campaigns against them.

Evicting The Indians

More than a thousand engagements were fought between Indians and whites in the late 19th century, killing at least 2,500 whites and twice as many Indians. On the Plains, most of the battles involved the Sioux, Cheyenne, Arapaho, Kiowa, and Comanche tribes. The Shoshone under Chief Washakie always remained peaceful. The final drama came in the 1870s,

beginning with the discovery of gold in the Black Hills of Dakota Territory. A flood of miners overwhelmed attempts by the government to keep them out of Sioux territory, and negotiations to purchase the land bogged down when Red Cloud demanded a $600 million payment.

In 1876, Gen. Sheridan led a three-pronged invasion to forcibly evict the Sioux from the Powder River region. They hadn't counted on two problems: the large numbers of Indians ready to do battle, and the rashness of junior officer Col. George A. Custer. At Little Big Horn on June 25, 1876, all of Custer's men were wiped out by a combined force of Indians led by Crazy Horse, Sitting Bull, and others. This massive Indian victory quickly became the rallying cry for whites anxious to "solve" the Indian problem by forcing them onto reservations. Within five years, the last of the tribes had given up the fight. The uprising that led to the infamous Wounded Knee Massacre of 1890 was a last dying gasp to regain the land that had once all belonged to the Native Americans.

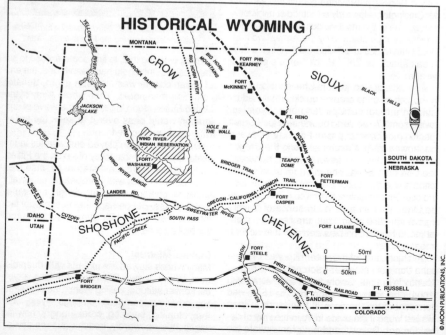

HISTORICAL WYOMING

© MOON PUBLICATIONS, INC.

TRAPPERS AND EXPLORERS

The first Europeans to explore Wyoming were a party of Frenchmen led by François and Louis-Joseph Verendrye who entered northern Wyoming in 1743. During the winter of 1807-08, John Colter—a trapper and former guide for the Lewis and Clark Expedition—explored northwest Wyoming in an attempt to develop the fur trade with Crow Indians. Colter was soon followed by other white trappers in search of beavers. It was a hazardous business, with the constant threat of Indian attacks, along with the many natural hazards such as angry grizzlies, disease, and injuries. Help was hundreds of miles away. The mountain men era (see "Wind River Mountain Country," p. 207) lasted only until 1840 when demand for the furs plummeted, but the trappers' knowledge of the terrain proved invaluable. Many became guides for civilian and military expeditions, wealthy hunters, and government explorations of the West. The mountain passes they found (or more likely had been shown by Indians) provided a route for the exodus westward in the 1850s.

WESTWARD HO

Oregon Trail

The great migration west began in 1843 when the first emigrants headed over the Continental Divide. By 1870, perhaps 350,000 people had traveled across Wyoming by wagon train, stagecoach, horseback, and foot. For most of them, this land seemed a worthless stretch of sagebrush, a barrier to the green lands farther west. The Oregon Trail is a general term used to describe a whole series of trails. At different times, and over different paths, this route encompassed the Oregon Trail (to both Oregon and Washington), the California Trail, the Mormon Trail (to Salt Lake City), and the short-lived Pony Express. Across Wyoming the route followed the North Platte and Sweetwater rivers upstream to the Continental Divide at South Pass. "Oregon Country" was not simply the area that would become the state of Oregon, but the entire region west of the Continental Divide. Thus, the hills just west of the divide in Wyoming became the "Oregon Buttes," and emigrants wrote of

entering Oregon as they crossed South Pass.

At the peak of migration in the early 1850s, hundreds of wagons rumbled by every summer day, each with its herd of cattle, horses, and mules. The grass quickly became overgrazed under this onslaught, and the scarce water badly polluted around popular campsites. Late summer travelers were forced to range far and wide for better conditions, creating even more paths. The Indians who had lived here were shocked by the migration, and began to realize not just what the whites were doing to their buffalo, but how overwhelmed they would be by the newcomers. (The entire Plains Indian population probably numbered 40,000 individuals at its peak, and disease and war greatly lessened these numbers.)

Emigrants were forced to travel as light as possible. Guide books (there were several; this was a big business even in the 19th century) described the crossings and camping places, and suggested provisions for the 2,000-mile journey. A wagon, harness, and eight oxen cost travelers around $400. The typical evening found the emigrant just 15 miles farther down the trail, and it generally took between four and six months to travel from Missouri to California or Oregon.

Because of the scarcity of wood, Oregon Trail travelers used dry grass, sagebrush, or buffalo chips for fuel. Meals were simple but hearty, often consisting of a few staples, plus whatever game might be found along the trail. Today when you drive across the state, it is easy to see how trying an experience this must have been for the emigrants, as gale force winds, dust, and lightning add to the parched ground, deceptively long distances, and the lack of shade. Wyoming can be a harsh and unforgiving land; it is not a place to wander into unprepared. Perhaps a tenth of the people who set out on the Oregon Trail never made it to their destination.

The Pony Express

On April 3, 1860, a lone rider galloped westward from the town of St. Joseph, Missouri. Nearly 2,000 miles away, another rider left the booming city of San Francisco, heading east. One of the most celebrated passages in American history had begun, the Pony Express. Although it only lasted 18 months and was a financial disaster, the Pony Express caught the national imagination, proved that rapid mail service was possible even in the winter, and helped keep California in the Union.

The Pony Express was the brainchild of William H. Russell, one of the great wheelers and dealers of the late 19th century, and director of the Central Overland California and Pike's Peak Express Company. Russell, along with partners Alexander Majors and William Bradford Waddell, managed the largest freighting company in the West, a business that at one time owned 50,000 oxen for its 3,500 wagons and employed 4,000 workers.

In 1855, the firm of Russell, Majors, & Waddell secured a monopoly to supply all U.S. government military posts west of the Missouri River. Because of Mormon raids on the supply wagons and the failure of the War Department to pay the company for its services, it was soon in financial trouble. To escape, the company needed the contract for mail service between California and St. Louis, a route then held by the Butterfield Overland Mail Company. Butterfield's route took mail along a circuitous 25-day trek through Texas and Arizona into southern California. With the nation slipping rapidly toward the Civil War, and Texas on the side of the South, there were fears that mail service would be halted and that California might join the Confederacy.

In 1859, the postmaster general signed a contract with Russell, Majors, & Waddell to operate coaches and horses along the central route to California. The Pony Express was born as a flamboyant symbol of the superiority of this route. Experienced young horsemen, some as young as 14, and none weighing more than 120 pounds, would ride the finest horses at a full gallop, carrying telegrams and mail through some of the most desolate land on earth. The trip was to take just 10 days.

Each horse had four mail pouches sewn into a leather *mochilla* that could be easily transferred between horses. (At $5 per half ounce, Pony Express mail was primarily urgent messages and newspapers.) Riders changed horses at relay stations—crude huts with a station keeper and stock tender—every 10 to 15 miles, continuing on for 75-100 miles before passing the precious package to another rider. After a short break, the rider would speed back to his home station with mail headed in the opposite direction. The whole operation required a military precision to keep the 119 relay and home stations stocked, make sure the horses were in good condition, and guard against the threat of attack. For their work, riders received $120 per month (including room and board).

The threat of Indian hostilities became real when Nevada Piutes, angry after decades of abuse and the theft of their land, began attacking white settlements, killing 16 of the men working at the relay stations, taking 150 horses, and burning seven stations. A full-scale war was avoided, but it took more than a month to get the Express back into operation, at a cost of $75,000. Already a money-loser, this helped ensure the collapse of the Pony Express. But it was not just money that brought down the Pony Express. Completion of the first continental telegraph line on October 24, 1861 caused the demise of the Pony Express. The Pony Express, its mission replaced by a much more rapid means of communication, ended just two days later. Riders had delivered 34,753 pieces of mail, losing only one *mochilla* (both horse and rider were killed) out of 616 cross-country runs.

The Overland Trail

Lesser known and shorter-lived than the Oregon Trail, the Overland Trail was established by Ben Holladay, owner of the Overland Stage Company. Although the Oregon Trail had served for many years as the primary route west, by the 1860s, a need was developing for a new path. Increasing Indian attacks made the Oregon Trail more dangerous, and the rapidly growing mining town of Denver was too far away. After Holladay was given the contract to deliver mail to the West, he quickly re-routed travel along a trail originally scouted by Jim Bridger.

The new route proved 60 miles shorter than the Oregon Trail, but it passed directly through the difficult desert country of western Wyoming, rather than along the relatively lush north Platte and Sweetwater rivers. Stage stations were established every 10-15 miles, where teams could be changed, and home stations were located every 50 miles where travelers could stop for meals or primitive lodging. The stages covered 100-125 miles in a 24-hour period, but were extraordinarily expensive for the time: $500 from Atchison, Kansas to San Francisco. Emigrants began using the new route instead of the Oregon Trail; in a single year (1864) some 17,584 men, women, and children used the Overland Trail, along with 50,000 stock and 4,264 wagons.

Although the new route remained relatively free from attacks for several years, the 1865 Sand Creek Massacre sent Indians on the warpath throughout the Plains. Stage stations were destroyed, stagecoaches were attacked, and many died on both sides. The attacks continued sporadically for the next two years. With completion of the transcontinental railroad in 1869, the Overland Stage rapidly faded in importance, and stagecoach service ended. The old Overland Trail continued to be used by wagons until the turn of the century.

CONNECTING THE COASTS

More than any other event, the transcontinental railroad led to the settlement and development of Wyoming. Most of its major settlements originated along the railroad lines. Not only did the railroad bring Wyoming within a couple of days of either coast, but it also led to the opening of coal mines to fuel the engines, development of the logging industry (for railroad ties and mine props), and made it easy to ship cattle to market. Settlers could order most anything—Sears Roebuck even shipped prefabricated houses that filled two boxcars. It was no coincidence that Wyoming became a territory just as the railroad was being pushed across its southern border. An enduring impact from the railroad is a checkerboard pattern of public and private land ownership along the Union Pacific's route across Wyoming.

Surveying The Route

The Union Pacific's route across the Rockies was planned by Gen. Grenville M. Dodge, a veteran of battles with the Sioux in the Powder River country. The traditional Oregon Trail route ran too close to Sioux country, was too far from the gold-mining city of Denver, and didn't have

the rich coal deposits of southwest Wyoming. The route Dodge chose headed almost straight across southern Wyoming, climbing the Laramie Mountains west of Cheyenne, and then cutting through the Laramie Plains and Red Desert before winding across the mountains of eastern Utah.

Despite Dodge's efforts to avoid direct confrontation with the Indians, and the government's diversionary tactic of building the Bozeman Trail through the Powder River country, the Arapaho did not take kindly to the presence of railroad survey and construction parties in their traditional hunting grounds. They pulled up survey stakes, stole horses, and killed surveyors and loggers, forcing Dodge to request military escorts. Three forts (Russell, Sanders, and Steele) were built in Wyoming to house these troops.

Working On The Railroad

To span the continent, the Union Pacific headed west from Omaha, while the Central Pacific worked east from Sacramento. By July 1867, tracklayers had reached the main division point that would become Cheyenne, and headed on west to found Laramie, Rawlins, Green River, and Evanston. Most of the Central Pacific's workers were Chinese contract laborers, while those on the Union Pacific were a mixture of Americans and emigrants, especially Irishmen. Great competition grew between the two groups, and a record was set as the tracklayers worked across the searing heat of Wyoming's Red Desert: the men laid 7 1/2 miles of track in a single day. Laborers were paid an extraordinary $2.50 an hour, but the work was equally dangerous; it is said that the transcontinental railroad was built at the cost of 10 men's lives per mile of track! Many were buried right in the roadbed. The tracklayers finally pushed their way into Utah, and met workers of the Central Pacific at Promontory Point on May 10, 1869.

The railroad brought with it a gang of men who seemed to thrive on corruption, thievery, prostitution, gambling, drunkenness, and murder. As construction moved westward, temporary towns sprang up along the way; many were gone as soon as the tracks were out of sight. The entire procession of construction workers and hangers-on quickly became known as Hell-on-Wheels.

railroad building on the Great Plains, from Harpers Weekly, 1875

WYOMING STATE MUSEUM

Worst of the temporary frontier towns was Benton, located a few miles east of present-day Rawlins. Those who passed through called it "nearer a repetition of Sodom and Gomorrah than any other place in America," or a "congregation of scum and wickedness . . . by day disgusting, by night dangerous." There was no grass, little water, and the alkali dust stood eight inches deep. Murders were a nightly affair at the 25 saloons and five dance halls. The big attraction was gambling, with hundreds of men crowding the big tent each evening, paying for whiskey, dancehall girls, or roulette wheels. Before the short-lived settlement could disappear in the alkali dust—just three months after its founding—more than 100 men lay buried in boot hill.

A rolling newspaper press tagged along with the flotsam and jetsam across Wyoming, printing the weekly *Frontier Index* in each new camp. Its editor, Legh Freeman, angered the primarily northern-born workers by constantly showing his support for the Confederacy; he once labeled Gen. Ulysses Grant, "the whiskey bloated, squaw ravishing adulterer, nigger worshipping mogul rejoicing over his election to the presidency . . ." In Bear River City (long gone, but near present-day Evanston), Freeman made the mistake of suggesting that several accused murderers then in jail should meet up with Judge Lynch. After a gang of vigilantes followed his suggestion by offering a necktie party for the three, other ruffians destroyed the *Frontier Index* office and chased its editor out of town.

STATEHOOD

Because of its difficult climate, a paucity of good agricultural lands, and no major deposits of gold, Wyoming was one of the last states to be settled. At various times, portions of Wyoming were part of Indian country, Mexico, Louisiana, Missouri, Texas, Nebraska, Dakota, Idaho, Oregon, and Utah. In 1868, Wyoming Territory was carved out of Dakota Territory, a move primarily intended to keep the Democratic voters building the Union Pacific Railroad from overwhelming the Republican power base in distant Yankton. The folks out West were equally happy to gain independence from such a tenuous governmental link. It was not until May 19, 1869, that an organized government was established in the new territory. The first census of Wyoming in 1870 found just 9,000 people (Indians were not counted).

The word Wyoming comes from the Leni Lanape Indians of Pennsylvania who used the word "Mecheweami-ing" to denote "At the Great

Plains." The term was first applied to the land that would become Wyoming in 1865 when Ohio's J. M. Ashley introduced a bill to form a "temporary government for the territory of Wyoming." Newspaper editor Legh Freeman has been credited with popularizing the name and having it inserted in the bill that created Wyoming Territory in 1868.

A triumvirate of politicians governed Wyoming for much of its first half century: Francis E. Warren (see "Southwest Wyoming," p. 53), John B. Kendrick and Joseph M. Carey. Carey, a Republican turned Democrat, was a founder of the powerful Wyoming Stock Growers' Association and the Cheyenne Club. He was a strong proponent of Wyoming statehood, and introduced the enabling legislation in the U.S. House. During the debate, he claimed a Wyoming population of something over 110,000 people, an exaggeration that helped sway enough House votes to pass the measure. (The U.S. census of the following year found just 62,555 people in Wyoming.) The act was signed into law by President Benjamin Harrison on July 10, 1890, making Wyoming the 44th state. Interestingly, this was the same year that the director of the U.S. Census Bureau declared that the "frontier of settlement" was no more.

The Equality State

Wyoming's first Territorial Legislature passed an act granting women the right to vote. The measure was signed into law by Gov. J.A. Campbell on Dec. 10, 1869, making this the first government in the world to grant women the right to vote. (Technically, Wyoming was not the first state to allow women suffrage; New Jersey widows already had limited voting rights.) The name "Equality State" comes from this bold step. It would be another 50 years before the 19th Amendment was finally passed, giving all women in America the right to vote. Not everyone looked upon women's suffrage as such a good step. In 1871, Democrats in the second Territorial Legislature repealed the measure, and then came within one vote of overriding Gov. Campbell's veto. (See "South Pass City," p. 89 for more on women's suffrage.)

Wyoming's status as the home for equal rights took another big step in 1925 after the death of Gov. William B. Ross. His wife, Nellie Tayloe Ross, was nominated to replace him, and won the special election on a sympathy vote. She made no effort to get elected, noting, "I shall not make a campaign. My candidacy is in the hands of my friends. I shall not leave the house." She served ably as the nation's first woman governor and achieved considerable national attention. Despite a good record, Ross lost her bid for re-election, primarily because she was a Democrat in a heavily Republican state. In 1933, President Roosevelt appointed her as director of the U.S. Mint, a title she held for the next 20 years. She died in 1967 at the age of 101.

CATTLE COUNTRY

Opening The Range

After the destruction of the bison herds and the eviction of the Indians, cattlemen found what seemed like the Garden of Eden in Wyoming. The land, grass, and water were essentially free for the taking. The cattle industry began innocently enough. In December, 1863, Tom Alsop was returning to Omaha with a train of 50 wagons when a snowstorm pinned them down near present-day Cheyenne. Alsop abandoned the oxen and wagons on the plains and led his men safely home on horseback. The following spring, they rode back to recover the freight and were startled to discover that the cattle they had left to die of exposure, had not only survived the winter, but were thriving. The discovery soon attracted a flood of ranchers.

The first cattle drive into Wyoming came around 1868, and millions more headed into or through the state in the 1870s and 1880s. Ranching looked like a simple business; dump a couple thousand head of cows and calves on the range in spring, and return a year later to round them up for market. What could be simpler? Investors from Omaha, New York, England, Scotland, and France quickly took note of the potential fortunes to be made.

By 1883, English and Scottish investors had poured some £6 million into Wyoming cattle, and had turned Cheyenne into a country club for the European gentry. Some were more gullible than others; stories are still told of an Englishman who watched as the cattle he was buying were driven by to be counted, not noticing that the same cattle had come around the hill a couple of times before. The use of "book counts" also inflated the value of the herds; frequently nobody bothered to make sure that numbers in the books equalled cattle on the range. The aristocracy were regarded with a mixture of humor and disdain by the hardened cowboys whose every other utterance came out a swear word. One British Lord rode up to a cowboy in his buggy, asking, "My good man could you tell me where your master is?" The cowboy glowered back, spat out his tobacco, and said, "The son-of-a-bitch ain't been born yet!"

During the early years of cattle ranching in Wyoming, cattle were allowed to roam at will, and not sorted out until the annual roundup. Sounds fine in theory, but in practice, a few

TOM HORN

The story of the Outlaw Tom Horn will always remain something of a mystery. Over the years, Horn worked as a stage driver, Army scout, deputy sheriff, Pinkerton investigator, and a stock detective for the Wyoming Stock Growers Association. When J.M. Carey (later Wyoming governor and senator) discovered that Tom Horn was out to murder, rather than bring in for trial the accused rustlers, he had Horn fired from the association. Other cattle barons quickly moved to hire him, however, paying $500 for each man murdered. Horn is generally blamed for ambushing and killing two ranchers (and suspected rustlers) in the Laramie Mountains in 1895, along with two others in Brown's Park, Colorado five years later.

Wherever Horn went, a trail of dead men was left behind. Nobody was able to pin the blame on him until 1901 when a 14-year-old boy was shot in the back and killed in the Laramie Mountains. It was a case of mistaken identity, since the boy had been wearing his father's hat and clothes. The older man was later shot from ambush, but survived. Horn was implicated in the boy's slaying by his trademark: a small stone placed under the victim's head.

Horn would probably have escaped even this heinous crime had he not bragged about it. The confession would never hold up in court today, however, since Deputy U.S. Marshal Joe LeFors had plied Horn with liquor and had a court stenographer listen through a crack in the door as he boasted of the slaying. Tom Horn had little money himself, but his supporters spent $100,000 in his defense, hiring the finest legal council, John W. Lacey, who had never lost any of his 50 previous murder trials (and who, not coincidentally, represented the Wyoming Stock Growers' Association and the Union Pacific Railroad). Despite this, Horn was adjudged guilty and sentenced to hang. Horn's supporters tried to free him with a dynamite blast, and he later did briefly escape from jail, but on November 20, 1903, he was hanged before a large crowd at the corner of Pioneer and 19th avenues in Cheyenne. Until the last minute, everyone expected a pardon, and many wealthy cattlemen feared what Horn might reveal about them, but in the end, his last words were to his friend T. Joe Cahill, "Joe, they tell me you are married now. I hope you're doing well. Treat her right."

BUFFALO BILL HISTORICAL CENTER

BRANDS

Branding dates back to the Egyptian Pharaohs who branded not only their cattle, camels, and donkeys, but even their slaves. (Slave branding was also practiced in America.) The American tradition of branding comes from the Spanish conquistadors and their vaqueros, but was adapted to the spacious Western plains. Because there were no fences, cattle belonging to various ranchers became intermixed, leading to inevitable questions of ownership. Brands helped clear up questions of ownership.

Brands appear almost anywhere on an animal, and a given ranch may have a half-dozen or more for its cattle, sheep, and horses. An individual animal often has several different brands or marks. To make them easier to identify on the hoof, cattle are frequently distinctively marked by cutting a notch in the ear, slicing the skin that hangs under the cow's throat (the dewlap), or hacking a flap of hide (a wattle) so that it hangs loose from the neck.

In Wyoming, having a brand is something of a status symbol, and the Wyoming Brand Book lists more than 27,000 currently in use. Not everyone who has a brand has stock; some are simply used for mailbox decorations on suburban ranchettes. The more complex ones aren't likely to appear on a cow since they become illegible as the scar heals. Brands that are hard to alter, or of historic significance may be worth more than $5,000 when sold. Getting a desired brand can be a problem since the state looks askance on brands that resemble others in the same area, or that might be easily altered by rustlers (they still exist). One 19th-century rancher became so fed up with having his brand suggestions rejected that he wrote the brand department, demanding, "Send me a brand P.D.Q." They complied by giving him the brand PDQ.

Branding usually takes place in the spring before cattle and calves are driven into the higher pastures or set loose on the Plains. A branding iron is heated to a dull red in a fire and then pressed against the calf as it is held down. Freeze branding is also often used. Most male calves are castrated at the same time. Reading brands is an art gained by years of experience. They are read from left to right, top to bottom, and outside to inside. Some brands simply represent the owner's initials, while others become symbols for all sorts of things.

flaws showed up, notably the problem of mavericks. (The term maverick refers to an unbranded calf or cow of questionable ownership, or, as writer Struthers Burt put it, "A calf whose mamma has died and whose father has run off with another lady cow.") Unbranded calves were generally divvied up among the ranchers on the basis of which herd they were with, but when herds became mixed together, conflicts were inevitable. In addition, multiple roundups meant that the first cowboys on the scene could pretty much decide for themselves which calves were theirs. Some even went so far as to slit the tongues of calves so they could no longer suckle and would not follow their mothers, thus becoming instant mavericks.

Cattle Barons And Rustlers

To curb the temptations for such "sooners," the powerful Wyoming Stock Growers Association—an organization dominated by the wealthiest of the cattlemen—gained the power to dictate when roundups could be held. The organization dominated the political landscape of Wyoming for many years. By the 1880s, a third of the state Legislature were association members. The 1882 Maverick Bill gave them control over all cattle roundups in the territory, with proceeds from the sales of mavericks going into the association's coffers. It could blacklist cowboys as "rustlers" on the basis of hearsay, and cattle shipped without their permission risked being impounded by inspectors in Chicago or Omaha.

Even worse, ranchers suspected of rustling (which seemed to include anyone except members) were sometimes ambushed and murdered by enforcers, the most notorious of whom was Tom Horn. Whole regions of Wyoming were terrorized by the practice of dry-gulching, in which suspected rustlers would be shot from behind and left in an out-of-the-way gulch.

Meanwhile, the large cattlemen—commonly called cattle barons—also ran into trouble, especially in the Powder River country. The fierce winter of 1886-87 decimated their herds; some lost all their cattle, while others had just 20 or 30 percent of the numbers the previous year. Big ranching outfits also found themselves hemmed in by homesteading settlers who fenced the land. (Fences created a hazard since cattle often moved with the winter winds until they hit the fences and then piled up there to die.)

The big cattlemen accused these "nesters" of not only fencing the land, but also of taking stray cattle for themselves. Using a "long rope" and a "running iron" they could easily alter the brands, and soon have their own herd. The cattle barons decided to put an end to this thievery once and for all with the infamous Johnson County War of 1892, but the invasion proved a complete fiasco. Two men died on each side in pitched battles between the "barons" and the "rustlers." Although the invaders managed to escape prosecution, the small nesters and rustlers had won the day. From that time on, the range would increasingly be fenced in.

SHEEP

Cattle arrived in most parts of Wyoming a decade or so before the first sheep munched their way across the grazing lands, but by 1902, the rangeland was crowded with close to six million sheep. Cattlemen considered the public land their own by right of previous use, though legally all this was open range owned by the government. As competition increased, cattlemen declared "dead lines" across which no sheep would be allowed. Conflicts quickly erupted, and the single herder and his dogs proved no match for a gang of cattlemen on horseback. Herders were murdered throughout the state,

and the violence escalated into the infamous Tensleep Raid of 1909 (see p. 356) in which three sheepmen died. After this, things quieted down as the land became increasingly settled, and as government policies divided up the areas. Some cattlemen even turned to raising sheep, but animosity still remains between sheepmen and cattlemen.

Over the years the number of sheep in Wyoming has steadily dropped; today there are around 837,000 at any given time. Sheep are generally moved up into the mountains each spring to graze in the high meadows, and then back down in the fall. The long drives along country roads are a sight straight out of the history books. Sheep are sheared in spring, generally just before lambing season. By fall the lambs are big enough to send to market, and the ewes are bred.

A good many of the first sheepherders in Wyoming were from the Basque region. Many preferred to take sheep instead of a salary, and so gradually gained a flock of their own. The frugal ones eventually became ranch owners in their own right. The herding business has not changed much over the years, however, and herders still spend weeks at a time alone, seeing nobody but the camp mover when he arrives to help move the outfit to new feedgrounds. Today many are Mexican, although some Basque and American herders are around. The life is a simple and quiet one.

ENERGY BOOM AND BUST

Wyoming's first oil well was drilled in 1884, and by 1908—the year of the first oil boom—production approached 18,000 barrels per year. Production continued to climb over the decades, reaching a peak in 1970 when more than 155 million barrels were pumped. Since then, the figures have dropped as older fields are exhausted and as low prices discourage exploration. In 1988, it had fallen to 104 million barrels. The decline in oil production has been offset somewhat by dramatic increases in two other energy sources: natural gas and coal. During the 1980s, both industries nearly doubled their production levels in Wyoming.

The Arab oil embargo of 1973 and subsequent price rises turned Wyoming upside down. The oil patch towns, particularly Casper, Rock Springs, Evanston, and Green River, turned into madhouses of pickup trucks, heavily muscled oil workers, honky-tonk bars, strip joints, fast food outlets, and trailer courts. Drugs, crime, prostitution, and gambling ripped across the state. The population of Rock Springs doubled in two years. In the heady rush of new workers and high-paying oil jobs, many towns embarked on ambitious construction projects such as schools and housing developments, while trailer parks sprouted up across the countryside. (Wyoming still holds top honors as the state with the highest percentage of mobile homes.)

This economic bubble collapsed with the sudden halving of oil prices in 1982, and Wyoming's population actually dropped by almost three percent during the 1980s. The bust left many towns struggling to survive as unemployment skyrocketed, the state government was forced into consolidation mode, and local residents were left with a bloated set of facilities. In the late 1980s, the economy began to slowly rebound, and recent years have seen efforts to diversify. Still, the inevitable booms and busts associated with the energy and mining industries will affect Wyoming for the foreseeable future.

ECONOMY AND GOVERNMENT

In recent years, Wyoming had ridden an economic bucking bronco as oil prices shot up and then suddenly dove, throwing this energy-rich state out of the saddle. A *Newsweek* article in 1989 called Wyoming "a Third World energy colony," noting that both the population and the economy had declined at the same time the national economy was growing rapidly. Wyoming's economy is gradually coming back as communities begin to emphasize tourism and small industries. When the inevitable next energy boom comes, perhaps folks won't be quite so anxious to put all their eggs in the energy basket.

Wyoming's economy is affected not only by private developments, but also by the government. The federal government owns almost 47% of the land, while the state government holds another 10%—leaving 43% in private hands. The largest public land agency, the Bureau of Land Management (BLM), owns nearly 18 million acres in Wyoming, but most of this exists in a checkerboard of small parcels with limited public access. The BLM manages only a few patches of wilderness scattered around Wyoming. The U.S. Forest Service has 8.7 million acres within nine national forests that cover the state's largest mountain ranges, and the National Park Service has another 2.3 million acres in five national parks, monuments, and recreation areas. Partly because of all this federal land, Wyoming residents are on the receiving end of generous federal monies; they are second only to Alaska in per capita federal aid.

Working For A Living

Today, Wyoming's economy is based on several industries: oil and gas extraction, coal and trona mining, cattle and sheep ranching, and tourism. Of these, the most important from a financial point is the oil and gas industry, contributing nearly half of the state's tax base. Some 1,000 fields annually produce 100 million barrels of oil (sixth in the nation) and 600 million cubic feet of natural gas (fifth in the nation). A quarter of the nation's coal reserves lie beneath Wyoming, and in recent years it has become the largest coal-producing state. Nearly all the 170 million tons extracted each year comes from enormous open-pit mines, primarily in the Powder River Basin. With perhaps a *trillion* tons of coal still below the surface, Wyoming is one of the largest energy storehouses anywhere on the planet. Vast deposits of trona (used primarily in glass and chemicals) occur in southwest Wyoming where mines produce 90% of the nation's supply. The state is also a major producer of bentonite, helium, and sulfur. Uranium was once an important industry—a third of America's reserves are in Wyoming—but since Three Mile Island, production had dropped to almost nothing.

Tourism contributes $800 million annually to the state's economy, and is particularly important in northwest Wyoming (Yellowstone and Grand Teton national parks). More than five million people come to enjoy the state's abundant recreational opportunities each year. The state's most obvious industry, and the one that encompass-

WYOMING LINGO

Absaroka—Alternatively pronounced ab-SOR-ka or ab-SOR-aka, the word means "People of the Large-Beaked Bird" (hence the name Crow Indians). The Absaroka Mountains lie east of Yellowstone National Park.

Arapaho—The word is often spelled Arapahoe. An Indian tribe of Algonquin stock originally living on the Canadian plains; the Northern Arapaho now live on the Wind River Reservation. The name comes from a Crow Indian term meaning "Tattooed People." They call themselves simply "Our People."

bentonite—A special kind of clay that originates from volcanic ash, bentonite absorbs large amounts of water, increasing in volume by 30 percent. Bentonite is used in oil drilling, to line ponds, and even in candy bars. Wyoming is the nation's largest producer of this mineral.

booshway—The boss at a mountain men rendezvous.

buck and rail fence—A fence consisting of X-shaped supports and connecting poles, these are the classic fences of Jackson Hole where the soils proved too rocky for ranchers to dig postholes. The abundant lodgepole pines made fine fences. Today, buck-and-rail fences are built more for beauty than function.

calcutta—The auctioning off of various rodeo teams or contestants; it's a popular way to wager bets on rodeo events. Rules vary.

cattle baron—A cattle owner with extensive holdings; primarily used during the heyday of the giant cattle spreads in the 1880s.

chaps—Pronounced "shaps," protective leather leg coverings, useful when riding horses through brush.

chislers—Ground squirrels, also called ground cougars. The lemmings of Wyoming; they seem to delight in waiting till the last minute and then dashing toward car wheels. Lots of them get nailed on dirt roads all across the state.

coup—Pronounced coo; a Plains Indian word that signified great skill and daring, it involved striking an enemy in the midst of a battle or some other deed of valor. "Counting coups" was similar to gaining today's military medals of honor. Those with many coups wore war-bonnets with many feathers.

coyotes—Fans of these ubiquitous critters call them "ki-O-tees," while those who regard them as "varmints" tend to pronounce the word "KI-oats."

creek—Everyone knows what it is, but old-timers in Wyoming pronounce the word "crik" in contrast to the East Coast synonym "stream."

dead line—A line established by turn-of-the-century cattlemen who feared competition from sheep. Those herders who brought sheep across the imaginary line risked death and the destruction of their flocks.

dogger—A rodeo term used for steer wrestlers; it originated from Will Pickett, an early wrestler who threw steers to the ground by biting their lips in the manner of a bulldog. The name stuck, even though the lip-biting part didn't.

dogie—A motherless calf. A famous old cowboy poem begins:

"As I walked out one morning for pleasure,
I spied a cowpuncher all riding alone;
His hat was throwed back and his spurs was
a-jingling,
As he approached me a-singin' this song,

Whoopee ti yi yo, git along, little dogies,
It's your misfortune, and none of my own.
Whoopee ti yi yo, git along, little dogies,
For you know Wyoming will be your new
home. . ."

dog-trot—A type of log cabin common on old Wyoming ranches. Two cabins were connected by a breezeway, making a favorite place for dogs to hang out on hot summer days. This cabin style actually originated in the southern Appalachians.

dude—This is a term that has changed in meaning over the years. Writer Nathaniel Burt called the original dudes, "any fancy-pants young man who wore a boutonniere and parted his hair in the middle." Later, the term came to mean a wealthy Easterner vacationing on a Western ranch, in contradistinction to "tourists" who were viewed as an inferior species. Today Wyoming's many dude ranches are more proletarian. The wealthy elite generally prefer "guest ranches" which are really luxury resorts with a few horses thrown in.

emigrants—The dictionary defines emigrants as people who leave one place to settle elsewhere, in contrast to immigrants who come into a new place. Guess it all depends on your perspective, but for some reason folks heading west on the Oregon Trail were almost always called emigrants, not immigrants.

hazer—A rodeo term used in steer wrestling. It refers to a cowboy who rides beside the steer to keep it in position for the dogger.

hog ranch—An establishment of ill repute where booze, gambling, and loose women were the primary attractions. The most famous were located near military forts in Wyoming, notably Fort Fetterman and Fort Laramie. The name is generally attributed to the appearance of the women, but may also refer to the tiny, squalid rooms where they plied their wares. Author David Lavender called them places offering "the poorest whiskey and women in the west."

hooey—A tie used in calf roping events at rodeos. Three feet are wrapped with a piggin' string and completed with a half hitch knot.

jackalope—An antlered jackrabbit found most commonly in the vicinity of Douglas, Wyoming, but proliferating throughout the West.

maverick—An unbranded cow or calf of questionable ownership. The term originated from Samuel Maverick, owner of a two-million-acre Texas ranch in the 1840s. Because many of his cattle were never branded, cowboys coming across unbranded cattle on the open range would joke that they were Maverick's. Eventually the term was applied to all unbranded cattle.

piggin' string—A short piece of rope used to tie a hooey around the feet of a roped calf or steer at a rodeo.

rendezvous—French for "appointed place of meeting." Between 1825 and 1840 the annual rendezvous was the big shin-dig for Rocky Mountain trappers, Indians, and traders. Modern-day versions try to re-create this trading and partying atmosphere.

runnin' iron—An improvised branding iron used by rustlers.

rustler—A cattle thief or someone accused of taking cattle from the cattle barons; during the "Johnson County War" the term actually became a badge of honor in parts of Wyoming. "Packing a long rope" became the common term applied to folks who rustled.

sage hen—Another name for the sage grouse, a common bird across Wyoming. The term was also a cowboy term for women.

scoria—A red rock commonly used on Powder River Basin roads. It was formed when coal beds caught fire and burned underground, baking adjacent shales and sandstones to create a bright red slag. The red comes from iron oxide. Clinker is another word commonly used for scoria.

Shoshone—An Indian tribe on Wyoming's Wind River Reservation. The word is also frequently spelled Shoshoni, and is generally pronounced with a long e at the end.

Sioux—The word was derived from a derogatory Chippewa Indian term meaning "enemy" or "snake" and used to describe the Indians who lived just to their west. The Sioux actually called themselves "Dakota," meaning an "Alliance of Friends."

trona—A mineral (sodium sesquicarbonate) used in glass, detergents, baking soda, and other products; mined in huge underground mines west of Green River.

varmint—Any animal you don't like; especially used for prairie dogs, ground squirrels, and coyotes.

wapiti—Pronounced WOP-a-tee. The Indian word for elk. It is occasionally used by biologists who consider it a more precise term.

es 90% of its land base, is agriculture. Surprisingly, however, grazing and farming employ less than six percent of the population. Wyoming is third in the nation in terms of sheep and lamb production, and has 1.3 million cattle and calves. It takes 35-40 acres to support a single cow, which is why the average Wyoming farm is 4,000 acres (versus a national average of 463 acres). Only four percent of the state is cultivated, with sugar beets, barley, alfalfa hay, wheat, oats, and dry beans the primary crops. These are mainly grown within the Bighorn Basin, Wind River Basin, and along Wyoming's eastern plains. The state has no truly large manufacturing plants, though every town has its own specialty, from cheese-making to computer printer manufacturing.

Wyomingites take their right to vote seriously, with turnout during presidential election years sometimes topping 80% of registered voters. Wyoming has 64 elected Representatives who serve two-year terms, along with 30 Senators elected for four-year terms of office. The elected statewide officials—governor, secretary of state, auditor, treasurer, and superintendent of public instruction—all stand for office every four years. Republicans have controlled both houses almost since statehood, although Democrats have retained the statehouse since 1975. Governor Mike Sullivan easily won re-election in 1990, but the congressional delegation has been staunchly Republican for quite a while, and appears set to stay that way. The two U.S. Senators are Malcolm Wallop and Alan Simpson, while the state's lone U.S. Representative is Craig Thomas, elected to fill the shoes of Dick Cheney who went on to head the Deptartment of Defense under President Bush.

POLITICS

Unlike many states where apathy reigns,

OUTDOOR RECREATION

Fishing And Hunting
Outstanding fishing opportunities abound throughout Wyoming, and a number of places—notably the Yellowstone country—have attained recognition as some of the finest in America. Cutthroat, brown, rainbow, brook, and lake trout are favorites of many anglers, but the state's waters also contain mountain whitefish, kokanee, grayling, channel catfish, small-mouth bass, large-mouth bass, and others. Non-resident fishing permits cost $15 for five days, $20 for 10 days, or $35 for a season. Youths pay $10 for a season permit. Get permits at most sporting goods stores or at Game and Fish offices. For detailed hunting and fishing information, contact the Game and Fish office at 5400 Bishop Blvd., Cheyenne, WY 82002, tel. 777-7735.

Skiing
Downhill skiing enthusiasts will be pleased to find developed facilities at 11 different Wyoming locations. The finest are in the Jackson area: Jackson Hole, Grand Targhee, and Snow King.

Other ski areas are: Snowy Range (west of Laramie), Hogadon (near Casper), Sleeping Giant (west of Cody), and Antelope Butte (east of Greybull). More limited facilities can be found at High Park (east of Worland), Eagle Rock (near Evanston), Pine Creek (east of Cokeville) and Snowshoe Hollow (near Afton). See appropriate chapters for descriptions. Cross-country skiers will discover an overwhelming choice of places to ski. The only developed Nordic areas are around Jackson Hole, but any of the mountain ranges fill with deep snow, providing an inexhaustible opportunity for discovery. (See "Jackson Hole," p. 226 for more on cross-country skiing opportunities and precautions.)

Snowmobiling
Wyoming has some of the most extensive snowmobile trails in America, covering more than 1,100 miles. The most popular snowmobile areas are in the mountains of northwest Wyoming, the Medicine Bows, the Wind River Range, the Big Horn Mountains, and the Lar-

amie Range. Snowmobile trail maps are available from the Wyoming Recreation Commission, 122 W. 25th, Cheyenne, WY 82002, tel. 777-7695. For snow conditions around the state, call the snowmobile hotline in Cheyenne at 777-6503. See specific areas for snowmobile rental information.

GETTING INTO THE WILDERNESS

To get a real feel for Wyoming, you need to abandon your car, get away from the towns, and head out into the vast undeveloped public lands. Wyoming's most popular backcountry areas are in the Wind River Mountains, the Medicine Bows, the Big Horn Mountains, and the entire northwest corner of the state, including Yellowstone and Grand Teton national parks. The Yellowstone region contains one of the largest nearly natural ecosystems and most remote country in the lower 48 states. Many campers prefer to use horses for the longer trips, but backpacking is very popular on the shorter trails, especially in the Wind Rivers and the national parks. Backcountry permits are required only within Yellowstone and Grand Teton. It is, however, a good idea to check in at a local Forest Service ranger station to get a copy of the regulations since each place is different in such specifics as how far your tent must be from lakes and trails and whether wood fires are allowed. Be sure to take insect repellent along on any summertime trip, since mosquitoes, deer flies, and horse flies can be quite thick, especially in July and early August.

A number of hiking trails, mostly two or three day hikes, are described for each of Wyoming's best known backcountry areas. For more detailed hiking information on Yellowstone, Grand Teton, the Big Horns, or the Wind Rivers, see the "Booklist," p. 413. A decent overall guide is *The Sierra Club Guide to the Natural Areas of Idaho, Montana, and Wyoming,* by John Perry and Jane Greverus Perry (Sierra Club Books, San Francisco). The National Park Service and Forest Service can also provide specific trail information.

Horses
For many people, the highlight of a Wyoming vacation is a chance to ride horseback into wild

---

STANDING BEAR

"We did not think of the great open plains, the beautiful rolling hills, the winding streams with tangled growth as wild. Only to the white man was nature a wilderness, and only to him was the land infested with wild animals and savage people. To us it was tame. Earth was bountiful, and we were surrounded with the blessings of the Great Mystery. Not until the hairy man from the east came, and with his brutal frenzy, heaped injustices upon us and families we loved, was it wild to us. When the very animals of the forest began fleeing from his approach; then it was that for us, the 'wild west' began."

—Sioux Chief Standing Bear

---

country. Although a few folks bring their own horses, most visitors leave the driving to an expert local outfitter instead. (If you've ever worked around horses in the backcountry, you'll understand why.) Horsepacking is an entirely different experience from backpacking. The trade requires years of experience in learning how to properly load horses and mules with panniers, which type of knots to use for different loads, how to keep the packstrings under control, which horses to picket and which ones to hobble, and how to awaken when the horses decide to head down the trail on hobbles at three in the morning. Add to this a knowledge of bear safety, an ability to keep guests entertained with campfire tales and ribald jokes, a complete vocabulary of horse-cussing terms, and a thorough knowledge of tobacco chewing, and you're still only about 10% of the way to becoming a packer.

Dozens of outfitters are scattered across Wyoming, but especially in the Jackson Hole, Pinedale, Cody, and Dubois areas. For a listing of outfitters in a given region, contact the local chamber of commerce office. The **Wyoming Outfitters Association**, Box 2284, Cody, WY 82414, tel. 527-7453, can provide a statewide listing.

Backcountry Ethics
Wyoming's wilderness areas represent places to escape the crowds, to enjoy the beauty and peace of the countryside, and to develop an understanding for nature. Unfortunately, as more

and more people head into the backcountry, these values are becoming endangered. To keep the wild places wild, you need to practice minimum-impact hiking and camping. This means using existing campsites and fire rings, locating your campsite well away from trails and streams, burning only dead and down wood, extinguishing all fires, digging latrines at least 100 feet from lakes or streams, and hanging all food above the reach of bears. Your tent site should be 100 yards from the food storage and cooking areas to reduce the likelihood of bear problems. Wood fires are not allowed in many areas, so be sure to bring along a portable gas stove. And, of course, haul your garbage out with you. Burning cans and tinfoil in the fire lessens their weight (and the odors that attract bears), but be sure to pick them out of the fire pit before you depart.

Trail Etiquette

Because horses are so commonly used in Wyoming, hikers should follow a few rules of courtesy. Horses and mules are not the brightest critters on this planet, and can spook at the most inane thing, even a bush blowing in the breeze or a brightly colored hat. Hikers meeting a pack string should move several feet off the trail and not speak loudly or make any sudden moves. If you've ever seen what happens when just one mule in a string decides to act up, you'll appreciate the chaos that can result from sudden noises or movements. Anyone hiking with a dog should keep it well away from the stock and not let it bark. Last of all, never walk closely behind a horse, unless you don't mind spending time in a hospital. Their kick is definitely worse than their bite.

BACKCOUNTRY SAFETY

Beaver Fever

Although Wyoming's lakes and streams may appear clean, you may be risking a debilitating sickness by drinking the water without treatment. The protozoan *Giardia duodenalis* is found throughout the state, spread by both humans and animals (including beaver). Although the disease is curable with drugs, it's always best to carry safe drinking water on any trip or to boil water taken from creeks or lakes. Bringing water to a full boil is sufficient to kill Giardia and other harmful organisms. Another option is to use the new (and expensive) water filters such as "First Need," available

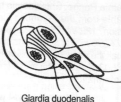

Giardia duodenalis

from backpacking stores. Note, however, that these may not filter out other organisms such as Campylobactor bacteria that are just 0.2 microns in size. Chlorine and iodine are not always reliable, taste foul, and can be unhealthy.

Hypothermia

Anyone who has spent much time in the outdoors will discover the dangers of exposure to cold, wet, and windy conditions. Even at temperatures well above freezing, hypothermia—the reduction of the body's inner core temperature—can prove fatal. In the early stages, hypothermia causes uncontrollable shivering, followed by a loss of coordination, slurred speech, and then a rapid descent into unconsciousness and death. Always travel prepared for sudden changes in the weather. Wear clothing that insulates well and that holds its heat when wet. Wool and polypro are far better than cotton, and should be worn in layers to provide better trapping of heat and a chance to adjust to conditions more easily. Always carry a wool hat since your head loses more heat than any other part of the body. Bring a waterproof shell to cut the wind.

If someone in your party begins to show signs of hypothermia, don't take any chances, even if the person denies needing help. Get the victim out of the wind, strip off their clothes, and put them in a dry sleeping bag on an insulating pad. Skin-to-skin contact is the best way to warm a hypothermic person, and that means you'll need to also strip and climb in the sleeping bag. If you weren't friends before, this should heat up the relationship! Do not give the victim alcohol or hot drinks, and do not try to warm the person too quickly since it could lead to heart failure. Once the victim has recovered, get medical help as soon as possible. Actually, you're far better off keeping close tabs on everyone in the group, and seeking shelter before exhaustion and hypothermia set in.

BEAR COUNTRY

Old-timers joke that bears are easy to differentiate: a black bear climbs up the tree after you, while a grizzly snaps the tree off at the base. Black bears are found in forested areas throughout Wyoming, but grizzlies exist only in Yellowstone National Park and surrounding country. Although grizzlies are generally a much greater threat to humans, black bears can also be dangerous, and backcountry travelers need to take precautions.

Grizzlies once ranged across the entire Northern Hemisphere, from Europe, across what is now the USSR, and through the western half of North America. Unfortunately, as white settlers arrived, they came to view these massive and powerful creatures (average adult males weighing 500 pounds) as a threat to themselves and their stock. The scientific name, *Ursus arctos horribilis*, says much about human attitudes toward grizzlies. They were shot, trapped, and poisoned nearly to the brink of extinction in the lower 48 so that today they now exist in only a few of the most remote parts of Montana, Wyoming, Idaho, and Washington. Wyoming has perhaps 200 grizzlies.

Avoiding Bear Hugs

Bear encounters are rare, but frightening experiences. Although there is considerable variability among individuals, most bears hear or smell you long before you realize their presence, and hightail it away. Surprising a bear, especially a sow with her cubs, is the last thing you want to do in the backcountry. Before heading out, check at a local ranger station to see whether there have been recent bear encounters. Larger groups are less likely to have problems. Make noise in areas of dense cover or when coming around blind spots on trails. Some people tie bells to their packs for this purpose, while others regard this as an annoyance to fellow hikers. Before camping, take a look around the area to see if there are recent bear tracks or scat. If so, you should find another spot. Keep a clean camp, and be sure to hang all food and other items that may smell at least 12 feet off the ground and four feet from tree trunks. Bears are attracted to odors of all sorts, including food, horse feed, soap, toothpaste, deodorants, and menstruation. If you discover an animal carcass, be extremely alert since a bear may be nearby and may attack anything that might threaten its food. Get away from such areas. Other potential problem areas are along streams where fish are spawning and in grassy or brushy areas where a resting bear may be hidden from your sight.

If you do happen to encounter a bear and it sees you, try to stay calm and not make any sudden moves. Do not run, since you could not possibly outrun a bear; they can exceed 40 mph for short distances. If a good-sized tree is nearby, climb it as high as you can with safety and stay there until you're certain that the bear has left the area. If no tree is close, your best bet is to remain still or back away slowly. Sometimes dropping something like a hat or jacket will distract the bear, and talking also seems to have some value in convincing bears that you're a human. If the bear does attack, curl up face-down on the ground in a fetal position with your hands wrapped behind your neck and your elbows tucked over your face. Your backpack may help protect you somewhat. Remain still even if you are attacked since sudden movements may incite further attacks. Many people have survived such attacks, despite being bitten and clawed. Recently, capsicum (pepper) sprays such as "Counter Assault" (Bushwacker Backpack & Supply Co., Box 4721, Missoula, MT 59806) have proven useful in fending off bear attacks. They are not, however, a cure-all or a replacement for being careful in bear country.

BOB RACE

ACCOMMODATIONS

Lodging in Wyoming covers the complete spectrum, from the very finest of luxury accommodations where a king would feel pampered, all the way down to flophouses so tawdry that even town drunks think twice. In general, visitors will find motel costs considerably less than what they might pay in other parts of America. This is especially true in the smaller towns and in places where the economy is weak from the bust following the oil boom. During the summer, rates at the mom-and-pop motels that line the streets of every Wyoming town start around $20-25 for one person or $25-30 for two people. Tack on another $10 for slightly fancier places with the AAA sign out front. Come wintertime, rates may drop 25% or more. The exception to these low rates is the northwest corner of the state, notably Cody, and most egregiously, Jackson. Expect to pay at least $40 s or $50 d during peak summer or winter season in Jackson Hole. Also beware that rates for Cheyenne motel and hotel rooms skyrocket during Cheyenne Frontier Days (late July).

The annual *TourBook* for Idaho, Montana, and Wyoming (free to members of the American Automobile Association) is a helpful guide to the better hotels and motels, offering current prices and accurate ratings. For a complete listing of motels, hotels, bed and breakfasts, dude ranches, and camping places in Wyoming, request a copy of the free *Wyoming Accommodations Directory* from the Wyoming Travel Commission, I-25 at College Dr., Cheyenne, WY 82002, tel. 777-7777 or (800) 225-5996. The booklet lists lodging and campgrounds in every part of the state. Throughout this book I have listed only two prices for most lodging places: one person (single or s) and two people in one bed (double or d). The accommodations charts are arranged from least to most expensive.

Hotels

Most of the traditional hotels that once offered lodging for weary Wyoming travelers have either fallen to the wrecking ball or have been turned into residence flophouses. Only a few of these historic gems have been restored to their glory; they include Cheyenne's Plains Hotel, Cody's Irma Hotel, Jackson's Wort Hotel, Medicine Bow's Virginian Hotel, and Saratoga's Wolf Hotel. Yellowstone National Park offers some of the finest old-time luxury accommodations: Old Faithful Inn, Lake Hotel, and Mammoth Hot Springs Hotel.

Motels

The various motel chains—Days Inn, Holiday Inn, La Quinta, Motel 6, and Super 8—all operate motels across the state, primarily in the larger towns. These cinderblock monuments to the bigger-is-better school of lodging stand on the edges of town, their towering signs acting as glaring eyesores. Each chain publishes its own brochure, listing locations and rates. Pick up a copy at a chain motel near your home or call their toll-free numbers. Every town in Wyoming has its locally owned small motels, generally run by an elderly woman with a yip-dog slightly larger than a small shrew (and twice as feisty). These motels vary widely in quality and price, but tend to offer the best rates and friendliest service.

Bed And Breakfasts

Bed and breakfasts are a relatively recent addition to Wyoming's lodging picture. These range from remote places where the accommodations are not unlike a guest ranch to historic Victorian homes in the center of town. Some of the best are found in Big Horn, Cody, Jackson Hole, Rawlins, and Wheatland.

Dude Ranches

An old and respected Western tradition is the dude ranch, most of which began as a sideline to the business of raising cattle. Friends from the East would remember old Jake out there in wild Wyoming where the buffalo roam and the antelope play, and would decide it was time for a visit. So off they would head, living in the ranchers' out buildings and joining in the chores. The "dudes" as they became known, soon told their friends, and Jake found his ranch inundated. After a couple of years of this, the next step was obvious, get those Eastern rascals to fork over some cash for the privilege of visiting. Pretty soon the dude ranching business had been born. At its peak in the 1920s, dude ranching spread through much of Wyoming and the West. Dude ranching saved many cattle ranches from extinction by providing a second source of income, and it simultaneously brought this magnificent land to the attention of people who had the money to prevent its development (most notably Grand Teton National Park).

At the older ranches, generations of families have returned year after year to vacation in the Wild West. Many dude ranches now call themselves guest ranches, a term that reflects both the suspicious way some people view the word dude, and the changing nature of the business. Many city folks today lack the desire or skill to actually saddle up their own horse, much less push cattle between pastures. As a result, guest/dude ranches tend to emphasize grand scenery, horseback riding, campfires, hearty meals, chuckwagon cookouts, sing-alongs, and evenings around the fireplace. Some folks even camp overnight out there in the fearful wilderness where the coyotes howl and the mice chew into your stash of potato chips. There aren't too many places left where you actually work alongside the cowboys. Playing is a lot more fun.

Wyoming has literally dozens of dude ranches and ranch resorts, offering accommodations ranging from Spartan to so sumptuous that they bear absolutely no resemblance to ranch life. Not all dude ranches are created equal—some are slick and modern with tennis courts and hot tubs while others are funky and old-fashioned with delightful rough edges. Dude ranch rates generally start around $650 pp (double occupancy) for a one-week stay, including everything from fine meals to horse rides. The fanciest resorts will set you back over $2,000 a week.

Ask plenty of questions ahead of time, such as what activities are available, what to bring in the way of clothing, what sort of meals to expect (vegetarians may have a hard time on many ranches), if there are additional charges, what the living accommodations are like, and how many other guests are likely to be there at the same time. Note that it is considered proper to tip the ranchhands, kitchen help, and others who work so hard to keep the ranch running. For many of them, this is a way to fund their college education.

Camping

Wyoming has dozens of public campsites scattered across the state, primarily on Forest Service and Park Service lands. Most of these have running water, garbage pickup, and outhouses, but no showers. The fee is generally $5-7 per night, and most are open from early June to mid-September. It's generally legal to camp for free on undeveloped Forest Service or BLM land throughout the state, but check at local offices for specifics. Every town of any size has at least one private RV park and

Horseback riding is a popular activity at many Wyoming dude ranches.

so-called campground. Most of these are little more than a vacant lot with shower and toilet facilities. These private campgrounds generally charge $2-4 for showers if you're not camping there. A better deal in many towns is to use the shower in the local public swimming pool, where you get a free swim thrown in for the entrance charge.

FOOD AND DRINK

Wyoming is not a state known for its haute cuisine. This is cattle country, the land of the free and the home on the range, where juicy steaks and the finest prime rib can be found in every podunk town in the state. (The two best steakhouses may well be in the don't-blink-or-you'll-miss-it town of Hudson.) Or if you don't like that, try chicken-fried steak, the house specialty at every truckstop and greasy spoon in Wyoming. Wash it down with a beer, and then sit back for a big hunk of apple pie. For breakfast, it's pretty much standard all-American fare, accompanied by a dark brew that folks in these parts call coffee. Real cowboy coffee, made only over an open smoky fire and not available within 20 miles of any town, is a potent medicine, not advised for children and the weak-kneed. Check local outfitters for the prescription.

Unfortunately, in Wyoming—like the rest of the nation—the real dining-out kings are McDonald's, Wendy's, Domino's, Dairy Queen, and all the other fast food outlets that are turning regional differences into a bland mediocrity of frozen burgers and whipped-shortening "milkshakes." For Mexican fare, most folks head to the appropriately named Taco John's, a Wyoming chain that will hopefully never be unleashed on the rest of America.

Actually, Wyoming food is not quite as uniformly bland as might be imagined, and travelers will discover several innovative and surprisingly reasonable restaurants in Laramie, Jackson, and Cody, fine Mexican eateries in Rawlins and Cheyenne, authentic Chinese food in Cheyenne, a soul-food restaurant in Rock Springs, and nouvelle cuisine restaurants scattered around the state. The most creative (and pricy) food can probably be found in the tourist town of Jackson.

On The Town

In many Wyoming towns, drinking and carousing hold as much interest as eating, especially on Friday and Saturday nights. Every burg of any size has its resident country-western band, and saloon dance floors fill up with duded-up cowboys and cowgirls out for a night on the town. Many of these bands also play Eagles-style rock tunes for variety. The larger cities and tourist towns have several nightclubs, some with disc jockeys, others with basic rock and roll fare. Don't expect a steep cover charge to get in the door—most places are free.

"Astronomical eclipses are of infrequent occurrence, but there is an eclipse taking place on Eddy Street daily and nightly. It is Professor McDaniel's Museum, which eclipses every other place of amusement in Cheyenne. The more money you invest with the Professor the greater equivalent you receive. Call upon him, imbibe one of those Tom and Jerrys, etc., and if not satisfied we pronounce you incorrigible. 'Ye Gods!' What nectar the Professor concocts in those little china mugs. Better than the dew on a damsel's lips. Speaking of damsels just step into the museum and you'll see 'em large as life, besides 1,001 other sciences, embracing every known subject. It is an awe-inspiring view."

—ad for McDaniel's Theater and Museum in the 1860s, quoted in The Magic City of the Plains: Cheyenne 1867-1967

EVENTS AND ACTIVITIES

During the summer months, every town in Wyoming has its own main event, generally centered around a morning parade, an afternoon rodeo, and an evening of country music and dancing. Rodeos are the definitive Wyoming activity, reflecting an enduring nostalgia for cattle and cowboys. During the summer, daily rodeos can be found in Cody and Jackson, and weekly rodeos in Laramie and Ten Sleep. Wyoming's biggest event is the famed **Cheyenne Frontier Days**, a 10-day bash that fills every hotel for a hundred miles and makes Cheyenne streets look like a miniature Los Angeles. It starts the last full week of July each year. Don't miss this one! The **Cody Stampede** (early July) is another very popular rodeo, parade, and all-round chance to party. For a complete calendar of Wyoming events, contact the Wyoming Travel Commission, I-25 at College Dr., Cheyenne, WY 82002, tel. 777-7777 or (800) 225-5996.

MODERN-DAY RENDEZVOUS

In recent years the mountain men rendezvous has become a major summertime attraction in Wyoming. The biggest and best rendezvous are held on Labor Day weekend at Fort Bridger and in early July in Pinedale. Also of note are those in Lander (early June), Riverton (early July), and Jackson (mid-July). These are rather strange affairs, attracting both tourists and locals to gawk at guys in buckskin pants or breechcloths and women in tanned leather skirts. Unlike the original rendezvous, you won't see many Indians at these get-togethers. The participants are a mixture of Joe Blow businessman who likes a little diversion, Wendy Waitress who dreams of simpler times, and a lot of folks who look like they're either former/current hippies or bikers and who find this a great way to live the simple life in a semi-legitimate way. More long hair, beards, braless women, and barefoot kids than you've seen in two decades.

Participants live in tepees, compete in black-powder contests, bake bread over fires, race horses bareback, and mug for the clicking cameras of tourists. Lots of beef jerky, Indian tacos, and fry bread for sale. This isn't a good place for the animal rights crowd, since many of the trade items at the modern rendezvous (as at the original ones) are from wild animals. Most of the people who attend a rendezvous have something to offer: old beads, leather clothing, tomahawks, knives, moccasins, woven crafts, tanned hides, and lots of fox, coyote, rabbit, ermine, and other furs.

Events at a rendezvous include black-powder shooting contests, storytelling, fiddle music, dancing, hide-tanning demonstrations, tomahawk and knife throwing, and foot races for the kids. In the evening when all the gawkers head back to their air-conditioned motel rooms, the rendezvous really comes to life with big campfires, storytelling, carousing, drinking, and a raucous good time for all. But woe be the one who shows up after dark in modern-day civilian clothes!

RODEO

It may come as a revelation to many people, but rodeo is one of the most popular sports in America; more people watch professional rodeos than attend NFL football games. In Wyoming—a state where even the license plate is graced with a cowboy astride a bucking bronc—it should come as no surprise that rodeo is king. Every small town in the state has a rodeo of some sort during the summer, and the larger cities have world-class rodeos attracting hundreds of riders and ropers from the Professional Rodeo Cowboys Association (PRCA). (By the way, in Wyoming, rodeo is always pronounced ROW-dee-oh.)

History

Although rodeo seems to have a few drops of Spanish bullfight in its blood, and many of the words—rodeo, bronco, lariat, arena, and honda—have Spanish origins, its true origins were in the days of cowboys and cattle in the Wild West. Gradually, groups of cowboys got together to show off their riding and roping skills and to compete with neighboring outfits. Everyone argues over the official origins of rodeo, but credit is generally given to a bucking and roping competition between the Mill Iron and Hash Knife outfits who met near Deer Trail, Colorado in 1869.

As the West began to become fenced in, the cowboy events moved into the nearby towns as organized "buckin' shows." Buffalo Bill Cody probably had more to do with popularizing the sport than any other person. For many years his Wild West Show traveled the world, providing a spectacle that included several of the events in present-day rodeos. Lander lays claim to the oldest rodeo in Wyoming. Begun in 1893, the Lander Pioneer Days rodeo still comes around each July. By far, the most famous Wyoming rodeo is the "Daddy of 'em All," Cheyenne Frontier Days, one of the top four rodeos in the world.

Over the years, rodeo has become more professional and less connected to the true cowboy. Many participants today come from cities and have never spent time herding cattle or working on a ranch—some of the finest have come from Harlem and the Bronx. Of course, many other cowboys still come from more traditional farming and ranching backgrounds, though they may work part-time at the local grocery store to fund their travels around the rodeo circuit. When they get enough money, they attend a week-long rodeo school, picking up pointers from past champions.

Those who make it to the top, do so the hard way. Grand National winners are decided on the basis of rodeo earnings, meaning that they must compete almost continuously, flying from one rodeo to another, staying in cheap motels, or living out of their RVs. Semi-pros and amateurs compete in the hundreds of smaller rodeos that dot Wyoming and the West, hoping to make it to the professional level. Most don't even come close, losing their stiff entry fees to more experienced competitors and taking home only bruises or broken bones.

Rodeo Today

The major rodeo events generally fall into two categories, riding and roping. Riding events include saddle bronc riding, bareback bronc riding, and bull riding, while roping events include steer wrestling, calf roping, and steer roping. Women's barrel racing, clown bullfighting, and chuck-wagon races complete the roundup. In most of the events, luck has much to do with who wins. Much of the scoring is based on the difficulty of the ride (the toughest broncs or bulls are favorites because they mean higher scores), and times for ropers are dependent upon the speed and behavior of the calf or steer they are trying to tackle.

Many rodeo riders are young, skinny-as-a-rail types, while ropers tend to be bulkier and older. The two groups don't mix much and generally have disparaging words to say about the "skinny cowboys on their rocking horses" or "those fat bulldoggers with no style and no skill." But behind this bluster, lies respect, especially for competitors in a cowboy's own events. Hang around the chutes awhile, and you'll discover a surprising generosity to fellow riders and ropers as they warn what to expect from a given bronc, help cinch down the straps, and joke over the new shiner from the horseshoe firmly planted in the bareback rider's face. And they party together late into the night, looking for the rodeo queens and the girls who like the smell of horse sweat. Small time winners often spread the loot back among the losers, buying drinks and renting a motel room where everyone can sneak in for a night's rest. Writer Fred Schnell, in *Rodeo! The Suicide Sport,* described a story that seems to epitomize rodeo life:

> *Once, when rodeo announcer Mel Lambert explained to the audience that a champion who had just made a good ride neither drank nor smoked and was a college athlete, Jim Shoulders, who has won 16 world titles, turned to a friend behind the chutes and said disgustedly, 'Isn't that the worst crap you've ever heard? What the hell is rodeo coming to?'*

One thing newcomers soon notice about rodeo cowboys is the clothes they wear—long sleeve shirts, cowboy hats, Wrangler jeans (never Levis—the seam is in the wrong place for riding), and cowboy boots. As writer Mary S. Robertson suggested, "In no other sport but rodeo do the players and the spectators dress alike." Interestingly, the PRCA actually has a rule requiring long sleeve shirts and cowboy hats; apparently at one time too many riders and ropers were wearing baseball caps and T-shirts, so the more traditional attire was made mandatory. And of course, there is one additional piece of attire worn by rodeo cowboys, the plate-sized silver and gold belt buckles. Top winners get these as awards for surviving a season of abuse; others buy them for flash and dash.

The Suicide Sport

A title occasionally used for rodeo is "the suicide sport." It is, unfortunately all too true. Accidents are very common and rodeos always have an EMT ready to tend the inevitable smashed legs, kicked-in ribs, and broken collar bones. Many cowboys are crippled for life and at least several die each year in the sport, including two at Cheyenne Frontier Days in the 1980s. Even the nation's top riders and ropers can be killed. Most dangerous of all are the bull rides, but just watching a "dogger" leaping off his horse onto the horns of a speeding steer can give the crowd pause. Rodeos are criticized by animal rights activists as unnecessary cruelty to animals—steers occasionally die from broken necks and broncs sometimes injure themselves (and their riders) by trying to jump out of the chutes—but the cowboys really do all they can to prevent injury to the animals they ride or rope.

Steer Wrestling

Steer wrestling, or bulldogging, involves leaping from a quarter horse onto the back of a 700-pound Mexican steer running at 25 miles an hour, grabbing his horns and wrestling him to the ground. If you think that sounds easy, try it some time! Steer wrestling originated in 1903 when Bill Pickett, a black Texas cowboy (many early cowboys were black), jumped on the back of an ornery steer, grabbed its horns, bent over its head and bit the steer's lower lip like an attacking bulldog. Soon he was repeating the stunt for the 101 Ranch Wild West Show. Others copied this feat, and though the lip-biting part has long-since disappeared, the name bulldogging has stuck.

Steer wrestling is a complex endeavor involving two men: a dogger and a hazer. When the steer hurtles into the arena, the two spur their horses in quick pursuit, with the hazer trying to force the steer to run straight ahead while the dogger gets into position to leap onto the steer's horns, wrestling him to the ground with his feet and head facing the same direction.

Since they are competing with other doggers on time, every second counts. Good doggers can get a steer down in less than seven seconds.

Calf Roping

Calf roping originated in the Old West when ropers would pull down a calf and quickly tie it up for branding. Today, this is the most competitive of all rodeo events, and there is often big money for the winners. Calf ropers chase a 200-350-pound calf on their expertly trained horses, roping it and then quickly throwing it on its side. After a quick wrap of the piggin' string around three ankles, followed by a half-hitch knot ("hooey"), the calf is allowed to try to break free. If it can't within six seconds, the time stands and an untie man rides in to free the calf. Time is of the essence in calf roping, and the most valuable asset for a roper is his horse. The best horses are in high demand, and are often rented to other riders for a cut of any winnings.

Steer Roping

The most controversial of all rodeo contests is steer roping, an event that has been banned from most rodeos because it is so hard on the animals. Cheyenne Frontier Days is one place it is still done. The procedure is essentially the same as calf roping, but with a much larger animal. When the 700-pound steer is jerked back by the rope and then thrown down with a thud, you can almost feel the impact. Fortunately, injuries to the tough old steers are uncommon.

Saddle Bronc Riding

When you say the word rodeo, many people immediately think of saddle bronc riding. The oldest of all rodeo sports, it originated from cowboys' attempts to train wild horses. Rodeo saddle bronc riding is more complex than this, however, requiring a special "association" saddle, dulled spurs, and very precise rules. It is a judged event, with points taken away for not being in the correct position or in control. Broncs are saddled-up in the chutes (fenced-in enclosures along the edge of the arena) and riders climb on, grabbing a thick hemp rope in one hand and sinking their boots into the stirrups. When the gate opens the bronc goes wild, trying to throw the rider off. The smooth back and forth motion of a good saddle bronc rider makes it appear that he is atop a rocking chair. Rides only last eight seconds (leading to lots of ribald cowboy jokes); when the horn sounds, a pickup man rides alongside the bronc and the rider slides onto the other horse.

Bareback Bronc Riding
Bareback riding is a relatively recent sport, arriving on the scene in the 1920s. The rules are similar to saddle bronc riding, but the cowboy rides with only a minimum of equipment—no stirrups and no reins. A small leather rigging held on by a leather strap around the horse is topped with a suitcase-like handle. A second wool-lined strap goes around the flank of the horse to act as an irritant so that they buck more. The cowboy holds on with one hand and bounces back and forth in a rocking motion, an effort akin to trying to juggle bowling pins while surfing a big wave. Eight seconds later it's over and a pickup man comes in to rescue the rider (if he hasn't been thrown to the ground).

Bull Riding And Rodeo Clowns
Bull riding is in a class of danger all its own. Unlike broncs who just want that man off their back, bulls want to get even. When a bull rider is thrown off (and this is most of the time, even with the best riders), the bull immediately goes on the attack, trying to gore or trample him. Many bull riders are seriously injured and some die when hit by this 2,000 pounds of brute force. There are no saddles in bull riding, just a piece of thick rope wrapped around the bull's chest with the free end wrapped tightly around the bull rider's hand. A cowbell hangs at the bottom of this contraption to annoy the bull even more. When the chute opens, all hell breaks loose as the bull does everything it possibly can to throw his rider off—spinning, kicking, jumping, and running against the fence.

If the rider hangs on for the required eight seconds (style isn't very important), the next battle begins, getting out of the way of one very angry bull. Here the **rodeo clown** comes in. Dressed in bright red and white shirts and baggy pants, they look like human Raggedy Andy dolls. In reality they are moving targets. Clowns use every trick in the book—climbing into padded barrels that the bulls butt against, weaving across the arena, mocking the bulls with matador capes, and simply running for their lives to

reach the fence ahead of the bull. Frequently, two clowns work in tandem to create confusion, one acting as the barrel man, and the other as a roving target. Rodeo clowns also play another role, that of entertainer between events. Their stock of supplies includes rubber chickens, trick mules, a series of pantomimed jokes with the announcers, and anything else that might keep folks from getting restless.

Other Events
One of the funniest of all rodeo events is the **wild horse race**, a zany event that since 1897 has always ended each day's events at Cheyenne Frontier Days. Twelve teams of three cowboys try to rope, saddle, and then race a collection of the wildest horses imaginable. If they manage to get on the broncs, their next problem is convincing the horse to run around the half-mile track in the right direction. It seems the definition of bedlam, with horses that break loose and start off in opposite directions, crashing into mounted riders and other horses. For sheer chaos, wild horse races would even put a Democratic Convention to shame!

Another crowd favorite at Frontier Days is the **chuckwagon race**, a Canadian invention with mostly Canadian teams. It is a confusing, fast-paced, chaotic, noisy, and dusty sport that involves four wagons, each pulled by four horses. Each team also has two "outriders," boys on horseback. At the sound of the starting gun, an outrider throws a 50-pound "cookstove" into the back of the chuckwagon and climbs back on his horse to chase the wagons. Then everyone takes off on a tight figure-eight course

TODD CLARK

around several barrels and then onto the half-mile circular track. The outriders ride in pursuit; they must cross the finish line near their chuckwagon. Needless to say, with four wagons pulled by 16 horses running at a full gallop, and another eight horses running alongside, the race is both exciting and dangerous. When the wagons come around the last corner, everyone in the stands is on their feet, yelling and cheering.

Barrel racing—one of the only female-dominated events—is found at nearly every rodeo, and consists of a triangular course of three barrels arranged a hundred feet apart. The event requires riding a fast horse in a set pattern around these barrels, trying not to knock any over. The fastest time wins. Some rodeos also have what is called the **calf scramble** (featuring dozens of children from the stands chasing a calf to get the ribbon off its tail) and the **colt race** where young colts are let loose in a race toward their mares. Both are real crowd pleasers.

INFORMATION AND SERVICES

Events and specific chamber of commerce information are listed for each town described in this book. There are large **state information centers** in Cheyenne, Evanston, Jackson, Laramie, Pine Bluffs, Sheridan, and Sundance. For a helpful overall guide to Wyoming, along with a listing of events, chamber of commerce offices, plus lodging and camping places, request a copy of the free *Wyoming Vacation Guide* from the Wyoming Travel Commission, I-25 at College Dr., Cheyenne, WY 82002, tel. 777-7777 or (800) 225-5996. For a complete listing of more than 225 **museums and galleries**, con-

tact the Wyoming Arts Council, 2320 Capitol Ave., Cheyenne, WY 82002, tel. 777-7742. The finest large museum—Cody's Buffalo Bill Historical Center—should not be missed, but a visit to the smaller and less-known museums is also well worth your time. Some of the best are found in Buffalo, Casper, Cheyenne, Douglas, Fort Laramie, Grand Teton National Park, Jackson, Lusk, South Pass City, and Thermopolis. The **area code** for Wyoming is 307. Throughout this book, summer is defined as Memorial Day to Labor Day, except when otherwise noted.

TRANSPORTATION

By Air
Commercial airline service to Wyoming is limited to the towns of Casper, Cheyenne, Cody, Gillette, Jackson, Laramie, Riverton, Rock Springs, Sheridan, and Worland. Four major airlines serve the state—United, Continental, Delta, and American—but most connections are via Denver or Salt Lake, even if you want to fly from one part of Wyoming to another. Deregulation at work!

By Land
Given the expansiveness of Wyoming and the small population, it comes as no surprise that the primary means of transportation in the state is the automobile, or in rural areas, the pickup truck. Greyhound covers the southern end of Wyoming along I-80, with Powder River Transportation, tel. (800) 442-3682, focusing on the rest of the state. Because fewer passengers

were being fed to Powder River by Greyhound's cross-country service, Powder River was forced to scale back, leaving some communities without bus service. Note: If you're planning to travel by Greyhound, and are coming from out-of-state, get an Ameripass, available only in New York, Miami, Los Angeles, or San Francisco. International travelers can knock approximately $100 off Ameripass rates by showing their passports.

In 1991 **AMTRAK** reinstated daily passenger train service across southern Wyoming following an eight-year hiatus. The Pioneer Line now connects Seattle and Chicago, with Wyoming stops in Evanston, Green River, Rock Springs, Rawlins, Laramie, and Cheyenne. For price and scheduling information, call AMTRAK at (800) 872-7245. This is an excellent way to reach Wyoming, and will almost certainly lead to the revitalization of the state's wonderful old train depots. Cars can be rented at all the larger towns, and those with airports generally have the national chains (Hertz, Avis, etc.). Because of Wyoming's small population and long distances, cyclists will find uncrowded roads to ride. The long distances between towns, windy conditions, and frequent summer thunderstorms add to the adventure. Many thousands of miles of gravel and dirt roads provide excellent places to explore on mountain bikes. Get the excellent BLM area maps (available at most BLM offices) before heading out. Off the Deep End Travels, tel. (800) 223-6833, has guided cycling tours of Wyoming.

Winter Travel

During the winter, Wyoming travelers need to take special precautions. Snow tires are a necessity, but you should also keep a number of emergency supplies, including tire chains, a shovel and small bag of sand in case you get stuck, first aid kit, booster cables, flares, flashlight, dehydrated food, water, ice scraper, and sleeping bag. Call the Wyoming Highway Department at one of the following 800 numbers for road and travel conditions in various parts of Wyoming: 442-7850 (western), 442-2535 (north-central), 442-2555 (northeast), 442-2565 (east-central), and 442-8321 (southeast).

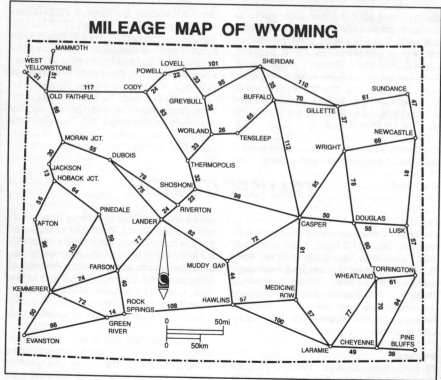

MILEAGE MAP OF WYOMING

CATHY CARLSON

SOUTHEAST WYOMING

Southeast Wyoming is farming and ranching country, part of the vast prairie region that drapes America's heartland. In many ways, it is indistinguishable from western Nebraska or eastern Colorado, one long continuum of grass, grain, and grazing. Folks drive big American cars and Ford pickups. Instead of the saddleries and oil companies elsewhere in Wyoming, you'll find farm equipment dealers and more feed caps than cowboy hats. They hold down better in the wind that seems never to stop blowing.

Buffalo roamed through southeast Wyoming for thousands of years, hunted by nomadic tribes of Plains Indians. Now sheep and cattle follow the same trails, and farmers grow wheat where Cheyenne Indian villages once stood. Alternating bands of wheat and fallow land give some areas a candy-striped appearance, while in others the expansive prairie extends in all directions. Old windmills, white farmhouses, hip-roofed barns, rusting retired farm machinery, and tall silos mark the old homesteads that became permanent farmsteads. The gravel roads cut straight across this gently rolling land, with sudden right-angled jags around the old home-

stead boundaries. Drive out on these roads and the pace slows to country speed. Folks raise a hand to wave as you pass, and stop to chat on the crest of a hill. Tune in the radio, and you're likely to hear country music, farm market reports, and Paul Harvey commentaries. This is Wyoming's most important agricultural region.

The capital city of Cheyenne dominates the economy of southeast Wyoming, one of only two real cities in the state (the other being Casper). The other major settlements—Wheatland, Torrington, and Lusk—are small agricultural focal points and governmental centers for their respective counties.

Southeast Wyoming experiences typical high-plains weather. It is hot and windy in the summer, cold and windy in the winter. The wind (averaging over 13 mph) is a given; great country for kites, but not much fun when the gales of winter slice through like a knife. Partly because of this wind, however, Cheyenne has some of the cleanest air in the nation. Explore the back roads, and you'll find busy cattle ranches, abandoned mining towns, remnants of many historic trails, archaeological sites, dinosaur bones, and old sod homesteads. Hiking through the gently undulating plains is a delightful experience, for vast expanses of this land remain almost un-

changed from the time when bison roamed the great grasslands of the West.

CHEYENNE

As you drive west toward Cheyenne (pop. 55,000), the Colorado Rockies loom like whitecaps on the southwestern horizon, apparitions in this land of barely rolling plains, snow fences, stunted grass, and the highway slashing toward the boundary of sight. You catch quick glimpses of the great mountain ranges that ramble across Wyoming, like tantalizing flashes like a burlesque show. Gradually they grow larger, and finally you know that the Great Plains will soon be left behind. It's easy to imagine how this must have looked to the railroad passengers who passed this way in the 1860s, watching the mountains loom on the horizon as they rolled into Wyoming. Suddenly you're shaken into the present by the highway sign, "Cheyenne Next 4 Exits." Suburban homes crowd over the gentle hillsides, and the state capitol gleams in the setting sun. You have arrived at Wyoming's political and transportation fulcrum.

The city of Cheyenne hunkers down in the southeastern corner of Wyoming, just 10 miles from Colorado and 40 miles from Nebraska. Cheyenne perpetually runs a horse race with arch rival Casper over who has the most people. Right now Cheyenne is in front. Its wide, tree-draped urban streets form a gridwork through downtown, while rampant suburbia spreads its tentacles over the surrounding prairie. Cheyenne is remarkably similar to another state capital— Lincoln, Nebraska, and for many visitors, it offers a taste of the West without leaving the Midwest. Folks in Casper or Cody view Cheyenne as the capital of eastern Wyoming, and as a city whose ties are really closer to the markets of Denver or Omaha than to the sagebrush, oil, and coal of Wyoming. People in Cheyenne brush aside these criticisms. They know everyone else is just jealous.

As the state capital, the largest city, home for a strategic military base, a center for various governmental agencies, and a major transportation hub, Cheyenne is a big fish in the small pond called Wyoming. The city has one of the most stable economies in the state. Its largest

employer (nearly 5,000 people) is giant Francis E. Warren Air Force Base, with several thousand other folks working for the federal, state, and local government agencies around town. Railroad tracks of the Union Pacific and Burlington Northern railroads head to the four points of the compass, and Cheyenne is right at the junction of two of the primary transportation routes across the Plains and Rockies: I-25 and I-80. Some 800 folks work for Union Pacific, with hundreds more employed in trucking, communications, and shipping firms.

HISTORY

Like so many other Wyoming cities, Cheyenne is a creation of the railroad. It is the oldest of Wyoming's railroad towns, established as the Union Pacific was racing westward in 1867. When Gen. Grenville M. Dodge was planning the new railroad's route, he decided to establish a major rail terminal in the plains just before the long climb over the Laramie Mountains. He named the new settlement Cheyenne, for the Indians who lived in this country. The word is from a Sioux Indian term Shey an nah, meaning "People of a Strange Tongue." (Some have suggested a less complimentary origin for the word, the French term chienne, meaning in genteel English "female dog.") While he was there, Indians attacked a Mormon grading crew, killing two men. The graveyard was started before the first building was up. By November of that year the new town of Cheyenne had swollen to 4,000 people, earning the nickname "Magic City of the Plains." It was easily the largest town in Wyoming, and has remained that way for nearly all the state's history.

At first Cheyenne consisted of the usual hell-on-wheels railroad settlement of tents and hastily erected buildings. Railroad workers and Army men from nearby Fort D.A. Russell turned the town into a rip-roaring place—at first, every second building was a saloon, and burlesque shows were the rage. At center stage stood a 36 by 100 foot tent housing Headquarters Saloon. Reporter James Chisholm noted:

"The wildest roughs from all parts of the country are congregated here, as one may see by glancing into the numerous dance-houses and gambling hells—men who carry on the trade of robbery openly, and would not scruple to kill a man for ten dollars."

Settling Down
Within a decade, however, Cheyenne had settled into a more urbane stage. The railroad provided access to the East, not only allowing cattle to be shipped, but also keeping the town abreast of the latest fashions and furnishings, and bringing news of world events. With the discovery of gold in the Black Hills, Cheyenne becoming the primary shipping center for supplies to the Black Hills and gold bullion from the smelters.

By the 1880s, Cheyenne had grown to a cosmopolitan small city of 14,000 people, and was declared the wealthiest city per capita in the world. It was one of the first cities in the West to have electric lights —a powerplant charged batteries during the day and then delivered them by wagon to the various establishments in time for the evening's use. In 1882, the elaborate Cheyenne Opera House opened with great fanfare. With seating for up to 1,000 people, luxurious furnishings, and a huge 52-light gas chandelier overhead, it was regarded as the equal of those in New York, and attracted such performers as Lily Langtry, Sarah Bernhardt,

P.T.Barnum, Buffalo Bill Cody, and the Royal Opera Company.

Rule Of The Cattle Barons
Destruction of the once-vast herds of bison and

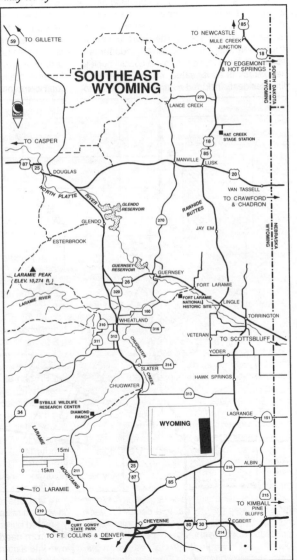

© MOON PUBLICATIONS, INC.

the decimation of Indians who had lived in Wyoming suddenly opened up nearly all the territory to cattle grazing. Cheyenne became the focal point for hundreds of cattlemen who rushed in to make a killing on the booming cattle market. (At the time, Laramie County extended all the way to the border with Montana, so it was logical that Cheyenne would be the center of ranching activity in the state.) The most famous of these men was Alexander Swan, founder of a spread so large that it required a special book to keep track of all its cattle brands. Other part-time residents included members of English no-

bility such as Moreton Frewen (nephew of Sir Winston Churchill) and Sir Oliver H. Wallop, seventh earl of Portsmouth.

Despite its edge-of-the-state location, Cheyenne was the logical place for Wyoming's territorial capitol. The railroad was here, along with Fort D.A. Russell and most of the wealthy cattlemen. In 1869, the first territorial governor, John A. Campbell, made it the temporary capital, with the Legislature meeting in rented quarters. Five years later it almost lost that title to Laramie in a rump session of the Legislature, but after completion of the capitol building in 1888,

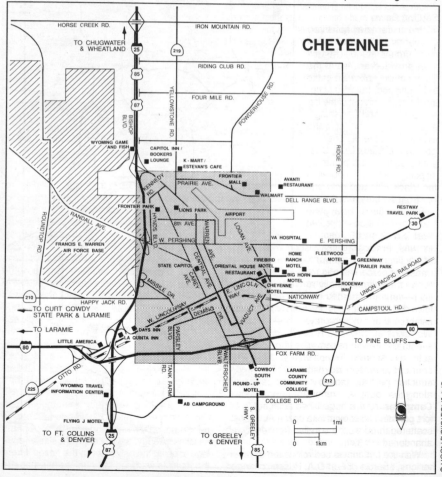

© MOON PUBLICATIONS, INC.

FRANCIS E. WARREN

One of Wyoming's best-known politicians was Francis E. Warren (1844-1929). A life-long Republican, Warren served as both a territorial and state governor before being elected to the U.S. Senate in 1890. A millionaire, his ranch once had more than 100,000 sheep. This land would later get him in trouble when he was charged with fencing public land for his own gain; his friendship with President Theodore Roosevelt helped keep him out of prison. While territorial governor in the 1880s, Warren was an ardent agitator for statehood. His 37 years in the U.S. Senate made him one of its most powerful members; newspapers labeled him the "Boss of Wyoming." With Warren's backing, Fort D.A. Russell always got more than its share of the pork barrel, and after his death, it was renamed in his honor. Cheyenne's old **Warren Mansion** at 222 E. 17th St. was once owned by Francis E. Warren. President Theodore Roosevelt stayed here as a guest of Warren, and its ornate interior features are still intact. The building was built in 1889 from stone rejected for use in the state Capitol building. Over the years the stone began to deteriorate and the outside walls had to be covered with stucco.

WYOMING STATE MUSEUM

it became obvious that the governmental seat would remain in Cheyenne.

Fort D.A. Russell

In 1862, President Lincoln approved creation of a military fort to guard the then-proposed transcontinental railroad from Indian attacks. When the railroad finally arrived—five years later—the Army established a fort near the new town of Cheyenne. (Both the town and fort were established on the same day.) Named for a Civil War general, David A. Russell, the new fort eventually grew to become the largest cavalry outpost in America. Troops from the base were sent out to protect railroad survey and construction parties, and later served as guards along the route. An important supply depot, **Camp Carlin**, was established adjacent to the fort, providing equipment for a dozen Army posts scattered throughout the Indian frontier. It was abandoned in 1890.

With the Indians' forced relocation to reservations, the role of Fort D.A. Russell changed into a training center and strategic garrison for the Rockies. New brick barracks and officers' quarters were completed in 1885, and the dusty parade ground was planted with grass and trees. Wyoming's Senator Francis E. Warren had long "brought home the bacon" by gaining all sorts of political plums for his constituents, one of the biggest being continued support for the fort in Cheyenne. After his death in 1929, the fort was renamed in his honor. The base served as a training center and POW camp in WW II, and was transferred to the newly created Air Force in 1947.

The old fort's current role, a Strategic Air Command base, began in 1958 when the arrival of Atlas missiles made Warren the nation's first nuclear missile base. The event was greeted with glee by Cheyenne's then-mayor Worth Story, who exclaimed, "Cheyenne is proud to be the nation's number one target for enemy missiles." Today, the city enjoys a similar privilege at being the only place in the nation where the multiple-warhead MX nuclear missiles are based. Cheyenne even has a Missile Drive. Warren Air Force Base controls 150 Minuteman III and Midgetman missiles, plus all 50 MX missiles in existence, making it one of the most important intercontinental ballistic missile (ICBM) centers in America. The missiles themselves are dispersed over a 150-mile radius in Wyoming, Nebraska, and Colorado, creating an attractive bullseye target centered on Cheyenne. The military owns land in other parts of Wyoming today (notably the Camp Guernsey training area north of Wheatland and a Naval Petroleum Reserve at Teapot Dome), but Warren AFB is the state's only major military installation.

SIGHTS

State Capitol
Capitol Avenue—one of the primary streets in Cheyenne—seems to symbolize the city's history. State government buildings line the street, and at either end are the two main reasons for Cheyenne's existence: the Union Pacific depot to the south, and the State Capitol to the north. The Capitol is open Mon.-Fri. 8:30-5 and Sat. 9-5 (closed on Sat. in winter). Visitors can watch a short slide show about the building or go on a guided tour during the summer. There is no charge. Call 777-7220 for more info.

Wyoming's Capitol building falls in the tradition of ostentatious political structures, and is modelled after the Capitol in Washington, D.C. The initial structure was authorized by a $150,000 appropriation from the territorial Legislature in 1886. The cornerstone was laid on May 18, 1887, and the central portion was completed the following year. Later additions were the two wings. When completed in 1917, the building measured its present 300 feet in length. The 146-foot-tall dome has been reguilded with gold four times, most recently in 1986. Don't bother trying to climb up to steal any; the entire dome is covered with less than an ounce of gold. The Capitol was completely renovated between 1974 and 1980 at a cost of $7 million.

The Capitol's central rotunda has a checkered marble floor with cherrywood staircases leading to the second floor. Directly overhead is a beautiful blue stained-glass window imported from England. The senate chambers are in the west wing, with the house meeting in the east wing. You can view the Legislature from the third-floor balconies when it is in session. Inside the legislative chambers are four Western murals painted by Allen T. True (designer of Wyoming's bucking bronco symbol), along with others by Joseph Henry Sharp and Bill Gollings. Look upward in each chamber to see the large Tiffany stained-glass ceilings with the state seal.

From the outside, the Capitol dome seems strangely tall; rumor has it that architects once voted it the nation's ugliest state capitol. Out front is a bronze statue of **Esther Hobart Morris**, the person incorrectly credited with making Wyoming the first state to grant women the right to vote. Directly behind the Capitol building is the sparkling new **Herschler Building**, named for the only Wyoming governor to serve three terms, Ed Herschler. It has an attractive interior atrium and houses the offices of various state agencies. In between the two buildings is an 18-foot-tall, 4,500-pound bronze statue by Edward Fraughton, *Spirit of Wyoming*. In it, a bucking horse and rider seem almost suspended in space. It is perhaps fitting that the two mottos of Wyoming—the Equality State and the Cowboy State—are symbolized by statues on either side of the State Capitol. Wander around the grounds and you'll discover a monument to the Spanish American War, a bison, and a copy of Philadelphia's Liberty Bell.

Historic Governors' Mansion
Located at 300 E. 21st St., tel. 777-7878, the old governors' mansion is open Tues.-Fri. 8-5 year-round, plus Sat. 9-5 during the summer. There is no charge. A video provides information about its inhabitants, including the nation's first woman governor, Nellie Tayloe Ross, who lived here from 1925 to 1927. The two-story brick building was completed in 1905 at a cost of $33,000, and is in the Georgian style with four concrete columns out front. Inside are furnishings from a variety of periods. (The current governors' mansion was completed in 1976 near the intersection of Central Ave. and I-25.)

Wyoming State Museum
The free Wyoming State Museum is in the Barrett State Office Building at 24th and Central, tel. 777-7022, and is open Mon.-Fri. 8-5, and Sat. 9-5, plus Sun. 1-5 during the summer. It is not large, but does have a number of good dis-

DOWNTOWN CHEYENNE

Map labels:

GOVERNOR'S MANSION (NEW)
MUNICIPAL GOLF COURSE
PRAIRIE AVE.
POWDERHOUSE RD.
FRONTIER MALL
DELL RANGE BLVD.
25
85
87
KENNEDY RD.
YELLOWSTONE RD.
CENTRAL AVE.
SWIMMING POOL
FRONTIER DAYS OLD WEST MUSEUM
SLOANS LAKE
LIONS PARK
FRONTIER PARK
BOTANIC GARDENS
8th AVE.
AIRPORT
7th AVE.
OWL INN
6th AVE.
5th AVE.
4th AVE.
3rd AVE.
HYNDS BLVD.
MCCOMB AVE.
CRIBBON AVE.
PIONEER
CAREY
CAPITOL
CENTRAL
2nd AVE.
1st AVE.
W. PERSHING
E. PERSHING
FIRST DAY COVER MUSEUM
THOME AVE.
CAREY AVE.
CAPITOL AVE.
LIBRARY
VAN LENNEN
SEYMOUR AVE.
MAXWELL AVE.
PEBRICAN AVE.
RUSSELL AVE.
MORRIE AVE.
BRADLEY AVE.
DUFF AVE.
ALEXANDER AVE.
RANDALL AVE.
HOSPITAL
30th ST.
29th ST.
28th ST.
27th ST.
26th ST.
25th ST.
24th ST.
23rd ST.
22nd ST.
21st ST.
20th ST.
DILLON AVE.
SNYDER AVE.
REED AVE.
BENT AVE.
O'NEIL AVE.
EVANS AVE.
HOUSE AVE.
STATE CAPITOL
STATE MUSEUM
HISTORIC GOVERNORS' MANSION
19th ST.
18th ST.
17th ST.
HOLLIDAY PARK
80
30
E. LINCOLN WAY
POST OFFICE
ST. MARK'S EPISCOPAL CHURCH
FIRST UNITED METHODIST CHURCH
CIVIC CENTER
TWIN DRAGON RESTAURANT
WHIPPLE HOUSE RESTAURANT
WARREN MANSION
EMANUEL'S
PLAINS HOTEL
CHAMBER OF COMMERCE
BUS DEPOT
UNION PACIFIC RAILROAD YARD
UNION PACIFIC DEPOT
MISSILE DR.
HAPPY JACK RD.
DEY AVE.
AMES AVE.
W. LINCOLNWAY
WESTLAND RD.
SANDS MOTEL
GUEST RANCH MOTEL
FRONTIER MOTEL
UNION PACIFIC RAILROAD
10th ST.
9th ST.
8th ST.
7th ST.
6th ST.
5th ST.
4th ST.
3rd ST.
2nd ST.
1st ST.
ATLAS MOTEL
LUXURY DINER
DEMING DR.
LUXURY 8 MOTEL
STAGE COACH MOTEL
HITCHING POST INN
MOTEL 6
SUPER 8 MOTEL
LOS AMIGOS
STANFIELD AVE.
0   0.5mi
0   0.5km
MOON
LARIAT MOTEL
HOLIDAY INN
80
85
FOX FARM RD.

© MOON PUBLICATIONS, INC.

plays on the Plains Indians, sheepherding, cattle ranching, and rustling. Also here are an art gallery with changing displays and a gift shop containing books and crafts from Wyoming.

Frontier Days Old West Museum
Located right next to the rodeo grounds in Frontier Park, this is one of the nicest museums in Wyoming. It's open Sun. 10-6 and Mon.-Sat. 8-7 June-Sept., and Mon.-Fri. 9-5 and Sat.-Sun. 11:30-4:30 the rest of the year. During Frontier Days the doors are open daily 8 a.m. to 9 p.m. Admission is $2 for adults, $1 for seniors, $5 for families, and kids under 12 free. The museum's primary focus is on horse-drawn transportation. Inside the main room is a marvelous collection of 35 different carriages, many of which appear in the annual Frontier Days parades. The collection includes everything from a buckboard (the name came from the lack of springs on the axles) to an 1860s overland stage and a Yellowstone coach. The helpful museum brochure ($1) describes each coach in detail. A small room in the museum houses memorabilia from Cheyenne Frontier Days, and includes an eight-minute video of rodeo action. Other rooms have Indian clothing and headdresses, railroad items (including a wonderful stained-glass window), and a variety of Old West paraphernalia, such as saddles and drugstore items. The gift shop sells various Frontier Days souvenirs, while a small art gallery displays Western paintings.

Botanic Garden
One of Cheyenne's lesser-known attractions is the fine city-run Botanic Garden in Lions Park, tel. 637-6458. Hours are Mon.-Fri. 9-3:30, Sat. and Sun. 11-3:30; no charge. The botanic gardens provides training and garden vegetables for troubled kids, handicapped people, and seniors. Visitors find it a pleasant place to relax, especially during the winter when the warmth and the showy flowers are a delightful surprise. Inside the passively solar-heated greenhouse (look for the black metal drums filled with water) are three sections containing everything from vegetables to cacti. The central portion of the greenhouse has tall banana plants and tropical flowers, and a pond contains Koi goldfish and turtles. A small library has various gardening magazines and books.

F.E. Warren Air Force Base
For something different, try a visit to Wyoming's primary military base. The entrance to Warren Air Force Base is flanked by three missiles, but the buildings are actually quaint, with hundreds of two- and three-story brick buildings set back from the tree-lined streets. Expansive green lawns give it a country club feeling. This is essentially a self-supporting city, with childcare facilities, schools, stores, a veterinary clinic, and of course, that old neighborhood standby, nuclear warheads. During Frontier Days, jets take off constantly from the airport, suddenly screaming overhead in a sharp climb that brings gasps from the crowd. A small **Base Museum**, tel. 775-1110, is open to the public Wed.-Sat. 1-4 during the summer. Tours are available on Thurs. at 7:30 a.m. Call 775-3381 for details. You'll need to stop at the gate for permission to enter.

Whipple House
Located at 300 E. 17th St., tel. 638-1883, this wonderful Victorian home was built in 1883 by Ithamar C. Whipple, a wealthy merchant, cattleman, mayor, and state legislator. The home was later occupied by attorney and one-time Wyoming Territorial Supreme Court Justice John W. Lacey. Lacey defended both the notorious outlaw Tom Horn and the equally infamous oilman Harry Sinclair. Lots more interesting history in this old home; it was even the site of an exorcism to remove a bothersome ghost! The building is now on the National Register of Historic Places and is run as a gourmet restaurant.

First Day Cover Museum
Stamp collectors will enjoy a visit to the free First Day Cover Museum, 702 Randall Blvd., tel. 634-5911. The museum is open Mon.-Sat. 9-5, and houses First Day Covers worth close to $1 million, including Great Britain's 1840 Penny Black and many others. (First Day Covers are released only on the first day of issue for new stamps and are postmarked at just one location.) Pretty obscure stuff, but interesting if you are into philately.

Historic Churches

Cheyenne has several of Wyoming's most ostentatious and interesting churches. **St. Mark's Episcopal Church**, 1908 Central Ave., tel. 634-7709, is the oldest, begun in 1886, but not completed until 1893. It has an exterior of red lava stones with traditional stained-glass windows, including one by Tiffany. This was the home church for many of the transplanted British and Scottish cattle barons, so it is fitting that the funeral for the notorious hired gunman Tom Horn (who worked for some of them) was held here in 1903. Two other impressive churches are **St. Mary's Catholic Cathedral**, 2107 Capitol Ave., tel. 635-9261, built in 1907 of native standstone in the Gothic Revival style, and the **First United Methodist Church**, 18th and Central avenues, tel. 632-1410, also made from sandstone, and completed in 1894. The previous Methodist church on the same site was where marshal, gunman, and gambler, Wild Bill Hickok, married a circus performer, Agnes Lake Thatcher in 1876. The officiating clergyman wrote in the registry, "Don't think they meant it." Just five months later Wild Bill was shot in the back in a Deadwood saloon.

Railroad Paraphernalia

The railroad business reached its peak in the 1940s, when Cheyenne had the finest equipment and service anywhere in America. Despite a slow decline in subsequent years, and the ending of Amtrak service in 1983, the railroad is still an important part of Cheyenne's economy, with freight trains rumbling through town day and night. Drop by the gorgeous old **Union Pacific Railroad depot** at the south end of Capitol Ave. to see one of the finest remaining depots in the West. Built of red and gray sandstone in 1886, the structure was for a time the largest building in the territory, and the most elaborate depot between Omaha and San Francisco. (The depot was a reward to Governor Francis E. Warren for restoring order after the 1885 massacre of Chinese workers at the Union Pacific's vital Rock Springs coal mines.) It occupies an entire block, with the clock tower and Romanesque arched openings adding a sense of class. Holliday Park along E. 17th St. has a **Big Boy locomotive**, one of only 25 ever made and one of the largest steam locomotives ever built. It was used to haul freight over the mountain tracks between Cheyenne and Ogden, Utah. A couple of blocks east of here is a boxcar from the **French Merci Train**, given as a thank you for food Americans had given the French after World War II.

Wyoming Hereford Ranch

In 1883, cattle barons Alexander and Thomas Swan, backed by European investors, formed the Wyoming Hereford Association, placing 400 purebred Hereford bulls and cows on a ranch near Cheyenne. This was the first real attempt to bring quality cattle to the state, and was at one time the world's largest herd of thoroughbred cattle. Gradually other ranchers followed this lead, as the rangy longhorns of Texas were replaced by the more manageable Herefords (now the dominant breed in Wyoming). The 60,000-acre Wyoming Hereford Ranch has survived for more than a hundred years and has many historic structures. It is five miles east of Cheyenne on Campstool Road. Call 778-1401 for tours.

Other Sights

Cheyenne has quite a number of interesting old Victorian buildings. Stop by the chamber of commerce for a brochure ($1) that takes you on a **walking tour** of historic downtown. Of particular note are the Victorian homes of "Cattle Baron's Row" on 17th Street. Between mid-May and mid-Sept., the visitors bureau provides excellent **trolley tours** of Cheyenne. These 1 1/2-hour tours cost $5 ($2.50 for kids), and include visits to several historic buildings. Get tickets at the chamber of commerce on weekdays or the Wrangler Store, 1518 Capitol Ave., tel. 634-3048, on weekends. The **Wyoming Department of Game and Fish** at 5400 Bishop Blvd., tel. 777-7735, has a small museum with wildlife dioramas, an aquarium with trout, and wildlife photographs; open Mon.-Fri. 8-5 year-round and Sat.-Sun. 9-5 during the summer.

ACCOMMODATIONS

Motels

Choose from more than two dozen different lodging places in Cheyenne. Generally, space is not a problem, but when Frontier Days comes to town, motel rates often double or even triple, with motels and campgrounds booked up six months in advance. Even towns as far away as Torrington are affected, so be sure to plan well ahead during this time.

Cheyenne is fortunate in having one of Wyoming's only remaining historic lodging places, the **Plains Hotel**. Built in 1911, the hotel was completely refurbished in 1986. For many years this was the political center of Cheyenne, with politicians retiring to the bar to discuss whatever politicians discuss. Note the tile mosaic of Chief Little Shield in the sidewalk along Central Avenue.

Campgrounds
Cheyenne's closest public campgrounds ($4) are in **Curt Gowdy State Park**, 26 miles west on State 210, tel. 632-7946. There are also campsites ($5) within the scenic Pole Mountain area of Medicine Bow National Forest (see p. 101). **Greenway Trailer Park**, 3829 Greenway St., tel. 634-6696, has paved RV lots for $10 and showers for $2. Open year-round. **AB Camping**, 1503 W. College Dr., tel. 634-7035, charges $10 for tents and $12 for RVs; open all year. The most complete local camping facility is **Restway Travel Park**, 4212 Whitney Rd., tel. 634-3811, (800) 442-2854 (in Wyoming), or (800) 443-2751 (outside), which charges $12

CHEYENNE ACCOMMODATIONS

Name	Address	Phone	Rates	Features
Pioneer Hotel	209 W. 17th St.	634-3010	$14 s, $17 d	flophouse
Big Horn Motel	2004 E. Lincolnway	632-3122	$16 s or d	kitchenettes available, tawdry
Plains Hotel	1600 Central Ave.	638-3311 (800) 341-8000	$20 s, $25 d	airport shuttle, historic place
Round-Up Motel	403 S. Greeley Hwy.	634-7741	$21 s, $25 d	kitchenettes available
Frontier Motel	1400 W. Lincolnway	634-7961	$21 s, $30 d	
Lariat Motel	600 Central Ave.	635-8439	$24 s, $26 d	
Motel 6	1735 Westland Rd.	635-6806	$24 s, $30 d	pool
Cheyenne Motel	1601 E. Lincolnway	778-7664	$25 s, $29 d	kitchenettes available
Capitol Inn	5401 Walker Rd.	632-8901 (800) 876-8901	$25 s, $30 d	pool, airport shuttle
Atlas Motel	1524 W. Lincolnway	632-9214	$26 s or d	kitchenettes available
Sands Motel	1100 W. 16th St.	634-7771	$26 s, $30 d	
Fleetwood Motel	3800 E. Lincolnway	638-8908 (800) 634-7763	$27 s, $34 d	AAA approved, pool
Sapp Brothers Big C Motel	six miles east	778-8878	$27 s, $31 d	AAA approved
Home Ranch Motel	2414 E. Lincolnway	634-3575 (800) 999-7188	$28 s or d	AAA approved
Stage Coach Motel	1515 W. Lincolnway	634-4495	$29 s or d	AAA approved, kitchenettes available

*handwritten: Firebird   1905 E Lincolnway   307-632-5505 $25-33   Mobil *, NS*

*handwritten: mob.1 *, WS*

for tents and $14 for RVs. Showers for non-campers are $3; open all year. Restway offers shuttle-bus service ($3 RT) to Frontier Days and also has horseback rides, chuckwagon dinners, and other activities. Friendly folks.

FOOD

The city of Cheyenne offers a surprisingly diverse choice of eateries, from greasy spoons to gourmet continental cuisine. In addition to all the places listed below, Cheyenne is jammed with all the fast food chains, particularly along E. Lincolnway.

Breakfast And Lunch
One of the real treats in Cheyenne is the down-home **Lexie's**, 216 E. 17th St., tel. 638-8712. Great breakfasts and the best burgers in town. The place gets crowded with locals most days. **Driftwood Cafe**, 200 E. 18th St., tel. 634-5304, is also popular. The huge **Little America** coffeeshop, 2800 W. Lincolnway, tel. 634-2771, is open 24 hours a day, offering better than average truckstop food. The restaurant here has a fine Sunday brunch. Also open at all hours is **Sunrise Cafe** at the Capitol Inn, 5401 Walker Rd., tel. 632-9978. **Ruthies Sub Shoppe**, 1651 Carey Ave., tel. 635-4896, makes good sandwiches for lunch. For a taste of the East Coast,

CHEYENNE ACCOMMODATIONS (CONT.)

Name	Address	Phone	Rates	Features
Super 8 Motel	1900 W. Lincolnway	635-8741 (800) 848-8888	$32 s, $36 d	pool
Flying J Motel	2245 Etchepare Dr.	638-7202	$36 s, $39 d	AAA approved, pool
Rodeway Inn	3839 E. Lincolnway	634-2171 (800) 228-2000	$36 s, $41 d	AAA approved, pool, airport shuttle
Luxury 8 Motel	1805 Westland Rd.	638-2550	$37 s, $39 d	AAA approved
La Quinta Inn	2410 W. Lincolnway	632-7117	$37+ s, $45+ d	AAA approved, pool
Hitching Post Inn	1700 W. Lincolnway	638-3301	$38+ s, $45+ d	AAA approved, pool, jacuzzi, sauna, airport shuttle, exercise facility
Holiday Inn	204 W. Fox Farm Rd.	638-4466 (800) 465-4329	$45+ s or d	AAA approved, pool, jacuzzi sauna, airport shuttle, exercise facilities
Little America	2800 W. Lincolnway	634-2771	$45+ s, $52+ d	AAA approved, pool, airport shuttle, excercise facilities
Days Inn	2360 W. Lincolnway	778-8877 (800) 325-2525	$49 s, $54 d	jacuzzi, sauna, exercise facilities, continental breakfast

try a Philly steak sandwich or pierogie from **Little Philly**, 1013 Logan, tel. 632-6824. The cheapest meal deal in Cheyenne is the state government cafeteria in the **Herschler Building** (directly behind the Capitol), where lunch will set you back just $3. The indoor atrium is spacious and very pleasant. Open Mon.-Fri. 7-4, with limited service after 2 p.m. Get pastries at **Cookie Jar Bakery**, 3219 Snyder Ave., tel. 632-2488.

International Eats
Several places in town make very good south-of-the-border food. Favorites are: **Los Amigos**, 620 Central Ave., tel. 638-8591; **Emanuel's Mexican Cuisine**, 1607 Carey Ave., tel. 632-1744; and **Estevan's Cafe**, beside the K mart on Yellowstone Rd., tel. 632-6828. Wyoming is not known for its Chinese food, but Cheyenne has two relatively authentic Chinese restaurants that are worth a visit: **Twin Dragon Restaurant**, 1809 Carey Ave., tel. 637-6622, and **Oriental House**, 1602 E. Lincolnway, tel. 635-1411. Twin Dragon's lunchtime buffet is a very good deal.

Stuff yourself at **Avanti Restaurant**, 4620 Grandview Ave., tel. 634-3422, where an all-you-can-eat Italian-American evening buffet is just $7 including dessert. **Pete's Pizza**, 1801 Warren Ave., tel. 632-2267, claims to make "the world's best pizza," but most folks in Cheyenne seem to prefer **Pizza Hut**, 2215 E. Lincolnway, tel. 635-4151. For gourmet cuisine, don't miss the historic **Whipple House**, 300 E. 17th St., tel. 638-1883, where you can taste everything from veal shank Milanese to buffalo crepes! Entrees start around $11, with homemade French-style pastries for dessert. The patio makes for pleasant summertime dining.

Dinner
Owl Inn, 3919 Central Ave., tel. 638-8578, has been around since 1935, and is one of the most popular family dining establishments in Cheyenne. The homemade chicken noodle soup is famous. It's also a good place for a quiet drink with friends. Another favorite is **Albany Restaurant**, 1506 Capitol Ave., tel. 638-3507. **Poor Richard's**, 2233 E. Lincolnway, tel. 635-5114, has Cheyenne's only Saturday brunch. The prime rib and seafood are excellent and reasonably priced, and the salad bar is one of the best around. Enjoy a drink at the fireside

lounge. **Carriage Court** at Hitching Post Inn, 1700 W. Lincolnway, tel. 638-3301, is the place to go for fresh fish or oysters. If you're looking for mass quantities of food, head to **Wyatt's Cafeteria** in Frontier Mall, tel. 634-5292, where all-you-can-eat lunches are just $4.50 and dinners only $5.50. **Little Bear Inn**, three miles north on I-25, tel. 634-3684, is quite an experience. Good steaks, but the rest of the menu sometimes varies in quality. For prime rib, fly up to **Cloud 9 Restaurant** at the airport (300 E. 8th Ave.), tel. 635-1525.

ENTERTAINMENT AND EVENTS

All summer long, visitors gather alongside the chamber of commerce building on Lincolnway to watch the **Cheyenne Gunslingers** put on a Hollywood-style shoot-'em-up. The good guys invariably win. Pretty tacky, and absolutely no relationship to Cheyenne's history. Check with the chamber of commerce for times. During July and August, tourists fill the historic Atlas Theatre at 211 W. 16th St. to watch comic melodramas by the **Little Theatre Players**. Lots of audience participation, plus popcorn, pizza, and beer for sale. Tickets for the nightly shows are $6, or $4 for kids and seniors. Call 635-0199 for details.

Nightlife
Cheyenne is a hopping town when it comes to nightlife, especially during Frontier Days when every C&W band this side of the Mississippi finds a place to play. **Cowboy South**, 312 S. Greeley Hwy., tel. 637-3800, is the biggest and best country music bar in town. Another favorite, especially with the Air Force crowd, is the similarly spacious **Cheyenne Club**, 1617 Capitol Ave., tel. 635-7777. **Hitching Post Inn Lounge**, 1700 W. Lincolnway, tel. 638-3301, and **Little Bear Inn**, three miles north of Cheyenne, tel. 634-3684, are also popular C&W hangouts, as is **Mayflower Tavern**, 112 W. 17th, tel. 634-2761, where the rodeo cowboys jingle their spurs. (Cowpokes have been known to ride horses through its doors.) **Cristy's** at Holiday Inn, 204 W. Fox Farm Rd., tel. 638-4466, has a lounge with Top-40 DJ music most nights, while **Little America**, 2800 W. Lincolnway, tel. 634-2771, sometimes has easy-listening music. Also check at **Shenanigans Bar**, 222 W. 16th, tel.

637-5043, and **Mingles**, 1318 Stillwater, for rock music. For something more risqué, head 10 miles south of town to the Wyoming-Colorado border where **The Clown's Den**, tel. 635-0765, features topless performers with names like Amber, Candy, Tiffany, Passion, and Pricilla. Cowgirl wet T-shirt contests every night.

FRONTIER DAYS

Cheyenne Frontier Days, the "daddy of 'em all," is Wyoming's largest and most famous annual event, with all sorts of entertainment, from professional rodeos to parades. Festivities begin the last full week of July and continue for 10 action-packed days. There is something for everyone at this memorable event, but the rodeo is the main attraction for the 300,000 visitors from all 50 states and many other nations. The largest number commute in from Denver, a hundred miles away, while others jam the campgrounds and motels for a hundred miles in all directions.

History
There are several versions for the origin of Cheyenne Frontier Days, the most plausible being that it was inspired when a Union Pacific employee, F.W. Angier, watched a group of cowboys from the Swan Land and Cattle Company trying to load an ornery horse into a railroad car. The show he saw sparked his imagination, and when he suggested the idea of a Wild West buckin' and ropin' contest, others quickly jumped on the bandwagon. Just one month later (September, 1897), the first Cheyenne Frontier Days celebration began. It was a rip-roaring success, with 15,000 people in attendance. In addition to various cowboy contests, Frontier Days included several events that you won't see today—a staged battle between Sioux Indians and the U.S. Cavalry, Pony Express demonstrations, and a mock stage holdup and hanging by vigilantes. Obviously, the production had been influenced by Buffalo Bill's Wild West Show, then touring Europe. Most amusing of all was the dog and hare event, where a rabbit was released to be chased by dogs. Unfortunately, the dogs in the race were quickly joined by many more from the stands, so no winner was declared, although the loser was obvious. Cheyenne Frontier Days has grown over the years to a 10-day celebration (two weekends), and is regarded as one of the top-four rodeos in the world (the others being the Salinas California Rodeo, Calgary Stampede, and Pendleton Round-Up). Local enthusiasts call it the world's largest outdoor rodeo.

Activities
Frontier Days centers around the daily rodeos, with the nation's top rodeo cowboys showing their stuff. The rodeo has all the standard contests: bareback bronc riding, saddle bronc riding, Brahma bull riding, steer roping, calf roping, and steer wrestling. Other events include exciting and dangerous chuckwagon races, chaotic and amusing wild horse races, quarterhorse racing, and a real crowd pleaser, the colt race (where young colts race toward their mares). With a purse of more than $400,000 (largest regular season payoff in rodeo), Frontier Days attracts more than 1,000 contestants, so many of the timed events must begin at 7 each morning!

Frontier Park is the center of all sorts of other activities during Frontier Days, including daily performances by the **Southern Plains Indian Dancers**, and a **tipi village** on the south end of the parking lot. Each evening brings musical performances, including some of the top names in country music. A large and well-run **carnival** provides stomach-churning rides, sugar and grease in all forms (cotton candy, candy apples, ice cream, corn dogs, burgers, etc.), plus thousands of stuffed animal prizes, stretched-out coke bottles, velvet paintings, and other necessities. Other entertainment includes country music performers, balloon "sculptors," Indian dancers, magicians, and cloggers. After all this debauchery, try attending the **cowboy church services** held nightly at 7 p.m. on the rodeo grounds. Also in Frontier Park is the Cheyenne Frontier Days Old West Museum (see description above), where the annual **Governor's Invitational Art Show** offers the chance to view or purchase works from nearly 50 different Western artists.

Not everything happens in Frontier Park. On Mon., Wed., and Fri., during Frontier Days the Kiwanis Club puts on a free **pancake feed** for close to 10,000 folks. The feeding frenzy lasts from 7-9 a.m. Check out the cement mixer used to stir up 3,600 pounds of pancake batter or the Boy Scouts trying to catch the furiously flying flapjacks. Visitors sit on bales of hay and are treated with performances by Indian dancers and musicians of all stripes. For many children, the four **parades** (held at 9:30 a.m. on both Saturdays, as well as on Tues. and Thurs.) are a special treat. The 1½-hour parades display the largest collection of horse-drawn vehicles in the nation. You'll see everything from popcorn wagons to hearses. Other events during Frontier Days include square dances, chili cookoffs, and an **open house** at Warren Air Force Base where you can check out Air Force jets of all types (including the C-130 Hercules, a plane big enough to hold seven busses), demonstrations by military bands, tours of historic homes and the missile launch control center, plus a hair-raising air show by the USAF Thunderbirds. Ride the shuttle bus to the base from Frontier Mall. In addition to Frontier Days, Cheyenne plays host each November to the **Mountain States Circuit Finals Rodeo** at Laramie County Community College. Another popular event is the **Laramie County Fair**, held the first full week in August.

Specifics

For information on Frontier Days, including a schedule of events, call 778-7222, (800) 227-6336 (outside Wyoming), or (800) 543-2339 (inside Wyoming). Rodeo tickets cost $8-$12 pp, while tickets to night shows are $8-$17. A package ticket includes rodeo entrance, a night show, and admission to Old West Museum for $16.

Get tickets from the ticket office, south of the main grandstand, or from TicketMaster, tel. (303) 290-8497. Entrance to the midway is $1 for adults and 50¢ for children ages 6-12, but persons holding tickets to Frontier Days events are admitted free. Parking costs $2 per vehicle in the huge lot along Carey and 8th avenues. (Note, however, that overnight camping is not allowed here.) Because of the large number of participants in the calf roping, steer roping, and steer wrestling contests, preliminary events are held each morning from 7-10 a.m., with no entrance fee charged. The main rodeo events start promptly at 1:30 p.m. and last three hours. Information wagons are near the Old West Museum and at the ticket office.

OTHER PRACTICALITIES

Recreation

One-hour horseback rides ($10) are available at **Blue Ribbon Horse Center**, 406 N. Fort Rd. (two miles west of Cheyenne), tel. 634-5975. They also offer chuckwagon suppers. Swim at the indoor pool in **Lions Park** for $1 (75¢ for seniors and kids). The park also has a flower garden, an 18-hole **municipal golf course** (tel. 637-6418), picnic areas, playgrounds, and ponds that turn into skating rinks in the winter. Sloans Lake is a popular swimming hole in the summer. Private golf courses surround Cheyenne.

Shopping

Cheyenne is an automobile town, so most folks shop at one of the big malls scattered around the edges of the city. **Frontier Mall** at 1400 Dell Range Blvd. is one of the state's largest, with more than 75 stores. Walmart and a mega-K mart add to the shop-til-you-plop allure. Cheyenne has several good bookstores. **City News**, 18th and Carey streets, tel. 638-8671, has many Wyoming titles, while **Waldenbooks** in Frontier Mall, tel. 634-7099, is another good-sized shop. For used books, head to **Book & Record Exchange**, 318 W. 17th, tel. 635-2665, or **Book Rack**, 3321 E. Pershing, tel. 632-2014. Downtown Cheyenne has two of the largest Western clothing stores in the state: **Wrangler** (owned by Corral West), 1518 Capitol Ave., tel. 634-3048, and **Cheyenne Outfitters**, 210 W.

16th, tel. 775-7550. Both are great places to pick up a cowboy hat or cowboy boots. The latter also publishes a national catalogue for mail orders, tel. (800) 234-0432.

Peoples Sporting Goods, 217 W. 16th, tel. 638-8981, and in the Frontier Mall, tel. 638-8985, rents and sells a wide variety of outdoor gear, from fishing tackle to skis. Check out the $60,000 gun collection downtown. For cheap clothes, stop by the large **Salvation Army Thrift Store** at 1401 E. Lincolnway, tel. 637-8073. Cheyenne has quite a few art galleries, including **Gallery West**, 122 W. 16th, tel. 632-1258; **Manitou Gallery**, 1715 Carey Ave., tel. 635-0019; **Wyoming Western Art Gallery**, 205 W. 17th, tel. 632-1100; and the very nice **Child Gallery**, 1623 Capitol Ave., tel. 634-2235. **Cheyenne Artists Guild**, 1010 E. 16th St., tel. 632-2263, is the state's oldest art guild (since 1949), and has a nonprofit gallery in Holliday Park.

Information And Services

The **Cheyenne Chamber of Commerce** office is in the historic Tivoli Building (once a speakeasy brothel) at 301 W. 16th, tel. 638-3388, and is open Mon.-Fri. 8-5 (and on Sat. during Frontier Week). Ask about the ghost that inhabits the building. A **"Howdy Wagon"** out front is staffed Sat. 8-6 and Sun. noon-6. The state also maintains a spacious **Wyoming Information Center** at the College Dr. exit along I-25, tel. 777-7777 or (800) 225-5996. For information on Cheyenne and Laramie County from other states, call the **Cheyenne Area Convention and Visitors Bureau** at (800) 426-5009. The large **Laramie County Public Library**, 2800 Central Ave., tel. 634-3561, is open Mon.-Thurs. 10-9, Fri. and Sat. 10-6. Mid-Sept. through May it is also open Sun. 1-5. **Laramie**

County Community College, 1400 E. College Dr., tel. 778-5222, has both day and night classes for some 3,500 students. Founded in 1968, it focuses primarily on technical fields, although there are two-year degrees in everything from accounting to wildlife conservation. The 271-acre campus has 18 buildings, most of the ugly concrete-box style common in the early 1970s.

Transportation

The Cheyenne Airport is just south of Dell Range Blvd., with the entrance at the east end of 8th Avenue. **United Express**, (800) 241-6522, and **Continental Express**, tel. (800) 525-0280, have daily flights to Denver. **Airport Express**, tel. (303) 482-0505, offers shuttle service between Denver's Stapleton International Airport and Cheyenne for $25 OW or $38 RT. Four local taxi companies to choose from in town: **A-1 Veterans Cab**, tel. 634-4444; **Ace Taxi**, tel. 637-4747; **Checker Cab**, tel. 635-5555; and **Yellow Cab**, tel. 633-3333.

At the airport you can rent cars from **Hertz**, tel. (800) 654-3131, **Budget Rent-A-Car**, tel. (800) 527-0700, **National Car Rental**, tel. (800) 227-7368, **Avis**, tel. (800) 331-1212, or **Sears Rent-A-Car**, tel. (800) 527-0770. Both **Second Hand Rose**, 1009 E. 7th St., tel. 632-4237, and **American West Rentals**, 120 Greeley Hwy., tel. 634-0665, have used cars for $20/day with 50 free miles. The bus depot is right in front of the downtown train station. **Greyhound**, tel. 634-7871, provides connections east and west along I-80, and south to Denver, while **Powder River Transportation**, tel. (800) 442-3682, has daily bus service from Cheyenne north to Wheatland and much of northern Wyoming. **Denver Express**, tel. (800) 658-3231, has daily van runs to Denver and Torrington.

Packer Jeff Benkowsky relaxes after a hard day on the trail in the Teton Wilderness.

CURT GOWDY STATE PARK

The 1,645-acre Curt Gowdy State Park is located 26 miles west of Cheyenne along State 210, the scenic "back way" to Laramie. Here, two small lakes offer recreation for anglers, boaters, snowmobilers, and cross-country skiers. The lakes are a part of Cheyenne's water supply (no swimming), and were constructed between 1904 and 1910. An elaborate Rube Goldberg scheme completed in 1964 now carries 12 million gallons of water from the west, crossing the Continental Divide, the Sierra Madre, the Snowy Range, and the Laramie Range to bring it to thirsty Cheyenne. In 1971, the two lakes at the eastern end were set aside as a state park and named for Wyoming native Curt Gowdy, a Hall of Fame baseball player and well-known TV sportscaster. Camping here costs $4 per day at any one of five sites. Pleasant hiking in the surrounding pine-covered countryside, but by late summer the lakes tend to get drawn down rather severely. There are some interesting granitic formations to explore and climb. Also in the park is the historic Hynds Lodge, a stone structure completed in 1923 and available for families and groups to rent. For details, call park headquarters at 632-7946.

Happy Jack Mountain Music Festival comes around the first weekend in July at Curt Gowdy, offering a fun chance to listen to bluegrass tunes, sample the wares at a crafts fair, or participate in a fishing derby. Tickets are $6 per day. On Labor Day weekend, the park is the scene of a **mountain men rendezvous**.

PINE BLUFFS

Pine Bluffs (pop. 1,100) is a small agricultural and transportation center on Wyoming's eastern border. It is so close to Nebraska that one gas station—Smitty's Stateline Truckstop—straddles the border, with a line painted down the middle of the building. Pine Bluffs feels like western Nebraska, with ponderosa pines crowding the long ridge south of town. Wheat fields and irrigated potato fields surround Pine Bluffs. The spuds head to the potato chip factory here; look for Rocky Mountain brand in Wyoming stores. The town itself is middle America, with spreading shade trees along the main streets.

Sights

The most interesting sight in Pine Bluffs is the ongoing **archaeological excavation** near a major Indian occupation site that dates back for 8,000 years. Indians pitched their tipis atop the pine-covered bluffs here and headed down to the fertile valley below to hunt and collect berries. Their tipi rings are still visible. Each summer, University of Wyoming students under the direction of Dr. Charles Reher come here to slowly dig through the soil to find a buried treasure trove of prehistory. The staff will be happy to answer your questions. The site is located right next to the tourist information center at the I-80 rest area. Also here is a display of approximately 20 painted tipis; pick up the brochure describing the various designs.

The free **Texas Trail Museum** at 3rd and Market streets, tel. 245-3513, houses a Conestoga wagon, old photos, and a small collection of homesteading and ranching items. It's open daily 9-5 during the summer, or by appointment (stop by the town hall) at other times. The town of Pine Bluffs lay right along the great Texas Trail; at its peak in 1871, more than 600,000 cattle were trailed north from Texas past this point. Pine Bluffs became not just a watering place for cattle, but also a vital shipping point. For several years, more cattle were shipped from the railroad station at Pine Bluffs than anywhere else in the world. A monument to the Texas Trail stands in the adjacent park. Next to the museum is the **University of Wyoming Archaeological Education Center**, a summeronly trailer with displays and artifacts from various archaeological digs. Tiny **Albin** (pop. 130) is 18 miles north of Pine Bluffs and has an interesting old sod house. The annual event here is Albin Days, held in July each year. Call 246-3444 for details.

1↗

2↗

3↘

4↘

5↘

6↘

WELCOME
M.T.W. 6A.M-8P.M
THUR. 6A.M-2P.M
FRI+SAT.6A.M-9P.M
SUN. 4P.M-9P.M
FAT ED'S

OPEN

Practicalities

Travelyn Motel, 515 W. 7th, tel. 245-3226 or (800) 453-4511, has comfortable rooms starting for $25 s or $28 d. **Pine Bluff Mobile Village**, is a half mile east of town, tel. 245-3665, with tent spaces (no shade) for $9, and RV sites for $14. Showers are $3 for non-campers. Open mid-April to mid-October. **Linda's Cafe**, 111 E. 2nd St., tel. 245-9238, is the friendly local coffeehouse, specializing in homemade pies and pecan rolls. **Wild Horse Cafe**, 600 Parsons, tel. 245-9365, is another local eatery with all-American fare. **Pizza Place**, 715 Parsons, tel. 245-3443, makes good sandwiches and fast food. **Fiddler's Restaurant**, 711 Parsons, tel. 245-3548, is the sit-down dinner restaurant in Pine Bluffs, with a steakhouse and lounge. Very good food. They sometimes have live music here, as does **Jim's Bar**, 104 Main St., tel. 245-3521.

The primary hangout in Pine Bluffs is the local bowling alley, **Pine Bowl**, 3rd and Pine, tel. 245-3622. No chamber of commerce office in town, but the state-run **Tourist Information Center** at the I-80 rest area has both local and statewide info. It is open late May-September. The **library** is at 110 E. 2nd, tel. 245-3646. Pine Bluffs has a free outdoor **swimming pool** (summers only) at 200 E. 8th, tel. 245-3783.

Trail Days comes around the first weekend in August, with rodeos, barbecues, a parade, a melodrama, and dancing. A few mountain men types rendezvous in the bluffs above town. There are also **calf and team roping** events at the rodeo grounds on Tuesday and Thursday evenings and Sunday afternoons through the summer. **Greyhound**, tel. 634-7744 (in Cheyenne), stops at L&M Auto in Pine Bluffs, with connections in both directions along I-80.

CHUGWATER

Chugwater (pop. 200) was once headquarters for the giant Swan Land and Cattle Company, the greatest of Wyoming's cattle spreads during the 1880s. The town itself was founded in 1913 on land sold by the Swan Company. Today it is best known for Chugwater Chili, though it is not actually packaged in town. The chili mix is a creation of Dave Cameron, who calls himself a "hunting guide, chili cook, and real estate broker, in that order." Chugwater has to have one of the strangest origins of any town name in America, coming from the Indian practice of driving buffalo over cliffs into the creek. The "chug" sound they made as they hit the water led Indians to call it "Water at the Place Where the Buffalo Chug."

Practicalities

Chugwater has a free small **museum** with an

impressive collection of brands, open Sat.-Sun. 1-5 only. **Buffalo Grill**, tel. 422-3458, makes home-cooked meals served with gusto. The **Diamond Guest Ranch/Chugwater KOA**, tel. 422-3567, is located on a historic 75,000-acre cattle ranch 15 miles west of town. The ranch was begun in 1884, and for many years a breeding center for Clydesdale and Morgan horses. It has been a guest ranch since 1968. All sorts of outdoor recreation here, including hayrides, swimming, and trail rides. Also here are a restaurant and bar. Cabins run $36 d, while campsites cost $11 for tents or $16 for RVs. The annual **Chugwater Chili Cookoff** is held at Diamond Ranch each June, attracting several thousand fire-breathing chili-eaters. **Powder River Transportation**, tel. (800) 442-3682, has daily bus service north and south from Chugwater.

1. Eddie Abraham and Schwope with sugar beets in Bighorn Basin; 2. Craig Abraham and Antonio Acosta with their hogs at Abraham Farms near Byron in Bighorn Basin; 3. sheepherder John Abyta with some of his 1,700 sheep near Bald Mountain in Bighorn National Forest; 4. Jason Schutterle at the Whiskey Mountain Rendezvous in Dubois; 5. Roustabouts James Lock and Avon Shakespeare work a drilling rig on the Wind River Indian Reservation; 6. Nobody goes away hungry from Fat Ed's Cafe in Douglas.

WHEATLAND

With a name like Wheatland (pop. 3,900), it should be pretty obvious that you're in farming country. Actually, wheat is not the primary crop grown here; sugar beets, dry beans, and barley are. The 1,650-megawatt coal-fired Laramie River Station powerplant, built in the 1980s, is five miles north of town, and supplies electricity to a grid that feeds an eight-state area. It's the biggest local employer. Another substantial employer is a local marble quarry operation that mines dolomite in the Laramie Mountains and crushes it for use in everything from aquarium gravel to cattle feed. Don't let on that I told you, but Wheatland has Minuteman III nuclear missiles out in the country near the powerplant. Perhaps for this reason, Wheatland claims to have of the highest per capita number of churches anywhere; 23 different houses of worship crowd the town.

History

Wheatland is a creation of the Wyoming Development Company, founded in 1883 by a number of individuals, including senators Joseph M. Carey and Francis E. Warren. In one of the few successful applications of the famous Carey Act in Wyoming, the company built a dam on Big Laramie River and canals to carry the water to some 50,000 acres where homesteaders formed the Wheatland Colony. In 1905 the town of Wheatland was incorporated, becoming the hub of activity for the region, and later the Platte County seat. During the late 1970s and early '80s, Wheatland followed the boom pattern common to other Wyoming towns, with oil and gas exploration nearby and construction of the giant powerplant attracting thousands to town. When things went bust, Wheatland was pulled down; it still has not really recovered. That old standby, agriculture has gained increasing importance.

SWAN LAND AND CATTLE COMPANY

The most famous of all Wyoming ranches was the Swan Land and Cattle Company, Ltd., founded in 1883 by Alexander and Thomas Swan with enormous financial backing from Scottish investors: £600,000 the first year and an additional £1.6 million spread over the next three years. At its peak in the mid-1880s, the company's holdings reached from its headquarters along Chugwater Creek westward for 120 miles to the North Platte River near Rawlins. More than 110,000 cattle ranged across this vast expanse. The company bought 550,000 acres of Union Pacific Railroad land (and therefore controlled the checkerboard of public land in alternating sections), and purchased government land along major creeks in the area. By doing this, it controlled access to water in this semi-arid country, thus keeping others from settling on surrounding public lands. All told, the Swan Land and Cattle Company had its tentacles over nearly a million acres with more than 30 different ranches. The company had dozens of different brands, but locals knew it as the "Two Bar." Cowboys loved the company, for it always provided good wages ($20 a month to start) and working conditions, plus the best food around.

In the mid-1880s things began to turn sour, and by 1886 the Scottish investors were getting worried about what looked like fraud and misrepresentation by Alexander Swan. Apparently the reported 110,000 cattle shown on the books did not all exist on the hoof. A lawsuit eventually led to his firing, but another factor caused considerably more devastation: the severe winter of 1886-87 which killed off thousands of the firm's cows and calves, pushing the company to the brink of bankruptcy. Amazingly, the reorganized company managed to survive for more than 50 years, though it began raising sheep instead of cattle after 1903. It was quite prosperous during the World War I when wool prices soared, but gradually declined as the economy turned down. By 1950, the vast operation had been entirely liquidated. Some folks claim that a wild bronc from the old Two Bar Ranch, Steamboat, was the inspiration for Wyoming's bucking horse symbol (as appears on license plates). Many of the historic ranch's buildings are still intact, and the complex has been designated a National Historic Landmark.

WHEATLAND

TO GLENDO & DOUGLAS

TO POWERPLANT AND GUERNSEY

MR. C'S RESTAURANT

ROMPOON RD.

SWANSON RD.

NORTH RD.

FRONT RD.

TORCHLIGHT INN

J.J.'S BROWN DERBY

ROWLEY ST.

16th ST. 15th ST. 14th ST. 13th ST. 12th ST. 11th ST. 10th ST. 9th ST.

OAK ST.

E. OAK ST.

FARM & MARKET RD.

CEDAR ST.

WYOMING MOTEL

BLACKBIRD INN

SPRUCE ST.

PINE ST.

LIBRARY

POST OFFICE

WALNUT ST.

W. WALNUT ST.

MAIN CANAL

MAPLE ST.

CHAMBER OF COMMERCE / CITY HALL

GILCHRIST ST.

WHEATLAND CREEK

PLATTE COUNTY FAIRGROUNDS

AIRPORT

WATER ST.

8th ST.

WEST WINDS MOTEL

WESTERN MOTEL

ANTELOPE GAP RD.

W. SOUTH ST.

SOUTH ST.

PARKWAY MOTEL

PLAINS MOTEL

JOHNSTON ST.

LEWIS PARK (CAMPING)

VIMBO'S MOTEL AND RESTAURANT

SHIEK ST.

HOSPITAL

ZORN ST.

W. MARIPOSA PKWY.

BRICE ST.

SWIMMING POOL

LOOMIS ST.

COLE ST.

E. COLE ST.

OLD LARAMIE RD.

OLD U.S. 87

GOLF COURSE

COLORADO - SOUTHERN RAILROAD

V - O RANCH RD.

W. COZAD RD.

TO SYBILLE CANYON AND LARAMIE

TO CHUGWATER & CHEYENNE

COZAD RD.

NOT TO SCALE

© MOON PUBLICATIONS, INC.

Sights

The **Laramie Peak Museum** on 16th St. is open Tues.-Sat. 11-5. No charge. It houses a variety of historical flotsam and jetsam. Call 322-9601 for tours of the huge **Laramie River Station** powerplant just north of Wheatland. Approximately 30 miles southwest of Wheatland on State 34 is the Wyoming Game and Fish Department's **Sybille Wildlife Research Center** (pronounced suh-BEEL) which houses elk, moose, deer, mountain sheep, and black-footed ferrets. A new visitor center here is open daily during the summer and Mon.-Fri. the rest of the year, and includes exhibits and videos on the endangered black-footed ferret. TV monitors show activity in the adjacent ferret facility, where more than 140 of these cute little furries live. This is a unique opportunity to glimpse one of the rarest mammals on earth.

Accommodations

Blackbird Inn Bed & Breakfast, 1101 11th St., tel. 322-4540, rates near the top of my list of places to stay in Wyoming. Run by a friendly local schoolteacher, Dan Brecht, this old Victorian home (built in 1912) has been lovingly restored. Excellent full breakfasts served during the summer months, but even the continental breakfast offered the rest of the year will fill you up. Rates are an incredible $20 s or $25 d ($5 cheaper in the winter months). **Mill Iron Spear Ranch**, 2612 Palmer Canyon Rd., tel. 322-5940, also offers fine B&B accommodations in a country setting. The lowest motel rates in Wheatland are at **Parkway Motel**, 1257 South Rd., tel. 322-3080, for $20 s or $24 d, and **Western Motel**, 1450 South Rd., tel. 322-9952, with rooms for $20 s or $25 d (same price for kitchenettes). Lodging at **Wyoming Motel**, 1109 9th St., tel. 322-5383, costs $24 s or $28 d. **Torchlight Inn (Best Western)**, 1809 N. 16th St., tel. 322-4070 or (800) 528-1234, has rooms starting for $31 s or $35 d. **Vimbo's Motel**, 203 16th St., tel. 322-3842, is one of the nicest places to stay in town, with rooms for $30 s or $34 d. **West Winds Motel**, 1756 South St., tel. 322-2705, costs $25 s or $29 d, while **Plains Motel**, 208 16th St., tel. 322-3416, has rooms with refrigerators for $24 s or $27 d. You can camp for free at 40-acre **Lewis Park**, right in Wheatland, or pay to stay at **Squaw Mountain R.V. Camp**, 2005 N. 16th, tel. 322-3253.

Food

Granny's Goodie Shop, 719 9th St., tel. 322-5321, makes good sandwiches for lunch, and hot coffee and donuts for a quick breakfast. Tolerable pseudo-Mexican food at **El Gringo's**, 705 10th St., tel. 322-4402, and standard family dining at **Vimbo's Restaurant**, 203 16th St., tel. 322-3725. The fanciest place in Wheatland is **Mr. C's Restaurant**, 28 Rompoon Rd., tel. 322-9229, where you'll find excellent steak and

BLACK-FOOTED FERRETS

On September 25, 1981, near Meeteetse, Wyoming, a dog walked up to its master with a strange creature in his mouth. It was a black-footed ferret, a sleek, black-masked animal last seen in 1972 and feared extinct. Biologists soon discovered that a nearby prairie dog colony housed the only living population of ferrets, the world's rarest mammal. Ferrets eat prairie dogs, and were once found in their colonies from Saskatchewan to Texas. The colonies were huge—one along the Cheyenne River in eastern Wyoming stretched for a hundred miles—but the prairie dogs went the way of many other animals, hunted and poisoned by settlers and their land taken over by plowed fields. Although still present in Wyoming, prairie dog colonies are now much smaller and more isolated. The population of ferrets declined with their shrinking food source.

With the discovery of ferrets living near Meeteetse, national attention focused on saving the population from extinction. In 1986, an outbreak of canine distemper threatened to kill all the remaining wild ferrets, so they were captured and taken to the Wyoming Game and Fish Wildlife Research Unit at Sybille. After inoculations, an ambitious captive breeding program was begun. It proved so successful that in 1989 the population was split up (to reduce the chance that all would be killed in an accident such as a tornado), with some sent to the National Zoo in Virginia and others to Omaha's Henry Doorly Zoo. There are plans to re-introduce the ferrets to prairie dog colonies in Shirley Basin (south of Casper) and to the original Meeteetse site in the near future. Interestingly, reports continue to come in of black-footed ferret sightings. Perhaps these hard-to-find creatures are still living in some remote prairie dog colonies.

seafood in a pleasant atmosphere. Quite reasonable for lunches. Wheatland's surprise is **J.J.'s Little Brown Derby**, 1707 9th St., tel. 322-4257. Located in a 1950s-era trailer house with appropriately tacky decor, it has great food, reasonable prices, and huge portions. The burgers and chicken-fried steak are famous.

Information And Services
The **Wheatland Chamber of Commerce** office is downstairs in the city hall at 600 9th St., tel. 322-2322, and is open Mon.-Fri. 8-4. **Platte County Library**, 904 9th St., tel. 322-2689, is open Mon.-Thurs. 10-8, Fri. 10-5, and Sat. 10-2. There is a fine outdoor **swimming pool** in Lewis Park, open only during the summer. The local nine-hole **Wheatland Golf Course**, 1253 Cole, tel. 322-3675, costs $8. For something unique, stop by 1556 Cedar, where Lucy Gorman makes woven wheat wall hangings. **Powder River Transportation**, tel. (800) 442-3682, has daily bus service to Cheyenne and most of northern Wyoming. The **Platte County Fair and Rodeo** comes to town the second week of August, offering a street breakfast, barbecue, parade, professional rodeo, and entertainment, plus all the usual fun of a country fair. Most enjoyable of all is the pig wrestling. Two other local events are worth noting: **Community Fest** in mid-July has bake sales, homemade crafts, and a carnival, plus amateur rodeo events at **Miles Mitchell Memorial Day Rodeo**.

GUERNSEY AND VICINITY

Guernsey (pop. 1,700) is a scenic railroad and ranching town along the once mighty North Platte River. The river is now just a trickle in late summer, thanks to all the upstream dams. Guernsey was named after Charles A. Guernsey, a prominent local rancher and legislator who came here in the late 19th century. The town is right at the heart of the Oregon Trail, with Fort Laramie just 11 miles east, and numerous other markers from that interesting era. The Wyoming Army National Guard maintains Camp Guernsey, a large troop training facility just north of town.

Emigrant Trail Sights
The Oregon Trail ran just on the other side of the North Platte River from Guernsey. One mile south of town are some of the deepest **Oregon Trail ruts** anywhere along the historic route. A short gravel road heads to a parking area where a short trail leads up a small hill to five-foot-deep gouges cut into the soft rock. The paths of bullwhackers are visible alongside. The old wagon trail is easy to follow in both directions, and the surrounding landscape has probably changed but little since the last wagon train rolled past. Not far away is a white obelisk marking the grave of Lucindy Rollins, one of the thousands who died on the hard road west.

The hundred-foot-tall **Register Cliff** is three miles south of Guernsey. Here the soft limestone made a perfect place for passing emigrants to carve their names, and thousands took the time to do so. The oldest—dating to the 1850s—are now behind a chainlink fence to keep folks from defacing them further. Thousands of swallows nest on the cliff here. North of Guernsey, ruts of the historic Mormon Trail are visible along **Emigrant Hill** where Mormon pioneers struggled to hoist their wagons up this steep slope. Another important nearby site was **Emigrants' Washtub**, a warm springs where weary travelers stopped to bathe and wash clothes.

Practicalities
Guernsey has a small **visitor center/museum** that is open during the summer months. Stay at **Sage Brush Motel**, tel. 836-2331, for $26 s or $30 d. No bunkhouse accommodations at the **Bunkhouse Motel**, tel. 836-2356, but standard motel rooms for $27 s or $30 d. **Annette's White House**, 239 South Dakota, tel. 836-2148, has bed-and-breakfast accommodations for $30 s or d. Camp for free at the **town park**, including showers. For meals, **Papa Tony's** has very popular Saturday night Italian dinners and Sunday buffets. **S & S Cafe**, tel. 836-9301, has homemade baked goods and very good breakfasts. The best steaks in Guernsey are at **Trail Inn**, tel. 836-2573. **Casa de Nueve** dishes up authentic Mexican fare, or try **Burrito Brothers** for fast food. Get groceries at the **Jack and Jill Food Center**. A town swimming pool is

open during the summer, and a local golf course provides a place to putt around. Rent canoes from **Quick Canoe Rentals**, tel. 836-2039. They will even drive your car downstream to the take-out point. Each 4th of July, the **Old Timer's Rodeo** comes to Guernsey, offering all the standard small town fun: a parade, rodeo, barbecue, street dance, and fireworks.

HARTVILLE AND SUNRISE

Six miles north of Guernsey on State 270 is the picturesque old mining community of Hartville (pop. 100). Established in 1884, it is the oldest incorporated town in Wyoming. The town is named for Colonel Verling Hart, an officer at nearby Fort Laramie and owner of a copper mine here. The Hartville Uplift region (as it is known by geologists) is one of the most mineral-rich in Wyoming. Indians used the iron as pigment to make war paint, and some of their tunnels stretched 20 feet into the hills. During the

1870s, prospectors found gold, silver, copper, onyx, and iron ore in these scenic pine- and juniper-dotted hills. Copper brought the first miners, but by 1887 it had been mostly mined out, and they turned to iron ore. Hartville arose as a shopping, gambling, boozing, and whoring center for the miners; many of the historic stone and false-front buildings still stand.

Of note is the old stone jail and **Miners Bar**, the state's oldest drinking establishment. The cherrywood back bar was made in Germany in 1864 and shipped to Fort Laramie, moving to Hartville in 1881. Also in Hartville is **Venice Bar**, famous for homemade Italian dinners on Saturday evenings. Meals by reservation only; call 836-2881. The local cemetery is crowded with the bodies of men who died wearing their cowboy boots—this was one town where gunfights really did take place on Main Street—so it is logical that the local annual festivities are **Boot Hill Days.** Drop in on Labor Day weekend for all sorts of activities, including a melodrama, street games, mock shootouts, and plenty of food.

© MOON PUBLICATIONS, INC.

The mining ghost town of Sunrise is located just a mile east of Hartville. An extraordinarily rich body of iron ore was discovered here in 1887, and a dozen years later the Colorado Fuel and Iron Corp. established an open-pit iron mine, a mine that would eventually become the largest glory hole in the world. (In 1986, mine-reclamation work attempted to restore the gaping glory hole to a more natural contour.) The company hired some 750 predominantly Italian and Greek emigrants to dig the ore, which was shipped to a smelter in Pueblo, Colorado. To house the workers, the clean, well-planned company town of Sunrise sprang up. The mine was closed in 1980 due to a lessened demand for ore, and its brick buildings now stand abandoned. Sunrise claims a miniscule footnote to trivial history: *Ripley's Believe It or Not* noted that the town had the longest string of car garages in the world. They are still standing.

The Hartville area is part of the so-called **Spanish Diggings**, an extensive archaeological site that covers hundreds of square miles. The area was originally believed to be the site of a Spanish gold mine (hence the name), but was later found to have been used by Indians to gather flint for arrowheads. They mined quartzite, jasper, moss agate, and chalcedony here for perhaps 10,000 years. Stone flakes and countless old pits (up to 15 feet deep and 50 feet across) abound in this region. Hundreds of tipi rings and rock chips can be found here, and the material mined was carried all the way to the Missouri River. One of the most important aboriginal places in Wyoming is in this area, an 11,000-year-old paleo-Indian site called **Hell Gap**. Excellent three-hour tours of Hell Gap, the Spanish Diggings, the Cheyenne-Deadwood Stage Route, and historic ranches leave from the Conoco Station in Fort Laramie, tel. 837-2724. This is a not-for-profit operation run by a local rancher and archaeologist, George Ziemens. A donation is requested.

GUERNSEY STATE PARK

Two state parks are found along the North Platte River in eastern Wyoming. Guernsey is the smaller of the two (about seven miles long, and covering 6,538 acres), but it is considerably more interesting than its sister, Glendo State Park. Guernsey State Park is a mile northwest of Guernsey, off U.S. 26. The park surrounds Guernsey Reservoir, backed up behind a 105-foot-tall, 560-foot-long earthen dam completed in 1927. Originally, the dam stored 74,000 acre feet of water, but half of that capacity has been lost due to siltation. To reduce this problem, the reservoir is now drained down each summer, killing off many of the fish. Don't bother bringing your fishing pole. Guernsey is surrounded by scenic grass- and sage-covered hills topped with juniper and pine, while steep sandstone cliffs drop to the water in places. There is a pleasant sandy beach five miles west along the southern shore, and seven campgrounds; each costing $4 per night. The water is quite warm, making this a popular swimming hole.

Other than the water, the main attractions in Guernsey State Park are the wonderful stone structures built by the Civilian Conservation Corps during the 1930s, some of the best examples of CCC craftsmanship in existence. **Guernsey State Park Museum** is the finest of all, with an arched-stone entrance that faces impressive Laramie Peak, 35 miles to the west. Inside are enormous hand-hewn timbers, wrought-iron light fixtures, and flagstone floors. This place was built to last! The museum (tel. 836-2900) is open daily noon-8, May 15-Labor Day (closed winters), and houses 14 displays created by the CCC to illustrate the geology and human use of the surrounding country. Take a look at the historical slide show. Other park structures built of native material include roads, overlooks, rock walls, culverts, bridges, picnic shelters, and the famous "million-dollar privy." Also within Guernsey State Park are eight miles of hiking trails and a short nature trail near the museum. Pick up a trail guide inside.

GLENDO STATE PARK

Located 25 miles east of Douglas, and 32 miles north of Wheatland, 10,000-acre Glendo State Park surrounds Glendo Reservoir. A 167-foot-high and 2,096-feet-long earthen dam backs up the water for 14 miles, and generates some 24,000 kilowatts of electricity. This is one of the largest reservoirs on the North Platte River, with almost 80 miles of shoreline. (Note, however, that drought years have sometimes reduced the reservoir to little more than a puddle.) The surrounding country is treeless and windy, but the towering 10,272-foot summit of Laramie Peak dominates the skyline to the west. The surprisingly warm water at Sandy Beach makes this a favorite play area for families. Other attractions are the Red Cliffs where cliff divers agonize over the long drop, and Muddy Bay where anglers look for walleye, perch, or trout (lunker walleyes here). Dozens of small coves can be explored by boat, or you can float down the river below the dam. The wind can really blow, making for good windsurfing conditions, but also creating hazards for folks who go out in small boats.

Practicalities
There are seven state park campgrounds ($4) on the eastern end of Glendo Reservoir. Get permits from park headquarters (tel. 735-4433) near the dam. The little town of **Glendo** (pop. 300) is just two miles from Glendo State Park, near the site of the old **Horseshoe Creek Stage Station**. Built by Mormons in the 1850s, the station was later burned by them to keep it out of government hands. A small **Glendo Historical Museum** is open seasonally, with Indian and early settlers' gear. Lodging is available at **Howard's Motel**, 106 A St., tel. 735-4252, for $16 s or $19 d. **Glendo Marina** near the dam, tel. 735-4216, has rustic motel accommodations overlooking the lake for $28 s or $35 d, plus a restaurant, grocery store, and RV hookups. Rent fishing boats here for $60 a day and up. The marina is open year-round, but the other facilities are closed in winter. **Glendo Days** comes around each July with a rodeo and street dance.

FORT LARAMIE NATIONAL HISTORIC SITE

One of the most important historic sites in all Wyoming is old Fort Laramie, located three miles south of the town of the same name. The fort played a changing series of roles as the West was developed: Indian trading post, emigrant way station, and military center. Fort Laramie stood at the crossroads of history. The budding territory's first school and post office opened here, and nearly every famous citizen from the frontier era—from Jim Bridger to Mark Twain—stopped in. Today Fort Laramie is one of the most popular stopping points for visitors who want a taste of the rich history of this region.

HISTORY

In 1834, trader William Sublette halted along the banks of the Laramie River near its confluence with the North Platte. With him were 35 mountain men, their pack animals weighted down with trade items for the annual rendezvous along the Green River. Sublette had a bold plan, to build a permanent trading post here, one that would make it easier to bring supplies west and beaver furs and buffalo robes back east, a place where Indians and whites could parlay, with both profiting. He left behind a dozen men to begin work on what would become Fort William

(as in William Sublette), and hurried west to the rendezvous. The men threw up a cottonwood stockade, with blockhouses on the corners, and a tunnel to the outer gate for trading with the Indians.

Over the next two years the post changed hands a couple of times (and names—to Fort Lucien), becoming an important trade center for Pierre Chouteau's American Fur Company. By 1841, competition from another trading post —built just a mile away—forced the company to start again. This time they spent $10,000 building a whitewashed adobe fort near the old one that was already rotting. Fort John-on-the-Laramie was the official name given to the second fort, but this was quickly shortened to Fort Laramie.

Over the next eight years, Fort Laramie emerged as a strategic center for the Indian trade, with more than 10,000 buffalo robes purchased each year. (Traders generally paid the equivalent of $1 per robe in the form of gunpowder, hatchets, tobacco, coffee, sugar, blankets, and of course, liquor; the robes were sold in St. Louis for $4 each.) But trade with the Indians was gradually supplanted by a new role for the fort: the growing migration of people westward. Fort Laramie stood right along the main trail to Oregon and California. It was a third of the way to the Columbia River mouth, and provided a much-anticipated break before the long, desolate trek over the Continental Divide. In 1843, nearly a thousand people passed the fort, and the numbers increased each year, reaching a crescendo after gold was discovered in California in 1849. Soon thereafter, more than 50,000 emigrants were trudging into Fort Laramie each summer. They stopped to repair wheels at the carpentry and blacksmith shops, purchase food and whiskey at the store, or trade tired stock for fresh oxen and horses. The latter was the best deal for traders at the fort; all they had to do was put the oxen and horses they had gotten in trade (generally a two-for-one deal) out to pasture for a couple of weeks and then trade them as fresh stock to subsequent emigrants.

The Army Takes Over

The great migration westward had its negative consequences. Indians complained that buffalo were being shot and forced away from their traditional migration routes, and that the thousands of stock brought by the emigrants were destroying the grass. The inevitable conflicts began as young warriors halted wagon trains demanding "tolls" in the form of tobacco, coffee, or sugar. Quickly, this escalated into attacks against the emigrants, and a great hue and cry went up for protection from the "savages." Thus it was that Congress gave Fort Laramie a new role: as a military garrison to protect the Oregon Trail.

In 1849, the Army purchased Fort Laramie for $4000, establishing the first military post in what would become Wyoming. Some 180 men—both cavalrymen and infantrymen—were assigned to the post. A rapid expansion program was begun, with the old adobe fort serving as temporary quarters while more elaborate facilities were built. The Army's Fort Laramie did not fit the Hollywood stereotype of a frontier fort; having no log perimeter or blockhouses. The fort was instead laid out around a central parade ground, with clapboard and "lime grout" concrete buildings forming a loose perimeter. In case of attack, the Army was prepared to retreat to a single heavily fortified building. Despite this general lack of protection, the fort was never attacked by Indians (though the horses were brazenly driven off one time), and most soldiers never engaged in battle with the Indians.

Fort Laramie was essentially a male bastion, though a few officers' wives were present. The only exceptions were laundresses, hired generally on the basis of their physical appearance (the less attractive the better), so as to not appeal to the soldiers' prurient interests. A small group of Indians (termed derisively "Laramie Loafers") soon attached themselves to the fort, camping nearby and providing scouts, interpreters, errand boys, and paramours. Fort Laramie was not a pleasant place. The food was deplorable, discipline so strict that even the smallest infraction could land a man in the brig, and sanitary conditions were so bad that by 1880 it was getting hard to find a place to dig latrines that had not already been contaminated. The infrequent paydays turned into drunken brawls. No wonder so many men deserted their post and slipped off for the promising gold fields of California! The inevitable "hog ranch" also grew up near the fort, offering an escape from the day to day monotony of the soldiers' lives. In 1877, Lt. John G. Bourke, described the ranches as

"tenanted by as hardened and depraved a set of witches as could be found on the face of the globe. Each of these establishments was equipped with a rum-mill of the worst kind and each contained from three to half a dozen Cyprians, virgins whose lamps were always burning brightly in expectance of the coming of the bridegroom, and who lured to destruction the soldiers of the garrison. In all my experience I have never seen a lower, more beastly set of people of both sexes."

For the next four decades, Fort Laramie served as the nerve center of this part of the plains, providing troops and cavalry to retaliate against Indian attacks, and serving as a meeting place for treaty arrangements when the political wind shifted toward negotiation instead of confrontation. The first of these treaties came in 1851, under the forceful leadership of Indian agent Thomas Fitzpatrick, a former mountain man. More than 10,000 Indians attended, representing the Sioux, Cheyenne, Arapaho, Shoshone, Crow, Gros Ventre, and Assiniboin tribes. The treaty consisted essentially of annual bribes (annuities) to be given to the Indians to compensate them for their losses to whites. The various tribes would be assigned to distinct territories, but could hunt in other areas. After signing the treaty, a mountain of presents awaited, the first of the $50,000 in annuities for each of the next 50 years. Shortly thereafter, the federal government reneged on the promise, increasing the annual amount to $70,000 per year, but cutting the time to just 10 years. Peace lasted but a short while.

Grattan Massacre

One of the few Indian-white conflicts to occur in the vicinity of Fort Laramie took place in 1854. It began innocently enough when a Mormon emigrant's lame cow wandered off and was butchered by a hungry Miniconjou Indian waiting for the government to dispense annuities. A hot-headed young lieutenant, John Grattan, was sent out to bring in the Indian. Unfortunately, Grattan's interpreter was drunk, and began immediately shouting insults at the Sioux in whose village the man was camped. Grattan himself was anxious for a fight, hoping to gain a piece of fame, so when the Sioux refused to give up the man—offering instead to pay for the cow with two horses—Grattan would have nothing of it. His soldiers opened fire, and were immediately themselves attacked by a vastly superior force of Sioux. All 29 soldiers died in the massacre that followed, and Fort Laramie itself stood in danger of being destroyed. But the Indians instead raided local storehouses for the promised annuities, and headed out. The Army used the Grattan Massacre as proof that the Indians could not be trusted. In reality, the entire incident was one of utter stupidity on the part of the Army.

More Trouble

One of the least distinguished post commanders at Fort Laramie was the hard-drinking and ill-tempered Colonel Thomas Moonlight. In 1865, he publicly hanged two Sioux subchiefs who had brought in two white women captives for reward. Their bodies were left dangling in chains for several days, an act that brought condemnation from the Eastern press. In retaliation, the Sioux killed several soldiers, and then managed to drive off most of the horses from Colonel Moonlight's cavalry. A sullen Moonlight led his almost horseless cavalry in the 120-mile-long hike back to the fort. Shortly thereafter, he was stripped of his command. (Moonlight later served as a politically appointed territorial governor of Wyoming.)

With the decline in importance of the Oregon Trail, Fort Laramie became a staging area for military expeditions against the Indians. In the Treaty of 1868, signed at Fort Laramie, the Sioux were guaranteed the Powder River country "as long as the grass shall grow and the buffalo shall roam." But the discovery of gold in the Black Hills abruptly changed the picture, for now whites wanted the land itself, not just a road through it. They eventually got it, but not before the massacre of Custer and his men at Little Big Horn in 1876. After this, with the Indians tucked away on reservations, most of the hostilities died down, and the fort lost its strategic importance. The railroad had long since supplanted the Oregon Trail as the primary route west, and for the decade of the 1880s, Fort Laramie served as a way station along the Cheyenne to Deadwood stage road. During this time the fort grew more genteel, with the planting of trees and completion of numerous substantial homes.

The Army Departs

By 1889, it was clear that Fort Laramie had outlived its usefulness, and it was ordered closed. The following year the 35,000 acres of military land was opened to homesteaders, with the buildings auctioned off. Because of the scarcity of wood in the area, many were stripped and hauled away to become cabins or other structures. Others remained on the site, used as homes, businesses, or barns. For the next half century the historic fort slowly deteriorated, but in 1937, the state of Wyoming purchased the site and donated it to the federal government. The following year it was declared a national monument, to be managed by the National Park Service. A lengthy and difficult restoration process managed to stabilize the ruins and restore a dozen of the historic structures, but it was not until 1964 that the fort was restored to something approaching the conditions in the 1880s.

FORT LARAMIE TODAY

More than 90,000 visitors come to historic Fort Laramie each year for a rewarding traipse back in time. The clear, tree-lined Laramie River still flows close by, and the large parade ground engenders a feeling of this fort's importance, while the bleak, windswept setting speaks of its hardships.

Visiting The Fort

Buildings and grounds of the 830-acre Fort Laramie National Historic Site are open year-round from sunrise to sunset. Entrance costs $1 (kids under 16 free). No camping, but there is a pleasant picnic area. For a good orientation to Fort Laramie, head to the **visitor center/park headquarters** building (tel. 837-2221) that houses excellent displays, including a scale model of the fort and many photos. The center is open daily 8-7 June-Aug., and daily 8-4:30 the rest of the year. Movies about the fort are shown hourly during the summer, and the bookstore has a good selection of Wyoming and frontier history books. Ask about the daily interpretive talks and tours. Every summer day at 12:30 p.m., an artillery crew fires a blank round through the mountain howitzer, a gun used to drive off Indian attacks.

The **living history** program helps bring Fort Laramie to life each summer, with employees dressed in a variety of period costumes. They will be happy to explain their roles at the fort. Buy a root beer or apple cider at the enlisted men's bar and taste fresh bread in the bakery. If you're in the area in early July, be sure to drop by Fort Laramie for an **Old Fashioned 4th of July Celebration** with all sorts of festivities, including a traveling medicine show and fiddlers. Many locals join in by dressing up in period clothing and taking part in the activities that range from cannon salutes to fashion shows.

Historical Buildings

By the time it was abandoned in 1890, Fort Laramie had approached the size of a small town, with 60 buildings of all types and ages scattered around the grounds. The remains of 21 of these old buildings are still visible, some simply lime grout concrete ruins, maintained in a state of arrested decay. A dozen have been completely restored and refurbished, with authentic period pieces behind Plexiglas doors. The Park Service has an informative Historic Buildings Guide for 20¢, available at the visitor center. See it for descriptions of the various buildings. Several of these are particularly noteworthy: the cavalry barracks, Old Bedlam, the bakery and the guardhouse.

Most of the men who soldiered out of Fort Laramie lived under crowded conditions with little privacy. Sometimes this even meant living in tents for long periods. The **cavalry barracks** (on your left as you enter the fort) were not much of an improvement. Walk up to the restored second floor to find row upon row of cots where an entire company of 60 men slept. Then try to imagine all the snoring and the smelly feet after being out on duty for weeks at a time! Baths were taken (in theory) every Saturday night in a half barrel.

The oldest and most prominent building at Fort Laramie is **Old Bedlam**, an attractive clapboard structure that dominates the west end of the parade grounds. Built in 1849, it was the center of life at the fort. Old Bedlam served a variety of roles: as post headquarters and officers' quarters for the first 19 years, then as a hotel of sorts for bachelor officers, and after 1881 as a duplex for Army families. The name apparently comes from the bedlam that existed with so many folks jammed together, particularly after payday, when parties raged. Old Bedlam is now refurnished to represent two different periods. Upstairs are displays representing the living quarters of Lt. Colonel William O. Collins, while the bachelor officer's quarters are downstairs.

The old stone **guardhouse** on the east side of the fort could house up to 40 prisoners, ranging from soldiers who had violated minor conduct rules to those charged with murder. The basement jail had no furniture, toilet, or light, and no heat even in the dead of winter. Stop by the historic **bakery**—one of four built here at different times—for a taste of bread. One loaf of bread, along with greasy salt pork, beans, rice, and rot-gut coffee, was the typical daily allotment for soldiers. Fresh vegetables were often unavailable for months at a time, and scurvy was a constant threat. In the field, the rations were even worse, generally consisting of salt pork, beans, and wormy hardtack.

One of the less-visited sights in the area is **Old Bedlam ruts** two miles northwest of Fort Laramie. A gravel road leads to the location; get a map from park headquarters. The ruts (marked by posts) climb up into the gentle hills west of the old fort, offering a marvelous panorama of a landscape that has not changed much in the last century. From here, it's easy to imagine emigrants looking back on the fort, their last touch with civilization for hundreds of miles. Nearby is the grave of Mary Homsley, one of the thousands who died along the difficult trek west. The ruts can be traced all the way to Guernsey, where they grow even deeper. A similar series of ruts extends eastward from the fort.

Fort Laramie (The Town)

The town of Fort Laramie (pop. 400) is three miles north of the historic fort and across the North Platte River. Wyoming's oldest post office is here, begun in the 1880s when the Army was occupying the nearby fort. A mile south of town is an **iron bridge** built in 1875. It doesn't look like much—and has been superseded for more than 30 years by a concrete span just up-

river—but was of historic importance. Funded by a $15,000 congressional appropriation, the bridge ensured the creation of the Cheyenne-Deadwood Stage and Express through here. It remained the major route north for many years thereafter. A highway monument east of the town of Fort Laramie along U.S. 26 notes the site of the **Grattan Massacre** (see above).

Margaret's Cafe serves home-style meals, or if you're in a hurry head to **Chuckwagon Drive-In** for fast food. Pitch tents for free at the town park, just across the railroad tracks on the south side of town, or stay at the friendly **Bennett Court Campground**, tel. 837-2270, where tent sites cost $7 and RV sites $9. Showers for non-campers are just $1; open year-round. **Chuckwagon Campground**, tel. 837-2828, is open April-Nov. only, and charges $9 for RVs or tents.

TORRINGTON

Torrington (pop. 6,100) is a quiet farming town located just eight miles from the Nebraska border. It is the county seat for Wyoming's most important agricultural county, Goshen (alias "The Land of Goshen"). Lots of sugar beets, alfalfa, oats, dry beans, corn, and hay are grown here. The tree-lined North Platte River drifts lazily through town. Torrington's economy is relatively stable, with a Holly Sugar factory (the biggest local employer) on the edge of town, and many productive farms in the surrounding countryside. Two long waterways—Fort Laramie Canal and the Interstate Canal—provide irrigation water to much of this farmland. Trains filled with coal from Campbell and Weston counties constantly rumble through toward the south and east; a stench from the sugar beet factory hangs in the air; and the livestock auction is the big daily event. A walk along Main St. is a trek through the American heartland. But bring your earplugs along; loudspeakers on Torrington's downtown street corners blare muzak!

History

Although several hundred thousand emigrants passed through Goshen County on their way to Oregon, California, or Utah, none

bothered to stop. The area was not settled until cattlemen came in the 1880s, followed by homesteaders around the turn of the century, including many from Russia and Germany. Many of the "soddies" and wooden shacks these emigrants built still stand in the fields around the county. Named for Torrington, Connecticut, the town was incorporated in 1907 as a ranching and farming center. Completion of the Interstate Canal in 1915 and the Fort Laramie Canal in 1924 brought North Platte River water, making it possible to grow a wide variety of crops. The Burlington Railroad arrived from the east in 1900, but it was not until 1926 that the Union Pacific built a line connecting Torrington with Pine Bluffs to the south. That year proved a pivotal one, for it brought a new train depot and the Holly Sugar Company plant. The town has grown slowly over the years, and except for a brief flirtation with oil and gas in the 1970s, has remained true to its farming and ranching roots.

Sights

Located right at the crossroads of the Oregon Trail, the Cheyenne to Deadwood Stage Route, the Mormon Trail, and the Texas Cattle Trail, the **Homestead Museum** seems to sit atop history. It is housed in the old brick and ma-

TODD CLARK

TORRINGTON

HOSPITAL

EASTERN WYOMING COLLEGE

GARRETT ST.

WESTERN MOTEL
MAVERICK MOTEL

ROUSE ST.

GOSHEN COUNTY FAIRGROUNDS

WEST VALLEY RD.

TO FT. LARAMIE & GUERNSEY

25th AVE.
TORRINGTON LIVESTOCK COMMISSION CO.

CHAMBER OF COMMERCE
CITY HALL
BRONCO BAR

POST OFFICE
LIBRARY
THE BAKE HAUS

SUPER 8 MOTEL
JACK & JILL FOOD STORE

KING'S INN
ST. JOSEPH CHILDREN'S HOME

GOLF COURSE RD.

PIONEER PARK (CAMPING)

GOLF COURSE

14th AVE.
11th AVE.
KELLY'S SUPER MARKET

BLUE LANTERN MOTEL
TRIPLE M BIKE SHOP

TRAVELERS COURT
IDEAL GROCERY

HOLLY SUGAR FACTORY

NORTH PLATTE RIVER

NOT TO SCALE

HOMESTEADERS MUSEUM

SOUTH MAIN ST.

1st AVE.
2nd AVE.
4th AVE.
5th AVE.

UNION PACIFIC RAILROAD

TO CHEYENNE

SHOEMAKER ST.

JIRDON PARK / SWIMMING POOL

GRASS ROOTS TRAIL

29th AVE.
28th AVE.
27th AVE.
26th AVE.
24th AVE.
23rd AVE.
22nd AVE.
21st AVE.
20th AVE.
19th AVE
16th AVE.
15th AVE.
13th AVE.

MAIN ST.

AIRPORT RD.

18th AVE.
17th AVE.

BURLINGTON NORTHERN RAILROAD

EAST VALLEY RD.

TO SCOTTSBLUFF, NEBRASKA

© MOON PUBLICATIONS, INC.

sonry Union Pacific depot just south of town, built in 1926. The last train stopped at the depot in 1964. The museum, tel. 532-5612, is open Sun. 1-4 and Mon.-Sat. 10-5 during the summer, and Mon.-Fri. 10-4 in winter. Although it contains a substantial paleo-Indian collection, the museum focuses on the thousands of turn-of-the-century homesteaders who flocked to eastern Wyoming. Displays include artifacts from the 4A Ranch on Bear Creek and Bordeau Trading Post near Fort Laramie, an interior reconstruction of a local homestead, plus a marvelous collection of old black-and-white photos. Sit down and spend some time looking through these pictures; they will quickly transport you back to a simple era where pioneers scratched

out a hardscrabble life on the mixed-grass prairie in wooden or sod shacks. Once you are through these, check out the box of freebees: pieces of old stone knives and scrapers from a nearby archaeological dig. Outside is an excellent modern replica of a Concord stagecoach (considered the Rolls Royce of travel at that time), an old homestead cabin, and a windmill.

Over 120,000 cattle are raised in Goshen County each year—more than in any other Wyoming county—so it is logical that Torrington should also be at the center of the livestock trade. Each year more than a quarter million cattle are marketed at Torrington's two livestock sales barns. These are fascinating places to visit, offering an authentic taste of ranching life

Torrington Livestock Auction, on U.S. 26 at W. E St., tel. 532-3333, has auctions beginning at noon every Friday, with additional Wednesday load lot auctions in the fall. **Stockman Livestock Auction**, tel. 532-7079, is two miles south of Torrington on U.S. 85, then a half mile west on State 154. Here you'll find cattle sales every Thursday at 11 a.m., with additional fall sales of feeder cattle on Tuesdays. Tours of nearby cattle ranches are available through a local women's group, the **Goshen County Cow-Belles**, tel. 532-5231 or 532-2809. For just $1, they provide two-hour tours of nearby ranches. Advance arrangements are necessary. For a nice walk, saunter along the **Grassroots Trail**, built atop an old irrigation canal that slices along the northern edge of Torrington.

Motels

The cheapest lodging in Torrington is at **Blue Lantern Motel**, 1402 S. Main St., tel. 532-9986, costing just $16 s or $19 d. It is primarily a residential motel. **Oregon Trail Lodge**, east of town on U.S. 26, tel. 532-2101, has rooms starting for $20 s or $26 d. **Maverick Motel**, 1 1/2 miles west on U.S. 26-85, tel. 532-4064, charges $23 s or $25 d. **Western Motel**, 1 1/2 miles west on U.S. 26-85, tel. 532-2104, has some of the nicest rooms around for $30 s or $32 d. The local **Super 8 Motel**, 1548 S. Main St., tel. 532-7118 or (800) 848-8888, costs $29 s or $33 d. **King's Inn**, 1555 S. Main St., tel. 532-4011, has pleasant rooms and an indoor pool for $33 s or $36 d.

Camping

Camp for free in **Pioneer Park** along the North Platte River on the edge of town. Open year-round, but during the winter you'll need to get water elsewhere. **Travelers Court**, 750 Main, tel. 532-5517, has shady riverside tent sites for $8, with RV sites for $13. Open year-round. **Kountry Kids Kampground**, three miles east of Torrington on U.S. 26, tel. 532-2356, charges $8 for tents and $10 for RVs. Open all year. Also here are all sorts of other recreation, from go-carts and miniature golf to cookouts and canoe float trips down the North Platte River ($22 and up). Popular with families.

Food

For great breakfasts (try the buttermilk hotcakes) and fresh baked goods, head to **The Bake Haus**, 1915 Main St., tel. 532-2982. Lots of locals hang out here in the morning. Good sandwiches and fast food at **Burgers-N-More**, on West U.S. 26-85, tel. 532-4333. Get standard American fare, served in quantity, at **Deacons Restaurant**, 1558 S. Main St., tel. 532-4766, or homestyle country cooking at **Wagwell's Cafe**, 530 W. Railroad Ave., tel. 532-5847. **Kings Inn**, 1555 S. Main St., tel. 532-4011, has prime rib specials on Friday and Saturday nights. For reasonably priced steaks and seafood, head to **Little Moon Lake Supper Club** on the stateline, eight miles east on U.S. 26, tel. 532-5750. Two grocers are in Torrington: **Kelly's Super Market** on S. Main, tel. 532-3113, and **Jack & Jill Food Store**, 1542 S. Main, tel. 532-3401.

Entertainment And Events

Broncho Bar, 1924 Main St., tel. 532-4285, has live country music, while **The Jungle**, 1914 Main, and **Southside Tote-Away**, 1934 W. A St., tel. 532-9822, offer rock and roll. Many locals also head over to the **Stateline Oasis**, just across the Nebraska line, for the chance to dance to rock or C&W tunes. The biggest annual event in Torrington is the **Goshen County Fair**, held the second full week in August with everything from a parade to pig wrestling. It's a good place to check out all the 4-H hogs and sheep on display. The **Sugartime Harvest Fest**, held the last week in October, includes a pancake feed, bike race, street sales, live music, and dancing.

Information and Services

The **Torrington Chamber of Commerce** office, 350 W. 21st Ave., tel. 532-3879, is open Mon.-Fri. 9-noon and 1-5. The **public library**, 2001 E. A St., tel. 532-3411, is open Mon.-Sat. 10-5 in summer with reduced Sat. hours (10-noon) in winter. **The Christmas Store**, 119 E. 19th Ave., tel. 532-7433, has some used books for sale. **Eastern Wyoming College**, 3200 W. C St., tel. 532-7111, is one of the oldest junior colleges in the state, first established in 1948 as an extension of the University of Wyoming (but now independent). The hilltop campus has 1,800 full- and part-time students studying in nearly 60 vocational and academic fields. **Denver Express**, tel. (800) 658-3231, has daily van runs to Scottsbluff, Nebraska, as well as Cheyenne and Denver. **Triple M Bike Shop**, 1112 S. Main St., tel. 532-7833, rents bikes, while cars can be rented from **Platte Valley Motor Co.**, 510 W. Valley Rd., tel. 532-2114. Torrington has an outdoor **swimming pool** (tel. 532-7798) in Jirdon Park that is open summers only. Kids will love the 180-foot water slide. There is also an 18-hole municipal **golf course** north of town, tel. 532-2418.

TORRINGTON VICINITY

The town symbol for Torrington is the ringnecked pheasant, a fitting one in this farming country. **Downar Bird Farm**, 17 miles south on U.S. 85, raises some 7,000 pheasants each year. It is run by the Wyoming Game and Fish Department, which releases them each fall for area hunters. This is basically a release-and-shoot operation, since the birds are let go in unfamiliar territory just in time for hunting season. The farm is an interesting place to visit, with 27 different pheasant breeds. (By the way, the ringnecked pheasant so common in the Midwest is a native of China.)

Heading North
Ten miles northwest of Torrington is the farming crossroads called **Lingle** (pop. 500). Here you'll find two fine places to eat. **Lira's**, tel. 837-2826, offers authentic Mexican food that attracts folks from many miles around. Also here is **Stagecoach Inn**, tel. 837-2614, with all-you-can-eat dinner specials on Thursday and Friday evenings and the largest salad bar in the area. Lingle's **Harvest Festival** takes place each August. North of Lingle on U.S. 85, the irrigated pastures and green fields give way to endless prairies. This is a land of sandy hillocks carpeted with short grasses, similar to the sandhill country of western Nebraska that lies just a dozen miles eastward.

Halfway between Lingle and Lusk, the road passes the almost ghost town of **Jay Em** (pop. 15), named for the cattle brand of rancher Jim Moore. Just to the north lies his old Jay Em Ranch. A few people still live in the old wooden houses of Jay Em, and the post office becomes a meeting place each morning, but the town is otherwise deserted. It's a peaceful spot to stop and walk along narrow Rawhide Creek among the cottonwood trees and tall grass. The rustic old buildings (a National Historic District) are a photographer's treat. Continuing north to Lusk, the country again opens into grassland, windmills, and cattle, with a few tree-topped hills and small rocky buttes.

LUSK

Lusk (pop. 1,700) is the county seat of Wyoming's least-populated county. Just 3,200 people live in rural Niobrara County—an average of almost 524 acres per person! It's remote grassland country here, with long, straight highways leading from Lusk in the compass directions. As a ranching town, Lusk has a relatively stable, albeit limited, economic base. The oil industry that once was so prominent here has faded considerably in recent years.

History
The first settlers in this part of Wyoming were miners in search of copper, silver, and gold. They built a small settlement around the Silver Cliff Mine, but moved a mile east when the Fremont, Elkhorn, and Missouri Valley Railroad arrived in 1886. Lusk was named for Frank Lusk, a local rancher who donated land for the new townsite. In 1917, oil was discovered along Lance Creek, 20 miles north of here, and almost overnight, Lusk became a boomtown, reaching more than 10,000 residents during the peak years of oil production. Pipelines were built to the 200 producing wells, and a refinery was added in Lusk. By the 1940s, Lance Creek had become Wyoming's largest oil field. More recently, oil production has declined, and the old standby of ranching has regained prominence. In 1984, the town succeeded in getting a women's correctional center built in Lusk. This is now the second-largest employer in the county (after the local school district).

Lusk has seen its share of lust over the years. The Yellow Hotel brothel occupied a place of local importance until the 1970s; rumor has it that the madam, Del Burke, was allowed to keep it open because she owned most of Lusk's water bonds. Ten miles southwest of Lusk is a marker to **Mother Featherlegs** (so named because she often rode horseback with her red pantaloons blowing in the wind). A well-known madam, she was murdered in 1879, apparently for money. Some claim that a fortune in gold she had buried nearby is still waiting to be claimed. A marker 10 miles southwest of Lusk notes the site of her old place of entertainment, and is said to be the nation's only historical marker commemorating a prostitute. In 1990, Lusk locals swept into a Deadwood saloon and recovered her famous pantaloons which had been stolen from the historic site in 1964.

Sights

Lusk has one of the nicer historic collections in the state, the aptly named **Stagecoach Museum**, 342 S. Main. It's open daily 10-5 and 7-9 p.m. in July and Aug., and Mon.-Fri. 1-5 during May, June, Sept., and October. Climb up the steep, narrow stairs to find the reason for this name, an old coach built by Abbott & Downing of Concord, New Hampshire in the 1860s. Used for many years on the famed Cheyenne and Black Hills Stage and Express Line, the stagecoach is one of only two in existence; its sister resides in the Smithsonian Institution. The museum also houses a treasure chest broken open during the Canyon Springs Stage robbery of 1879. (It contained gold bullion from the Black Hills destined for Cheyenne.) Other items in the Lusk museum are more standard fare—an old buggy, a sulky, a dray wagon, and covered wagons, along with various Indian artifacts and arrowheads. Notice the collection of photos from Niobrara County's many old one-room schoolhouses, and above the staircase, a 31-star U.S. flag from 1876. Try to not snicker at the kitschy doll collection dressed up as the wives of various presidents. Out back is an old one-room schoolhouse. Another sight of minor historical interest is on the east side of town along the railroad tracks. Here you'll find a **redwood water tank** built in 1886 to supply water for steam engines of the Chicago and Northwestern Railroad. It is one of only six still standing in the nation.

Motels

The least expensive lodging in Lusk is at **Hospitality House Motor Hotel**, 201 S. Main, tel. 334-2120, with rooms upstairs for $18 s or $21 d. **Townhouse Motel**, 565 S. Main, tel. 334-2376, has rooms starting for just $24 s or d, while **Rawhide Motel**, 805 S. Main, tel. 334-2440, charges $26 s or $28 d. **Pioneer Court (Best Western)**, 731 S. Main, tel. 334-2640 or (800) 528-1234, has pleasant rooms for $28 s or $34 d and up. **Covered Wagon Motel**, 730 S. Main, tel. 334-2836 or (800) 341-8000, offers the nicest accommodations in Lusk starting for $36 s or d (including pool, jacuzzi, and sauna). **Trail Motel (Budget Host)**, 305 W. 8th, tel. 334-2530 or (800) 333-5875, charges $37 s or d.

Camping

Camp for free in **Northside Park**, right along the Niobrara River. **BJ's Campground**, 902 S. Maple St., tel. 334-2462, has clean campsites at $11 for tents and RVs, and is open year-round. **Pink Panther Campground**, two miles west of Lusk on U.S. 18-20, tel. 334-2827, charges $11 for tents and $12 for RVs. Showers for non-campers are $4. Open April-November.

Food

The best breakfasts in town are at **Coffee Cup Cafe**, 206 S. Main, tel. 334-3303, and **Crazy Charlie's Truck Stop**, 1025 S. Main, tel. 334-2200. **Ducks Restaurant**, 625 S. Main St., tel. 334-2322, serves steaks, seafood, and Mexican dinners. Check out the amusing collection of duck memorabilia. **The Diner**, 234 S. Main, tel. 334-3606, offers basic greasy-spoon fare: good pancakes for breakfast and decent Friday night tacos. **Ranger Cafe**, 302 S. Main, tel. 334-2028, is another popular spot with locals. **Fireside Inn**, 904 S. Main, tel. 334-3477, is a bit expensive, but has very good family-style meals. The Sunday brunch is a bargain, and the soup-and-salad bar offers an inexpensive way to pig out. Live C&W music at the downtown **Cowboy Bar**, 904 S. Main, tel. 334-3634. Lusk has a **Safeway** store at 405 S. Main.

Information And Services

The **Lusk Chamber of Commerce**, 218 S. Main, tel. 334-2950, is open during the summer Mon.-Fri. 10-noon and 1-3, and Sat. 10-noon. Winter hours are hit or miss. Swim at the **Lusk Plunge** on the north side of the tracks during the summer. The local country club offers a free round of golf to anyone showing a current receipt from a local motel or campground. **Wyoming Whale Ranch** near Lusk provides wagon camping tours of historic sites along the Cheyenne-Deadwood Stage Route. Call 334-3598 for specifics. Lusk has an **Octoberfest** in mid-September (Septemberfest?) with German food, beer, polkas, and games. The **Niobrara County Fair** comes to Lusk in early August. The major local event, however, is the *Legend of Rawhide*.

LEGEND OF RAWHIDE

In 1946 the town of Lusk was looking for an event to attract visitors; something, say, along the lines of Cheyenne Frontier Days, only different. A local doctor, Walter Reckling, faintly remembered a tale that had been passed down for generations—the legend of Rawhide Buttes. It was one of the enduring yarns of the Old West, an event claimed to have occurred in half a dozen different states, and with probably a thousand different versions. In the story an emigrant wagon train headed west to the California goldfields, carrying along a young man who boasted that he would shoot the first Indian he saw. He killed an innocent Indian girl (a princess, of course) and her tribe retaliated by attacking the wagon train and forcing the young man to surrender. He was skinned alive in revenge. Nobody has ever been able to substantiate the tale, but then again, nobody has proved it didn't happen either.

Dr. Reckling managed to stir up considerable interest in Lusk for the idea, and then found a local col-

lege student, Eva Lou Bonsell, who was studying theater in Colorado. She wrote a play to be pantomimed as a narrator described the scenes, and the *Legend of Rawhide* was off and running. The first production gained a measure of reality by being staged in the midst of a thunderstorm. The crowd of 10,000 loved it. The *Legend of Rawhide* made the covers of *Life* and *Look* magazines at various times, and ran from 1946 to 1966. It was revived again in 1986. Today, the annual production is still a decidedly local affair with a cast of 200 folks from the surrounding area. The spectacle has evolved over the years with the addition of 13 "soiled doves," Father DeSmet, and Jim Bridger, along with some 15 wagons and several dozen Indians on ponies. The skinning alive of bad guy Clyde Pickett is the gory climax. (It's also quite a trick, but I won't give away the secret.)

The *Legend of Rawhide* is put on the second weekend in July every year, and begins at 8 p.m. on Fri. and Sat. nights. General admission is $5, or $3 for kids under 12, with reserved seats in the covered grandstands for $8. Other activities include afternoon parades and an art show. For more information, call 334-2950 or 334-3764. Whether or not the story is true, **Rawhide Buttes** actually do exist; they are 10 miles south of Lusk. (Some stories give a less interesting version for the origin of the name Rawhide Buttes: that they were the site where raw buffalo hides were prepared for shipment east.) A highway marker notes the Cheyenne and Deadwood Stage Station that once stood here.

TODD CLARK

HEADING NORTH

U.S. 18-85 heads due north from Lusk toward Newcastle, passing through mile after mile of rolling and windy grassland with scattered rocky buttes, a few wearing a top hat of ponderosa pines. For the first dozen miles the road parallels the historic Cheyenne-Deadwood Stage Route. Bottomland creeks curl through, with cottonwoods and willows on both sides. This is gorgeous Big Sky country; the land seems almost an afterthought. It's about as remote a place as you'll find, with just a few ranches, windmills, and cattle for company.

Some 13 miles north of Lusk is a sign noting the old **Fort Hat Creek Stage Station**, mistakenly built (in 1876) along Sage Creek, Wyoming instead of Hat Creek, Nebraska! Easy to see how the country could start to blend together in the endless hills here. The old stage station itself is two miles east of here on a paved road and then one mile southwest on a gravel road. It is an impressive two-story log structure built in 1887 to replace the original buildings that had burned. The small fort garrisoned 40 soldiers who rode out to protect the Cheyenne–Deadwood Stage from attack. Hat Creek was typical of other stage stations along the route. One writer of the time, Leander P. Richardson, noted: "At any of these places a traveler can purchase almost anything, from a glass of whiskey to a four-horse team, but the former article is usually the staple of demand."

Tiny **Lance Creek** (pop. 180) lies in the middle of Niobrara County and is surrounded by the Lance Creek oil fields. An oil boom peaked here during World War II, but more recently, production has declined and the community ekes out a minimal survival. The Lance Creek area is famous as the site for discoveries of horned dinosaurs (Ceratopsians) and other fossils. Beginning in the 1880s, scientists found an incredible number of fossil plants, dinosaurs, and ancient mammals, including at least 75 different species of vertebrates, many of which were previously unknown. There are no signs or facilities to mark the location. Halfway between Lusk and Newcastle is **Mule Creek Junction**, consisting of a state rest area along with a combination gas station/cafe/junk-food shop. A couple of miles north of this U.S. 85 crosses Cheyenne River, near the site of the aptly named **Robber's Roost Stage Station**. Here outlaws sometimes attacked the Cheyenne-Deadwood Stage when it slowed to cross the river. In an 1878 robbery attempt an outlaw was killed here by the shotgun messengers, but the others managed to escape with the mail sacks.

MEDICINE BOW COUNTRY

West from Cheyenne, I-80 climbs a long, gentle ramp into the Laramie Mountains, reaching the highest point on its 3,000-mile trek across America, and then abruptly beginning a steep descent onto the spacious Laramie Plains. A distinctly frontier feeling envelops this land: mountains rim the valley, and as you continue west the grass is intermixed with more and more sagebrush. You are entering the real West of mountains, sage, and sky.

Medicine Bow Country consists of Albany County, with Laramie and the Laramie Plains at its center and the Laramie and Medicine Bow mountains on either side, along with Carbon County, where Rawlins is the main town and the Sierra Madre dominate the southern horizon. The name Medicine Bow has a convoluted origin. The mountains in southern Wyoming were considered a sacred place, and each year Indians gathered nearby to celebrate powwows and to build bows from the cedar wood. The Indian term for medicine means something spiritually powerful, as symbolized by the mountains, by the cedar that made fine bows, and by the annual powwows. Whites combined the various tribal activities into "Medicine Bow," and

applied the name to a river, a mountain range, a national forest, and a town.

The land is remarkably diverse in terms of both topography and vegetation. Laramie Basin contains the highest short-grass prairie in the world, some 7,200 feet above sea level. Three mountain ranges cross through this region: the Laramie Mountains, Medicine Bow Mountains (also called the Snowy Range), and the Sierra Madre. Mountain slopes are covered with lodgepole pine, Engelmann spruce, and subalpine fir, while alpine meadows, tundra, and rock dominate at the highest elevations. To the north and west of these mountain ranges, the country is a dry landscape of sage and desert.

Economy

The economy of the Medicine Bow region is much like the rest of Wyoming, heavily dependent upon grazing and energy. More than 170,000 cattle and 75,000 sheep graze over this land of sage and grass, while mines near Hanna produce large amounts of low-sulfur coal. Wells in Carbon County pump more than 37 million cubic feet of natural gas each year. Other important pieces of the regional economy are the

MEDICINE BOW COUNTRY

© MOON PUBLICATIONS

University of Wyoming in Laramie and tourism, particularly in the Snowy Range and Upper North Platte River Valley. Transportation has long been a vital factor in the region. Ben Holladay's stage traversed the desolate plains on the Overland Trail, followed by the Union Pacific Railroad, and eventually by I-80, the primary artery across America for truckers and travelers.

The remote stretch of I-80 between Laramie and Elk Mountain is commonly called the "Snow Chi Minh Trail," a joking reference to the ceaseless blowing snow that sometimes shuts down traffic for days at a time during the winter. Gale-force winds have even been known to blow semis over!

LARAMIE

The countryside around Laramie (pop. 27,000) differs little from much of Wyoming—arid plains abruptly broken by rugged mountain ranges—but the town itself offers a real change of pace. True, Laramie does have rodeos, restaurants with names like The Cavalryman, and great C&W tunes at the ever-popular Cowboy Saloon, but it also seems to violate one's expectations of a Wyoming town. Take a stroll along downtown's Ivinson Ave. and you'll discover The Chocolate Cellar, with fancy chocolates from all over, and Whole Earth Grainery, selling bulk organic foods in a hippie decor. Nearby are vegetarian restaurants that serve cappuccino, and a bar that attracts reggae bands.

Laramie is one of my favorite cities in Wyoming, a place with a sense of intelligence without being stultified, where culture mixes with fun and games. Tourist brochures call Laramie "Gem City of the Plains." It has the laid-back college town feel of a Chico or Fort Collins. The students add a playful, educated atmosphere—there are bikes on the streets, heady conversations over beers, and lots to do, from rock concerts to theatrical productions. Laramie has both crowded fast food outlets and sophisticated restaurants offering more substantial fare. It is probably the only place in the state (other than Jackson) where a restaurant would have the temerity to put descriptions of wines on the menu: "An excellent varietal aroma of apples and butter. It has a full rich flavor and a nicely balanced, clean finish . . ."

The Union Pacific Railroad splits Laramie into two distinct parts. The campus, the more stately older homes, and nearly all the city lie on the east side, while less pretentious quarters lie on "the other side of the tracks." Long freight trains roll through every few minutes at all hours of the day and night, piled high with double-deck containerized freight boxes destined for Chicago, Denver, or Las Vegas.

Located close to the Medicine Bow Mountains (hiking, skiing, etc.), Vedauwoo Rocks (rock-climbing), Lake Hattie (windsurfing), and the Colorado Rockies, Laramie is a haven for those who love the outdoors. The only problem is the wind that in midwinter makes life in this part of the state difficult. Temperatures may be relatively mild—in the low 20s—but add in a 30 mph wind and it feels like 20 below. Bitter, gale-force winds can howl through for days on end in this open country.

HISTORY

The city of Laramie—along with all sorts of other places in eastern Wyoming—has the name of a French-Canadian trapper who was killed by Arapaho Indians in the mountains now named in his honor. Nearly everything else about the man is open to question. Jacques LaRamee (or was it Joseph De la Ramie?) was killed in 1820 (or 1821) by Arapahos (or another tribe) who stuffed his body under the ice in a beaver pond (or left his body in his cabin). Be that as it may, in death he had a far more lasting legacy than anything he did while alive.

Fort Sanders

The first permanent settlement in the Laramie area was Fort Sanders (originally known as Fort John Buford), built in 1866. Located approximately two miles south of present-day Laramie, it served to protect emigrants and stagecoaches along the Overland Trail, and later to protect Union Pacific Railroad construction workers. At its peak, Fort Sanders housed nearly 600 soldiers. As with other posts on the frontier, desertions were rampant; 41 men went AWOL in a single month, taking with them whatever supplies they could grab. As the threat from Indian attacks lessened over the years, so did the value of Fort Sanders. It was abandoned in 1882.

The Union Pacific Arrives

Laramie City (as it was first called) was named and established by Gen. Grenville Dodge, the man in charge of planning the Union Pacific's route westward. The location was chosen because of a major spring that still produces millions of gallons of water, and because ties could be cut in the mountains to the west and brought down the Laramie River. The proximity of Fort Sanders also influenced the location. By the time the first train rolled into Laramie City on May 10, 1868, many "sooners" had already set up business in tents. The first passengers were met with 23 saloons, one hotel, and no churches. Within three months, Laramie had 5,000 people.

Many of the earliest to arrive were the usual end-of-the-track types: hoodlums, gamblers, prostitutes, and others out to make a fast buck. When the tracks headed on westward, the riffraff stayed behind, kept busy by the soldiers. Within a short time, a saloon owner named Asa Moore gained the support of various gambling houses, brothels, and other bars to create a rump town government with him as mayor. The

man they appointed town marshall had recently left Cheyenne after being acquitted on a murder charge, and his assistant was caught stealing mules. Laramie quickly became one of the wildest towns on the frontier, with murders almost daily. Men who were arrested often faced a trial in a back room of Asa Moore's saloon, where his men robbed and then killed them, burying their bodies out on the plains. Stories tell of up to 10 men disappearing in a single night.

Seeing that the law was in the hands of criminals, the more respectable citizens decided to put an end to the mayhem. More than 500 men joined a vigilance committee that swept into the saloons, brothels, dance halls, and casinos on

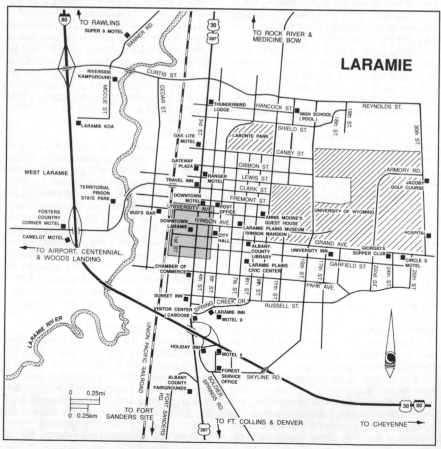

the night of Oct. 18, 1868. Three men died in gun battles (including a musician and a vigilante) and dozens of others were wounded. Another three were hanged by vigilantes, including Asa Moore. The next day, outlaw Big Steve Young met the same fate, and more than a hundred crooks were piled into railroad cars and sent west. These actions calmed things down rather quickly, and thereafter Laramie City became something of a model town. It is perhaps fitting that, four years later, Laramie would be awarded the territorial prison.

For many years the main reason for the existence of Laramie was the presence of the railroad and the operations it established, including a round house, iron foundry, tie-treating plant, machine shops, and a mill for reprocessing old rails. Gold discoveries in the Snowy Range to the west helped Laramie's economy grow, but the railroad remained the larges. employer in Laramie until the 1950s when it was supplanted by the university.

Women's Suffrage

Laramie was the site of two of the most notable events in the history of women's rights. On September 6, 1870, Louisa Gardner Swain ("Grandma Swain") became the first woman in the nation to vote in an open and public election. A few months before this, a judge in Laramie established the world's first jury to have women members. (Reporters noted that the female jurors hid behind heavy veils and held crying babies on their laps.) The women brought about a change in the jury system: breaks for boozing and gambling were ended, while smoking and chewing tobacco in the jury box were halted. The women also proved more likely to convict men of murder than their male peers who regarded killing humans a less serious crime than rustling cattle. A stone monument near 1st and Garfield streets marks the location where the first all-woman jury met.

The University

In 1886, Laramie received a gift from the state Legislature that would eventually transform it from a cow town into a college town. Under the leadership of Col. Steph-

en W. Downey ("Father of the University"), the Legislature voted to establish the new University of Wyoming. It was part of a deal that carved up Wyoming: Cheyenne became the capital city, while Rawlins landed the prison, and Evanston the state asylum. The bill was signed into law by Gov. Francis E. Warren in 1886, four years before Wyoming achieved statehood. The school opened the following year with a single building—now called Old Main—built at a cost of $49,000. The new program had five professors and 42 students (both men and women) who paid $7.50 each to attend. Over the years, the railroad gradually lost in importance while the university added more and more to the local economy, until it became the biggest local employer. It remains so today. Because of the university, Laramie has never really experienced the economic booms and busts common to much of Wyoming.

WYOMING STATE MUSEUM
Women's Suffrage, Frank Leslie's Newspaper, 1888

UNIVERSITY OF WYOMING

Wyoming is unique as the only state to have just one baccalaureate-granting institution. The University of Wyoming campus in Laramie thus gains the state's undivided financial support, much to the chagrin of the two-year colleges. The university lays claim to being the highest university campus in the nation; at 7,200 feet, it makes Denver's mile-high claim to fame look puny. Although not a major research institution, the school has respected research programs in atmospheric sciences (ozone depletion studies), aquatic toxicology, oil recovery technology, water management, agricultural research, and infrared astronomy. Approximately 10,000 students attend the university.

BILL NYE

Laramie lays claim to one of the most popular humorists of the 19th century, Edgar "Bill" Nye (1850-1896). Born in Maine and raised in Wisconsin, Nye arrived in Laramie in 1876, and soon began writing columns for the *Laramie Daily Sentinel*. His sharp wit and wry sense of humor quickly began to show through the news, and local Republicans backed him in publishing his own paper, the *Laramie Boomerang* (named for a flea-bitten gray mule that kept returning no matter how hard Nye tried to get rid of him). The paper first rolled off his "lemon-squeezer" press in 1881. When the news wasn't all that interesting, Nye would "write up things that never occurred with a masterly and graphic hand. Then, if they occur, I am grateful; if not, I bow to the inevitable and smother my chagrin."

AMERICAN HERRITAGE MUSEUM

In 1883, an attack of spinal meningitis forced him to leave high-elevation Laramie for a lower climate. By the time he departed, Nye's newspaper was in dire financial condition, but it managed to survive under new, more responsible, management. The *Boomerang* is still published today, and is one of the state's few daily papers. The old livery stable where it was published is on the corner of 3rd and Garfield; Nye's office was on the second floor.

Bill Nye's witty *Boomerang* columns gained him something of a national following, and by the 1890s, Nye had become the best-paid humorist in America, making $30,000 a year. Nye would eventually author 14 books of humor, the best known being *Bill Nye and Boomerang*, *Forty Liars and Other Lies*, and *Baled Hay*. *Bill Nye's History of the United States*, published in 1894, sold an incredible 500,000 copies. Unfortunately, the intense stress of being constantly on the road helped shorten his life. Nye died of a stroke when just 45 years old.

The following commentary on Wyoming agriculture and "reclamation" efforts is typical of Nye's tongue-in-cheek writing:

> I do not wish to discourage those who might wish to come to this place for the purpose of engaging in agriculture, but frankly I will state that it has its drawbacks. In the first place, the soil is quite course, and the agriculturist, before he can even begin with any prospect of success must run his farm through a stamp-mill in order to make it sufficiently mellow. This, as the reader will see, involves a large expense at the very outset. Hauling the farm to a custom mill would delay the farmer two or three hundred years in getting his crops in, thus giving the agriculturist who had a pulverized farm in Nebraska, Colorado, or Utah, a great advantage over his own, which had not yet been to the reduction works . . .

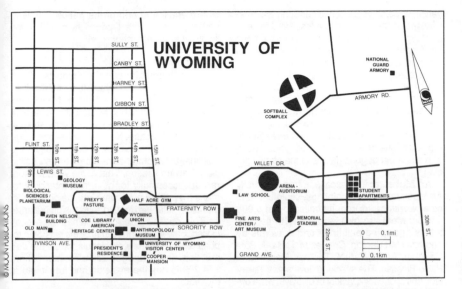

The university provides a wide spectrum of degree programs, some 110 at the undergraduate level along with 125 graduate programs. It operates on a semester system with a summer session open to visiting students. A summertime Elderhostel provides classes for folks over 60, and various noncredit classes are also offered throughout the year, covering the spectrum from ballroom dancing to LSAT preparation. For a copy of the school's *General Bulletin,* call the Admissions office at 766-5160 or (800) 342-5996 or write: University of Wyoming Admissions Office, Box 3435, Laramie, WY 82071.

Campus Sights

Head to the Coe Library's **American Heritage Center** for a real treat. The library itself offers the finest collection of books about Wyoming in existence, and is the hub of an eight-unit library system containing nearly a million volumes. The Rare Book Room on the third floor houses displays on various writers, along with Alfred Jacob Miller's famous *The Rendezvous Near Green River—Oregon Territory,* valued at $750,000. (Miller was the only artist to ever witness a mountain men rendezvous.) Also here are displays on Owen Wister, the Johnson County War, and various outlaws.

The Heritage Center, tel. 766-4114, is on the fifth floor, and is open Mon.-Fri. 7:30-4:30 during the summer, and Mon.-Fri. 8-5 the rest of the year. A gorgeous saddle presented to actor Tim McCoy by the Shoshone Indians in 1918 is here, along with other Hollywood film memorabilia such as the six-guns worn by Hopalong Cassidy, and even Jack Benny's violin. Of far more value are the prints by George Catlin, who spent five years in Indian country (1832-1837), etchings and watercolors by Yellowstone painter Thomas Moran, and oil paintings by W.H. Jackson, Bill Gollings, and Henry Farny. Hidden away in the director's office is a Frederic Remington painting. All told, a stunning display that almost nobody seems to notice.

Anthropology Museum: A small portion of the Anthropology Department's extensive cultural collection can be seen on the main floor of the Anthropology Building (tel. 766-5310, open Mon.-Fri. 8-5). The primary focus is on Plains Indians. A mammoth skull is here, along with a display on the Vore Site buffalo jump in northeastern Wyoming.

Geology Museum: One of the more interesting campus sites is the Geology Museum, tel. 766-4218, open Mon.-Fri. 8-5 and Sat.-Sun. 10-1. Free tours are available. A life-size bronze Tyrannosaurus rex greets visitors at the entrance, while dinosaur bones surround the door-way. Inside the museum are fossil and mineral displays from around the state. An enormous mammoth skull found near Rawlins is one of the most impressive fossils, but the museum's centerpiece is a 75-foot-long and 15-foot-tall skeleton of an Aptosaurus excelsus, better known as a Brontosaurus. Excavated along Sheep Creek in Albany County, it's one of just five mounted specimens in the world. Right next door is the **Wyoming Geological Survey Building**, with tons of fun maps of all types, along with a number of good guides to the state's geology.

Art Museum: The excellent, free University Art Museum exhibits paintings, sculpture, and other works of art from its collection of 5,000 pieces. Most are by 19th- and 20th-century artists, including paintings and drawings by Thomas Hart Benton, Charles M. Russell, Paul Gauguin, Andy Warhol, Thomas Moran, and Pablo Picasso. The spacious downstairs gallery provides space for a variety of displays, while up-stairs is a small gallery with student and faculty works. The museum is located in the Fine Arts Center, tel. 766-2374, and is open Tues.-Fri. 11:30-5 and Sat.-Sun. 1:30-5. Another place to see artwork on campus is **Gallery 234**, which exhibits student pieces. It is located in the Wyoming Union building.

Other University Sights: The first building built on the campus was **Old Main**, completed in 1887 and now housing the administrative offices. The prominent tower that once adorned the building was removed in 1915. Look for Wyoming's territorial seal over the west entrance. Located in the basement of the Science Complex near the Science Library, the **Planetarium** offers Wednesday programs during the school year at 7:30 p.m. It specializes in the history of astronomy with a recorded tape and slide show on the solar system. In the Agriculture Addition building is the **Entomology Museum** that houses thousands of insect specimens. Although primarily for research, it is open to the public. Also in the same building is the **Range Herbarium**, considered one of the most complete collections of grasses in the western states. It is open Mon.-Fri. 7:30-4:30. More impressive is the **Rocky Mountain Herbarium**, on the third floor of the Aven Nelson building, tel. 766-2236, where you'll find one of the nation's largest herbarium collections. Open to the general public by prior arrangement.

Other Laramie Sights

Laramie Plains Museum: Although its official name is the Laramie Plains Museum, this historic site is known to most folks as the Ivinson Mansion. Located at 603 Ivinson, the home is a delightful example of the Queen Anne style of Victorian architecture. Now on the National Register of Historic Places, it was built in 1892 for a millionaire merchant-turned-banker and politician, Edward Ivinson. That same year, Ivinson ran unsuccessfully for governor, intending to make his palatial new home into the governor's mansion. After his death, the mansion became an Episcopalian girls school. When the school closed, Safeway planned to raze the old home to build a grocery store, but locals fought the demolition and managed to raise more than $74,000 to buy the mansion and turn it into a museum.

The Ivinson Mansion spreads over an entire city block, with a carriage house out back. Few of the original furnishings remain, but much of the interior woodwork (including a free-standing stairway built without nails or screws) is still here. The museum has been furnished with antiques, including some elaborate hand-carved furniture built at the Wyoming Penitentiary in 1901, handmade toys (including a 160-year-old doll), a piano that arrived by covered wagon, and a number of Indian artifacts. More unusual are such items as a quilt that took 60 years to complete (listed in *Ripley's Believe It or Not*), a seven-headed shower that looks like a medieval torture chamber, and some 300 different Madonnas! Look for the horsehair quirt made by Bill Carlisle, the "gentleman train robber" (see p. 112). In the back carriage house, be sure to buy a couple of the amusing postcards from 1907.

The museum, tel. 742-4448, is open Sun. 1-5 and Mon.-Sat. 9-8, June-Aug., and Mon.-Sat. 1-3 the rest of the year. Guided tours are given throughout the day. It costs $2 for adults, $1.50 for seniors, $1 for ages 6-15, and free for children. During the summer, the museum has free programs (tel. 766-3031) for children every Wednesday morning.

Territorial Prison

In 1872, the territorial Legislature voted to construct a penitentiary at Laramie. (Wyoming prisoners had previously been housed in the Detroit House of Correction at a cost of $1.25 a week.) The imposing three-story stone building was dedicated to "evil doers of all classes and kinds"; fittingly enough, a bottle of bourbon was deposited in the cornerstone. It remained a prison until 1902 when the inmates were transferred to a new facility in Rawlins. The most famous prisoner to spend time here was the outlaw George Parker, better known as Butch Cassidy. (Both Calamity Jane and Jack McCall—the man who killed Wild Bill Hickock—spent time in the Laramie jail, but not in the prison.)

After the prisoners were moved out in 1902, the building was turned over to the university for use as a stock farm, with the cells becoming cattle stalls and the prison broom factory becoming a sheep barn. In 1986, the state declared the site Wyoming Territorial Park. Since then, the prison restoration has become part of a massive development to create the largest historical theme park in the Rockies. Various attractions will be opening over the next several years, with the full $60 million project to be completed by 1995. Look out Disneyland! The Territorial Prison (tel. 745-6161) is open daily, with tours every half-hour during the summer. The cost is $2 for adults, $1 for ages 8-18, and free for kids under 8.

Laramie Plains Civic Center

A couple of places are worth visiting at the civic center, 710 Garfield. The **Wyoming Children's Nature Center and Museum**, tel. 745-4732, is open Sat. 10-4 during the summer or by appointment the rest of the year, and provides kids a hands-on experience with the natural world. Admission is $1 for adults or 50¢ for children. Also on the grounds is the **East Side School**. Built in 1878, this is the oldest stone schoolhouse in Wyoming. Inside the civic center theater are the six **murals**, painted in the early 1930s by noted muralist Florence E. Ware.

Art Galleries

Laramie has a number of small art galleries in addition to the fine one at the university. **El Cuero Del Toro**, 205 Grand Ave., tel. 721-8893,

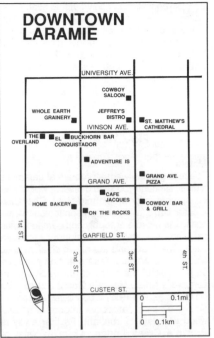

sells South American baskets, hats, and woven wall hangings, as well as other crafts from around the world. Other local galleries worth a look are **Gallery West**, 121 Ivinson Ave., tel. 742-3245, **Artisans' Gallery**, 213 S. 2nd, tel. 745-3983, and **Mitchell's Frame Studio**, 209 S. 3rd, tel. 742-9755.

Other Sights

A granite monument to **Fort Sanders** is two more miles south of town on Kiowa Street. Not much remains of the fort other than the ruins of the old stone guardhouse and the powder house. One of Fort Sanders' wooden buildings was moved to LaBonte Park, at 9th and Canby streets in Laramie, and is now used as a recreation center. **St. Matthew's Cathedral**, at the corner of 3rd and Ivinson, is one of Wyoming's more interesting churches. The limestone church was built in 1868 and funded by banker Edward Ivinson. Laramie's downtown is on the National Register of Historic Places with many buildings dating from the 19th century. Along Ivinson Ave., a major renovation turned what had been a collection of sleazy flophouses and bars into a lively and enjoyable section of Laramie. The chamber of commerce office provides a city map that includes a **walking tour** of town. **Hutton Lake National Wildlife Refuge** is six miles south of Laramie on State 230, then three miles south on County Rd. 37. It is a quiet, peaceful place to look for ducks, shorebirds, and migratory birds.

PRACTICALITIES

Motels

Space is generally not a problem at Laramie's motels, although you should reserve well ahead during graduation week (mid-May), Cheyenne Frontier Days (mid-July), and on football weekends. The old rule of supply and demand holds here, so rates also rise considerably at these times. The best deals are at two chain motels: Motel 8 and Motel 6 (see chart on opposite page). One of the homiest places to stay in Laramie is **Annie Moore's Guest House.** The old house (built in 1912) is now a bed and breakfast, and has an attractive interior of natural wood with lots of sunlight. Farther away is **Brown's Creek Lodge**, 17 miles west of Laramie, tel. 745-8700. Near here is the historic stone ranch home of Henry Bath, built in 1875. **Vee Bar Guest Ranch** is 20 miles west on U.S. 130, tel. 745-7036, with daily or weekly accommodations. **Two Bars Seven Ranch**, tel. 742-6072, is in the tiny town of Tie Siding, 27 miles south of Laramie on State 287, and provides daily or weekly accommodations.

Camping

The closest public campground ($5) is in the scenic Pole Mountain portion of **Medicine Bow National Forest**, approximately 10 miles east of Laramie. Other public campsites are 30 miles west in the Snowy Range. See below for details on both areas. **Curt Gowdy State Park**, 22 miles east of Laramie on State 210 (Happy Jack Rd.), has campsites for $4. **Riverside Kampground**, I-80 at Curtis, tel. 742-2129, charges $7 for tents and $9 for RVs. Located along the Laramie River, it's open year-round. **Laramie KOA**, 1171 Baker, tel. 742-6553, charges $9 for tents and $15 for RVs. Showers cost $3 for non-campers. Open mid-March through mid-November. **N-H Trailer Ranch**, 1360 N. 3rd., tel. 742-3158, charges $10 for RV parking with hookups. Open year-round.

Food

If you like reasonable prices, creative cooking, and a wide selection (who doesn't?), you're bound to appreciate all that Laramie has to offer in the way of dining out. You'll discover some of the best food in Wyoming here. For earthy breakfasts and hearty dinners, visit **The Overland**, 100 Ivinson Ave., tel. 721-2800, a very popular cafe with a wine list of more than 125 different varieties. **Philly West** , 105 Grand Ave., tel. 742-8951, specializes in genuine Philadelphia cheese-steak sandwiches.

Several places offer Mexican food in town; best is **El Conquistador**, 110 Ivinson Ave., tel. 742-2377. The great margaritas and all-you-can-eat Sunday dinners at **Cafe Olé**, 519 Boswell Dr., tel. 742-5522, make it a popular place. **Chelo's**, 357 University Ave., tel. 745-5139, is a tiny greasy spoon that locals rave over. Judge for yourself. Two places offer decent Chinese food: **Hong Kong West**, 1665 N. 3rd, tel. 742-8138, and **The Mandarin**, 1254 N. 3rd, tel. 742-8822. The latter serves up more spicy and authentic fare. **Giorgio's Supper Club**, 2312 Grand Ave., tel. 745-7676, serves a fine Italian dinner, and has a good salad bar. **Grand Avenue Pizza**, 301 Grand Ave., tel. 721-2909, bakes some of the best homemade pizzas in Wyoming.

Jeffrey's Bistro, 123 Ivinson Ave., tel. 742-7046, is a personal favorite. The menu is on the light side and includes vegetarian specialties, with some creative combinations such as East Indian Bryani or feta walnut chicken. Great homemade bread and a pleasant brick, oak, and brass atmosphere. For a fine night on the town, locals head to **Cafe Jacques**, 216 Grand Ave., tel. 742-5522, where the varied menu emphasizes high quality and nouvelle cuisine. Dinner entrees start around $12, with lunches for $6 and up. Highly recommended. **Roundhouse Restaurant**, 1560 N. 3rd, tel. 745-4948, features elegant dining at reasonable prices. The Sunday brunch and Friday seafood buffet are favorites. For more traditional steaks and seafood, **The Cavalryman**, 4425 S. 3rd, tel. 745-5551, is considered the best around. Also well-liked is **Cowboy Bar & Grill**, 309 S. 3rd, tel.

LARAMIE ACCOMMODATIONS

Motel	Address	Telephone	Rate	Features
Motel 8	501 Boswell Dr.	745-4856	$15+ s, $27+ d	
Motel 6	621 Plaza Lane	742-2307	$18 s, $24 d	
Thunderbird Lodge	1369 N. 3rd St.	745-4871	$24 s, $27 d	
Ranger Motel	453 N. 3rd St.	742-6677	$25 s, $29 d	
Circle S Motel	2440 Grand Ave.	745-4811	$28 s, $32 d	pool
Travel Inn	262 N. 3rd St.	745-4853	$28 s, $32 d	AAA approved, pool
University Inn	1720 Grand Ave.	721-8855	$30 s, $32 d	
Super 8 Motel	1987 Banner Rd.	745-8901 (800) 848-8888	$30+ s, $33+ d	AAA approved
Camelot Motel	523 Adams	721-8860 (800) 876-6788	$30+ s, $36+ d	AAA approved, Budget Host
Downtown Motel	165 N. 3rd St.	742-6671	$34+ s, $37+ d	AAA approved
Annie Moore's Guest House	819 University Ave.	721-4177	$35+ s, $45+ d	B&B
Gas Lite Motel	960 N. 3rd	742-6616 (800) 528-1234	$36+ s, $39+ d	AAA approved, pool, Best Western
Laramie Inn	421 Boswell	742-3721	$38+ s, $40+ d	AAA approved, pool
Sunset Inn	1104 S. 3rd St.	742-3741	$38+ s, $45+ d	AAA approved, pool, jacuzzi
Foster's Country Corner Motel	1561 Jackson St.	742-8371 (800) 526-5145	$42 s, $48 d	pool, spa, Best Western
Holiday Inn	I-80 and U.S. 287	742-6611 (800) 465-4329	$49+ s or $55+ d	AAA approved, pool, airport shuttle

742-3141, where a fun atmosphere makes this popular with families. Good burgers and steaks. For inexpensive cafeteria food, as well as pizza, ice cream, and deli food, head to the **University Cafeteria**, downstairs in the Wyoming Union building on campus.

Australian bakers Allison and Kim Campbell crank out delicious homemade breads and pastries at **Home Bakery**, 304 S. 2nd, tel. 742-2721. This building served as the second office of Bill Nye's *Boomerang* newspaper. A bakery has been on the premises since 1901. **The Chocolate Cellar**, 115A Ivinson Ave., tel. 742-9278, sells imported chocolates from all over the world. **Ideal Foods**, 1575 N. 4th, tel. 742-2188, has a good deli counter and salad bar. **Whole Earth Grainery and Truck Store**, 111 Ivinson, tel. 745-4268, is a funky hippie-style grocery with all sorts of organic produce, dried foods, teas, spices, and coffees. Not many places like this in Wyoming! For an authentic Western cookout, ask at the chamber of commerce about the twice-monthly (summer only) **CowBelle Cookouts**, put on by local ranches. Just $5 brings a tour of a ranch, along with a BBQ beef dinner and entertainment.

Entertainment

Lots of night action in this vigorous, youthful town. Each year, the university puts on a **summer theater** with lighthearted productions at the Laramie Plains Civic Center, 710 Garfield. Call 742-6641 for details. During June and July, **band concerts** are held at the Washington Park Bandshell on Wednesday evenings. Laramie's oldest saloon (dating to 1890) is the **Buckhorn Bar**, 114 Ivinson Ave., tel. 742-3554. The Buckhorn packs in an odd mix: bikers during the day and the granola/tree hugger crowd at night. Mounted heads of all types and an antique bear trap adorn the walls. Notice the bullet hole in the mirror behind the bar. The Buckhorn is a popular place for TV sports, and most every night during the school year the back room thumps to rock or reggae.

For hot C&W music, duded up cowboys and cowgirls head to **The Cowboy Saloon**, 108 S. 2nd, tel. 721-3165. It's a spacious place with a big dance floor, two bars, and several pool tables. **Ranger Lounge**, 463 N. 3rd Ave., tel. 745-9751, offers blues, jazz, and reggae tunes, but not all the time. **Mingles**, 3206 Grand Ave., tel. 721-2005, cranks up the Top-40 tunes to a young crowd, and is a popular place to shoot pool at any of the 14 tables. **The Drawbridge/ TD's/Little Brown Jug/Minidome** (they can't seem to agree on the name) is right across from campus at 1622 Grand Ave., tel. 745-3490. It offers more DJ music on the big dance floor, and alcohol-free teen dances on Tuesday and Friday nights. Also check the **Holiday Inn**, I-80 and U.S. 287, tel. 742-6611, which sometimes has live music or comedy acts. **Bud's Bar**, 354 W. University Ave., tel. 745-5236, is the big hangout for sports enthusiasts. Everyone goes there before and after university football or basketball games, sort of like the "Cheers" bar (or so claims *Sports Illustrated*). Students head to the **Beergarden** in the basement of the Wyoming Union building, which has live music during the school year. Also check out **The Gallery**, 107 Grand, tel. 745-9782, for weekend tunes.

Events

Laramie Jubilee Days rolls around in mid-July, with rodeos, parades, barbecues, a free pancake breakfast, a street dance, melodramas, square dancing, a quarter horse show, and other activities to celebrate Wyoming's statehood.

The **Albany County Fair** is held in early August. In early September, "Queen Elizabeth" opens a three-day **Elizabethan Faire** on campus. There are all sorts of folks in period costumes, offering comedies, Shakespearean plays, puppets, folk dancing, music, jousting, minstrels, as well as arts and crafts displays.

Sports And Recreation

The biggest attraction in Laramie comes each fall with the arrival of football season. Half the state seems to turn out to join in the festivities at War Memorial Stadium, with tailgate parties, rooting sections, and rock 'em sock 'em helmeted soldiers battling it out against other citadels of higher learning. Up to 30,000 fans crowd the stadium Saturday afternoons to cheer on the Wyoming Cowboys (better known as the "Pokes," as in "Cowpokes"). The football team has a mixed record over the years—a Cody rodeo announcer once joked that Nebraska and Wyoming were uniting so that Nebraska could share Yellowstone, while Wyoming would have a real football team! Needless to say, the crowd did not appreciate the humor. The university also competes in a number of other sports, with men's basketball being the primary draw. The athletic facilities are among the finest in the nation and include a modern 15,000-seat arena-auditorium for basketball games, concerts, and other events. For tickets, call 766-4850 or (800) 442-8322.

The public **swimming pool** at 11th and Reynolds charges $1 for adults or 50¢ for kids. Square dancers should check out the twice-monthly dances in Laramie at the **Quadra Dangle Club**, 3905 Grays Gable Road. See the chamber of commerce for details. **Jacoby Park Golf Course** on N. 30th, tel. 745-3111, is an 18-hole public course. Rent skis from **Fine Edge Ski Shop**, 1657 Jackson, tel. 745-4499; **Lou's Sport Shop**, 217 Grand Ave., tel. 745-8484; and **Cross-Country Connection** in West Laramie, tel. 721-2851. **West Laramie Fly Store**, 1657 Snowy Range Rd., tel. 745-5425, is the place to go for fishing gear. **Adventure Is**, 209 S. 2nd, tel. 742-3191, offers beginning windsurfing classes at windy **Lake Hattie**, 20 miles southwest of Laramie on State 230. During the summer, this shallow lake is a good place to swim or fish for kokanee or rainbow trout.

Shopping

The spacious **University Bookstore**, in the student union, tel. 766-3264, has many regional titles and lots of travel books. **Books a-Go-Go**, 408 University Ave., tel. 745-5835, is one of the largest bookshops in the state, with hundreds of magazines and an enormous selection of paperback novels. **Chickering Bookstore**, 307 S. 2nd, tel. 742-8609, is a small and friendly bookshop in downtown Laramie. **Personally Recommended Books**, 107½ Ivinson, tel. 745-4423, is a relaxing place to look over local literary favorites, while **High Country Books**, 306 S. 2nd, sells both new and used books, along with rare titles.

On the Rocks, 305 S. 2nd, tel. 721-2163, is a fine climbing, hiking, and ski shop with friendly, knowledgeable folks. Other good outdoor shops are **Lou's Sport Shop**, 217 Grand Ave., tel. 745-8484, and **Adventure Is**, 209 S. 2nd, tel. 742-3191. For custom-designed outdoor clothes, head to **Bradley Mountain Wear**, 213 S. 1st, tel. 742-9490. For a different type of clothing, **The Hourglass**, 210 S. 2nd St., tel. 745-3288, claims to have the largest selection of lingerie in the Rockies!

Information And Services

The **Laramie Chamber of Commerce**, 800 S. 3rd St., tel. 745-7339 or (800) 445-5303, is open Mon.-Fri. 8-5. Look for the summer-only visitor center in the caboose on the south end of town; open Mon.-Fri. 9-6 and Sat.-Sun. 10-5. On campus, head to the **University of Wyoming Visitor Information Center**, 1408 Ivinson Ave., tel. 766-4075. It's open during the summer Mon.-Fri. 7-6 and Sat. 7-1, or Mon.-Fri. 9-5 and Sat. 9-1 the rest of the year. No tours of campus, but they can provide maps and complete info on the school. Right next door is the historic Cooper Mansion, built in 1920 in the Mission/Pueblo style and now on the National Register of Historic Places. There is also an **information center**, tel. 766-3160, in the Wyoming Union building that is open Mon.-Fri. 8-7:30. Check the ride board here if you're looking for or offering transportation. Also stop by for a listing of campus activities.

The modern **Albany County Library**, 310 S. 8th, tel. 745-3365, is open Mon.-Thurs. 10-9, and Fri.-Sun. 1-5 (closed Sun. in summer). Much more impressive are the university libraries that house nearly a million volumes, 150,000 maps, and 13,000 periodicals. Most of these are in the **William Robertson Coe Library**, tel. 766-5312, which also has a map room, a rare book room, an extensive depository of government publications, and the outstanding Hebard Collection of historical books about Wyoming and the West. Also of note are the **Geology Library** in the Geology Building, tel. 766-4264, the **Science and Technology Library** in the Science Complex, tel. 766-3374, and the **Law Library** in the College of Law, tel. 766-2210.

Transportation

Laramie Airport is just west of town on State 130. **United Express**, tel. (800) 241-6522, has daily flights from Laramie to Denver, while **Airport Express**, tel. (303) 482-0505, provides van service to Denver's Stapleton Airport for $30 OW or $45 RT. **Greyhound**, 1358 N. 2nd, tel. 742-0896, runs daily buses along I-80 in both directions, and northwest to Rock River and Medicine Bow. Rent cars from **Avis**, tel. (800) 331-1212, or from **Burman Motors**, 3600 Grand Ave., tel. 745-8961. **Laramie Taxi Service**, tel. 745-8294, provides local cab service.

Wyoming/Colorado Scenic Railroad

Wyoming's only remaining passenger train provides day-long excursion trips between Laramie and Walden, Colorado, 110 miles to the southwest. The trains run May-Sept.; reservations are suggested. Stop by the Greyhound bus station, 1358 N. 2nd, tel. 742-0896, for tickets. Rates start at $20 for adults or $16 for children for the roundtrip ride between Laramie and Fox Park. The conductor describes landmarks and the railroad's history along the way. The tracks head west across the Laramie Plains and then climb up sharp switchbacks into the beautiful Snowy Range, before crossing a 9,600-foot pass and dropping down into Colorado's North Park area. Ever wanted to stop a train? This one will do so to let you take photos.

POLE MOUNTAIN AREA

Heading east from Laramie on I-80, the freeway climbs steadily up into second-growth ponderosa and lodgepole pine forests of the Pole Mountain area. It's a scenic land punctuated by unusual and colorful rock formations. For many years much of the land here belonged to the military, and was used as a target and maneuver area for the Army's version of off-road vehicles, tanks. Amazingly, the land seems to show little sign of all this abuse today.

Ten miles east of Laramie is the Summit Rest Area (local info available), located on the highest point (8,640 feet) along I-80. A 12-foot-tall bronze bust of **Abraham Lincoln** looks over the freeway from atop a stone base. It was created by Robert I. Russin, an art professor at the university, and Wyoming's best-known sculptor. The old road through this pass was known as the Lincoln Hwy. and the sculpture was placed here in 1959, the 150th anniversary of Lincoln's birth. (The Lincoln Hwy.—completed in 1923—was the first transcontinental highway.) The sculpture was moved to the present location in 1969 when the interstate highway came through.

Choose from five Forest Service campgrounds ($5, open May-Oct.) in the Pole Mountain area, or camp for free on land away from the roads. **Headquarters National Recreation Trail** extends five miles from the Summit Rest Area to the Headquarters Road. During the winter, Pole Mountain becomes a popular cross-country ski area. Many others come to play on the tubing and tobogganing hill near the Happy Jack Trailhead.

East of the summit, I-80 follows a long open plateau and then drops very gradually into the short-grass prairie of southeast Wyoming via

"The Gangplank." The Colorado Rockies form a jagged southern horizon line. This gentle crossing of the Laramie Range was discovered by General Grenville Dodge in 1865. While exploring the railroad's new route, an attack by a party of Indians forced his men to flee eastward. In the process they discovered this gentle ramp to the plains of Cheyenne. Unfortunately, today the route is marked for miles by a domino-like line of billboards advertising everything from McDonald's to Giant Western Fireworks. Too bad the billboards could not all be toppled like dominoes to reveal the expansive grassland beyond!

Vedauwoo
Just five miles east of the summit is the turnoff to strange rock formations known as Vedauwoo (pronounced VEE-dah-voo), a name meaning "Earthborn" in Arapaho. The area was considered a sacred place where young Indian men went on vision quests. These oddly jumbled rocks form all sorts of shapes—mushrooms, balancing rocks, feminine curves, rounded knolls, lizards, faces, turtles, and anything you might dream up. Imagine it as a Rorschach test. Indians believed that the rocks were created by animal and human spirits. Today, Vedauwoo is considered one of the best places to practice rock-climbing in Wyoming. Climbs go from a difficulty level of 5.0 all the way up to 5.14, with many easy places to practice crack climbs. Nonclimbers come just to view the rocks, to ride mountain bikes along the dirt roads, to hike in the countryside, or to scramble up for marvelous vistas of the surrounding land. Vedauwoo Glen Rd. connects with Happy Jack Rd. for a nice loop trip.

Pyramid Power
Head two miles south from the Vedauwoo exit to one of the strangest monuments in Wyoming: a 60-foot-tall pyramid in the middle of nowhere. The monument commemorates Oakes and Oliver Ames, two of the most influential figures in the building of the transcontinental railroad. As a U.S. congressman, Oakes Ames gained passage of a bill that allowed the railroad to sell bonds equal to the amount loaned by the federal government, some $60 million. The company they established to handle this financing was the infamous Credit Mobilier of America. Later it

POLE MOUNTAIN AREA

TO ROCK RIVER
TO RAWLINS
TO CENTENNIAL
FORT SANDERS (SITE)
LARAMIE
TO CURT GOWDY STATE PARK & CHEYENNE
TO WOODS LANDING
SUMMIT REST AREA
HAPPY JACK RD.
VEDAUWOO
HUTTON LAKE NATIONAL WILDLIFE REFUGE
AMES MONUMENT
SHERMAN (SITE)
TO FT. COLLINS & DENVER
TIE SIDING
TO CHEYENNE
0 3mi
0 3km

© MOON PUBLICATIONS

1. Eastern Shoshone Indian Days in Fort Washakie attracts powwow dancers from across the West;
2. One of the most popular events at Cheyenne Frontier Days is bareback bronc riding; 3. Oil pumpjacks of the giant Salt Creek Oil Field completely surround the town of Midwest; 4. the ghost town of Piedmont in southwest Wyoming;
5. Laurie Ihm greets visitors to the historic mining town of South Pass City in period costume.

would be learned that Oakes had bribed fellow congressmen with discount railroad stock and had greatly exaggerated construction costs for his own gain. A congressional investigation labeled Oakes "King of Frauds," and censured him, but he died before he could stand trial. The money was never recovered.

Despite this bit of infamy, the monument to the Ames brothers was built in 1882 at a cost of nearly $65,000. It was originally located at the highest elevation of the transcontinental railroad route near the town of Sherman, a place where trains halted to check their brakes before the long descent on either side. In 1902 the tracks were re-routed a couple of miles to the south, leaving the grandiose pile of rocks by itself. Nothing remains today from the Sherman townsite except a cemetery. The Ames Monument seems to bring out two conflicting emotions, dismay at the obscenity of this monstrosity, and amusement at the irony that so much money was wasted on a self-aggrandizing monument that was soon abandoned even by the railroad that the Ames brothers had helped build.

MEDICINE BOW VICINITY

Two roads head west from Laramie. Most people follow I-80 straight to Rawlins, but U.S. 30-287 (the old Lincoln Hwy.) gets you there in about the same time and provides a strong flavor of the Old West. The little town of **Rock River** (pop. 400) has two bars, a general store, a cafe, a church, a motel, and not much else. **Longhorn Lodge Motel**, 362 N. 4th, tel. 378-2226, has rooms for $19 s or $23 d.

West from Rock River, the road sails through desolate treeless country, with sagebrush to the horizon, and the impressive summit of Elk Mountain rising to the southwest. The Union Pacific Railroad parallels the highway most of the way, and antelope glance up at the passing trains. Anyone coming through in the winter will appreciate the miles of snow fences along the south side of the highway. Still, the snow streams over the roadway almost constantly.

COMO BLUFF

Halfway between the towns of Rock River and Medicine Bow on U.S. 30-287 is a long low ridge known as Como Bluff. Not much to distinguish this from countless other buttes in the West, but paleontologists consider it one of the most important sites ever discovered, a place one author likened to Darwin's *Origin of the Species* in terms of its impact on scientific thought. This was the first large discovery of dinosaurs anywhere, and the first place where Diplodocus dinosaurs—the largest ever found—were discovered. At Como Bluff thousands of bones were found from all sorts of dinosaurs, ranging all the way up to the some of the largest ever unearthed. The mammals discovered here are prized around the world, and include all but three of the 250 known Jurassic mammals found in North America. Combined, the dinosaur and mammal fossils from Como Bluff make up a major part of the collections of Yale's Peabody Museum, the Smithsonian Institution, the New York Museum of Natural History, and the National Museum in Washington, D.C., as well as many others around the world.

History

In July of 1877, Professor Othniel Charles Marsh of Yale College received a letter from two Wyoming men calling themselves Harlow and Edwards. They told of finding "a large number of fossils, supposed to be those of the Megatherium, although there is no one here sufficient of a geologist to state for a certainty." Marsh was in stiff competition with other paleontologists around the country, and his rival, Professor E. D. Cope from the Philadelphia Academy of Sciences had just scooped him on a major dinosaur discovery in Colorado. The letter from "Harlow and Edwards" piqued Marsh's curiosity. An assistant sent to investigate wrote that the find was indeed substantive, and suggested that Marsh immediately hire the two discoverers—they were actually two railroad employees, William Reed and William Carlin—to keep them from revealing the secret. Reed would later work for many years as a collector for the University of Wyoming, and eventually as an instructor in geology and curator of the Geology Museum on the Laramie campus.

Work began almost immediately and continued right through the blizzards of winter, but despite efforts to keep the find a secret, Professor Cope soon had his own men working at Como Bluff. The rivalry almost came to blows, and Marsh's men made it a point to smash any bones left behind after their digging was complete and to backfill the quarries with rocks, even if their rivals were working below. Excavations continued until 1889 when most of the finest specimens had been unearthed.

Today geology and paleontology classes still come to Como Bluff, but the quarries where the bones were found are now abandoned and can't be seen from the road. Como Bluff itself is visible a little over a mile north of U.S. 30, and a sign describes the site. Travelers will want to stop at **"the world's oldest building,"** at Como Bluffs ($1, or 50¢ for kids), a small rundown museum/gift shop built from dinosaur bones, and run by friendly downhome folks. Inside are more bones and some jewelry for sale. It's open daily 9:30-7 in summer. Quite amusing.

MEDICINE BOW

The little town of Medicine Bow (pop. 400) is the sort of place where headlines in the weekly *Medicine Bow Post* complain of dogs getting into garbage or barking at kids. For the most part it's a run-down, nondescript town with old box-like houses and newer box-like trailers. Medicine Bow differs very little from hundreds of similar places all over the West, but it was here that novelist Owen Wister had his legendary cowboy hero, the Virginian, face off with Trampas. Over a game of cards, Trampas called the Virginian a "son-of-a-bitch" leading to the famous encounter where the Virginian pulls his pistol and says, "When you call me that, smile!" It remains one of the classic lines in American folklore.

History
The town of Medicine Bow began in the 1870s as a Union Pacific pumping station along Medicine Bow River, and grew into a local supply point and minor Army garrison. It has always been a center for the ranchers who run thousands of livestock in the surrounding countryside, so it was a logical place to base Wister's

cowboy hero. During the 1930s, Medicine Bow prospered because it lay along the Lincoln Hwy. (U.S. 30), but with the completion of I-80, it has lapsed into decay. The coal mines of Hanna (20 miles west) and uranium and oil explorations in Shirley Basin led to temporary energy booms, but the economy is now back to its ranching base.

Sights
Medicine Bow's main attraction is the boxy, three-story **Virginian Hotel** built in 1909 (seven years after *The Virginian* came out). At the time, it was the largest hotel between Denver and Salt Lake City. It is still a marvelous building, with the upstairs rooms lovingly restored to Victorian elegance. Take a look around, even if you aren't planning on staying here. Just down the street is the modern **Diplodocus Bar** (alias the "Dip"), containing the largest jade bar in existence, cut from a 4¹/2-ton jade boulder discovered near Lander. Look down for the only hand-painted dance floor west of the Mississippi. While you're here for a beer, be sure to ask owner Bill Bennett to show his unusually intricate woodcarvings.

Across from the hotel is the **Medicine Bow Museum**, housed in the old wooden railroad depot (1913). Out front is a cabin built by Owen Wister that stood in Jackson Hole until being moved here in 1976, along with a petrified wood monument to Wister. The museum contains the typical things found in small town museums—various homesteading items, a lamb warmer, a coyote scare (made from sawdust and firecrackers), and old fire equipment. Kind of like wandering through an old attic, where you wonder how half the stuff was ever used. There is an old caboose on the side. The museum, tel. 379-2383, is open summers daily 10-6. The rest of the year it's open Mon.-Thurs. 10-3:30.

Five miles south of windy Medicine Bow is a giant **wind turbine** built in 1982 for the U.S. Department of the Interior. The largest wind generator in existence, it's located in one of the windiest spots in America. Originally there were two such windmills here, each one producing 5 million kilowatt hours of electricity a year. Supporters envisioned an enormous wind farm with perhaps another 50, but these 400-foot-tall monsters proved unwieldy embarrassments, and were abandoned by the government when it

> *Town, as they called it, pleased me the less, the longer I saw it. But until our language stretches itself and takes in a new word or closer fit, town will have to do for the name of such a place as Medicine Bow. I have seen and slept in many like it since. Scattered wide, they littered the frontier from the Columbia to the Rio Grande, from the Missouri to the Sierras. They lay stark, dotted over a planet of treeless dust, like soiled packs of cards. Each was similar to the next, as one old five-spot of cards resembles another. . . . Yet this wretched husk of squalor spent thought upon appearances; many houses in it wore a false front to seem as if they were two stories high. There they stood, rearing their pitiful masquerade amid a fringe of old tin cans, while at their very doors began a world of crystal light, a land without end, a space across which Noah and Adam might come straight from Genesis. Into that space went wandering a road, over a hill and down out of sight, and up again smaller in the distance, and down once more, and up once more, straining the eyes, and so away.*
>
> —From Owen Wister's *The Virginian*

was discovered that repairs would be prohibitively expensive. One of the $6 million turbines was blasted over with dynamite and sold for $13,025 on the scrap market in 1988. The remaining turbine is now privately owned and still produces electricity.

State 487 heads north from Medicine Bow into remote **Shirley Basin**, some of the finest cattle rangeland in the state. Lots of wildlife here too, especially deer and antelope. Extensive deposits of uranium have been found in Shirley Basin—some of the largest and richest in the world—but low prices and an oversupply have all but halted the uranium-mining business. The basin is the site of some of the largest remaining prairie dog towns in existence. Because of this, it will be one of the first areas where the endangered black-footed ferret will be released back into the wild. Shirley Basin also contains an extensive petrified forest; ask directions in Medicine Bow. Nearly every yard in Medicine Bow has a piece out front.

Practicalities

Rooms at the historic **Virginian Hotel**, tel. 379-2377, are remarkably inexpensive, starting at just $20 s or $22 d with a bath down the hall. If you miss your TV and private bath, try the rooms in the annex next door. The downstairs restaurant provides good home-cooking, and most Saturday nights will find country bands in the bar. **Trampas Lodge**, tel. 379-2280, also has rooms for $24 s or $26 d. Pitch your tent or park RVs at the town park. Groceries are available from **Bow Market**, and pastries at **Pearle's Kitchen**. The town has an indoor swimming pool on the east side. **Bow Days** is the annual celebration in Medicine Bow, held each July and including rodeos, black-powder shoots, parades, live music, and dancing. The **Greyhound** bus, tel. 325-6525, connects Medicine Bow with both Rawlins and Laramie.

HANNA

The growing town of Hanna (pop. 1,300) lies at the center of one of the state's major coal fields. Lots of mobile homes and company housing in Hanna, but there is nothing particularly interesting about the town, unless you care to check out the Miners Monument or the enormous Union Pacific snowplow. Near Hanna are two large coal mines: the Medicine Bow strip mine 23 miles west, and the larger Cyprus Shoshone mine five miles north. The latter is Wyoming's only remaining underground coal mine. Mining has been a mainstay of the local economy since coal was discovered here in the late 1800s. Two disastrous mine explosions in 1903 and 1908 killed 228 miners, but the mines remained open until 1954. They were reactivated in the 1970s. The mining ghost town of **Carbon**—established in 1868 as the state's first coal town—once stood a few miles east of here. The coal ran out in 1902, and today only a few ruins and the graveyard remain.

Practicalities

Golden Rule Motel, tel. 325-6525, charges $20 s or $22 d. Very friendly owners. This is the de facto chamber of commerce office. The **Greyhound** bus stops out front, connecting Hanna with both Rawlins and Laramie. Standard American and Mexican food at **Hacienda Cafe**, 600 Front, tel. 325-9900. **The Tucker Box**, 624 Madison, tel. 325-6353, serves very good breakfasts and lunches on weekdays. Use Hanna's

Rock Creek Stage
Station, 1861

fine **recreation center** with sauna, pool, jacuzzi, and gym for $2.50.

ELK MOUNTAIN

The I-80 crossroads settlement of Elk Mountain (pop. 300) sits in the rolling grasslands at the foot of the rounded, snow-topped 11,162-foot peak of the same name. Elk Mountain is unusual in its solitary location, and remains topped with snow almost year-round. It is one of the most prominent natural landmarks anywhere along I-80. Unusual clouds frequently hang off its peak, making it a valuable site for the University of Wyoming's atmospheric research program. **Elk Mountain Hotel**, tel. 348-7774, built in 1905, has been completely refurbished with Victorian-style accoutrements for $25 s or $28 d (bath down the hall). Relax in the hot tub here. The hotel also runs a bar and restaurant with homemade soups, pasta, and steaks, or you can try **Noon Camp Cafe**, tel. 348-7478. Elk Mountain once contained the Garden Spot Pavilion, a dance hall that attracted all the big name orchestras, including Louis Armstrong, Tommy Dorsey, and Lawrence Welk. Five miles west of town, a stone monument marks the site of **Fort Halleck**, a short-lived military post built in 1862 to guard the Overland Trail. With the arrival

of the transcontinental railroad, it was abandoned in 1866, and its fixtures moved east to Fort Buford (later called Fort Sanders) near present-day Laramie

ARLINGTON

Approximately 30 miles west of Laramie is a freeway town with lots of history, Arlington. Stay at the **Arlington KOA**, tel. 378-2350, where tents are $11, RVs $16. In Arlington are several buildings from the **Rock Creek Stage Station** that stood along the Overland Route, including a log cabin built around 1860, one of the oldest buildings in Wyoming. Also here is a combination blacksmith shop/dance hall/gambling palace. In 1865, Indians attacked a wagon train near the Rock Creek Stage Station and captured two girls, Mary and Lizzie Fletcher. Mary was eventually sold to a white trader, but Lizzie remained with the Arapahos for the rest of her life. It wasn't until 35 years later that Mary discovered that her sister was alive and living on the Wind River Reservation. Having grown accustomed to the Arapaho way of life and enjoying a high status in the community, Lizzie chose to stay in her home. She is buried next to her husband, Broken Horn, in the St. Stephens Mission Cemetery.

MEDICINE BOW MOUNTAINS AND VICINITY

Medicine Bow National Forest is scattered over four disjunctive areas in Wyoming. The northern portion—the Laramie Mountains—is discussed in "Central Wyoming" (p. 154), while the Pole Mountain section is described on p.95. The other two mountainous areas are west of Laramie: the Medicine Bow Mountains (locally called the Snowy Range) and the Sierra Madre Range. Most of this has been Forest Service land since 1902, although the name and boundaries have changed over the years. Mining was the big attraction in the late 1800s, but the major gold and copper deposits were quickly mined out, and logging became the primary use of this mountainous country. Between 1867 and 1940, millions of railroad ties were brought out of the Laramie and Medicine Bow mountains by tie hacks who logged almost every driveable creek they could get their hands on. The area provided ties for not only Wyoming, but western Nebraska and Colorado as well. Logging for lumber

is still important in the Medicine Bow National Forest, but recreational use is increasing each year as more and more people discover this very scenic country. The Supervisors Office for Medicine Bow National Forest is in Laramie (605 Skyline Dr., tel. 745-8971), with district offices in Saratoga (212 S. 1st, tel. 326-5258), and Encampment (204 W. 9th, tel. 327-5481). Pick up a copy of the Medicine Bow National Forest Map ($2) at any of these offices before heading out.

LARAMIE PLAINS VICINITY

Heading west from Laramie on State 130, the country is some of the most desolate in Wyoming, with flat grassland stretching in all directions, interrupted by mountains to the east, south, and west. An enormous windswept bowl here—**Big Hollow**—was created by howling

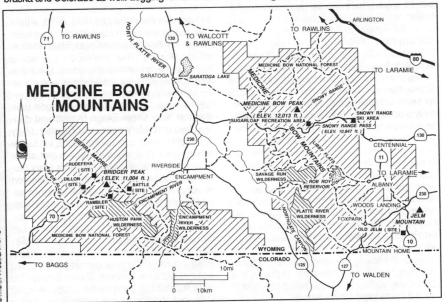

winds during the last ice age. The only other place like this is in the Soviet Union. Laramie Basin is also unique in having the highest short-grass prairie in the world, some 7,200 feet above sea level. Eleven miles west of Laramie, State 130 crosses the historic **Overland Trail** that carried emigrants, mail, and freight west between 1862 and 1868 when the railroad replaced it. The wagon ruts are still visible, with markers tracing the old route. As you approach the Medicine Bow Mountains, the highway dips down to sample the tree-lined beauty of Little Laramie Creek, and then begins the long ascent to Snowy Range Pass.

Albany

State 11 heads south along Little Laramie Creek to the foothills town of Albany, passing rolling grass and sagebrush country, with pine-topped hills. Old ranches are sprinkled around this gorgeous little valley. Rooms at the **Albany Lodge**, tel. 745-5782, are $22 s or d, and the bar has hundreds of baseball caps tacked to the ceiling. On Saturday nights, this is a popular place, with tasty $10 steak dinners. A dirt road continues south from Albany to Woods Landing, but it is often closed by blowing snow in the winter. Albany is a very popular base for snowmobilers.

Centennial

Thirty-five miles west from Laramie, State 130 widens to include the funky old mining town of Centennial (pop. 50). Situated at the foot of the Snowy Range, Centennial was founded in 1875 and gained its name the following year, the centennial of the founding of America. (James Michener claims to not have known of the town when wrote his book of the same name about an early Rocky Mountain town.) Prospectors came here in search of gold. That first year the Centennial Mine produced more than $90,000 worth, but when the vein ran out, only a few stayed around. A short boom created by infusions of cash from a Boston financier brought a fish hatchery, hotels, mining explorations, and an exclusive country club to Centennial, but the bubble again burst when the expected gold deposits failed to materialize. Eventually, Centennial became a minor ranching center and train stop. Today, it is a tourist way station with a devil-may-care mix of old log homes and house trailers.

The small **Nici Self Museum** in the old railroad depot building (built in 1907) contains exhibits on the area's mining and logging history, and is open Sat.-Sun. 1-4 from July 4 to Labor Day or by appointment the rest of the year (tel. 742-7158 or 742-8612). Out front is a Union Pacific caboose and various old farm implements. Check out the "police car" as you roll through town. **Pat's Old Corral Motel**, tel. 745-5918 or (800) 678-2024, has rooms for $30 s or $35 d; open year-round. The restaurant here serves outstanding sirloin steaks in a comfortably rustic atmosphere, and has live music during the summer. **Friendly Motel**, tel. 742-6033, has rooms for $22 s or $27 d.

A mile west of Centennial is a small **Forest Service Visitor Center** where you can get maps and info. **Mountain Meadow Guest Ranch**, tel. 742-6042, is three miles west of town, and sometimes has rustic cabins starting for $33. Two-hour horseback rides cost $17. Cross-country skiing opportunities abound nearby, making this a nice place to stay during the winter. The ranch was originally built in 1924-25.

SNOWY RANGE

In between the Laramie Plains and the valley created by the upper North Platte River lie the Medicine Bow Mountains, locally called the Snowy Range. The latter is an appropriate name; it can snow here at any time of the year, and 10-foot drifts are not uncommon in the winter, with snow remaining on high passes until late summer. The Snowy Range contains the **Savage Run Wilderness** (15,260 acres) and the **Platte River Wilderness** (22,363 acres), both lying along the southwestern end of the range just above the Wyoming-Colorado border. Most visitors simply enjoy the drive over the mountains and the chance to camp beside an alpine lake with a 12,000-foot mountain as a backdrop. Numerous short hiking trails make this a favorite spot for locals.

Scenic Drives

The 40-mile drive on State 130 over the Snowy Range is one of the most dramatic in Wyoming, designated as a National Scenic Byway. The pass is closed by snow from late Oct.-Memorial Day, but is open to just beyond the Snowy

Mountain Ski Area on the east side and 20 miles up from the west side year-round. Higher elevation parts of the road are very popular with snowmobilers and cross-country skiers. West of Centennial, the highway climbs sharply through the lodgepole and spruce forests to beautiful Snowy Range Pass at 10,847 feet (second highest in the state).

Be sure to stop at **Sugarloaf Recreation Area**, just east of the pass. Sharp glacially carved spires rise above the small lakes, and islands of stunted Engelmann spruce dot the alpine country. Trails head out to nearby lakes and flower-covered alpine meadows. At the summit, a viewing platform provides panoramic vistas of Libby Flats, massive Medicine Bow Peak, and the valleys on both sides. Nearby Mirror Lake and Lake Marie are two of the most photographed spots in Wyoming, with a spectacular backdrop of steep mountain faces reflecting in the dark blue lake waters. Campgrounds and picnic areas are all along here. On the western side, the highway drops steadily down through the forest, eventually reaching the sage and grass of the Upper North Platte River Valley.

Another route west is State 230. While this highway is not as dramatic as the Snowy Pass trek, it is open year-round, and is still quite scenic. The road curves around the southern end of the Snowys, passing through **Woods Landing** en route to the Colorado border. Woods Landing is simply a gas station/country store, but it represents the only real settlement between Laramie and Encampment, a distance of 87 miles. Excellent fishing for brown trout along the Big Laramie River. The mining ghost town of **Old Jelm** is four miles south of Woods Landing, and contains a number of old clapboard buildings. Ask locally for permission to visit. The university's **Jelm Mountain Observatory** is up a five-mile dirt road from here. Call the university in advance (tel. 766-6150) for a tour of the largest infrared telescopes in the continental U.S.

Beyond Woods Landing, State 230 dips south, passing several mountain lodges, including **WyoColo Lodge**, just north of the state line, tel. 742-4230, where rustic cabins cost $20. There is also a bar and a few food items available. Open year-round. The road continues into Colorado for nine miles along Colorado 127,

then back north on Colorado 125 for another nine miles before again crossing into Wyoming on State 230. Much of this is open rangeland with hills on either side. Only a few abandoned cabins and fences mark the presence of humans on this vast land. The huge white hip-roofed barn of the Big Creek Ranch is one of the most beautiful in all Wyoming. Turn around for outstanding views of the Colorado Rockies.

Camping

There are 27 different Forest Service campgrounds ($5-6 per site; open June-Sept.) within the Snowy Range portion of Medicine Bow National Forest. Because of heavy use during the summer, you should arrive at the most popular sites early in the day. Ten of these campgrounds may be reserved by calling (800) 283-2267 ($6 extra). In addition to the official campgrounds, dispersed camping is permitted in most areas as long as you're off the main roads. Check with the Forest Service for specifics.

Trails

The three-mile-long **Medicine Bow Peak Trail** climbs 1,600 feet to the summit of this 12,013-foot mountain, highest in southern Wyoming. Extraordinary vistas from the top. The trail leaves from the Lake Marie picnic area, and is in exposed alpine most of the way. Also at Lake Marie, the **Lakes Trail** follows along the shore, continuing to Lewis Lake 1 1/2 miles away. This is an easy, almost level path with excellent panoramic vistas. From here you can continue up **North Gap Lake Trail** for another four miles. This trail departs from the Lewis Lake parking lot in the Sugarloaf Recreation Area, and follows a gentle grade past several mountain lakes. This entire area is crisscrossed with a number of other alpine trails. Get a topographic map for details, and stop by any Forest Service office for trail descriptions.

Savage Run Trail crosses the wilderness area of the same name. It is nine miles long and follows Savage Run Creek, dropping 2,400 feet along the way. **Platte River Trail**, a five-mile-long path, parallels the river through North Gate Canyon, a long stretch of whitewater in the Platte River Wilderness. The banks are lined with ponderosa pines and Douglas firs. Access is from the south via Sixmile Gap Campground. The trail is on the western bank of the river, but by late summer the river can usually be forded, allowing hikers to continue another 1½ miles northward to Pickaroon Campground.

River Rafting
Two companies offer rafting trips down the North Platte near the Wyoming-Colorado boundary, generally run May-June when the water level is highest. **Out West River Co.**, 1st and Bridge in Saratoga, tel. 326-5114, has day-long whitewater trips through North Gate Canyon (class III and IV water) for $60 per person. Scenic float trips down the more mellow stretches are $40 for all-day (including lunch), or $25 for half-day voyages. The company also offers a variety of historic tours, fishing trips, and nature treks. **Highlands Rafting Company**, 4402 Cheyenne Dr. in Laramie, tel. 742-2294, provides whitewater trips in North Gate Canyon at $60 for one-day or $150 for two-day voyages. Scenic, day-long float trips are $45. Fishing trips, raft rentals, and shuttle services are also available.

Snowy Range Ski Area
Located in the mountains 32 miles west of Laramie on State 130, the Snowy Range Ski Area has four lifts and 23 different runs. Outside of Jackson Hole, this is the best place to ski in Wyoming, with a good variety of skiing conditions, uncrowded slopes, and soft powder snow. Snowy Range is open mid-Nov. through April, and charges $18.50 for adults ($14 half day) and $8.50 for kids under 12 and seniors ($6.50 half day). It's open Wed.-Sun. 9-4, with ski rentals and lessons available. The lodge has cafe food and a fireplace. For more information, call 745-5750 or (800) 462-7669.

Other Winter Sports
The Forest Service maintains many miles of Nordic ski trails in the mountains around the Snowy Range Ski Area, with a wide variety of loops and longer treks available. An overnight ski hut is available for rent (tel. 745-8971) near the Libby Creek Trail. Snowmobiling is one of the most popular winter activities in the Snowy Range, and parking lots on all sides of the range fill with vehicles on winter weekends. More than 200 miles of groomed trails follow summertime roads. For details on both cross-country skiing and snowmobiling, stop by the Laramie Forest Service office. Historic **Medicine Bow Lodge**, just inside the western Forest Service boundary

along State 130, tel. 326-5439, offers cross-country ski rentals, along with lodging and meals. Cabins are $30 s or $35 d. The lodge first opened in 1917, and the main building is still in use. After a long day, soak those tired muscles in the hot tub.

SARATOGA

The friendly, laidback town of Saratoga (pop. 1,800) is one of two towns in Wyoming that centers around hot springs (the other is Thermopolis). The name was borrowed from another well-known spa: Saratoga, New York. Wyoming's version of Saratoga straddles the North Platte River, and putters along on a mixed economy. Louisiana Pacific Company has a large lumber mill in town, the Jack Alexander company manufactures furniture, and many cattle graze in the river bottom country along the scenic North Platte. Saratoga is also something of a bedroom community for coal miners who work in Hanna but prefer the country around Saratoga. Others commute as far as Rawlins to work.

Like many places in Wyoming, Saratoga has long depended upon various extractive industries for a livelihood, and is only now discovering how attractive the land itself is. With mountains on both sides, "blue ribbon" trout fishing, river float trips, a free hot springs, a rich history, and lots of wildlife, it is almost certain that tourism will grow increasingly important.

History
Indians called Saratoga Hot Springs "Place of the Magic Water"; a place of healing where various tribes could mingle without fear of attack. When whites arrived and first bathed in these waters, the Indians noted that they boiled more violently than before, indicating an evil spirit. Thereafter most shunned the hot springs, but an 1874 smallpox epidemic forced some to desperation, and they returned. Patients were soaked in the hot water in an attempt to boil out the disease, and then dipped in the cold river water. When all the patients died, the Indians decided that whites had turned the waters from good medicine to bad medicine. The area was littered with the graves of smallpox victims. Thereafter the Indians moved even farther away from the hot springs.

In 1877, William H. Cadwell homesteaded near the springs and built a wooden bathhouse on the site, offering hot baths, meals, and a place for travelers to stretch out for a night's sleep. People flocked here from all over the region, and some even came from England to soak in the waters that were claimed to cure "rheumatism, eczema, paralysis, stomach trouble, kidney disease, nerves, and all forms of blood and skin disease." The copper mining boom in the Sierra Madre brought prosperity as miners came to Saratoga to relax, and freighters used it as a way station and supply center. A spur route from the Union Pacific line was built south to Saratoga in 1907 to haul ore from the mines, but they closed shortly thereafter, and the town was forced to turn to other pursuits, becoming a ranching and logging center.

Sights
The main attraction in Saratoga is **Hobo Pool**, on the east end of Walnut Ave., where an outdoor concrete pool is fed by the odorless 114-128° F water of Saratoga Hot Springs. It's open 24 hours a day and is handicapped-accessible. No charge. A larger swimming pool (not mineral water) is adjacent, and is open daily 1-4 and 7-9 p.m. during the summer; $1.50 per swim. A heated changing room has showers. The mineral baths attract both old and young, with more adventurous types sprinting down to the adjacent North Platte River to cool off. Other hot springs feed directly into the river, keeping some stretches open year-round. Because of this, **Odd Fellows Park** at River and Main streets is a good place to see ducks and geese at all times of the year.

Saratoga's wonderful **Wolf Hotel**, 101 E. Bridge St., was built in 1893 by a German emigrant named Frederick Wolf. The old brick building with steeply gabled windows served for many years as a stage stop along the road to the mines of the Sierra Madre. It was restored with antique furnishings during the 1970s and '80s, and offers an enjoyable taste of the past. Ask at the bar to see their photo of Superman at the Wolf.

The **Saratoga Museum**, 106 Constitution Ave., tel. 326-5511, is housed in the old railroad depot and contains a hands-on archaeological display and historical exhibits on ranching, early emigrants, and sheepherding. Open daily 1-5 during the summer or by appointment the rest of the year. The **North Platte River** from the Wyoming-Colorado border to the mouth of Sage Creek (65 miles north) is the only "blue ribbon" trout fishery in southern Wyoming, with outstanding fishing for rainbow and brown trout. Indian petroglyphs can be found along the bluff above the river just north of town. (As a trivial aside, the North Platte is one of the only rivers in the U.S. that flows north for a good portion of its length.) Fish are raised at the **Saratoga National Fish Hatchery**, four miles north of town, tel. 326-5662; open daily 8-4. Constructed in 1915, the hatchery produces fingerling cutthroat, brown, and lake trout for Wyoming rivers and lakes.

Lodging
The classic **Wolf Hotel**, 101 E. Bridge St., tel. 326-5525, has refurbished rooms for $29 s or $35 d, along with a few older rooms (bath down the hall) with very plain fixtures for $17 s or $23 d. The friendly **Riviera Lodge**, 303 N. 1st St., tel. 326-5651, $25 s or d, is right on the river, with a BBQ area out back. **Silver Moon Motel**, 412 Bridge St., tel. 326-5974, has rooms for $24 s or $26 d, while **Sage and Sand Motel**, 311 S. 1st St., tel. 326-8339, charges $28 s or $32 d. The elaborate **Saratoga Inn**, E. Pic Pike Rd., tel. 326-5261, has its own mineral springs and nine-hole golf course ($10). Rates start at $34 s or $38 d. The hot springs here is generally open to the public as well (no charge). **Hacienda Motel**, a half mile south of town, tel. 326-5751, charges $35 s or $40 d and up. **Hood House Bed & Breakfast**, 214 N. 3rd, tel. 326-8901, costs $30 s or $40 d. This old Victorian home is beautifully furnished with antiques.

Camping
Saratoga Lake Campground, 1 1/2 miles north of town, has campsites around this small lake for $5 ($7.50 with RV hookups). No trees or showers. The closest Forest Service campground is 25 miles to the east, with many more campgrounds ($5-6) as you continue up State 130 over Snowy Range Pass. **Saratoga Trailer Park**, 116 W. Farm Ave., tel. 326-8807, has tent spaces for $7 and RV sites for $10. Showers are $2 for non-campers. This is a pleasant riverside location with lots of shade. **Saratoga**

Inn, E. Pic Pike Rd., tel. 326-5261, has RV and tent sites for $13-15.

Food And Entertainment

Mom's Kitchen, 402 S. 1st, tel. 326-5136, is a good family-style breakfast place. **Wally's**, 110 E. Bridge, tel. 326-8472, is the place to go for steak sandwiches on homemade bread, Italian food, and pizzas (the specialty). The **Wolf Hotel** serves up hearty (and pricey) steaks, prime rib, and seafood in an atmosphere with Victorian charm. The bar is the local hangout and offers live C&W music periodically. **Saratoga Inn Restaurant** (closed in winter) also delivers fine steaks and seafood. This is a popular place for Sunday brunches, and their bar (open year-round) has live country or rock music on weekends. Get groceries at **Super Valu Foods** on the south end of town. The deli here has baked goods, or you can hang out with the locals over coffee and donuts at **Billy's Donuts** on W. Bridge Street.

Events

No major summertime events in Saratoga, although the 4th of July brings out the standard fireworks show. The **Ice Fishing Derby** each January is considered one of the top derbies in the nation. The following month brings **Cutter Races** and draft-horse pulls. Lots of excitement as two-horse teams race down the straightaway.

Recreation

Out West River Co., 1st and Bridge, tel. 326-5114, has a variety of float trips on the North Platte River, and rents canoes or rafts for $40/day. **Great Rocky Mountain Outfitters**, 216 E. Walnut, tel. 326-8750, and **Elk Mountain Safari Inc.**, E. Pic Pike Rd., tel. 326-8773, also offer fishing trips and scenic river floats.

Information And Services

The **Saratoga Chamber of Commerce**, 114 S. 1st St., tel. 326-8855, is open Mon.-Fri. 9-5. Another source for information is the small kiosk in front of the **Forest Service Ranger Station**, 212 S. 1st, tel. 326-5258. The office is open daily in summer. The **library**, 503 W. Elm St., tel. 326-8209, is open Mon. and Fri. 2-5, and Tues.-Thurs. 11-8. **Eaton's**, 117 E. Bridge, tel. 326-5314, is a delightfully funky and friendly old

Western clothing store. The aisles are packed with so much stuff that you have to dig through them to find anything. **Blackhawk Gallery**, 100 N. 1st., tel. 326-5063, sells Western artwork, and the **Jade Shop**, 124 E. Bridge, has reasonably priced items of all sorts, even a jade-head golf putter. A real surprise in Saratoga is the airport with its 8,400-foot runway. No commercial service, but during the summer and fall, wealthy businessmen (alias "the conquistadors") flock here for a rendezvous at local dude ranches, jamming the tarmac with corporate jets, and turning Shively Field into the third busiest jetport in Wyoming. There is no bus service to Saratoga.

ENCAMPMENT AND RIVERSIDE

The small logging and tourism town of Encampment (pop. 600) lies in the foothills of the Sierra Madre, lovely country that was once home for thousands of copper miners. Today the area abounds with ghost towns from that era. Encampment's twin settlement of Riverside (pop. 100) lies just a mile to the east. This is a very popular area with hunters who come for deer, antelope, and elk, as well as photographers who enjoy the colorful autumn leaves, and anglers who try the outstanding fishing.

History

Encampment takes its name from the Grand Encampment of French-Canadian trappers who rendezvoused along the Encampment River in 1838. Miners had long suspected that the Sierra Madre contained a wealth of minerals, but it was not until 1896 that the first significant gold strike was made. It was another mineral, however, that transformed the region. Encampment itself began in 1897 when British sheepherder Ed Haggerty discovered a rich vein of copper in the Sierra Madre to the west. The mine he developed was named Rudefeha, a word concocted from the letters of the various partners' names—J.M. **Ru**msey, Robert **De**al, George **Fe**rris, and Ed **Ha**ggerty. In the first three months of digging, miners recovered $300,000 worth of copper ore. Haggerty took his 10% share and returned to England.

As the wealth of the discovery became known, Chicago promoter and newspaperman

Willis George Emerson purchased the mine and built a 16-mile-long aerial tram to haul the ore up over the 10,600-foot Continental Divide and then down to the Boston-Wyoming Smelter at Encampment (elevation 7,200 feet). The tram consisted of 304 wooden towers with buckets supported on thick steel cable that each held 700 pounds of ore. The buckets moved at four miles an hour and could carry almost 1,000 tons of ore a day. The whole operation was an engineering marvel. Thousands of men flocked to the mines, creating almost overnight the settlements of Elwood, Battle, Copperton, Dillon, Halfway House, and Rambler. A railroad was completed from the smelter to the main Union Pacific line at Wolcott in 1905, and by 1908 more than 23 million pounds of copper had been produced.

The main regional settlement was Encampment, located at the foot of the mountains and numbering 1,500 rough and hardened souls at its peak. Nearby Riverside served as a shipping center for the mines. (Originally known as Dogget, the name was changed to Riverside after folks began calling it "Dog Town.") Another 1,500 people lived in the other mining towns. The mining boom came to an abrupt halt after two disastrous fires destroyed the concentrating mill, smelter, boiler room, and powerhouse. Combined with falling copper prices, the company was forced into bankruptcy. Soon, all sorts of illegal actions surfaced, including overcapitalization and fraudulent stock sales.

All but a few diehards left the area, and what had once been the town of Grand Encampment was eventually relegated to a lesser status, simply Encampment. Logging, first for ties and mine supports, and later for lumber, became an important part of the economy; today the Hammer Sawmill is the largest local employer. Tourism is becoming increasingly important in the area, and a ski resort in the Sierra Madre is on the drawing board.

Museum

The excellent **Grand Encampment Museum** includes artifacts from turn-of-the-century mining camps that filled the Sierra Madre. Displays include historic photographs, 19th-century clothing, Indian artifacts, Forest Service memorabilia, and even a folding bathtub from the 1890s. Most interesting of all are the 14 authentic historic buildings set up as a frontier town with wooden boardwalks. The oddest of all is a two-story outhouse from the mining ghost town of Dillon. The lower level was used in summer, with the upper floor reserved for wintertime when the snows drifted many feet deep. The Australian term for privies, "long drop," has especial applicability here! Also at the museum are parts of the 16-mile-long aerial tramway that brought ore from the Rudefeha mine. The museum is open daily 1-5 p.m. during the summer, and weekends during Sept. and October. Open by special appointment (tel. 327-5205) in the winter. There is no charge. On Memorial Day weekend the museum has turn-of-the-century living history demonstrations.

Lodging

Elk Horn Motel, 508 McCaffrey, tel. 327-5110, has rooms for $19 s or $23 d, while **Bear Trap Cafe** in Riverside, tel. 327-5277, has rustic cabins for $20 and modular units for $25 s or d. **Riverside Cabins** in Riverside, tel. 327-5361, rents rustic four-person cabins with kitchenettes for $25. **Lorraine's Bed & Breakfast Lodge**, 1016 Lomax, tel. 327-5200, is a modern log home with full breakfasts. Rates are $25 s or $38 d. **Platts Guides & Outfitters**, 12 miles south of Riverside, tel. 327-5539, also offers B&B accommodations on a working cattle ranch.

Camping

Pitch your tent for free at **Grand View Park** next to the Encampment museum, where locals have begun a Japanese garden! The nearest Forest Service campsite ($5) is Bottle Creek Campground, seven miles southwest of town on State 70. Several more campgrounds lie west of here in the Sierra Madre. Ask locally for directions to three BLM campgrounds: Bennett Peak, Corral Creek, and Encampment River (the closest). Bennett Peak costs $3, while the others are free. **Lazy Acres RV Park** in Riverside, tel. 327-5968, has shady RV and tent sites for $7 and RV sites for $10. Showers for non-campers are $1.50. Open May-October.

Food

Encampment has two restaurants: **The Oasis**, 706 Rankin, tel. 327-5129, and **Grand Encampment Cafe**, 623 Freeman, tel. 327-5207. An interesting old two-story brick building at 706

Freeman houses both **Kuntzman's Cash Store** and the **Sugar Bowl**, tel. 327-5271, which has an old-fashioned soda fountain. **Bear Trap Cafe** in Riverside, tel. 327-5277, serves standard American food.

Entertainment And Events
Both **Pine Lodge Saloon**, 518 McCaffrey, tel. 327-5203, and the **Mangy Moose** in Riverside, tel. 327-5117, have live music periodically throughout the summer. One of the most popular events in Wyoming is the **Woodchoppers Jamboree and Rodeo** at Encampment in late June. Begun in 1961, this is the state's largest loggers' show, with all sorts of events, including tree-felling, chainsaw log bucking, hand-sawing, pole-throwing, and axe-throwing contests. Other activities include a fun amateur rodeo, parade, barbecue, and melodrama. The town erupts with lots of drunk-and-rowdy behavior at night, befitting such a festival. Each February, the **Sierra Madre Winter Carnival** includes dog sled and snowmobile races, snow sculptures, broom ball, a casino night, a melodrama, dances, and other activities.

Information And Services
Encampment's **city hall** is in the historic Opera House, a wooden building with a bell tower that looks like a lighthouse. The **Forest Service Ranger Station** is at 204 W. 9th, tel. 327-5481, and the **Encampment Library** is at 202 Rankin Ave., tel. 327-5775.

SIERRA MADRE

The historic Sierra Madre cover a small section of Wyoming, a finger from the Medicine Bow Range that stretches south into Colorado. It is one of the lesser-known parts of the state. Worth a visit are the many mining ghost towns and historic mine sites, plus quite a few miles of wilderness trails. The highest mountain in the range is the 11,004-foot Bridger Peak, named for mountain man Jim Bridger. The Sierra Madre contain two recently created wilderness areas: **Huston Park Wilderness** (31,400 acres) and **Encampment River Wilderness** (10,400 acres). Both are readily accessible by road. (Despite the current wilderness status for these areas, much of this land was actually logged

over at the turn of the century to supply railroad ties and mine timbers for the Union Pacific Railroad.)

Sights
Battle Hwy. (State 70) crosses the Sierra Madre from Encampment on the east to Baggs on the west, a distance of 57 miles. Approximately 28 miles of this is gravel, though it will be upgraded to pavement within a few years. During the winter, State 70 is closed at the forest boundary, although snowmobilers and skiers may continue up the road. Approximately 10 miles west of Encampment is **Battle**, one of many old ghost towns that cap the Sierra Madre. A 4WD road heads north from here to the summit of Bridger Peak and then down the western side of the Continental Divide to the Ferris-Haggerty mine site at the ghost town of **Rudefeha**, where remains of the tramway towers are still visible. A mile to the west are the remains of **Dillon**, established after the company town of Rudefeha banned saloons. The owners simply moved a short distance away and started anew, and in no time at all Dillon was the largest town in the Sierra Madre. Many buildings remain here, hidden in the trees.

Just across the Continental Divide on State 70 lies beautiful Battle Lake, where you'll find a monument to **Thomas A. Edison**. While vacationing in the Sierra Madre in 1878, Edison was pondering over what substance to use as a filament for electric lights, but when he looked down at the frayed ends of his bamboo fly rod, he realized carbonized bamboo would make a fine non-conducting and substance. The story has been passed down as fact through the years, but in reality Edison didn't come up with the idea until a year later. (Maybe he remembered the old fly rod at the time.) The town of **Rambler** once stood along the lake shore, with the Doane-Rambler copper mine nearby. The mine operated from 1879 to 1902, producing a half million tons of copper. Another six miles west are a few remains from the settlement of **Copperton**.

The western slopes of the Sierra Madre are carpeted with extensive old stands of quaking aspen trees that came up after fires swept this region during the mining era. A favorite of photographers, especially in fall, is **Aspen Alley**, the aspen-lined gravel road (Forest Rd. 801) that heads north from Little Sandstone Campground. Another off-the-beaten-path sight is the old fire tower (no longer in use) at **Blackhall Mountain**, approximately 15 miles south of Riverside on Forest Rd. 409. The last several miles are narrow, but passable. From the top are long vistas into the mountains of Wyoming and Colorado.

Camping

The Forest Service maintains seven campgrounds ($5-6, open mid-June to mid-Sept.) in the Sierra Madre, five of which are located along the main road across the mountains, State 70. These campgrounds are not nearly as crowded as those in the Snowy Range to the east.

Trails

The Sierra Madre contain a number of hiking or horsepacking trails, particularly within the two wilderness areas. **North Fork Encampment Trail** takes you two miles up North Fork Creek to Green Mountain Falls. Get to the trailhead by driving west from Encampment to Bottle Creek Campground, and then south on Forest Rd. 550 for 1 1/2 miles. This is one of the few waterfalls in the area. **Encampment River Trail** is a well-maintained 15-mile-long path that follows this wild and scenic river through the heart of the new Encampment River Wilderness. Access is from the IOOF Camp two miles south of Encampment or from Hog Park near the Colorado state line.

Huston Park Trail provides an enjoyable high-elevation trek along the Continental Divide. This 16-mile-long trail traverses the Huston Park Wilderness, with access one mile south of the Battle townsite or from a trailhead located 2 1/2 miles west of Hog Park Reservoir. **Baby Lake Trail**, a six-mile path through alpine country, is accessed from just south of the Lost Creek Campground. At the upper end along the Continental Divide, access is from the end of a two-mile gravel road that heads south from Battle townsite.

During the winter months, the Forest Service maintains more than a dozen miles of **cross-country ski trails** around the Bottle Creek Campground, 5 1/2 miles west of Encampment. A parking area at the forest boundary provides access. Many forest roads in the Sierra Madre are used extensively by snowmobilers.

LITTLE SNAKE RIVER VALLEY

The Little Snake River Valley is one of the most isolated parts of Wyoming. It lies right along the Colorado border, with the desolate Red Desert to the west and the Sierra Madre to the east. Here, three tiny towns spread out along the irrigated farmland the follows Savery Creek: **Baggs** (pop. 380), **Dixon** (pop. 70), and **Savery**. Baggs was named for rancher George Baggs and his notorious wife Maggie; this was a gathering place for outlaws. Butch Cassidy helped build a place in Baggs known as Matthew's House. It is still standing. An unusual two-story log blockhouse built by mountain man Jim Baker is in Savery next to the **Little Snake River Museum**. Also of note is the amateur rodeo held each June in Dixon. Stay at **Drifters Inn**, tel. 383-2015, in Baggs for $29 s or d.

FORT FRED STEELE

History

Fort Fred Steele—named for Civil War hero Maj. Gen. Frederick Steele—was built in 1868 as one of three Wyoming posts established to protect the transcontinental railroad from Indian attacks. Soldiers from the fort fought against the Utes in northern Colorado during their 1879 uprising against tyrannical Indian agent Nathan C. Meeker. The troops also helped reestablish peace after the 1885 anti-Chinese riots in Rock Springs. After the fort was abandoned by the Army in 1886, civilians took over the buildings, turning this into a major supply base for ranchers and sheepherders. It was headquarters for the Carbon Timber Company, a company that controlled the enormous tie market for the Union Pacific Railroad in the Rockies and owned nearly 25,000 acres of timberland. Lodgepole pine were felled in the Medicine Bow Mountains and floated down the North Platte River during high flows each spring. At Fort Steele, they were caught by a log boom and loaded onto railway cars or used in the sawmill or box factory. The tie industry remained important well into this century, with 300,000 ties being sent down the North Platte River in 1938 alone, but when the Union Pacific stopped using hand-hewn ties in 1940, the town of Fort Steele suffered. With the loss of its main industry and the moving of the Lincoln Hwy. (in 1939), all but a few people moved away.

Fort Steele Today

Fort Steele is now a 137-acre state park located nine miles east of Sinclair on I-80. A summer-only visitor center in the old bridge tender's house provides historical info on the fort and on the Carbon Timber Company. Historical plaques describe the place, but not much remains from what had been a substantial settlement, just a couple of clapboard buildings, some sandstone foundations and chimneys, and the walls of a house once owned by Fenimore Chatterton (who served as governor from 1903 to 1905). Stone walls from the military quartermaster's corral are just west of the parade grounds, but a disastrous arson fire on New Year's Eve 1976 destroyed two enlisted men's barracks that had stood here for more than a century. Just up the hill from the fort site is a square stone ordnance magazine (1881) with an adjacent cemetery containing the graves of civilians who died in the area. Only a few headstones remain. The slow-moving North Platte River right next to the fort is a great place for picnics (no camping, alas). Despite the paucity of historical buildings, there is something rather nice about the authenticity of the site. Stop in at dusk on a summer evening, and you'll hear the distant rumble of freight trains, while coyotes howl from nearby hills, and the North Platte River rolls quitely away from this lonely place.

SINCLAIR

Sinclair (pop. 500) is one of the more distinctive small settlements in Wyoming. In 1923, the Producers Oil and Refining Company (Parco) established a 50,000-barrel-a-day oil refinery here and built a town to house its employees, naming the town Parco. When the Sinclair Oil Company bought the refinery in 1934, the town's name changed. Today, the refinery still lights up the night sky for miles around, and hundreds of giant oil tanks stand behind the facility. Interstate 80 passes right by Sinclair, and most folks don't bother to stop, except to fill up at the Burns Brothers Truckstop a mile east of town (a Sinclair station of course). Actually, the town is a pleasant little resting place. When Parco built the company town, everything was constructed in Spanish mission style, including the large Parco Inn at the center. An elaborate unused fountain and a nice small park stand across from the now almost-abandoned building. Only the bar is still open at the inn. Of note in Sinclair is **Su Casa Cafe**, tel. 328-1745, which makes genuine Mexican food. No motels in town, but the road north of Sinclair leads to popular Seminoe and Pathfinder reservoirs where camping is available (see "Central Wyoming," p. 170). Sinclair also has a nine-hole golf course, site of the biggest 4th of July fireworks display in the area.

RAWLINS

The small city of Rawlins (pop. 9,500) sits right in the middle of southern Wyoming. To the east and south lie mountain ranges and rich grazing land; to the west is the Great Divide Basin and a vast expanse of desert country. During the late 1970s and early '80s, Rawlins was a hub of development as the "Oil Patch" blossomed and energy companies pumped petro-dollars into the economy. But like so many other Wyoming towns, the inevitable bust that followed was traumatic. Layoffs affected everyone in town in one way or another, and Rawlins still shows signs of being down in the dumps. Not everyone packed up and left, however. Most of the people who lived here before the oil boom stayed around when the bust hit, scraping by on traffic from the freeway, local ranchers, and energy companies. In addition, the coal industry continued to thrive through the '80s. Quite a number of Rawlins workers now commute the 40 miles each way to work in the Hanna coal mines. With restoration of the old state prison, Rawlins is trying to broaden its limited tourism base.

HISTORY

Rawlins is named for Gen. John A. Rawlins, the secretary of war under President Grant. In 1867, as the railroad route was being surveyed westward, the crew of Gen. Grenville Dodge met up with soldiers under Rawlins' command. When they discovered a clear, alkali-free spring at the base of a hill, Rawlins remarked, "If anything is ever named after me, I hope it will be a spring of water." Dodge immediately decided

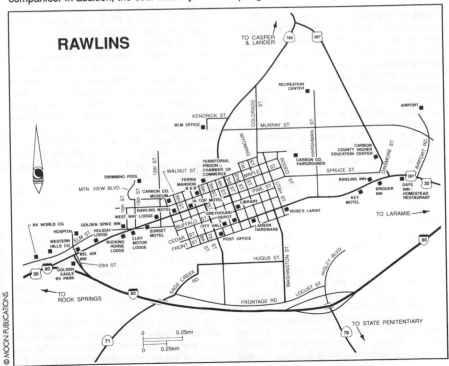

© MOON PUBLICATIONS

to name this Rawlins Spring. When a division point on the Union Pacific was established here in 1868, the town was also named Rawlins Spring. It was later shortened to Rawlins.

In 1886, the Wyoming Legislature appropriated $100,000 for a state penitentiary in Rawlins. Two years later, construction began, with enormous slabs of sandstone cut and hauled by wagon from a quarry south of town. Because of inadequate funding, the new prison was not completed and occupied until Dec. 1901, some 13 years after it was begun. By that time the town had grown, and what had been a relatively remote location was now in central Rawlins. For the next eight decades, this would be Wyoming's only state prison, housing its most hardened criminals. The prison was finally abandoned in 1981, when the inmates were transferred to a new facility south of Rawlins.

SIGHTS

Frontier Prison

Rawlins' main attraction is the Frontier Prison at 5th and Walnut streets, first opened in 1901, and in use until 1981. (Actually, it was a state prison for all of its existence, but locals prefer to call it a frontier prison since construction began while Wyoming was still a territory.) During the summer months, the prison is open Mon.-Sat. 8:30-4:30 and Sun. 10:30-4:30, with guided tours every hour. These excellent, hour-long tours cost $3 for adults or $2 for seniors or kids, children under six free. During the rest of the year, tours are only by appointment; check at the chamber of commerce office next door, tel. 324-4111. Be sure to bring a sweater or coat with you, since the stone prison is a chilly place, even in midsummer. **Outlaw Mercantile** in front of the old prison sells gifts (T-shirts, leather belts, paintings, and other items) made by inmates at the new state prison just south of Rawlins.

The most famous inmate to spend time here was William Carlisle, the "gentleman train robber." During three Union Pacific train robberies in Wyoming, Carlisle netted barely $1,000. He never took money from female passengers and was reported to have bought gifts for children with the money. After the third robbery, he was caught and sentenced to life in prison. Carlisle

was sent to Rawlins in 1916, but escaped in a shirt crate three years later. During another train robbery Carlisle was shot and wounded, but still managed to remain free for two weeks before a posse caught up with him. The last conviction landed him with another life sentence, but the governor pardoned Carlisle in 1936. He walked out a changed man and eventually became a respected Laramie motel owner and author of a book about his life, *The Lone Bandit.* Carlisle died in 1964.

The imposing turret towers and stonework of the prison's exterior give it the oppressive appearance of a medieval castle. Inside, conditions for the inmates were almost as primitive, bordering on ghastly. There was no plumbing or electricity for the first 15 years, and it was 1978 before hot water was installed in one block of cells. A special dungeon house was built for uncooperative inmates, and beatings were common in the early years. Nine prisoners were hanged (one by fellow inmates), and another five were executed in the gas chamber in Rawlins, the last dying in 1965. The gallows were a uniquely gruesome device in which the victim actually hung himself through an elaborate mechanism by which his weight displaced a water counterbalance, thus releasing a trap door and leaving him hanging by a noose. It was built to hang notorious cattle detective and murderer Tom Horn in 1903 (see "Introduction," p. 30) and moved into the prison later. (Tom Horn was never in this prison.) The instrument did not always work; one man had to be strangled by the "humane" guards. Death row inmates in Wyoming now face lethal injection instead. Science marches onward!

The old prison was the scene of several escape attempts, including one in which four death row inmates tunneled out as far as the west wall before being caught. The dirt was secreted away in the ceiling panels; it's still visible there. Two other breakouts were successful—one involved 28 men—although all the escapees were later caught or killed in the surrounding community. In later years the penitentiary housed 325 prisoners and employed 100 guards and other workers.

In 1987, the grade-B movie *Prison* was filmed on location here, with a number of locals as extras. Parts of the movie set are still visible, and some of the prison floors are still red from the fake blood. If you missed it in the theaters, don't despair; this is one of those god-awful flicks that will eventually make it to the 4 a.m. movie dregs slot on some obscure cable TV station.

Carbon County Museum
Housed in an old Mormon church at 9th and Walnut streets, tel. 324-9611, the Carbon County Museum is open Mon.-Fri. 1-4 year-round, plus Mon.-Fri. 7-9 p.m. June-August. There is no charge. The museum is a mixed bag, containing a few Indian items, a 1920 hook and ladder truck, along with various stage station and civil war artifacts. Easily the strangest object in the Carbon County Museum is a pair of two-tone shoes made from the skin of Big Nose George Parrot, a train robber and murderer. These were made by Dr. John E. Osborne, who also decided to saw open George's skull to see if the brains of desperadoes differed from common men. (This is the same Dr. Osborne who would serve as governor of Wyoming from 1893 to 1895!) The bottom of the skull is also on display here, along with Big Nose George's death mask and a photo of the old whiskey barrel that Osborne decided to store the body in. The barrel wasn't discovered until 1950 when a construction crew found it while digging at an old Rawlins drugstore.

Larson Hardware
Hardware stores don't generally fit in the category of local attractions, but Larson Hardware at 208 W. Cedar is an exception. The old store houses several thousand arrowheads that have been picked up over the years by J.W. Larson. It is one of the largest arrowhead and artifact collections anywhere in Wyoming, with 44 different display cases surrounding the walls. Drop in and talk to the friendly folks here.

Buildings
Quite a number of interesting old sandstone buildings are scattered around downtown, built from stone quarried around Rawlins. Notable ones include the Shrine Temple at 5th and Pine (completed in 1909), the Elks Club at 4th and Buffalo (completed in 1909), and the Presbyterian church at 3rd and Cedar (built in 1882). The Union Pacific Railroad depot at 400 W. Front was built in 1901 of granite and brick and was in use until 1983. It's still in good condition.

One of the most attractive buildings in Rawlins is the Ferris Mansion at 607 W. Maple, built for the widow of an early mining pioneer, George Ferris.

"Rockology"
The country around Rawlins is a geologist's and rock hound's paradise, with jade, petrified wood, agate, and other minerals to be discovered. Of course, oil, gas, and coal are what geologists are most interested in around here. The **Rawlins Uplift** (a thrust-faulted anticline) rises immedi-

---

BIG NOSE GEORGE PARROT

George Manuse, better known as Big Nose George Parrot, was one of the most notorious outlaws in the West. In 1878 his gang attempted to derail a Union Pacific train by pulling up a piece of track and waiting in ambush. Unfortunately for the outlaws, an alert UP employee discovered the missing rail before the train arrived, and a manhunt ensued. A posse followed the gang's tracks into Rattlesnake Canyon and then stopped in a camp that had been recently deserted. As a deputy sheriff bent over to check the coals, he commented, "They're hot as hell." Immediately, a voice came from behind the bushes, "We'll show you how hot hell is." Two deputies were shot dead.

Two years later, the law finally caught up with Big Nose George in Montana, and he was taken back to Rawlins in shackles. When the train pulled into town, 15 armed men forced the sheriff to release the prisoner to them, and hauled him off to be hanged. Big Nose George managed to avoid fate this time by noting that, "Dead men tell no tales," but he was convicted of the murders the following spring and sentenced to hang. In an escape attempt shortly after the trial, George cracked the skull of a guard with his shackles before finally being subdued. When word of the escape attempt spread through Rawlins, a mob of masked men broke into the jail. Big Nose George was hauled out and lynched in the street, though it took two tries—the rope was too long the first time. The Rawlins jail register notes that Big Nose George Parrot "Went to join the angels via hempen cord on a telegraph pole in front of Fred Wolf's saloon."

ately north of town, providing a textbook example of stratigraphy. Plenty of fish and invertebrate fossils here too. Alex Semryck (tel. 324-3566), a retired geologist, provides half-day tours of the Rawlins Uplift during the summer months, an excellent way to learn geology from a local expert. Rawlins has a number of jade shops, the largest being **Indian Joe's**, 1810 E. Cedar, tel. 324-9552. As a side note, the paint known as "Rawlins Red" originated from ironoxide mined just north of the town. The color is still used for barns and buildings in the eastern U.S., and this was the color originally chosen by Gen. Rawlins to paint the Brooklyn Bridge—as secretary of war, he approved the bridge plans.

PRACTICALITIES

Accommodations

Given its relatively small size, Rawlins has a surprising number of places to stay. Part of this is a holdover from the boom era when housing was tight and many workers lived in motels and mobile homes. Prices are quite reasonable (see chart below). Of particular note is **Ferris Mansion Bed and Breakfast**, a classic Victorian home built in 1903, and on the National Register of Historic Places.

Campgrounds

The nearest public campground (free; open June-Oct.) is at **Teton Reservoir**, 17 miles south of Rawlins. More public facilities ($4; open year-round) in Seminoe State Park, 28 miles north of Sinclair. See "Central Wyoming," p. 170, for details. A number of pretty dreadful parking lot/campgrounds can be found in Rawlins. Great places to swelter in the simmering heat of summer. Cheapest ($7 tents or $9 RVs) is **Western Hills Campground**, 2500 Wagon Circle Rd., tel. 324-2592. Others include **RV World Campground**, 2401 Wagon Circle Rd., tel. 328-1091, and **Golden Eagle RV Park**, 2346 W. Spruce, tel. 324-2011.

Food

No real standouts on the Rawlins breakfast

RAWLINS ACCOMMODATIONS

Motel	Address	Telephone	Rates	Features
West Way Lodge	1219 W. Spruce	324-3535	$14 s, $16 d	
Bucking Horse Lodge	1720 W. Spruce	324-3471	$20 s, $22 d	
Holiday Lodge	2011 W. Spruce	324-7878	$20 s, $22 d	
Cliff Motor Lodge	1500 W. Spruce	324-3493	$22 s, $24 d	
Hi Top Motel	713 W. Spruce	324-4561	$20 s, $26 d	clean
Golden Spike Inn	1617 W. Spruce	324-2271	$22 s, $25 d	
Sunset Motel	1302 W. Spruce	324-3448	$26 s, $30 d	AAA approved
Bridger Inn	1902 E. Cedar	328-1401	$29 s, $32 d	AAA approved
Rawlins Motel	905 W. Spruce	324-3456	$30 s or d	AAA approved
Key Motel	1806 E. Cedar	324-2728	$30 s, $32 d	AAA approved
Days Inn	2222 E. Cedar	324-6615 (800) 325-2525	$36+ s, $43+ d	
Rawlins Inn	1801 E. Cedar	324-2783	$41 s, $45 d	
Ferris Mansion Bed and Breakfast	607 W. Maple	324-3961	$45 s or d	AAA approved, historic place
Bel Air Inn	23rd and Spruce	324-2737 (800) 528-1234	$51+ s, $58+ d	AAA approved, pool, sauna, Best Western

scene, but **Square Shooter's Eating House**, 311 W. Cedar, tel. 324-4380, has standard American fare served in an enjoyable downtown place with animal heads on the walls. Good for lunches and dinners too. Fast service and decent truckstop grub at **Gay Johnson's Restaurant**, west of Rawlins, tel. 324-3463, and **Rip Griffin's Truckstop**, I-80 at Higley Blvd., tel. 328-2103. **Rocky's**, 1915 E. Murray, tel. 328-0308, is the local sandwich joint, or head to the deli counters at **Ideal Foods** or **City Market**.

The economic shakeout that hit Rawlins in the 1980s has meant that several of the nicest restaurants are now gone. Fortunately, one of Wyoming's real gems remains: **Rose's Lariat** at 410 E. Cedar, tel. 324-5261. The ads claim, "Best Mexican food in town. Ask anyone!" Some folks claim that this is one of the best and most authentic Mexican restaurants in Wyoming. Not to be missed. For pizza, try **Cappy's**, 18th and W. Spruce, tel. 328-9957; **Shakey's**, 1602 Inverness Blvd., tel. 324-7138; or **Pizza Hut**, 506 Higley Blvd., tel. 324-7706. The last two usually have lunchtime meal deals too. For an all-you-can-eat buffet, head to **Homestead Restaurant**, 2222 E. Cedar, tel. 324-6615. **Bel Air Inn Restaurant**, 23rd and Spruce, tel. 324-2737, is the nicest eatery in Rawlins, and grills the finest steaks around. If you just want cheap greasy-spoon fare 24 hours a day, try **Downtown Coffee Shop**, 401 W. Cedar, tel. 328-0205.

Entertainment And Events
The lounge at **Days End**, 2222 E. Cedar, tel. 324-6615, has Top-40 DJ tunes most nights and occasional rock bands. For live country/rock tunes, traipse on down to the **Golden Spike Inn**, 1617 W. Spruce, tel. 324-2271. The main local event is the **Carbon County Fair and Rodeo**, held the second full week of August each year. In early July, **Old West Summerfest** includes booths, races, local tours, and country music.

Recreation
The **Rawlins Family Recreation Center**, 1616 Harshman, tel. 324-7529, has racquetball, basketball, and volleyball courts, along with a weight room and other facilities for $2 ($1 for seniors or kids.) Swim at the high school pool year-round or during summers at the Washington Park pool.

Roll-On Skate Center, 3rd and Cedar, tel. 324-7850, has evening skating for $2, including skates.

Shopping
Cedar Chest Gallery, 416 W. Cedar, tel. 324-7737, is a gift shop and art gallery with a small collection of Wyoming books. **Trails Unlimited**, 105 4th St., tel. 324-6144, rents cross-country skis and other gear. Owner Keevin Mitchell also leads local backpacking trips. Check out **West Way Flea Market**, 1219 W. Spruce, tel. 324-3535, for all sorts of old junk at cheap prices.

Information
The **Rawlins-Carbon County Chamber of Commerce** is right in front of the old prison at 5th and Walnut, tel. 324-4111, and is open Mon.-Fri. 8-5. During the summer, guides to the prison are here on weekends too, and can provide local info. **Carbon County Public Library**, 3rd and Buffalo, tel. 328-2618, is open Sept.-May on Mon., Wed., and Fri. 9-6, Tues. and Thurs. 9-5 and 7-9, and Sat. 9-noon. **Carbon County Higher Education Center**, 600 Higley Blvd., tel. 328-9204, provides night classes and a variety of two-year degree programs. The **BLM district office** is at 1300 N. 3rd, tel. 324-7171.

Transportation
No commercial air service to Rawlins. **Greyhound**, 301 W. Cedar, tel. 324-5496, has bus service along I-80 in both directions, but no direct connections between Rawlins and Casper or other cities in the northern part of Wyoming; the nearest connection is via Cheyenne or Rock Springs. **BJ Taxi Service**, tel. 324-7251, is the local public transit system. Rent cars from **McGee Murphy Ford**, 7th and Spruce, tel. 324-3434, for $26 per day plus 26¢/mile.

HEADING NORTH

U.S. 287-State 789 points north from Rawlins into Wyoming's heartland, crossing the Continental Divide twice along the way as it dips into the Great Divide Basin and then back out again. Once inside the basin, the highway throws itself straight across this sandy land from point A to point B, with not much in between to deflect it.

No need to touch the steering wheel here. The fences collect both tumbleweeds and bits of miscellaneous junk. To the northeast the tilted face of 10,037-foot Ferris Mountain rises, but your sense of distance falters in the featureless desert land where only fences and a few gullies halt the relentless horizontal geography. Geologist love this place: long, eroded ridges, and scarps in the distance that appear so parched of water their barren slopes could be the bleached rib cages of some prehistoric monster. Some amazing badlands formations are here as well.

Forty miles north of Rawlins, the highway climbs through **Whiskey Gap**, with Green Mountain to the west and the Ferris Mountains to the east. The gap got its name in 1862 when Maj. Jack O'Farrell caught his soldiers drinking from an illegal barrel of whiskey in a trader's wagon. The whiskey was dumped on the ground, but some flowed into a spring that one soldier later called the "sweetest water he had ever tasted." Another five miles north is the junction of U.S. 287-State 789 and State 220 at **Muddy Gap**. Not much here other than a run-down motel, gas station, and store, but travelers will enjoy stopping to talk with Frank Erickson at the store. The road diverges, with one fork leading northeast to Casper, passing the Oregon Trail landmarks of Devils Gate and Independence Rock along the way, and the other heading northwest to Lander, with Split Rock and Jeffrey City along the way. In either direction you will find stereotypical Wyoming countryside—sagebrush, grass, cattle, and sky.

BOB RACE

SOUTHWEST WYOMING

Southwest Wyoming is the state's forbidden quarter, a place seen most frequently from I-80. Most folks consider it a stark, barren, and worthless chunk of earth. In 1866, Gen. William T. Sherman wrote, "The Government will have to pay a bounty for people to like it up here." Others said people wouldn't come, no matter how many incentives the government might offer. But despite the lack of trees, the broiling hot summers, and the wind-iced winters, people *have* settled here, primarily to extract the area's immense energy and mineral resources. Southwest Wyoming contains both the state's largest county (Sweetwater) and its smallest (Uinta), along with Lincoln County, seemingly named for its L-shape. The Green River cuts across this part of Wyoming, eventually joining the Colorado River in Utah.

History
When whites first arrived in southwest Wyoming, they found the Shoshone and Ute Indians hunting buffalo and antelope in this desert country. The first mountain men rendezvous took place here, and many of the vital emigrant routes passed through, including the Oregon, Mormon, and Overland trails, along with the Pony Express and the transcontinental telegraph. But it was the Union Pacific Railroad that opened the land to settlement. Completion of the railroad in 1869 brought about the establishment of Rock Springs, Green River, and Evanston, while coal mines were developed in the Rock Springs, Evanston, and Kemmerer areas to fuel these trains. Men of all nationalities came to work the mines, creating a racial diversity still visible.

Just as the coal mines began to close in the 1950s, enormous trona deposits were developed in western Sweetwater County, and many miners simply switched employers. Other mines extract phosphates and coal, while the natural gas fields of Sweetwater and Uinta counties are the most productive in Wyoming. Southwest Wyoming has the world's biggest coal mine, coke-producing plant, trona mine, and helium plant. Put all this together, and it is obvious that despite the desert setting and small population, southwest Wyoming is in some ways the most industrialized part of the state.

THE RED DESERT

The eastern half of Sweetwater County contains a vast treeless area known as the Red Desert, so named because of the brick-red soil that stretches in all directions. It is a place not to be trifled with. With less than nine inches of precipitation a year, and summertime temperatures frequently over 100° F, this forbidding, lonely place is the largest stretch of unfenced land in the lower 48. Some of the biggest remaining herds of wild horses roam here, along with desert elk, and one of the last wild herds of bison. Antelope are found throughout this country along with a few cattle and lots of sheep. The signs of humans are few and far between: dirt roads, oil and gas wells, and old wind-scoured buildings.

The Red Desert lies within the **Great Divide Basin**, a 90-mile-long region where the little water that falls never makes it to either ocean. Red Lake—a salty playa—fills with water during rare rainy spells, only to soak into the sandy soil or evaporate in the summer sun. The Continental Divide splits south of Great Divide Basin, and then rejoins on its northern margin, leaving a bowl in the middle. Highway travelers thus cross the Continental Divide twice.

As you head west from Rawlins toward Rock Springs (108 miles away), the only town worth noting—and marginally so—is **Wamsutter** (pop. 600). Natural gas wells now sprinkle the country to the west and south. Butch Cassidy's Hole-in-the-Wall gang robbed a Union Pacific train near here in 1900. At **Point of Rocks**, 25 miles east of Rock Springs, the state has restored an Overland Stage station built in 1862. Ruins of the stables are nearby. The station served as a jumping-off point for a road to South Pass City during the gold rush years. The historic stone building is well worth the brief sidetrip from I-80. Coal is pulled out of the ground at two large strip mines not far away. The Jim Bridger Mine feeds directly into the enormous Jim Bridger Power Plant, built in the early 1970s to supply power for Utah and Wyoming. North of here are the **Natural Corrals**, an area where caves reach into the volcanic hills and often contain ice even in midsummer. Check with the Rock Springs BLM office for directions and precautions.

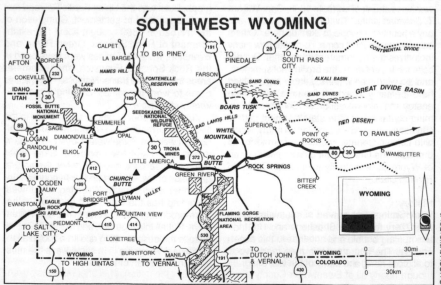

Killpecker Dunes

North of Rock Springs, White Mountain rises like a cresting wave over the valley through which U.S. 191 passes. Approximately 11 miles up is the turnoff to Tri-Territory Rd. (County Rd. 4-17), providing access to the Killpecker Sand Dunes, the largest active dunes in North America. Hikers will enjoy the dunes, reaching to 150 feet high, but be sure to come prepared for a desert climate and to bring a compass and topographic map. Deep pools of water are on the lee side of some dunes, and you may spot desert elk, wild horses, or deer (along with gas wells and pipelines to the east). One of the most distinctive features is **Boars Tusk**, a prominent rocky spire (actually a volcanic plug) that's a favorite of local rock climbers. The area north and east of Boars Tusk contains both active and stabilized sand dunes, while Shoshone petroglyphs can also be found nearby. This whole area is very interesting to explore, but be aware that ORVs roar through the stabilized eastern dunes. See the BLM office in Rock Springs for details.

ROCK SPRINGS

As an energy and transportation center, Rock Springs (pop. 20,000) is western Wyoming's largest city. It's also Wyoming's whipping boy, the place people joke about and consider the local version of hell-on-earth. No pretense of civilization here, just a crazy patchwork of dead-end roads with missing street signs, boarded-up motels, ugly condos, prefab houses, trailer parks, and split-levels sprawling out in all directions. The town is cut in half by the tracks of the Union Pacific.

Like most other mining and energy towns, Rock Springs has always experienced booms and busts. The underground coal mines are long closed, but today they create a hazard as they gradually settle, dropping the overlying buildings down as they go. The subsiding mines are perhaps a symbol of what happened to Rock Springs in the late 1980s as the energy-dependent economy collapsed and the oil field workers fled for greener pastures. A recent survey suggested that the city might turn to tourism, but that may be a real challenge given the current conditions. Rock Springs will probably remain a blue-collar city where workers in the mines, the powerplant, and the oil fields can relax.

HISTORY

Rock Springs began as a stage station along the Overland Trail, but grew because of the Union Pacific's need for coal to run its trains. The Railway Act granted the Union Pacific rights to all coal along the transcontinental route. Although nearly all of Sweetwater County is underlain with coal, in Rock Springs the coal was close to the surface and easily accessible; the mines actually ran underneath the tracks in many places. Eventually the mines would spread over a mile in various directions, creating a honeycomb of tunnels under Rock Springs.

Water And Coal

Despite the fact that Rock Springs is named for flowing water, the lack of water has always been a problem. Rock Spring dried up once coal mining began, and Bitter Creek provided only muddy, bitter water. Killpecker Creek, a sometimes-stream that flows through Rock Springs, was named by soldiers who noted the alkaline water's rather disconcerting biological effects (!) after they drank it. Honest. In the early years, Rock Springs was so short on drinking water that it had to be brought by train from the Green River and stored in barrels. Baths were a once-a-week event despite the coal dust that blackened everyone in Rock Springs.

Although various companies mined coal for decades, it was the Union Pacific Coal Co. that really owned Rock Springs and its miners. And it was the UP that was to blame for many of the problems: the filth, the poor housing, the lack of water, and the working conditions that spawned racial hatred. After the Union Pacific switched from burning coal to diesel in the 1950s, the underground mines were closed. An open-pit mine located east of Rock Springs now provides coal for the gigantic Jim Bridger Power Plant, built in 1971, while the Black Buttes strip mine in the same area feeds power plants elsewhere in the nation. The latter mine may even-

ROCK SPRINGS

Map labels:

TO FAIRGROUNDS,
FARSON, & PINEDALE

191

AMERICAN
FAMILY INN   OUTLAW INN
EXIT 104

NOMAD INN

30

80

TO AIRPORT
& RAWLINS

ELK ST.

SPRING'S
MOTEL

SADDLE
LITE MOTEL   SANDS
CAFE
CAMP PILOT
BUTTE SITE
KNOTTY
PINE LODGE   MOTEL THUNDERBIRD
EXIT 107

ELK ST. MOTEL

KILLPECKER CREEK

LYLE BLVD.   BUTTE AVE.

PILOT

BRIDGER AVE.
CENTER ST.   NORTH FRONT ST.
CODY
MOTEL

RECREATION
CENTER

COLLEGE DR.

MADISON DR.

WESTERN
WYOMING
COLLEGE

SWEETWATER DR.

JAMES DR.

G ST.

FOOTHILL BLVD.

DEWAR DR.

PARK HOTEL   MUSEUM

POST OFFICE   SKYLINE DR.

MOTEL 6   HOSPITAL   LIBRARY

2nd ST.

SOUTH MAIN ST.

BROADWAY

A ST.

B ST.

C ST.

D ST.

E ST.

NEW HAMPSHIRE ST.

WHITE MT. MALL

LA QUINTA MOTOR INN
EXIT 102   INN AT ROCK SPRINGS

LAMPLIGHTER
MOTEL

GATEWAY BLVD.

MOTEL 8

KILLPEPPERS

DEWAR DR.

CLEAR VIEW DR.

SUNSET DR.

HOLIDAY
INN

PLAZA
MALL

CEDAR ST.

WALNUT ST.

BLAIR AVE.

430

30

80

COMFORT INN   CHAMBER OF
COMMERCE

BLM DISTRICT
OFFICE

TO GREEN
RIVER   BITTER CREEK

W. 2nd ST.

SOUTH CIRCUMFERENTIAL

BLAIRTOWN · FLAMING GORGE RD.

QUEALY RD.

0   0.5mi

0   0.5km

MOON

© MOON PUBLICATIONS

---

tually spread its tentacles over 60 square miles of desert land.

Boom And Bust

The late '70s and early '80s brought turmoil to Rock Springs in the form of a boom that attracted the same on-the-edges crowd that followed the transcontinental railroad workers west more than a hundred years earlier. The population doubled in the first four years of the 1970s, and by 1982, high-paying energy and construction jobs had made Rock Springs the wealthiest city in the nation on a per capita basis. Simultaneously, however, crime reports shot up more than a thousand-fold, and the city gained a reputation as "sin city." The late 1980s were even less kind to Rock Springs, as oil companies fled town and as the economy collapsed simultaneously with the collapse of the mines under Rock Springs. Left behind were abandoned motels and restaurants where weeds now grow through the asphalt. Rock Springs is slowly resurfacing as trona and coal mines are developed and as the oil and gas industry rebounds.

Sights

The **Rock Springs Museum** in the old city hall, 201 B St., tel. 362-3138, is open summers Mon.-Sat. 1-9, and Fri.-Sat. 1-6 during the winter. No charge. The attractive sandstone building (built in 1894) looks more like a medieval castle than a city hall. Inside, the local memorabilia spreads over two floors. The site of **Camp Pilot Butte** (see "The Chinese Massacre" below) is now occupied by the Saints Cyril and Methodius Catholic Church at 633 Bridger (a major Slavonian center in the community). Only one of the original buildings remains, a soldiers' barracks now used as a parish school. Chinatown was just north of here. Another interesting building—once a butcher shop—is at 432 Main. It was while working here that Robert LeRoy Parker (Butch Cassidy) acquired his nickname "Butch." The second J. C. Penny store ever opened was located in the building at 531 N. Front Street.

Several miles northwest of Rock Springs is **Pilot Butte**, a prominent spire visible for miles in all directions, and a marker for emigrants along the Overland Trail. Today a cable ladder makes it easy to climb. **Western Wyoming College**, 2500 College Dr., tel. 382-1600, is a two-year college in attractive brick buildings with fine views of town. Inside, find a small art gallery, a surprising display of dinosaur bones, plus a museum containing archaeological and natural history collections. Check out the giant pendulum and the spacious atrium in the student center.

Accommodations

Rock Springs has quite a number of reasonably priced places to stay; see the chart on p. 122. The nearest public camping (free; open mid-May to mid-Sept.) is at **Firehole Campground**, 27 miles southwest of Rock Springs in Flaming Gorge National Recreation Area. A **KOA Kampground** two miles west of town on North Service Rd., tel. 362-3063, provides great scenic vistas of the oil storage tanks. If you still want to stop, tent sites are $10, RVs $12. Open June-September. **Albert's Trailer Court**, 1560 Elk St., tel. 382-2243, is mainly for RVs ($12), but you can pitch a tent for $2.50. Open year-round.

THE CHINESE MASSACRE

Rock Springs has the dubious honor as the site of one of the most infamous incidents in Wyoming history, the Chinese Massacre. In 1875, the Union Pacific Railroad tried to step up coal production at its Rock Springs mines, but the miners refused when they found their wages simultaneously being cut. To fill the gap, the company brought in Chinese contract laborers who would work for less money. They immediately became targets of harassment. The railroad hired more and more Chinese at the same time whites were turned away, and within a decade, more than 500 Chinese miners were in Rock Springs.

Things came to a head on Sept. 2, 1885, when the supervisor of one of the mines began assigning Chinese workers to locations where whites had previously been working. Whites attacked the Chinese, first with picks and shovels, then with rifles. The violence spread, and Chinatown—a ramshackle assemblage of shacks along what is now Ahsay Ave.—was burned to the ground. A mob of 60 men swept after the defenseless Chinese workers, robbing and then murdering them. Twenty-eight Chinese died in the melee and many more fled and may have died while trying to cross the desert. The sheriff came down from Green River to protect the whites, but did nothing to stop the murders in Chinatown. No one ever faced trial for the attacks.

The riots spawned similar anti-Chinese violence and strikes all over the West, and led Gov. Francis E. Warren to call for federal troops to protect the remaining Chinese workers. As a result, Camp Pilot Butte was established to serve as a buffer between the Chinese and whites. (This is said to be the only place in America where an international treaty post was established.) Some 250 soldiers remained here until the Spanish-American War forced the fort's abandonment in 1899.

The workers—both white and Chinese—gradually filtered back. By December, the mines had 85 whites and 457 Chinese workers. The massacre led the U.S. to pay the Chinese government $149,000 in compensation (used to fund Chinese student scholarships in America). In 1920s and '30s, the Union Pacific Coal Company finally rewarded the few remaining Chinese workers with passage back to their homeland and endowments to pay for their retirement. Only one of the men remained in Rock Springs all his life. The bones of others who died were shipped home to China.

ROCK SPRINGS ACCOMMODATIONS

Motel	Address	Telephone	Rates	Features
Saddle Lite Motel	1411 9th St.	362-1846	$18 s, $21 d	
Cody Motel	75 Center St.	362-6675	$18 s, $23 d	
Park Hotel	19 Elk St.	362-3701	$18 s, $24 d	
Motel Thunderbird	1556 9th St.	362-3739	$19 s, $25 d	
Motel 8	108 Gateway Blvd.	362-8200	$21 s, $31 d	
Elk Street Motel	1100 Elk St.	362-3705	$22 s, $26 d	
Motel 6	2615 Commercial	362-1850	$23 s, $29 d	pool
Lamplighter Motel	1004 Dewar Dr.	362-6673	$30 s, $35 d	AAA approved, kitchenettes
Springs Motel	1525 9th St.	362-6683	$30 s, $35 d	AAA approved
Nomad Inn	1545 Elk St.	362-5646 (800) 341-8000	$33+ s, $37+ d	AAA approved, pool
The Inn at Rock Springs	2518 Foothill Blvd.	382-9600	$34+ s, $39+ d	AAA approved, pool, jacuzzi, exercise facility
American Family Inn	1635 N. Elk St.	382-4217	$34 s, $39 d	AAA approved, pool, jacuzzi
La Quinta Motor Inn	2717 Dewar Dr.	362-1770 (800) 531-5900	$35+ d $43+ d	AAA approved, pool
Comfort Inn	1670 Sunset Dr.	382-9490 (800) 221-2222	$37+ s, $41+ d	AAA approved, pool, jacuzzi, continental breakfast
Outlaw Inn	1630 Elk St.	362-6623 (800) 528-1234	$49+ s, $55+ d	AAA approved, pool, Best Western
Holiday Inn	1675 Sunset Dr.	382-9200 (800) 465-4329	$51+ s, $57+ d	AAA approved, pool, jacuzzi

Food

Ask someone in Rock Springs where they go for meals, and they're likely to say, "Green River." Interestingly, the same question posed to someone from Green River elicits the response, "Rock Springs." Something strange is going on here. **Outlaw Inn**, 1630 Elk St., tel. 362-6623, has a good all-round family restaurant serving a varied menu. Recommended. More good family cooking at **Killpeppers**, 1030 Dewar Dr., tel. 382-8012, and **Lew's Family Restaurant**, 1506 9th St., tel. 382-9894. **Renegade Cafe**, 1610 Elk St., tel. 362-3052, has downhome cooking in a greasy-spoon atmosphere. For cheap lunches and a very pleasant atrium setting overlooking Rock Springs, head to the cafeteria at **Western Wyoming College**, 2500 College Drive. Fast food enthusiasts should drive in to **Grub's Drive In**, 415 Paulson, tel. 362-6634, where the grease-drenched Shamrock burgers are a favorite. Be sure to drip-dry the french fries first. **El Matador Restaurant**, 126 K St., tel. 382-4971, serves Mexican fare. **Sands Cafe and Bar**, 1549 9th St., tel. 362-5633, has a big-bellied Buddha out front and Chinese and American food inside. This is probably the best all-around meal deal in Rock Springs.

One of the biggest surprises in the Rock Springs area is **Sweet's Bar and Cafe**, five miles west of town, tel. 362-3125, open Fri. and Sat. nights only. The menu includes catfish, ribs, and other southern specialties served in a less-than-fancy atmosphere. There are three excellent steak and seafood places located west of town: **Log Inn Supper Club**, tel. 362-7166; **Ted's Supper Club**, tel. 362-7323; and **White Mountain Mining Co**, tel. 382-5265.

Entertainment

At one time 40% of the businesses in Rock Springs were bars, and even during Prohibition, the "soft drink parlors" dispensed Kemmerer moonshine. Quite a few places still offer nightlife, although many are on the sleazy side, particularly those places along the railroad tracks. The two nicest places are **Killpeppers**, 1030 Dewar Dr., tel. 382-8012, where rock and pop bands can be heard most nights, and **Saddle Lite Saloon**, 1704 Elk St., tel. 362-8704, where cowboys dance to C&W tunes. On weekends, head to **White Mountain Mining Co.**, west of Rock Springs, tel. 382-5265, or **Mingle's**, 1635 Elk St., tel. 382-4217, for more live music. For something a bit more risqué (topless dancers), try **Astro Lounge**, 822 Pilot Butte Ave., tel. 382-9876.

Events

Two rodeos attract contestants to Rock Springs: the **All Girl Rodeo** in early May, and **Red Desert Round Up** in early August. The latter is the second-largest professional rodeo in Wyoming, and is the main summertime event in Rock Springs. A Saturday morning pancake breakfast in downtown is followed by a parade. The **Sweetwater County Fair** is held here in early August, right after the Round Up. **Sweetwater Downs** at the fairgrounds has quarter horse and thoroughbred races every weekend in June. In late August, the **Rocky Mountain Polka Festival** attracts folks from all over the nation.

Recreation

The fine **Rock Springs Recreation Center**, 3900 Sweetwater Dr., tel. 382-3265, has an indoor pool and gym, racquetball and tennis courts, weightroom, sauna, and jacuzzi. Entrance is $3 for adults or $1.50 for children. Similar facilities and prices are at the **civic center**, 410 N. St., tel. 362-6181. The Western Wyoming College swimming pool is open most days for just $1. **White Mountain Golf Course**, tel. 382-5030, has an 18-hole course three miles north of town.

Information And Services

The **Rock Springs Chamber of Commerce**, 1897 Dewar Dr., tel. 362-3771, is open Mon.-Fri. 8-5. The **library** at 400 C St., tel. 362-6212, is open Mon.-Thurs. 10-9 and Fri.-Sat. 10-5. Inside, you'll find a good collection of Wyoming books, along with an **art gallery** that includes a painting of the Chinese Massacre. Artists with works here include Conrad Schwiering, Hans Kleiber, Grandma Moses, and Norman Rockwell! **White Mountain Library** at 2935 Sweetwater Dr., tel. 362-2665, has the same hours. The **BLM** has two offices in Rock Springs: 79 Winston Dr., tel. 362-6422, and north of town on U.S. 191, tel. 382-5350. They can provide info on buying a wild horse from one of their Red Desert roundups. The biggest bookstore in town is **B. Dalton** in White Mt. Mall, tel. 382-4900, or you can buy books at the **Campus Bookstore**, tel. 382-1600, at the college.

Transportation

Rock Springs airport is eight miles east of town and has daily service to Denver on **Continental Airlines**, tel. (800) 525-0280. Rent cars at the airport from **Hertz**, tel. (800) 654-3131, or **Avis**, tel. (800) 331-1212. **Greyhound Bus**, 1005 Dewar Dr., tel. 362-2931, has I-80 service in both directions. The **Rock Springs-Jackson Bus Line**, 913 2nd, tel. 362-6161, provides daily summertime van service to Pinedale and Jackson. In the winter, it drops back to Mon., Wed., and Fri. runs.

GREEN RIVER

Green River (pop. 13,000) is a prosperous trona-mining and transportation town that straddles the river of the same name. It is the seat for Sweetwater County. Interstate 80 cuts a swath just north of town, plunging through tunnels beneath memorable badlands topography. The large Union Pacific Railroad yard slices the town in half. Rundown buildings crowd the railroad tracks, but elsewhere Green River appears vibrant. Wander through the older parts of town to find small but tidy wooden frame homes, while ranch-style suburbs spread to the south. The economy of Green River is relatively stable now, after the turbulent swings in the late 1970s and '80s.

History
Green River was established in 1868 as the Union Pacific Railroad was being constructed across southern Wyoming. In May 1869, Maj. John Wesley Powell brought fame when his expedition of 10 men climbed off the train at Green River City and began their long float down the Green and Colorado rivers. They made it all the way through the Grand Canyon in stout wooden boats. Seven men survived; three who decided to hike out rather than face the treacherous rapids were never seen again. Powell returned in 1871 for a second voyage that included a large contingent of scientists who helped map this region. Powell would later direct the U.S. Geological Survey.

Trona Mining
Wyoming leads the world in the mining of an obscure but important mineral known as trona. With processing, trona—sodium sesquicarbonate—becomes soda ash, and is used in glass, detergents, pulp and paper, metal refining, and baking soda. Trona is found in a few widely scattered places around the globe, but mined commercially only in a thousand-square-mile area located 25 miles west of Green River. Most trona occurs in a 10-foot thick bed some 1,500 feet underground. No chance of running out soon; there's enough here to supply the world for several thousand years. The world's largest trona mine is run by FMC Corporation, and has 2,000 miles of tunnels, more than all the streets

of San Francisco! The tunnels are 14 feet wide and eight feet tall, big enough to use as two-lane roads. During the 1970s and '80s, Green River saw an enormous growth surge as the trona mines expanded their operations, and as oil and gas explorations attracted thousands of roustabouts. The population jumped from less than 5,000 in 1970 to almost 13,000 in 1980, and has been holding steady since then.

Sights
Sweetwater County Historical Museum in the county courthouse at 80 W. Flaming Gorge Way, tel. 875-2611, is open Mon.-Fri. 9-5 and Sat. 1-5 July-Aug., and Mon.-Fri. 9-5 the rest of the year. Inside, find dioramas showing prehistoric Indian life, Indian artifacts, photographs from the Powell expedition, plus an impressive Tyrannosaurus rex footprint found in a nearby coal mine. There is even a very rare dugout canoe discovered along the Green River. Also of interest are the brass gong, ceremonial drum, and other items that were once part of the Chinese Joss House in Evanston.

The most distinctive feature of the country around Green River is **Castle Rock**, the stunning rocky butte that rises above the freeway north of town. Other unusual buttes are Tollgate Rock on the northwest end of town and Mansface Rock behind the post office. **Expedition Island**—a National Historic Site—is where John Wesley Powell began expeditions down the Green River. A small plaque memorializes these voyages of discovery.

Motels
Green River's least expensive lodging place is **Mustang Motel**, 550 E. Flaming Gorge Way, tel. 875-2468, where rooms are $19 s or $22 d and up including an indoor pool. **Flaming Gorge Motel**, 316 E. Flaming Gorge Way, tel. 875-4190, charges $20 s or $22 d. **Desmond Motel**, 140 N. 7th, tel. 875-3701, has rooms starting at $24 s or $26 d. Two very good bargains are **Coachman Inn Motel**, 470 E. Flaming Gorge Way, tel. 875-3681, with rooms starting for $25 s or $28 d, and **Western Motel**, 890 W. Flaming Gorge Way, tel. 875-2840, where rates are $24

GREEN RIVER

s or $28 d and up. At **Super 8 Motel**, 280 W. Flaming Gorge Way, tel. 875-9330, rooms begin for $25 s or $29 d.

Camping

The closest public camping is at **Buckboard Crossing** ($5; open mid-May to mid-Sept.), 25 miles south of Green River on State 530. **Tex's Travel Camp**, four miles west on State 374, tel. 875-2630, is right along the river and has some shade trees. Tenters camp for $11, RVs for $16. Showers cost $5 for non-campers. Open May-September.

Food

Some of the most popular local restaurants lie on the way east; see "Rock Springs" above for details. **Ember's Family Restaurant**, 95 E. Railroad Ave., tel. 875-9983, has good breakfasts, homestyle cooking, and delicious prime rib. Have a cup of coffee at **Cowboy Cafe**, 580 E. Flaming Gorge, tel. 875-4770, the local greasy spoon hangout. Good sandwiches and lunch deals at **Downtown Deli**, 176 E. Flaming Gorge, tel. 875-8743. For fast food—including tasty buffalo burgers and onion rings served by car hops—head to **Burger A Go Go**, east of town, tel. 875-2794. Their Maxi Burger could feed a small nation! Open summers only. The best local pizza is at **Pizza Hut**, 615 E. Flaming Gorge Way, tel. 875-4562. Try **Rita's Mexican Food**, 520 Wilkes Dr., tel. 875-5503, for authentic and cheap (but very greasy) south-of-the-border fare. **Red Feather Inn**, 211 E. Flaming Gorge Way, tel. 875-6625, has Greek specialties.

The real surprise in Green River is **Trudel's Restaurant'e**, 3 E. Flaming Gorge Way, tel. 875-8040. The cook (Trudel Lopez) is German, but her husband (Armando Lopez) is Mexican, and the menu shares a similar eclecticism. Most of the time you'll find Mexican (not spicy) and American cookery, but two Saturday nights a month Trudel's has hearty German fare. Get groceries and baked goods at **City Market**, 400 Uinta Dr., tel. 875-2577, or **Smith's Food Store**, 905 Bridger Dr., tel. 875-6900. Both are open 24 hours.

Entertainment And Events
Given its blue-collar base, it's no surprise that Green River has lots of bars. You'll find half a dozen along Railroad Ave., including **The Brewery**, 50 W. Railroad Ave., tel. 875-9974, housed in an amusing castle built in 1900. **Cowboy Bar**, 580 E. Flaming Gorge, tel. 875-4770, has C&W music on Fri. and Sat. nights. **Mast Lounge**, 24 E. Flaming Gorge Way, tel. 875-9990, is a biker hangout with rock music, go-go dancers, and striptease artisans. **Flaming Gorge Days** in early July, featuring a parade,

country music, horseshoe contests, a flea market, and other activities. The **Antique Car Show** follows in late July, attracting participants from throughout the Rockies.

Recreation
The excellent **Green River Recreation Center**, 1775 Hitching Post Dr., tel. 875-4772, has an Olympic-size pool, a gym, weight room, and even nursery services. Entrance costs $3. During the winter, rent cross-country skis here for $10 a day to use in the nearby Uinta Mountains. **Fergy's River Rats**, tel. 875-2754, offers Green River float trips and raft rentals. This is a rather gentle float.

Information And Services
The **Green River Chamber of Commerce** office at 1450 Uinta Dr., tel. 875-5711, is open summers daily 9-5, and Mon.-Fri. 9-5 the rest of the year. Be sure to stop here to see the large relief map of Flaming Gorge and to purchase Forest Service maps or local books. **Consignment Corner**, 550 E. Flaming Gorge, tel. 875-7702, sells used books. There is a small bookstore in the Green River campus of **Western Wyoming College** on College Way, tel. 875-2278. The school sits atop a hill just south of town, and offers a fine view of the surrounding badlands. **Sweetwater County Library**, 300 N. 1st East, tel. 875-3615, is open Mon.-Thurs. 10-9 and Fri.-Sat. 10-5. **Greyhound Bus**, 178 E. Flaming Gorge Way, tel. 875-4577, has service east or west along I-80.

GREEN RIVER VICINITY

LITTLE AMERICA

Find Little America approximately 20 miles west of Green River. From either direction along I-80, billboards announce, "Little America, only 350 (250, 150, 100 . . .) miles ahead!" And then, out in the desolate, windblown landscape, drivers suddenly come to this oasis of consumption where you can cozy up to cable TV or enjoy fresh produce trucked in from California. The repair bays can hold half a dozen semis at once, and often do. Ten bright red fuel tanks have "LITTLE AMERICA" emblazoned on their

sides, flanked by two emperor penguins.

Little America had its origins in the mind of S.M. Covey, a sheepherder who spent a fearful winter near here in the 1890s. Covey resolved to build a way station for travelers, a place to escape from the blizzards and wind. Many years later, he saw a photo of Admiral Byrd's "Little America" in Antarctica, and was inspired in 1932 to create his own Little America, adding over the years a restaurant, motel, and dozens of gas pumps. He died in the 1960s, and the operation was bought by Earl Holding. Other Little America stations are flung across the West—Cheyenne, Sun Valley, Flagstaff, Salt Lake City, and even San Diego—but this is the real thing, and the only one that rates a name on the map.

Practicalities

Little America Motel, tel. 875-2400 or (800) 634-2401, has immaculate rooms starting for $38 s or $44 d. The coffee shop is always open, and good, reasonably priced meals can be had here or in the restaurant. Get a 25¢ ice cream cone to go. But the real reason for Little America's existence is fuel to propel you on down the road. It seems fitting that a place with such an all-American name should be built to worship the internal combustion engine. There are 65 gas pumps out front (OK, one of them is a propane tank.)

West of Little America, I-80 lies across colorful badlands country, passing a temple of a different kind—**Church Buttes**. Brigham Young and his Mormon pioneers held religious services under these church-like spires in 1847. Access today is via a gravel road north of the interstate.

SEEDSKADEE NATIONAL WILDLIFE REFUGE

The 13,812-acre Seedskadee National Wildlife Refuge is 37 miles northwest of the town of Green River on State 372. The word comes from the Shoshone's Seeds-kee-dee, meaning "River of the Prairie Hen." The refuge stretches 35 miles along the Green River, containing marshes and riparian areas that provide outstanding waterfowl and wildlife habitat. It is one of the finest birding areas in the state; over 200 species have been sighted. Canada geese are common, along with sandhill cranes, coots, shorebirds, great blue herons, and a variety of ducks. Good fishing here, and canoeists and rafters will see quite a few moose, deer, and antelope along the banks. Refuge headquarters (tel. 875-2187) is just northwest of the intersection of State highways 372 and 28.

NAMES HILL

There are three well-known places in Wyoming where Oregon Trail travelers paused to carve their names into the rocks: Register Cliff, Independence Rock, and the westernmost of the three, Names Hill. The latter is six miles south of the tiny oil and gas town of **La Barge** (pop. 800) near the Lander Cutoff of the Oregon Trail. Hundreds of old names are carved in the sandstone cliff, along with far too many recent additions. A fence surrounds one carving that says, "James Bridger 1844 Trapper." It's authenticity is dubious since Bridger always signed his name with an X; he could neither read nor write. (Give him the benefit of the doubt, maybe a companion carved it for Bridger while he watched.) **Fontenelle Reservoir** lies just west of Names Hill, and backs up behind a 137-foot earthen dam on the Green River. As you head north from here, the red and yellow badlands rise along the east side of the Green River, while oil pumpjacks punctuate the land in all directions.

FLAMING GORGE NATIONAL RECREATION AREA

The 94,308-acre Flaming Gorge National Recreation Area lies south of the town of Green River, reaching across the Utah border. Flaming Gorge is named for the impressive red gorge fight that Maj. John Wesley Powell described in his famous 1869 expedition:

At a distance of from 1 to 20 miles a brilliant red gorge is seen, the red being surrounded by broad bands of mottled buff and gray at the summit of the cliffs, and curving down to the water's edge on the nearer slope of the mountain. This is where the river enters the mountain range . . . We name it Flaming Gorge.

Flaming Gorge Reservoir backs up behind a 502-foot-high concrete arch dam completed in 1964, and located 15 miles south of the Wyoming border. The reservoir extends for 91 winding miles upstream, almost to the town of Green River. The dam has three enormous generators, each producing 50,000 megawatts of power. The reservoir also provides irrigation water for Utah farmers, and recreation for boaters, waterskiers, and anglers. Many osprey nest on the rocky pinnacles and cliffs around the edges, while below the dam is a river-runners funhouse.

ACCESS AND SIGHTS

The landscape surrounding the Wyoming portion of Flaming Gorge is typical high desert country, but once you cross into Utah, the road climbs into mountains covered with forests of pinyon pine, juniper, lodgepole, and ponderosa pine. This area was a favorite hideout of Butch Cassidy and other outlaws, who operated out of nearby Brown's Hole. Flaming Gorge Reservoir is encircled by roads—total loop distance 160 miles—providing a pleasant overnight break from the grinding I-80 routine. The main roads don't come particularly close to the dramatic gorge itself (except at the dam), but side roads do provide access.

Flaming Gorge National Recreation Area is administered by the U.S. Forest Service. Get information and topo maps at the Ashley National Forest offices in Dutch John, Utah, tel. (801) 885-3838, or Manila, Utah, tel. (801) 784-3228. The latter is open summers every day 7:30-5. The Bureau of Reclamation maintains a **visitor center** atop the dam that is open daily 9-4 all summer. Self-guided dam tours are available April-October. A second visitor center at **Red Canyon Overlook** is open daily 9-4 in summer, and offers breathtaking canyon views.

U.S. 191 heads south from the Rock Springs area over the dry sage and juniper landscape. Take the paved turnoff to **Firehole Canyon** where there is a campground ($8 including showers; open May-Sept.) and some interesting geological treats, including the two fingerlike

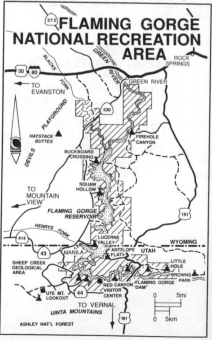

1↙ 2↘

1. The Dubois area contains some of the most interesting badlands formations in Wyoming;
2. The Red Hills of the Gros Ventre Range live up to their name.

projections known as North and South Chimney Rocks. Look for sheepherders tending huge flocks. A dirt road continues south along the canyon to the Wyoming border, or you can return to U.S. 191 to eventually reach the dam. Utah 44 crosses the top of the dam and climbs through the scenic mountain country to the west before dropping down to the town of Manila where it joins State 530 heading north.

Sheep Creek Geological Area is a side loop from the southwestern end of the NRA, and has all sorts of craggy rock formations of interest to geologists and rock hounds. It's a good place to witness a billion years of history and to look for bighorn sheep. A road leads west from here to **Ute Mountain Fire Tower**, a restored and accessible old wooden lookout with grand vistas. Approximately 14 miles west from Manila along State 414 is the site of the first mountain men rendezvous, held in 1825. Just northeast of Manila and barely in Wyoming are a number of unusual Indian petroglyphs; ask at the Forest Service office for directions. As you continue north along the western side of Flaming Gorge (State 530), the road passes **Haystack Buttes**, a series of beehive-shaped rocky mounds, followed by the barren, eroded badlands of **Devils Playground**, where sagebrush, sand, and cactus extend as far as you can see.

PRACTICALITIES

Accommodations And Food

Flaming Gorge Lodge is four miles south of the dam, tel. (801) 889-3773, and has motel rooms for $39 s or $45 d. The town of Manila, Utah is just three miles south of the Wyoming border on the west side of the reservoir, and has several lodging places. Cheapest is **Steinaker's Motel**, tel. (801) 784-3363, where rooms are $22 s or $25 d (closed winters). **Grubb's Motel**, tel. (801) 784-3131, charges $28 s or d for rooms, and also has a cafe. **Vacation Inn**, tel. (801) 784-3259, has condos for $36 s or $42 d. Very clean and nice, but open only April-October. **Niki's Motel**, tel. (801) 784-3117, is a modern and comfortable place to stay for $35 s or $44 d. Get groceries at the small **Crossroads Market**, tel. (801) 784-3392.

Camping

The Forest Service maintains 16 different roadside campgrounds in the Flaming Gorge NRA ($5-7; open mid-May to mid-September). Most are on the Utah side, particularly around the dam. Reservations (extra charge) can be made for several of the campgrounds by calling (800) 283-2267. It is also possible to camp for free in undeveloped parts of the Flamingo Gorge. There is a **KOA Kampground** in Manila, Utah, tel. (801) 784-3239, with tent sites for $11, RV sites for $14. Open May-September.

Hiking

Two trails are noteworthy. The **Little Hole Trail** parallels the river along the north bank from just below the dam to Little Hole, seven miles away. The steep **Hideout-Carter Creek Trail** is a 10-mile route leading to Hideout Boat Camp. The wonderful **High Uinta Wilderness** lies 30 miles west of Manila, Utah, and includes Kings Peak, highest mountain in Utah. This area is very popular with hikers and cross-country skiers from the Evanston and Green River areas. Several access roads come in from the north; see the Forest Service office in Evanston for details.

Fishing

Flaming Gorge Reservoir is famous for its monster fish, including a record 51-pound Mackinaw and a 33-pound brown trout. In addition to these two species, anglers catch lake and rainbow trout, kokanee, small-mouth bass, and large-mouth bass. **Flaming Gorge Fishing Derby** in mid-May is one of the biggest such events in Wyoming. The reservoir has three places where you can rent boats and fishing gear, or hire a fishing guide: **Buckboard Marina**, tel. (307) 875-6927; **Cedar Springs Marina**, tel. (801) 889-3795; and **Lucerne Valley Marina**, tel. (801) 784-3483. Below the dam, the Green River is considered the finest fishing in Utah. Because the reservoir lies in both Utah and Wyoming, be sure you have the appropriate fishing license for that part of the lake.

Float Trips

One of the most popular summertime activities is floating down the Green River below Flaming Gorge Dam. An entry station below the dam has safety information. The first several miles of the river are relatively gentle (although there are a half-dozen small rapids) and can be run without a guide, but life jackets are mandatory. Most folks put in just below the spillway and take out at Little Hole, seven miles downriver. Plan on three hours for the run. Overnight camping is not allowed along this stretch, but campsites are available below Little Hole. It is also possible to continue on down the river to Gates of Lodors, 31 miles beyond Brown's Park. Check at the various visitor centers for details and precautions for these longer float trips.

Rafts can be rented ($35 for a six-person raft) from **Flaming Gorge Recreation Services** in Dutch John, (801) 885-3191, **Flaming Gorge Lodge**, four miles south of the dam, (801) 889-3773, and **Flaming Gorge Flying Service** in Dutch John, tel. (801) 885-3338. All these companies offer guided fishing trips or shuttle services ($30 for up to eight people from Little Hole). Flaming Gorge Flying Service also has hot showers for $2. Note that river levels may fluctuate due to varying releases from the dam, pushing the river up or down by three to four feet in a matter of 15-30 minutes. For more information on river-running, see *Dinosaur River Guide* by Laura Evans and Buzz Belknap (Westwater Books, Boulder City, Nevada).

BRIDGER VALLEY

Beautiful Bridger Valley is a large splotch of green in the midst of desert country, nourished by numerous irrigation ditches off the Blacks Fork River. This was the first place in Wyoming to be farmed, having been settled by Mormons in 1853. (By the way, the various branches of the Green River—Smiths Fork, Blacks Fork, Henrys Fork, La Barge, and Hams Fork—are all named for trappers in Jedediah Smith's party of mountain men who first spread over this country in 1824. It was considered the richest beaver-trapping waters ever discovered.)

LYMAN AND MOUNTAIN VIEW

Lyman (pop. 2,500) consists of a wide main street and not much else. The town was named for a Mormon leader, and many of those who settled here were members of that religion. Lyman's pretentious new town complex is the only building of note, although more because of its size than any architectural merit. Stay at **Valley West Motel**, tel. 787-3700, where comfortable rooms (including some kitchenettes) are $26 s or $28 d. For meals, try **Golden Eagle Cafe**, tel. 787-3822, or buy groceries at **Foodtown**, tel. 787-3344. There is a **KOA Kampground**, tel. 786-2762, just north of town. The charge is $11 for tents or $14 for RVs. Open mid-May to mid-October. **Greyhound Bus**, tel. 787-6192, stops at Paramount Dry Goods, 110 N. Main in Lyman. Since this is a Mormon town, July 24 has a special meaning; it was on this date in 1847 that pioneers first reached Salt Lake City. Lyman's **Days of '47 Celebration** includes a rodeo, parade, and dance.

The town of Mountain View (pop. 1,400) is appropriately named; to the south, the Uintas form a rough-edged horizon line. Mountain View is in the heart of farming and ranching country. Not much to see in the town itself, and the best food can be found at the local **Pizza Hut** or the **Thriftway** grocery store. For entertainment, well, there's always the bowling alley. **Hoedown on the Smiths Fork** comes to Mountain View the third weekend in July, with early American performances by fiddle, banjo, and hammer dulcimer enthusiasts. The closest public campground is 22 miles away along the Wyoming-Utah line. For details, stop by the Wasatch National Forest district office in Mountain View, tel. 782-6555. Both Lyman (tel. 787-6333) and Mountain View (tel. 782-3525) have public swimming pools.

PIEDMONT

The ghost town of Piedmont is a rarely visited part of Wyoming, but worth the seven-mile drive south from I-80. Take the LeRoy Rd. exit (mile 24) and head west on County Rd. 128, following an old railroad grade south. Continue straight at the intersection, and keep your eyes open for the herd of wild buffalo that roam this country.

Around 1869, Moses Byrne built five **charcoal kilns** near Piedmont, each 30 feet high and 30 feet across and made of stone and mortar. Wood was sealed in the ovens and slowly burned until it turned into charcoal for Utah's Pioneer smelter. Three of these massive kilns still stand, like three over-sized breasts emerging from the plains. A half mile south are a dozen buildings from the ghost town of Piedmont, abandoned when the railroad tracks were moved farther north in 1901. The last store closed in 1940. A local legend claims that Butch Cassidy buried loot from one of his bank holdups near here. The father of Calamity Jane is buried in an unmarked grave in the small Piedmont cemetery, shot down in a saloon.

FORT BRIDGER

The most interesting historic site in Southwest Wyoming is Fort Bridger, located in the town of the same name. The Uinta Mountains form a majestic backdrop to the south, and the Blacks Fork River winds through. The old fort is just three miles off I-80, providing an easy diversion from the Interstate-highway blahs.

History
Fort Bridger was built in 1843 by the famed mountain man Jim Bridger and his Mexican partner, Louis Vásquez. The location—right on the Oregon and Mormon trails—quickly made this a vital stopping point for emigrants heading west to California, Oregon, or Salt Lake. The new "fort" consisted of a few crude log huts and a corral surrounded by a log stockade, while the lush riverside country provided pasturage for stock. Conflicts quickly developed between Bridger and the Mormon emigrants, who eyed his prosperous trade with envy and his good relations with the Indians as competition for their own efforts to turn them against the U.S. government. Under the pretext that Bridger was supplying weapons to Ute Indians, Brigham Young ordered Bridger arrested, sending 150 men to do the job. Bridger managed to escape, hiding in a nearby eagle nest while the men searched in vain. He finally fled with his Indian wife to Fort Laramie, but lost all his merchandise, livestock, and buildings to the invaders. The Mormons then built their own base, **Fort Supply**, located 12 miles south of Bridger's trading post, and established the first agricultural settlement in Wyoming. Soon Fort Supply had more

than 100 log buildings surrounded by a palisade. In 1855, they purchased Fort Bridger from Vásquez (without Bridger's knowledge or consent), and added a variety of structures. When the so-called "Mormon War" began two years later, the Saints decided to leave nothing for the U.S. Army. They burned both the forts and fled to Salt Lake City.

Jim Bridger leased his land to the Army in 1858 for $600 a year. They rebuilt the fort with room for the 350 troops who called this home. A Pony Express station was established in 1860, followed later by an Overland Stage station. The fort was the site of the first newspaper published in Wyoming (1863). It also served as a base for Chief Washakie's band of Shoshone Indians until a treaty signed here in 1868 set aside the Wind River Reservation. Fort Bridger was abandoned by the military in 1890, with many of its buildings sold at auction. Thirty years later, the state of Wyoming brought the site and has since restored or reconstructed many of the structures.

Sights
Fort Bridger, tel. 782-3842, is open daily 9-6 May 15-Oct. 15 and Sat.-Sun. 9-4:30 the rest of the year. No charge. A number of buildings are open to the public during the summer, although only the museum is open the rest of the year. The grounds themselves are open year-round from 8 a.m. to sunset. Between June and Aug., the staff dresses in 1880s costumes and provides living history demonstrations and historical information. Various activities take place throughout the year, including a mountain men rendezvous (see below) and special midnight tours (mid-August).

The attractive grounds are sprinkled with aspen and cottonwood trees, and beautifully restored buildings. First stop is the **museum/visitor center**, housed in the enlisted men's barracks. Inside, find a model of the old fort, displays of Army uniforms and weapons, Indian artifacts (including a bowl made from a buffalo hump), a chuckwagon, and even a working telegraph to practice your Morse code. Be sure to look for Jim Bridger's old powderhorn. Visitors can watch a slide show on the fort's history.

Practicalities
The town of Fort Bridger contains **Wagon**

Wheel Motel, tel. 782-6361, where rooms start for $18 s or $26 d. There is a restaurant on the premises. Camp for free across from the state historic site. Get groceries at **Fort Bridger Cash Store**, tel. 782-6744. Wagon coach rides are offered during the summer by **Black's Fork Stageline**, tel. 782-3945.

Fort Bridger Rendezvous—held on Labor Day weekend—is the largest modern-day mountain men rendezvous in Wyoming. Tents and tipis sprawl across the fort grounds. Events include cannon shoots, muzzle-loading shoots, Indian dances, archery contests, knife- and tomahawk-throwing, and clothing contests, plus all sorts of trading and food. The brochures also promise shooting challenges and whip fights, along with eye-gouging and ear-biting contests. Sounds like fun. It attracts 400 buckskinners, squaws, hunters, and pilgrims, along with over 10,000 spectators.

EVANSTON

Evanston (pop. 12,000) is just six miles from the Utah border along I-80, and only 85 miles from Salt Lake City. Evanston's economy depends upon natural gas and oil wells, ranching, transportation, and a state hospital. It is a typical small town, with a mixture of prosperity and difficulty. On the outskirts of Evanston, fireworks stands crowd the freeway off-ramps, waiting to lure Utahans. Others cross the border for fun in the bars.

History
As the transcontinental railroad construction crews raced across Wyoming in 1868, the settlement of Evanston was established as the last division point before the Wasatch Range. The town received its name from the railroad's surveyor, James A. Evans. By 1887, it had 1,500 people, many of whom worked at the Union Pacific car and machine shops, at an ice plant, or on the tracks. Others logged railroad ties in the mountains or raised sheep and cattle. Rich deposits of coal were discovered four miles north of Evanston, and several mines soon opened, creating the town of **Almy**. In 1869, hundreds of Chinese miners were hired as strike breakers at the mines, creating tensions that would later erupt into race riots, and force the temporary abandonment of Evanston's Chinatown. The Almy mines became notorious for deadly methane gas explosions. At least 60 whites and uncounted Chinese miners were killed in blasts in 1881, 1886, and 1895. The mines closed in 1906, leaving many of the fires unextinguished. Not much remains of Almy today. In 1886, the territorial Legislature offered Uinta County representatives the choice of either the university or the insane asylum. They chose the latter, and Evanston is still home to the Wyoming State Hospital.

The Overthrust Belt
Evanston lies at the center of the energy-rich Overthrust Belt that extends from Canada to Mexico. This 40-mile-wide uplift was formed when two land masses smashed together, thrusting the western portion atop the eastern half, and creating folds that trapped oil and gas. It was long believed to contain rich energy deposits, but hundreds of dry holes were drilled before they finally hit home. In 1976, the Yellow Creek Oil Field was discovered, producing both oil and natural gas, and unleashing a boomtown atmosphere. Many more oil and gas fields have been discovered since then. Although Uinta County is Wyoming's smallest, it is easily the largest in terms of natural gas production. In 1988, more than a third of the state's production came from here, some 173 million cubic feet of gas.

Sights
Uinta County Museum, 36 10th St., tel. 789-2757, is open Mon.-Fri. 8-5 year-round, plus Sat.-Sun. 10-4 during the summer. Outside are various old wagons and a 1944 Union Pacific dining car. Inside, look for the Coletti Still, said to have made the nation's finest Prohibition-era moonshine. Also of interest here are various Chinese items—including opium pipes, a gong, a Buddha figure, and lanterns—along with hundreds of historic photos. The historic **Evanston Depot** is next door. Built in 1900, it was one of the finest along the line, and had separate waiting rooms for men and women. Last used in 1983—when Amtrak stopped running across

JIM BRIDGER

Legendary figures fill the history of the West, but only one man—Jim Bridger—ranks as the uncrowned king of the mountain men. Like many other frontiersmen from the 19th century, Bridger never learned to read or write, but his deep knowledge of the mountains and Indians gained him the name "Old Gabe." His skills seemed to rival those of the angel Gabriel. Jim Bridger has 21 different Wyoming places named for him, more than any other individual.

Bridger was born in 1804 in Virginia, moving with his family to Missouri. When both his parents died, he was sent off to apprentice with a blacksmith, but the wild country beckoned, and when William Ashley advertised for "Enterprising Young Men" to go into the Rockies to trap beaver, Bridger quickly joined up. He was on the first keelboat that headed out in 1822, and wintered that year on the Bear River of southern Idaho. When men began speculating on where the Bear River led, Bridger volunteered to find out, thus becoming the first white man to discover Great Salt Lake. Bridger took any challenge in stride. When Ashley needed a volunteer to test the possibility of running furs down the Bighorn River, Bridger stepped forward. He nearly died taking his log raft through the wild waters of Bighorn Canyon, but the adventure added to his growing reputation.

Bridger entered the fur trading business in 1830 when he and four others bought the Rocky Mountain Fur Company from Ashley. They in turn, sold the business to William Sublette five years later. Bridger continued to lead trapping parties until the last rendezvous in 1840, then turning his attention to the growing tide of emigrants heading west to California and Oregon. Together with partner Louis Vásquez, Bridger built a trading post (Fort Bridger) along the Blacks Fork of the Green River. He later served as a scout for the U.S. Army in the Powder River, although his sage advice was often ignored.

Like many other mountain men, Jim Bridger had several wives. His first was a white Mormon woman, but when Jim refused to join her religion, they separated. He later married three different Indian women. The first two died early, but the last one—daughter of the great Shoshone Chief Washakie—would live to return to Missouri with him. Bridger's knowledge of sign language was legendary; he once kept an audience of Sioux and Cheyenne Indians in rapt attention for over an hour as he recounted a lengthy adventure entirely in signs. In one of his yarns told to a naive British army captain, Bridger described how the Indians had him trapped in a canyon with his only escape up a 200-foot waterfall. When the captain insisted upon discovering how he escaped this predicament, Bridger wryly went on, "Oh bless your soul, Captain, we never did get out. The Indians killed us right there!" Partly because of such stories, few believed Bridger's true accounts of the geysers and hot springs he had found in Yellowstone or of the stream that split along the Continental Divide, with waters flowing in both directions. Bridger died on his Missouri farm in 1881 at the age of 77.

BUFFALO BILL HISTORICAL CENTER

Jim Bridger

Wyoming—it is still in prime condition. The **Beeman-Cashin Implement Depot** across the road is used for dances and community activities. Built around 1886 and restored in 1986, this unique wooden structure has no supporting posts.

During the early part of this century, Evanston had a prominent Chinatown located along the north side of the tracks. Life centered around the **Joss House**, a sacred temple built in 1870, and one of just three in the nation. After the Chinese workers returned to their homeland, the building was destroyed in a suspicious 1922 fire. A replica of the Joss House was completed in 1990 and furnished with a new dragon and various Chinatown artifacts.

Accommodations

Quite a few inexpensive places to stay in Evanston; see the chart (opposite) for specifics. The homiest lodging in Evanston is at **Pine Gables Inn B&B**, built in 1883, and used as a European-style bed and breakfast during the 1920s and '30s. The house was restored in 1981, furnished with antiques, and reopened as a delightful bed and breakfast. No nearby public campgrounds, but **Sunset RV Park**, 196 Bear River Dr., tel. 789-3763, charges $8 for tents or $11 for RVs. Non-campers can shower for $2. **Phillips RV Trailer Park**, 225 Bear River Dr., tel. 789-3805, charges $10 for tents or $12 for RVs. Both places are open year-round.

Food

Meet the Evanston cops over coffee and donuts at **Main Street Deli**, 1025 Main St., tel. 789-1599. A great breakfast bargain is the tortilla, eggs, and home fries for under $3. **Lotty's Restaurant**, 1925 Harrison Dr., tel. 789-9660, also makes good breakfasts (served anytime). Waffles are the specialty, and there is a weekend breakfast bar. Get lunchtime sandwiches at

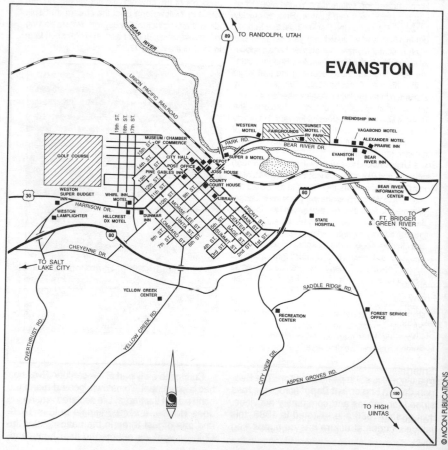

© MOON PUBLICATIONS

EVANSTON ACCOMMODATIONS

Motel	Address	Telephone	Rates	Features
Hillcrest DX Motel	1725 Harrison Dr.	789-1111	$16 s, $24 d	
Whirl Inn Motel	1724 Harrison Dr.	789-9610	$17+ s, $25+ d	
Alexander Motel	248 Bear River Dr.	789-2346	$18 s, $24 d	
Vagabond Motel	212 Bear River Dr.	789-2902	$19 s, $22 d	
Weston Super Budget Inn	1936 Harrison Dr.	789-2810 (800) 333-7829	$20 s, $25 d	
Bear River Inn	261 Bear River Dr.	789-0791	$25 s, $30 d	
Friendship Inn	202 Bear River Dr.	789-6830	$25 s, $30 d	AAA approved, jacuzzi
Super 8 Motel	70 Bear River Dr.	789-7510	$27 s, $31 d	
Pine Gables Inn	1049 Center St.	789-2069	$29 s, $37 d	AAA approved, historic B&B
Evanston Inn	247 Bear River Dr.	789-6212	$30 s or d	AAA approved
Prairie Inn	264 Bear River Dr.	789-2920	$30 s or d	AAA approved
Weston Lamplighter	1983 Harrison Dr.	789-0783 (800) 333-7829	$40 s, $45 d	AAA approved, pool, jacuzzi
Dunmar Inn	1019 Lombard	789-3770 (800) 528-1234	$52+ s or d	AAA approved, pool, Best Western

Subs Unlimited, 92 Yellow Creek Rd. (next to Smith's), tel. 789-3343. **Legal Tender Dining Room** in the Dunmar Inn, 1019 Lombard, tel. 789-3770, is an attractive and popular local establishment offering standard steakhouse fare. **Last Outpost**, 205 Bear River Dr., tel. 789-3322, is another very good local restaurant. **New Paris Cafe**, 933 Front, tel. 789-2882, offers not French, but Chinese cooking with a strong American influence. Fittingly enough, it is directly across from the rebuilt Joss House. The Friday night buffet is a good bargain. Best pizza around is at **Pizza Hut**, 134 Yellow Creek Rd., tel. 789-1372, although **Shakey's**, 350 Front St., tel. 789-8281, offers a reasonable lunchtime special.

Entertainment

Evanston is jam-packed with liquor stores and lounges, here to quench the parched thirst of Utahans who cross the border in droves. **Legal Tender Lounge** at Dunmar Inn, 1019 Lombard, tel. 789-3770, has two bars: an upstairs disco and a downstairs saloon where you can dance to C&W tunes most nights. The lounge at **Weston Lamplighter**, 1983 Harrison Dr., tel. 789-0783, has country or rock bands on weekends. Two other places sometimes offer live music: **Last Outpost**, 205 Bear River Dr., tel. 789-3322, and **Lotty's Lounge**, 1925 Harrison Dr., tel. 789-9662.

Events

In late June, stop in Evanston for the **Chili Cook-off**. **Bear River Rendezvous** is held in late August and includes all the standard mountain men trading and other activities. The big event in Evanston is, predictably, the annual rodeo, here known as **Cowboy Days**. Labor Day weekend festivities pack all the motels in town as folks come from Wyoming, Idaho, and Utah to watch professional cowboys show their stuff at "the biggest little rodeo in the world." It is a three-day event with musical entertainment, dances, a large arts and crafts fair, a parade, pancake breakfast, spaghetti dinner, and clowns. The **Uinta County Fair** in early August includes competitions, stock sales, music, and dancing.

Recreation

The excellent **Evanston Recreation Center**, 275 Saddle Ridge Rd., tel. 789-1770, features a swimming pool, gyms, racquetball courts, weight room, and hot tub. Entrance costs $2 for adults or $1 for seniors or youths. **Eagle Rock Ski Area**, tel. 789-1770, is a small city-run area 10 miles east of Evanston on County Rd. 180. It has one chairlift and two rope tows, and is open weekends 10-4, Dec.-March. The vertical drop is a whopping 430 feet, and the cost is a remarkable $8 for adults or $5 for kids. Rent skis from **PowderHound Ski & Cycle**, 52 Park Rd., tel. 789-5142. Cross-country skiers head to the **Lily Lake Touring Area**, 30 miles south of Evanston in the Uintas. Call 789-7588 for details. **Purple Sage Golf Course** is a nine-hole public course on Country Club Lane, tel. 789-2383. During the summer, **Wyoming Downs Racetrack**, 12 miles north of Evanston on State 89, tel. 789-0511, has horse racing with pari-mutuel betting. In winter, there is a small ice rink (free) on 6th St. above Summit.

Information And Services

Evanston has two places to go for information. If you're entering the state from the west, be sure to stop at **Bear River Information Center** at Exit 6, just off I-80, tel. 789-6540. The center has a wealth of statewide information, along with a pleasant picnic area and short trails. Open summers daily 7-7 and winters daily 8-5. The Bear River, just a creek here, flows northward through the grounds, eventually draining into Great Salt Lake. It's the largest river in the Western Hemisphere that doesn't reach the ocean. The **Evanston Chamber of Commerce**, 36 10th St., tel. 789-2757, is housed with the county museum, and has more local info. Hours are Mon.-Fri. 8-5, plus Sat.-Sun. 10-4 in the summer.

Uinta County Library, 701 Main, tel. 789-2770, is open Mon.-Thurs. 9-8, Fri. 9-6, and Sat. 10-6. **Curiosity Book Shoppe**, 927 Main St., tel. 789-7855, is a friendly little place located in the restored **Blyth-Fargo Building**, site of the first hardware/grocery store chain in the West. **Mountain View Ranger Station**, 1565 S. State 150, tel. 789-3194, has maps of Wasatch National Forest, but not much else. A tiny corner of the forest comes into Wyoming.

Transportation

Greyhound, 1025 Front St., tel. 789-2571, runs buses both east and west on I-80. **Evanston Taxi**, tel. 789-8222, has 24-hour service. Rent cars from **Evanston Motor Co.**, 2000 U.S. 30 W, tel. 789-3145, for $28/day, or from **Affordable Used Car Rental**, 101 U.S. 30, tel. 789-3096, for $30/day. No commercial service at the airport.

KEMMERER AND VICINITY

The twin towns of Kemmerer (pop. 3,000) and Diamondville (pop. 900) are at the center of the coal industry in southwest Wyoming. Kemmerer is the Lincoln County seat, and is located on the Hams Fork River; Diamondville lies just a few yards away. The surrounding country is dotted with mining and energy plants of various types. The world's largest strip mine is a few miles south, and a nearby Exxon plant is the world's largest manufacturer of helium (and the state's largest consumer of electricity). Another major employer is the FMC Coke Plant providing coke for a phosphorous plant in Pocatello, Idaho. It too, is the largest such operation in the world. Natural gas, oil, and sulfur are also very important locally.

HISTORY

Coal Mining

Explorer John C. Frémont first chanced upon coal here in 1843, but it wasn't until 1881 that the Union Pacific opened the first underground mine. Things really began to boom when Patrick J. Quealy and his partner Mahlon S. Kemmerer established the Kemmerer Coal Company. Hundreds of men died in mine accidents; worst was a 1923 explosion that killed 99 miners, mostly emigrants. The operation moved above ground in 1950, and the Kemmerer mine became the Pittsburg & Midway Coal Company, now a subsidiary of Chevron. Located six miles south of Kemmerer along U.S. 189, it is the world's largest open-pit coal mine, an 800-foot-deep monstrosity. Two-thirds of the coal is used at the adjacent Utah Power & Light Naughton Plant, that produces 710 megawatts of power. The mine and powerplant are the largest employers in the region, and the longest continuously operating mine in Wyoming. Call 877-9081 for tours.

Moonshine And Shady Ladies

During the 1920s, Kemmerer became a national center for bootlegging, gaining the title "Little Chicago." Kemmerer "moon" was a favorite of speakeasies, with winemakers ordering grapes by the trainload. A 1931 bust near Kemmerer found 24,000 gallons of liquor! All this ended when Prohibition was repealed in 1933.

With all the coal miners, the ratio of men to women in Kemmerer was nearly 50 to one, prime pickings for the world's oldest profession. Into these conditions stepped Madam Isabelle Burns, fresh off the train from Salt Lake City, with considerable experience in the "sporting" trade. She arrived in 1896, looking for somewhere to invest the $28,500 inheritance from her husband's suicide. With $5000 in cash she bought a dance hall with convenient side rooms, enough to house 50 prostitutes. In a short while, the Green House was a roaring success, allowing Madam Isabelle to build the most elegant house in town (still standing at 301 Ruby Street). Madam Isabelle quit the business in 1926, left town, and married a New Orleans physician. Her business went on in fresh hands.

Several deaths took place at the Green House, leading to a grand conflagration when a man whose sons had been murdered there burned one of the women to death, igniting the building in the process and leaving it a pile of ashes. After the 1926 fire, it was replaced as the Southern Hotel. The county sheriff finally shut things down in the late 1960s, despite pleas from locals that the loss of all the Utah and Idaho clients would hurt business in town. For more on this tantalizing bit of history, see Ray Essman's *Only Count the Sunny Hours* (Apollo Books, Winona, MN).

SIGHTS

The most unusual sights in Kemmerer relate to **James Cash Penney**, founder of the J. C. Penney chain. Penney moved to Kemmerer in 1902 from Evanston to open a dry goods store for the booming mining town, and his Golden Rule Store quickly achieved a reputation for quality and honesty. By 1912 there were 34 Golden Rule stores, and the following year the name was changed to J. C. Penney.

The **J. C. Penney Home** is a six-room cottage where Penney lived between 1903 and 1909. The house is right behind the chamber of commerce office downtown, and is open summers Sun. 12-4 and Mon.-Sat. 9-6. During the rest of the year, ask at the chamber for a tour. No charge. Guides are ready to show you around or to put on a video about the company's history. The J. C. Penney "mother store" is also in Kemmerer, just a few doors up the street.

Fossil Country Frontier Museum, 400 Pine Ave., tel. 877-6551, is open Mon.-Fri. 10-6 and Sat. 10-4, no charge. It contains a variety of art and archaeological exhibits, but more interesting are dozens of kinds of barbed wire dating from the 19th century.

PRACTICALITIES

Accommodations

Chateau Motel, 601 Pine Ave., tel. 877-3701, offers the least expensive lodging in town: $18 s or $21 d. **Antler Motel**, 419 Coral St., tel. 877-4461, has rooms starting at $20 s or $23 d. **Burnett's Motel**, 1326 Central Ave., tel. 877-4471, has rooms for $20 s or $24 d, while **Fossil Butte Motel**, 1424 Central Ave., tel. 877-3996, charges $22 s or d. Laze around at the comfortable **Lazy U Motel**, 521 Coral Ave., tel. 877-4428, for $28 s or d and up. **Energy Inn**, 360 N. U.S. 30 in Diamondville, tel. 877-6901, charges $27 s or $32 d; same price for kitchenettes. **Fairview Motel**, 501 N. U.S. 30, tel. 877-3938, has rooms starting at $30 s or $44 d.

The closest public campground (free) is along **Fontenelle Reservoir**, 25 miles northeast of Kemmerer. **Riverside Trailer Park**, 216 Spinel St., tel. 877-3416, has RV spaces for $11. Open mid-May to mid-October.

Food

Diamond Inn Restaurant, 1006 Spring Valley Ave. in Diamondville, tel. 877-3663, is the local breakfast hangout. For a reasonably priced Chinese-American lunch, head to **Nishi's Corner**

Cafe, 801 S. Main, tel. 877-4007. **Kirkwood Kitchen**, 1433 Central Ave., tel. 877-6633, serves all-American fare, or head to **Polar King Drive In**, U.S. 189, tel. 877-9448, for burgers. **Luigi's Supper Club**, 819 Susie Ave. in Diamondville, tel. 877-6221, has excellent Italian-American cooking. **Lake Viva-Naughton Marina**, 15 miles north of Kemmerer on the reservoir, tel. 877-9669, is famous hereabouts for its excellent seafood and steaks. More steaks and seafood at **Frontier Saloon & Restaurant**, north of town on State 233, tel. 877-9922.

Entertainment And Events
Luigi's Supper Club, 819 Susie Ave. in Diamondville, tel. 877-6221, sometimes has live music, but the best bet is **Lake Viva-Naughton Marina**, 15 miles north of Kemmerer, tel. 877-9669. **Turn of the Century Days** comes around the last weekend in July and includes a chili cook-off, carnival, Little Buckaroo Rodeo, parade, bed races, and other activities.

Recreation
Kemmerer Recreation Center, 1776 Dell Rio Dr., tel. 877-9641, has racquetball courts, a gym, weight room, jacuzzi, and sauna. Entrance costs $1.50 for adults, 75¢ for seniors and youths. Swim at the outdoor pool in Archie Neil Park or the indoor pool at the high school, tel. 877-6256. The town's nine-hole golf course is north of town on U.S. 189, tel. 877-6954.

Information And Services
The **Kemmerer Chamber of Commerce** is housed in a log cabin in Triangle Park at the center of town, tel. 877-9761. (Locals joke that Kemmerer is too small to have a town square, so it has a town triangle instead.) Open summers Mon.-Sat. 9-6 and Sun. 10-4, and the rest of the year Mon.-Fri. 10-2 (plus additional weekend hours in Sept. and October). Inside are displays of fossils and historical pictures. **Tynsky's Fossil Shop**, 201 Beryl St., tel. 877-6885, has fossil fish for sale. Ask about quarrying your own. **Warfield Fossil Quarry**, tel. 883-244, south of Kemmerer on U.S. 189, charges $22 per day. Check at the chamber of commerce for other nearby fossil quarries. The **Forest Service district office** is in Diamondville at U.S. 189 and 30, tel. 877-4415, and the **BLM office** is on U.S. 189 N, tel. 877-3933.

FOSSIL BUTTE NATIONAL MONUMENT

Established in 1972, Fossil Butte is an 8,180-acre natural area managed by the National Park Service and located 11 miles west of Kemmerer. The dominant feature is a 1,000-foot-tall escarpment rising above the arid plains. Within this butte exists the largest deposit of freshwater fish fossils in the Western Hemisphere; rivaled only by a similar deposit in Solenhofen, Germany. Fossil fish include perch, herring, paddlefish, stingray, and catfish. Fossilized insects, snails, turtles, birds, and plants have also been found here. The Green River Formation fossils were first collected by geologist Dr. John Evans in 1865, but the site now known as Fossil Butte was not discovered until a Union Pacific Railroad grade was cut through this country, exposing the fossils.

Origins
Fossil Butte is not unlike countless other buttes throughout Wyoming: an exposed rocky cliff lit with the red, yellow, and buff colors representing millions of years of deposition and erosion. Despite the arid conditions today, this land once supported a subtropical climate and was covered by an enormous body of water. During the Eocene Epoch (50 million years ago), the lake was filled with millions of fish. As water levels fluctuated over the millennia, fish died in large numbers and dropped to the deep lake bottom where they were slowly covered with a blanket of fine sediment. Eventually, they were fossilized, and when the lake dried up, the sedimentary deposits were gradually thrust skyward by geological forces.

Sights
The sparkling new **Fossil Butte Visitor Center**, tel. 877-4455, is open daily 8:30-4:30 (8-5:30 in summer). It is 3 1/2 miles off U.S. 30 (follow the signs), and houses a variety of displays on the area's geology, paleontology, and natural history, along with a room where you can watch experts preparing fossils. Two short videos on the area are available for viewing, along with a collection of books. Continue down the paved road past the visitor center another two miles to a picnic area. Here the road becomes gravel

and you can continue on several miles to a crossing of the historic Sublette Cutoff (the ruts are noticeable), Emigrant Springs (many names carved in the rocks), and the grave of one of the emigrants, Nancy Hill. The Kemmerer BLM office has more info on these areas.

The 2½-mile (RT) **Quarry Trail** on the south side of the monument provides access to a historic fossil quarry (600 feet up), and has various interpretive signs along the way. It is illegal to take fossils or other items. Another mile-long trail leads from the visitor center to an area where partially excavated fossils can be viewed. Other than these two, you're on your own, although the open country makes hiking relatively easy. (Watch for rattlers, however.)

During the summer, rangers lead walks from the visitor center each Sat. and Sun. at 10 a.m., and give Mon. evening "campfire chats" at Archie Neil Park in Kemmerer. Check the visitor center for other programs and walks. Camping is not allowed at Fossil Butte, and the nearest lodging is in Kemmerer. **Fossil Discovery Day** in mid-July offers a variety of family activities, tours, and talks at Fossil Butte.

Ulrich's Fossil Gallery, tel. 877-6466, located just outside the national monument, has fossil fish for sale. Out front are enormous dinosaur tracks found in a nearby coal mine. The Ulrich family (one of the leaders in creating the national monument) has a nearby quarry on state land where you can dig your own fish fossils for $35. You're allowed to keep a wooden pallet full of the most common species, although the state gets any rare specimens that might turn up. The quarry is open daily 8 a.m. to 9 p.m. through the summer.

COKEVILLE

Cokeville (pop. 560) is situated in a long, fertile valley along the Idaho border and south of Star Valley. The country is punctuated with small white farmhouses. Cokeville was founded in 1874, and is named for the coal that proved good for making coke. Directly behind the town is an impressive triangular mountain, Rocky Point. This is ranching and farming country, but many locals commute to work at the coal mine and power plant near Kemmerer. Nearly everyone is Mormon here. **Valley Hi Motel**, tel. 279-3251, has rooms for $25 s or $28 d, while **Hideout Motel**, tel. 279-3281, charges $20 s or d and up. Get home-cooked meals at **Midway Cafe**, tel. 279-3480, or fast food at the summer-only **Hideout Drive-In. Pine Creek Ski Area**, six miles east of Cokeville, tel. 279-3201, consists of a chairlift and rope tow with a vertical rise of 1,200 feet. Ski rentals and instruction are available. Open Tues., Sat., and Sun., Jan.-March.

Lake Alice

Take an enjoyable side trip to Lake Alice, a pristine mountain lake at the end of a 1½-mile trail in Bridger-Teton National Forest. Three-mile-long Lake Alice was created many centuries ago when a mountain slid across the valley, damming the creek. Get here by heading northeast from Cokeville on State 232 and bearing right at the Y where the pavement ends (12 miles up). The gravel road continues another 13 miles to the trailhead where you'll find the very nice **Hobble Creek Campground**. Good fishing both in the creek and at Lake Alice. The country around here is some of the only unroaded land left in the Wyoming Range.

Fossilized herring are the most common specimens found at Fossil Butte National Monument.

BOB RACE

STAR VALLEY

West of the Wyoming Range, the mountains seem exhausted as they dip into a broad, fertile farming valley that stretches across the Idaho border. This is Star Valley, a place with closer ties to Idaho—in terms of geography, farming, sheep ranching, transportation, and even religion—than to Wyoming. The valley reaches 10 miles across and 40 miles from north to south; an early settler labeled it "The Star of all Valleys." It is a very pretty place, with the Salt River (so named because of salt deposits and saline springs along its banks; the water is not salty) creating an oasis of greenery, and the mountains establishing a grand backdrop. Irrigation ditches flow alongside the roads and dairy cows stand in the velvet green farm fields. The houses are spacious, built to house large Mormon families. A single main road, U.S. 89, heads north across the full length of Star Valley, with all sorts of side roads and scattered pinprick settlements.

the number of wives a man could have. Polygamy, while outlawed by the federal government in 1882, was winked at by Wyoming authorities for many years; they needed all the settlers they could get, especially the hardworking Mormons. A large brick LDS church still stands in every podunk town in Star Valley.

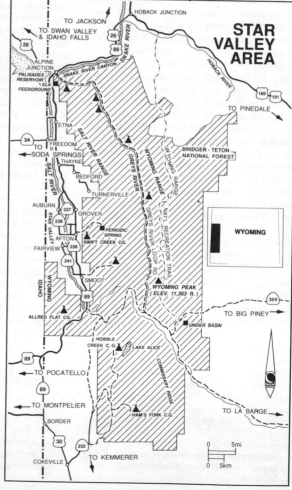

History

The **Lander Cutoff** of the Oregon Trail cuts through the southern half of Star Valley, following the Salt River as far as the Auburn area and then cutting northwest along Stump Creek. The trail, built in 1858 under the direction of Frederick W. Lander, was the first federal road built west of the Missouri River. It is readily visible along the south end of Greys River Rd. where it is marked by concrete posts and emigrant graves.

The first white settlers came to Star Valley from Idaho in the 1880s, fleeing laws restricting

Pitts Specials, made in Afton, are world-famous stunt planes.

BOB RACE

AFTON

Afton (pop. 1,600) is the primary settlement in Star Valley. It is a typical small American town, the sort of place where parents complain of kids partying with kegs and making-out on the backroads. Meanwhile the high schoolers complain of nothing to do. The local economy has suffered in recent years as farmers struggle on fertile land in a marginal climate. The Tricon Timber sawmill belches smoke from its plant that processes much of the 4.5 million board feet of timber cut annually on adjacent Forest Service lands. Christen Industries, also in Afton, manufactures a variety of aircraft, including the Pitts Specials, considered the finest aerobatic planes made. Quite a few workers also commute by bus to Jackson Hole—69 winding miles each way—where jobs are plentiful.

Sights
Afton's best-known attraction is the world's largest **elk antler arch**, an 18-foot-high arch that extends over the main street. Built in 1958, it contains 3,000 antlers. The small **Pioneer Museum** at 46 5th Ave. is open Mon.-Sat. 1-5 June-August. No charge. Inside are various items collected by the Daughters of the Utah Pioneers, including a loom, spinning wheel, and other miscellaneous memorabilia.

One of the most distinctive sights around Afton is **Periodic Spring**, located in Swift Creek Canyon, six miles east of town (take 2nd Avenue). It's one of only three intermittent springs known to exist. During late summer, icy water gushes from a gaping opening in the cliff for approximately 18 minutes, then stops for an equal period of time, only to resume flowing. The spring is reached via a 3/4-mile trail and across two rather shaky bridges. Periodic Spring feeds Swift Creek, the water source for Afton, and is so pure that no chlorination is needed. The Shoshones regarded this as a sacred place of healing, and said that a powerful medicine man was able to turn the waters on and off by command. Today, hydrologists believe that a large underground chamber periodically fills and then empties of water through a natural siphon in the porous limestone rock. The spring loses its intermittent flows in spring when it flows constantly. Best time to see it in action is in the early fall.

The town of Auburn, eight miles north and west of Afton, contains **Auburn Hot Springs**, a rather astounding area that covers several acres. The water is 144° F—some of the hottest in Wyoming—and flows out from 100 different vents, mud pots, small geysers, pools, and travertine terraces. Sort of a mini-Yellowstone without the fame.

Accommodations
Both **Corral Motel**, 161 Washington, tel. 886-5424, and **Lazy B Motel**, 219 Washington, tel. 886-3187, have rooms for $30 s or $34 d. The former is open April-Oct. only. **Mountain Inn**, one mile south of town, tel. 886-3156, has rooms for $40 s or $45 d, including a swimming pool and hot tub. **Hi Country Inn (Best Western)**, 3/4 mile south of town, tel. 886-3856, charges $40 s or $45 d. North of the wide spot in the road called **Grover** (pop. 120), the road enters a narrow canyon, known appropriately enough as The Narrows. One and a half miles up is **Silver Stream Lodge**, tel. 883-2440, which charges $28 s or d. The Forest Service's **Swift Creek**

Campground ($5; open mid-May to mid-Sept.) is only 1½ miles east of Afton. Periodic Spring is farther up the same road.

Food
DJ's Cafe, 323 Washington, tel. 886-3609, is popular with local coffee drinkers and smokers. Decent breakfasts and inexpensive chicken dinners. **Red Baron Drive-In**, 838 Washington, tel. 886-3745, is the hangout for burgers and fries. **Elkhorn Restaurant**, 465 Washington, tel. 886-3080, has very good homemade lunch specials and a big salad bar. The lunchtime smorgasbord at **Pizza Hut**, 228 Washington, tel. 886-9794, is popular. **Silver Stream Lodge**, seven miles north of Afton, tel. 883-2400, has a popular steak and seafood restaurant and cocktail lounge. **Colter's Bar**, 355 Washington, tel. 886-9597, has good steaks and burgers, served in a rustic Old West atmosphere. Eat outside on the patio during the summer. **Homestead Restaurant**, just south of town, tel. 886-3878, serves the area's finest prime rib. Try the double fudge desserts. Get groceries at **Thriftway**, just north of Afton, tel. 886-5550.

Entertainment And Events
For live C&W or rock music, head to **Colter's Bar**, 355 Washington, tel. 886-9597, where the young crowd hangs out, or **Valley Vineyard**, 967 Washington, tel. 886-9215. The **Lincoln County Fair** is held in Afton during early August.

Recreation
Country Gardens Pool, just north of town, tel. 886-5507, is open May-Sept., and costs $2.50 for adults or $1.50 for kids, including hot tub. Golfers will find the nine-hole **Afton Golf Course** south of town, tel. 886-3338, and two more at Star Valley Ranch in Thayne. During the winter, the town operates **Snowshoe Hollow**, tel. 886-9831, a small ski area just east of Afton. The hill has a rope tow and snack bar. Groomed cross-country ski trails are at Fish Creek, in the same vicinity.

Information And Services
Afton has a tiny summer-only **visitor center** at 2nd and Washington that is open Tues.-Sun. 10-6. **Star Valley Branch Library**, 261 Washington St., tel. 886-3158, is open Mon., Wed.,

and Fri. 10-6, Tues. and Thurs. 10-8, and Sat. 10-2. Lots of genealogy titles. **Book Corral**, 431 Washington, tel. 886-5246, has a small collection of Wyoming books. The **START Bus**, tel. 733-4521 (in Jackson), has daily summer and winter runs between Afton and Jackson for only $3 RT. This is primarily used by workers, but is a great, inexpensive way to get to or from Jackson Hole.

GREYS RIVER LOOP ROAD

Star Valley is bordered on the west and south by a portion of Bridger-Teton National Forest that crosses both the Salt River Range and the Wyoming Range. The Greys River flows between the two, paralleled by an 80-mile-long gravel road that is popular with vacationers, hikers, anglers, and hunters. The road begins south of Afton, and goes all the way to Alpine Junction. Excellent fishing for cutthroat, rainbow, brown, and brook trout in the river, and good opportunities to see deer and moose. Considerable logging still takes place in the mountains, and many thousands of sheep and cattle graze the open areas.

Camping And Hiking
Camping ($4-5; open mid-June to mid-Sept.) is available at seven places along the Greys River Rd.; nicest are ones at Murphy Creek and Forest Park. More than 450 miles of trails cut across this country, including the 75-mile-long **Wyoming Range National Recreation Trail** along the crest of the mountains. A side road off the Greys River Rd. leads to a two-mile trail that climbs 11,363-foot **Wyoming Peak**, tallest in the range. During the winter, cross-country skiers will find four groomed ski trails, while snowmobilers can cruise on 100 miles of groomed routes. See the **Greys River District Office**, 125 Washington St. in Afton, tel. 886-3166, for a map of this area and recreation information. The chamber of commerce has a listing of local guides and outfitters.

OTHER TOWNS

Thayne And Bedford
Thayne's (pop. 280) claim to fame is the **cutter**

races, a sport invented here in the 1920s. In it, horses pull "chariots" over a frozen field at breakneck speeds. Races are held on weekends Dec.-February. **Bedford Mercantile,** tel. 883-2136, sells handmade quilts made by local seamstresses, and is located in a landmark structure built in 1900.

Thayne's **Sunset Motel,** tel. 883-2462, wins the prize for some of the cheapest rooms in Wyoming. Weekday rates are $10 s or $20 d, rising to a lofty $15 s or $20 d on weekends. Take a look at the rooms first. **Swiss Mountain Motel,** tel. 883-2227, charges $32 s or $36 d. **Flat Creek RV Park** south of Thayne, tel. 883-2231, charges $10 for RVs. Nice cabins with kitchenettes are $25. Tenters can find a spot for free; $3 for showers. Open year-round. Just north of Thayne is **Star Valley Ranch Resort,** tel. 883-2457, an obscenely elaborate place with summer homes, a restaurant, RV park, two golf courses, and tennis courts. Ugly billboards announce its presence for miles in both directions.

Star Valley Cheese, tel. 883-2510, is one of the most unusual eating places in Wyoming. The restaurant—an old-fashioned place straight out of the 1950s—serves good sandwiches, burgers, homemade pies, and other fare, or you can buy fresh cheeses from the coolers. Open daily May-October. The cheese is made in the plant right behind the shop (take a look through the window), generally mozzarella, provolone, and ricotta. Some 60,000 pounds of cheese emerge each day; it takes just 32 hours to make cheese. Everything here gets the Star Valley label, although the plant is now a part of Western Dairymen Cooperative. Well worth a stop. **JH Ranch Cafe,** tel. 883-2357, has homemade breads and pastries, along with "The Thing." **Dad's Bar,** tel. 883-2300, offers live music on weekends and the best steaks in the area. This is also home to a small cutter racing museum. (The sport was established by "Dad" Walton.)

Freedom And Etna

Freedom (pop. 100), Star Valley's oldest settlement, straddles the Idaho-Wyoming border. The town was established by Mormons in 1879, and offered an escape from Idaho Territory's efforts to ban polygamy. Arthur Clark named the town for his freedom to have multiple wives. Today, Freedom has a small country store just a few feet from the border where you are free to buy Idaho lottery tickets. Freedom is famous in gun circles for a small factory, **Freedom Arms,** tel. 883-2468, that makes handguns, including the monstrous .454 Casull, the world's most-powerful revolver (and one of the most expensive at $1,100 apiece). Don't ever get on the wrong end of this deadly instrument.

Etna lies near the northern end of Star Valley, and has a small country store, and an outsized brick LDS church that looks big enough to house the entire population of 200. In late summer, the sweet scent of new-mown hay hangs in the air. **Horse Shoe Inn Motel and Cafe,** tel. 883-2281, has rooms for $25 s or $30 d, but is closed during the winter.

Alpine Junction

The crossroads settlement called Alpine Junction (pop. 180) consists of several motels, restaurants, and bars strung out in all directions along U.S. 26 and 89. The vicinity is known as Lower Valley and borders on Palisades Reservoir. Everything here is aimed at tourists en route to Jackson Hole. Approximately 800 elk gather each winter at the **Elk Feedground,** located a mile south of Alpine on U.S. 89. The elk can be viewed from the parking area here, and they often approach parked cars rather closely.

Alpen Haus, tel. 654-7545, has rooms starting for $30 s or $40 d, including a whirlpool. Check out the fossil fish at the reception desk. Also here is a restaurant and bar. **Flying Saddle Lodge (Best Western),** tel. 654-7561, has rooms starting for $32 s or d, including a swimming pool. Open June-Oct. only. **Three Rivers Motel,** tel. 654-7551, has rooms for $30 s or $38 d, while **Palisport Motel and Campground,** tel. 654-7540, charges $32 s or $34 d. Tent sites are $9, $13 for RVs. Showers for non-campers cost $3. **Lakeside Motel and Restaurant,** tel. 654-7507, charges $34 s or d, and has a restaurant featuring homemade food. **Bette's Coffee Shop,** tel. 654-7536, serves delicious, reasonably priced breakfasts and lunches on weekdays, plus dinners Fri.-Sun. nights. Recommended. **Jeep's Bar,** tel. 654-7585, has live music (mostly C&W) on weekends, and is one of the most popular weekend hangouts in the Star Valley vicinity. **Greys River Lodge,** on the Greys River Rd., tel. 654-7777, has very nice bed and breakfast accommodations in a modern log home. Contact **Alpine Riding & Rafts**, tel. 654-9900, for horseback rides in the area, and raft trips down the Snake River Canyon. Many similar operations are run in nearby Jackson.

SNAKE RIVER CANYON

Above Alpine Junction, the country abruptly changes as U.S. 89-26 enters Snake River Canyon, paralleling it all the way to Hoback Junction, 23 miles away. In places, the highway hangs high over the river, with only a guardrail blocking the way (and sometimes not even that). This is a delicious way to enter Jackson Hole, offering numerous pullouts where you can view the roiling rambunctious rapids of the sinuous Snake River as it slithers through millions of years of rocky cliffs. At sunset, the river glows a silver ribbon of light. A big, powerful river, the Snake eventually feeds into the Columbia River in Washington state. Riverbanks are lined with ancient cottonwoods, while the higher slopes exude lodgepole pines.

The whitewater of Snake River Canyon is a favorite of recreationists, and during the summer you're bound to meet cars with kayaks on their roofs and vans filled with happy rafters heading back to Jackson. See "Jackson Hole" p. 243 for details on the many river-running options. River access is generally via the West Table Creek and Sheep Gulch boat ramps. A half-dozen Forest Service **campgrounds** ($5; open late May to mid-Sept.) are scattered all along the way. Many fill up early in the day during midsummer. Undeveloped camping spots along the way are also used by many travelers.

Boar's Tusk

BOB RACE

BOB RACE

CENTRAL WYOMING

The counties of Natrona and Converse enclose definitive Wyoming country: sage- and grass-carpeted plains, desolate badlands, impressive tree-draped mountainsides, and the big, lazy North Platte River. This is grazing country; each year nearly a quarter of the sheep raised in Wyoming, along with 120,000 cattle, come from these two counties. The dominant industry, however—and the one that dictates the region's economy—is oil. It means jobs for roughnecks in dozens of oil fields, but it also greases the wheels of city life, offering refinery and transportation work, government positions, and a wave of other impacts in the local community as the wages pass on to construction workers, shop owners, and school teachers. Without oil, Casper—Wyoming's second-largest metropolitan area—would be little more than a cattletown crossroad on the way to Yellowstone.

The Land
Geographically, central Wyoming is quite diverse. The north portion is an open, expansive place. Driving across the long, straight highways that divide this land is like sailing a boat over an ocean of gentle rollers, with mountains

so far in the distance that they could well be islands. Golden eagles spin giant loops in the sky, and the coal-black clouds of distant summertime thunderheads are pierced by brilliant slashes of lightning. The wind blows on, bending the grass as it passes in waves of motion, whirling the old windmills that pump water to sheep, cattle, and deer. This is rolling mixed-grass prairie and sagebrush country, with sharp ridges appearing suddenly, topped by narrow bands of ponderosa pine and juniper.

South of this rangeland lies the North Platte River, carving a slow curve first to the north, then east, and finally southeast toward Nebraska. Giant dams hold back the water for irrigation and electricity. A green stripe of riparian forests and irrigated fields borders the river. South of the Platte, the land changes, with the Laramie Mountains rising in a rough-edged jumble of rugged canyons and pine-covered peaks. Elk stand along mountain meadows, bugling in the cool air of late fall. Pickup trucks slow down as wild turkeys speed-walk across the gravel roads. Clear mountain brooks filled with trout cascade down mountain slopes. West of here, central Wyoming becomes drier and more desolate, wrinkled by the badlands of Hells Half Acre and the barren crests of desert mountain ranges.

Casper dominates the central Wyoming economy with oil refineries, the only statewide newspaper, the state's largest junior college, and its biggest shopping mall. The towns of Douglas and Glenrock go their own ways, with a mix-ture of ranching, oil, coal, and tourism. Farther north, the tiny settlements of Midwest and Edgerton cap the vast Salt Creek oil field. Between these few outposts of civilization lie hundreds of square miles of sagebrush and grass, jackrabbits, and rattlers. Only the scattered roads, oil pumpjacks, windmills, and old ranch houses mark the presence of humans.

DOUGLAS

Douglas (pop. 5,100) epitomizes life in small-town America. It's the sort of place where the big summertime events are the state fair and week-ly drag races, where a night on the town means joining a bowling league or doing the two-step at the LaBonte Inn, and where men hang out in the Corner Barber Shop to talk politics, retiring next door to the historic College Inn Bar for a beer. On both ends of Douglas are more modern slices of Americana—suburban ranch-style homes cover the hills. It's a friendly, conservative town with pickup trucks, dense American food, and an unusual history.

HISTORY

Douglas came into existence with the arrival of the Fremont, Elkhorn, and Missouri Valley Railroad. Platted in 1886, the town was named for Stephen A. Douglas, the senator from Illinois best known for his debates with Abraham Lincoln. It quickly boomed to 1,600 people that first year, boasting three newspapers, several restaurants and hotels, two dance halls, 12 stores, and 21 saloons (easy to see where priorities lay). Once the railroad construction had moved

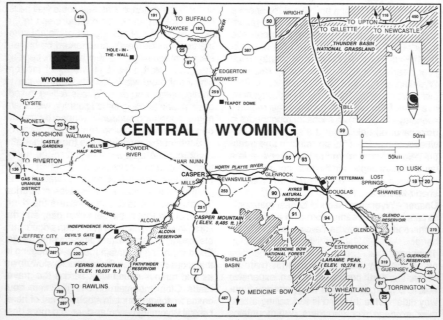

© MOON PUBLICATIONS

Map of Douglas showing streets and points of interest including: AIRPORT, TO GILLETTE (59), NORTH PLATTE RIVER, LAW ENFORCEMENT ACADEMY, KEITH RIDER PARK, HOLIDAY INN / CHUTES EATERY, GRUMPY'S, RIVERSIDE PARK, YELLOWSTONE HWY., CHAMBER OF COMMERCE, LABONTE INN, SUPER 8 MOTEL, TO FORT FETTERMAN (93), PIONEER MUSEUM, CITY OFFICE BUILDING, LIBRARY, POST OFFICE, HOME BAKERY, HOSPITAL, CEDAR ST., WALNUT ST., CENTER ST., OAK ST., WASHINGTON PARK, ELM ST., PINE ST., DOUGLAS PARK CEMETERY, RIVERBEND DR., TO CASPER (91), JACKALOPE KOA CAMPGROUND, WYOMING STATE FAIRGROUNDS, BROWNFIELD RD., DOUGLAS MOTEL, ASH ST., BIRCH ST., HAMILTON ST., HIGH SCHOOL & RECREATION CENTER, FOREST SERVICE OFFICE, PLAINS MOTEL AND RESTAURANT, VAGABOND MOTEL, FAT ED'S, POW CAMP SITE, SMYLIE RD., RICHARDS ST., CHIEFTAIN MOTEL, DOUGLAS INTERNATIONAL RACEWAY, PIZZA HUT, VILLAGE INN, PARK DR., MESA DR., BIG HORN TAXIDERMY, CLEMENTINE'S, ALPINE INN, BIG WHEEL TRUCKSTOP / BUS STOP, TO I-25, TO ESTERBROOK & JACKALOPE PLUNGE (94), BIKEPATH, GOLF COURSE, TO GLENDO STATE PARK & CHEYENNE, NOT TO SCALE, MOON, 2nd ST., 3rd ST., 4th ST., 5th ST., 6th ST., 7th ST., 8th ST., 9th ST., 10th ST., 11th ST., 12th ST., 87, 26, 20, 25

© MOON PUBLICATIONS

on down the line to Casper, the population dwindled, becoming a sleepy little ranching center for the next 70 years. Only the late-summer state fair brought Douglas to life each year.

World War II

One of the strangest pieces of Douglas history is its prisoner-of-war camp, built in 1943 along the North Platte River. The camp contained 180 barrack-style buildings, and housed up to 3,000 prisoners of war. The camp was surrounded by an electrified fence, watch towers, German shepherds, and Army guards. One prisoner was shot by a guard, and a few others escaped, but they didn't get far in this remote country, 2,000 miles from the sea. Though some of the prisoners at Douglas were German Nazi and SS officers, the majority were Italians, many of whom were happy to be away from the war.

The prisoners worked in local agricultural fields, harvesting potatoes and sugar beets for $4 a day, or at a variety of art projects in the camp. Most impressive was the work of several Italian artists who painted the interior of the U.S. officers' club with 15 murals of Old West scenes. After the war, the prisoners returned home, though some have returned to visit in later years. The land was sold to Converse County for $1, and the barracks were dismantled or bought by locals who moved them to other parts of town. Today the POW camp site is an open meadow on the west bank of the North Platte and south of Richards Street.

Boom And Bust

Like much of Wyoming, Douglas has watched its fortunes wax and wane over the years. In the 1950s, with the Cold War at fever pitch, prospectors combed Wyoming with Geiger counters, discovering major uranium deposits just north of Douglas. Others found oil, gas, and coal. A giant coal-fired power plant opened in nearby Glenrock, and by the late '70s the region was one of the most prosperous in the state. At the peak of the oil and uranium orgy in the early 1980s, the town of Douglas had doubled to over 10,000 people.

The tourist brochures claim "growth has leveled off," but in reality it fell off a cliff, dropping perhaps 50% in a couple of years. Longtime locals had mixed feelings when the balloon suddenly burst in the mid '80s—happy to see the rabble leave town, but suddenly burdened with paying for all the new schools, roads, and other facilities ordered up in the heady heyday. Today, the economy of Douglas is back to its old mixture of ranching and energy, with some people commuting 60 miles each way to coal mines near Wright. Most folks are happy to live a simpler life. Of course, the next energy boom could be just around the corner.

SIGHTS

Pioneer Museum

The people of Douglas point with pride to their local museum, easily one of the finest in Wyo-

---

JACKALOPES

Definition: Jackalope—a mammal that moves by bounding, found originally in Converse County, Wyoming, but now distributed throughout the western states. It has the horns of an antelope and the body of a jackrabbit. First observed by trapper Roy Ball in 1829, and later noted by cowboys and others after too little sleep, too many days in the saddle, and too much cheap whiskey. A nocturnal animal, jackalopes are never seen during the day. They are reputed to attain speeds approaching 90 mph and often sing just before thunderstorms. Powerful and vicious when attacked. The hornless does are commonly seen by tourists, while the bucks remain elusive. Westerners feel that the federal government is hushing up the true story of these dangerous critters to make cowboys look like liars.

OK, I admit to liking plastic pink flamingos and tacky postcards, but jackalopes are another story. The first time you see a mounted jackalope specimen, they are mildly amusing, but with each tourist junk shop west of the Mississippi offering more jackalopes, the originality quickly fades. The town of Douglas takes credit for this hare-brained idea, though its claim is a bit suspect. In the 1920s, a Douglas resident saw a jackalope mounted in a store in Buffalo, Wyoming. He described the creature to his grandson, Douglas Herrick, who was intrigued by the animal. In 1941, he attached the antlers of a deer to the head of a large jackrabbit he had shot and sold the specimen to the LaBonte Hotel. The rest—as they say—is history. Douglas Herrick's son, Jim Herrick, follows in his father's

BOB RACE

footsteps, offering everything from fighting jackalopes to jackalope "love mounts" at Big Horn Taxidermy on Smylie Road.

In 1960, the State of Wyoming gave the Douglas Chamber of Commerce "jackalope" as a registered trademark. Today jackalopes are everywhere in Douglas: the town symbol contains one, an eight-foot-tall jackalope statue greets visitors to the fairgrounds, another statue has hopped atop the LaBonte Hotel, a roadside sign warns "Watch Out For Jackalope," cans of jackalope milk are sold in the stores, you can drink "Rabbit Punch" at a local bar, jackalope hunting licenses are available around town, and of course, the critters multiply like rabbits on the shelves of local shops.

ming. Located just inside the fairgrounds, the spacious museum, tel. 358-9288, is open Tues.-Fri. 8-7 and Sat.-Sun. 1-5 in summer, and Tues.-Fri. 9-5 in winter. Free. The main room is filled with old rifles and saddles (including one that belonged to outlaw Tom Horn). Check out the special "running irons" used by rustlers to alter cattle brands. Fittingly enough, the rifle of Nate Champion—a rustler murdered in the Johnson County Wars—is also here. Look around the other rooms and you'll discover the bison-fur mittens worn by Portugee Phillips on his ride to get help for Fort Kearny, and an Army trumpet and bullets from the Custer battlefield.

On a kinder and gentler note, take a look at the large doll collection and many unusual women's fans, along with a description of "fan language." Downstairs are several wonderful old quilts, and an extraordinary collection of Indian artifacts, including a Sioux wooden flute, beaded moccasins, an Indian bow from the Wagon Box Fight, hundreds of arrowheads and other implements from the "Spanish Diggings" site, and even a stone war club from the Black Hills. Outside are seven old train cars in various stages of disrepair, along with a schoolhouse built in 1886.

More Sights

The old **officers' club** from the Douglas POW camp is now an Odd Fellows Hall at 115 S. Riverbend Dr., tel. 358-2421. Ask to take a look inside at the wall-to-wall murals painted by Italian artist/prisoners during World War II. One of Wyoming's oldest churches is the **Christ Episcopal Church**, built in 1896 and now on the National Register of Historic Places. The attractive white structure is located at 411 Center, tel. 358-5609. The **Plains Complex**, 628 E. Richards, tel. 358-4489, has several historic structures, hauled in from all over this part of Wyoming. Included are the old officers' quarters from Fort Fetterman, and a POW camp building. The ice cream parlor served at various times as a barn, boarding house, and maternity center. Check out the ceiling doors. The **Douglas Park Cemetery**, on the east end of Pine St., has a number of interesting old graves, including that of horsethief "Doc" Middleton. Also here is the grave of George W. Pike.

PRACTICALITIES

Accommodations

There are 10 motels and hotels to choose from in Douglas; see below for specifics. For a homier stay, visit **Akers Ranch B&B**, 81 Inez Rd., tel. 358-3741, where cabins are $35 s or $40 d. Two other local ranches operate as bed and

DOUGLAS ACCOMMODATIONS

Motel	Address	Telephone	Rates	Features
Douglas Motel	539 S. 4th	358-2472	$16+ s or d	kitchenettes
Four Winds Motel	615 Richards	358-2322	$18 s, $20 d	
Vagabond Motel	430 Richards	358-9414	$20 s, $24 d	
Plains Motel	628 E. Richards	358-4484	$22 s, $24 d	
Chieftain Motel	815 Richards	358-2673	$25 s, $29 d	AAA approved
LaBonte Hotel	206 Walnut	358-9856	$25 s, $30 d	
I-25 Inn	2349 E. Richards	358-2833	$25 s, $30 d	AAA approved
Super 8 Motel	314 Russell Ave.	358-6800 (800) 843-1991	$28 s, $32 d	
Alpine Inn	2310 E. Richards	358-4780	$29 s, $34 d	
Holiday Inn	1450 Riverbend Dr.	358-9790 (800) 465-4329	$44+ s, $50+ d	AAA approved, pool, whirlpool, sauna, excercise room

breakfasts: **Two Creek Ranch**, 800 Esterbrook Rd., tel. 358-3467, and **Wagonhound Ranch**, 1061 Poison Lake Rd., tel. 358-5439. Note that when the state fair arrives each August, everything books up weeks ahead. Many locals rent out rooms in their homes to visitors while the fair is going on; get a list from the chamber of commerce. Dormitories are also available for temporary lodging on the fairgrounds; call 358-2398 for details.

Camping
Pitch tents or park RVs for free at **Riverside Park** along the North Platte River. The free showers have an amusing western-decor bathroom covered with "branded" wood. Camping is limited to two nights, and the sprinklers come on at 8 a.m., so get up early! Two nearby camping places—Ayres Natural Bridge Park and the Laramie Mountains—are described on pp. 154-156 The RV crowd heads to **Jackalope KOA**, tel. 358-2164, west of Douglas on State 91. Rates are $11 for tents or $16 for RVs. Open year-round.

Food
Restaurant food in Douglas is pretty standard Wyoming fare. Breakfast time means bacon and eggs at **LaBonte Inn**, 206 Walnut St., tel. 358-9856, or big portions at the **Big Wheel Truckstop**, just east of town, tel. 358-4446. Lunchtime attracts locals to **Breeze's Sandwich Shop**, 117 N. 8th, tel. 358-9456, for a sub and salad, or to **Pizza Hut**, 1830 Richards, tel. 358-3657. **Clementine's**, 1199 Mesa Dr., tel. 358-5554, has all-you-can-eat lunch specials. The **Plains Complex**, 628 E. Richards, tel. 358-4489, has a so-so coffee shop (open 24 hours) and an old-fashioned ice cream parlor. For fast food, head to **Grumpy's**, 1213 Teton Way, tel. 358-5702, where locally raised beef is used in their big burgers.

Come dinner time, there are several choices. Clementine's has steak and prime rib, pizza, and Mexican food in a pleasant atmosphere. **Fat Ed's**, on the corner of E. Richards and 10th streets, tel. 358-6330, is run by neighborly "Fat Ed" Rogina. It's a Douglas favorite straight out of the 1950s, the sort of place your dad probably loved. Car-hop service for burgers, or sit down inside for something more substantial. Try a huge plate of gravy-drenched turkey, white

bread, and potatoes, and top it off with a fat slice of homemade pie. For a classier meal of steak and salad, try **Chute's Eatery** in the Holiday Inn, 1450 Riverbend Dr., tel. 358-9790. Their soup-and-salad buffet is a good deal. Also popular is the elegant **Country Inn**, 2341 E. Richards, tel. 358-3575. It has a nice salad bar.

Douglas has three grocery stores: **Peyton Bolln Grocery**, 100 S. 3rd, **Decker Food Center**, 1100 Richards, and a **Safeway**, 130 S. 4th. For fresh-baked pastries, head to **Home Bakery**, 119 N. 3rd, tel. 358-9251.

Recreation
The town has a free summer-only outdoor **swimming pool** ($1.50 adults, 75¢ under 19) in Washington Park, and an indoor pool (open year-round) at the high school, 1701 Hamilton, tel. 358-4231. Other free facilities here include gyms, racquetball courts, sauna, and weightroom. Seven miles south of Douglas on Esterbrook Rd. (State 94) is **Jackalope Plunge Swimming Pool**, tel. 358-2820, fed by the 84° F water of Douglas Warm Spring. No chlorine. This is a fun place to play volleyball, enjoy a picnic, or practice your diving. Entrance is $3 adults, $2 under age 10. Open summers only, Thurs.-Sun. 11-7. A couple of miles south of Jackalope Plunge, you can see ruts of the old Oregon Trail; ask at the chamber of commerce for directions. An 18-hole **golf course**, tel. 358-5099, is southeast of Douglas. **Riverside Park**, along the western bank of the North Platte River, contains a two-mile-long paved bike path that makes for a pleasant evening stroll. Take along your fishing pole to try for trout, walleye, or channel catfish. If you have your own raft or canoe, the river provides pleasant, leisurely float trips.

Entertainment
Chutes Lounge in the Holiday Inn, 1450 Riverbend Dr., tel. 358-9790, has lounge-lizard tunes six nights a week, a big-screen TV, and free hors d'oeuvres on weeknights. **LaBonte Lounge**, 206 Walnut, tel. 358-5210, is the place for weekend bands. Farther afield, you can dance on summer weekends at **Esterbrook Lodge**, 32 miles south of Douglas. The historic **College Inn Bar**, 103 N. 2nd, tel. 358-9976, is a favorite place for major league drinking with the locals.

Wyoming State Fair

In 1905, the Wyoming Legislature appropriated $10,000 for a Wyoming State Fair in Douglas. With land donated by the Chicago and Northwestern Railroad, the "Show Window of Wyoming" opened that summer, offering a variety of agricultural exhibits, plus horseback wrestling, Roman races, and concerts. To top it off, two cavalry soldiers added their own drama by putting on an impromptu gunfight. Later, auto polo and motorcycle-riding events were added, but the big hit was Professor Carver's High Diving Girl who leapt with her horse off a 40-foot platform into a pool of water.

The Wyoming State Fair is held the third week of August each year, drawing thousands of visitors from all over the nation. The 113-acre fairgrounds is right next to town, and includes a 4,300-seat grandstand, an arts and crafts building, cafeteria, arena, open-air pavilion, livestock barns and stalls, and of course, plenty of carnival rides, cotton candy, and stuffed animal prizes in the midway. Keep yourself entertained at the market swine evaluation, the 4-H vegetable judging, the demolition derby, or the sheep-to-shawl contest. A free "people shuttle" (tractor-pulled wagon) takes folks around the fairgrounds and into town. Other attractions include evening C&W concerts and a Saturday morning parade. Since this is Wyoming, the biggest events at the fair are the PRCA rodeos held the final three days.

Other Events

Both locals and visitors enjoy the **High Plains Oldtime Country Music Show & Contest** held in mid-April. Plenty of hot fiddle, guitar, and banjo players offer entertainment. **Fort Fetterman Days**, held the third weekend in June at the old fort, attracts a troop of soldiers and other folks dressed in costumes from the 1870s. There are black-powder contests, old-time music, and games. In late June, **Jackalope Days** offers a small carnival and street fair. All summer long, the grandiosely named Douglas International Raceway on the southeast edge of town hosts **drag races** of all types. It's considered one of the top quarter-mile strips in the nation. The biggest races come in mid-July.

Information And Services

The **Douglas Area Chamber of Commerce** office, 318 1st St., tel. 358-2950, is open Mon.-Fri. 8-12 and 1-5. **Converse County Library**, 300 Walnut St., tel. 358-3644, is open only Mon., Tues., and Fri. 10-6, and Thurs. 12-8. **R-D Pharmacy**, 206 Center, tel. 358-3266, sells Wyoming books. Visit the **Meadowlark Gallery** at 300 S. 4th St., tel. 358-3808, for local arts and crafts, and check **Yesterday's**, 123 S. 2nd, tel. 358-3509, for unusual flea-market novelties. The U.S. Forest Service **Laramie Peak District Office**, 809 S. 9th St., tel. 358-4690, has maps and info on both Medicine Bow National Forest and Thunder Basin National Grassland. **Powder River Transportation** buses (tel. 800-442-3682) stop at Big Wheel Truckstop, just east of Douglas, provide connections to most of Wyoming.

DOUGLAS VICINITY

FORT FETTERMAN

Seven miles northwest of Douglas on State 93 is Fort Fetterman State Historic Site. The fort was named for Lt. Col. William J. Fetterman, who was killed by Indians in the Fetterman Massacre of 1866 (see "Powder River Country," p. 382). Begun in 1867, this was the last fort built in the Rockies. With the signing of the Fort Laramie Treaty of 1868, forts Casper, Reno, Phil Kearny, and C.F. Smith were all closed, leaving Fort Fetterman as the only Army base in northern Wyoming. The hilltop location afforded commanding views along the infamous Bozeman Trail in both directions, but the location proved inhospitable. A report to headquarters the first winter noted "officers and men were found under canvas exposed on a bleak plain to violent and almost constant gales and very uncomfortable." Even after the buildings were completed, the fort remained a dreaded, windswept, lonely place, and many soldiers deserted as soon as they could get to the nearest railroad. The regimen was strict, with daily parade drills and the prospect of long rides to fight Indians in the surrounding country. Soldiers called the place "Hell Hole," while the Sioux derisively labelled it "Fort Fetterman Reservation." Not far away stood the "Hog Ranch"—sin city on the plains—where gambling, drinking, and women offered a choice of ways to spend the $13 a month calvarymen received.

Fort Fetterman served as a supply base for the Army during the mid-1870s, and both Gen. Crook and Col. MacKenzie led expeditions from here to attack the Sioux, but the fort itself was never the scene of any conflicts. After the battles had finally died down, the fort was abandoned in 1882. Instead of immediately disappearing, however, "Fetterman City" became the center of ranching and trade in the area. For a while, at least, it was a wide-open town with enough gunfights, hangings, whoring, gambling, and drunkenness to give "Miami Vice" a run for the money. In his novel *The Virginian,* Owen Wister used Fetterman as the basis for his rough-and-tumble town of "Drybone."

The Fort Today

After the railroad arrived in 1886, Douglas became the new center for trade, and Fetterman quickly faded from the scene. Most of the buildings were torn down or moved to Douglas, and only two of the original buildings remain, an adobe ordinance warehouse and a log officers' quarters. Inside the officers' quarters is a small state-run **museum** (free) that includes historic displays on the fort, Indians battles, and Fetterman City. The buildings are open daily 9-6 in summer, or by appointment (tel. 358-2864) the rest of the year. You can visit the grounds at any time. The surrounding country still exudes a sense of barren loneliness, and it's easy to see how much the soldiers must have hated this windswept post. Ask the museum staff to point out the faint tracks of the "Bloody Bozeman" Trail to the south.

THUNDER BASIN NATIONAL GRASSLAND

Thunder Basin National Grassland is an expansive blend of high rolling plateaus, steep rocky escarpments, and gentle plains. It's one of the few places in Wyoming where mountain ranges are not visible, giving the countryside a North Dakota feel. Most of the grassland is covered with a mixture of western wheatgrass, blue grama grass, and big sagebrush, but some of the ridges have stands of ponderosa pine and juniper, while creek bottoms contain cottonwood trees or greasewood. There are 170 known golden eagle nests on Thunder Basin—one of the biggest concentrations in Wyoming—along with abundant populations of sandhill cranes, turkeys, antelope, mule deer, elk, and coyotes. Many bald eagles winter here. Look out for the jackalopes, too; lots of the antlerless variety get hit by cars.

Thunder Basin National Grassland covers 1.8 million acres within Powder River Basin. The land is a checkerboard of private ranches, along with property belonging to the Forest Service, the BLM, and the state. The federal government owns 572,000 acres of the total, with headquarters at the Forest Service office in Douglas, 809 S. 9th St., tel. 358-4690. Get a copy of the detailed Thunder Basin map here for $2.

History

Thunder Basin came about during the glory days of the New Deal, and remains today an enclave of pseudo-socialism within the rock-ribbed Republican state of Wyoming. Although ranchers had grazed sheep and cattle in the area since the mid-19th century, the arrival of homesteaders caused the land to be divided into smaller parcels. In the arid mixed-grass prairies of eastern Wyoming, it was nearly impossible for a family to survive—the rains fell too infrequently for farming, and profitable cattle or sheep operations required more than 640 acres of grazing land.

Overgrazing, soil erosion, and five consec-utive drought years in the 1930s combined to force many families off the land. Counties risked bankruptcy because of lost tax revenue. The Agricultural Adjustment Administration finally began purchasing homesteads in 1934, giving money to the counties in lieu of taxes. Programs were begun to re-establish grasses to protect the soil and to develop water sources for livestock, while private land ownership was consolidated into larger, more economically manageable units.

Management

Today, local ranchers use the grassland in a cooperative grazing scheme that allows 21,000 cattle and an equal number of sheep on the federal land. Improvements such as dams, wells, and fences are cooperatively developed. In addition to livestock grazing, practically every acre

PRAIRIE DOGS

Prairie dogs are cat-sized rodents that live in underground communities and feed on roots and plants. Prairie dog towns sometimes cover thousands of acres, with burrow holes spaced every 50 feet or so. Two species occur in Wyoming; the white-tailed and black-tailed prairie dogs. The latter are found in at least 180 "towns" covering more than 28,000 acres within Thunder Basin National Grassland. Local ranchers complain of lost grazing range due to digging by the "dogs" and injuries from horses and cattle stepping into their holes. Because of this, the Forest Service for many years systematically poisoned prairie dog colonies for "range improvement" (translation: cattle grazing).

Sightings of the endangered black-footed ferret on the national grassland helped end most of this poisoning in the 1970s, and prairie dog populations have rebounded dramatically. Unfortunately, the Forest Service continues its poisoning program in places. In addition, because prairie dogs are still considered varmints, "sport" hunters aren't limited on how many they can shoot. Hunters from South Dakota—having already decimated prairie dog populations in their own state—are coming to the prairie dog colonies of Wyoming, shooting as many as they can. Meanwhile, the Department of Game and Fish is raising a covey of once-

wild ferrets (a predator of prairie dogs) at its Sybille Canyon facility, hoping to someday return them to such places as the national grassland (see p. 68 for more on the black-footed ferret). By trying to contain the prairie dog population to small areas, the hunters, Forest Service, and private ranchers may well be endangering the long-term survival of the world's rarest mammal, the black-footed ferret. If you're interested in seeing prairie dogs, ask at the Douglas Forest Service office for a copy of their prairie dog town map. The largest area—covering at least eight square miles—is along Horse Creek in the Rochelle Hills. Smaller prairie dog colonies lie along North Antelope Road.

BOB RACE

of Thunder Basin has been leased for petroleum exploration. Currently, over 450 oil and gas wells pump from 58 oil fields. Vast deposits of sub-bituminous coal underlie almost the entire area, and five gigantic strip mines cover 27,000 acres of land. Included is Black Thunder Coal Mine, the largest coal producer in the U.S.. Revenues from oil and coal developments on the grassland bring in nearly $20 million a year to the federal treasury, a figure unmatched anywhere else in the Forest Service system. Bentonite—a lubricant and absorptive clay used in everything from oil-drilling muds to candy bars—is also mined on the grassland, and major uranium deposits wait for the public to forget about Three Mile Island and Chernobyl.

Recreation

A network of over 775 miles of gravel and dirt roads crisscross Thunder Basin National Grassland, but there are no developed trails, campgrounds, or other facilities. You can, however, camp for free anywhere on the public lands. A couple of areas are popular with hunters, birdwatchers, photographers, and others looking for a chance to get out and about. The **Rochelle Hills**, a forested volcanic escarpment near the corner of Converse, Campbell, and Weston counties, is one of the prettiest parts, though a recent fire has blackened some of the trees. A scenic gravel road takes you in a long loop north of the tiny settlement of **Bill** (the name came from four early homesteaders, all of whom had the same first name—Bill), and then for 50 miles through the Rochelle Hills, before dropping back to State 59, eight miles south of Wright. Check the grassland map for specifics. The Upton-Osage area also contains miles of ponderosa pine-topped hills and many small ponds that attract birds.

Because of the patchwork quilt of land ownership on the grassland, many federal parcels are accessible only across private property, and you may need to get permission from the landowners first. Ask at the Douglas Forest Service office for access information. As with much of Wyoming's rangelands, you need to be on guard for prairie rattlesnakes, especially around rockpiles and prairie dog towns. Also, beware of thunderstorms and the lightning that can strike in this open country—they don't call this Thunder Basin for nothing.

LARAMIE MOUNTAINS

The Laramie Peak portion of Medicine Bow National Forest lies approximately 30 miles south of Douglas, cutting from northwest to southeast along the Laramie Mountains. The mountains are draped with stands of ponderosa, lodgepole, and limber pine, along with Engelmann spruce and subalpine fir at higher elevations. Lower elevations are dominated by grass and sagebrush. It is pretty, but rugged country, with deep valleys dividing the high granitic ridges and peaks. Several exceed 9,000 feet. Deer, elk, antelope, and wild turkeys are commonly seen in the Laramie Mountains, and rainbow, brook, and brown trout are found in the creeks. Public and private lands are intermingled here, with only a few large tracts of Forest Service property, the biggest being around Laramie Peak, an impressive mountain clearly visible from Douglas, and a landmark for travelers along the old Oregon Trail. (They called this country the Black Hills.) There is some logging around Esterbrook and Albany Peak, especially in insect-killed forests, but Laramie Peak is de facto wilderness.

The **Esterbrook** area, 32 miles south of Douglas on State 94, began as a copper mining town in 1886, but never really had much to show for the effort. Esterbrook is famed for an old log church whose rear window frames snowcapped Laramie Peak. It's a very popular place for weddings. A fine campground is close by, along with **Esterbrook Lodge**, offering small cabins, a restaurant, and bar with summertime live music on weekends.

Camping And Hiking

Free camping at four small campgrounds (open June to mid-Oct.) in the Laramie Mountains. See the map (opposite) for access. Some of the finest hiking in central Wyoming is found along the **Laramie Peak Trail**, a 5½-mile path that climbs to the top of 10,272-foot Laramie Peak. The trail begins right behind Friend Park Campground, 36 miles south of Douglas, and passes a small waterfall two miles up. Periodic forest openings offer dramatic vistas as you continue up the mountain, gaining 2,500 feet along the way. On top find expansive vistas in all directions. (Communication buildings and towers are

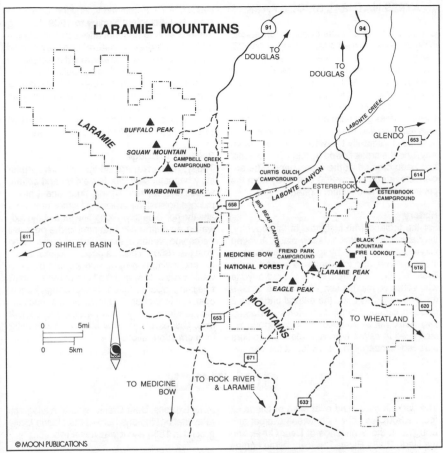

LARAMIE MOUNTAINS

91

TO
DOUGLAS

94

TO
DOUGLAS

LABONTE CREEK

TO
GLENDO

653

LARAMIE

BUFFALO PEAK

SQUAW MOUNTAIN

CAMPBELL CREEK
CAMPGROUND

CURTIS GULCH
CAMPGROUND

614

WARBONNET PEAK

658

LABONTE CANYON

ESTERBROOK

ESTERBROOK
CAMPGROUND

611

TO SHIRLEY BASIN

BIG BEAR CANYON

MEDICINE BOW

FRIEND PARK
CAMPGROUND

BLACK
MOUNTAIN
FIRE LOOKOUT

618

NATIONAL FOREST

LARAMIE PEAK

EAGLE PEAK

MOUNTAINS

620

653

TO WHEATLAND

0   5mi

0   5km

671

TO MEDICINE
BOW

TO ROCK RIVER
& LARAMIE

633

© MOON PUBLICATIONS

also here.)

Another good climb is up the 4WD road to
Black Mountain Lookout, one of the last operating fire towers in Wyoming, open June-
September. Great views down pristine Ashen-
felder Creek. Get there by following Forest Rd.
633 south of Esterbrook Campground for six
miles to the Laramie Peak Scout Camp. The
4WD road is just beyond this on the right.

Two other hikes follow old jeep roads from
the Curtis Gulch Campground, 38 miles south of
Douglas. One of the more scenic treks in the
Laramie Mountains is up the steep-walled
LaBonte Canyon. The two-mile-long **LaBonte**

Creek Trail offers both pleasant hiking and excellent fishing for brook trout. Keep your eyes
open for bighorn sheep and elk as you hike up
the canyon. The nearby **Big Bear Canyon Trail**
climbs along Big Bear Creek for three miles.

Come winter, the Laramie Mountains offer
excellent cross-country skiing opportunities, with
many miles of scenic country and untracked
snow. Over 20 miles of groomed trails surround
the Esterbrook area, used primarily by snowmobilers, but also by skiers. A warming hut is
also here. Pick up a map of snowmobile trails
from the Douglas ranger station.

AYRES NATURAL BRIDGE PARK

One of the most unusual geologic formations in Wyoming is 14 miles west of Douglas on I-25. Take Exit 151 and go five miles south to the tiny 22-acre Ayres Natural Bridge Park. The main attraction is a 150-foot-long and 50-foot-high rock arch over LaPrele Creek. This natural arch was formed when a meander bend in LaPrele Creek gradually eroded the base of the rock face, leaving the upper part of the cliff unscathed. Eventually the weakened rock gave way, and the creek flowed through the hole that had been created at the creek bend. The ancient creek bed is now 300 feet away from the present creek and 50 feet higher.

History

For the Indians who first lived in this country, the natural bridge was a deadly place. A young brave had been struck by lightning while hunting in the canyon, and thus began a legend that a beast inhabited the area, ready to grab anyone who ventured into his lair. When white settlers realized this, they used the natural bridge as a place to escape from Indian attacks, knowing they would not be pursued. Early day mountain men lived in caves here and Mormon settlers built cabins nearby in the 1850s. It took an ex-

pedition by Dr. Ferdinand V. Hayden, director of the U.S. Geological Survey in 1869, to bring the rock arch to national attention. He found it odd "that so great a natural curiosity should have failed to attract the attention it deserves." In 1881, Alva Ayres (or Ayers; spelling tends to get mangled in Wyoming) bought the land here and used the lush LaPrele Creek country as headquarters for a freighting business. The natural bridge and surrounding land were donated to Converse County in 1920 by Ayres' heirs.

Seeing The Bridge

Today, Ayres Natural Bridge offers a surprisingly beautiful side trip. Boxelders and cottonwoods line LaPrele Creek, fluorescent green patches against the brilliant red sandstone rocks and the rich blue sky. Along one face of the red-walled amphitheater that circles the park are the carved names of many visitors, some dating from the 1880s. This is a popular weekend picnic and swimming spot, and a great place to watch birds or to spend a quiet night at the small free campground. Ayres Natural Bridge Park is open April-October. A gate blocks the road during the winter, but you can walk in the last half mile. Call caretaker Ray Morton at 358-3532 for more information.

GLENROCK

The podunk cattle and coal town of Glenrock (pop. 2,300) lies halfway between Casper and Douglas at the confluence of Deer Creek and the North Platte River. The town name comes from Rock in the Glen, a large rock just to the west. Deer Creek was a favorite camping spot along the Oregon Trail, a place to rest up, do a little fishing, and let the stock graze on the lush creekside grass. Starting in 1847, Mormon emigrants mined the coal visible along the north bank of the river; this proved to be the first coal mined in Wyoming. The first bridge to span the North Platte River was built here in 1851, but was washed out in a flood the following year. Deer Creek Station was established in the 1850s, operating first as a trading post and later as a relay terminal for the Overland Stage and as a home station for the short-lived Pony Express. Later, when telegraph wires replaced the

Pony Express, Deer Creek became a telegraph relay station. Indians burned the station to the ground in 1866 and it was never rebuilt.

Boom And Bust

Around the turn of the century, several underground coal mines opened, transforming the quiet settlement of Glenrock into a raucous mining town. They closed in 1916, just as oil was discovered west of Glenrock. Some 5,000 oil workers flooded the town, along with a raft of less-honorable professions. Two oil refineries were built, fed by 200 Big Muddy oil wells. One refinery closed in the 1920s, the other in the '50s. More oil was found in 1949, and again in 1973, leading to temporary booms. The massive coal-fired Dave Johnston Powerplant became one of the largest local employers when it opened in 1958, and the discovery of uranium

25 miles northeast of Glenrock attracted hundreds of people to the area when several large uranium mines opened. In the late 1980s they began to shut down, and Glenrock has experienced hard times. Downtown shows this decline in a number of boarded-up old storefronts.

Sights

Rock in the Glen, a half mile west of Glenrock, has the carved names from a few of the 19th century emigrants who passed by on their way to Oregon, California, or Utah. Several **graves** from this era are scattered around Glenrock, sad reminders of the thousands who never made it. One is that of A.H. Unthank, just east of the Dave Johnson Powerplant on Tank Farm Rd., who died of cholera just a week after carving his name in Register Cliffs near present-day Guernsey. Four miles west of town is the grave of Ada Magill, a young girl who died of dysentery in 1864 as her parents headed west in a wagon train. Stones were piled on top of the grave to keep wolves from digging up her body.

In Glenrock City Park is a granite monument to **Dr. Ferdinand V. Hayden**, a physician who devoted his life to explorations of the West. Hayden helped found the U.S. Geological Survey and led the famed Hayden Yellowstone Expedition of 1870. The Indians considered Hayden a bit wacky, calling him "Man-who-picks-up-stones-running." Hayden used the Deer Creek Station at present-day Glenrock as a base of operations for several of his expeditions around Wyoming; hence the monument, placed here in 1931 by his photographic partner on these trips, William H. Jackson.

The country around Glenrock is laced with energy projects of all types. Immediately west of town is the Big Muddy oil field, where more than 2.6 million barrels have been pumped out over the last 40 years. The giant **Dave Johnson Powerplant** is six miles east of Glenrock along the North Platte River. It's one of the largest coal-fired powerplants in the Rockies, generating 810,000 kilowatts of electricity for the Pacific Northwest. A private railroad feeds coal to the plant from the Glenrock Coal strip mine, 16 miles to the north.

Lodging And Food

Glenrock has two motels and a wonderful old hotel. **The Coachman Motel**, 108 S. 3rd, tel. 436-2281, charges $24 s or $27 d. Kitchenettes are $28 and up. **Vee Tee Motel**, 500 W. Aspen, tel. 436-2772, has rooms for $24 s or $28 d, and kitchenettes starting for $30. **Higgins Hotel**, 416 W. Birch, tel. 436-9212, doesn't look like much on the outside—pale green asbestos shingles on a building built in 1916—but the inside is a real surprise. The entire hotel has been lovingly furnished with antique brass beds, wardrobes, lamps, and a ticking old grandfather clock. Rooms cost $26 s or $35 d, ($36 s or $51 d including breakfast). The owners, Jack and Margaret Doll, also run a fine gourmet restaurant here, **The Paisley Shawl**, named after the delicate old Scottish shawl—a family heirloom—in the dining room. The restaurant (Tues.-Sat. only) has a statewide reputation for its lunches, as well as its prime rib, steak, and veal dinners.

Other Glenrock eating establishments are **Ole's Pizza Plus** on W. Birch St., **Four Aces Dining Room**, 316 W. Birch, tel. 436-9010, and **El Diablo Supper Club**, east of town, tel. 436-8210. Country-western bands play on weekends at **Four Aces**, **El Diablo**, and/or **Deer Creek Lounge**, 13 S. 3rd, tel. 436-9909. Get groceries at **Williams' Town & Country Food Center**, 218 W. Cedar, tel. 436-2344.

Info And Services

Stop by the **First Insurance Agency**, 217 W. Birch, tel. 436-2564, for local information. There is a free indoor **swimming pool** at the monumental high school (a heritage of early 1980s boomtimes), 225 Oregon Trail, tel. 436-9201, and roller skating at **Glenrock Skate and Rec Center**, 585 W. Birch, tel. 436-5427. **Glenrock Library** is at 518 S. 4th, tel. 436-2573. **Real Wyoming Gifts**, 302 W. Birch, tel. 436-8604, sells all sorts of locally made items.

The big annual event is **Deer Creek Days**, a mid-July carnival with parades, games, a mountain men rendezvous, dancing, and lots of drinking. For something tamer, visit the livestock and horse auctions at the **Glenrock Livestock Exchange**, just east of town, tel. 436-5327, held on Wed. and Sat. during the summer months. This is an enjoyable way to learn about ranching and to rub shoulders with local cowboys.

CASPER

The city of Casper (pop. 44,700) trails out along the North Platte River with I-25 cutting a right angle through town. The outlying settlements of **Evansville** (pop. 2,600), **Mills** (pop. 2,100), and **Bar Nunn** (pop. 800) surround Casper, while more suburbs fill the intervening land. Casper is at the center of numerous oil fields, with three refineries and a giant oil tank farm. Oil-related manufacturing and service industries crowd the city; the Casper yellow pages contain 33 different types of oil-related listings, from oil well casing services to oil well surveyors. As "Oil Capital of the Rockies," the city is chained to the fortunes of oil. When oil prices soared following the OPEC oil embargo in 1973, Casper grew so fast that planners predicted its population could rival Denver's by the year 2000.

These optimistic (or apocalyptic, depending upon your point of view) predictions failed to materialize when oil prices plummeted in the 1980s. Sales tax receipts dropped by 50% between 1982 and 1987, and by the mid-'80s, many of downtown Casper's storefronts were covered with plywood. Even in 1990, it was still possible to buy a repossessed two-bedroom Casper home from HUD for as little as $6,000! The economy has gradually improved in recent years, as Casper has diversified its industrial base. Today, the two downtown movie theaters still offer $1.50 tickets to all shows, and vacant buildings line streets on the western end of town; but downtown is thriving, the suburbs are once again creeping over the countryside, and Eastridge Mall (Wyoming's largest shopping mall) is packed with chainstores.

With its central location, substantial population, convention facilities, and ties to the state's energy and ranching industries, Casper considers itself the true heart and soul of Wyoming. The only statewide newspaper, the *Casper Star-Tribune,* is based here, along with one of the state's premier medical centers. To Casperites, arch-rival Cheyenne is just a Nebraska city that happened to sneak into Wyoming. (The rest of Wyoming, however, views Casper with equal suspicion; in 1904 Casper aspired to become the state capital, but failed miserably, coming in third behind Cheyenne and Lander in a statewide vote.) A working-class town, Casper will never become a major tourist destination. Despite this, there are outstanding recreational opportunities on nearby Casper Mountain, at local reservoirs, and along the North Platte River, plus a variety of cultural activities at the brand-new Nicolaysen Art Center and the spacious Casper Events Center.

HISTORY

The Astorians
Although Casper is identified today with oil, the city began as a way station along the Oregon Trail. Seven of John Jacob Astor's fur traders led by Robert Stuart first traveled through this area in 1812 on their return from Oregon, arriving in late October. Knowing they could not make it back to St. Louis in their emaciated condition, the explorers constructed a rock-walled cabin (the first Anglo building in Wyoming), and covered it with buffalo hides. Game proved amazingly plentiful. They returned from a hunting trip with 47 bison, 28 deer and bighorn sheep, and a bear! But five weeks later, a band of 23 Arapaho warriors appeared, on their way to raid the Crow Indians farther north. Intimidated, the Astorians invited them in for a meal. They stayed for a day and a half, promising to return in two weeks. The Astorians quickly decided discretion was the better part of valor and moved to a new camp just across the border of what is now Nebraska. They finally reached Missouri the following spring.

Ferries And Bridges
The route pioneered by the Astorians eventually became a virtual highway to the West. The North Platte River was one of the main barriers to this migration, with many emigrants choosing to ford near what is now Casper. In early summer when the river ran dangerously high, people often died trying to cross. Others lost their wagons, or watched as their oxen and horses were swept downriver. When Brigham Young's party of Mormon emigrants arrived here in 1847, they built a 23-foot-long raft and floated

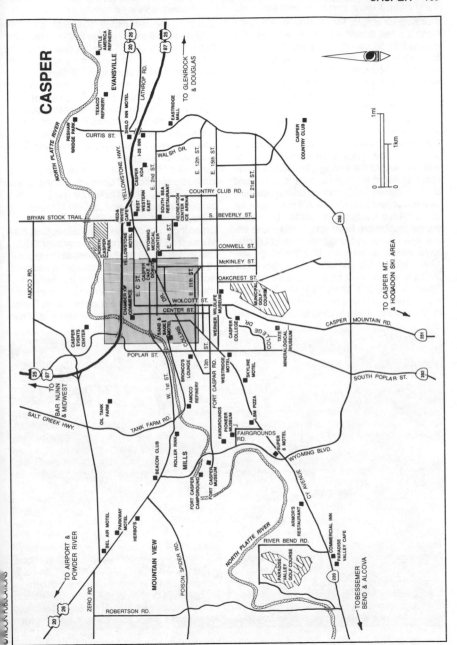

1. Mt. Moran rises over String Lake in Grand Teton National Park; 2. Autumn on Teton Pass turns aspens to a flaming yellow; 3. Midsummer flowers create a garden of color in high meadows within the Jedediah Smith Wilderness.

their wagons across. The Mormon ferry became Casper's first business venture, with Gentiles charged $1.50 per wagon. Business boomed. By 1849, several different ferries were competing with the Mormon ferry, but there were still delays of up to a week as wagons waited in line to cross. (This has to rate as one of Wyoming's only recorded traffic jams!)

In 1852, a French-Canadian trader named John Reshaw built a long wooden toll bridge at present-day Evansville, charging up to $5 in gold per wagon (less when the river was low and folks would risk fording). To stifle competition, he bought the Mormon ferry for $300 and shut it down. In 1859, another bridge was built six miles upriver by Louis Guinard to compete for the lucrative Oregon Trail traffic. Guinard's bridge must have been one of the most impressive structures along the entire 2,000-mile route. Built at a cost of $40,000, the bridge was 17 feet wide, 1,000 feet long, and supported by 28 log and rock cribs. It soon became the preferred crossing point along the North Platte, and the old Reshaw bridge was torn down, with the lumber used to build a fort (Platte Bridge Station)

to protect the new bridge. (Guinard made so much money at the toll station that he reportedly threw handfuls of gold into the river, exclaiming, "You have given me all my wealth; I now give back to you a tithe!")

Red Cloud's War

Platte Bridge Station served as a trading post for travelers, a Pony Express mail stop, and later a telegraph office. A volunteer force of up to 50 soldiers was posted to protect the telegraph and those traveling along the Oregon Trail from Indian and Mormon attacks. In retaliation for a massacre of Indians at Colorado's Sand Creek in 1865 (see p. 195), a full-scale war broke out between Indians and whites. One of these battlegrounds that July was Platte Bridge Station. Expecting a wagon train with vital supplies and ammunition, 20 men under the command of Lt. Caspar Collins left the fort to escort the expected convoy. Once across the bridge, the soldiers found themselves surrounded by Red Cloud and 3,000 of his Sioux warriors. In their flight back across the bridge, five soldiers died. Collins was killed when he stooped to rescue a fellow

Emigrant Train Crossing the Platte in Early Days.

wagon trains crossing the Platte River

1 ↗   2 ↗   3 ↘

1 ↗

2 ↗

3 ↗   4 ↘   5 ↘

soldier and his horse bolted, carrying him into the onrushing warriors. Other soldiers said that when last seen, he had his reins in his teeth and was firing pistols from both hands. Caspar's body was found two days later with 24 arrows in it.

A second battle followed that afternoon—the Custard's Wagon Train Fight. When the supply wagons of Sergeant Amos Custard came within sight of the fort, the soldiers tried to warn them with cannon fire. Three men from an advance guard made it to safety within the fort. The others quickly corralled the three wagons together, and put up a fierce fight, but within hours Red Cloud's men had killed and mutilated the 23 defenders and burned the wagons. In honor of Caspar Collins, Platte Bridge Station was renamed Fort Caspar. (Fort Collins, Colorado is named for his father William Collins.) Due to a spelling error by an Army telegraph operator that was never corrected, the town that eventually grew up nearby was misspelled Casper, rather than Caspar. Two years later, when most traffic on the Oregon Trail had been re-routed south to avoid conflicts with the Indians, Fort Caspar was abandoned. Shortly thereafter, the bridge and fort were burned by the Sioux.

Lawless Days And Nights

In 1888, the Fremont, Elkhorn, and Missouri Valley Railway extended its line up the North Platte River to the site of old Fort Caspar. A tent city quickly sprang up, followed by more permanent buildings, and for the next 17 years the town of Casper lay at the end of the tracks. It was an exceptionally violent place; employees of the first grocery store surrounded their beds with sacks of flour for protection from stray bullets. Casper's first public building was a jail. Even the Casper mayor got in the act, murdering his business partner in an 1890 gun duel on main street. The jury let him go free. When the ruffians became too much to tolerate, a street trial was held. Those who refused to leave town, faced the prospect of being strung up in a "necktie party." Pinned to the shirt of one murderer lynched by a vigilance committee was the following note: "Process of law is a little slow, so this is the road you'll have to go. Murderers and sinners, Beware! People's Verdict."

Oil Changes Everything

In 1851 Jim Bridger, Cy Iba, Kit Carson, and Basil Cimineau Lajeunesse discovered an oil spring just west of Casper at Poison Spider Creek. The oil was mixed with flour and sold as axle grease for wagon trains. By 1889, when the first oil well was drilled near Casper, it was clear that much more oil lay beneath the ground. Land speculators and claim jumpers flocked to Wyoming, and battles quickly broke out over who had staked the first claim; the winner generally had more burly men, guns, and lawyers. Soon the massive Salt Creek oil field (40 miles north of Casper) was producing, with wagons towed by teams of up to 20 horses hauling the oil back to Casper. A small refinery was built in 1895, the first in Wyoming. It was later replaced by more modern facilities, including the Standard Oil (now Amoco) plant, at one time the largest refinery on earth, handling 25,000 barrels of oil per day. Over time, Casper became the center of oil and refining in the Rockies.

Boom And Bust

Casper grew into a major industrial town with the development of the Salt Creek and other oil fields. So many roustabouts flooded Casper that they had to sleep in shifts at the tents, motels, garages, basements, or shacks. Dozens of illegal gambling houses and speakeasies helped make a trip to town memorable, while more than 2,000 prostitutes pursued their own boomtimes in the Sandbar district. (Prostitution was blatant until the 1950s.) Oil production peaked in the 1920s, but the crash of 1929 ruined this economic bubble. Casper's population plummeted from 30,000 in 1925 to 15,000 just five years later. World War II sent oil prices and Casper's economy soaring. An Army air base—home to 4,000 men—opened nearby; it's the site of Casper's airport. In the late '50s new technology—injecting water to force the remaining oil to wellheads—helped boost recovery dramatically at Salt Creek, and there followed another boom for Casper. The discovery of massive uranium deposits in the Pumpkin Buttes, Gas Hills, and Shirley Basin also fueled this growth.

The roller coaster ride has continued in recent decades: down in the late '60s, back up in the '70s. By the early 1980s, Casper was experiencing an orgy of growth, but almost overnight

DOWNTOWN CASPER

TO EVENTS CENTER

PLANETARIUM

POPLAR ST.

OVERLAND TRAIL

HILTON INN

FRONTIER AVE.

RODEWAY INN
EL JARRO'S
MOTEL 6

HOLIDAY INN /
DRAKE'S LOUNGE
SHOWBOAT MOTEL

E. G ST.

BENHAM'S RESTAURANT

E. F ST.

87
25

DOWNTOWNER HOTEL

LA QUINTA INN

CHAMBER OF COMMERCE

NORTH PLATTE RIVER

MOON

E. C ST.

DURBIN ST.
BEECH ST.
KIMBALL ST.
PARK ST.
GRANT ST.
LINCOLN ST.
JEFFERSON ST.
McKINLEY ST.
JACKSON ST.

POWDER RIVER TRANSPORTATION

CITY HALL

POST OFFICE

IMPERIAL INN

TOPPER MOTEL

PEKING RESTAURANT

E. A ST.

BOSCO'S RESTAURANT

VIRGINIAN MOTEL

DAVID ST.

CENTER ST.

WOLCOTT ST.

TRAVELIER MOTEL

TWENTY - SIX
TWENTY MOTEL

W. 1st ST.

E. 1st ST.

BOOK PALACE

0   0.25mi

0   0.25km

APPLE'S CORNER /
MEKONG RESTAURANT

WYOMING ARTISTS COMPANY

E. YELLOWSTONE HIGHWAY

E. 2nd ST.

W. 2nd ST.

ANTHONY'S RESTAURANT

TAUBERT RANCH OUTFITTERS

NICOLAYSEN ART MUSEUM

E. 3rd ST.

20
26

MIDWEST AVE.

E. 4th ST.

COLLINS DR.

MOUNTAIN SPORTS

E. 5th ST.

CHICAGO & NORTHWESTERN RAILROAD

ASH STREET

7th ST.

LA CASACITA

8th ST.

9th ST.

SPRUCE ST.

OAK ST.

the boom turned to severe recession. More than 5,000 people moved away in a single year, leaving overbuilt schools and half-empty shopping malls. By 1985, Rand-McNally rated Casper one of the 10 worst places in America to live. Times change; the city is rebounding with a more diverse economy.

SIGHTS

Fort Caspar

Although the original fort had long since disappeared, in 1936 the WPA reconstructed a half-dozen of Fort Caspar's log buildings and walls. Included are a blacksmith shop, overland stage station, commissary storehouse, trading post, and sutler's store (now a gift shop). Many supports from Guinard's long bridge across the North Platte are still visible as mounds of rock, and a small section of the bridge has been reconstructed. During summer months, two guides, dressed as 1860s cavalrymen, answer questions for visitors.

A newer brick building at the fort houses an excellent small museum (free) where you'll find a variety of items including a marvelous Indian headdress, a reconstructed Mormon handcart, and a painting by W.H. Jackson of Platte Bridge Station. Summer hours for the museum, tel. 235-8462, are Sun. 12-5, Mon.-Fri. 9-6, and Sat. 9-5. The rest of the year, it's open Sun. 2-5 and Mon.-Fri. 9-5. The fort buildings are open only during the summer, but you can wander around the grounds at any time of year.

Reshaw Bridge Park in Evansville contains a partial reconstruction of the wooden toll bridge used between 1852 and 1865 by thousands of Oregon Trail emigrants, along with a replica of the old **Mormon ferry** that operated here from 1847 to 1853. Look across the river to find a narrow seam of coal on the cutbank, coal used for fuel by early settlers and emigrants.

Nicolaysen Art Museum

One surprising aspect of Casper is an emphasis on art and culture that is exemplified by the Nicolaysen, Wyoming's finest contemporary art exhibition space. The permanent collection includes 1,900 drawings by German-American illustrator Carl Link, a collection of 400 dolls, and a variety of Native American paintings, pottery, and rugs. Children of all ages love the fine **Discovery Center** here, the only children's museum in Wyoming. The "Nic" is located at 400 E. Collins, tel. 235-5247, and is open Tues., Wed., and Fri.-Sun. 10-5, and Thurs. 10-8. No charge.

More Art

One legacy from Casper's oil boomtimes is an abundance of outdoor **sculptures**, including three pieces by Laramie sculptor Robert Russin. His energetic bronze *Prometheus* livens the library entrance at 307 E. Second St., while *Man and Energy* at the chamber of commerce, 500 N. Center, symbolizes Casper's ties to oil and coal. Neither is as controversial as *The Fountainhead*, a $230,000 red and blue metal sculpture placed in front of the new city hall in 1981. A statue of Caspar Collins on horseback guards the Casper Events Center, while a monument to sheepherders stands in front of the Wyoming Wool Growers Building at 117 Glenn Road.

Fora fine selection of arts and crafts, step into **Wyoming Artists Company**, a cooperative gallery at 232 E. 2nd St., tel. 577-0965, or **West Wind Gallery**, 1040 W. 15th, tel. 265-2655. Casper College has a student art gallery.

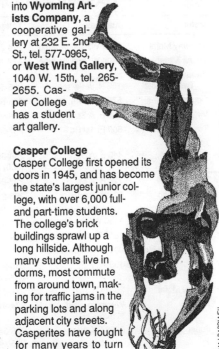

BRIAN BARDWELL

Casper College

Casper College first opened its doors in 1945, and has become the state's largest junior college, with over 6,000 full- and part-time students. The college's brick buildings sprawl up a long hillside. Although many students live in dorms, most commute from around town, making for traffic jams in the parking lots and along adjacent city streets. Casperites have fought for many years to turn their college into a four-year school, but the University at Laramie has successfully fended off all such moves. A fine 78,000-volume **library** on campus includes a rare book room with unusual Wyoming titles. Hours are Sun. 2:30-10 p.m., Mon.-Thurs. 7:30 a.m.-10 p.m., and Fri. 7:30-4:30. An **Elderhostel** program runs at Casper College during the summer, and the excellent **Fitness Center** is open to the public. In the College Center building you'll find a cafeteria, a small bookstore, and other facilities.

Visitors will enjoy a stop at two Casper College museums. **Tate Mineralogical Museum**, tel. 268-2110, is open Mon.-Fri. 10-5 during the summer, and Mon.-Fri. 2-5 during the school year. Entrance is free. Inside, you'll find one of the largest mineralogical collections in the Rockies, including several meteorites, various types of petrified wood, Indian artifacts, and fossils. Purchase polished stones at the entrance. The

Werner Wildlife Museum, 405 E. 15th, tel. 235-2108, is open daily 10-5 during the summer and Mon.-Fri. 2-5 in winter; no charge. The museum houses the usual stuffed critters from Wyoming—dozens of antelope heads, deer mounts, bears, bison, and many birds—along with several African trophies.

More Sights And Sounds
The free **Pioneer Museum** at the fairgrounds, tel. 266-4228, is open summers, Mon.-Sun. 9-4:30. Housed in an old Episcopal church, the small museum includes all the standard pioneer artifacts, from quilts and dolls to old telephones. One of Casper's minor claims to fame is having Wyoming's largest convention and performance center. Located on a hill overlooking the city, the **Casper Events Center** is a spacious, modern building with room for over 10,000 people. Check at the chamber of commerce for

CASPER ACCOMMODATIONS

Motel	Address	Telephone	Rates	Features
Parkway Motel	5102 W. Yellowstone	234-2162	$10 s, $12 d	tawdry
Bel Air Motel	5400 W. Yellowstone	472-1930	$14 s, $16 d	
Twenty-Six Twenty Motel	152 N. Jefferson	235-5828	$17 s, $19 d	
Commercial Inn	5755 CY Ave.	235-6688	$18 s, $22 d	kitchenettes
Virginian Motel	830 E. A St.	266-9731	$18 s, $22 d	
Travelier Motel	500 E. 1st St.	237-9343	$19 s, $20 d	AAA approved, clean and friendly
Imperial Inn	440 E. A St.	234-3501 (800) 368-4400	$19 s, $22 d	
Topper Motel	728 E. A St.	237-8407	$19 s, $23 d	
Rodeway Inn	621 N. Poplar	266-2400 (800) 228-2000	$19 s, $24 d	
Motel 6	1150 Wilkins Circle	234-3903	$20 s, $26 d	
Yellowstone Motel	1610 E. Yellowstone	234-9174	$21 s, $24 d	
Sand & Sage Motel	901 W. Yellowstone	237-2088	$21 s, $28 d	
Showboat Motel	100 W. F St.	235-2711 (800) 341-8000	$23 s, $29 d	AAA approved
Skyline Motel	2037 CY Ave.	234-9171	$24 s, $26 d	kitchenettes
I-25 Inn	Wyoming Blvd. at I-25	234-9125	$25 s, $30 d	AAA approved
Super 8 Motel	3838 CY Ave.	266-3480 (800) 843-1991	$27 s, $31 d	

upcoming events. **Casper Planetarium**, 904 N. Poplar, tel. 577-0310, is open Wed.-Sun. 7:30 p.m.-9 p.m. during the summer, with star-gazing programs. Explore the real sky through a telescope afterward. Admission is $2. **Stage III Community Theatre**, 4080 S. Poplar, tel. 234-0946, puts on plays Sept.-July. The **Casper Symphony Orchestra**, tel. 266-1478, is Wyoming's only professional orchestra, with winter performances. Tours of Casper's **Amoco Refinery** are available by appointment; call 265-3390 for details.

ACCOMMODATIONS

Casper motels cover the complete quality spectrum from dumpy little hole-in-the-walls to an elaborate Hilton Inn. In general, you'll find prices in Casper to be among the cheapest in Wyoming. Two dozen of the city's lodging estab-lishments are listed in the chart below. Better take a look at the rooms before plunking down any money at the cheapest places; some of these are marginal at best.

Camping

The nearest public camping ($4) is in the pines on Casper Mountain, 10 miles south of Casper and 3,000 feet higher in elevation. See "Casper Mountain," below, for details. Casper's three private campgrounds are open year-round and have swimming pools. The **Fort Caspar Campground**, tel. 234-3260, is on the river and just beyond the old fort site. Anglers will enjoy the trout pond here. Sites are $10 for tents or $14 for RVs. Showers for non-campers cost $3. **Casper KOA**, 2800 E. Yellowstone, tel. 237-5155, charges $11 for tents and $14 for RVs. **PM Campgrounds**, 1101 W. Prairie Lane, tel. 577-1664, in Bar Nunn has RV sites for $13.

CASPER ACCOMMODATIONS (CONT.)

Motel	Address	Telephone	Rates	Features
Westridge Motel	955 CY Ave.	234-8911 (800) 356-6268	$28+ s or d	AAA approved
La Quinta Motor Inn	301 E. E St.	234-1159 (800) 531-5900	$28+ s, $36+ d	AAA approved, pool
Bessemer Bend B&B	11 miles south	265-6819	$35 s, $45 d	
Best Western East	2325 E. Yellowstone	234-3541 (800) 528-1234	$37+ s or d	AAA approved, pool
Downtowner Motor Hotel	I-25 at Center	235-5713	$37 s, $43 d	
Shilo Inn Motel	739 Luker Lane, Evansville	237-1335	$39 s, $45 d	AAA approved, pool, whirlpool, sauna, continental breakfast
Days Inn	400 Frontier Ave.	235-6666 (800) 325-2525	$41+ s, $46+ d	AAA approved, pool, airport shuttle
Holiday Inn	300 W. F St.	235-2531 (800) 465-4329	$46+ s, $56+ d	AAA approved, pool, whirlpool, sauna, airport shuttle
Casper Hilton Inn	I-25 and Poplar	266-6000 (800) 445-8667	$52+ s, $62+ d	AAA approved, pool, jacuzzi, airport shuttle

FOOD

Casperites have white-collar incomes and blue-collar appetites, meaning quantity wins out over quality at most local eateries. Fortunately, there are several good exceptions to this rule. For a homestyle, reasonably priced breakfast, visit **Paradise Valley Cafe**, 5755 CY Ave., tel. 266-9914. On the other end of town is the **Red and White Cafe**, 1620 E. Yellowstone, tel. 234-6962, a popular greasy spoon hangout. **Herbo's**, 4755 W. Yellowstone, tel. 266-2293, is one of the local restaurants where big servings win out over quality. Packed with Casperites. For tasty, earthy breakfasts and lunches, head to **Apple's Corner Restaurant**, 152 S. Center, tel. 235-2775. It's one of Wyoming's only no-smoking-allowed restaurants. If you're looking for good pizza in Casper, give up. The best of a bad lot is probably at **Little Big Men Pizza**, 3350 CY Ave., tel. 235-0786. During the school year, visitors will find Casper's cheapest eats at the **Casper College cafeteria**.

International Eats

Casper has two good Italian restaurants; locals argue over which is best. **Anthony's**, 241 S. Center, tel. 234-3071, is more centrally located and a bit fancier, but the down-home **Bosco's**, 847 E. A St., tel. 265-9658, really packs them in, particularly over the lunch hour. For dinner, try the house specialty, shrimp scampi. For Mexican food, everyone in Casper goes to **El Jarro's**, 500 W. F St., tel. 577-0538. Their second restaurant at 2807 CY Ave., tel. 234-4818, has the same food but doesn't attract the crowds. Be ready for a long wait most any evening. The El Jarro's phenomenon exists for a number of reasons: inexpensive prices, big margaritas, crispy chips, tangy salsa, and mass quantities of food. Besides, the bleached-blond hostesses and the beefy waiters (who gather around tables to sing happy birthday at least a dozen times each hour) make for lots of ogling. Be forewarned, however, that this is Americanized Mexican food; we're talking something that looks like mushroom soup over the chile rellenos! For more authentic Mexican fare, try **La Casacita**, 633 W. Collins, tel. 234-7633.

A real surprise in Casper is the large number of Asian restaurants that dot the town—eight

places at last count. The food has suffered a bit from Americanization, but two of these places are quite good. **South Sea Chinese Restaurant** has two locations: 2025 E. 2nd, tel. 237-4777, and 116 W. 2nd, tel. 265-9711, and offers the more authentic fare. Also good is **Peking Chinese Restaurant**, 333 E. A, tel. 266-2207. The **Mekong**, 144 S. Center, tel. 237-6728, has a reputation for its Vietnamese cuisine. You may also want to try **Susie's**, 132 N. Ash, tel. 234-9715, Wyoming's only Japanese restaurant.

Steak And Seafood

Casper's old-time steakhouse is **Benham's**, 739 N. Center, tel. 234-4531. A bit pricey, but the varied menu of steak, seafood, and ribs is a palate-pleaser. The popular Pump Room, in the same building, has Mexican food, "gourmet hamburgers," and mixed drinks. **Armor's Restaurant**, 3422 Energy Lane, tel. 235-3000, is another popular steakhouse with a pleasant atmosphere and good food. In the same vein is **Goose Egg Inn**, nine miles southwest of Casper on State 220, tel. 473-8838, where prime rib, seafood, and pan-fried chicken are house specialties. Well worth the drive!

Groceries And Bakeries

Casper has a number of giant grocery stores scattered across the city—Albertson's, Buttrey, Safeway, and Smith's—and even a small Asian food store, **Wilson's Oriental Mart**, 382 W. Collins Dr., tel. 237-3715. If you're looking for fresh produce, be sure to check out the **Farmers Market** at the fairgrounds each Saturday morning. For fresh-baked goods, head to **Casper Cake and Donut**, 604 E. 2nd, tel. 234-1180. They have another bakery outlet in Eastridge Mall. All the big grocery chains also have in-store bakeries and delis. For espresso coffees, visit **Spirits Lounge** in the Casper Hilton Inn, I-25 at Poplar, tel. 266-6000.

ENTERTAINMENT

The biggest and best-known place for live music in Casper is the **Beacon Club**, 4100 W. Yellowstone Hwy., tel. 577-1503k, with country tunes and a fun, trendy crowd. **Drake's Lounge** in the Holiday Inn, 300 W. F St., tel. 235-2531, has live top-40 music most evenings and free hors d'oeuvres on weeknights. **Bronco's Lounge**, 1200 W. Collins Dr., tel. 266-5111, offers oldies, rock, and Western music most nights. Out in Evansville at **Shilo Inn Motel**, 739 Luker Lane, tel. 237-1335, you'll find live C&W on Friday and Saturday nights, plus old oldies for oldsters on Sunday night. Other places to check for musical entertainment and dancing are the **Colonial Lounge**, 4370 S. Poplar, tel. 265-9988; **Bourban House** (Hilton Inn), I-25 and Center, tel. 235-5713; **Goose Egg Inn**, 10580 Goose Egg Rd., tel. 473-8838; **Little Big Men Pizza**, 3350 CY Ave., tel. 234-0786; and the **Viking Restaurant and Lounge**, 2740 E. 3rd, tel. 234-5386.

EVENTS

In early June, the **Mountain Man Rendezvous** draws dozens of costumed mountain men and Indians to old Fort Caspar. Another June activity in Casper is the **Cowboy State Games**, an Olympic-style multi-sport festival with teams from all over Wyoming competing in everything from archery to wrestling. On **Midsummer's Eve** (June 21), be sure to be in Crimson Dawn Park for a mystical celebration of Casper Mountain's witches and spirits. Hundreds of Casperites will also be there, along with a few Bible-thumping protestors.

The **Casper Classic Bike Races** attract nearly a thousand of the top cyclists in America with a $50,000 purse. Beginning in late June and continuing up to the 4th of July, it encompasses six different events, including a grueling 15-mile-long climb up Casper Mountain. The last two days attract mountain bike racers. The annual **Wyoming Governor's Cup Regatta** at nearby Lake Alcova in late July is the biggest sailing event in the state. For a glimpse of the city's past, come to Fort Caspar for the **Platte Bridge Encampment** in late July. This taste of history includes period fashion shows, living history demonstrations, military drills, cannon and black powder contests, and mock battles between Indian warriors and Army troops. Not surprisingly, a military funeral follows. The **Casper Troopers Drum and Bugle Corps** also performs for the encampment. Established in 1957, it consistently ranks in the top 20 in national competitions.

Casper's biggest annual event is the **Central Wyoming Fair and Rodeo**. The various arts and crafts displays, farm animals, rodeos, and midway attract both locals and visitors. Rodeo events (including exciting chuckwagon races and clown "bullfighting") are $5 for adults (kids free). For more laid-back action, try the twice-weekly rodeos ($3) at North 40, located 10 miles north of Casper on I-25. Call 265-9619 for specifics. **Pari-mutual horse racing** comes to the fairgrounds later in August, lasting through mid-September.

RECREATION

The **Casper Recreation Center**, 1801 E. 4th St., tel. 235-8383, provides racquetball and volleyball courts, a weightroom, gym, and game room. Next door is **Casper Ice Arena**, tel. 235-8484, where public skating is just $2 on weekdays, including skate rentals. Wyoming's largest roller skating palace, **Wagon Wheel Roller Rink**, is in Mills at 305 Vanhorn Ave., tel. 265-4214.

The 18-hole **Casper Municipal Golf Course**, tel. 234-1037, charges $8.50 on weekdays. Two private courses include: **Paradise Valley Golf Course**, tel. 234-9146, and the **Casper Country Club**, tel. 235-5777. Casper is one of the nation's windiest cities; winds averaging 13 mph make this a great place for kite flying, hang-gliding, and **windsurfing**. Pathfinder and Alcova Reservoirs are both popular windsurfing spots. **Mountain Sports**, 543 S. Center, tel. 266-1136, may have rental equipment and lessons. While there, take a look at the various rock-climbing maps and books.

Mountain bikers will find many miles of roads and trails on Casper and Muddy mountains, south of town. For maps and info, contact **Casper Wheelmen**, 548 E. A, tel. 577-9117, or **The Bike Stop**, 515 W. Collins, tel. 577-0115. **Off the Deep End Travels**, tel. (800) 223-6833, offers six-day mountain bike trips along the old Oregon Trail for $335 pp. **Adventures West**, tel. 266-4868, runs three-day **horseback trips** along the Oregon Trail, plus a variety of other daily trail and wagon rides on Casper Mountain, complete with meals.

Water Sports

If you're looking for a little water activity, check out one of Casper's half-dozen **swimming pools**. Five outdoor pools (tel. 235-8403) are scattered throughout the city, and are open summers for $2 ($1 over the noon hour). The Paradise Valley pool also has a water slide. An indoor pool at the YMCA, 315 E. 15th, tel. 234-9187, is open year-round. Swim for $2, or use the complete facilities for $6 per day. (Trivia buffs will be interested to know that the Casper High School was the first in the nation to have an indoor swimming pool, built in 1929.)

The **North Platte River** flows right through the city of Casper, offering both the city's drinking water and a variety of recreational opportunities. The Platte's slow current and shallow depth (2-4 feet in most places) make for a gentle and scenic float trip with plenty of wildlife along the way: beaver, muskrats, ducks, geese, hawks, eagles, mule deer, and antelope. For a map and brochure describing public landings, camping, and parking areas along the 45-mile stretch of the Platte between Alcova Reservoir and Casper, contact the BLM at 1701 E. E St., tel. 261-7600. **Wyoming River Raiders**, 601 Wyoming Blvd., tel. 235-8624, has two-hour float trips ($20 pp) with a barbecue at the end. Ask about canoe and raft rentals here, too. Fishing is excellent for both German brown and rainbow trout; we're talking more than 11,000 pounds of trout per mile! Locals call it one of the West's largest and finest trout fisheries. For guided fishing trips ($100+/day), contact **Rainbow River Guides**, 5120 Alcova Route, tel. 473-1196. **Edness Kimball Wilkins State Park**, six miles east of Casper on State 256, is a 1,420-acre riverside park that is perfect for quiet picnics among the cottonwoods and fishing from the banks. There are fine views of Casper Mountain to the south. No camping, however.

GETTING MALLED

Casper is Wyoming's version of shop-till-your-car-dies. Sprawling suburbia, frantically feckless fast food, and a half-dozen park-anywhere malls combine to make Casper indistinguishable from Modesto, California or Columbus, Ohio. This is the sort of place where even the Highland Park Community Church is housed in what looks like an old K mart store. **Eastridge Mall** is Wyoming's largest shopping mall, with 93 (count 'em) stores, including most of the big chains. If Norman Rockwell were alive today he would have paintings of the high school girls eyeing the hunks on parade and the over-60, post-heart attack crowd doing their fast-walks around the mall.

OK, so not all of Casper's stores are in shopping malls. Downtown at 125 E. Second St., tel. 234-2500, is the impressive **Lou Taubert Ranch Outfitters**, a four-level department store with everything from cowboy boots (10,000 pairs in stock!) to gourmet coffee. It's a great place to try on a new cowboy hat. **Mountain Sports**, 543 S. Center, tel. 266-1136, has a good collection of outdoor supplies of all sorts, from windsurfing equipment to sleeping bags. Get topo maps and local hiking and climbing books here too. In the market for books? Head to Eastridge Mall for **B. Dalton**, tel. 247-0793, and **Waldenbooks**, tel. 235-2046, for new books, or to **Book Palace**, 225 W. 1st, tel. 577-1325, for a fine selection of used books. The latter is a great place to browse. The **Book Nook**, 918 E. 2nd, tel. 237-2211, also sells used books. **Westerner News**, 245 S. Center, tel. 235-1022, sells paperbacks and magazines.

INFORMATION

The friendly **Casper Chamber of Commerce**, 500 N. Center, tel. 234-5311 or (800) 852-1889, is the place to go for tourist paraphernalia. Summer hours are Mon.-Fri. 8-7, Sat.-Sun. 10-7; come winter, hours are Mon.-Fri. 8-5. The **Natrona County Library**, 307 E. 2nd, tel. 237-4935, is open Mon.-Wed. 10-8, Thurs.-Fri. 10-6, and Sat.-Sun. 1-5.

TRANSPORTATION

Natrona County Airport is eight miles northwest of Casper on U.S. 20-26. Two airlines provide commuter service (prop planes) to Denver: **Continental Express**, tel. (800) 525-0280, and **United Express/Mesa Airlines**, tel. (800) 241-6522. **Delta/Sky West**, tel. (800) 221-1212, has daily commuter service to Salt Lake City. The airport is an official Foreign Trade Zone. Call **RC Cab**, tel. 235-5203, for taxi service. **Powder River Transportation**, 315 N. Wolcott, tel. (800) 442-3682, has daily bus service to Douglas, Gillette, Buffalo, and other towns in northern Wyoming.

Rent cars at the airport (around $35/day) from **National Car Rental**, tel. (800) 227-7368; **Avis**, tel. (800) 331-1212; **Budget Rent-A-Car**, tel. (800) 527-0700; or **Hertz**, tel. (800) 654-3131. In town, car rentals are cheaper at **Dollar Rent A Car**, 804 N. Poplar St., tel. (800) 421-6878. All these car rental places include 100 free miles. **Affordable Used Car Rentals**, 131 E. 5th St., tel. 237-1733, has new small cars for $21/day plus 15¢/mile.

CASPER VICINITY

CASPER MOUNTAIN

Scenic mountain country is just a hop, skip, and a jump away from Casper. When the thermometer tops 100° F in summertime, Casper folks escape to the cool mountains, just a 15-minute drive from town. Snow often lingers until July. Rotary Park, seven miles south of Casper, has eight miles of scenic trails climbing through the steep canyon cut by Garden Creek. The creek drops for 50 feet over **Garden Creek Falls**, one of the few waterfalls in this part of Wyoming.

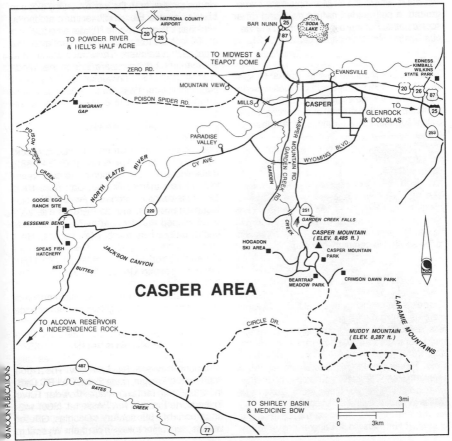

The steep, winding drive up Casper Mountain has turnouts offering panoramas that stretch all the way to the Big Horn Mountains, 125 miles to the north. Casper Mountain's flattened 8,100 foot-summit is carpeted by ponderosa pine trees and pleasant grassy meadows. Several county parks (Casper Mountain, Crimson Dawn, Beartrap Meadow, and Ponderosa) offer very popular getaways where deer and elk are found. The five **campgrounds** on Casper Mountain cost $4 per night; three of them are open year-round. Water is available only at Beartrap (the nicest) and Casper Mountain campgrounds. Red Valley separates Casper Mountain from its neighbor five miles to the south, **Muddy Mountain**. The gravel road climbs up Muddy Mountain, where the BLM maintains a campground, a self-guided nature trail, and other scenic paths. For more information on the various Casper Mountain parks, call 234-6821.

Trails

The short **Lee McCune Braille Trail** on Casper Mountain has 39 stations with plaques describing the natural world in braille and English. Even sighted people find the trail eye-opening. Nearby is a summer camp for the blind. Another un-

usual feature is **Crimson Dawn Museum**, open Sat.-Thurs. 10-7, tel. 472-0452. Inside the old log cabin home of Neal Forsling (built in 1929) is a small collection of artwork along with artifacts from Casper Mountain. Children enjoy wandering along nearby woodland trails where 20 shrines reveal the good witches, magical creatures, and forest spirits who haunt this land. Get here by heading 12 miles south of Casper along State 251. A sign marks the turnoff to Crimson Dawn.

Hogadon Ski Area

First opened in 1959, the small city-run Hogadon Ski Area is nine miles south of Casper near the top of the mountain. A family area, it includes slopes ranging from the easiest bunny slope to black diamonds. Eleven different runs are fed by two chair lifts and a poma lift, with a vertical rise of 600 feet. Ski rentals and lessons are available, along with a cafeteria. The slopes are open to telemarkers. Lift tickets are $13 on weekends ($9 half-day), or $11 on weekdays ($9 half-day). Hogadon is open Wed.-Sun. 9-4. Call 235-8499 for information, or 235-8369 for snow conditions.

Cross-country Skiing

Casper Mountain often has surprisingly good powder conditions. The county (tel. 234-6821) maintains 28 km of groomed cross-country ski trails, along with a warming hut. Daily passes are $2. Cross-country lessons are available through Mountain Sports. In addition, there are extensive undeveloped areas where more adventurous backcountry skiers practice telemarking. Rent cross-country skis on Casper Mountain or from **Mountain Sports**, 543 S. Center, tel. 266-1136; **Dean's Sporting Goods**, 260 S. Center, tel. 234-2788; or **Bundy's Ski & Cycle**, 3201 CY Ave., tel. 237-2509. Casper Mountain also has more than 52 miles of groomed snowmobile trails.

BESSEMER BEND

The bucolic Bessemer Bend area—10 miles southwest of Casper along State 220—abounds in history, both real and imagined. A lazy curve in the North Platte River, Bessemer Bend was an important 19th-century crossing point for wagon trains. Rock walls from a shelter built in

WYOMING STATE MUSEUM
Joseph M. Carey

1812 by the Astorians are still visible on a knoll overlooking the river. Between 1860 and 1861, the Red Butte Pony Express station stood at the river bend, site of the longest of all Pony Express rides, a 320-mile gallop by Buffalo Bill Cody that lasted a grueling 21 hours and 40 minutes. The nearby Red Buttes were also where Custard's Wagon Train Fight took place (see p. 161). Bessemer City sprang up along the bend in 1888, calling itself "Queen City of the Plains." It lasted only a couple of years, and when Casper was voted the Natrona County seat, Bessemer City quietly faded away. Many of its buildings were moved to Casper, and today Bessemer City is a just field of alfalfa hay.

Along the east side of the North Platte River at Bessemer Bend is the site of the famed **Goose Egg Ranch**, once one of Wyoming's largest cattle spreads. In *The Virginian,* Owen Wister used Goose Egg Ranch for a memorable scene

where two drunken cowboys switch blankets on a dozen babies while their parents are dancing, creating havoc when the ranch families drive home with the wrong children. Owned for many years by the Carey family—both father Joseph M. Carey and son Robert Carey served as a governor and U.S. senator—it was later renamed the CY Ranch. The southern half of Casper is built on what was once CY land; hence CY Ave., one of the city's main thoroughfares. Ironically, the old Goose Egg ranch house died partly because of the fame brought to it in *The Virginian.* The abandoned stone buildings gradually deteriorated as tourists chipped away for momentos. Fearing that the buildings might collapse, the owners finally tore down the ranch in 1951. John Wayne's oil field fire movie, *Hellfighters,* was filmed not far away in 1968.

Today folks come to Bessemer Bend to enjoy a steak at Goose Egg Inn or to watch wintering golden and bald eagles in nearby Jackson Canyon (named for famed Yellowstone photographer William H. Jackson). Another five miles down State 220 is **Dan Speas Fish Hatchery**, tel. 473-8890, Wyoming's largest trout-rearing facility. Open daily 8-5.

THE "LAKE DISTRICT"

The 655-mile-long North Platte River rises in Colorado, heads north into Wyoming, and then curves a long lazy loop to the east, cutting across western Nebraska, and finally joining with the South Platte River near the city of North Platte. The entire basin covers 32,000 square miles, and in Wyoming, is fed by the Sweetwater, Medicine Bow, and Laramie rivers. The name "Platte" is French for "Broad"; Indians called the river "Nebraska," meaning "Flat." Both are appropriate titles along much of its path. Cottonwood trees line the banks, and the river offers an essential watering hole for wildlife.

Once one of the most impressive rivers in the Plains states—at flood stage it ran 150 yards wide and 10-15 feet deep—the North Platte has been reduced to little more than a creek through much of Wyoming. Near Fort Laramie, where wagon trains in the 1850s found a treacherous crossing, the river today sometimes ceases to flow at all, lying in shallow puddles in the late

LAKE DISTRICT

TO INDEPENDENCE ROCK
TO CASPER
BISHOP POINT CAMPGROUND
ALCOVA HOT SPRINGS
ALCOVA RESERVOIR
INTERPRETIVE CENTER
PATHFINDER MOUNTAIN CAMPGROUND
FREMONT CANYON
PATHFINDER RESERVOIR
PEDRO MOUNTAINS
SEMINOE MOUNTAINS
"MIRACLE MILE" (CAMPING)
RED HILLS CAMPGROUNDS
KORTES RESERVOIR
SHIRLEY MOUNTAINS
SAND DUNES
SAND DUNES
HORSESHOE RIDGE
SEMINOE RESERVOIR
MEDICINE BOW RIVER
HAYSTACK MOUNTAINS
HANNA
NORTH PLATTE RIVER
SINCLAIR FORT STEELE
TO LARAMIE
TO RAWLINS

summer sun. A look at the map makes it obvious what has happened to the water—agriculture has siphoned it all away.

Reclamation

Without irrigation, farming was difficult or impossible in much of the arid West, and the thousands of homesteaders who tried to survive on 640 acres soon saw their hopes and dreams fade in the withering summer heat. Irri-

gation seemed natural for these desert lands. John Wesley Powell's idea of "arid lands reclamation" through dams and irrigation canals gradually gained favor, and by the 1890s, Wyoming's politicians were claiming that irrigation could turn 12 to 15 million acres of the state into productive farmland. The Carey Act—named for Wyoming's Senator Joseph M. Carey—tested these claims by having the federal government donate land to the states to be reclaimed by settlers. Wyoming became the first state to try out the new law, but only 10% of the two million acres in the program were finally patented. The costs were simply too high and the return too low; funding for the massive dams and irrigation canals could only come from the federal government. The Reclamation Act of 1902 was designed to do just that.

When the Reclamation Act's money started flowing, the North Platte was one of the first to be dammed (or damned, depending upon one's perspective). It seemed a potential godsend for farmers who had long used water wheels to lift water from the river into adjacent irrigation ditches. Today, eight giant dams hold back the river and its tributaries in Wyoming: Seminoe, Kortes, Pathfinder, Alcova, and Gray Reef all above the city of Casper, along with Glendo, Guernsey, and Grayrocks farther downstream. Two long irrigation canals—the Interstate Canal and the Fort Laramie Canal—supply water to farms east of Wheatland. Ironically, nearly 80% of the water behind Wyoming dams on the North Platte goes to fields in neighboring Nebraska. This is also true at most of the other large reclamation projects in Wyoming: Bighorn Canyon water goes to

Montana, Keyhole Reservoir water to South Dakota, Jackson Lake water to Idaho, and Flaming Gorge water to Utah. Meanwhile, more than a hundred-thousand acres of once-valuable farming and grazing land in Wyoming lie under these massive reservoirs. Wyoming, one of the driest states in the nation, has become an exporter of huge quantities of water to grow crops in surrounding states.

Seminoe Reservoir

Completed in 1939, Seminoe Dam is a 295-foot-high concrete arch dam. It is the farthest upstream of the North Platte dams, and holds back more than a million acre-feet of water. A powerplant produces 45 megawatts of electricity. The reservoir is bounded by the 3,821-acre **Seminoe State Park**, a name that comes from the nearby Seminoe Mountains, which in turn were named after the French trapper, Basil Cimineau Lajeunesse. (Folks apparently had a hard time spelling his middle name.) The reservoir stretches almost 20 miles south of the dam, through desolate, rocky mountains and gigantic dunes of white sand. Sandy beaches along the shoreline attract swimmers in late summer. Juniper and ponderosa pine trees dot the hills, while sagebrush, greasewood, yucca, and salt sage grow on the lower slopes. The steep 500-foot knife edge of Horseshoe Ridge is visible on the eastern shore. Golden eagles nest along the southern arm of Seminoe Reservoir, and bighorn sheep and elk have been reintroduced. The area also abounds with sage grouse.

Seminoe has two state park **campgrounds** ($4, open year-round) along its northwest shore. Water and toilets are available. You can also camp for free on Bureau of Reclamation sand dunes along the lake's southern arm. The reservoir is popular for fishing (rainbow, brown, and cutthroat trout, along with walleye) and water-skiing. Gas and limited provisions are available at Seminoe Boat Club. Access from Rawlins and Sinclair to the western shore of Seminoe is relatively easy via a 34-mile-long paved road, but the 70 miles of mixed pavement and gravel from

Casper are a bit harder to take. The eastern shore is even less accessible.

An overlook at the dam site provides views into the steep rocky canyon and the dam that spans the chasm. North of this, the road drops steeply into the canyon, and then climbs up through Morgan Creek Canyon where big ponderosa pines, willows, and cottonwoods line the creek. A few miles beyond this, the road descends over a pass and then down through Hamilton Creek Canyon, finally emerging into open sagebrush country near the **"miracle mile"** of the North Platte River. There is free camping here among the cottonwoods that line the riverbank, and excellent trout fishing. More free camping at Sage Creek Rd., a half mile north of the river crossing. The name Miracle Mile—actually three miles of free-flowing river—refers to this popular "blue ribbon" fishery, maintained by regulated flows from the 244-foot-high **Kortes Dam** powerplant, just upstream. In reality, the miracle is that any stretch of the North Platte still has anything resembling natural flows.

Pathfinder Reservoir

Pathfinder Reservoir is 30 miles southwest of Casper on State 220 and then another 10 miles in along County Rd. 409. In 1905, the federal government provided funds for this, the first dam in eastern Wyoming, to be built near the junction of the Sweetwater and North Platte rivers. Proponents claimed that the reservoir would irrigate more than 700,000 acres, primarily in Wyoming, but instead, just 130,000 acres were irrigated, nearly all of this in Nebraska.

Completed in 1909, Pathfinder Dam is considered an engineering marvel for its time, and is listed on the National Register of Historic Places. The 214-foot-high arched structure is made up of large granite blocks quarried from adjacent hills and held together with cement and steel hauled by wagon teams from Casper, 45 miles away. (The trip sometimes took three weeks.) Pathfinder is named after explorer John C. Frémont, "Pathfinder of the West." In 1842 he ventured down the river, and—against the advice of his guides—decided to run the canyon below the present dam site (now Fremont Canyon). They narrowly escaped alive.

Pathfinder Reservoir splits into two arms, following the upstream path of the Sweetwater and North Platte rivers. **Pathfinder National Wildlife Refuge** covers 16,807 acres of land around scattered parts of the reservoir, and is home to many mammals and birds. Canada geese nest along the shore, and white pelicans nest on an island here. **Camping** is available at Pathfinder Mountain and Bishops Point ($4; April to mid-Sept.), or you can camp for free along much of the lake's hundred-mile shore (except within the refuge). The deep-blue lake is a popular place for anglers in search of cutthroat, brown, and rainbow trout, or walleye. Windsurfers find some of Wyoming's finest sailing conditions. **Pathfinder Marina** has rental boats, fishing gear, gas, and a snack bar.

Not far from the dam is an old stone building that once housed the damtender, but is today used as an **interpretive center**. Summer hours are Sat. 11-5 and Sun. 10-4; ask at the adjacent frame house for a peek inside at other times. A pleasant 1 1/2-mile loop trail crosses the dam, follows Fremont Canyon (lined with hundreds of cliff swallow nests), and then recrosses the river over an impressive swinging footbridge, before returning to the interpretive center. The interpretive center has a brochure describing sights along the path.

Alcova Reservoir

Although much smaller than Pathfinder or Seminoe Reservoir, Alcova is a favorite recreation spot for the people of Casper. Windsurfing, sailing, water-skiing, and ice fishing are all popular sports on this windy lake, located 30 miles southwest of Casper. The upper portion of the reservoir reaches into famed **Fremont Canyon**, a mini-Grand Canyon whose red vertical cliffs reach 500 feet above the river. Access is via dirt roads from both sides. The water makes for exciting river running if you have a kayak and the skills. Golden eagles nest here. It is also very popular with rock-climbers. There are dozens of climbs up to a rating of 5.12. For details, stop by Mountain Sports in Casper for a copy of Steve Petro's *Climbers Guide to Fremont Canyon*. Anglers try their luck with the rainbow and cutthroat trout and walleye.

The name Alcova comes from **Alcova Hot Springs** (129° F water), so named because of its location within a series of coves. At the turn of the century, developers tried to turn the hot springs into a spa, but the propensity of Wyomingites to take baths but once a week made the venture a failure. The springs were covered by the reservoir, but an artesian well below the dam pours forth the naturally heated water. Bring your swimsuit!

The 265-foot-high Alcova Dam, part of the depression-era Kendrick Project, was completed in 1938, with a 36-megawatt powerplant added in the 1980s. Facilities here include picnic areas, swimming beaches, four campgrounds ($4), and the **Alcova Lakeside Marina**, tel. 472-6666, where you can rent boats and buy gas or supplies. Water leaves Alcova Dam and flows into the small **Gray Reef Reservoir** used to control the fluctuating discharges from Alcova and to generate more power. From here some of the water is diverted into the 62-mile Casper Canal, irrigating 24,000 acres of alfalfa hay, barley, oats, and corn west of Casper.

OREGON TRAIL LANDMARKS

Three of the most famous landmarks along the entire Oregon Trail lie within Natrona County: Independence Rock, Devil's Gate, and Split Rock. Travelers anticipated these landmarks, for they marked the start of a long, gentle approach to the Continental Divide, 80 miles to the west. The route past these landmarks paralleled the Sweetwater River, a ribbon of lush grass in a rugged, desolate landscape. The names applied to adjacent mountains and creeks offer a clue to the land's harshness: Rattlesnake Mountains, Poison Spider Creek, Greasewood Creek, Sulfur Creek, and Stinking Creek. Steamboat Lake, just a few miles north of Independence Rock, was a source of bicarbonate of soda used to bake bread. Cattle that drank the lake's putrid water died, while bread made with this baking soda took on a greenish cast. But along the Sweetwater, horses and oxen could find forage, firewood was available, and the clean mountain water offered a relief from the alkaline springs to the east. (The name Sweetwater arose when a mule team carrying sugar lost its load in the river.) Today, State 220 crosses the old Oregon Trail several miles east of its junction with U.S. 287 at Muddy Gap. The highway parallels the trail for the next 45 miles west.

Independence Rock

Head southwest from Casper along State 220 for 55 miles till the granitic dome of Independence Rock rises above the flat surrounding plain. The rock is 1,950 feet long by 850 feet wide; its smoothly rounded top reaches to 193 feet. Travelers could not resist the chance to note their passing on this gigantic billboard; an estimated 50,000 names were carved, chipped, or painted on Independence Rock during the mid-19th century. Father Jean Pierre DeSmet, a famed Jesuit missionary, labeled it "the Great Register of the Desert." His initials, along with the names of Captain Bonneville, John C. Frémont, and many other explorers were etched into the rock face.

Independence Rock apparently received its name from explorer and mountain man William Sublette, who arrived here on July 4, 1830, leading the first wagon train across the overland route. Oregon Trail emigrants tried to reach the rock around July 4 to be on schedule for Oregon. When the rock came into view, it was a source of rejoicing, for it offered a welcome place to rest alongside the Sweetwater River. During the heyday of migration along the Oregon Trail, dozens of wagon trains would find themselves at the rock on Independence Day, and the celebrations included patriotic flag-waving, the firing of guns, big dinners, and other festivities. Many people did not make it beyond Independence Rock; dozens of unmarked graves surround the rock.

Today, hundreds of the original names carved into Independence Rock are still visible, though weathering and lichen have obliterated many more. Unfortunately, more recent travelers have added their names, sometimes covering up names over a hundred years old. Independence Rock can be climbed from a number of points along the perimeter, providing fine views of the surrounding countryside. Some of the oldest and best-preserved names are on top. An old road circles the rock, making for an interesting mile-long hike. Names can be found on all sides, and you're bound to see deer and other wildlife along the Sweetwater River. A small footbridge crosses the still-visible Oregon Trail route here.

Devil's Gate

Visible from Independence Rock and just seven of miles to the southwest is another famed Oregon Trail landmark, Devil's Gate. Over the centuries, the Sweetwater River has gradually sliced a giant cleft through the Rattlesnake Mountains, leaving 370-foot cliffs on both sides of a 1,500 foot-long canyon. (An Indian legend offers an alternative origin for Devil's Gate: a gigantic tusked beast had roamed Sweetwater Valley, and when the Indians finally managed to mortally wound the animal, it gouged out the nearby mountains in its death agony.) Devil's Gate was another favorite emigrant campsite. The cut is hard to miss, especially from the east, the direction of most Oregon Trail travelers. Today, the BLM maintains a historic site along State 220, with a short loop trail and signboards. At least 20 emigrant graves are nearby. The **Tom Sun Ranch**, visible from here, was established in 1872 by a French-Canadian trapper, Thomas De Beau Soleil (Thomas Sun). His original cabin is a National Historic Landmark, and the ranch is still owned by the Sun family. A museum ($3) at the Sun Ranch is open by reservation only, tel. 324-6925. The ranch also provides a number of historical tours of the area.

Martin's Cove, just two miles northwest of Devil's Gate, is the site of the most disastrous experience along the Oregon and Mormon trails. In 1856, a group of 1,620 British converts to the Mormon religion sailed from Liverpool for America, intent upon reaching Salt Lake City before winter. (Total cost of the trip to Utah, including ship passage from England, was just $45 pp.) The converts left Missouri in several groups; last to leave were 576 people under the direction of Edward Martin. They headed out in late August, crossing the North Platte at present-day Casper on October 19. Instead of the usual wagons, many of these poor emigrants pushed or pulled small handcarts that held their few possessions. Soon the weather turned bitterly cold and a blizzard dumped 18 inches of snow on them and temperatures dropped to -14° F. The elderly and children died first; eventually even the strongest began to die. A rescue wagon from Salt Lake City finally arrived in late October, with rescuer Daniel W. Jones writing:

There were old men pulling and tugging their carts, sometimes loaded with a sick wife or children, women pulling along sick husbands; little children six to eight years old struggling through the mud and snow . . . The provisions

we took amounted to almost nothing among so many people, many of them now on very short rations, some almost starving.

The survivors were escorted 65 miles to Martin's Cove, a protected area near Devil's Gate. The company of foolhardy emigrants finally reached Salt Lake City in late November, but 145 members had died along the way. Another Mormon handcart company, led by James G. Willie, suffered a similar fate that same year, losing 67 people to the elements.

Split Rock
The final of the three geologic landmarks that lined the Oregon Trail through present-day Natrona County is Split Rock, a bite taken out of a solid granite mountain. The cleft was visible for two days as emigrants trudged along; it seemed a gunsight aimed toward the west. In the early 1860s, a Pony Express station, overland stage station, telegraph station, and garrison of troops were located nearby. Today, Split Rock is noted at a turnout 10 miles west of Muddy Gap Jct. along U.S. 287. Tourists sail past in minutes what took the emigrants many long and treacherous days.

NORTH OF CASPER

Salt Creek Oil Field
Forty miles north of Casper is the Salt Creek Oil Field, considered the largest light oil field in the world. The 10-mile-long field covers a land of sage, sand, and rock that has produced over 600 million barrels of oil and 700 million cubic feet of gas. Much more oil has been found nearby. A drive up State 259 is a trip through a bizarre alien world of desert land carpeted with giant grasshopper-like electric pumpjacks spaced every couple hundred feet to the horizon. (Actually, they look more like the little plastic ostriches sold in tourist shops—the ones that keep tipping down to a bowl of water to "drink.") The pumpjacks don't run all the time, allowing the oil to accumulate in the well before pumping resumes. West of the company town of Midwest, things get even stranger, with an incredible grid of pumpjacks, dirt roads, powerlines, and storage tanks crisscrossing the harsh land.

To a geologist, this famed oil field occupies a classic anticlinal structure that trap oil; hundred-foot cliffs surround the field. Wyoming's territorial geologist, Samuel Aughey, discovered these unusual structures and brought the first speculators here to file placer claims in 1884. The first well in the area was drilled in 1889 by a Pennsylvania oilman, M. P. Shannon. The oil was hauled by horse-drawn wagon, to Casper, 50 miles away. In 1904, Shannon sold his small Casper refinery and 105,000 acres of Salt Creek leases to European speculators for $350,000.

BRIAN BARDWELL

Four years later the real boom came when a Dutch-financed company struck black gold at 1,050 feet in the Salt Creek Field, spouting oil in a massive gusher. The news hit like a shark in a school of fish. Battles over land claims quickly escalated to the shouting and shooting stage. The Midwest Oil Company was formed, building the first pipeline to Casper in 1911, feeding the new Midwest refinery there. The Fransco Company added another refinery the following year, and Standard Oil of Indiana built a cracking plant to retrieve more gasoline from the crude.

As WW I steamed over the horizon, the field suddenly gained a vital national importance; oil shipped to the allies from Salt Creek was considered an important factor in the defeat of Kaiser Wilhelm. After the war, Standard Oil (now Amoco) bought out all of Midwest's Salt Creek properties, but the 14 remaining companies competed with each other for the crude, with oil derricks within spitting distance of each other.

Production declined as the companies attempted to pump the oil too fast, trying to get it before it flowed into neighboring wells. Finally in 1939, Salt Creek became the first oil field in America to run as a unitized operation, with joint management of the various wells for greater efficiency and conservation. Production in Salt Creek reached a peak in 1923 (when it produced 5% of the nation's oil), but the introduction of gas injection in the 1920s and water flooding in the 1950s helped push more oil to the wellheads. Although just a third of the oil at Salt Creek has been recovered even today—more

than 100 years after its discovery—retrieving the remaining oil will require more sophisticated techniques such as flooding with carbon dioxide. Salt Creek, with 12 thousand barrels per day still accounts for two-thirds of Natrona County's oil production. It's Wyoming's third-largest producing field.

Midwest And Edgerton

The twin oil towns of Midwest (pop. 600) and Edgerton (pop. 350) lie near the center of the Salt Creek Field. A paved road north of Midwest leads to the Shannon Pool oil field, where oil was first discovered. Thousands of drill holes surround the towns, laced together by a grid of dirt roads, powerlines, and pipes.

The company town of Midwest is named for Midwest Oil Company, now a part of Amoco. Its four straight streets contain rows of identical wooden houses built in the Roaring '20s, but now showing their age. The stench of sulfur from a gas recovery plant south of town permeates the air. Midwest's golf course is dotted with oil pumps, and folks attending Mass at the Catholic church can hear the quiet, rhythmic "ker-thunk" from a couple of pumpjacks just a hundred feet away. Midwest was especially hard hit by the slide in oil prices in the '80s; assessed valuation plummeted from $9.2 million in 1987 to $1.5 million in 1989! The impact is obvious in a walk around town: peeling paint on the small wooden box houses, boarded-up buildings, aging cars, and a sense of defeat.

The dumpy little town of Edgerton isn't much better. Edgerton's Derrick Drive-In is no more, though the sign still stands as a monument to the depressed oil economy. Try eating instead at **Edgerton Cafe** or Midwest's **Derrick Cafe**. The only lodging place is **Tea Pot Motor Lodge** in Edgerton, tel. 437-6541. Edgerton claims a bit of baseball trivia: it was the first place in America to have a baseball game played under lights.

Tempest In A Teapot

Twenty-five miles north of Casper along U.S.

87 is a distinctively shaped butte, Teapot Rock. Until a 1962 windstorm knocked down the "spout" that bent away from one side, the rock resembled a teapot. In the first decades of this century, rapid growth in the oil industry sent prospectors and speculators all over the West in search of black gold. To ensure adequate fuel supplies for the Navy's ships after WW I, the government set aside three large oil reserves— Elk Hills and Buena Vista in California, and Wyoming's Teapot Dome Oil Field (named for Teapot Rock).

In 1921 and 1922, Secretary of the Interior Albert B. Fall secretly leased Teapot Dome to Edward Doheny and Harry Sinclair, owners of Mammoth Oil Company. (Could anyone have ever come up with a more fitting name for a corrupt corporation?) Although the action was technically legal, the $100,000 bribe paid by Doheny to President Harding's interior secretary was decidedly not legal, and Fall was forced to resign. The action brought a plethora of charges against the giant oil companies, and political cartoonists had a heyday with Teapot Dome. Interior Secretary Fall was convicted of accepting bribes and spent a year in prison. Harry Sinclair (for whom both the oil company and the Wyoming town are named) hired detectives to spy on a jury investigating Teapot Dome, and was sent to jail in 1929 for contempt of court. He also spent three months in jail for refusing to testify before a Senate committee investigating the scandal. Today, the U.S. Navy still owns thousands of acres at Teapot Dome, and there are hundreds of oil wells a few miles east of the highway. A sign points out "Naval Petroleum Reserve Number 3," but you won't find any historical signs mentioning this rather sordid piece of Wyoming history. The mailboxes and nearby white buildings of Teapot Dome Ranch mark the site of Teapot Rock.

HEADING WEST

Powder River
The tiny settlement of Powder River (pop. 50) lies along U.S. 20-26 where it crosses this famous river, 35 lonely miles west of Casper. Not much here today; writer James Conaway called the town, "little more than a Texaco station and a bunch of pronghorn antelope looking at it."

On the third weekend in July, however, several hundred people flock (pun intended) to town for the annual **Sheepherder's Fair**. It features dog trials, sheep roping, and sheepherding demonstrations of all sorts. A band plays C&W favorites late into the evening for a happy throng of dancers.

Hell's Half Acre
Head west from Casper on U.S. 20-26 for 45 miles to one of the freaks of nature, Hell's Half Acre. Actually covering 320 acres, the area includes a strange collection of deeply eroded and colorful badlands surrounded by featureless sage-covered plains. Ancient coal deposits within the badlands caught on fire and burned for many years, and when explorer Captain Bonneville passed by in 1833, he labeled it Devils Kitchen because of these sulfurous fumes. The name Hell's Half Acre was a later title. Indians used these badlands as a buffalo trap, driving herds of them to their deaths over the canyon walls. In the late 19th century, after whites had slaughtered the bison to the brink of extinction, bone pickers gleaned thousands of these bones from Hell's Half Acre for eastern fertilizer plants. Archaeologists later discovered more bones here, along with arrowheads and other artifacts. Hell's Half Acre is well worth a stop, but be forewarned that a kitschy souvenir shop, cafe, motel (tel. 472-0018), and RV park detract from the view. It's a great place to meet busloads of tottering tourists from hell.

Lysite And Lost Cabin
This area is decidedly off the beaten track, located eight miles north of another nowheresville town, Moneta (pop. 10). At one time the main route into the Bighorn Basin and Yellowstone lay along the Lysite road, but with completion of a highway through Wind River Canyon in 1927, traffic bypassed this area. Slow-paced Lysite has an old-time country store, and is the sort of place where horses are still a means of transportation. Lysite library is housed in a building slightly larger than a shoe box.

Three miles to the east is Lost Cabin, named for a gold mine in the Big Horn Mountains. Miner Allen Hulburt and two partners discovered a stream filled with gold, but Indians killed his partners and partially burned their cabin. The dazed miner scooped up as much gold as he could carry and fled to Casper where his tale pricked more than a few ears. Despite repeated efforts by Hulburt and others, the Lost Cabin mine was never again found. (This is only one of many such tales about the fabled mine.)

The fly-speck of a town called Lost Cabin is centered around an elaborate mansion by John B. Okie. He came to Wyoming as a cowboy with only the clothes on his back, decided sheep were a better bet, and gradually became a millionaire. Okie once ran 30,000 sheep through the surrounding country, gaining the title "The Sheep King." His mansion—called "The Big Tipi" by local Indians—was built in 1900 for $30,000, and filled with carved fireplaces, Asian chandeliers, imported furniture, stained glass, and Persian prayer rugs. Surrounding it were a greenhouse filled with flowers tended by Japanese gardeners, a roller rink, a dance hall, and even an aviary housing 140 exotic birds. A powerplant was built to supply electricity for Okie's town. In 1930 Okie drowned in a nearby reservoir while hunting ducks. The old mansion is not open to the public but is visible from the gate.

Castle Gardens

A remote and little-known archaeological site is Castle Gardens, located 21 miles south of Moneta on a gravel road and then another six miles east on a rough dirt road. Not recommended for RVs or after rains when the road turns into a quagmire. Signs at Moneta and at the turnoff keep you from getting lost. Castle Gardens is a desolate area with all sorts of odd sandstone formations: toadstools, spires, and various creatures seem to appear. It's easy to see how this would be a sacred spot for the Indians who came here centuries ago. Small juniper and limber pines grow amid the grey rocks and sand, creating a garden in the castles of Castle Gardens. No camping at the site, but there are picnic tables and an outhouse.

Dozens of Indian pictographs (presumably Shoshonean in origin) have been sharply incised into the soft rock walls. They include many in the shield motif, believed to represent the round shields of Indian warriors. While they may be up to 900 years old, these figures are probably more recent than the pecked style of pictographs present in the Dinwoody Creek and Legend Rock areas. Castle Gardens' figures that show horses or tipis are clearly from the period after A.D. 1700. The most elaborate shield found here—the figure of a turtle painted green, yellow, and red—is now in the State Museum in Cheyenne. The remaining pictographs are protected by chain-link fences, but vandals have marred many of these priceless artifacts with graffiti. The site leaves you with mixed emotions: a multitude of questions about what the images represent, a feeling of closeness to the natural world in this remote and fascinating place, and an utter disgust for those who would destroy this cultural heritage.

West To Shoshoni

The 85 miles of highway (U.S. 20-26) that connect Casper with Shoshoni cross an almost featureless plain, a place that seems to define the word "bleak." No trees in sight, and the clouds throw moving shadows across a landscape of sage and grass. This is antelope country. Even the ranches are few and far between out here, and cattle take slow, desultory steps in the summer heat or brace against the bitter winds of winter. For many travelers this is pedal-to-the-metal country, a place to crank up the country tunes and sail on west.

BOB RACE

WIND RIVER MOUNTAINS COUNTRY

The Wind River Mountains—Wyoming's highest and longest range—form a dramatic divide between two of the state's most important rivers. The east side drains into the Wind River, eventually reaching the Atlantic Ocean, while the western slopes drop into the Green River and eventually down to the Pacific. The name Wind River Mountains originated as a Crow Indian reference to the warm Chinook winds that blow down the Wind River Valley. (Writer Joe Kelsey noted that "Wind River Mountains" contains three of the ancient Greek's four elements: earth, air, and water.)

The Land

This chapter covers Sublette and Fremont counties, named for two of the state's most famous explorers. Fremont County is a land of sharp contrasts. The eastern end consists of a spacious arid landscape of sage, grass, and antelope, while to the west are the fluorescent green irrigated fields along the Wind River and the pastel badlands near Dubois. Along the southern and western borders rise the snow-crested Wind

River and Absaroka mountains. At almost six million acres, this is Wyoming's second-largest county (after Sweetwater).

The centerpiece of Fremont County is the Wind River Reservation, home to both the Eastern Shoshone and the Northern Arapaho peoples. Within the reservation itself are the tiny towns of Fort Washakie, Ethete, and Arapahoe. The much larger non-Indian settlements of Riverton and Lander border it on the east, while on the south are the historic mining towns of South Pass and Atlantic City. West of the reservation, the town of Dubois provides an entry point into the Absarokas, the Tetons, and Yellowstone.

The Wind River Valley is farming and ranching country, with nearly half of Fremont County's people employed in agriculture. Some 150,000 acres of alfalfa hay, feed and malt barley, sugar beets, and oats are under irrigation each year. This is Wyoming's second-biggest dairy county, eclipsed only by Park County, and it has the largest number of horses in the state. There is also a substantial amount of oil and natural gas

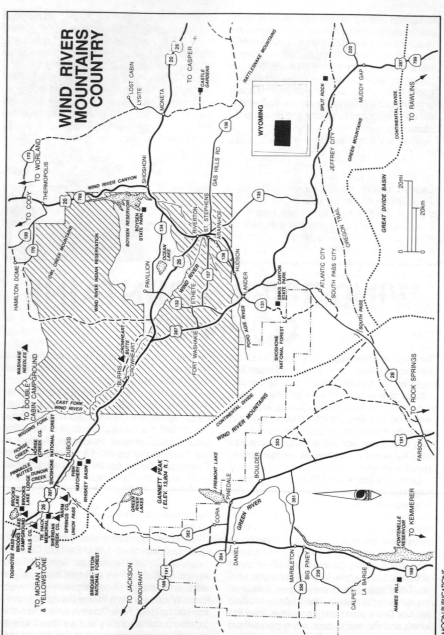

WIND RIVER MOUNTAINS COUNTRY

© MOON PUBLICATIONS

production on the Wind River Reservation where energy royalties bring in millions of dollars each year. Uranium was discovered in the Gas Hills area east of Riverton during the 1950s and grew into a major industry in the 1960s and '70s, before plummeting when the Three-Mile Island accident of 1981 brought the dangers of nuclear power to the forefront. Today the main work in the uranium mines is an effort to clean up the abandoned sites.

Sublette County has fewer people than any other county in Wyoming, just 4,500 individuals spread over 10,495 square miles. Cattle exceed people by a 16:1 margin, and there is only one town of any size: Pinedale. A few folks live in the little burgs of Big Piney, Marbleton, Boulder, and Daniel. Not surprisingly, the big industry here is ranching, although tourists are increasingly attracted to the area for its scenic beauty. There are magnificent vistas of the Winds all along the western front—far more dramatic than from the eastern side.

RIVERTON

Located near the confluence of the Big Wind River and Little Wind River, aptly named Riverton (pop. 9,500) is the largest settlement in Fremont County, and the eighth-largest city in the state. It's a mid-America suburbia sort of place where K marts and McDonald's dominate the outskirts. Cheap gas and low-priced hotels make visiting easier. The modern Central Wyoming College attracts students from throughout the area. The Wind River Reservation surrounds Riverton on all sides.

History

The Riverton area was the site of two trapping and trading rendezvous, in 1830 and 1838. The land became part of the Wind River Reservation in 1868, but a portion was ceded by the Shoshone and Arapaho tribes in 1904. Almost overnight, the town of Riverton sprang up as would-be farmers drew lots for prime farmland. It still has the state's largest dairy. Canals were dug and fields planted to crops; more than 100,000 acres of irrigated farmland surround Riverton today.

During the 1960s and '70s enormous uranium deposits were developed in the nearby Gas Hills area. Hundreds of millions of dollars poured into the local economy, creating rapid growth, but when nuclear power suddenly lost its luster, so did Riverton. After the bust that followed, the town began to diversify and has been slowly rebounding. Today the largest private employer is DHPrint, a manufacturer of computer printers. Other major employers are a soda ash hauling company, Bonneville Transloaders, the Brunton Co. (the nation's only compass manufacturer), and various government-supported programs.

Sights

The **Riverton Museum**, 700 E. Park Ave., tel. 856-2665, is open Tues.-Sat. 10-5 between May and Sept., and Tues.-Sat. 11-4 the rest of the year. No charge. Local historical exhibits include a tipi that contains a buffalo robe and powwow drum, an Indian cradle board with saddle, a model of the Carissa mine at South Pass, various old farm and mining equipment, and an interesting exhibit on oil drilling. Take a gander at Desert Demon, a stuffed wild mustang that proved untamable (hence his current more sedate condition; a bullet helped in the "taming" process). While here, also check out the photos of Leslie King, the father of former President Gerald R. Ford and a prominent Riverton area rancher. (President Ford's parents were divorced and his mother later married a man whose last name was Ford.) Gerald Ford worked as a ranger in Yellowstone after graduating from college in Michigan, as did his son Jack Ford many years later. **Riverton Livestock Auction**, located on Fairgrounds Rd., tel. 856-2209, is Wyoming's second-largest livestock auction barn (after Torrington). The monthly horse sales are the most enjoyable.

Accommodations

Riverton has some 15 different places to bed down for the night, all priced quite reasonably. See the chart (p. 183) for specifics. Camp for free in the small city campground next to the fairgrounds. Free hot showers, and you can pitch your tents on the grass beneath the cottonwood trees or park RVs in the gravel lot. Although the Wind River flows nearby, the hectic location is not exactly idyllic. **Owl Creek Kampground**, six miles northeast of Riverton on U.S.

26, tel. 856-2869, has tent sites for $10, RVs for $14, and showers for non-campers for $3. Open mid-May to mid-September.

Food

The best local breakfast eatery is, surprisingly, **Airport Cafe** at the airport, tel. 856-2838. Homemade cinnamon rolls and pies are specialties. **Claimsteak Restaurant**, 1616 N. Federal, tel. 856-6503, has a Mexican buffet on Wednesday night, along with a seafood buffet on Friday and champagne brunch on Sunday. **Broker Restaurant**, 203 E. Main, tel. 856-0555, also has good Mexican food, along with prime rib, steak, seafood, and roast duck. **Valley View Supper Club**, 4911 Valley View Rd., tel. 856-2447, is the favorite place for steaks and prime rib. (See "Hudson," p. 185, for the very best steaks in this part of Wyoming.) **Trade Winds**,

302 N. Federal, tel. 856-7666, serves Americanized Chinese dishes. The biggest salad bar in Riverton is at **Golden Corral**, 400 N. Federal Blvd., tel. 856-1152. Get groceries at **Woodward's IGA**, 619 N. Federal and 906 W. Main, or **Smith's**, 1200 W. Main.

Entertainment And Events

Good Time Charlie's Lounge, 502 E. Main St., 856-4285, has rock music on weekends. **Club El Toro**, tel. 332-4627, in nearby Hudson also has live tunes. Summer kicks off with a **Mountain Man Encampment** the first weekend in July near the site of a similar gathering in 1838. The next two weekends are reserved for the **Riverton Rendezvous**, which includes an arts and crafts festival, stock car races, rodeos, outdoor dancing, a melodrama, and all sorts of other activities. The festival ends with a **Hot Air**

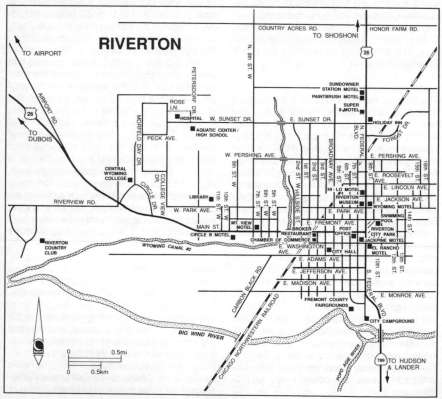

RIVERTON ACCOMMODATIONS

Motel	Address	Telephone	Rate	Features
Jackpine Motel	120 S. Federal	856-9251	$16 s, $20 d	
Mountain View Motel	720 W. Main	856-2418	$20 s, $22 d	
El Rancho Motel	221 S. Federal	856-7455	$20 s, $24 d	
Wyoming Motel	319 N. Federal	856-6549	$21 s, $25 d	
Driftwood Inn	611 W. Main	856-5811	$22 s, $26 d	
Thunderbird Motel	302 E. Fremont	856-9201	$25 s, $30 d	AAA approved
Paintbrush Motel	1550 N. Federal	856-9238	$28 s, $30 d	AAA approved, friendly
Hi-Lo Motel	414 N. Federal	856-9223	$28 s, $31 d	AAA approved
Tomahawk Motor Lodge	208 E. Main	856-9205 (800) 341-8000	$29 s, $31 d	AAA approved, jacuzzi, sauna
Circle B Motel	909 W. Main St.	856-9677	$29 s, $32 d	AAA approved
Cottonwood Ranch B&B	951 Missouri Valley Rd.	856-3064	$30 s, $35 d	working ranch
Super 8 Motel	1040 N. Federal	857-2400 (800) 848-8888	$33 s, $38 d	
Holiday Inn	789 N. Federal	856-8100 (800) 465-4329	$36+ s, $38+ d	AAA approved, pool, exercise facility
Sundowner Station Motel	1616 N. Federal	856-6503 (800) 874-1116	$37 s, $39 d	pool, jacuzzi, sauna, very nice

Balloon Rally on the third weekend in July, where you're likely to see more than two dozen colorful balloons lifting off at sunrise. The event attracts celebrities from the world of ballooning. **Fremont County Fair and Rodeo** comes to the Riverton Fairground in mid-August, with stock dog trials, a demolition derby, parade, and PRCA rodeos. Other **rodeos** are held every Tuesday night mid-June to August. In mid-August, the Riverton Museum sponsors a **Folk Festival** with demonstrations of pioneer skills and arts such as story-telling, old-fashioned cooking, and folk music. Meet all sorts of people in turn-of-the-century costumes and on horse-drawn carriages. More fun at the **Cowboy Poetry Roundup** in October where the cow-pokes spin tales.

CATHY CARLSON

Shopping

Books and Briar, 313 E. Main, tel. 856-1797, is a surprisingly nice book shop in downtown Riverton, with quite a few Wyoming and Indian titles. Also check out the bookstore on the CWC campus. **Beaver Creek Stitchery**, 415 E. Main, tel. 856-5303, sells authentic Western dusters, scarves, and other locally sewn items. **Wind River Trading Post**, 924 S. Federal Blvd., tel. 856-6141, has locally made beadwork and jewelry, along with turquoise jewelry from Arizona. Royce Brown, a local Arapaho craftsman, makes miniature Indian war bonnets for $35 each. Call **Lone Bear Crafts**, tel. 856-1521, for details.

Recreation

Riverton has an outdoor summer-only pool in City Park at

Main and Federal, and an indoor **Aquatic Center** at the high school on W. Sunset Dr., tel. 856-4230, with a sauna and whirlpool. Both are free. The (18-hole golf course) **Riverton Country Club** is at 4275 Country Club Dr., tel. 856-4779.

Information And Services
Riverton Chamber of Commerce is in the old railroad depot at 1st and Main, tel. 856-4801 or (800) 325-2732, and is open Mon.-Fri. 9-5. The attractive 109-acre campus of **Central Wyoming College** (CWC), tel. 856-9291 or (800) 442-1228, is on the west edge of town along U.S. 26. Founded in 1966, it offers two-year programs in more than 50 fields for nearly 1,000 full-time students. Students run Wyoming's only PBS television station and an excellent National Public Radio station (FM 88.1). The brand new **public library**, 1330 W. Park Ave., tel. 856-3556, is open Mon., Tues., and Thurs. 1-9, Wed. 9-1 and 5-9, Fri. 9-4, and Sat. 9-1. CWC also has a good-sized library.

Transportation
The **Riverton Airport**, located two miles northwest of town, has daily connections to Denver on **Continental**, tel. (800) 525-0280. **J C Cab**, tel. 856-7079, is the local taxi company. Rent cars at the airport from **Avis**, tel. (800) 331-1212, or **Hertz**, tel. (800) 654-3131. **Powder River Transportation** has in the past offered bus service to Riverton. Call (800) 442-3682 for the latest scoop.

RIVERTON VICINITY

SHOSHONI

Shoshoni (pop. 800) is one of the saddest hunks of desolation in Wyoming; only Jeffrey City beats it for top honors in this rather dubious category. During the late 1970s and early '80s this was a booming oil and uranium town, but today three-quarters of Shoshoni seems abandoned, with tall grass, peeling paint, and plywood windows. Tumbleweeds tumble down Main St., and locals joke that no one wants to be the last to "turn out the lights" because they're afraid of getting stuck with the electric bill! Fittingly enough, Shoshoni is bordered on the north by Badwater Creek and on the south by Poison Creek. East of Shoshoni is an arid landscape of badlands topography.

Practicalities
The main attraction in town is **Yellowstone Drug Store**, tel. 876-2539. During the summer months, scads of tourists stop here for delicious malts and ice cream floats at the old-time soda fountain. Peek in the windows of Gamble's store across the street, a crowded, funky old store that was closed by the fire marshal several years ago. Also in Shoshoni is the interesting little **CU Rock Shop**. Tipi rings northwest of town are still visible.

Aside from Yellowstone Drug and the Rock Shop, Shoshoni's only redeeming value is its reasonably priced accommodations. **Motel Dor-Ray**, 550 W. 2nd, tel. 876-9358, charges $20 s or $30 d, while **Desert Inn Motel**, 605 W. 2nd St., tel. 876-2273, has rooms for $20 s or $24 d. **Shoshoni Motel**, 503 W. 2nd, tel. 876-2216, charges $20 s or $23 d, but is the poorest of the lot. **Boysen State Park** is just a few miles north of here, with camping facilities for $4 a night.

BOYSEN STATE PARK

Established in 1956, Boysen State Park, tel. 876-2796, surrounds a reservoir named for Asmus Boysen, a Danish emigrant who built the first dam here in 1907-08. When the water from his dam covered tracks of the Burlington Railroad, they sued and had his dam blown up. The dam that now backs up the Wind River is a 230-foot-high earthen structure completed in 1961, and located at the entrance to Wind River Canyon. Boysen Reservoir is a motorboat playground popular with water-skiers and anglers. Its relatively warm waters attract swimmers to the beach near park headquarters.

Boysen Reservoir lies primarily within the Wind River Indian Reservation and is surrounded by open desert country. A nearly straight highway (U.S. 20) rolls north from Shoshoni over the arid hills and rocky buttes, providing a few good vistas across the lake. Southwest of Shoshoni, U.S. 26 crosses an arm of the reservoir. **Boysen Lake Marina**, on the north end near the entrance to Wind River Canyon, tel. 876-2772, has a restaurant, grocery store, and RV spaces ($13). The reservoir is surrounded by 10 different state park campsites ($4; open year-round). **Wyoming Winter Carnival** comes to Boysen in mid-Feb., featuring souped-up snowmobile races, ice golf, ice-bowling, ice sculpture, dog-sled races, and even a "snodeo." The main event is the high altitude speed run in which funny sleds (more like rockets with runners) reach speeds topping 160 mph.

GAS HILLS

The paved, but almost-untraveled Gas Hills Rd. (State 136) leads east from the Riverton area to several now-closed open-pit uranium mines, including the Lucky McMine, discovered in 1953 by Neil and Maxine McNeice, and mined for many years. Perhaps a third of the nation's uranium reserves remain in these arid hills. Today signs warn trespassers of the nuclear hazard in the abandoned mines. Dirt roads from the end of the pavement (approximately 45 miles east of Riverton) lead south to Jeffrey City, northwest to tiny Waltman, and east to Casper along Poison Spider Road. This is some of the most remote and desolate country you will ever find, with nary a tree in sight. The antelope love this sage and grass landscape. Castle Gardens (see "Central Wyoming," p. 177) can also be accessed from Gas Hills Road. A sign on the road (easy to miss) points out the turnoff.

HUDSON

It would be easy to drive through Hudson (pop. 300) without paying any attention to this rather rundown little place. That would be a mistake. Big Red's Cafe has a sign proclaiming "Homemade Pie Soup," (I think it needs a comma somewhere). Other attractions include Bob's Gun and Ammo, Drive In Liquors, Riviera of Hudson Beauty Salon, and an old Sinclair sign painted on the side of a brick building. Hudson has a distinct sense of decay, with boarded-up shops along the main drag, but off the main drag are quiet, cottonwood-lined streets and simple frame homes. This place is full of character and characters.

Hudson was established in 1905 and became a major coal-mining center in the early part of this century before the mines closed. Most of those who settled were European emigrants, and the town still maintains a strong ethnic flavor; the old fire truck says "Dago Red" on the front. Nowhere is this ethnic heritage as evident as in the two Yugoslavian-run steakhouses that attract folks from all over the state. **Svilar's**, tel. 332-4516, is the oldest, and its owners are staunchly Republican. Mama Bessie Svilar founded the restaurant in the 1920s to serve the hungry local miners, but soon travelers began going out of their way to visit tiny Hudson. Restaurant critic Red Fenwick noted that Svilar's "put Hudson on the map in big red letters that dripped with gravy and honey and meat juices." Mama Svilar died in 1981, but the food is still great, and the bar remains a popular place for drinks.

Just across the road is **Club El Toro**, tel. 332-4627, owned by the Vinich family and offering similarly fine steaks and other hearty fare. The homemade ravioli hors d'oeuvres are a specialty. John Vinich is a gadfly Democratic state senator who ran for the U.S. Senate in 1988, losing to Malcolm Wallop by only 1,165 votes out of nearly 180,000 cast. The Vinich family also owns **Union Bar**, just across the street, another very popular local hangout. El Toro has live C&W music on weekends. The empty building next to El Toro says "All Political Signs Welcome," offering something of a neutral zone between the Democrats and Republicans. After stuffing yourself at Svilar's or Club El Toro, ask about the badlands country east of Hudson. Some fascinating eroded formations are just a few miles out.

LANDER

Friendly Lander (pop. 7,700) lies along the banks of the Popo Agie River, with the majestic Wind River Mountains rising just to the west. The town has a state training school for the retarded that employs more than 600 people. Also important are government, ranching, and construction-related jobs. Lander is smaller and more homey than nearby Riverton, and has become something of a center for those who love the outdoors. The relatively mild winters here make it an attractive place to retire, and Lander's proximity to the Popo Agie Wilderness (see p. 214) makes it a jumping-off place for mountain treks into the high country.

History

Lander began in 1869 when the Army established a small military post, Camp Augur (later Camp Brown), to protect Shoshones from attacks by the Sioux and Arapaho. The rich valley

Main St., Lander, ca. 1883 LANDER PIONEER MUSEUM

along the Popo Agie River proved easy to irrigate and grew ample crops to feed hungry miners in nearby South Pass. Settlers moved here from the dying gold mines of South Pass in the late 1870s, creating the crossroads settlement of Pushroot (later renamed Lander after Colonel Frederick W. Lander who had surveyed the Oregon Trail's Lander Cutoff.) During the 1960s and '70s, Lander became a mining boomtown as hundreds of workers commuted to the Columbia-Geneva iron mine and mill near Atlantic City. When the mine closed in 1983, many businesses followed suit, leaving downtown pockmarked with abandoned storefronts.

Sights
The **Pioneer Museum**, 630 Lincoln St., tel. 332-4137, is open Mon.-Fri. 10-6, and Sat.-Sun. 1-4 from June to mid-September. The rest of the year its doors are open Mon.-Fri. 1-4:30 and Sat. 1-4. No charge. Pioneer Museum first opened in 1915, and the original log cabin still comprises its core. The museum houses an outstanding collection of Indian artifacts, including buffalo robes, beaded gloves, painted buffalo hides, and a squaw saddle. The skull of Harvey Morgan—a local farmer killed in an 1870 Indian raid in Deadman Gulch (east of Lander) —is also in the museum, with the 10-inch wagon bolt still gruesomely driven through it. A skilled marksman, he had fired off more than 200 rounds from his rifle before his death. For something completely different, peek in the tiny wedding chapel, popular for spring nuptials. Another room, the One-Shot Antelope Hunt Memorial Room, is devoted to this bizarre sport with its own celebrities.

Accommodations
See the chart (on p. 188) for Lander's motels and bed and breakfast places. Free camping at **Lander City Park**, 405 Fremont St., right along the banks of the Popo Agie River. Pitch tents on the shady grass here or park vehicles in the lot. Local high schoolers often park here for a bit of extracurricular activity, so don't expect a quiet night. **Sinks Canyon State Park**, 10 miles southwest of Lander on State 131, has a nice campground ($4); see p. 190 for details. There are three private campgrounds in the Lander area. **Rocky Acres Campground**, five miles northwest on U.S. 287, tel. 332-6953, charges $9 for tents and $13 for RVs. **Ray Lake Campground**, nine miles northwest on U.S. 287, tel. 332-9333, charges $9 for tents or $13 for RVs; open June-October. **K-Bar Ranch Campground**, 10 miles southeast on U.S. 287, tel. 332-3836, has tent sites for $7 and RV hookups for $11. Non-campers can use the showers for $2, open year-round.

LANDER ACCOMMODATIONS

Motel	Address	Telephone	Rate	Features
Downtown Motel	569 Main St.	332-5220	$22 s, $24 d	open June-Sept.
Western Motel	151 N. 9th St.	332-4270	$24 s, $26 d	kitchenettes
Maverick Motel	808 Main St.	332-2821	$24 s, $26 d	
Pioneer Court Motel	6th and Lincoln	332-2821	$24 s, $26 d	
Teton Motel	586 Main St.	332-3582	$25 s or d	kitchenettes
Horseshoe Motel	685 Main St.	332-4915	$26 s, $28 d	
Country Fare B&B	904 Main St.	332-9604	$27+ s, $42+ d	historic
Holiday Lodge	210 McFarlane Dr.	332-2511	$30 s, $39 d	AAA approved, kitchenettes
Black Mountain Ranch B&B	9 miles NW	332-6442	$30 s, $50 d	horseback rides
Silver Spur Motel	340 N. 10th St.	332-5189	$32 s or d	pool, continental breakfast
Pronghorn Lodge	150 E. Main St.	332-3940 (800) 999-5233	$35 s, $37 d	AAA approved, jacuzzi

Food

Two places in Lander attract locals for breakfast: **Highwayman Cafe** on the south end of town, tel. 332-4628, and **The Commons**, 170 E. Main, tel. 332-5149. The Commons also has a big salad bar. **Marguerita Ville**, 5th and Lincoln, tel. 332-3933, serves up pseudo-Mexican fare. **Tony's Pizza Shack**, 637 Main, tel. 332-3900, makes very good pizzas using homemade dough; their breadsticks are a local favorite. For lunches, head to **The Breadboard**, 125 E. Main, tel. 332-6090, where the sandwiches are a bit on the pricey side, but worth it. **Judd's Grub Drive-In**, 634 Main, tel. 332-9680, has the best fast food in town (including an enormous one-pound burger, as the high school kids will attest. **The Hitching Rack**, half a mile south on U.S. 287, tel. 332-4322, has a big salad bar and home-made soups. This is the place locals go out for dinner. Actually two of the most popular night-out places are 10 miles northeast in Hudson: Svilar's and Club El Toro (see p. 185).

Recreation

When most folks think of recreation in Lander, they think of the wonderful mountain country just a few miles away. See below for more on the Popo Agie area (p. 190) and the Wind River Mountains (p. 207). Lander's Olympic-size **swimming pool**, 450 S. 9th, tel. 332-4653, is open year-round, and costs $1.75 for adults, kids $.75-1.25, and seniors free. **Freewheel Sports**, 149 Main, tel. 332-6616, rents mountain bikes. The nine-hole **Lander Golf and Country Club** is on Capitol Hill, tel. 332-4653. During the winter, skate for free at City Park, where you'll also find a warming hut and skate rentals. **Great Divide Tours**, 336 Focht Rd., tel. 332-3123 or (800) 458-1915 (outside Wyoming), provides guided horseback rides for $5/hour. All-day 4WD tours of the surrounding country (wild horses guaranteed) are $45, ($25 for kids).

NOLS

Because of its proximity to the glorious Wind River Mountains, Lander has become a center for the environmental movement in Wyoming. The best known organization is the **National Outdoors Leadership School** (NOLS), located in a brick building at 288 Main St., tel. 332-6973. NOLS was founded in 1964 by Paul Petzoldt who participated in the 1938 attempt on K2, setting an American altitude record.

NOLS was established to offer classes in wilderness living skills that would lead people to respect their environment, and that would go beyond the Outward Bound emphasis upon survival. Over the years, NOLS folks have achieved a reputation as the purists in the field, emphasizing low-impact camping and respect for the land. Today the school offers classes all over the world, lasting from two weeks to three months, and covering everything from wilderness horsepacking to East African mountaineering. They are not cheap, starting around $1,600 for a two-week natural history class in Prince William Sound, and rising to $5,700 for a 65-day exploration of Kenya (not including air transportation). Equipment can be rented from NOLS for the classes. College credit is available, as is a limited amount of financial aid. For more info and a catalog of classes, write NOLS at P.O. Box AA, Lander, WY 82520.

Other Environmental Groups

Also in Lander is the **Wyoming Outdoor Council**, an organization founded in 1967 that emphasizes conservation education and environmental lobbying, especially on such issues as wilderness, wildlife, growth impacts, and waste management. Tax deductible memberships start at $15 a year. Their address is 201 Main (P.O. Box 1449), tel. 332-7031. **The Nature Conservancy** has its Wyoming state office at 258 Main, tel. 332-2971. Most of its 17,000 acres are conservation easements or cooperative projects rather than preserves. None are currently open to the public.

Entertainment

Nemo's Long Branch Saloon, 432 U.S. 287, tel. 332-7742, often has country tunes or DJ music on weekends, while **One Shot Lounge**, 695 Main, tel. 332-2692, occasionally offers rock and roll. Also check **The Hitching Rack**, half a mile south on U.S. 287, tel. 332-4322, and Hudson's **Club El Toro**. As a side note, the present **Stockgrower's Bar** at 202 Main (not the original name), was a hangout for the outlaw Butch Cassidy. It was built in 1886.

Events

Lander hosts the **Wyoming State Winter Fair** the last weekend in January, with livestock exhibits, dog weight pulling contests, horse shows, entertainment, and dancing. In early June the **Popo Agie Rendezvous** commemorates the 1829 rendezvous held near here. **Pioneer Days**, a three-day party in early July, is Lander's big event. There is a big parade with dozens of floats, marching bands, vintage autos, and performers, along with Indian dancing, street dances, and evening fireworks. The primary event is the **rodeo**, the oldest paid rodeo anywhere on earth, first established in 1893. Other roping events are held every Wednesday night between late June and August. The **Apple Festival** in late August is another popular Lander event.

The **One Shot Antelope Hunt** attracts hunters each August as teams of three head out to see how quickly they can bring down an antelope with just one shot. The governors of Wyoming and Colorado are "team captains," and celebrities sometimes participate. All sorts of convoluted rules and ridiculous ceremonies make this akin to fraternity initiation rites: hunters have their bullet blessed by Shoshone tribal members, and the losers dress as Indian squaws to dance with the winners. Old men find strange ways to amuse themselves.

Jade

The Jeffrey City area (60 miles east of Lander) is world-famous for its nephrite jade, a mineral found only in Asia, British Columbia, and Wyoming. The jade comes from Crooks Mountain, and much of it was discovered in the 1930s and '40s by Bert Rhoads who owns **Rhoads' Rocky Mountain Jade Shop**, 423 Main, tel. 332-4439. Rhoads' wife Verla discovered the largest piece of jade ever found, a 3,366-pound boulder that required heavy mining equipment to haul out. Wyoming jade varies greatly in value depending upon the color and the rarity. Some of it sells for around $7.50 a pound, while Wyoming emerald jade can sell for several thousand dollars per karat. Warning: Much of the jade jewelry sold as "Wyoming jade" actually comes from British Columbia. Buy only from reputable dealers.

Information And Services

The **Lander Chamber of Commerce** office is in the old railroad depot at 160 N. 1st St., tel. 332-3892 or (800) 433-0662 (outside Wyoming), and is open Mon.-Fri. 9-5. **Fremont County Library**, 2nd and Amoretti, tel. 332-5194, is open

Mon., Tues., Thurs. 1-9, Wed. 9-1 and 5-9, Fri. 9-4 throughout the year, plus Sat. 9-1 in winter. The **BLM District Office** is at 125 Sunflower St., tel. 332-7822, and the **Lander District Forest Service** office is at 600 N. U.S. 287, tel. 332-5460. **The Booke Shoppe**, 160 N. 2nd, tel. 332-6221, has a selection of books on Wyoming, while **Kottage Krafts**, 343 Main, tel. 332-9722, sells handmade gifts. The closest airport is in Riverton. Call (800) 442-3682 to see if Powder River Transportation is currently running buses to Lander. Rent cars from **Fremont Motors**, 161 State 789, tel. 332-4355, for $25/day plus 20¢/mile.

LANDER VICINITY

EAST ON U.S. 287

A few miles east of Lander on U.S. 287, you pass an impressive vermillion sandstone butte and a beautiful old red rock barn that once stabled horses along the stage route through here. In 1884, Wyoming's **first oil well** dug was drilled not far away. The site—now called the Dallas oil field—was known to Indians and had been described in Washington Irving's *Adventures of Captain Bonneville* as the Great Tar Springs. Nineteenth-century emigrants used the oil to grease wagon axles. As you continue eastward, the Wind River Mountains gradually diminish in magnitude. Stop to look up at them for a while. It is easy to see how the pioneers from the east—where a mountain is anything over 1,000 feet—would watch these mountains grow closer with each day's travel, and wonder at their rugged crowns. It's also easy to see why they would choose to cross around the southern end of this range (South Pass) instead of over it. Forty miles east of Lander, the highway passes a marker describing **Ice Slough**, one of many landmarks along this portion of the Oregon Trail. Dense grasses in a small marsh kept ice all through the summer, a real treat for emigrants on a hot summer day.

Jeffrey City

The bleak, almost-ghost town of Jeffrey City (pop. 600) is a casualty of the bust that followed the uranium mining boom of the 1970s. First called Home on the Range, the town was renamed for a Rawlins philanthropist, Dr. Charles W. Jeffrey. The town was built on the nuclear industry, and as a company town, its survival was tied to the fortunes of Western Nuclear Company. By 1980, the population had swollen to 3,000, and all sorts of new buildings were tossed up. Today, weeds grow through the concrete sidewalks around the empty bunkhouses, and Home on the Range Restaurant, Coats Motel, Drillers' Delite Lounge, and Jeffrey City Grocery are all closed. Only a gas station and bar remain on this remote stretch of highway. The modern grade school looks rather forlorn in all this desolation. Ranching, oil, and gas keep Jeffrey City from drying up and blowing away. Rockhounds should ask for directions to the famed jade deposits around Jeffrey City, but make sure you're on public land or have permission from landowners.

East of Jeffrey City lies definitive Wyoming country with rolling sage and grassland, a few weathered old homesteads, and distant mountains on all sides. **Cottonwood Campground** ($4; open June-Oct.), a BLM facility, is six miles east of Jeffrey City and then eight miles south on Green Mountain Loop Road. You aren't likely to meet many folks here. See "Central Wyoming," p. 173, for more on the country east of Jeffrey City.

SINKS CANYON AND THE LOOP ROAD

State 131 climbs south from Lander through the fascinating country of Sinks Canyon and then over the mountains to Atlantic City. A popular loop trip is to follow this road to Atlantic City, returning to Lander via State 28, a total distance of 56 miles. (See map on p. 214.) Plan to spend all day if you want to savor the many sights along the way. Locally this is known as the Loop Rd., and it is very popular with both visitors and residents. Bighorn sheep were transplanted into Sinks Canyon in 1987, and are common sights along the road. Rock climbers practice their skills on the steep cliffs of the canyon. Several campgrounds are here, along with lots of lakes, trails, and big mountain country. Get to State 131 by heading south on Lander's 5th Street. Sinks Canyon begins seven miles away.

The Sinks

The Popo Agie River (pronounced po-PO-zha) begins in the snowfields of the Wind River Mountains, dropping northeast to its junction with the Wind River near Riverton. **Sinks Canyon State Park** is one of Wyoming's geological wonders. Here the Middle Fork of the Popo Agie plunges into a cave (the "Sinks"), only to emerge again a half mile down in a gigantic spring. The river's name—Popo Agie—is a Crow Indian word meaning "Beginning of the Waters." The stream originally flowed above ground, and still does during high spring runoff, but over time a cave formed in the water-soluble Madison Limestone that underlies this region, allowing the water to disappear underground. Near the "rise of the sinks" is a diversion dam built at the turn of the century. Lots of large rainbow trout congregate in the pool, and visitors toss them bits of food. No fishing allowed.

The **Sinks Visitor Center**, tel. 332-3077, houses displays of fish and animals, along with geological exhibits. Open daily 8-7 during the summer only. Two **campgrounds** are nearby: the Forest Service's Sinks Canyon Campground ($5; open mid-June to mid-Sept.), and just up the road, the state-run Sawmill and Popo Agie campgrounds ($4; open year-round). Get brochures at the visitor center for the mile-long nature trail near the Popo Agie campground. More interesting is the **Popo Agie Falls Trail**, which takes off from the Bruce Picnic Ground, a mile above Popo Agie Campground. This 1½-mile trail climbs 600 feet in elevation to a series of attractive waterfalls, the largest being 60 feet. Horses and mountain bikes are allowed on the trail. During the winter, skiers enjoy groomed cross-country trails in the canyon.

Into The Mountains

Beyond the state park, the road turns to gravel and switchbacks steeply up the canyon's south face. The Owl Creek Mountains—50 miles to the north—are visible from the overlook. The road is washboarded in sections, so be ready for a buckin' bronc ride and lots of traffic. The rough ride is made worthwhile by excellent vistas and several attractive lakes (enlarged by dams). This is primarily lodgepole and limber pine country, but around Louis Lake you'll discover some huge old Engelmann spruce and subalpine fir trees.

The Forest Service maintains four fine campgrounds ($5) at **Fiddler's Lake, Worthen Meadows, Little Popo Agie Creek,** and **Louis Lake.** Fiddler's Lake has handicapped-accessible facilities and is the highest (9,400 feet). Louis Lake is easily the most popular, made more scenic by a sharp granite cliff that rises directly behind the lake. Good fishing for brown and Mackinaw trout, and moose are commonly seen around the lake's margins. **Louis Lake Lodge,** tel. 332-4324, rents very rustic four-person cabins (oil lanterns and handmade furnishings) for $35. You can also rent horses ($7.50/hour) or canoes and boats ($5/hour). Open only in summer. Other folks car camp around Frye Lake or off the road. A number of hiking trails head west from Loop Rd. to the lake-dotted Popo Agie Wilderness (see p. 214).

South from Louis Lake the road opens into a high plateau with limber pine trees and widespreading vistas south to the Oregon Buttes. Antelope are common in the sagebrush country, while moose are seen in the aspen stands along the road and in the marshes around Fiddler's Lake. The Loop Rd. meets State 28 beside the now-abandoned U.S. Steel iron ore mine. From here you can continue back to Lander on the highway, or visit the historic South Pass area (see p. 215).

WIND RIVER RESERVATION

At 2.2 million acres, the Wind River Reservation is one of the largest Indian reservations in the nation. It is home to both the Northern Arapaho and Eastern Shoshone tribes, and reaches some 70 miles from north to south, and 55 miles from east to west. You'll find some of the most unforgettable vistas in Wyoming here: fabulous badlands on the western edge; the beautiful Wind River where the cottonwoods glow a brilliant yellow in the cool fall air; deep green irrigated pastures where horses, sheep, and cattle graze; and desolate, wide-open spaces where only cactus, sagebrush, jackrabbits, and rattlesnakes grow. Bright yellow sunflowers add color to the roadsides in late summer. All this is set against a backdrop of the enormous snow-capped Wind River Mountains.

The Wind River Reservation was the scene for the classic Zane Grey western, *War Paint,* a film that featured both Tim McCoy and hundreds of Arapaho and Shoshone Indians. Today, hundreds of people, both Indian and nonnative, come to watch a different form of entertainment: the many powwows that occur throughout the summer months on the Wind River Reservation. The annual sun dance ceremonies are more intense, spiritual events where outsiders are only tolerated. The Shoshone and Arapaho peoples maintain separate sun dances and pow-wows; absolutely no cameras or tape recorders are allowed during the sun dances.

One of the most heated legal battles in recent Wyoming history focused on water from the Wind River. In 1989, the U.S. Supreme Court awarded the Shoshone and Arapaho tribes rights to nearly half the river's flow, based upon an 1868 treaty. The tribes then dedicated a substantial portion of the water to in-stream flows to develop a world-class fishery. Farmers dependent upon this water are angry they may be left high and dry in some years, but the tribes counter that for years that is exactly what the farmers were doing to the local fish. Don't bring the topic up in a Riverton bar.

Despite the close proximity of the reservation to Lander and Riverton, very little interaction goes on between Indians and nonnatives except in business situations. After more than 120 years, the various cultures—Arapaho, Shoshone, and Anglo—are still like oil and water. Whites regard the Indians as disorganized, drunken, and lazy. Indians view whites as pushy, materialistic, selfish, and disrespectful. Relations are not a whole lot better between the

1↗ 2↗ 3↗ 4↗ 5↘ 6↘

1. the travertine terraces of Mammoth Hot Springs; 2. Old Faithful Geyser; 3. Roaring Mountain; 4. Obsidian Creek flows below the Sheepeater Cliffs; 5. Snowcoaches prove a popular means of travel when winter comes to Yellowstone; 6. the Old Faithful Inn

CHIEF WASHAKIE

The history of Wyoming during the 19th century is one of constant battles between Indians and the invading white settlers. Only one tribe—the Shoshone—provided an exception to this rule. The reason for this stems from Chief Washakie (pronounced WASH-a-key), a man whose life spanned the entire tumultuous century. Washakie was born around 1798 of Shoshone and Flathead parents. His birth name was Pina Quanah, but later in life he gained the name Washakie—literally, "The Rattler"—a reference to a rawhide buffalo rattle he used to scare Sioux ponies during his daring raids. Because his father was killed by the Blackfeet tribe, Washakie lived something of an orphan's existence, growing up among both the Lemhi and Bannock tribes. He eventually joined the Eastern Shoshones and quickly proved himself as a fearless and extraordinary warrior.

In the 1830s, Washakie—fluent in sign language—met and became a close friend of famed mountain man Jim Bridger. One of Washakie's daughters became Bridger's third wife. From Bridger, Washakie learned a few words of English, and realized that a union with whites against his enemies was wiser than trying to fight the countless hordes coming across the plains from the east. Around 1843, after the death of the previous chief, Washakie gained control over a band of Shoshones based in the Upper Green River. As their lifelong chief, he was recognized as an extraordinarily intelligent, kindhearted, and forceful leader. Because of his consistent support, Washakie was sought out by white settlers whenever trouble appeared with other tribes.

In 1876, Washakie's Shoshones joined with General Crook against the Sioux and Cheyenne in the Battle of the Rosebud. The battle was a standoff, but Washakie's sage advice almost certainly prevented Crook's troops from facing the same fate met by General Custer one week later. When President Chester A. Arthur visited Wyoming in 1883, he asked Chief Washakie to meet him at a reception in Fort Washakie. The proud chief demured, instead insisting that the president come to him. They met in Washakie's tipi.

Chief Washakie died on the Wind River Reservation on Feb. 22, 1900, and was buried with full U.S. military honors, the only Indian chief to ever be so honored. He was 102 years old, and had led his people for over 60 years. With Washakie's death died the tradition of having one man as chief of the Shoshones. Although his name is not nearly as well-known today as that of Red Cloud or Crazy Horse, Washakie deserves a place in history as one of the great warriors and peacemakers. A dozen different Wyoming places are named in his honor, including the Washakie Wilderness and Mount Washakie.

Chief Washakie

Shoshones and Arapahos who still view each other with an animosity born of constant warfare during the 19th century.

SHOSHONE HISTORY

Originally peoples of the Great Basin, the Shoshones first entered southwestern Wyoming in the 16th century, gradually pushing northward until they controlled most of the land now known as Wyoming, along with territory all the way into Canada. As they moved onto the Plains, and with the acquisition of the horse, Shoshone life changed drastically, from a simple stone age culture of grubbing for roots and eating whatever they could catch by hand to a sophisticated buffalo-centered livelihood. Because Shoshone culture extended far to the south, they came into contact with Spanish traders, and were some of the first Indians to have horses. The Shoshone introduced horses to the northern plains region around 1700, forever transforming Plains Indian culture. To the trappers and traders who first encountered the Shoshone, they were known as the Snakes, because of their serpentine-like hand signals used to signify their tribal name. The word "Shoshone" refers to the simple willow and sagebrush lodges in which they lived before the great flowering of their culture in the 18th and 19th centuries. The Eastern Shoshone occupied western Wyoming, while their cousins, the Western Shoshone lived in Idaho.

In the late 18th century, the expanding Shoshone culture was halted when their enemies—the Sioux, Crow, and Arapaho—forced the Shoshone west of the Laramie Mountains. The Wind River and Fort Bridger vicinities became wintering areas. After a spring sun dance and buffalo hunt, the various tribal members would move into the mountains of northern Utah to hunt, fish, and gather berries and roots. Each fall the entire tribe would gather in the Great Divide Basin and head across the Continental Divide for the fall buffalo hunt in the Wind River and Bighorn basins. Led by Chief Washakie, the Eastern Shoshones—unlike most other Plains Indians—maintained an unbroken friendship with the invading whites.

Onto The Reservation

The Shoshones were not recognized in the great Fort Laramie Treaty of 1851, and the Wind River Basin and Bighorn Basin where they had long lived were assigned to the Crows. The Fort Bridger Treaty of 1863 gave the Shoshones and Bannocks a reservation covering parts of Colorado, Utah, Wyoming, and Idaho. In 1868, this enormous 45-million-acre spread was whittled down to just the Wind River region (with the Bannocks given a separate Idaho reservation).

Several years later, the government lopped off 600,000 acres around the rich gold region of South Pass City, giving Chief Washakie $500 a year, and $5,000 worth of cattle for five years (around four cents an acre). More land was ceded to the government in 1897 (Thermopolis

Hot Springs) for $60,000, and in 1905, 1.4 million acres were opened to homesteaders north of the Wind River. In exchange for the latter, the Shoshones and Arapaho received per capita payments, schools, payment for water rights, and an irrigation system on what remained of their reservation. This area is now one of the state's most important agricultural regions.

In 1878, Wyoming's territorial governor asked Chief Washakie if the destitute Arapahos—archenemies of the Shoshone—could be allowed to stay temporarily on the Wind River Reservation. Washakie's sympathetic heart finally gave in:

It is plain they can go no further now. Take them down to where Popo Agie walks into Wind River and let them stay until the grass comes again. But when the grass comes again take them off my reservation. I want my words written down on paper with the white man's ink. I want all you to sign as witnesses to what I have said. And I want a copy of that paper. I have spoken.

Despite this agreement, the "temporary" became permanent, and urgent pleas by Washakie went unheeded. Once again the government had abused its most loyal friend.

Many years after Chief Washakie's death, the Shoshones sued over this gross injustice. In 1937, the tribe was awarded $6.4 million for the land given to the Arapahos, minus the expenses for every building ever built by the government on the fort and services rendered. The cheapskate federal government even deducted $125 for a silver saddle given by President Grant to Chief Washakie as a token of appreciation! What was left amounted to a total of $2,350 per capita, distributed almost entirely in various BIA-run programs.

ARAPAHO HISTORY

The Arapaho—a Blackfeet Indian term meaning "Tattooed People"—always called themselves simply "Our People." They originally lived a farming life in what is now central Minnesota, but the arrival of whites on the East Coast created a domino effect among eastern Indians, pushing tribes westward on top of each other. Because of this pressure, the Arapaho, along with the Sioux and Crow, migrated onto the Great Plains in the late 18th century. They quickly adopted the nomadic life associated with Plains Indian culture, a life centered around the buffalo, and made possible by the horse. Pressure from the Sioux (who numbered perhaps 25,000 individuals versus 3,000 Arapaho) forced the Arapahos to join with the Cheyenne and move south to the Arkansas and Platte river regions.

Around 1830, the Arapaho split into northern and southern divisions, due in part to the establishment of Fort Laramie on the Laramie River (Wyoming) and Bent's Fort on the Arkansas River (Colorado). For many years, the Northern Arapaho wintered in northern Colorado, scattering along the North Platte River with the coming of spring, and then gathering again in late summer to hunt buffalo and prepare for winter. In the 1851 Fort Laramie Treaty, the Arapaho and Cheyenne tribes were assigned the area east of the Rockies between the Arkansas and North Platte rivers, but as gold was discovered in the Rockies, whites began to push the Arapaho off this land.

After Cheyenne and Arapaho warriors began raiding white ranches in Colorado during the early 1860s, the governor demanded action. In the Sand Creek Massacre of 1864, a peaceful Cheyenne and Arapaho village was viciously attacked by U.S. cavalry soldiers under Colonel John M. Chivington. The action sparked a massive retaliation as Arapaho, Sioux, and Cheyenne warriors sacked Julesburg, Colorado, tore down miles of telegraph wire, stampeded cattle herds, and burned ranch and stage stations throughout the Rockies.

After this, the Arapahos shifted their living patterns, spending winters along Wyoming's Powder River and summers in the Medicine Bow country to the south. They continued to attack Shoshones on the Wind River Reservation, emigrant trains along the Overland Trail, and miners around South Pass until the early 1870s, but gradually lessened their raids as the futility of their condition became more apparent.

The end came in the Bates Battle of 1874 when the Shoshones and the U.S. Army attacked the Arapaho, leaving them demoralized and without horses or supplies. In the late 1870s, many Arapaho served as Army scouts, and some even joined an Arapaho unit of the Army during the 1880s. Best known of the Arapaho scouts was Friday, an orphan Arapaho boy adopted by mountain man and Indian agent Thomas Fitzpatrick and taught in eastern schools. He returned to his tribe, becoming their most important translator, and a force for peace. It was probably Friday's friendship with Chief Washakie that led Washakie to finally tolerate Arapahos on his reservation.

Onto The Reservation

With the buffalo gone and their way of life under constant pressure from white settlers and the deadly diseases they brought, the Arapaho were in desperate straits, shuttling from one temporary home to another. The government refused to set aside a separate reservation, insisting that they live with the Cheyenne in Oklahoma or with the Sioux in South Dakota, far from their Wyoming home.

In 1878, the Northern Arapaho were shoe-horned onto the Wind River Reservation with their hated enemies in what was to be a "temporary" stay. Only 913 Arapaho remained—mostly women and children—from the tribe that had once been so powerful. (Interestingly, the Arapaho now outnumber the Shoshones on the reservation.) The two bands of Arapaho that settled on the Wind River Reservation were led by Chief Black Coal (whose people settled in present-day Arapahoe) and Chief Sharp Nose (whose people settled around present-day Ethete).

The two tribes continue to jointly occupy the Wind River Reservation, with the Arapahos holding the eastern half (the towns of Ethete and Arapahoe) and the Shoshones in the west (the towns of Fort Washakie, Burris, and Crowheart). In 1891, the Arapahos were given equal rights on the reservation, despite Shoshone Chief Washakie's continued attempts to have them removed. Although Chief Washakie's son mar-

CATHY CARLSON

ried an Arapaho woman, there is still very little intermarriage between the tribes and almost no blending of the two cultures, even after more than a century.

RESERVATION LIFE

In the early reservation years every effort was made to break the spirit of the "savages" and to make them into red-skinned Europeans. Even that most basic attribute, one's name, was taken away in the 1890s by the Commissioner of Indian Affairs. Thus, Yellow Calf became George Caldwell and Night Horse became Henry Lee Tyler. Even William Shakespeare and Cornelius Vanderbilt suddenly became tribal members! (The effort was not entirely successful since William Shakespeare was credited with bringing Peyotism—an important Native American religion today—to the Wind River Reservation.) Other measures helped weaken the culture, including the repression of Native religious practices, indoctrination by Christian missionaries, banning of face painting, and the forced cutting of young boys' long black hair. Today, the nation is paying the price for these all-too-successful attempts to destroy Native American culture.

Most of the 4,500 Arapahos and 3,000 Shoshones live in housing built by the tribal council or in the hundreds of mobile homes that dot the reservation. From a non-Indian point of view, they are decidedly untidy, with junk of all sorts piled outside; but then, the folks who live here really don't care what outsiders think. Older log cabins can be found all over the back roads, their sod roofs collapsing and their log walls slowly returning to the earth. A number of missions are scattered throughout this area, marked by attractive log or stucco churches.

POWWOWS

CATHY CARLSON

The Indian "powwow" (an Algonquian term meaning "medicine man") is a colorful celebration of Native American culture that cuts across tribal boundaries. Nobody knows the exact origin of powwows, but they may have developed from the Grass Dance of the Omaha and Pawnee Tribes who passed the dance on to various Plains tribes. The dance was used as a way of communicating with the Great Spirit, and the rhythmic beat of the drum helped send prayers skyward. Buffalo Bill Cody first introduced Indian dancers to audiences all over America and Europe, and in 1887, the Ponca Tribe began the first Indian fair and powwow. Other tribes joined in the fun, and powwows became increasingly popular with the coming of the 20th century. The creation of "fancy dancing" allowed more personalized costumes and dances. Women were allowed to dance, and by the 1940s, Indians began traveling long distances to join other tribal powwows.

Dancers perform to a beat set up by different groups of drummers. who sing a repetitious song as they beat out the rhythm. The chant evokes images of somber ceremonies far out on the Plains, and of a lost culture. The dances originated from different tribes, but have been adapted using the more colorful synthetic fabrics and beads of today. Professional dancers travel a circuit throughout the Western states, and even non-Indians take part in powwows. Contestants wear numbers similar to those at

Oil and gas revenues from a number of major fields on the reservation provide millions of dollars each year in the form of monthly per capita payments. These royalties, along with various Bureau of Indian Affairs (BIA) assistance programs, ranching, farming, and tribal-owned businesses are the main source of income. A Business Council acts as the manager of tribal income. The Arapahos tend to emphasize communal sharing and a purity of race much more than the Shoshones who are more likely to marry whites and to own private land.

Most people on the reservation are poor, and many are unemployed, having lost their jobs when the uranium mines closed down and oil companies left. Pawn shops in Lander and Riverton often acquire valuable cultural items from desperate individuals when the money runs out before the month does. For many on the reservation, sports are the way out. Every

kid, it seems, plays basketball, and there are hoops outside all the trailer homes and government-built houses. For older folks, bingo is a major source of entertainment, with games almost every night of the year.

Despair And Hope

The Wind River Reservation has severe problems with drugs and alcohol; a third of the children are born with fetal alcohol syndrome. Many young people (and older folks too) die in alcohol-related car accidents or fights, while suicide rates and infant mortality are distressingly high. Despite all the problems, there is a genuine sense of pride in the cultural history of the Arapaho and Shoshone peoples. To attack the problems of alcoholism and the loss of self-identity, young people learn their native tongue in special classes, and take part in powwows, sun dances, and personal vision quests. The warrior

trackmeets or rodeos, and compete for cash awards.

Two main styles of powwow dance exist. In **traditional dancing**, the movements are slow and graceful, with an adherence to more authentic costumes and traditional dance steps. Male dancers wear a bustle of eagle feathers, representing the birds of prey that once gathered over battlefields to feed on dead warriors. They also wear a head roach made from porcupine guard hairs. **Fancy dancing** is more casual, sort of an anything-goes dance where the steps are decided by the individual dancers. It generally involves lots of spins, bows, and head movements. Men's costumes are equally freeform, with all sorts of gaudy additions, particularly colorful bustles added to the shoulders and arms. Women's costumes for both traditional and fancy dancing are not as showy as the men's, although they do include bells, elk teeth (or plastic copies), and shell decorations on the dresses, along with shawls, and necklaces of hairpipe.

The Wind River Reservation has a half dozen powwows throughout the year, all but one of which are held outdoors. Tipis are set up, and the event becomes a joyful celebration of life and culture. These are three-day weekend events that involve not just singing and dancing, but traditional games, parades, and a "giveaway ceremony." Activities last all day and late into the evening. Things generally begin with a festive parade that includes a military color guard and a powwow queen seated atop a car hood. Visitors are welcome at powwows and photos are

not usually a problem, although this is less true at Arapaho powwows. For general information on powwows and other events on the reservation, call 332-3040.

tradition is expressed in a high enlistment in the nation's armed forces.

The reservation is a center for fine beaded clothing and moccasins that are prized by collectors. Arapaho patterns are geometric in nature, with rectangles and triangles appearing frequently. Arapaho women generally use red, black, blue, yellow, orange, and white as the main colors, with mountains, tipis, and butterflies as common themes. Eastern Shoshone patterns tend to be more circular, with the rose as a popular theme.

ARAPAHOE AND ST. STEPHENS

The town of Arapahoe (known locally as Lower Arapahoe) is a small village on the southeastern edge of the reservation. It came into existence because of animosity between the tribes, as a subagency where annuities could be distributed to the Arapahos without their having to face the taunts of "beggar" or "dog eater" from the Shoshones at Fort Washakie. A prominent white water tower is visible for many miles. The **Northern Arapaho Powwow** (oldest on the reservation) is held here in early Aug., followed by the **Labor Day Powwow**.

St. Stephens Mission
In 1884, the St. Stephens Mission was established by Father John Jutz, a Jesuit missionary. Chief Black Coal consented to allow a mission to be built, and later proved an ardent supporter of the school for Arapaho children. Until 1939, the Catholic Church operated a boarding school here, replaced by a day school that ran until the 1970s when it became increasingly difficult to find priests and nuns to run the mission.

As you enter St. Stephens Mission, you pass a modern grade school built in 1983, and run by a private non-religious corporation with an entirely Indian leadership. The most interesting sight at the mission is **St. Stephens Church,** built in 1928. The white stucco exterior is covered with colorful Arapaho geometric symbols. Note

the right panel in which a black-robed figure appears to be preaching to a crowd. This is taken from an Indian pictograph at Castle Gardens (see p. 177), and is believed to have been etched into the rock by an Indian who had watched Father Pierre DeSmet baptize 305 Arapahos during the great council of 1851 at Fort Laramie.

The excellent quarterly magazine **Wind River Rendezvous** is published by the mission and is available for just $10 a year; write them at Box 278, St. Stephens, WY 82524. Although this is a religious organization, the magazine deals with all sorts of historical and social issues. A cemetery near the mission contains the graves of Chief Lone Bear, Francis Setting Eagle, and John Broken Horn, along with that of his wife, Sarah Broken Horn—a white woman (born as Lizzie Fletcher) who had been captured as a child and raised as an Indian. See "Arlington," p. 99, for more on this story.

The **North American Indian Heritage Center,** tel. 856-4330, is open Mon.-Fri. 9-4, and includes an art gallery with historic photos, plus a fine gift shop containing Arapaho paintings, belts, moccasins, hair ornaments, earrings, necklaces, and other works. Some of the most interesting items for sale are miniature mannequins in tribal costumes. The center also runs **Singing Horse Tours,** tel. 856-6688. For $20, visitors are given a 30-minute orientation lecture and walking tour of the St. Stephens Mission, and a cassette tape and map describing other reservation sites.

ETHETE

Ethete (pronounced EEE-thuh-tee) is the primary Arapaho settlement on the reservation. People live in trailer homes scattered on small plots around town or in ticky-tacky box houses built by the BIA. (The prefabricated houses are

known as the "Easter Egg Village" because of the bright colors.) Tipi poles lean against the barns, and the bright tribal colors and geometric patterns dominate the laundromat/video store.

BOB RACE

"Downtown" Ethete consists of a stoplight surrounded by a grocery store (with a few handicraft items), gas station, community hall, high school, and the above-mentioned laundromat. All this is entirely forgettable, except for nearby St. Michael's Mission. The **Ethete Community Powwow** is held in mid-June, and the annual **Ethete Celebration** is held in late July. In mid-July the Ethete powwow grounds come alive with the **Northern Arapaho Sun Dance** ceremony (no cameras).

St. Michael's Mission

Established in 1887 by Rev. John Roberts of the Episcopal Church, this mission is the town's reason for existence. When Chief Sharp Nose was asked for his approval to build here, the response was "Ethete," meaning "Good." The buildings here were constructed between 1910 and 1917, and are arranged in a circle around a grassy lawn. Most are built from cobblestones, with Arapaho designs on the doors, but the **Church of Our Father's House** is of log. Inside this fascinating building (built in the shape of a cross) are rustic handmade benches from local wood and a central Arapaho drum. Altar seats are made of elk antlers, and the back window faces the great Wind River Mountains. The **Arapaho Cultural Center** at the mission houses a variety of Arapaho cultural artifacts from the late-19th and early-20th centuries.

FORT WASHAKIE

Fort Washakie is the center of activity on the Wind River Reservation. The BIA compound is here (locals insist the initials stand for Boss Indians Around), along with headquarters for the tribal council. Fort Washakie was the home of Chief Washakie, the longtime leader of the Shoshones. Behind Chief Washakie's town are a series of sharp escarpments, and through a gap in the hills you look into the mighty Wind River Mountains.

In 1869, the U.S. Army established a fort, Camp Augur (later Camp Brown), along the Popo Agie River to protect the Shoshones from attacks by Arapaho and Sioux warriors. The fort was later moved a dozen miles west and renamed Fort Washakie, making this one of the only forts ever named for an Indian chief. It remained open until 1909 when the threat of conflict between the Shoshones and Arapahos had diminished. A few buildings still stand, including a **stone guardhouse**. They are now used by the BIA.

Sights

Despite its miniscule size, Fort Washakie has an array of interesting sights. **Warm Valley Arts and Crafts**, tel. 332-7330, sells handmade Indian beadwork, jewelry, garments, and other items from the reservation. Also on display are Chief Washakie's headdress, leather shirt, and suitcase. It is owned and operated by the Eastern Shoshone tribe, and is open Mon.-Fri. 8-4:45 all year, plus Sat. 9-3 June-August. **Hines General Store**, tel. 332-3278, has more beadwork, moccasins, and baskets. **El Ranchito**, next door, sells delicious Indian tacos. The **Shoshone Cultural and Resource Center**, tel. 332-9106, is in the "White House" on the BIA compound. Built in 1913, it now serves as an information and heritage center. Upstairs are some historic photos along with a video about powwows. Young people take cultural and Shoshone language classes here. It's open Mon.-Fri. 8-5.

Just off U.S. 287 in Fort Washakie is a **Living History Indian Village** where you'll see hide-tanning, beading, Indian dancing, tipi erecting, and other demonstrations. For sale are locally made beadwork and Indian foods. Open June-Oct., Sun. 1-8 p.m., and Mon.-Sat. 9 a.m.-8 p.m.; $1 for adults, 50¢ for children.

South Fork Rd. west from Fort Washakie passes the **Washakie Graveyard**. A substantial granite memorial notes that Washakie was, "Always loyal to the government and his white brothers. A wise ruler." Directly across the road is the **R.V. Greeves Art Gallery**, tel. 332-3557, open by appointment only. Greeves is one of America's best-known sculptors; his *The Unknown* is in the Buffalo Bill Historical Center.

Continue another mile along this road (stay left at the "Y") to the **Sacagawea Cemetery**. The remote setting offers views of the Wind River Mountains. Sacagawea's gravesite (or at least the Wyoming version) is marked by an impressive granite headstone, and one of her sons, John Baptiste, is buried alongside. The graveyard also contains an old log church and a number of old bed frames over graves, a burial

SACAGAWEA

Fictional books about Sacagawea (pronounced sah-cah-gah-WEE-ah), describe her as a beautiful Indian maiden, guide, peacemaker, heroine, and mother—sort of the original Superwoman. Historian James Truslow Adams declared her one of the six most important women in American history. The reality is a bit less romantic, but still fascinating. Sacagawea—her name meant "Bird Woman" in Shoshone—was born around 1788 in what is now eastern Idaho. As a child, she was captured by the Minnetaree tribe and later sold to a French-Canadian trapper and interpreter named Toussaint Charbonneau. He eventually made her one of his many wives.

The Lewis And Clark Expedition

In 1803, President Thomas Jefferson negotiated the Louisiana Purchase from the French. For the fire-sale price of $16 million he suddenly doubled the size of the young nation called America. Captains Meriwether Lewis and William Clark were selected to lead a secret exploration of this vast land. They left St. Louis in late 1804, camping that first winter in North Dakota, where they met Sacagawea and her husband Charbonneau. Lewis and Clark didn't think much of the ill-tempered and untrustworthy Charbonneau, but realized the value in having a Shoshone woman who also spoke English and French. Charbonneau was hired, with the stipulation that his wife come along.

Over the winter, Sacagawea gave birth to a baby boy, and when the troupe headed out two months later, the child was on her back in a cradle board. Contrary to the romanticized novels, her role was not so much as "The Guide," but as an interpreter, as one who knew the edible plants along the way,

and as a symbol of the expedition's friendly intentions. When the expedition reached the Continental Divide, they met up with Sacagawea's sister and brother, whom she had not seen since being kidnapped six years before. The Shoshones agreed to provide guides and horses to cross the Rockies.

They reached the Pacific Ocean that fall, and built a fort near the mouth of the Columbia River for winter quarters. They recrossed the mountains the following summer, and Sacagawea, Charbonneau, and their son returned to their old existence in Mandan country. The rest of the expedition party reached St. Louis on September 23, 1806, long after everyone but President Jefferson had given them up for dead. The trip proved a vital step in bringing the Northwest under the U.S. flag.

Later Years

From here, the story of Sacagawea becomes murkier. Some researchers claim she died in 1812 of "putrid fever" at Fort Mandan in North Dakota. This version is generally told by Dakota folks. Wyoming partisans prefer another story: that the woman who died so young was one of Charbonneau's other wives, and that Sacagawea continued to live for many more years. After leaving her abusive husband, she wandered all over the West, finally ending up on the Wind River Reservation with fellow Shoshones. She served a crucial role as translator for Chief Washakie in negotiations to establish the reservation. The "Bird Woman" (or at least the Wyoming version) died on April 9, 1884, and was buried near Fort Washakie in a cemetery overlooking the Wind River. The 13,569-foot Mt. Sacagawea in the Wind River Mountains is named for the Bird Woman.

BOB RACE

practice that was common for many years on the reservation.

The historic **Shoshone Episcopal Mission** is on Trout Creek Rd., 1 1/2 miles southwest of Fort Washakie, and was founded in 1883 by Rev. John Roberts, a Welsh missionary known as "White Robe." A boarding school for Indian girls was built in 1891. The two-story brick and stone building still stands,

though the school closed in 1945. A simple log mission church is nearby. Three miles east of Fort Washakie on the way to Ethete is **Chief Washakie Hot Springs**, where 110° F water flows into a public swimming pool ($1.50). This was a favorite place of Chief Washakie. Maybe these mineral waters helped him live to age 102!

Practicalities

Ray Lake Campground, two miles southeast of Fort Washakie on U.S. 287, tel. 332-9333, charges $9 for tents or $13 for RVs. Tipis are also available for rent. Open June-October. There is no other lodging available on the reservation, although many places are available in nearby Lander, Riverton, and Dubois. **Little Wind River Outfitter**, tel. 332-2409, provides guided horsepacking trips in the Little Wind River drainage on the reservation. They also offer special three-day Indian encampments where you learn skills such as beadwork, archery, and arrow-throwing, and get to hear Shoshone and Arapaho legends.

Fishing on the Wind River Reservation requires a special permit ($7-35), available from the Tribal Fish and Game Office in Fort Washakie, tel. 332-7207. This permit also allows hiking, camping, and boating access. Restrictions apply, and a number of areas (including the entire northern end of the reservation) are closed to the non-Indian public. The map that comes with the permit shows open areas. Hunting by outsiders on the reservation is strictly verboten.

Events

In late June, Fort Washakie is home to the **Treaty Day Celebration** that includes Indian games, dancing, and a feast. It is immediately followed by the **Eastern Shoshone Powwow and Rodeo** that attracts Indians from all over the West. The all-Indian rodeo features Indian relays where bareback riders rocket around the track in a chaos of flying dirt and colliding horses. Another Shoshone powwow is held in Crowheart in early June, and an Eastern Shoshone Sun Dance takes place near Hamilton Dome in late July. In late December, another Shoshone powwow is held at Fort Washakie, but this time inside the local gymnasium.

WEST TO DUBOIS

As you head northwest along U.S. 26-287, the Wind River Mountains and Absarokas grow ever closer, and the Wind River Valley begins to narrow. Crowheart Butte dominates the skyline to the north for many miles, and then you drop over a rise to discover a stunning landscape of red rock badlands accented by the green of cottonwoods along the Wind River. For the next 20 miles, travelers are treated to a constantly changing panorama of gloriously colorful badlands topography. It is a geologist's dreamworld. Several reservoirs provide irrigation water along with recreation on the Wind River Reservation. Largest is **Bull Lake**, along the western margin. The Shoshones say that it is haunted by a supernatural water buffalo. The aquamarine waters of **Ocean Lake** are well-known for bass and crappie fishing. Other people come to swim or waterski.

Crowheart Butte

The tiny settlement of **Crowheart** consists of an old-fashioned country store and gas station surrounded by irrigated fields and grazing cattle. A couple miles northeast of the store—and visible for many miles in either direction—is a regal summit, Crowheart Butte, looking like a pyramid whose top got caught in a giant lawn mower.

The name comes from an 1866 battle over hunting rights in the Wind River Valley between the Shoshones and Bannocks against their enemy, the Crows. The Crows had been "given" the valley in the Fort Laramie Treaty of 1851, while the Shoshones and Bannocks had been "given" the same land in the 1863 Fort Bridger Treaty. Four days of intense fighting led to a standoff, and to prevent further bloodshed, the chiefs declared a winner-takes-all fight atop this butte. Charging each other on horseback with lances drawn, both were thrown in the collision, and the fight turned to a hand-to-hand struggle. In the battle, Shoshone Chief Washakie killed Crow Chief Big Robber and then reputedly ate the vanquished leader's heart (or at least carried it around on a spear). Thus the name, Crowheart Butte. When Chief Washakie was later asked about the story, he replied, "When a man is in battle and his blood runs hot, he sometimes does things that he is sorry for afterwards. I cannot remember everything that happened so long ago."

Crowheart Butte is regarded as something of a sacred place by local Indians, and is used as a place of spiritual renewal for young men on a vision quest. A small rock shelter stands on the top, used for this purpose. It is illegal for non-Indians to climb Crowheart Butte, and legends claim that those who do so may disappear.

Broken Wheel Ranch

The Broken Wheel Ranch, located near Dinwoody Creek (10 miles west of Crowheart), offers an amusing taste of the Hollywood frontier.
During the 1980s, Lee Kozell—a onetime Wyoming cowboy and retired Pittsburgh bartender—
built this miniature Wild West town, including a
saloon, jail, church, general store, bank, and
brothel. Get here by turning south on the dirt
road just beyond Dinwoody Creek, and following
the road 1 1/2 miles to the buildings.

Whiskey Basin

The highway continues its slow, scenic climb
to Dubois, crossing the cottonwood-lined Wind
River three times en route. Approximately 25
miles west of Crowheart (five miles east of
Dubois), a gravel road leads to a state fish hatchery and a bighorn sheep wintering range in
Whiskey Basin. A sign points the way. The road
is easy at first, but approaches the 4WD status
within a couple of miles as it follows Torrey
Creek up past a string of four small lakes. State
Game and Fish **campsites** (free) are located
along Ring and Trail lakes. A trailhead at the
end of the road (12 miles) provides access to the
primary route up to Dinwoody Glacier and
13,804-foot Gannett Peak. (See p.207, for more
on the Glacier Trail.)

A number of large Indian pictographs are on
large boulders in the Trail Lake vicinity. The figures—some four feet tall—are elaborate other-
worldly creations with horns and headdresses.
Evidence points to their use in shamanistic ceremonies produced under altered states of con-
sciousness. While the age is unknown, they are
probably at least 2,000 years old, and from Atha-
paskan (a Canadian tribe) rather than Shoshonean origins. This is some of the oldest rock art in
Wyoming.

During the winter months, Whiskey Basin
Habitat Area contains the largest population of
Rocky Mountain **bighorn sheep** anywhere on
earth. At times more than 1,200 sheep congregate here because of the mild winters and the
lack of deep snow. Best time to find them here is
Dec.-Feb., but some stick around till April.
Bighorn sheep are also sometimes seen in the
meadows along the highway or in the hills just
above Dubois.

DUBOIS

Approaching Dubois (pop. 1,000) from either direction, you drive through the red and yellow badlands that set this country apart. The luxuriant Wind River winds its way down a narrow valley where horses graze in the irrigated pastures, and old barns and newer log homes stand against the hills, while the tree-covered Absaroka Mountains ring distant views. The town of Dubois consists of a long main street that makes a sharp elbow turn and then points due west toward the mountains. It has an authentic frontier feel, with many log buildings, and even a few snatches of wooden sidewalks. Locals live in cabins, trailer homes, and simple frame houses. Dubois weather is famously mild (warm Chinook winds often melt any snow that falls) and grand scenery reigns in all directions. Snowmobilers, hunters, and anglers have begun to discover that Dubois provides a good place to relax in Wyoming's "banana belt," while at the same time remaining close to the more temperamental mountains. By the way, Dubois is pronounced DEW-boys; other pronunciations will reveal your tenderfoot status. (Actually, locals sometimes jokingly call it "Dubious.")

History
Dubois began in the 1880s when pioneer ranchers and homesteaders settled in the area, followed by Scandinavian hand-loggers who cut lodgepole for railroad ties. The town that grew up along the juncture of Horse Creek and the Wind River was first known as Never Sweat, but when citizens applied for a post office, the Postal Service refused to allow the name. The agency suggested Dubois instead, the name of an Idaho Senator who just happened to be on the Senate committee that provided funding for the post office.

Dubois is a town in transition. For most of its existence, Dubois served as a logging and ranching center. In 1987, the Louisiana Pacific sawmill shut down, throwing many loggers and millworkers onto the unemployment roles. Loggers blamed environmentalists and the Forest Service for sharply reducing the timber available, but environmentalists countered that the company was simply using the reductions as an excuse to close an aging mill. After everyone ran out of mud to sling, they decided to look at what Dubois had to offer and discovered that lo and behold, they just happened to be sitting in an almost-undiscovered recreational and retirement gold mine. In the last few years Dubois has leapt full-force into the tourism business. The transformation of Dubois to a visitor-oriented economy certainly has its downside— elaborate log summer homes are beginning to overrun the lush pastures on both ends of town —but it also means that much of the surrounding country will remain undeveloped.

Sights
The **Dubois Museum**, 909 W. Ramshorn, tel. 455-2284, is open daily 9-5 May-Sept., no charge. It houses exhibits on the Sheepeater Indians and various cultural artifacts, plus displays on ranch life, fossils, natural history, and the tie hacks. Just west of Dubois is a signed turnoff to a **scenic overlook**. The gravel road climbs sharply (no RVs) for approximately a mile to this point, where signs note the surrounding peaks. Marvelous views of 11,635-foot Ramshorn Peak from here. **Rocky Mountain bighorn sheep** crowd the Dubois area in the winter. Many are visible on the hills just south of town, with hundreds more gathered in the Whiskey Basin Habitat Area, five miles east (see p. 202).

The historic **Welty's General Store**, 113 W. Ramshorn, tel. 455-2377, was built in 1889. The real surprise inside is a Colt .44 with "Butch Cassidy" carved in the handle. The gun was found by Dubois rancher Leon Warnock in 1936 while hunting in the Wind River Mountains. Rock hounds will find all sorts of petrified wood, agates, and other colorful rocks up the Wiggins Fork and Horse Creek drainages; ask at the chamber of commerce for directions.

Accommodations
Dubois makes an excellent stopping point on the way to Yellowstone and Grand Teton national parks, with lodging prices far below those in Jackson Hole. See the chart (following page) for Dubois area motels and lodges. Ten different

DUBOIS ACCOMMODATIONS

Motel	Address	Telephone	Rate	Features
Red Rock Motel	3 miles east	455-2337	$20 s, $22 d	quiet location
The Line Shack	13 miles west	455-3232	$20 s, $25 d	rustic
Twin Pines Lodge & Motel lodge	218 Ramshorn	455-2600	$23+ s, $25+ d	cabins, historic
Trail's End Motel	511 Ramshorn	455-2540	$24+ s or d	AAA approved, pool, cabins, open May-Sept.
Branding Iron Motel	401 Ramshorn	455-2893 (800) 341-8000	$24 s, $28 d	AAA approved, cabins, kitchenettes, jacuzzi
Stagecoach Motor Inn	103 Ramshorn	455-2303	$25+ s, $32+ d	AAA approved, pool, kitchenettes, very nice
Wind River Motel	519 W. Ramshorn	455-2611	$26 s, $30 d	open May-Sept.
Black Bear Country Inn	505 W. Ramshorn	455-2344 (800) 873-2327	$30 s, $32 d	AAA approved, kitchenettes, jacuzzi
Rendezvous Motel	1 mile west	455-2844	$35 s, $40 d	
Geyser Creek B&B	4 miles west	455-2702	$50 s, $65 d	very nice

dude ranches are also found in the area. The closest public campground is **Horse Creek Campground** ($5; open June-Oct.), located 12 miles north of Dubois on Horse Creek Road. **Circle-Up Camper Court**, 225 W. Welty, tel. 455-2238, charges $10 for tents (some shade) and $15 for RVs. Tipis are $15; they sleep up to six. Non-campers may use the showers here for $3. Open mid-April to mid-Nov., this is one of Wyoming's nicer private campgrounds.

Food
Ziggy's Whisker Pete's Cafe, 318 W. Ramshorn, tel. 455-2656, is the place to go for breakfasts; be sure to get the country hash browns. **Cowboy Cafe**, 115 E. Ramshorn, tel. 455-2595, also has good breakfasts with big helpings of biscuits and gravy. For a real artery-clogger, try the steak and eggs. For lunchtime sandwiches, homemade soups, and salads, head to **Wild West Deli**, 128 E. Ramshorn, tel. 455-3354. The **Pizza Pub**, 308 S. 1st, tel. 455-3480, has tolerable Mexican food (everything seems to be deep fried), and much better pizzas. Open

summers only. **Village Cafe**, 515 W. Ramshorn, tel. 455-2122, is an interesting place, offering donuts and coffee in the mornings and steak dinners each evening. Both **Ramshorn Inn**, 202 E. Ramshorn, tel. 455-2400, and the **Rustic Pine Steakhouse**, 119 E. Ramshorn, tel. 455-2772, serve good charbroiled steaks and seafood, along with a Sunday smorgasbord. **The Line Shack**, eight miles west and then five miles up Union Pass Rd., tel. 455-3232, is a popular place for Friday or Saturday night all-you-can-eat prime rib and shrimp dinners ($12). **Red Rock Lodge**, 13 miles east of Dubois, tel. 455-2944, has Friday night prime rib specials. Get groceries at **Ramshorn Food Farm**, 610 W. Ramshorn. For outstanding fresh-baked pastries, breads, and tasty hardtack (made from a special Swedish recipe), be sure to stop by **Circle-Up Camper Court**, 225 W. Welty, tel. 455-2238.

Entertainment
Dubois is a hopping place during the summer, especially on weekends. **Outlaw Saloon**, 204

W. Ramshorn, tel. 455-2387, often has rock tunes, while both **Ramshorn Inn**, 202 E. Ramshorn, tel. 455-2400, and **Rustic Pine**, 119 E. Ramshorn, tel. 455-2430, offer C&W bands. The Rustic Pine also has square dancing on Tuesday nights in July and August. This classic Western bar has elk and moose heads, plenty of old wood, and a pool table. Check out the ash trays that note, "God spends his vacation here." Dudes from local ranches often invade Dubois one night of the week; ask around if you don't want to be overwhelmed with visitors.

Events
The Dubois calendar of events kicks off in early May with the **Tie Hack Dinner**, a smorgasbord of Swedish cookery. Later that month, Dubois hosts a series of enjoyable cowboy **Pack Horse Races**. An **Old Time Country Fair** arrives in early July, with a street dance, ice cream social, carnival, parade, and rubber-ducky races down the river. The bars stay open all night long. A few days later comes **Tie Hack Days** with tie hack exhibitions, demonstrations of butter churning and soap making, and other activities. Two mountain man rendezvous take place during the summer. In early June the **Little Fawn Rendezvous** is for kids only, and includes tipi living and frontier skills training. **Whiskey Mountain Buckskinners Wind River Rendezvous** in mid-August is for the oldsters and includes some impressive black-powder marksmanship contests. Don't miss the Dubois firemen's buffalo BBQ during rendezvous weekend.

Recreation
There is a nine-hole **golf course** on the western end of Dubois. The Absarokas and Wind River Mountains around Dubois are extremely popular with snowmobilers during the winter months, and several places rent 'biles in town. Most of the activity centers around **The Line Shack**, eight miles west and then five miles up Union Pass Rd., tel. 455-3232. You can rent snowmobiles here ($80-100/day), stay in the motel ($30 s or $35 d), and get meals at the restaurant. More than 100 miles of trails head out in all directions. Another base of operations is **Diamond Bar E Ranch**, 15 miles west of Dubois, tel. 455-3415. Snowmobile rentals are available, and lodging is $40 s or $64 d including

breakfast and dinner. **Cross-country skiers** find trails near Falls Campground and Brooks Lake (both 23 miles west of town), and Togwotee Mountain Lodge (40 miles west), along with an enormity of backcountry areas off limits to snowmobiles.

Information And Services
The **Dubois Chamber of Commerce**, 616 W. Ramshorn, tel. 455-2556, is open daily 8-7, May-Aug., and Mon.-Fri. 9-5 the rest of the year. Check here for a listing of local horsepacking outfitters, and about the "pony express" mail service run by a local boy. Also ask for a map showing old logging flumes, tie hack cabins, and other historic structures. Stop by the **Forest Service Ranger Station** at 209 E. Ramshorn, tel. 455-2466, for maps of Shoshone and Bridger-Teton national forests ($2) and info on local trails. See "Bighorn Basin," p.328, for more on the Washakie Wilderness. See p. 212, for more on the Fitzpatrick Wilderness. **Trapline Gallery**, 120 E. Ramshorn, tel. 455-2800, sells Indian-crafted beadwork, jewelry, and artwork, as well as furs. **Water Wheel Gift Shop**, 113 E. Ramshorn, tel. 455-2112, has a small selection of regional books.

DUBOIS VICINITY

Anyone who loves the outdoors will discover an abundance of pleasures around Dubois. There is good fishing in the Wind River (rainbow, cutthroat, brown, and brook trout) or in the many alpine lakes (generally rainbow, brook, and Mackinaw trout), plus lots of deer, elk, and bighorn sheep. Hikers and horsepackers will find hundreds of miles of Forest Service trails in the area. Photographers love the brilliantly colored badlands that frame Dubois on both the east and west sides. And each winter, hundreds of 'bilers climb on their sleds and cross-country skiers strap on their boards to enter the world of deep powder in the Absarokas. The map on p. 180 shows attractions in the Dubois area.

Horse Creek Area
Horse Creek Rd. heads north from Dubois, providing scenic views of the Absarokas. **Horse Creek Campground** ($5; open June-Oct.) is 12 miles north. Forest Rd. 504 continues an-

other five miles, providing access to the Washakie Wilderness via Horse Creek Trail. Forest Rd. 508 splits off near Horse Creek Campground and leads another 17 miles to **Double Cabin Campground** ($5; open June-October). Several trails head into the wilderness from here; most popular are Frontier Creek Trail and the Wiggins Fork Trail. You'll find remnants of a petrified forest six miles up the Frontier Creek Trail, but they have been rather picked over by collectors. (It's illegal to remove petrified wood from a wilderness area.) For other Washakie Wilderness trails info, ask at the Dubois Ranger Station.

Union Pass

The first road across the Absarokas headed through Union Pass, southwest of Dubois. The pass forms a divide between the waters of the Columbia, Colorado, and Mississippi rivers, and marks the boundary between the Absaroka, Wind River, and Gros Ventres mountain ranges. Nearby is an interpretive exhibit and nature trail through a flower-filled meadow. Union Pass Rd. (gravel) leaves U.S. 26-287 approximately nine miles northwest of Dubois, and climbs across to connect with State 352 north of Pinedale. A side road takes off from the Union Pass Rd. a couple of miles up and heads along Warm Springs Creek to the Forest Service's **Warm Springs Campground** ($5), eventually re-connecting with U.S. 26-287 near the **Sheridan Creek Campground** ($5). The remains of an old tie hack logging flume are visible near here and the warm springs (85° F) flow into the creek.

OVER TOGWOTEE PASS

The enjoyable drive west from Dubois first cuts through the colorful badlands, playing tag with the Wind River as it begins a long ascent to 9,644-foot Togwotee Pass, (pronounced TOE-go-tee). The pass is named for a subchief under Chief Washakie. Togwotee was one of the last independent Sheepeater Indians (a branch of the Shoshones), and the man who guided a U.S. government exploratory expedition over this pass in 1873. He even guided President Chester Arthur on his month-long visit to Yellowstone in 1883. Togwotee Pass is one of the most scenic drives imaginable, with Ramshorn Peak peeking down from the north for several

miles, until the road plunges into dense lodgepole forests (Shoshone National Forest) with lingering glimpses of the Pinnacles. At the crest it emerges into grass, willow, and flower-bedecked meadows with Blackrock Creek winding through. Whitebark pine and Engelmann spruce trees cover the nearby slopes. As the highway drops down the eastern side (Bridger-Teton National Forest), another marvelous mountain range—the Tetons—dominates the horizon in dramatic fashion. There is snow along the roadsides until early July; notice the high posts along the road used by wintertime snowplows. Togwotee Pass is a complete shock after all the miles of sagebrush and grassland that control the heartland of Wyoming. It is like entering another world, a world of cool, forested mountains and lofty peaks instead of the arid land, with vistas reaching to the horizon.

Pinnacle Buttes Area

Dominating the view along U.S. 26-287 for perhaps 15 miles are the Pinnacle Buttes. Twenty-three miles west of Dubois, you come to the turnoff to Brooks Lake, elevation 9,100 feet. Take it, even if you don't plan on camping here. A five-mile gravel road leads to the cliff-rimmed lake, and a clear creek flows east and south from here. The Forest Service maintains two excellent **campgrounds** ($5, open mid-June through Sept.) along the lake shore. Facing the lake is historic Brooks Lake Lodge (see below). Back on the main highway, you'll want to stop at **Falls Campground** ($6; open mid-June to early Sept.), where Brooks Creek tumbles into a deep canyon. Reservations ($6 extra) may be made for campsites here by calling (800) 283-2267. In wintertime, cross-country skiers will find an easy ski trail (signed but not groomed) that heads out two miles from here. Wind River Lake is another five miles up the hill, just below the pass. It's a gorgeous place for picnics, with deep blue water and the sharp cliffs of Pinnacle Buttes behind.

Mountain Lodges

Diamond Bar E Ranch, 15 miles west of Dubois, tel. 455-3415, has rustic cabins starting for $20 s or $25 d, and B&B accommodations for $65 d. RV sites are $12. In the summer, most visitors stay by the week at the dude ranch here. **Pinnacle Motor Lodge**, 20 miles west of Dubois on U.S. 26-287, has rooms starting for $29 s or $35 d. There are also RV campgrounds at two other dude ranches: **Rawhide Ranch**, 14 miles west of Dubois, tel. 455-2407, and **Triangle C Ranch** (once a tie hack camp), 18 miles west of Dubois, tel. 455-2225.

Brooks Lake Lodge, tel. 455-2121, provides some of the most incredible scenery in Wyoming, with both Brooks Lake and the Pinnacles for a backdrop. The main hall (on the National Register of Historic Places) is filled with big-game trophies from all over the world. Built in 1922, this classic Western lodge served travelers en route to Yellowstone. It was completely restored in the late 1980s. The lodge is 23 miles west of Dubois and then five miles in from U.S. 26-287 along the Brooks Lake road. It's open mid-June to mid-Sept. and then mid-Dec. to mid-April. During the summer, lodging costs $125/day pp, including meals, horseback rides, canoes, and guided fishing. Cabins are $20 pp extra. Come winter, Brooks Lake Lodge is a popular ski-in or snowmobile-in destination for lunch or evening cocktails. Overnight winter accommodations ($100 pp including breakfast and dinner) are available, along with special all-inclusive weekend packages for $425 per couple. See "Jackson Hole and the Tetons," p. 234 for info on Togwotee Mountain Lodge, a few miles west of Brooks Lake.

WIND RIVER MOUNTAINS

The Wind River Mountains begin near South Pass and continue 100 miles northwest to Union Pass, forming part of America's Continental Divide backbone. The range is visible for more than a hundred miles across the sagebrush country of central and southwestern Wyoming, its rugged snowcapped peaks gleaming in the light. The Shoshones traversed this range each spring and fall, and Sheepeater Indians hunted in the high country, but to most of the white pioneers whose wagon trains rolled across South Pass, the peaks represented a forbidding, mysterious place. In 1868, writer James Chisholm offered a description of the range that still rings true today:

I think the best inspired painter that ever drew would fail in attempting to describe these mighty mountains. He may convey correctly enough an impression of their shape, their vast extent and sublime beauty. But there is a something always left out which escapes all his colors and all his skill. Their aspects shift and vary continually. Their very shapes seem to undergo a perpetual transformation like the clouds above them. There is a mystery like the mystery of the sea—a silence not of death but of eternity.

Today, the Wind River Mountains are considered Wyoming's premier backpacking area, offering perhaps 800 miles of trails. Much of the country is well above timberline, with glacially carved mountains and countless small lakes.

Mountain climbers enjoy practicing moves on thousands of granitic precipices representing all degrees of difficulty. The Winds contain Gannett Peak—at 13,804 feet it's the tallest in Wyoming—along with all but one of the state's 15 other highest peaks. There are over 150 glaciers in the Winds, including seven of the 10 largest glaciers in the lower 48. All of these formed during the Little Ice Age between A.D. 1400 and 1850. The glaciers that actually carved these mountains were far larger, so massive in fact, that they covered the mountaintops to great depths and spilled over to create the hanging valleys, cirques, alpine lakes, U-shaped valleys, and steep cliffs of today.

Three different Forest Service wilderness areas cap these mountains; largest is Bridger Wilderness on the western side of the Continental Divide (in Bridger-Teton National Forest), with Popo Agie and Fitzpatrick Wilderness areas east of the crest (in Shoshone National Forest). Add in the BLM's Scab Creek Wilderness for a total of more than 735,000 roadless acres. The lower elevations of the Wind Rivers are also national forest lands, but are managed for other purposes, primarily timber-harvesting and grazing. On the northeast border is the Wind River Reservation which includes some of the high mountain country, but access is restricted. Contact the **Tribal Fish and Game Office** in Fort Washakie, tel. 332-7207, to purchase a limited hiking, fishing, and camping permit.

Wildlife

Most of the streams and larger lakes in the Winds have been planted with rainbow, cutthroat, California golden, brook, German brown, or Mackinaw trout, along with grayling and mountain whitefish. Although grizzlies no longer roam these mountains, black bears are still here (mainly below treeline), and food should always be hung out of their reach. Actually other creatures—mosquitoes—are more likely to be a problem. Be sure to bring insect repellant during July and August when they are at their worst. Other critters you're likely to see include bighorn sheep, moose, elk, mule deer, and coyotes. Pikas and yellow-bellied marmots are common in the high-country boulder fields.

Access

Three highways circle the Wind River Range: U.S. 26-287 on the northeast, U.S. 191 on the southwest, and State 28 on the southeast. (See p. 180.)The mountains are traversed by only one road, the gravel Union Pass Road. Most people cross the relatively gentle southern slopes at South Pass or over Togwotee Pass to the northeast. Access to the three wilderness areas can be gained from either side, but the high passes and long distances keep many hikers on one side or the other. See descriptions of the three different wilderness areas (below) for specific access points.

Most trails in the Winds are relatively free of snow by late June and remain so until mid-October, but the high passes may not open until mid-July. Be prepared for afternoon thunderstorms and the possibility of snow at any time in this mountain country; night temperatures can drop below freezing even in midsummer. Be aware that there is not a lot of wood in many parts of the Winds, so be sure to bring a gas stove to cook on. In addition, wood fires are prohibited at many of the most heavily used sites.

Unlike the mountain country farther north, most of the people who head into the Winds do so on foot rather than atop a horse. Horses are used by a quarter of the people, and "spot-packing" (in which horses bring in supplies for base camps but everyone hikes in on foot) is a popular way to get into the backcountry without carrying everything on your back. Many outfitters offer these services; check with nearby chambers of commerce. Permits are not required within the Winds except for commercial groups or those using stock. **Lander Llama Co.**, 327 Washington St. in Lander, tel. 332-5624, provides guided llama trips into the Popo Agie Wilderness, as well as the Absarokas near Dubois. For something even more unusual, **Wind River Rent-A-Goat**, Box 250, Rt. 62 in Lander, provides goat-packing trips.

More Info

Forest Service ranger stations in Lander (Popo Agie Wilderness), Dubois (Fitzpatrick Wilderness), and Pinedale (Bridger Wilderness) can provide information for their respective areas. An area map ($2) of Southern Shoshone National Forest covers the Fitzpatrick and Popo Agie wilderness areas, while a Pinedale Area map ($2) covers the Bridger Wilderness. These maps are available at most Forest Service offices in Wyoming.

Briefly described below are a number of the most popular hikes. There are literally hundreds of possible treks one can take in the Winds, so don't think these are your only options. In fact, if you want to avoid the crowds, you should probably pick up a few topo maps and discover your own trails. Finis Mitchell's *Wind River Trails* (Wasatch Publications, Salt Lake City) is a folksy, inexpensive guide by a man who has hiked this country since 1909. Mitchell personally planted trout in dozens of high country lakes during the 1930s, and even has a mountain named for him. Pick up this guide if you plan to do any fishing. *Climbing and Hiking in the Wind River Mountains* by Joe Kelsey (Sierra Club Books, San Francisco) has accurate information on most of the hiking trails, and describes hundreds of technical climbs. Topographic maps are available from sporting goods stores in the surrounding towns. The most up-to-date Wind River Mountains maps are from Earthwalk Press, 2239 Union St., Eureka, CA 95501, and can be found in most area bookstores and sporting goods shops.

GREEN RIVER LAKES AREA

The long drive to Green River Lakes is one of the most popular getaways in the Wind River Mountains. The road parallels the Green River

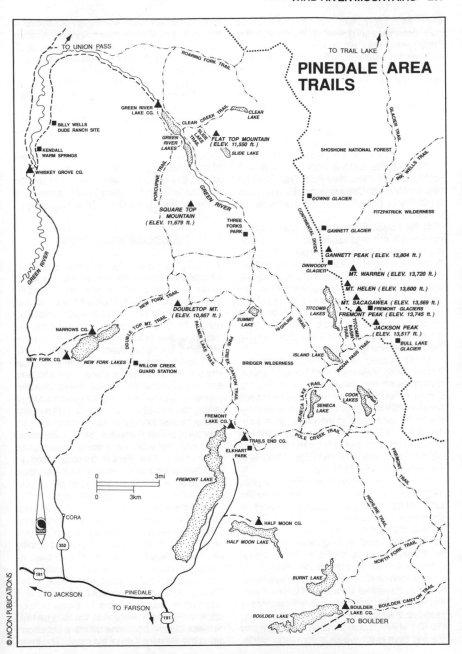

TO UNION PASS

ROARING FORK TRAIL

PINEDALE AREA TRAILS

TO TRAIL LAKE

BILLY WELLS DUDE RANCH SITE

GREEN RIVER LAKE CG.

CLEAR CREEK TRAIL

CLEAR LAKE

GLACIER TRAIL

KENDALL WARM SPRINGS

CLEAR LAKE

SLIDE LAKE TRAIL

FLAT TOP MOUNTAIN (ELEV. 11,550 ft.)

SHOSHONE NATIONAL FOREST

WHISKEY GROVE CG.

GREEN RIVER LAKES

SLIDE LAKE

INK WELLS TRAIL

PORCUPINE TRAIL

SQUARE TOP MOUNTAIN (ELEV. 11,679 ft.)

THREE FORKS PARK

DOWNS GLACIER

FITZPATRICK WILDERNESS

GREEN RIVER

CONTINENTAL DIVIDE

GANNETT GLACIER

GANNETT PEAK (ELEV. 13,804 ft.)

DINWOODY GLACIER

MT. WARREN (ELEV. 13,720 ft.)

NEW FORK TRAIL

DOUBLETOP MT. (ELEV. 10,867 ft.)

MT. HELEN (ELEV. 13,600 ft.)

MT. SACAGAWEA (ELEV. 13,569 ft.)

FREMONT GLACIERS

SUMMIT LAKE

TITCOMB LAKES

FREMONT PEAK (ELEV. 13,745 ft.)

TITCOMB BASIN TRAIL

JACKSON PEAK (ELEV. 13,517 ft.)

NARROWS CG.

DOUBLE TOP MT. TRAIL

PINE CREEK CANYON TRAIL

HIGHLINE TRAIL

BULL LAKE GLACIER

NEW FORK CG.

NEW FORK LAKES

PALMER LAKE TRAIL

ISLAND LAKE

INDIAN PASS TRAIL

WILLOW CREEK GUARD STATION

BRIDGER WILDERNESS

SENECA LAKE TRAIL

SENECA LAKE

COOK LAKES

FREMONT LAKE CG.

TRAILS END CG.

POLE CREEK TRAIL

FREMONT TRAIL

ELKHART PARK

CORA

FREMONT LAKE

352

HALF MOON CG.

HALF MOON LAKE

HIGHLINE TRAIL

191

TO JACKSON

PINEDALE

TO FARSON

191

BURNT LAKE

NORTH FORK TRAIL

BOULDER LAKE CG.

BOULDER CANYON TRAIL

BOULDER LAKE

TO BOULDER

0 — 3mi
0 — 3km

© MOON PUBLICATIONS

as it drifts first northward, then makes a U-turn to meander across southwestern Wyoming, eventually joining the Colorado River in Utah. Willows line the riverbanks in this open valley, while sagebrush and aspen cover the hills. Cattle and horses graze on the lush grasses. Get to Green River Lakes by heading to **Cora** (six miles west of Pinedale), and then north on State 352. Little Cora has a delightful old log general store. The first 26 miles of the road to Green River Lakes are paved and kept plowed all winter. Approximately 15 miles up, a sign points the way to **New Fork Lake**, located four miles away on a cobblestone (!) road. **New Fork Trail** takes off from the **Narrows Campground** ($5; open June to mid-Sept.), providing one of many routes into the Winds.

At the Forest Service border, state maintenance ends and the road becomes gravel, getting rougher as you go the remaining 18 miles. Watch the weather, since this upper portion can become a quagmire after heavy rains. The fantastic scenery makes the trip worthwhile, despite the washboarded conditions. Look for some enormous "erratic" boulders a couple of miles up the road from here, evidence of the glaciers that once scoured this valley, carrying the boulders along with them.

Approximately three miles beyond the Bridger-Teton National Forest border, a gravel road splits off and heads over Union Pass to Dubois. Although this route was used by Indians and mountain men, today it probably sees more use by snowmobiles in the winter than summertime cars. The Forest Service's **Whiskey Grove Campground** ($5; open mid-June to mid-Sept.) is just across the bridge at the site of the old logging town of Kendall.

Back on Green River Lakes Rd., you pass **Kendall Warm Springs** 1½ miles above the turnoff to the campground, its 85° F waters issuing from a few hundred feet up the hill. This is the only place in the world where the Kendall dace can be found. Fully grown, they are just two inches long, or, as the Forest Service notes, shorter than their scientific name (*Rhinichthys osculus thermalis*). The water drops over a 12-foot-high travertine terrace into Green River. The terrace has been built up over thousands of years, at the same time the river was cutting into its banks, thus separating these fish and allowing them to survive away from larger preda-

tors. To protect them, wading is not allowed in the waters of Kendall Warm Springs. Another two miles up the road are the log and red sandstone remains of the **Gros Ventre Lodge**, one of Wyoming's first dude ranches.

The road ends at the popular **Green River Lake Campground** ($5; open mid-June to mid-September). Weekends and the July 4th holiday may fill the campground to overflowing. A number of other unofficial campsites are just off the road below the lake. **Square Top Mountain** stares back across the lake, one of the most photographed spots in Wyoming. It is especially beautiful at sunrise when the water is calm and the first light catches its cliff faces. See below for trails in the Green River Lakes area.

BRIDGER WILDERNESS

The 428,169-acre Bridger Wilderness reaches 90 miles along the western side of the Wind River Mountains, encompassing 27 active glaciers, 1,300 alpine lakes, and 600 miles of trails. It is named for famed mountain man and guide, Jim Bridger, and was first designated a "primitive area" in 1931, gaining wilderness status with the original Wilderness Act of 1964. Despite this status, a considerable amount of sheep grazing still takes place in the southern end of the Bridger Wilderness; it was "grandfathered-in" with the wilderness legislation. We're talking close to 20,000 sheep in the wilderness. These "hoofed locusts" or "range maggots" (pick your term) pollute the waters, trample the meadows, and leave behind a barren overgrazed moonscape. The Forest Service office in Pinedale has been notoriously lax in enforcing controls on high-country grazing by sheep, and shows little signs of changing its ways.

Unlike sheep, humans must camp at least 200 feet from lakes or trails in the wilderness. Bridger Wilderness has special regulations that prohibit campfires in seven of the most heavily used areas between July 1 and Labor Day, including those around Green River Lakes, Island Lake, Big Sandy Lake, and Cirque of the Towers. Pick up a map showing the sites and listing other regulations from the Forest Service office in Pinedale. Access to the Bridger Wilderness comes from nine different entrances along the western side of the range. The three most popular points of entry are described below, along with a number of the favorite trails. If you're looking for solitude, you may want to avoid these popular paths.

Green River Lakes Trails
Easily the most scenic entry into the Winds is from Green River Lakes, located on the end of a paved-then-dirt road that leads north from Cora. (See "Pinedale Vicinity," p. 186, for sights along the Green River Lakes Road.) The road ends at a campground ($5) facing onto Lower Green River Lake, where the unforgettable 11,679-foot summit of Square Top Mountain dominates the view.

For an easy five-mile day hike, follow the trails that circle Lower Green River Lake (Highline Trail on the east and Lakeside Trail on the west). Excellent views of Flat Top Mountain (not to be confused with Square Top Mountain) from the Lakeside Trail, and of the Clear Creek Falls along the Highline Trail. Keep your eyes open for moose and osprey. An interesting side trip is the short hike to Upper Green River Lake where Square Top proves even more startling. Another side trip heads up **Clear Creek Trail**—it takes off from the southeastern end of Lower Green River Lake, climbs two miles to a natural bridge, and then continues an equal distance to Clear Lake. Some of this country was burned in a 1988 fire. Flat Top is relatively easy to climb; see Finis Mitchell's Wind River Trails for the route.

Those interested in longer hikes will find several trails in the Green River Lakes area. **Roaring Fork Trail** climbs up to Faler Lake, 14 miles away, and 2,200 feet higher. The **Highline Trail** follows the northeast shore of Lower Green River Lake and then continues south to the uppermost headwaters of the Green River. From there, the trail stays in the alpine much of the way to its destination at the Big Sandy Trailhead on the southern end of the Bridger Wilderness. The total distance is 72 miles, but few people actually follow this path that far, preferring to branch off to other sights. Another popular trek is up **Porcupine Trail** to Porcupine Pass and then down **New Fork Trail** to New Fork Lake (a total of approximately 17 miles). Porcupine Trail begins at the upper end of Lower Green River Lake, splitting off from Lakeside Trail.

Elkhart Park Trails
Elkhart Park Trailhead lies at the end of a 15-mile-long paved road that heads northeast from Pinedale along the east shore of Fremont Lake. During the summer, the Forest Service generally has someone here to answer questions. There is a campground here, too ($5). An overlook provides excellent vistas over Fremont Lake and Bridger Wilderness, with a big parking area that fills with cars in July and August.

Trails head out from Elkhart in two directions. **Pine Creek Canyon Trail** heads north, providing a relatively direct connection with Summit Lake (13 miles) and then down into Green River Lakes (30 miles total). The main drawback with this trail is that it loses 2,000 feet by dropping into Pine Creek Canyon, elevation that must be regained to reach Summit Lake. Also note that Summit Lake has outfitters' camps that distinctly lessen the area's remote aura. A nice loop can be made by heading east from Summit Lake along the Highline Trail to Elbow Lake and Seneca Lake, where you follow the Seneca Lake and Pole Creek trails back to Elkhart Park. This loop takes you through some of the more scenic areas in the wilderness, and covers approximately 31 miles.

The most popular destination from Elkhart is **Titcomb Basin.** Access from Elkhart Park is via a series of connected trails: the Pole Creek, Seneca Lake, Indian Pass, and Titcomb Basin trails. Many hikers and climbers overnight at Island Lake, making for very crowded conditions much of the summer. It is 15 miles from Elkhart Park to Upper Titcomb Lake, a mountain cirque with abundant wildflowers. The lakes have been planted with golden trout. A side hike goes up through gorgeous Indian Basin to Indian Pass (three miles). Mountaineers can then descend to the Knife Point and Bull Lake glaciers within the Popo Agie Wilderness.

The valley above Titcomb Basin is open, giving climbers access to the west side of a whole row of peaks, including Mt. Helen (13,620), Mt. Sacagawea (13,569 feet), Jackson Peak (13,517 feet), and **Fremont Peak** (13,745 feet). The last two can be climbed without technical expertise, although Fremont does require some rough scrambling in places. It is most easily climbed from the southwest side; see a topographic map to find the route. There are many outstanding opportunities for those with greater expertise to try their skills on the cliff faces here.

Fremont Peak is named for **John C. Fré-mont,** the son-in-law of Senator Thomas Hart Benton, the biggest promoter of the "Manifest Destiny" that would lead Americans all the way to the Pacific. Because of this familial association, Frémont was given the task of exploring and mapping the western territories, work that brought him the nickname, the "Great Pathfinder." Some of his ventures—such as floating through the wild waters of Fremont Canyon on the North Platte River, or crossing the Rockies in the dead of winter—were downright stupid, and his guides tried to stop him. Frémont's best asset was his wife who painted his adventures in such a heroic light that his presidential ambitions were nearly realized.

In 1842, Frémont and his men climbed what appeared to be the highest mountain in the Wind River Range, a summit they called Snow Peak, now Fremont Peak. From the west, it is obvious why Frémont and his men would mistake this for the highest: Gannett Peak (59 feet taller) is barely visible from a distance, hidden behind other summits. It was not until years later that the mistake was discovered.

Big Sandy Trails

One of the most popular entry points into the Bridger Wilderness is from Big Sandy Trailhead. Access is from a number of different directions (see map, p. 213), but all require long stretches of gravel road. Easiest access is from the north. From the town of Boulder, take State 353 where it turns west off U.S. 191 and follow it till it turns to gravel (16 miles). Bear left at the intersection a half mile up, and go another nine miles to another junction (signed) where you again turn left and go seven more miles to the turnoff (left) to the Forest Service's Dutch Joe Guard Station and then on to Big Sandy Opening. The road ends at **Big Sandy Campground** (free; open mid-June to mid-Sept.), where the trails begin. The Forest Service generally has someone stationed here.

Big Sandy Lodge is just to the left near the end of the road, and provides guided trail rides ($50/day) and rustic cabins ($35). The historic lodge (built in 1929) contains a trophy-filled lounge and two stone fireplaces. Spot-pack trips are $50/day, while guided-pack trips cost $100/

day. Write the lodge at Box 223, Boulder, WY 82923, for more info and reservations.

A maze of trails depart from Big Sandy Opening. The **Highline Trail** heads north, extending across the Bridger Wilderness to Green River Lakes, and continuing from there to Union Pass, a hundred miles away. The trail connects with numerous other paths, including **Shadow Lake Trail,** a 2½-mile route to this alpine lake. More adventurous types can continue up through Texas Pass and down to Lonesome Lake in the Cirque of the Towers, a distance of 15 miles. Another side route off the Highline Trail is the **Washakie Trail,** a path used by this famous Shoshone chief during his people's biannual migration between the Wind River Valley and the Green River country. This trail goes into the Washakie Lakes area of the Popo Agie Wilderness, where you can connect with the Bears Ears Trail (see below).

The most popular trail out of Big Sandy Opening is **Big Sandy Trail,** a 5½-mile trek to crowded Big Sandy Lake, where it meets a spider web of trails and cairn-marked paths to other high-country lakes. Beyond the lake, **Big Sandy Pass Trail** climbs up North Creek over Big Sandy Pass (shown as Jackass Pass on some maps) before dropping into Lonesome Lake and Cirque of the Towers (total distance 8½ miles). Big Sandy Pass Trail is a long slog. A strenuous loop trip consists of the Big Sandy Trail-Big Sandy Pass Trail route combined with the Texas Pass-Shadow Lake Trail-Highline Trail route described above. Total distance is 24 miles.

FITZPATRICK WILDERNESS

The 198,838-acre Fitzpatrick Wilderness occupies the northeast side of the Wind River Mountains, sandwiched between the Bridger Wilderness just over the Continental Divide and the Wind River Indian Reservation to the east. The wilderness is a rugged landscape of rock and ice, with dozens of mountain lakes and cascading mountain brooks. Wyoming's highest mountain, Gannett Peak, forms part of the western border, and 44 active glaciers crowd against the summits; the largest covers 1,220 acres. The Fitzpatrick is a favorite of folks with considerable backpacking or mountaineering experience.

BIG SANDY AREA TRAILS

Although long maintained as a "primitive area," the Fitzpatrick Wilderness was officially established by Congress in 1976, and is named for Tom Fitzpatrick, a respected mountain man, guide, head of the Rocky Mountain Fur Company, Army scout, and Indian agent. To the Indians, he was "Broken Hand," a name received after he lost three fingers in a rifle accident while being pursued by Blackfeet Indians; despite this he still managed to kill two of his attackers.

Access
The primary entrance point into the Fitzpatrick Wilderness is from **Trail Lake**. Head four miles southeast from Dubois on U.S. 26-287 and turn right (south) onto a gravel road. The road leads into Whiskey Basin, with a rutted dirt road continuing to the left past a string of small lakes,

the last being Trail Lake. The trails begin here, 12 miles off the highway. (Note that the Cold Springs/Burris and St. Lawrence Basin trailheads mentioned in the Wind River Mountain guidebooks are now closed to the general public.) Forest Service regulations in the Fitzpatrick prohibit camping within 50 feet of trails or lakes. In addition, no campfires or horses are allowed at the confluence of Dinwoody and Knoll Lake creeks and the base of Dinwoody Glacier.

Trails
Three major trails lead from Trail Lake into the high country. The **Whiskey Mountain Trail** climbs over the peak of the same name and then on to heavily used Simpson Lake, a dozen miles away. From here it's possible for experienced hikers to continue over a pass above San-

dra Lake (another 3¹/₂ miles) and then down into the Roaring Fork drainage of the Bridger Wilderness. The **Bomber Basin Trail** leads from Trail Lake Trailhead to Bomber Lake, eight miles away and 2,600 feet higher, crossing the deep canyon created by Torrey Creek on a high bridge. The basin is named for a B-17 bomber that crashed here during WW II when its crew was practicing a strafing run on either a bear or bighorn sheep. The plane wreckage is still here. The upper portion of this trail (above Bomber Falls) is not maintained, but is passable.

A very popular moderately long hike is up **Glacier Trail** all the way to Dinwoody Glacier. It is a sweaty and difficult 23 miles, but passes lots of lakes and ruggedly beautiful alpine country. Bighorn sheep are often seen along the way. The first several miles are without water, so be sure to bring plenty with you. The trail ends at the glacier, providing access for mountaineers who want to scale 13,804-foot **Gannett Peak**, highest in Wyoming. (The peak is named for Henry Gannett, chief topographer for the Hayden Survey of the 1870s, and was first climbed in 1922 by Arthur Tate and Floyd Stahlnaker.) Because it is nearly surrounded by glaciers, most routes require roping up, particularly the popular one across the Gooseneck Glacier. (From the west side, there Is also a Class 3 gully scramble.) Many mountaineers come up this trail to climb Gannett and the cluster of peaks over 13,000 feet just to the south, including Mt. Woodrow Wilson, The Sphinx, Mt. Warren, Doublet Peak, and Turret Peak. See Joe Kelsey's *Climbing and Hiking in the Wind River Mountains* for details.

POPO AGIE WILDERNESS

The Popo Agie Wilderness is a 101,991-acre parcel of magnificent mountain real estate with jagged peaks, deep valleys, and more than 240 lakes. At least 20 peaks rise above 13,000 feet; Wind River Peak is the tallest at 13,225 feet. Popo Agie was first established as a primitive area in 1932, and enlarged and reclassified as wilderness in 1984. The Popo Agie is bounded to the west by the Bridger Wilderness and to the north by the Wind River Indian Reservation. Access to the Popo Agie Wilderness is generally from the east side in the Lander vicinity, although it is possible to cross the Continental Divide from the Bridger Wilderness. Camping is not allowed within 200 feet of trails, lakes, or streams.

Dickinson Park Access

The primary jumping off point into the Popo Agie Wilderness is the Dickinson Park area, northwest of Lander at an elevation of 9,300 feet. Get here by turning west on Moccasin Lake Rd. (paved) just south of Fort Washakie at the Hines Store. Stay right where the road turns to dirt and continue to Moccasin Lake/Dickinson Park junction, a total of 19 miles. Turn left here, and head another four miles to **Dickinson Creek Campground** ($5; open mid-June to mid-September). **Allen's Diamond Four Ranch**, tel. 332-2995, is here, offering a variety of trips, ranging from guided horsepacking trips to wagon rides (both $125/day). Many people opt for spot pack trips ($70/day). This is popular with those who want to hike while still enjoying the pleasures of a horse-packed base camp. The ranch also offers rustic cabin accommodations for $30 and up.

The Dickinson Park area has trailheads at the Dickinson Park Work Center and the Dickinson Creek Campground, a mile farther up the road. The **Bears Ears Trail** takes off from the work center, and climbs quickly into the alpine before going over Adams Pass. It passes Bears Ears Mountain (look for the "ears") and follows through the alpine before dropping into the lake-filled headwaters of the South Fork of the Little Wind River, 14 miles away. Along the way, are all sorts of connections to other trails, including a variety of loops. From the Dickinson Campground trailhead, the popular **Smith Lake Trail** heads south and then west to Smith and then Cathedral Lakes (eight miles). The **North Fork Trail** splits off the Smith Lake Trail approximately a quarter mile up. This trail will eventually (15 miles) take you straight to Lonesome Lake at the base of the soaring Cirque of the Towers. Unfortunately, the hike requires four different fordings of the North Fork of the Popo Agie River, a dangerous feat when the water is high. It's best to wait till late summer.

Loop Road Access

The Loop Rd. (State 131) cuts south from Lander through Sinks Canyon and then over the mountains to South Pass, providing a number of entry points into the Popo Agie Wilderness. (See "Lander," p. 186 for other sights along this interesting road.) **Middle Fork Trail** begins at **Bruce Picnic Ground**, 13 miles south of Lander on the Loop Rd., and follows the Middle Fork of the Popo Agie River upstream to Sweetwater Gap (16 miles), where you enter the Bridger Wilderness. Many people use this trail to reach the Cirque of the Towers area via the Pinto Park and North Fork trails (total one-way distance approximately 23 miles). The heavily used **Tayo Creek Trail** splits off from the Middle Fork Trail approximately 13 miles up, and continues another four miles to Tayo Lakes. **Sheep Bridge Trail** begins at **Worthen Reservoir**, 20 miles south of Lander on Loop Rd., and heads west for three miles to its junction with the Middle Fork Trail. Many people use this to cut distance and elevation off their trek into the Tayo Lake or Cirque of the Towers areas. (It starts 1,200 feet higher than the Middle Fork Trail.)

Cirque Of The Towers

This is one of the best-known and most visited places in the Wind River Mountains, an incredible semicircle of pinnacles at the headwaters of the North Fork of the Popo Agie River. **Lonesome Lake** is in the center, backdropped by peaks with such names as Warbonnet, Pingora, Sharks Nose, Camels Hump, Lizard Head, and Watch Tower. All of these are well known in the climbing community and attract folks from around the globe. Lonesome Lake is not so lonesome these days, and there is talk of restricting the number of hikers and climbers. On a typical day in early August you're likely to find a mini-town of tents. The water quality suffers from all these people. To lessen the visual impact, some hikers bivouac behind the larger boulders rather than pitching a tent. The most popular way to reach Cirque of the Towers is from the Big Sandy Opening Trailhead (see "Bridger Wilderness," below), but the longer North Fork Trail (described above) is also commonly used and does not require traversing any passes. The other popularly used route is the Sheep Bridge Trail (described above).

SOUTH PASS AREA

At the southern end of the Wind River Mountains, a broad, relatively gentle pass provides a corridor across the Continental Divide. This part of Wyoming is packed with history. Today, State 28 traverses South Pass, climbing south and then west from Lander, past scenic Red Canyon, and close to the almost-ghost towns of Atlantic City and South Pass, before starting the long descent into the Green River Basin and the junction town of Farson. Winters on the pass are long, cold, and windy—the snow fences stretch for miles along the highway.

Gold was first mined here during the middle 1860s, and a long series of booms and busts followed. For a brief time in 1867-68, the "Sweetwater Mines" attracted national attention, and thousands of men (and a few women) flocked to the area. The land was officially part of the Wind River Reservation at the time, but legalities didn't matter much when gold could be found. South Pass was ceded by the Shoshones in 1878. Prospectors still head out each spring in search of the elusive mother lode, and various schemes to reopen the old mines surface periodically. Today the area is enjoyed by thousands of tourists and others attracted by the rich historical and recreational opportunities.

Over The Pass

South Pass was first discovered by the game animals who traversed this country and the Indian hunters who followed them. The first whites to traipse through were the Astorians, fur traders led by Robert Stuart in 1812. The first wagon wheels rolled over South Pass in 1824, and between 1841 and 1866 more than 350,000 emigrants followed what had become the primary route west. Of all the sights along the Oregon Trail, South Pass must have been one of the most anticipated. West of here the waters flow to the Pacific Ocean, and the entire country became known as the Oregon Territory (hence the "Oregon Buttes" south of South Pass). Travelers took great pleasure in stopping at Pacific Springs, happy in the knowledge that its waters eventually reached the Pacific. An important stage and Pony Express Station stood here; some of the buildings from a later ranch are still standing.

Today, State 28 drapes a similar route across South Pass. Signboards denote various historic sites along the way. At the signboard that describes the Oregon Trail, a rough dirt road leads a mile back to the clear waters of Pacific Creek, where posts mark the historic route. Don't believe everything you read on the signs, however:

the "Parting of the Ways" monument actually marks the South Pass City-Green River stage road where it intersects the Oregon Trail rather than the famous point where the Sublette Cutoff took Oregon- and California-bound travelers west while Mormon voyagers (and others in need of supplies) diverged southwest to Fort Bridger. The true Parting of the Ways lies 10 miles southwest from this marker. The highway west to Farson rolls up and down the sage-carpeted hills, cutting straight as a carpenter's plumb line. To the north, the Wind River Mountains dominate, while to the south distant sand dunes become visible, part of the Red Desert country.

SOUTH PASS CITY

Located at 7,800 feet above sea level, South Pass City is one of Wyoming's highest settlements. Although commonly called a ghost town, the town never really died out. South Pass City is now a state historic site, providing one of the most interesting and authentic historical settings in the state.

Gold In The Hills

During the days of '49, many thousands of would-be miners streamed through South Pass on their way to California, little knowing that gold lay beneath their feet. Gold was first found in 1842, but its discoverer was killed by Indians; other miners faced similar fates. First to file a claim was Henry Reedal, who discovered what became known as the Carissa Lode in 1867. Shortly thereafter, the Miner's Delight Lode was discovered. The finds attracted an onslaught of miners, and by that fall the town of South Pass City had mushroomed to Wyoming's largest settlement; nearly 3,000 residents.

The discovery of gold at South Pass helped propel the effort to make Wyoming a territory separate from Dakota; a move that took place the following year. At its rip-roaring peak, there was even an effort to make South Pass the Wyoming Territorial capital. The town included six general stores, three butcher shops, several restaurants, two breweries, seven blacksmith shops, five hotels, and dozens of saloons and "sporting houses." The Carissa mine's shafts would eventually reach 400 feet down, and the mill would produce gold worth more than six

---

SINKS CANYON & SOUTH PASS AREA

287

789

TO FORT WASHAKIE & DUBOIS

TO HUDSON & RIVERTON

LANDER

131

POPO AGIE RIVER

TO JEFFREY CITY

SAWMILL CG.

SINKS CANYON S.P.

VISITOR CENTER

POPO AGIE FALLS TRAIL

POPO AGIE CG

SINKS CANYON CG

SWITCHBACK OVERLOOK

FALLS

FRYE LAKE

TABLE MOUNTAIN

SITE OF FIRST OIL WELL IN WYOMING

287

789

SHOSHONE

LITTLE POPO AGIE RIVER

RED CANYON

NATIONAL

FIDDLER'S LAKE

FIDDLER'S LAKE CG

LITTLE POPO AGIE CREEK CG

FOREST

LOUIS LAKE

LOUIS LAKE CG

LANDER CUTOFF

CONTINENTAL

ABANDONED U.S. STEEL MINE

BIG ATLANTIC GULCH CG

MINER'S DELIGHT

ATLANTIC CITY CG

FT. STAMBAUGH LOOP RD.

ATLANTIC CITY

CARISSA MINE

WILLIE HANDCART COMPANY MONUMENT

SOUTH PASS CITY STATE HIST. SITE

LEWISTON

28

DIVIDE

OREGON TRAIL

TO FARSON

OREGON BUTTES

0   4mi

0   4km

© MOON PUBLICATIONS

million dollars. But this was primarily hard rock mining requiring large capital investments and long hours. The lack of water in this arid country meant that placer mining was possible only in the spring, with summers spent toiling in the hard-rock mines for $5 a day.

The Sweetwater mines were a short-lived bubble that burst almost as quickly as it grew. Instead of the hoped-for mother lode, miners found only small pockets of gold. Within five years most of the miners gave up and moved away. By 1875, fewer than a hundred people remained. But South Pass City refused to die. There were more booms (followed by busts) in the 1880s, 1890s, 1930s, and 1960s. Miners still come to these hills in search of gold.

Women's Suffrage
Given the rough mining crowd that jammed the streets of South Pass City, it seems odd to find the town at the center of the effort to gain equal rights for women. In late 1869, the first territorial representative from South Pass City, William Bright, introduced a women's suffrage bill before the first territorial Legislature. It was a measure supported by his wife and a number of other South Pass women, but probably opposed by many of the local men. One of the most vehement opponents was another South Pass City resident and territorial legislator, Benjamin Sheeks. The measure surprised almost everyone by being passed and signed into law by Governor John Campbell. In anger, Benjamin Sheeks resigned his post as justice of the peace for South Pass City, only to be replaced by a woman, Esther Hobart Morris. She was the first woman judge in America. In her 8 1/2 months of service, Morris tried 26 cases, gaining recognition for her fairness, along with considerable national exposure.

A greater claim to fame for Morris as the "Mother of Women's Suffrage" is suspect. In 1869, she is supposed to have held a tea party in which the South Pass City women extracted a promise from then-candidate William Bright to introduce legislation granting women the right to vote. The tea party tale was concocted by her son (a newspaper editor) after her death, but gained entry into the history books as fact. A statue of Morris in front of the state capitol credits her with the bill. Morris herself never claimed any such thing, and in fact was not an active suffragist. According to Bright, the reason he introduced the legislation was not because of lobbying by local women but because, "If Negroes had the right to vote, women like his wife and mother should also."

South Pass Today
In 1965, South Pass City's buildings risked being carted off to southern California's Knott's Berry Farm theme park. With the help of "Flaming Mame" Alice Messick, a committee of Wyoming folks outbid the Californians for the buildings and managed to keep them. The following year, the state purchased the site and began the process of restoration. South Pass contains some 25 old buildings and 13,000 authentic artifacts, 90% of which actually came from the area. The buildings are open daily 9-6, May 15-Oct. 15, no charge. Call 332-3684 for details. The rest of the year, visitors can wander the streets and look in the windows, but many items are in storage. On summertime weekends the old town comes alive with gold-panning and blacksmithing demonstrations by costumed old-timers. Be sure to drop by the Morris cabin for fresh-baked cookies. The old-fashioned **4th of July** celebration at South Pass is great fun, with wagon rides, country dancing, a barbecue, exhibits, and lots of folks in old-time costumes. Bill Bates is here most summer days, offering 1 1/2-hour horseback rides ($20), complete with tall tales, cowboy poetry, and local history. Evening rides ($30) are longer and include a steak dinner. His company, **Trails West**, tel. 332-7801 or (800) 327-4052, also has two- to four-day wagon train treks ($250-$450) along the old Oregon Trail.

Head first to the **visitors center**—in what was once a South Pass store—for interpretive displays, old photos, and a video on the area's history. Pick up the brochure here that describes the buildings. Just to the west is the **Smith-Sherlock Store**, where you can check out the old items or buy licorice candy. Other interesting buildings that have been restored and furnished with original items include a blacksmith shop, butcher shop, hotel, miner's cabin, saloon, school, and dugout cave used to keep perishables cool. **Sweetwater County Jail**, built in 1870, is the oldest non military government building in Wyoming. The reconstructed **Esther Morris cabin** stands on the eastern end of the row of buildings. Out front is a granite marker from 1939 that credits her with originating women's suffrage. Next to it is a more recent disclaimer.

Just east from the Morris cabin is a half-mile-long **nature trail** along Willow Creek, with the chance to explore the Carie Shields Mine (it produced $35,000 worth of gold) and other mines, cabins, and mill sights. Be careful where you walk around these old structures. Along the creek you're likely to see all sorts of animals, from beavers to bighorn sheep, mule deer, and moose. The state also has a 10-km **volksmarch trail** for those who don't mind paying to hike. Look out for the little people, however. Indians told tales of these evil people (*nynymbi*) who could cause all sorts of problems for others, including shooting arrows at lone travelers. Sheepherders sometimes found themselves under a barrage of rocks from the dwarfs, and a few locals claim they still exist around South Pass. One must be careful not to step on their underground burrows.

ATLANTIC CITY

The funky little town of Atlantic City has dirt streets, old log and stone buildings, and a delightfully infectious country atmosphere. It's the sort of town where the old mercantile boasts "Museum Gals Steakhouse Bar Cabins," where many homes (and the church too) still have outhouses, and the big event is the volunteer fire department picnic (late August). Residents pile up cords and cords of firewood to make it through the long cold winters. The snow can get deep here near the top of the Continental Divide (elevation 7,660 feet). One winter, the drifts topped 27 feet and the snow plows didn't get in for several weeks! Most residents like the quiet beauty that winter brings to Atlantic City, depending upon snowmobiles and skis to get around. Note that groceries are not available in either Atlantic City or South Pass, so stock up elsewhere.

History

Atlantic City was formed in 1868 when gold mines had attracted thousands of miners to the Sweetwater Mining District. As miners arrived in South Pass, they spread out over the nearby country in search of other gold deposits, founding the settlements of Atlantic City, Miner's Delight, and Lewiston at promising locations. As with most frontier towns, saloons vastly outnumbered churches in early Atlantic City. The first county sheriff owned a local brothel! **Fort Stambaugh** was established a few miles to the east in 1870 to protect miners from Sioux and Arapaho raids. It lasted only to 1878, and the buildings were auctioned off in 1881.

In the 1880s, another mini-boom hit as French capitalist Emile Granier built a 25-mile-long ditch from the Wind River Mountains to Atlantic City for hydraulic mining. The effort failed when the money ran out before the gold could be found. Another boom hit in the late 1920s and '30s when a dredge worked its way down Rock Creek, leaving behind enormous piles of gravel. By the early 1960s, Atlantic City's population had been reduced to a handful of folks. Development of a U.S. Steel iron ore (taconite) strip mine nearby brought prosperity after 1962, but it too closed in 1983, leaving behind a gaping pit now filled with water. Atlantic City now depends upon tourism and summer homes. But as a local brochure notes, "The wind of this old gold town always whispers of another boom on its way."

Sights

Atlantic City's main attractions are its mining-era buildings, many dating from the turn of the century. **Atlantic City Mercantile** was built in 1893 out of adobe brick. Its false front is covered with old metal siding, while inside are dozens of historic photos and artifacts. Pick up a brochure inside describing the town's other historic buildings. The stone building a block to the east once housed the **McAuley Store**, later Hyde's Hall. Calamity Jane once provided the entertainment in the saloon here. Up the hill is **St. Andrews Episcopal Church**, a rustic old log church built in 1913. The **Gratrix Cabin**, a block east of the church, was built in the late 1860s and was home to Judge Buck Gratrix, a man who noted that he lived in three different counties, two territories, and one state while living in one place!

One of the most attractive structures in town is **Miner's Delight Inn**, a couple of old log buildings in mint condition. This was originally the Carpenter Hotel, built in 1904 and run as a boarding house for miners and others until 1961.

Rock Creek flows through Atlantic City, and on the west end of town the banks are lined with huge piles of boulders left behind by the gold dredging operations of the '30s.

Fort Stambaugh Rd. heads east from Atlantic City, following a 12-mile loop past the site of Fort Stambaugh (not marked) and the ghost town of Miner's Delight. A side road leads to **Lewiston**, another abandoned gold-mining town. The loop road is a very scenic drive with open grassland and scattered patches of young aspen and lodgepole. (The miners wiped out previous stands.) Antelope are sure to be seen along the way. **Miner's Delight** now consists of around a dozen log buildings in various states of decay. A small beaver pond and graveyard are also in Miner's Delight, with other old mining buildings visible just west of here.

The road west from Atlantic City to South Pass City passes more old gold mines, notably the **Duncan Mine** (two miles out) and the famous **Carissa Mine**, just before the road drops down to South Pass City. Most of the mines and buildings are on private land, and many contain hazardous structures and shafts without covers. Watch your step! A little over seven miles south of Atlantic City is a monument to the **Willie Handcart Company**. In 1856, a large group of Mormon emigrants led by James G. Willie, were caught in a series of early winter storms and camped here awaiting help and provisions from Salt Lake City. Sixty-seven of them died before they reached the promised land.

Practicalities
Atlantic City Mercantile, tel. 332-5143, has A-frame cabins that sleep six for $45. Open summers only. The bar here often has live music on Friday and Saturday nights, though it tends to be of the one-man-with-drum-machine-and-twangy-voice variety. The mirror behind the bar has a gunshot hole. The Merc's dinners are renowned throughout this part of Wyoming. In the front, munch on inexpensive but very good burgers, while back room guests are treated to an old-timey setting of oil lanterns and great aspen-grilled meats and seafood. A bit on the pricey side (entrées around $15), but worth it. Also in town is **Red Cloud Saloon,** which sometimes has live music. The big attraction here is the pool table. Next door is the mediocre **TNT Cafe,** where you get a dose of local gossip and

Calamity Jane

YELLOWSTONE NATIONAL PARK

dense cigarette smoke with your breakfast or lunch. **Miner's Delight Inn,** tel. 332-3513, provides antique-furnished rooms (twin beds) for $50 s or d including a continental breakfast. The six-course home-cooked dinners ($20) attract people from all over the country, although locals are less enthusiastic. Dinners are by reservation, and only during the summertime. Interested in trying a little prospecting? The **Old Hermit Gold Mine** south of Atlantic City provides tours of the underground mines and a chance to pan for gold in Rock Creek. For more info, stop by the **Old Rock Shop**, tel. 332-7396, on State 28 just north of South Pass City. The rock shop also has a cafe and bar. The BLM maintains two campgrounds ($4) in young aspen stands along the Fort Stambaugh Loop Rd.: **Atlantic City Campground** and **Big Atlantic Gulch Campground**. Big Atlantic Gulch doesn't have water.

FARSON AREA

Farson (pop. 320) stands at the busy highway junction where State 28 and U.S. 191 greet each other. Locals live in trailer homes—the modern version of log cabins—and work at a couple of local businesses. All around are long straight roads, flat sagebrush desert, a few irrigated pastures, and antelope. It's a long way from here to anywhere else, so almost everyone stops for a road break. In the simmering summer sun, **Farson Mercantile**, tel. 273-9511, is crowded with people buying ice cream cones to eat in the shade of the olive trees out front. The old brick two-story store is a classic country market. **Oregon Trail Cafe**, tel. 273-9631, is named for this historic trail that passed right through the center of Farson. It offers standard road grub, along with **Mitch's Cafe**, tel. 273-9606, where you're more likely to find locals. **Sitzman's Motel**, tel. 273-9246, charges just $21 s or $25 d.

Heading South

Four miles south of Farson is tiny **Eden**, where irrigated green fields bring the arid landscape alive. Of note here is the old **Oregon Trail Baptist Church**, with its brown log walls, quaint bell tower, and back window facing the Wind River Mountains. The view probably makes it hard to concentrate on the service. Kitty-corner across the road is the Eden Saloon where the view may not be as great, but after a few beers it really doesn't matter. South of Eden, U.S. 191 cruises into the bleak Bad Lands Hills country on its way to Rock Springs.

Heading North

Immediately north of Farson, the highway crosses Big Sandy River, little more than a creek much of the year, with Big Sandy Reservoir holding back much of its water for irrigation. Flat, irrigated fields of hay surround Farson. As you continue northward to Pinedale (58 miles), the jagged snow-topped crowns of the Wind River Mountains loom ever larger and the sagebrush grows more abundant on the arid landscape rolling away to the mountains. The highway crosses both the **Sublette Cutoff**—one of the original routes to Oregon Country—and the 1858 **Lander Cutoff**, the first federal road west of the Mississippi. Tune in to KQSW (96.5 FM) for country tunes to speed you on your way.

A gravel road that begins two miles east of Farson and heads north along Little Sandy Creek and then northwest to Boulder is even more dramatic, passing along the foothills of the Winds. It's used to access the Big Sandy Trailhead for the Bridger Wilderness. This is one of my favorite drives in Wyoming. Clouds often drape the distant mountains, but when they part—like curtains at a Broadway premier—they reveal the 13,000-foot crest of the Wind River Mountains in all their majesty. This is truly one of the classic Western vistas, with the interplay of land, light and sky creating an unforgettable scene.

The land knocks you out: mountains struggling up through the distant plain, bursting aside the sandy sod, crowning the eastern horizon with slanting patches of monstrous rock faces and snow-mantled slopes, reflecting back the light from a westering sun. Antelope glance up as you drive past; a rough-legged hawk hunches down on a fence post; several horses paw the ground. Periodically a narrow set of pickup truck tracks angles over the horizon to some remote ranch. In places like this, it is hard not to love the wildly beautiful state of Wyoming.

PINEDALE

Pinedale (pop. 1,200) is similar in many ways to its neighbor across the mountains, Dubois. Both towns were long dependent upon ranching and logging, but are now starting to appreciate the visitors who come to simply enjoy the landscape. Rich people from all over the nation (and the world) have bought up the old ranches and turned them into summer homes, and small jets crowd the tarmac (if it could be called that) at Pinedale's airport. Most of these folks are corporate bigwigs such as the head of PepsiCo, but others include John Barlow (lyricist for the Grateful Dead) and James Baker (Sec. of State under President Bush). Residents brag that Pinedale has all the beauty of Jackson Hole with none of the hassles. All around Pinedale are hay-filled meadows, grazing horses, and modern ranchettes. The Wind River Mountains are close and dramatic.

In addition to ranching and tourism, Pinedale is also a minor governmental center, with BLM, Forest Service, Game and Fish, and Sublette County offices here. The Upper Green River is still very important cattle country. Each fall, the cattle drift back down from their summer home in the mountains when cool October weather hits the high country. At Cora (10 miles northwest of Pinedale), cowboys from 20 different ranches sort out the 7,500 cattle that pile up against fences in the "Green River Drift."

History

The first inhabitants of the Upper Green River Valley were the Shoshone, Gros Ventre, Sheepeater, and Crow Indians who hunted buffalo, elk, and antelope in this rich country. Whites first came as explorers and fur trappers in the early 1800s, and by the 1830s this was the "capital" of the fur trade in the Rockies. Six different rendezvous were held along the Upper Green River. The first white settler arrived with his cattle in 1878, and within a few years a small trading center sprang up alongside Pine Creek. Pinedale was platted in 1899, later becoming the Sublette County seat.

Sights

Pinedale's excellent **Museum of the Mountain Men**, 700 E. Hennick St., tel. 367-4101, was completed in 1990. It's open Sun. 1-5 and Tues.-Sat 9-5 in summer, and Tues.-Sat. 9-5 in Sept.; closed the rest of the year. Entrance costs $2.50 adults, $1.50 seniors, and $1 kids. Located on a hill overlooking town, the museum provides artifacts and memorabilia from the fur-trapping era, along with interesting exhibits describing this fascinating time. Jim Bridger's rifle is here, along with a covered wagon, and a video about the fur trappers. A gift shop sells historical books. In the basement is a collection of items from Sublette County.

Accommodations

See the chart (following page) for a listing of motels and lodges in the Pinedale area. The closest public camping is at **Fremont Lake Campground** ($5, open June-late Sept.), seven miles northeast of Pinedale along the lake. **Half Moon Campground** ($5, open June to mid-Sept.) is on the northwest shore of Half Moon Lake, eight miles northeast of Pinedale. A dozen other Forest Service and BLM campgrounds are dotted all along the western side of the Wind River Mountains. **KOA Campground**, 204 S. Jackson Ave, tel. 367-2400, charges $9 for tents and $12 for RVs; open mid-May to mid-September. **Lakeside Lodge** at Fremont Lake, tel. 367-2221, charges $8 for tents and $12 for RVs. Open mid-May to early September.

Food

Wrangler Cafe, 310 E. Pine St., tel. 367-4233, is a popular place for breakfasts. Try the omelettes. **Sue's Bread Box**, 423 W. Pine, tel. 367-2150, serves fine, earthy breakfasts and lunches with homemade soups and sourdough bread. Be sure to get one of the sticky raison buns at the bakery here. **Calamity Jane's/Corral Bar**, 30 W. Pine, tel. 367-2469, is the place to go for delicious burgers and fries or for Mexican food and pizzas. Other places with standard American fare are **Stockman's Steak Pub**, 117 W. Pine, tel. 367-4563, and **Patio Grill**, 35 W. Pine, tel. 367-4611. **King Cone Drive In**, 513 S. U.S. 191, tel. 367-6404, (open summers only) is famous (infamous?) as "Home of the Road Kill

Burger." Funniest T-shirts in town.

McGregor's Pub, 25 N. Franklin Ave., tel. 367-4443, specializes in delicious prime rib, steak, and seafood, but also has great lunches served on an outside deck. Come evening, this is a favorite place for cocktails. Open summer only, and a bit on the pricey side. Eight miles east of town on Fall Creek Rd. is **Fort Williams Recreation Area**, tel. 367-6353, which has famous thick steaks, beans, and other hearty fare served on weekends June-October. **Sweet Tooth Saloon**, 128 W. Pine St., tel. 367-4724, is an old-fashioned ice cream parlor. Get groceries at **Faler's Thriftway**, 341 E. Pine, tel. 367-2131. Inside is one of the largest collections of critter heads anywhere, along with a deli.

Entertainment
Both the **Cowboy Bar**, 104 W. Pine, tel. 367-4520, and the **Stockman's Bar**, 16 N. Maybell Ave., tel. 367-4562, have live C&W tunes most weekends. **Fort Williams Recreation Area**, eight miles east of Pinedale, tel. 367-6353, is a popular place to unwind in a cozy atmosphere; open June-Oct. only. **The Place Bar**, tel. 367-2585, in Cora (10 miles northwest of Pinedale)

has a pool table along with lots of mounted animal heads.

Events
In mid-March, Pinedale livens up with a **Winter Carnival** that includes horse-pulls, hockey, softball in the snow, barefoot races, and general drunkenness. Meet locals afterward at the clinic for lessons in how to get over pneumonia. The big summertime event in Pinedale is the **Green River Rendezvous**, held the second weekend in July. Established in 1936, this is one of the oldest celebrations of the mountain men rendezvous era, and commemorates the raucous activities of the 1830s on nearby Horse Creek. A pageant attracts up to 15,000 visitors, and there are all sorts of other activities, including black-powder shoots, historic demonstrations, a parade, square dancing, cowboy poetry, a crafts fair, and rodeos. Late in July comes the annual **Fremont Lake Sailing Regatta.**

Recreation
Many nearby lakes and streams offer outstanding fishing for cutthroat, rainbow, brook, Mackinaw, golden and brown trout, plus grayling

PINEDALE ACCOMMODATIONS

Motel	Address	Telephone	Rate	Features
Sun Dance Motel	148 E. Pine	367-4336	$28 s, $30 d	AAA approved
Pine Creek Motel	650 W. Pine St.	367-2191	$28 s, $30 d	
Teton Court Motel	123 E. Magnolia St.	367-4317	$28 s, $30 d	open May-Oct.
Lakeside Lodge	4 miles north	367-2221	$28+ s, $30+ d	cabins, open May-early Sept.
Boulder Lake Lodge	24 miles southeast	367-2961	$28 s, $35 d	AAA approved, pack trips
Camp O' The Pines	38 N. Fremont Ave.	367-4536	$30 s, $34 d	kitchenettes, open June-Oct.
Rivera Lodge	442 W. Marilyn St.	367-2424	$32 s or d	kitchenettes, cabins, open May to mid-Oct.
Wagon Wheel Motel	407 S. U.S. 191	367-2871	$34+ s, $36+ d	AAA approved, very clean
Log Cabin Motel	49 E. Magnolia St.	367-4579	$35 s or d	kitchenettes, cabins, historic
Fort Williams B&B	8 miles east	367-6353	$35 s, $45 d	
ZZZZ Inn	327 S. U.S. 191	367-2121	$45 s or d	

and whitefish. A number of local outfitters provide float-fishing trips down the Green River; see the chamber of commerce for a listing. Canoeists or kayakers will also enjoy floating down stretches of the Green. Ask at the Forest Service office for details. There is an indoor **pool** in the high school, tel. 367-2832; rates are $1.25 (50¢ for kids).

The east slope of the the Wind River Mountains contains several large lakes, created when glaciers retreated after the last major ice age some 10,000 years ago. The terminal moraines they left behind acted as dams, although some have been enlarged with human-created dams in recent years. The lakes are very popular with anglers. **Fremont Lake** is Wyoming's second-largest natural lake, reaching 12 miles in length, a half mile across, and up to 600 feet deep. It's just three miles northeast of Pinedale, and is famous for the Mackinaw that approach 40 pounds. Other lakes of note are **Half Moon Lake, Willow Lake**, and **Boulder Lake**. See "Green River Lakes Area" (below) for info on the Green River Lakes and New Fork Lakes. All of these lakes mentioned have Forest Service campgrounds for $5 a night (some are free), and trails that lead into the Bridger Wilderness.

Cross-country skiers should pick up a copy of the **Skyline Drive Nordic Touring Trails** map from the Forest Service office in Pinedale. The trails are not regularly groomed, but are marked and the trail has generally been broken by others. More adventurous skiers will find all sorts of places to explore in the Bridger Wilderness just a few miles east of Pinedale. The lower elevations of the Wind River Mountains are also extremely popular with **snowmobilers**, and trails head out right from town. The Continental Divide Snowmobile Trail points north to Yellowstone or south to South Pass. Snowmobiles can be rented from several local dealers.

Information And Services

The **Pinedale Chamber of Commerce**, 35 S. Tyler, tel. 367-2242, is open Mon.-Fri. 8:30-5. A summer-only information kiosk on Pine St. near Fremont Ave. is open daily 8-6. The **Forest Service District Office** is located at 210 W. Pine St., tel. 367-4326, and the **BLM Office** is at 431 W. Pine St., tel. 367-4358. **Pinedale Office Supply**, tel. 367-2428, sells books on Wyoming. The **Public Library** is at 40 S. Fremont

Ave., tel. 367-4114. **Jackson-Rock Springs Bus Line**, tel. 362-6161, in Rock Springs, has daily summertime service through Pinedale, heading both north and south. In the winter, the service is Mon., Wed., and Fri. only.

NEARBY TOWNS

Boulder

A dozen miles south of Pinedale is **Boulder** (pop. 70), consisting of a gas station/grocery store. **Ox-Yoke Acres Campground**, tel. 537-5453, charges $10 for tents (no trees), $12 for RVs. Showers for non-campers are $3. Open May-October. **Meadow Lake Outfitting**, five miles east of Boulder, tel. 537-5278, has bed and breakfast accommodations for $50 d, including a warm springs pool. Halfway between Pinedale and Boulder is a roadside telephone pole topped by an active osprey nest.

Daniel

Head 11 miles west of Pinedale and then another mile south on U.S. 189 to tiny **Daniel**, where the country bar makes some of the best Bloody Marys in Wyoming. **Coulter's Campground**, tel. 859-8224, has tent or RV spaces for $12. Open May to mid-October. A roadside marker north of Daniel notes the site of **Fort Bonneville**, built in 1832 to serve as a base for the fur trading by Captain Benjamin Bonneville. It lasted only a year, but gained the nickname "Fort Nonsense" because of the severely cold and snowy winters that made life difficult for Bonneville's men. The fort consisted of two blockhouses guarding a perimeter of tall log posts. Two miles east of Daniel on a dirt road is a monument to Father Pierre Jean DeSmet, who performed Mass during the 1840 rendezvous. A small chapel marks the site. The Green River Valley was right in the heart of prime beaver-trapping country.

Big Piney

Big Piney (pop. 780) is what happens when the oil boom goes bust. The rundown little place has more boarded-up storefronts than active businesses. Stay at **Big Piney Motel**, tel. 276-3352, for $30 s or $36 d. **Frontier Hotel**, tel. 276-3329, charges just $15, but take a look at the rooms first. No TV or phones. **Lain's Sports**

Center & Motel, tel. 276-3303, has dirt-cheap rates of $15 s or d in dumpy old trailers. **Sage Cafe**, tel. 276-3068, serves good all-American fare, and has a nice salad bar. **Ye Olde Pizza Parlor**, tel. 276-3546, makes fine pizzas. The main annual event is the **Big Piney Chuckwagon Days** on the 4th of July.

Marbleton

Marbleton (pop. 700) is just a couple hundred yards up U.S. 189 from Big Piney, and consists of a few old log buildings. **Marbleton Inn**, tel. 276-5231, offers excellent dinners and the finest lodging accommodations in the area ($30 s or $36 d). **Country Chalet Inn**, tel. 276-3391, has pleasant rooms for $26 s or $30 d. Campers will be happy to know that the **Laundry Basket Laundromat** in Marbleton has hot showers for $1. The **Waterhole**, tel. 276-3796, is the center of nightlife in the area, offering all sorts of bizarre contests,

---

MOUNTAIN MEN

The era of the fur trapper is one of the most colorful slices of American history, a time when a rough and hardy breed of men took to the Rockies in search of furs and adventure. Romanticized in such films as *Jeremiah Johnson*, the trappers actually played but a brief role in history, and numbered fewer than 1,000 individuals. Their real importance lay in acting as the opening wedge for the West—as a vanguard for the settlers and gold miners who would follow their paths, often led by these same mountain men.

The Fur Business

Fashion is what sent men into the Rockies in the first place, since the waterproof underfur of a beaver could be used to create the beaver hat, all the rage in the early part of the 19th century. William H. Ashley, founder of the Rocky Mountain Fur Company, was one of the most important figures in the fur trade.

Ashley's company of men—along with $10,000 in supplies—made it up into the Yellowstone River country, where he left them the following year, promising to resupply them in 1825 on the Henry's Fork near its confluence with the Green River, along the present-day Wyoming-Utah border. Thus began the first rendezvous. They would take place every summer until 1840.

During the heyday of the fur trade, a common saying was "all trails lead to the Seedskeedee [Green River]." Six rendezvous were held here in the 1830s, with the others in the Wind River/Popo Agie River area, on Ham's Fork of the Green River, or in Idaho and Utah. Sites were chosen where there was space for up to 2,000 mountain men and Indians, plenty of game, ample grazing for the thousands of horses, and good water. It was no coincidence that all were held in Shoshone country rather than farther east or north where the hostile Sioux, Blackfoot, and Crow held sway. Despite such precautions, something over half of Ashley's men were scalped by Indians.

The Rendezvous

The rendezvous (a French word meaning "appointed place of meeting") consisted of a time when the trappers—both white and Indian—could sell their furs, trade for needed supplies and Indian squaws (the women had little say in the matter, but most took considerable pleasure in the arrangement), meet with old friends, get rip-roaring drunk, and engage in story-telling, gambling, gun duels, and contests of all sorts. Horse racing, wrestling bouts, and shooting contests were favorites. Debauchery reigned supreme in these three-week-long affairs, and by the time they were over, many of the trappers had lost their entire year's earnings.

The end of the rendezvous system—and most of the Rocky Mountain fur trapping—came about for a variety of reasons: overtrapping, the financial panic of 1837, and other materials—particularly the South American nutria and silk from China—were being used more often in hats. In addition, permanent trading posts such as Fort Laramie drew Indians away from the mountains to trade for buffalo robes instead of beaver furs. By 1840, when the last rendezvous was held on the banks of the Green River near present-day Pinedale, it was obvious there would be no more. One of the longtime trappers, Robert Newell, said to his partner, Joseph Meek:

We are done with this life in the mountains —done with wading in beaver dams, and freezing or starving alternately—done with Indian trading and Indian fighting. The fur trade is dead in the Rocky Mountains, and it is no place for us now, if ever it was. We are young yet, and have life before us. We cannot waste it here; we cannot or will not return to the States. Let us go down to the Wallamet and take farms.

1↗ 2↘ 3↘

1 ➘ 2 ➚ 3 ➘

including gopher races and "cowboy open golf." Ask about the Little Buckaroo Rodeo for children, complete with those ever-wild Shetland ponies. North of Marbleton, the enormous Wind River Mountains become more visible and the highway crosses the **Lander Cutoff**, its ruts now barely visible across the sagebrush. Built in 1858 by Col. Frederick W. Lander and his soldiers, it served two purposes: as a shorter route to California and Oregon, and as a way to bypass the Mormon communities in Utah. The route offered good grazing and water, as well as abundant game, and it quickly became the preferred route to California and Oregon.

TO JACKSON HOLE

U.S. 189-191 provides a scenic route to Hoback Junction and Jackson Hole, crossing the Green River and then slowly climbing into the hills. Aspens begin to appear on the hilltops and willows line the creeks. The 11,000-foot-tall Gros Ventre Mountains are visible to the northwest. Gradually, lodgepole pine and aspen begin to replace the sagebrush. At "The Rim," the road enters Bridger-Teton National Forest. West of here, the land drains into the Hoback River which joins the Snake River at Hoback Junction, 40 miles away. The road curves gradually down through this mountainous country, crossing the Hoback River again and again.

Bondurant

The spread-out town of Bondurant (pop. 100) straggles along the road through a gorgeous mountain valley, its pastures dotted with enormous piles of hay, creekside willows, and grazing horses. **Triangle F Lodge**, tel. 733-2836, has rustic log cabins for $20-35. A cafe here serves standard American fare. **Smiling S Motel**, tel. 733-3457, charges $22 s or d; campground rates are $6 for tents or $10 for RVs. Showers for non-campers are $2. Open mid-May to mid-September. **Hoback Village**, tel. 733-3631, has modern cabins (but no TV) for $40 s or d, open May-October. On the west end of "town," **Elkhorn Bar and Trading Post**, tel. 733-8358, has a general store and country watering hole. **Fall River Ranch**, eight miles southwest of Bondurant, tel. 733-1184, has B&B accommodations for $35 s or $45 d, including fresh breakfast milk from their cow. Full room and board (including horseback riding and fishing) costs $75 s or $100 d per day.

Hoback Canyon

A few miles west of Bondurant, the road clings to the walls of Hoback Canyon as it passes the high face of Battle Mountain, site of one of the few conflicts between Indians and whites in this part of Wyoming. It was here in 1895 that whites from Jackson Hole attacked Bannock Indians who had been hunting "out of season" along the Hoback River. (See "Jackson Hole" p. 226 for more on this sad story.) Immediately beyond Battle Mountain, you'll see the entrance of Granite Creek and a 10-mile gravel road that leads to **Granite Hot Springs**, a popular place to relax in both summer and winter. The Granite Canyon Rd. is not plowed in winter, but is used by both snowmobilers and cross-country skiers. Just before you reach Hoback Junction, a sign describes John Hoback, the trapper and guide who led the Astorian trappers of Wilson Price Hunt through here in 1811.

the
Summer
Rendezvous

JACKSON HOLE AND THE TETONS

Jackson Hole is one of the most-visited slices of wild country in North America. Each year more than two million travelers pass through, stopping to enjoy the energetic town of Jackson, to camp under the stars in Grand Teton National Park, to hike flower-bedecked trails into the mountains, to ride a sleigh among thousands of elk, to raft down the Snake River, to ski at one of the local resorts, or to simply stand in wonderment at the view from Snake River overlook. Many continue on north to Yellowstone National Park, another place on everyone's must-see list. Drive north from Jackson toward Yellowstone and you'll quickly discover why so many people are attracted to this place. The Tetons seem to act as a magnet, drawing your eyes away from the road and forcing you to stop and absorb some of their majesty. Welcome to one of the world's great wonderlands.

In the lingo of the mountain men, a "hole" was a large valley ringed by mountain ranges. Jackson Hole, on Wyoming's far western border is, justifiably, the most famous of all these intermountain valleys. Although Jackson Hole reaches an impressive 40 miles north to south, and up to 10 miles across, it is the magnificent range of mountains to the west that define this valley. Shoshone Indians who wandered through this country called the peaks Teewinot ("Many Pinnacles"); later explorers would use such labels as Shark's Teeth or Pilot Knobs, but the name that stuck came from lonely French-Canadian trappers who arrived in the early 1800s: les Trois Tetons ("Three Teats").

The valley, originally called Jackson's Hole, was named for a likeable trapper, David E. Jackson, one of the men who helped establish the Rocky Mountain Fur Company. When Jackson and his partners sold out in 1830, they realized a profit of over $50,000. Jackson's presence remains in names for both Jackson's Hole and Jackson Lake. Eventually, more polite folks began calling the valley Jackson Hole, in an attempt to end the ribald stories associated with the name Jackson's Hole. (It's easy to imagine the jokes with both Jackson's Hole and the Tetons in the same place.)

TO BOZEMAN

GALLATIN NATIONAL FOREST

287
191

HEBGEN LAKE

89
GARDINER

TO LIVINGSTON

MAMMOTH HOT SPRINGS

TOWER JUNCTION

SILVER GATE

COOKE CITY

TO RED LODGE

MONTANA
WYOMING

ABSAROKA - BEARTOOTH WILDERNESS

212

TO CODY

NORRIS JUNCTION

GRAND CANYON OF THE YELLOWSTONE

CANYON JUNCTION

NORTH ABSAROKA WILDERNESS

SHOSHONE NATIONAL FOREST

296

20

WEST YELLOWSTONE

MONTANA
IDAHO

MADISON JUNCTION

YELLOWSTONE NATIONAL PARK

YELLOWSTONE RIVER

LAKE JUNCTION

TO IDAHO FALLS

OLD FAITHFUL GEYSER

YELLOWSTONE LAKE

SYLVAN PASS

14 16 20

TO CODY

SHOSHONE LAKE

WEST THUMB

NORTHWEST WYOMING

LEWIS LAKE

191

287

TARGHEE NATIONAL FOREST

RIVER

ABSAROKA RANGE

JOHN D. ROCKEFELLER JR. MEMORIAL PARKWAY

TWO OCEAN PASS

TO ASHTON

32

JACKSON LAKE

TETON WILDERNESS

WASHAKIE WILDERNESS

33

GRAND TETON NATIONAL PARK

BRIDGER - TETON NATIONAL FOREST

ALTA

MORAN

MT. MORAN

26

TOGWOTEE PASS (ELEV. 9,658 ft.)

BROOKS LAKE

DRIGGS

TETON RANGE

GRAND TETON

89

191

BRIDGER - TETON NATIONAL FOREST

SHOSHONE NATIONAL FOREST

VICTOR

31

TETON VILLAGE

MOOSE

KELLY

GROS VENTRE WILDERNESS

DUBOIS

33

22

390

NATIONAL ELK REFUGE

26

WILSON

JACKSON

287

TO IDAHO FALLS

GRANITE HOT SPRINGS

26

HOBACK JUNCTION

GROS VENTRE RANGE

CONTINENTAL DIVIDE

WYOMING

IDAHO
WYOMING

ASTORIA HOT SPRINGS

89

SNAKE RIVER

HOBACK RIVER

ALPINE

89

BONDURANT

0   20mi

TO AFTON

TO PINEDALE

189
191

0   20km

34

© MOON PUBLICATIONS

HISTORY

The first people to cross the mountain passes into Jackson Hole probably arrived while the last massive glaciers were still retreating. Clovis stone arrowheads—a style used 11,000 years ago—have been found along the edges of the valley. These early peoples were replaced in the 16th and 17th centuries by the Shoshone, Bannock, Blackfeet, Crow, and Gros Ventre tribes who hunted bison from horses. When the first fur trappers tramped up the river valleys into Jackson Hole, they found Indian paths throughout the valley.

Explorers And Trappers

In 1806, as the Lewis and Clark expedition was returning from the west coast, they met two fur trappers heading up the Missouri River. John Colter, a respected scout, left the expedition to join the trappers. The following year, Colter headed out to establish a system of trade with the Indians. His wanderings in the winter of 1807-08 provided the first white exploration of this region. A map produced by William Clark in 1814 and based upon Colter's recollections shows an incredible midwinter journey around Yellowstone and Jackson lakes, crossing the Tetons twice, and up through Jackson Hole. He did not get back to the fort until the following spring, telling tales of huge mountain ranges and a spectacular geothermal area that others quickly laughed off as "Colter's Hell." (In 1931, an Idaho farmer plowed up a stone carved into the shape of a human face, and with "John

Colter 1808" etched into the sides. There is evidence that it was a hoax, carved by a man anxious to obtain a horse concession with Grand Teton National Park. He got the concession after donating the rock to the park museum.)

Because of the abundance of beavers along the tributaries of the Snake River, Jackson Hole became an important crossroad for the Rocky Mountain fur trade. No rendezvous was ever held in the valley, but many of the most famous mountain men spent time here. After the fur trade died in the late 1830s, few whites wandered into Jackson Hole since it lay away from the Oregon Trail and other paths west.

Settlers

The first Jackson Hole homesteaders arrived in 1884, followed quickly by those coming to escape the law. The settlers survived by grazing cattle, harvesting hay, and acting as guides for rich hunters from Europe and eastern states. Gradually they filled the richest parts of the valley with homesteads. Conflicts soon arose between the Bannock Indians who had been hunting in Jackson Hole for more than a hundred years and the new settlers who made money by guiding wealthy sportsmen.

By 1895, Wyoming had enacted game laws prohibiting hunting during 10 months of the year. Claiming that the Indians were taking elk out of season, Constable William Manning and 26 settlers arrested a group of 28 Indians (mostly women and children) who had been hunting in Hoback Canyon. When the Bannocks attempted to flee, an old Indian was shot four times in the back and died. Most of the others escaped.

The "Colter Stone," with Colter's name inscribed on one face, and the date 1808 on the other.

G. BRYAN HARRY/COURTESY OF GRAND TETON N.P.

THE WHITE SHOSHONE

The quiet little Jackson Hole settlement of Wilson is named after one of the West's most fascinating characters, "Uncle Nick" Wilson. Born in 1842, Nick grew up in Utah, where he made friends with a fellow sheepherder, an Indian boy, and learned to speak his language. Then, suddenly Nick's life took a strange twist. The mother of Chief Washakie (from Wyoming's Wind River Reservation) had recently lost a son, and in a dream she had been told that a white boy would come to take his place.

Unable to convince her otherwise, Washakie sent his men out to find the new son. They came across Nick and offered him a pinto pony and the chance to fish, hunt, and ride horses all he wanted. It didn't take much persuading, and for the next two years he lived as a Shoshone, learning to hunt buffalo, to use a bow and arrow, and to answer to his new name, Yagaiki. He became a favorite of Chief Washakie, but when word came (falsely) that Nick's father was threatening to attack the Shoshones with an army of men to retrieve his son, the chief reluctantly helped Nick return home.

At age 18, Nick Wilson became one of the first Pony Express riders, a job that nearly killed him when he was struck in the head during a Piute Indian attack. A doctor managed to remove the arrow point, but Wilson remained in a coma for nearly two weeks. Thereafter, Wilson always wore a hat to cover the scar, even inside buildings. He went on to become an Army scout and a driver for the Overland Stage, before returning to a more sedate life of farming. Many years later, in 1889, Nick Wilson led a party of five Mormon families over steep Teton Pass and down to the rich grazing lands in Jackson Hole. The town that grew up around them became Wilson. In later years, "Uncle Nick" recounted his early adventures in a book, *The White Indian Boy*.

Settlers in Jackson Hole feared revenge and called in the cavalry, but the Indians who had been hunting in the area all returned peaceably to their Idaho reservation. Astoundingly, the New York Times headlined the incident with "Settlers Massacred—Indians Kill Every One at Jackson's Hole—Courier Brings the News—Red Men Apply the Torch to All the Houses in the Valley." Although none of this was true, the attack by whites succeeded in forcing the Indians off their traditional hunting grounds, an action eventually upheld in a landmark U.S. Supreme Court case.

Jackson Hole Comes Of Age

By the turn of the century, the settlements of Jackson, Wilson, Kelly, and Moran had all been established. The towns grew slowly as people survived by ranching, guiding, and by running a strange new business, tending wealthy "dudes" from back east. Eventually tourism would vastly eclipse the importance of raising cattle, but even today Teton County has nearly as many cattle as people. Jackson, the largest town in Jackson Hole, was established in 1897 when Grace Miller (wife of the local banker known derisively as "Old Twelve Percent") bought a large plot of land and planned a townsite. In an event that should come as no surprise in "The Equality State," Jackson became the first town in America to be entirely governed by women. The year was 1920, and not only was the mayor a woman (Grace Miller), but all four councilmembers, the city clerk, treasurer, and even the town marshal. They remained in office until 1923.

Over the years Jackson has grown, spurred on by the creation of Grand Teton National Park and the development of Jackson Hole Ski Resort. During the 1980s Jackson Hole began to really boom as tourists flooded the region and as wealthy families built elaborate second homes and golf courses. Although much of the area is public land and will remain undeveloped, rapid growth on private land threatens to turn Jackson Hole into another Aspen or Vail.

JACKSON

The town of Jackson (pop. 5,200) lies near the southern end of Jackson Hole, hemmed in on three sides by Snow King Mountain, the Gros Ventre Range, and East Gros Ventre Butte. At 6,200 feet in elevation, Jackson experiences cold snowy winters, wet springs, warm sunny summers, and gorgeous falls. Jackson is quite unlike any other place in Wyoming. Sit on a bench in town square on a summer day and you're likely to see cars from every state in the Union. Tourists dart in and out of the many gift shops, art galleries, fine restaurants, Western-style saloons, and trendy boutiques. The cowboy hats all look as if the price tag just came off. This sure isn't Rock Springs! In fact, about the only thing the two towns seem to share are rumors that the Mafia owns a number of major businesses.

In other parts of Wyoming, Jackson is viewed with a mixture of awe and disdain: awe over its booming economy, but disdain that Jackson is not a "real" town, just a false front put up to sell things to outsiders. Yes, Jackson is almost wholly dependent upon the almighty tourist dollar, but as a result it has a cultural richness that is lacking in other parts of the state. Besides, if you don't like all the commercial foolishness, it's easy to escape to a campsite or remote trail in the wonderful countryside of nearby Grand Teton National Park or Bridger-Teton National Forest.

Keep your eyes open around Jackson and you're likely to see famous (or infamous, depending upon your perspective) residents such as actor Harrison Ford, former Secretary of the Interior James Watt (who resigned in disgrace in 1983), attorney Gerald Spence (of Karen Silkwood and Imelda Marcos fame or infamy), for-

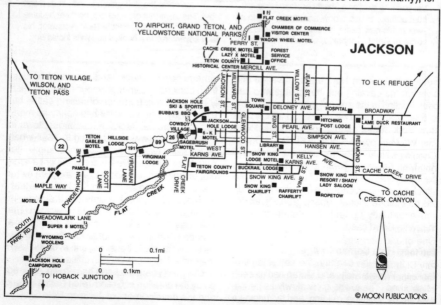

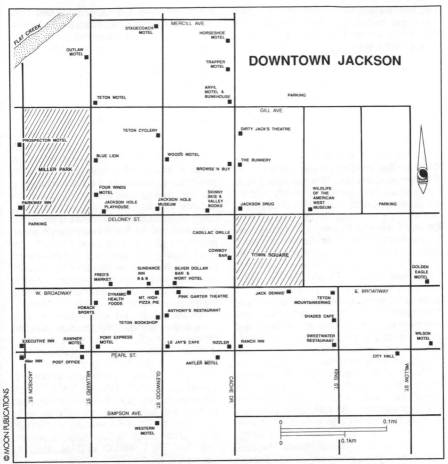

DOWNTOWN JACKSON

mer Wyoming governor Clifford Hansen, Yvon Chouinard (mountaineer and founder of Patagonia), along with members of the Rockefeller family.

SIGHTS

Town Square

One of Jackson's most distinctive and attractive features is its central town square. The Rotary Club planted trees here in 1932 and added four picturesque arches made from hundreds of elk antlers. Today these trees offer summertime shade, and at any time of day or night you'll find visitors admiring or getting their photo taken in front of the arches. During the winter, the town square's snow-covered arches and trees are draped with lights, giving them a festive atmosphere. Surrounded by dozens of boardwalk-fronted galleries, bars, restaurants, factory outlets, and gift shops, the square is the main focus of tourist activity in Jackson. Depending upon the season, horse-drawn carriages, stagecoaches, or sleighs ($3-5 pp) wait to transport you on a leisurely ride around town. During the summer, "cowboys" put on a free **shoot-out** for throngs of camera-happy tourists. The shoot-out starts every night except Sunday at 6:30

p.m. With stereotypical players and questionable acting, the "mountain law" system seems in dire need of reform. Most folks love the sham; Kodak loves it even more.

Museums

The small **Jackson Hole Museum**, 105 N. Glenwood, tel. 733-2414, has interesting displays and collections from the days of Indians, trappers, cattlemen, and dude ranchers who once made this magnificent valley their home. Check out the Paul Bunyan-sized bear trap and the old postcards. Admission is $2 for adults, $5 for families, and $1 for students and seniors. Summer hours are Sun. 10-4 and Mon.-Sat. 9-6. It is closed Oct. to early May. Ask here about the historical **walking tours** ($2) of Jackson's downtown, given Mon.-Fri. at 11 a.m. **Teton County Historical Center**, 105 Mercell Ave., tel. 733-9605, houses photo archives and many old books from the area, along with a fine exhibit on the fur trade and an impressive collection of Indian trade beads. A replica of the "Colter Stone" is also on display. Hours are Mon.-Fri. 9-5 during the summer, and Mon.-Fri. 1-5 Sept.-May; free admission. For a slice of Americana, visit the **wildlife museum** at 862 W. Broadway, tel. 733-4909. Pay $2 ($1 for kids) for the standard collection of stuffed big bears posed threateningly In front of background murals.

Wildlife of the American West Art Museum, 110 N. Center St., tel. 733-5771, houses more than 250 paintings and sculptures of Western wildlife, the largest such collection in the world. Featured artists include Ernest Thompson Seton, George Catlin, Conrad Schwiering, Charles M. Russell, Albert Bierstadt, Karl Bodmer, John Clymer, and many others. The upstairs gallery has oil paintings and bronzes by Carl Rungius. Admission is $2, or $5 per family; summer hours are Sun. 1-6 and Mon.-Sat. 10-6. Winter hours are Sun. 1-5 and Tues.-Sat. 10-5. Closed in parts of spring and fall.

Art In Jackson Hole

Artists have long been attracted by the beauty of Jackson Hole and the Tetons. Mount Moran, the 12,805-foot summit behind Jackson Lake, is named for Thomas Moran, whose watercolors helped persuade Congress to set aside Yellowstone as the first national park. The late Conrad Schwiering's paintings of the Tetons have at-tained international fame, and one was even used on the Postal Service's Wyoming Centennial stamp in 1990. Ansel Adams' photograph of the Tetons remains etched in the American conscience as one of the archetypical wilderness images. A copy of the image was included in the payload of the Voyager II spacecraft currently en route out of our solar system. Today many artists live or work in Jackson Hole, making this Wyoming's premier center for the arts.

More than 30 galleries crowd the center of Jackson, covering the spectrum from Indian art collections of questionable authenticity to impressive photographic exhibits and shows by nationally acclaimed painters. Unfortunately, many of these galleries offer recycled ideas that are now manufactured in mass quantity with every cliché thrown in. Particularly egregious examples are the Southwestern-style pastel pottery, the elk-antler lamps, and the paintings of noble-looking mountain men and Indians set against a Grand Teton backdrop. Local newspapers provide a complete rundown of current exhibitions and displays, along with maps showing gallery locations.

Several galleries are worth a visit, including the excellent Wildlife of the American West Art Museum (described above). One of the largest is **Wilcox Gallery**, a mile north of town on U.S. 89, tel. 733-6450, featuring paintings by Jim Wilcox. The spacious **Trailside Galleries**, 105 Center St., tel. 733-3186, has fine paintings, drawings, jewelry, glassware, and sculpture by contemporary artists. **Main Trail Galleries**, 90 N. Center St., tel. 733-4355, emphasizes Western paintings and sculpture, both contemporary and traditional. **The Robert Dean Collection**, 172 Center St., tel. 733-9290, specializes in authentic, high-quality Indian art and jewelry. **Rawson Galleries**, 50 King St., tel. 733-7306, features both traditional and avant-garde watercolors, etchings, and other artwork. If you're a fan of miniature bronze cattle stampedes, romanticized Indian portraits, and grandiose landscapes, visit the two locations of **Gallery of the West**: 60 and 110 E. Broadway, tel. 733-9211. For fine pottery, stop by **Fish Creek Pottery**, 86 E. Broadway, tel. 733-9181.

Many nationally known photographers live or work in Jackson Hole, exhibiting their prints in Jackson galleries. Thomas Mangelsen's **Images of Nature Gallery** at 125 N. Cache (up-

SAVING JACKSON HOLE

In recent years the town of Jackson has boomed as expensive homes spread across old ranchlands, huge retailers such as K mart moved in, and oil companies continue to salivate over oil and gas wells on nearby Forest Service land. Today, despite the fact that 97% of the land in Teton County is in the public domain, the 70,000 acres of private land that remain are rapidly being developed, and Jackson Hole is in grave danger of losing the wild beauty that has attracted visitors for more than a century. There is even talk of a four-lane highway through Spring Gulch, an area now traversed by a gravel road!

The **Jackson Hole Alliance for Responsible Planning**, 260 E. Broadway, tel. 733-9417, is a thousand-member environmental group that works to preserve the natural areas of Jackson Hole and to prevent the town from becoming just another trashy tourist mill. Membership is only $10/year and includes a bi-monthly newsletter and a chance to help control the many developments that threaten the valley. Another influential local group is the **Jackson Hole Land Trust**, Box 2897, tel. 733-4707, a nonprofit organization that purchases land and obtains conservation easements to maintain ranches and other land threatened by development. They now protect more than 6,000 acres in the valley, including the 1,740-acre Walton Ranch visible along the highway between Jackson and Wilson.

stairs), tel. 733-6179, displays a selection of his outstanding wildlife photos. **Eagle Photographics Gallery**, 35 E. Deloney, tel. 733-4016, includes many of Fred Joy's large-format visions of the American West.

The nonprofit **Arts Center**, tel. 733-3642, in Pink Garter Plaza houses the tiny Artwest Gallery. Also here is Actors Co-op, tel. 733-3426, which performs plays throughout the year, and Dancer's Workshop, tel. 733-6398, offering dance classes and performances. Each summer, the **Snake River Institute** (run by Gov. Sullivan's daughter) offers workshops and seminars on the arts and their connection to the natural world. One-day seminars start at $65. Teachers cover the spectrum from respected poets and writers to photographers and anthropologists. Contact the Institute at Box 7724, Jackson 83001, tel. 733-2214, for more information and a class brochure.

NATIONAL ELK REFUGE

Just a couple miles north of Jackson is the National Elk Refuge, winter home for thousands of these majestic animals. During the summer, these elk can be found up to 65 miles away, feeding on grasses, shrubs, and forbs in alpine meadows. But as the snows descend each fall, the elk move downslope, wintering in Jackson Hole and the surrounding country. The chance to view elk up close from a horse-drawn sleigh makes a trip to the National Elk Refuge one of the most popular wintertime activities for Jackson Hole visitors.

History
When the first ranchers arrived in Jackson Hole in the late 19th century, they moved onto land that had long been an elk migration route and wintering ground. The ranchers soon found elk raiding their haystacks and competing with cattle for forage, particularly during severe winters. The conflicts reached a peak early in this century when three consecutive severe winters killed thousands of elk, leading one settler to claim that he had "walked for a mile on dead elk lying from one to four deep."

Fortunately, a local rancher and hunting guide, Stephen N. Leek, had been given a camera by one of the sportsmen he had guided, George Eastman, inventor of the Kodak camera. Leek's disturbing photos of starving and dead elk found a national audience and helped pressure the state of Wyoming to appropriate $5,000 to buy hay in 1909. Two years later the federal government began purchasing land for a permanent winter elk refuge, a refuge that would eventually cover nearly 25,000 acres. Today it is administered by the U.S. Fish and Wildlife Service. Famed biologist, illustrator, and conservationist Olaus Murie came to Jackson Hole in 1927 to begin his studies of the elk, remaining here until his death in 1963. With his wife Margaret (Mardie) Murie, they chronicled their adventures in *Wapiti Wilderness* (Colorado Associated University Press, Boulder). Conservationist Mardy Murie still lives in Moose, holding near-sainthood status among Wyoming conservationists.

Today more than 7,500 elk—half the local population—spend Nov.-May on the refuge. Because the elk habitat in the valley has been reduced to a quarter of its original size by development, refuge managers try to improve the remaining land by seeding, irrigation, and prescribed burning. In addition, during the most difficult foraging period, the elk are fed pelleted alfalfa, paid for in part by sales of elk antlers collected on the refuge (see p.242). During this time, each elk eats more than seven pounds of supplemental alfalfa a day, or 30 tons per day for the entire herd. Elk head back into the mountains with the melting of snow each April and May. During the summer months only a few can be found on the refuge.

Visiting The Refuge

The refuge is primarily a winter attraction, although it is also an excellent place to watch birds and other wildlife in summer. Trumpeter swans nest and winter here. Get to the refuge by heading east on Broadway through town till it dead-ends. The signed dirt road curves left here and goes four miles to the refuge.

The **Elk Refuge Visitor Center**, tel. 733-9212, has displays, books, and pamphlets about elk, plus a slide show on elk and the refuge. Wait here for the **horse-drawn sleighs**, the refuge's real attraction. These sleighs offer a unique opportunity to ride among the 7,500 or so elk without disturbing them. (People on foot would scare them.) Sleighs run daily 10-4 between late Dec. and late March, heading out as soon as enough folks show up for a ride (generally just long enough to watch the slide show). The cost is $6 ($3 for children), and the rides last for 30-45 minutes. Highly recommended. **All Star Transportation**, tel. 733-2888, offers shuttle service to the Elk Refuge from Teton Village ($11 RT) and downtown Jackson ($7 RT). **Jackson Hole Transportation**, tel. 733-3135, charges $8 RT from several downtown locations. Four miles north of town and next to the elk refuge is the **Jackson National Fish Hatchery**, tel. 733-2510, which rears a half million cutthroat and lake trout annually. Open daily 8-4.

ACCOMMODATIONS

As one of the premier centers for tourism in Wyoming, Jackson Hole is jam-packed with hotels, motels, B&Bs, guest ranches, condominiums, and campgrounds. In Jackson alone there are more than 30 lodging places, plus many more in nearby Teton Village, Wilson, and Hoback Junction. (See the charts, opposite, and on following pages, for a complete listing. Other lodging can also be found in Grand Teton National Park, see p. 268.) Unfortunately, prices at these motels are considerably higher than rates in other parts of Wyoming. Expect to pay a minimum of $40 s or $45 d during the peak visitor seasons: July and Aug., and late Dec. to early January. Rates will be lower (by up to 40%) in the off-seasons. Because of Jackson Hole's popularity, reservations are highly recommended. For the Christmas/New Year's period you should probably reserve in summer to be ensured of getting a place. For up-to-date lodging rates in and around Jackson Hole, request the accommodations brochure from the Jackson Hole Visitors Council, tel. (800) 782-0011.

Jackson's least expensive lodging place, the **Bunkhouse**, costs just $15 pp, including kitchen facilities and a TV room. It is right in town and almost always has space. Facilities are similar to a hostel: bunk beds in dorm-type cubicles. No curfew. It should come as no surprise that jet-set Jackson Hole has a number of elaborate, pricey, and sumptuous places to stay. The oldest and best known is the Wort Hotel, but several other places offer equally high standards (and prices). For a homier visit to Jackson Hole, make reservations at one of the delightful B&Bs.

Condominium Rentals

Condominiums provide one of the most popular lodging options for families and groups visiting Jackson Hole. These privately owned places are maintained by a number of local real estate management companies, and range from small studio apartments to spacious five-bedroom houses. All are completely furnished (including dishes), and have fireplaces, cable TV, phones, and mid-stay maid service. The nicest also include access to a pool and jacuzzi, and have

JACKSON HOLE CONDOMINIUMS

Condominium Companies	Number of Units	Telephone	
BBC Property Management	20	733-6170	(800) 325-8605
Ely & Associates	30	733-8604	(800) 333-0914
The Inn at Jackson Hole	6	733-2311	(800) 842-7666
Jackson Hole Lodge	24	733-2992	(800) 642-4567
Jackson Hole Property Management	85	733-7945	(800) 443-8613
Jackson Hole Racquet Club Resort	120	733-3990	(800) 443-8616
Mountain Property Management	15	733-1684	(800) 992-9948
Real Estate of Jackson Hole	5	733-0205	(800) 443-6130
Spring Creek Resort	70	733-8833	(800) 443-6139
Teton Village Property Management	115	733-4610	(800) 443-6840

JACKSON HOLE ACCOMMODATIONS

Name	Address	Phone	Rates	Features
Bunkhouse	215 N. Cache	733-3668 (800) 234-4507	$15 pp	hostel with kitchen
Split Creek Ranch	8 miles north	733-7522	$32 s, $42 d	kitchenettes, cabins
Motel 6	1370 W. Broadway	733-1620	$33 s, $39 d	pool
Hillside Lodge	945 W. Broadway	733-3391	$35+ s or d	kitchenettes
Alpine Motel	70 S. Jean St.	733-2082	$36 s, $42 d	pool, kitchenettes
Super 8 Motel	South U.S. 89	733-6833 (800) 843-1991	$38 s, $48 d	
Hoback Motel	Hoback Jct.	733-5129	$34 s, $36 d	
The Hostel	Teton Village	733-3415	$39 s or d	very plain
Snow King Lodge Motel	470 King St.	733-3480	$42 s or d	kitchenettes
Wood's Motel	120 N. Glenwood	733-2953	$46 s or d	AAA approved, open May-Sept.
Teton Gables Motel	1140 W. Broadway	733-3723	$46+ s or d	
Wagon Wheel Village	435 N. Cache	733-2357 (800) 323-9279	$47 s, $52 d	AAA approved, jacuzzi, kitchenettes, cabins, open mid-May to mid-Oct.
Ranch Inn Motel	45 E. Pearl St.	733-6363	$48 s or d	jacuzzi, kitchenettes
Sagebrush Motel	550 W. Broadway	733-0336	$48+ s or d	kitchenettes

continues on following pages

balconies overlooking the spectacular Tetons. Many of the condominiums are in Teton Village, right next to the ski area, with others scattered around Jackson Hole.

During the winter holiday season, expect to pay $160/night for studios (one or two people). Two-bedroom units (up to four people) start around $270/night, while full four-bedroom and

JACKSON HOLE ACCOMMODATIONS (CONT.)

Name	Address	Phone	Rates	Features
Elk Refuge Inn	North U.S. 89	733-3582	$49 s, $56 d	AAA approved, kitchenettes
Rawhide Motel	75 S. Millward	733-1216	$49+ s, $50+ d	AAA approved
Buckrail Lodge	110 E. Karns Ave.	733-2079	$50 s or d	AAA approved, open May to mid-Oct.
Stagecoach Motel	291 N. Glenwood	733-3451	$50+ s or d	
6-K Motel	480 W. Pearl	733-2364	$52+ s or d	kitchenettes
Wilson Motel	292 E. Pearl	733-2956	$52+ s or d	pool, kitchenettes
Hitching Post Lodge	460 E. Broadway	733-2606	$52+ s or d	AAA approved, pool, open mid-May to Sept.
Western Motel	225 S. Glenwood	733-3291	$54 s or d	pool
Lazy X Motel	325 N. Cache	733-3673	$55 s, $65 d	
Prospector Motel	155 N. Jackson	733-4858	$55 s, $59 d	AAA approved, open June-Sept.
Teton Motel	165 W. Gill St.	733-3883	$55+ s or d	AAA approved, open May-Oct.
Virginian Lodge	750 W. Broadway	733-2792 (800) 262-4999	$55 s, $60 d	AAA approved, pool, kitchenettes
Horseshoe Motel	285 N. Cache	733-2287 (800) 541-5256	$57 s or d	
Village Center Inn	Teton Village	733-3155 (800) 735-8342	$58+ s or d	AAA approved
49'er Inn (Friendship Inn)	330 W. Pearl	733-7550 (800) 451-2980	$58+ s, $62+ d	AAA approved, jacuzzi, sauna
Golden Eagle Motor Inn	325 E. Broadway	733-2042	$59 s or d	AAA approved, pool, open June-Sept.
Cache Creek Motel	390 N. Glenwood	733-7781 (800) 843-4788	$59 s or d	AAA approved, kitchenettes
Crystal Springs Inn	Teton Village	733-4423	$60 s or d	AAA approved
Flat Creek Motel	1935 N. U.S. 89	733-5276	$60 s or d	jacuzzi, sauna, kitchenettes
Anvil Motel (Budget Host)	215 N. Cache	733-3668 (800) 234-4507	$60+ s or d	newly rebuilt
Jackson Hole Lodge	420 W. Broadway	733-2992	$60+ s or d	AAA approved, pool, jacuzzi, sauna
Antler Motel (Friendship Inn)	50 W. Pearl Ave.	733-2535 (800) 453-4511	$62 s, $66 d	jacuzzi,
Trapper Motel	235 N. Cache	733-2648 (800) 341-8000	$62+ s or d	AAA approved, jacuzzi

JACKSON HOLE ACCOMMODATIONS (CONT.)

Name	Address	Phone	Rates	Features
Pony Express Motel	50 S. Millward St.	733-3835 (800) 526-2658	$64 s, $68 d	AAA approved, pool
Outlaw Motel	265 N. Millward St.	733-3682	$64+ s or d	kitchenettes
The Inn at Jackson Hole	Teton Village	733-2311 (800) 842-7666	$65+ s or d	AAA approved
Four Winds Motel	150 N. Millward St.	733-2474	$66+ s or d	AAA approved, open May-Sept.
Sojurner Inn	Teton Village	733-3657 (800) 445-4655	$70+ s or d	AAA approved, pool, jacuzzi, sauna
Executive Inn (Best Western)	325 W. Pearl Ave.	733-4340 (800) 528-1234	$73 s, $75 d	pool,
Days Inn	1280 W. Broadway	739-9010 (800) 325-2525	$74 s, $79 d	jacuzzi, sauna
Cowboy Village Resort	120 Flat Creek Dr.	733-3121	$74 s or d	AAA approved,
Parkway Inn (Best Western)	125 N. Jackson St.	733-3143 (800) 247-8390	$75+ s or d	AAA approved, pool, jacuzzi, sauna
Alpenhof Lodge	Teton Village	733-3242 (800) 732-3244	$90+ s or d	AAA approved, pool, jacuzzi, sauna
Wort Hotel	50 N. Glenwood St.	733-2190 (800) 322-2727	$105+ s or d	AAA approved, jacuzzi, airport shuttle
Snow King Resort	400 E. Snow King	733-5200 (800) 522-5464	$115 s, $125 d	AAA approved, pool, jacuzzi, sauna, airport shuttle
Spring Creek Resort	Gros Ventre Butte	733-8833 (800) 443-6139	$160+ s or d	AAA approved, pool, jacuzzi, airport shuttle
Jackson Hole Bed and Breakfasts				
Eagle's Nest B&B	Wilson	733-2462	$60+ s or d	full breakfast, open May-Sept.
Teton View B&B	Wilson	733-7954	$60+ s or d	full breakfast
Sundance Inn B&B	135 W. Broadway	733-3444	$65 s, $69 d	continental breakfast, refurbished motel
Fish Creek B&B	Wilson	733-2586	$65 s, $75 d	full breakfast, jacuzzi, log home
Twin Mountain River Ranch	Hoback Jct.	733-1168	$55+ s or d	full breakfast, log home
Big Mountain Inn	Moose-Wilson Rd.	733-1981	$85+ s or d	full breakfast, jacuzzi
Teton Treehouse B&B	Wilson	733-3233	$85+ s or d	full breakfast, mountainside home
Heidelberg B&B	Wilson	733-7820	$$85+ s or d	cabin, summer only
Wildflower Inn	Moose-Wilson Rd.	733-4710	$100+ s or d	full breakfast, jacuzzi, log house

loft condos (sleeps eight) start at a lofty $500/day. Summer and off-peak rates tend to be approximately 30% lower, with off-season rates 50% off midwinter prices. Minimum stays of between two and seven nights are required. In fall or spring, condos offer a real bargain for traveling families. If you have the luxury of time, do a little comparison shopping before renting a con-

JACKSON HOLE PUBLIC CAMPGROUNDS

Most Forest Service campgrounds can be reserved ($3.50 extra) by calling (800) 342-2267.
Park Service campsites are first-come, first-served only.
The campgrounds below are listed by direction and distance.

Campground	Miles and Direction from Jackson	Approximate Season	Fee	Features
Jenny Lake	20 N	May 25-Sept. 25	$7	Park Service; tents only; fills by 8 a.m.
Signal Mountain	32 N	May 25-Oct. 15	$7	Park Service; on Jackson Lake; fills by 10 a.m.
Colter Bay	40 N	May 25-Sept. 25	$7	Park Service; on Jackson Lake; fills by noon
Lizard Creek	48 N	June 15-Sept. 10	$7	Park Service; on Jackson Lake; fills by 2 p.m.
Snake River	55 N	June 15-Sept. 10	$7	Park Service; near Flagg Ranch; fills by 2 p.m.
Curtis Canyon	7 NE	June 15-Sept. 15	$6	Forest Service; 6 miles of gravel road
Gros Ventre	10 NE	May 5-Oct. 25	$7	Park Service; along Gros Ventre River; fills by evening
Atherton Creek	18 NE	June 5-Oct. 30	$5	Forest Service; along Gros Ventre River; 5 miles of dirt road
Red Hills	22 NE	June 5-Oct. 30	$5	Forest Service; along Gros Ventre River; 4 miles of dirt road
Crystal Creek	23 NE	June 5-Oct. 30	$5	Forest Service; along Gros Ventre River; 5 miles of dirt road
Hatchet	40 NE	June 25-Sept. 10	$5	Forest Service; in Buffalo Valley
Turpin Meadow	50 NE	June 25-Sept. 10	$4	Forest Service; in Buffalo Valley
Cabin Creek	19 S	May 25-Sept. 5	$5	Forest Service; along Snake River
Elbow	22 S	May 25-Sept. 10	$5	Forest Service; along Snake River
East Table Creek	24 S	June 5-Sept. 10	$5	Forest Service; along Snake River
Station Creek	25 S	June 10-Sept. 10	$5	Forest Service; along Snake River
Wolf Creek	28 S	June 10-Sept. 10	$5	Forest Service; along Snake River
Hoback	22 SE	June 1-Sept. 30	$5	Forest Service; along Hoback River
Kozy	30 SE	June 1-Sept. 30	$5	Forest Service; along Hoback River
Granite Creek	35 SE	June 15-Sept. 15	$5	Forest Service; hot springs; 9 miles of gravel road
Trail Creek	20 W	June 15-Sept. 10	$5	Forest Service; west of Teton Pass
Mike Harris	21 W	June 15-Sept. 10	$5	Forest Service; west of Teton Pass

do. Things to ask about are whether you have access to a pool and jacuzzi, how close you are to the ski slopes, how frequent the maid service is, and whether the units include such amenities as free washing machines. Also be sure to find out exactly what sort of beds are in the rooms, since couples won't enjoy sleeping in twin bunkbeds.

Camping

Both the National Park Service and the Forest Service maintain campgrounds around Jackson Hole. The chart shows 20 public campgrounds within 50 miles of Jackson. For more specifics, contact Bridger-Teton National Forest in Jackson at 340 N. Cache, tel. 733-2752, or Grand Teton National Park in Moose, tel. 733-2880. In addition to these sites, many people camp informally on Forest Service lands.

The Jackson area has six private campgrounds, offering the standard RV hookups and other amenities. Four of these also include tent sites: **Green Acres Campground**, tel. 739-9703; **Jackson Hole Campground**, tel. 733-2927; **Wagon Wheel Campground**, tel. 733-4588; and **Teton Village KOA**, tel. 733-5354. Expect to pay $11-15 for a basic tent site and $16-20 for RVs at most of these. Showers for non-campers cost $3. All of these private campgrounds are closed Oct.-early May. The only decent in-town place (real trees!) is Jackson Hole Campground, on the southern border of Jackson along Flat Creek. Farther away are private campgrounds in Hoback Junction (12 miles south), Astoria (17 miles south), Moran (35 miles northeast), and at Colter Bay and Flagg Ranch in Grand Teton National Park. At **Astoria Mineral Hot Springs**, tel. 733-2659, you get the added treat of a naturally heated mineral pool with 95° F water ($4 for non-campers) and riverside camping.

FOOD

Jackson stands out from the rest of Wyoming on the culinary scene: chicken-fried steak may be available, but it certainly isn't the house specialty! You won't need to look far to find good food; in fact, the town seems to overflow with impressive (and even more impressively priced) eateries. To get an idea of what to expect at local restaurants, pick up a copy of the free

Jackson Hole Dining Guide at the visitor center or local restaurants. It includes sample menus and brief descriptions of most local establishments. If you don't find a place to your liking in those listed below, be assured that all the major fast food outlets line Jackson's streets, ready to grease your digestive tract.

Breakfast

The best breakfast place in Jackson isn't in Jackson. **Nora's Fish Creek Inn**, in Wilson, tel. 733-8288, attracts a full house each morning with great, reasonably priced food, friendly waitresses, and an authentically rustic atmosphere. Nora's also serves tried-and-true dinners at a very good price. Highly recommended. In Jackson, locals get their buns into **The Bunnery**, 130 N. Cache, tel. 733-5474, each morning. Tasty pastries, homemade breakfasts, and great sandwiches and Mexican dishes for lunch. Also very popular for breakfast is **Jedediah's House of Sourdough**, 135 E. Broadway, tel. 733-5671. The old-time crowd heads to Jackson's greasy spoon for breakfast and other meals: **LeJay's Sportsman's Cafe**, 72 S. Glenwood St., tel. 733-3110. Open 24 hours a day, this is the place to go when no other restaurant is open and your stomach is demanding all-American grub.

Lunch

Jackson Drug, established in 1912, and in the same location since 1937, has a wonderful old soda fountain, popular with both locals and visitors. Located right on town square at 15 E. Deloney Ave., tel. 733-2442, the fountain makes homemade ice cream, along with sandwiches, soups, and spicy chili (winter only). One of the most popular noontime spots in Jackson is the **Sweetwater Restaurant**, 85 King St., tel. 733-3553, where the lunch menu includes salads, homemade soups, and a variety of earthy sandwiches. For dinner, try roast leg of lamb or the moussaka. Climbers and ski bums wear their Vuarnets to the oft-crowded **Shades Cafe**, 82 S. King St., tel. 733-2015. The tiny log cabin has a summer-only patio on the side, and delicious salads and burritos, as well as espresso coffees. It's a great place to hang out. Teton Village, has a second (winter-only) Shades Cafe, tel. 733-7091. **Pearl Street Bagels**, 145 Pearl St., tel. 739-1218, serves more good coffees with their home-baked bagels. Get one with lox and cream cheese for $3.75. Pick up tasty sub sandwiches (on tangy homemade bread) at **New York City Sub Shop**, 25 S. Glenwood St., tel. 733-4414. Fastest sandwich-makers in the business. If you're looking for a substantial organic lunch, try the cafe at **Dynamic Health Natural Foods**, 130 W. Broadway, tel. 733-5418.

American

The most popular locals' eatery is **Bubba's Bar-B-Que Restaurant**, 515 W. Broadway, tel. 733-2288. Each evening the parking lot out front is jammed with folks waiting patiently for a chance to chew the marvelous BBQ spare ribs, taste the spicy chicken wings, or fill up at the impressive salad bar. Lunch is a real bargain. Head three miles south of town on U.S. 89 to find the finest steaks in Jackson Hole at the **Steak Pub**, tel. 733-6977. Dinners are served in a rustic log cabin setting. Another very popular place with both locals and ski bums is the **Mangy Moose** in Teton Village, tel. 733-4913, where you'll find a good salad bar along with decent prices on steak and seafood. **The Rendezvous Cafe**, 145 N. Glenwood, tel. 733-9148, is a small, down-home place with reasonable burgers, seafood, and steaks served in a casual atmosphere. More good burgers at the '50s-style **Billy's Burgers**, 55 N. Cache (on the square), tel. 733-3279. Wilson's **Stagecoach Bar**, tel. 733-4407, makes delicious nachos, burgers, and other pub grub. **Togwotee Mountain Lodge**, 16 miles east of Moran Jct., tel. 543-2847, has an excellent Saturday evening all-you-can-eat seafood buffet for $20.

Pizza

Two pizza places stand out in Jackson. You'll find **Calico Pizza Parlor**, tel. 733-2460, in a garish red-and-white building three-quarters of a mile north on Teton Village Road. During the summer, be sure to get a side salad, fresh from their big garden. The bar at Calico is a very popular locals' watering hole. **Mt. High Pizza Pie**, 120 W. Broadway, tel. 733-3646, offers free delivery in town, but uses frozen crust. During the winter, their stuff-yourself pizza buffet (Mon.-Fri. 11:30-1:30 and Tues. 5:30-9 p.m. for under $5) is the best meal deal in Jackson.

Continental/Nouvelle Cuisine

If you want fine continental dining, and aren't

scared off by entrees starting around $15, Jackson has much to offer. In a plethora of fine European restaurants, one stands out: **Stiegler's**, tel. 733-1071, in the Aspens on Teton Village Road. The menu has names big enough to eat —Pfeffer Steak Hasumanns Art, or Kalbspiccata Maximillian—but the dense Austrian cuisine is simply outstanding. An excellent continental restaurant in town is **The Blue Lion**, 160 N. Millward St., tel. 733-3912. The front patio makes for delightful summertime dining. Try one of the fresh seafood specials. Jackson's most popular nouvelle cuisine restaurant is **Cadillac Grille**, 55 N. Cache (on the square), tel. 733-3279. The food is artfully prepared and includes a constantly changing menu of seafood and unusual game meats. The art deco decor of the Cadillac helps make it one of the most crowded tourist hangouts in town. Portions tend to be on the small side.

In Teton Village, be sure to visit **The Range**, tel. 733-5481, where excellent fixed-price nouvelle cuisine dinners make this a favorite of out-on-the-town locals. If you enjoy German cooking, particularly game and veal, head to the **Alpenhof**, tel. 733-3462, in Teton Village. For views so spectacular that they make it difficult to concentrate on your meal, don't miss **The Granary**, tel. 733-8833, located atop East Gros Ventre Butte, west of Jackson. This is also a very popular place for evening cocktails.

International Eats

Cafe Montagna, 740 W. Broadway, tel. 733-9194, serves classic Italian cuisine in a pleasant atmosphere. A nice place for a quiet evening without spending a fortune. Recommended. One of the tried-and-true local restaurants is **Anthony's Italian Restaurant**, 62 S. Glenwood St., tel. 733-3717. Prices are very reasonable and vegetarians will find several good menu items. Guaranteed to fill you up. For cheap but tasty Mexican fast food (summers only), **The Merry Piglets**, behind Teton Mountaineering on King St., tel. 733-2966, is noteworthy. **La Chispa**, tel. 733-4790, downstairs from the Cowboy Bar on the square, serves a variety of distinctive Mexican dinner specials at reasonable prices. The largest and most popular Mexican restaurant is **Vista Grande**, tel. 733-6964, on the Teton Village Road. The biggest drawing cards here are the pitchers of margaritas. **Lame Duck**

Chinese Restaurant, 680 E. Broadway, tel. 733-4311, offers an extensive range of Asian dishes, including roast duck, dim sum, tempura, sushi, and even "Saigon surprise."

Groceries

The largest Jackson grocer is **Albertson's**, 520 W. Broadway, tel. 733-9222, but many folks prefer the more friendly **Fred's Super Market**, 185 W. Broadway, tel. 733-2656, or **Food Town** next to the Pamida store at 970 W. Broadway, tel. 733-0450. For health foods, head to **Dynamic Health Natural Foods**, 130 W. Broadway, tel. 733-5418, or **Here & Now Natural Foods**, 1925 Moose-Wilson Rd., tel. 733-2742.

ENTERTAINMENT

Nightlife

Barflies will keep buzzing in Jackson, especially during midsummer and midwinter, when visitors pack local saloons every night of the week. At least one nightclub always seems to have live tunes; check Jackson's free newspapers to see where. Cover charges are generally only a couple of bucks, and many times you'll get in free. **Shady Lady Saloon** (in the Snow King Resort), 400 E. Snow King Ave., tel. 733-5200, has raucous rock 'n' roll six nights a week. It attracts a young, party-down crowd in a shout-to-be-heard atmosphere. Come wintertime, they offer free tacos every Friday evening and champagne for the ladies on Monday evenings.

The famous **Million Dollar Cowboy Bar**, on the west side of town square, tel. 733-2207, is a favorite of cowboys and wanna-be cowboys. The four pool tables at the front are almost always in use. Inside the Cowboy you'll discover burled lodgepole pine beams, display cases with stuffed bears and other cuddly beasts, bars inlaid with old silver dollars, and saddles for bar stools. Until the 1950s, the Cowboy was Jackson's center for illegal gambling. Bartenders kept a close eye on Teton Pass, where messengers used mirrors to deliver warnings of coming federal revenuers, giving folks at the bar time to hide the gaming tables in a back room. Today the dance floor fills with honky-tonking couples as the bands croon lonesome cowboy tunes six nights a week. Want to learn swing dancing? Every Thursday, you can join a free beginners class at 7 p.m.; then dance up a storm when the band comes on.

Just across the square is the **Rancher Bar**, where the atmosphere is a bit more relaxed. There are still a few genuine cowboys here. Upstairs is a big room filled with pool aficionados. **J.J.'s Silver Dollar Bar and Grill**, in the Wort Hotel at 50 N. Glenwood St., tel. 733-2190, offers a setting that might seem more fitting in Las Vegas; gaudy pink neon lights curve around a bar inlaid with 2,032 (count-em!) silver dollars. You'll have to sing your own tunes at the Silver Dollar since bands don't play here. Four blocks away, at 385 W. Broadway, tel. 733-3853, is **Spirits of the West**, where folk and rock bands often play.

Three other popular bars are in Teton Village. Right next to the tram, the **Mangy Moose Saloon**, tel. 733-4913, attracts a hip skier/outdoorsy crowd with reggae, blues, or rock bands most nights of the week during the summer and winter. It's one of Jackson Hole's jumping-est pick-up spots. At **The Sojourner**, tel. 733-3657, you can sip a beer and munch on the free hors d'oeuvres while watching basketball games on the big TV. **Dietrich's**, in the Alpenhof, tel. 733-3242, has mellow music along with free tortillas and salsa during the winter.

Out in Wilson, **The Stagecoach**, tel. 733-4407, is the place to be on Sunday nights from 5:30-10 p.m. (Wyoming bars close their doors at 10 p.m. on Sunday.) In the early '70s when hippies risked getting their heads shaved by rednecks at Jackson's Cowboy Bar, they found The 'Coach a more tolerant place. Today tobacco-chewing cowpokes show their partners slick moves on the tiny dance floor as the Stagecoach Band runs through the country tunes one more time—the band has performed here every Sunday since Feb. 16, 1969! For more entertainment, try a game of pool on one of the three tables or a buffalo burger in the cafe.

Otto Brothers Brewery

Prior to Prohibition in 1920, nearly every town in Wyoming had its own brewery, making such local favorites as Hillcrest Beer, Schoenhofen Beer, and Sweetwater Beer. After repeal of "the noble experiment," breweries again popped up, but competition from industrial giants such as Anheuser-Busch and Coors forced the last Wyoming operation—Sheridan Brewing—out of busi-

ness in 1954. It was another 34 years before commercial beer-making returned. In 1988, Charlie Otto started Wyoming's only existing brewery, a tiny backyard operation in Wilson that cranks out Teton Ale, Pale Ale, and Moose Juice Stout. You'll also find Teton Ale on tap at many Jackson area bars and restaurants. Or, take some home in a "growler," a half-gallon re-fillable bottle available at local liquor stores. (Note: The so-called "Jackson Hole Beer" is a watery lager made in Montana and sold to gullible folks who think they're buying a local brew.)

Theatres And Chuckwagon Shows

In addition to the bar scene, summers bring a number of lighthearted acting ventures to Jackson. For musical melodramas with an Old West theme, head to **Dirty Jack's Wild West Theatre**, 140 N. Cache, tel. 733-4775; **Jackson Hole Playhouse**, 145 W. Deloney, tel. 733-6994; or **Pink Garter Theatre**, 49 W. Broadway, tel. 733-3670. These are family favorites. Families also flock to the all-you-can-eat cookouts and Western musical performances at two nearby ranches: **Bar J**, Teton Village Rd. near Teton Pines, tel. 733-3370, and **Bar T-5**, 790 Cache Cr. Rd., tel. 733-5386. Neither of these is particularly authentic.

EVENTS

Winter And Spring

Kick the year off by watching (or participating in) the annual **torchlight ski parades** on Christmas Eve and New Year's Eve at all three local ski areas. **Ski races** take place all winter long, ranging from elegant "Powder Eight" Championships to blazingly fast freestyle cross-country races. (Volunteer to work one of the gates at a downhill race and you get to ski free the rest of the day.) The ski season ends with the annual **Pole-Pedal-Paddle Race**, combining alpine skiing, cross-country skiing, cycling, and canoeing in a wild, tough competition. It is the largest such event in the West. Each January and February local Shriners hold horse-drawn **cutter races**—essentially a wild chariot race on a quarter mile of sheer ice—at Melody Ranch six miles south of Jackson.

In late May, the world's only public **elk antler auction** takes place on town square, attracting hundreds of buyers from all over the globe. Local Boy Scouts collect three tons of antlers from the nearby National Elk Refuge each spring, with the proceeds helping to fund feeding the elk. This may sound like an odd event, but the high demand for antlers in the insatiable (pun intended) South Korean and Chinese aphrodisiac markets have made antlers worth more than $14 per pound, so the bidding is highly competitive. There is more than a touch of irony in the Boy Scouts making money from the sale of sexual stimulants!

Summer

On Wednesday and Saturday nights during the summer you can watch bucking broncs, rodeo clowns, and hard-riding cowboys at the **Jackson Rodeo** on the Teton County Fair Grounds. Kids get to join in the calf scramble. Prices are $6.50 for adults, $4.50 for children under 12 (free under age 4), or $21 for families. The rodeo starts at 8 p.m. Call the ticket office at 733-2805 for details. Each August, the **Old Timer's Rodeo** features a special performance of past champions at the fair grounds.

Memorial Day weekend brings **Old West Days**, complete with parades, Indian dancing, rodeos, a mountain man rendezvous, and other festivities. The **4th of July** is another big event with a parade and an impressive fireworks show from Snow King Mountain. Don't miss the 30-year-old **Grand Teton Music Festival** at Teton Village, held June-August. Performances of classical and modern works by world-renowned musicians are the highlight of this extravaganza. Ticket prices range from $5 to $15, with student discounts available; call 733-3050 for details. Also in late July is the always-fun **Teton County Fair**. The demolition derby forms a bang-up finale to the festivities. In early September, the **Jackson Hole One-Fly Contest** attracts anglers from all over, including a number of celebrity competitors.

Fall

Jackson Hole is at its most glorious in the fall, as aspens and cottonwoods turn a fire of yellow against the Tetons. Most of the tourists have fled back home, leaving locals and hardier visitors to savor the cool autumn nights. The major autumn event is the **Jackson Hole Fall Arts Festival**, featuring exhibits by local galleries, concerts, dance performances, theatre productions, quilting and poetry seminars, and other events. The annual Arts for the Parks award ($50,000!) during the festival attracts thousands of paintings representing scenes from America's national parks.

RIVER RAFTING

Jackson Hole's most popular summertime recreational activity is running Wyoming's largest river, the Snake. Each year more than 100,000 people climb aboard rafts, canoes, or kayaks to float down placid reaches of the Snake or to blast through the boiling rapids of Snake River Canyon. (As an aside, the name Snake comes from the Shoshone Indians who used serpentine hand movements as sign language for their tribal name—a motion that trappers misinterpreted as a snake and applied to the river flowing through Shoshone land.) Many different rafting companies offer dozens of different raft trips each day of the summer, so it generally isn't necessary to make reservations until the day you plan to go. Prepare to get wet. You may want to ask around to determine the advantages of each company—some are cheaper but require you to drive a good distance from town; others offer more experienced crews; while others provide various perks such as fancy meals, overnight camps along the river, or smaller boats. Also be sure to ask if you get to do any of the paddling or not. Note that this is pretty far from being a wilderness experience, especially in mid-July when stretches of the river looks like a Los Angeles freeway with traffic jams of rafts, kayaks, inner tubes, and other flotsam and jetsam.

Float Trips

The most gentle way to see the Snake is by taking one of the many daily float trips. Along the way, you'll be treated to stunning views of the Tetons, plus glimpses of eagles, ospreys, beavers, and perhaps moose or other wildlife along the riverbanks. Many local rafting companies offer five- or 10-mile scenic float trips along the quiet stretch within Grand Teton National Park, generally putting in at Deadman's Bar or Schwabacher Landing and taking out in Moose. Prices run $15-25 for adults and $10-15 for children. Roundtrip transportation from Jackson is included for most companies. A wide variety of special voyages are also available, including overnight camping trips, and fishing/floating trips.

Call one of the following raft companies for details, or pick up one of their slick brochures at the visitor center or their tiny offices scattered around Jackson: **Barker-Ewing**, tel. 733-1800; **Barlow River Trips**, tel. 733-9392; **Flagg Ranch**, tel. 733-8761 or (800) 443-2311; **Fort Jackson Float Trips**, tel. 733-2583; **Grand Teton Lodge Company**, tel. 733-2811; **Heart Six Ranch**, tel. 543-2477; **Lewis & Clark Expeditions**, tel. 733-4022 or (800) 442-8640; **Lone Eagle Expeditions**, tel. 733-1090; **Parkland Expeditions**, tel. (800) 328-0290; **Signal Mountain Lodge**, tel. 733-5470; **Solitude Float Trips**, tel. 733-2871; and **Triangle X**, tel. 733-5500.

Whitewater Trips

Below Jackson, the Snake enters the wild Snake River Canyon, a stretch early explorers labeled "the accursed mad river." The usual put-in point for whitewater trips is West Table Creek Campground, 26 miles south of Jackson. The take-out point is Sheep Gulch, eight miles downstream. In between the two, the river rocks and rolls through the narrow canyon, pumping past waterfalls and eagle nests, and then over a series of big rapids with names like Rope and Champagne, before reaching the two biggest, Kahuna and Lunch Counter. (For a look at the action from the highway, stop at the paved pullout at milepost 124 where a trail leads down to Lunch Counter.) Whitewater trips last around 3½ hours (including transportation from Jackson), and cost $16-25 for adults, or $15-20 for children. Longer voyages, including overnight trips cost approximately $90 for adults and $75 for children. Most companies include roundtrip transportation from Jackson. Don't take your own camera along unless it's waterproof; bankside float-tographers will be happy to sell you pictures for a permanent record of your run.

For details on whitewater raft trips, contact one of the following companies: **Barker-Ewing Whitewater**, tel. 733-1000; **Dave Hansen Whitewater**, tel. 733-6295; **Jackson Hole Whitewater**, tel. 733-1007; **Lewis & Clark Expeditions**, tel. 733-4022 or (800) 442-8640; **Mad River Boat Trips**, tel. 733-6203 or (800) 458-6008; **Sands' Wildwater**, tel. 733-4410 or (800) 223-4059; and **Snake River Park Whitewater**, tel. 733-7078.

Float It Yourself

Grand Teton National Park in Moose, tel. 733-2880, has useful information on running the park portions of the river; ask for a copy of *Floating the Snake River*. Note that life jackets, boat permits ($5), and registration are required to run the river through the park, and that inner tubes and air mattresses are prohibited. Floating the gentler parts (between Jackson Lake Dam and Pacific Creek) is easy for even novice boaters and canoeists, but below that point, things get more dicey. The water averages two or three feet deep, but it sometimes exceeds 10 feet and flow rates are often more than 8,000 cubic feet per second, creating logjams, braided channels, strong currents, and dangerous sweepers. Peak flows are between mid-June and early July. Inexperienced rafters or anglers die every year in the river. Flow-rate signs are posted at most river landings, the Moose Visitor Center, and the Buffalo Ranger Station in Moran. If you're planning to raft or kayak on the whitewater parts of the Snake River, be sure to contact Bridger-Teton National Forest office in Jackson, tel. 733-2752, for more information.

Lessons And Boat Rentals

Rent canoes at **Hungry Jack's** in Wilson, tel. 733-3561, for $20/day including roof rack, paddles, and life jackets. **Snake River Kayak & Canoe School**, 145 W. Gill St., tel. 733-3127, offers kayaking classes of all lengths, for $70/day

including transportation, equipment, and lunch. All-inclusive canoe clinics are $165 for 2½ days. The school rents canoes ($25/day), kayaks ($40/day), inflatable kayaks ($40/day), and rafts ($50/day), all with roof racks included. Their free brochure describes conditions on various stretches of the Snake River. **Leisure Sports**, 1075 South U.S. 89, tel. 733-3040, also rents rafts ($45/day), canoes ($30/day), kayaks ($25/day), and windsurfing equipment ($20/day), along with all sorts of other outdoor equipment. They can also provide a shuttle service. **Riding and Rafts** in Alpine, tel. 654-9900, has six-person rafts for $35.

OTHER SUMMER RECREATION

Horsin' Around

Think of the Wild West, and one animal always comes to mind—the horse. A ride on old paint gives city slickers a chance to saunter back in time to a simpler era, and to simultaneously learn how ornery and opinionated horses can be. In Jackson Hole you can choose from brief half-day trail rides in Grand Teton National Park all the way up to week-long wilderness pack trips into the rugged Teton Wilderness. The visitor center has a brochure listing more than a dozen local outfitters and stables offering trail rides.

For short rides (around $12/hour or $50/day), try: **Jackson Hole Trail Rides** in Teton Village, tel. 733-6992; **Snow King Stables**, behind Snow King Resort, tel. 733-5781; **Spring Creek Resort**, Spring Gulch Rd., tel. 733-8833; or **Bar T-5**, 790 Cache Creek Rd., tel. 733-5386. For a different sort of trip, try llama packing with **Jackson Hole Llamas**, tel. 733-1617, or **Black Diamond Llamas**, tel. 733-2877. Half-day llama treks are just $30 per person.

On The Water

Jackson Hole has some of the finest angling in Wyoming, with native Snake River cutthroat (a distinct subspecies) and brook trout in the river along with Mackinaw, cutthroat, and brown trout in the lakes. The Snake is a particular favorite of beginning fly-fishing enthusiasts. Many local companies offer guided fly-fishing float trips down the Snake River, or you can fish from the riverbanks with lures or flies. Expect to pay approximately $220/day with guide, lunch, and boat. The boats hold up to three people. Rental equipment is also available from local shops. Jackson has half-a-dozen different fishing shops. Stop by **Jack Dennis' Outdoor Shop**, 50 E. Broadway, tel. 733-3270 or (800) 522-5755, and pick up a copy of the free *Western Fishing Newsletter* for descriptions of local fishing areas and what lures to try. The visitor center has an up-to-date listing of fishing guides. Note that Wyoming fishing licenses are valid within Grand Teton National Park, but not in Yellowstone.

Jackson Lake is a popular windsurfing place, with moderate winds (perfect for beginners) and an impressive Teton backdrop. **Alpine Windsurfing**, 365 N. Glenwood, tel. 733-4460, rents windsurfing equipment for $35/day including wetsuit and roof rack, and offers lessons on the lake. Advanced windsurfers looking for stronger wind conditions head to Slide Lake east of Kelly, or to blow-me-down Yellowstone Lake.

Biking

Jackson Hole offers all sorts of adventures for cyclists, particularly those with mountain bikes. **Teton Cyclery**, 175 N. Glenwood St., tel. 733-4386; **Hoback Sports**, 40 S. Millward St., tel. 733-5335; **Leisure Sports**, tel. 733-3040, 1075 South U.S. 89; and **Mountain Bike Outfitters** in Moose, tel. 733-3314, all rent bikes for $15-20/day. The last of these has a helpful free map of local mountain bike routes. Local mountain bike tours (one includes a chair lift ride to the top of Snow King) are available from **Fat Tire Tours**, tel. 733-5335, for $35/day. **Off the Deep End Travels**, tel. 733-8707 or (800) 223-6833, has guided cycling trips combined with rafting on the Snake River for $45/day. Deep End also offers dozens of other trips all over the world for adventure travelers.

Alpine Slide And Scenic Rides

During the summer, kids love to race down the 2,500-foot-long **Alpine Slide** at Snow King Mountain, right on the edge of Jackson. Rides cost $4 ($3 for kids under 12). Snow King's main chair lift is also in operation during the summer, taking folks to the top of the 7,751-foot mountain for $4 ($2 for kids under 12). On top is a short nature trail and panoramic views of the Tetons. Call 733-5200 for details on both of these rides. Out in Teton Village, you can ride the **aerial tram** to the top of Rendezvous Mountain (10,552 feet) for $11 ($9 seniors, $7 teens, and $3 children). Open daily June-Sept., this is a spectacular way to reach the alpine. On top is a small gift/snack shop and naturalists who lead free summertime hikes into nearby Rock Springs Bowl. Call 733-2292 for details. Over in Alta, you can ride the Grand Targhee **chair lift** to the 10,200-foot summit of Fred's Mountain for $5 (weekends only).

Other Activities

There are no public swimming pools in Jackson, but you can soak in a wonderful hot mineral pool (105° F) at **Granite Hot Springs**, tel. 733-6318. Head south to Hoback Junction and then up Hoback Canyon to the turnoff for Granite. The pool is another 10 miles along a dirt road (total of 35 miles), and costs $4 for adults, $1-3 for kids. **Jackson Hole Golf & Tennis Club**, a mile north of town, tel. 733-3111, has an 18-hole golf course, swimming pool, and tennis courts. The Arnold Palmer-designed 18-hole **Teton Pines Country Club**, on Teton Village Rd., tel. 733-1005, is Jackson Hole's second golf spot. **Jackson Hole Athletic Club**, 875 W. Broadway, tel. 733-8830, has a gymnasium ($7.50/day) with Nautilus and other equipment, along with a variety of exercise classes. **The Hole Hiking Experience**, tel. 733-7155, leads day-long treks into the mountains around Jackson Hole for $45 ($20 for children).

WINTER RECREATION

For details on the many opportunities for downhill and cross-country skiing in and around Jackson Hole, see "Skiing the Tetons," p.249.

Ice Skating And Snowshoeing

Each winter, the town of Wilson floods a hockey-rink-sized part of the town park for skating. A warming hut stands next to the rink and the floodlights are on most nights. Jackson maintains a smaller ice rink at the Intermediate School on S. Cache and a broomball rink in Snow King Ball Park. For $7, including skate rental, you can hit the ice at Aspens Athletic Club's indoor rink, tel. 733-7004. Grand Teton National Park has free naturalist-led snowshoe hikes every Tuesday and Saturday departing at 2 p.m. from the visitor center in Moose. Snowshoes are provided. Make reservations at 733-2880.

Slip-Slidin' Away

Jackson Hole Resort Service, tel. 733-6657, offers visitors a quaint step back in time. Each winter evening, horse-drawn **sleighs** pick up Teton Village guests for a romantic ride up to a rustic log cabin where they are served a complete prime rib dinner before heading back to civilization. Make reservations well in advance for this popular trip down memory lane. Prices are $38 for adults or $20 for children. If you don't have that kind of cash, try one of the sleigh rides offered at the Elk Refuge (see p. 234). **Freebird Alaskan Adventures**, tel. 733-7388, offers dog sled tours, along with special moonlight trips. Run by Frank Teasley, a musher in Alaska's famous Iditarod race, this is a great opportunity to see some wonderful country in a unique way. Rates are $120/day or $85/half day. Full-day trips include trout and steak dinners. Reserve well in advance.

Snowmobiling

One of the fastest-growing wintertime activities in Jackson Hole is snowmobiling. Hundreds of miles of packed and groomed snowmobile trails head into Bridger-Teton National Forest as well as Yellowstone and Grand Teton national parks. Some of the most popular places include the Togwotee Pass area (48 miles north of Jackson), Cache Creek Rd. (east of town), and Granite Hot Springs Rd. (25 miles southeast). At least a half-dozen different Jackson companies offer guided snowmobile trips into Yellowstone, with prices starting around $125/day. **Togwotee Mountain Lodge**, 16 miles east of Moran Jct., tel. 543-2847 or (800) 543-2847, is where the snowmobile companies photograph their ads and brochures. Guided snowmobile tours start for $89/day. Contact the visitor center for a listing of local snowmobile rental companies and maps of snowmobile trails.

In recent years, one of the most contentious issues in Jackson Hole has been the proposal to construct the Continental Divide Snowmobile Trail through Grand Teton National Park, thus connecting the Yellowstone road network with snowmobile trails within Bridger-Teton National Forest. If this does happen, it will not only mean far more machines entering the already over-

crowded Yellowstone area, but also an unfortunate emphasis upon mechanized travel in previously undeveloped areas. Hopefully, the snowmobiles will be kept out.

INFORMATION AND SERVICES

Anyone new to Jackson Hole should be sure to visit the impressive **Wyoming State Information Center** at 532 N. Cache, tel. 733-3316. Hours are daily 8 a.m-8 p.m. between mid-June and Labor Day, and Mon.-Fri. 8:30-5:30 and Sat.-Sun. 10-2 the rest of the year. The information center is a two-level, sod-roofed wooden building with displays on local history and sights, a blizzard of free leaflets extolling the merits of local businesses, and an upstairs rear deck that overlooks the National Elk Refuge. Ducks and trumpeter swans are visible on the marsh. There are direct phones to several dozen local motels and hotels, plus a signboard that lights up when the hotels are full. Check out posters over the entrance from some of the 15 movies filmed in Jackson Hole, including *Shane, Any Which Way You Can, Big Trail, Bad Bascomb, Big Sky, The Far Horizons, Spencer's Mountain, Jubal, Mountain Man,* and *Rocky IV.* If you want general information before coming to Jackson Hole, the **Jackson Hole Visitors Council**, tel. (800) 782-0011, will be happy to provide brochures and piles of info. The **Jackson Hole Chamber of Commerce**, also in the State Information Center, has more specific info on local businesses.

Books

The **Teton County Library** at 320 S. King St., tel. 733-2164, is a great place to spend a rainy or snowy day. Built in 1940, this cozy old log structure houses a substantial collection of books about Wyoming and the West. Hours are Sun. 1-5, Mon., Wed., and Fri. 10-5:30, Tues. and Thurs. 10-9, and Sat. 10-5. Unlike many Wyoming towns where the book selection consists of a few romance novels in the local drugstore, Jackson is blessed with three fine bookstores: **Grand Books**, 970 W. Broadway (next to Pamida), tel. 733-1687; **Teton Bookshop**, 25 S. Glenwood, tel. 733-9220; and the largest, **Valley Bookstore**, 125 N. Cache, tel. 733-4533.

Living In Jackson Hole

Jackson Hole is becoming an increasingly popular place to live and work. The surrounding country is grand, there are many things to do and places to explore, and you're likely to meet others with similar interests. Jobs such as waiting tables, operating ski lifts, driving tour buses, cleaning hotels and condos, and construction work are generally plentiful, but the wages are not high. Check local classified ads or stop by the Wyoming Job Service Center, 545 N. Cache, tel. 733-4091, to get an idea of available jobs. The best jobs are those that offer either such perks as a free ski pass or that give you lots of free time to explore the area.

Unfortunately, because of Jackson Hole's popularity, finding a place to live is quite difficult, especially during the peak summer and winter tourist seasons. Workers are even being bused in from Afton, 70 miles away! Land prices (and hence housing costs) have been rising at an astronomical rate—Teton Village land shot up more than 100% in 1989 alone! A few Jackson area restaurants include inexpensive housing as a way to attract workers, but this is the exception; many workers are forced to live under less-than-ideal conditions such as jamming many folks into an apartment, sleeping in a tent during the summer, or crowding in with others into a too-small apartment. The best times to look for a place to live are in April and November. Check the papers as well as local laundromat and grocery store bulletin boards for apartments or cabins. The "Trash and Treasure" morning program on radio station KMTN is another place to try.

SHOPPING

If you have the money, Jackson is a great place to buy everything from artwork to mountain bikes. Even if you just hitched in and have no cash to spare, it's always fun to wander through the shops and galleries surrounding town square. Factory outlet stores offer slightly discounted prices on such brand names as Pendleton, Ralph Lauren Polo, Benetton, and Fila. Buy used clothing and other items at **Browse 'N Buy Thrift Shop**, 139 N. Cache, tel. 733-7524, and **Orville's**, 285 W. Pearl, tel. 733-3165. Orville's has old Wyoming license plates for just a buck—a big hit with European tourists.

Outdoor Gear

Outdoor enthusiasts will discover several excellent shops in Jackson. Climbers, backpackers, and cross-country skiers head to **Teton Mountaineering**, 86 E. Broadway, tel. 733-3595, for quality equipment. They also rent tents, sleeping bags, packs, climbing shoes, cross-country skis and other gear. A few doors away at 50 E. Broadway, tel. 733-3270 or (800) 522-5755, is **Jack Dennis Sports**, a large upscale store that sells fly-fishing and camping gear in the summer and skis and warm clothes during the winter. They also rent almost anything, from skis and skates to backpacks and cameras. **Skinny Skis**, 65 W. Deloney Ave., tel. 733-6094, has more in the way of quality clothing and supplies, especially cross-country ski gear. The least expensive place to buy rugged outdoor wear, cowboy boots, and cowboy hats is **Corral West Ranchwear**, 840 W. Broadway, tel. 733-0247. The **County Parks and Recreation Department**, 181 S. King St., tel. 733-5056, loans out tents, sleeping bags, and sports equipment for a $50 refundable deposit. Don't expect the highest quality, but what do you want for free?

Wyoming Woolens, a local manufacturer of quality warm clothing (the plant is in Afton), has two stores in Jackson: a retail shop near the square at 20 W. Broadway, tel. 733-2991, and a factory outlet with great bargains at 870 South U.S. 89, tel. 733-2889. For high-quality, handmade lycra and polarplus clothing, as well as tent or backpack repairs, visit **Columbine**, tel. 733-7179, a small shop in Pink Garter Plaza at 49 W. Broadway.

TRANSPORTATION

Access to Jackson Hole has become easier in recent years with several airlines and summer-only daily bus service. Most summer visitors arrive by car, though a few more adventurous souls pedal in on bikes. If you're looking for or offering a ride, the local FM station, KMTN, tel. 733-5686, has a daily ride-finder announcement at 11:20 p.m. Other folks call in with rides on the station's 9:30 a.m. "Trash and Treasure" radio show.

By Air

At one time, Jackson was considered impossible to get to, but today daily jet service brings visitors from all over the world. Jackson Hole Airport is eight miles north of Jackson in Grand Teton National Park. The only commercial airport within any national park, it is a source of considerable tension, as plans to expand the runway conflict directly with the park's management for natural resource values. The airport is served by **Delta**, tel. (800) 221-1212; **American**, tel. (800) 433-7300; **United Express**, tel. (800) 241-6522; **Continental Express**, tel. (800) 525-0280; and **Skywest**, tel. (800) 453-9417. Delta and Skywest route all their flights through Salt Lake City, while United Express and Continental Express go via Denver. American Airlines flights go through Salt Lake City or Dallas, but during the winter they also offer direct service to Chicago. **All Star Transportation**, tel. 733-2888, provides airport shuttle service to and from motels in Jackson ($5 OW) and Teton Village ($11 OW or $17 RT). Add a couple bucks for similar services from **Jackson Hole Transportation**, tel. 733-3135. Both companies meet all commercial airline flights. Make outgoing reservations a day in advance. For taxi service ($15 to town or $25 to Teton Village), call **A-I Taxi**, tel. 733-5089; **Caribou Cab**, tel. 733-2888; or **Tumbleweed Taxi**, tel. 733-0808.

Car Rentals

Most of the national chains (Avis, Budget, Dollar-Saver, Hertz, National, and Rent-A-Wreck) have rental cars in town or at the airport, but the best deals are from the two used car companies. **Rent-A-Wreck**, 1250 S. Carol Lane, tel. 733-5014, has a few cars that go for $20/day. (Transportation from the airport is $3 extra.) Rates at **Dollar Saver**, 285 N. Cache, tel. 733-2222, start at $25/day, but you'll have to find your own way into Jackson from the airport. The least expensive new-car rental companies (around $35/day) are **Resort Rent-A-Car**, 345 W. Broadway, tel. 733-1656, and **Budget**, 400 E. Snow King Ave., tel. 733-2206.

START Buses

Local buses are operated by Southern Teton Area Rapid Transit (START) and serve Jackson and Teton Village most of the year. This is Wyoming's only true public bus system! START fares are 50¢ within town and $1 to Teton Village (seniors free). Discount coupons are available for multiple rides. During the summer, buses run seven days a week, every half-hour in town and every hour to the Village, with additional daily service to Moose, Gros Ventre Campground, and even Star Valley ($3 RT). Winter schedules offer more frequent service to Teton Village. There is no bus service at all between mid-April and mid-June, and between early Sept. and early December. Pick up bus schedules and route maps in the visitor center. Hours of operation are 7 a.m. to midnight. Buses stop near most Jackson hotels and motels, and are equipped to carry skis and bikes on outside racks. START buses do not run to the airport or to Wilson. Call 733-4521 for more information.

Buses And Tours

Given that two million tourists cram through Jackson each year, it's hard to believe how limited long-distance bus service is. There are no direct bus connections to Idaho Falls, Dubois, Casper, Lander, or Riverton, and summer-only service to Cody. The only year-round service is the **Jackson-Rock Springs Stage Line**, a van that connects the two towns for $18 pp. During the summer this is a daily service, dropping back to Mon., Wed., and Fri. runs the rest of the year. Once in Rock Springs, you can catch Greyhound on a roundabout routing to other parts of Wyoming. The van stops at **Teton World Travel**, 72 S. Glenwood, tel. 733-4740. **Grand Teton Lodge Company**, tel. 733-2811, offers a twice-daily summer shuttle bus between Jackson and Jackson Lake Lodge for $8.50 OW. Buses depart from 72 S. Glenwood St., with stops at the airport and Jenny Lake upon request.

Two companies offer daily summertime bus tours of Grand Teton and Yellowstone national parks: **Powder River Tours**, 565 N. Cache, tel. 733-4152 or (800) 442-3682, and **Gray Line**, 332 N. Glenwood, tel. 733-4325 or (800) 443-6133. Rates are around $40 (including park entrance fees) for these all-day loop tours. The Grand Teton tour includes a Jenny Lake boat ride. In Yellowstone, Powder River travelers can connect with other buses to West Yellowstone, Gardiner, or Cody. Four- and six-day guided tours of the parks are also available through Gray Line.

Powder River has winter-only daily bus runs to Flagg Ranch for $25 RT, arriving in time to meet the snowcoach departures for Yellowstone. Book Yellowstone lodging and snowcoach or snowmobile packages through them, saving yourself the long-distance call to TWR

Services in Mammoth. Powder River also runs daily wintertime trips to the Elk Refuge, Teton Science School, and Grand Teton National Park, including lunch at Gros Ventre River Ranch, for $60 pp.

SKIING THE TETONS

Until recently, Jackson Hole was primarily a summertime resort, filled with carloads of screaming children, French tourists snickering at the name "Grand Teton," and adventurous young people streaming into the mountains. As access has become easier and the facilities more developed, many people have discovered the wonders of a Jackson Hole winter, especially one centered around a week on the ski slopes. Three very different ski resorts attract the crowds: Grand Targhee for downhome, powder-to-the-butt conditions; Snow King for steep, inexpensive, edge-of-town slopes; and Jackson Hole for flashy, world-class skiing. All three places have rental equipment and ski schools, and allow snowboards and telemarkers on the slopes. This mixture, along with an incredible abundance of developed and wild places to cross-country ski, combine to make Jackson Hole one of the premier ski destinations in America. Tip: If you plan to spend more than a couple of days in the area, it may well be worth your while to join the **Jackson Hole Ski Club**. In return for a $25 annual membership you receive an impressive number of premiums, including half-price lift tickets, various freebies, and discounts at more than 70 local shops. Join up at any local ski shop. See your travel agent for package trips to any of the Jackson area resorts.

Ski Rentals
Rent or buy downhill skis from: **Hoback Sports**, 40 S. Millward St. (also at Snow King Resort), tel. 733-5335; **Ski and Sports**, 485 W. Broadway, tel. 733-4449; **Jack Dennis Outdoor Shop**, 50 E. Broadway, tel. 733-3270; **Wildernest Sports**, Teton Village, tel. 733-4297; or **Teton Village Sports**, tel. 733-2181. Rent or buy cross-country skis at **Skinny Skis**, 65 W. Deloney Ave., tel. 733-6094, or **Teton Mountaineering**, 86 E. Broadway, tel. 733-3595. All the local Nordic centers also rent equipment.

GRAND TARGHEE SKI RESORT

Until recently, Grand Targhee was considered something of a hick ski area, the sort of place where folks skied in overalls and headed back to their farms to feed the cows. The food was dreadful, the lodging facilities were funky at best, and the lift operators wore cowboy hats with plastic covers. But, skiers also discovered that Targhee had some of the most incredible snow in the known universe. With an annual snowfall of 504 inches (42 feet!)—most of which is champagne powder—Targhee became the secret spot where powder hounds got all they could ever want. In 1987, Mory and Carol Bergmeyer took over and began transforming Targhee into a first-class ski area, remodelling the facilities, adding new restaurants and services, and inaugurating snowcat skiing. The lift operators still wear cowboy hats. A 1990 fire led to a completely new and expanded lodge facility. On the drawing boards are all sorts of new developments that have brought major controversy and even litigation by locals anxious to keep their peaceful way of life.

The biggest drawback to Grand Targhee is the same thing that makes it so great—the weather. Lots of snow means lots of clouds, and because it snows so much, there are many days when the name cynics apply—Grand Foghee—seems more appropriate. Many folks who have returned to Targhee year after year have still not seen the magnificent Grand Teton backdrop behind the ski area! Be sure to bring your goggles.

Nuts And Bolts
Targhee has three double chair lifts and one surface lift on the prosaically named Fred's Mountain. The top elevation is 10,200 feet, with the longest run dropping 2.8 miles and 2,200 feet. Although only 300 acres are groomed, the

remaining 1,200 acres of ungroomed powder mean that you'll always find track-free skiing. And if that isn't enough, try snowcat skiing ($70/half day or $135/day including lunch, lesson, and guide) on adjacent Peaked Peak. You'll get 8 to 12 runs each day and miles of untracked powder (bring your snorkel), with runs up to three miles long. Lift tickets at Grand Targhee cost $26/day ($16/half day) for adults and $13/day for children and seniors.

A full 70% of Targhee's groomed runs are intermediate, but advanced skiers will find an extraordinary number of deep-powder faces to explore. Snowboarders are also welcome. The ski school offers lessons for all abilities, and children's programs make it possible for parents to leave their kids behind. NASTAR races are held every Tues., Fri., and Sat., and cross-country skiers enjoy the Everything Nordic center (see "Cross-Country Skiing," below). Rental skis ($12.50/day or $8.50 for children) and snowboards ($25/day) are available at the base of the mountain. The ski area usually opens in mid-Nov. and closes in late April. Lifts operate from 9:30 a.m. to 4 p.m. daily. Call (800) 443-8146 for more on Grand Targhee.

Food And Lodging

Targhee has three places to stay: motel-style rooms in Targhee and Teewinot lodges, as well as condominium accommodations in Sioux Lodge. Nightly rates start around $90 d during the holiday season, but a wide variety of ski/lodging package deals are also available. A heated outdoor pool and hot tub are available for lodge residents. Call Targhee at (800) 443-8146 to get brochures detailing all these options.

At the base of Grand Targhee you'll find a cafeteria and several restaurants. You can ride in a horse-drawn sleigh to a Mongolian-style yurt for a home-cooked dinner of steak, chicken, or fish. The price is $24 pp ($13 for kids). Grand Targhee's social center is the **Trap Bar**, with live music most nights. Other shops here sell groceries, ski equipment, and clothing. For another diversion, try dog sledding at $30 for an hour-long ride. On Christmas and New Year's, be sure to stay around for the impressive torchlit ski parade down the mountain. Each Memorial Day, balloon enthusiasts come to Targhee for the hot air-balloon festival. The Bluegrass Festival rolls around in early August.

Getting There

Grand Targhee is located 42 miles northwest of Jackson on the western side of the Tetons in Alta, Wyoming. Get there by driving over Teton Pass (occasionally closed by winter storms), north through Victor and Driggs, Idaho, and then east back into Wyoming. A **shuttle bus** provides transport from the Jackson or Idaho Falls airport to Targhee for $20 OW (minimum two people). Make reservations two days ahead by calling the ski area. The **Targhee Express** bus makes daily wintertime trips (90 minutes each way) to Grand Targhee from Jackson and Teton Village. Buses leave Jackson at 7:30 a.m. and return by 6:30 p.m. For $35 (same as a lift ticket at Jackson Hole Resort) you get roundtrip bus transportation to Targhee and a lift ticket.

JACKSON HOLE SKI RESORT

Just 12 miles northwest of Jackson is Jackson Hole Ski Resort, the largest and best-known Wyoming ski area. A true skier's mountain, Jackson Hole is considered the most varied and challenging of any American ski area. The powder is usually deep (average snowfall is 38 feet!), lift lines are short, the slopes are uncrowded, and the vistas are unbelievable. First opened in 1965, Jackson Hole Ski Resort has become one of the nation's favorite ski areas.

Superlatives

A recent magazine article referred to Jackson Hole Resort as a place "where the skiing gets tough and the tough go skiing." Half of the runs here are in the advanced category, including several of the notorious double-diamonds. And yes, those death-defying cliff-jumping shots are real; on the tram ride up, check out the infamous Corbett's Coulair, a rocky gully that requires a leap of faith and suicidal urges. With an unsurpassed 4,139-foot vertical drop, 2,400 acres of terrain spread over two adjacent mountains, runs that may exceed four miles in length, and 24 miles of groomed trails, Jackson Hole is truly a resort of superlatives.

Actually, the mountain is so large that even rank beginners will find plenty of bunny slopes on which to practice. Rendezvous Mountain (10,450 feet) is where experts strut their stuff, while adjacent Apres Vous Mountain (8,481 feet) is primarily for those who like friendlier slopes. Intermediate skiers could spend all day exploring the various runs here. The most enjoyable way to the top of Rendezvous Mountain is aboard one of the new, 63-passenger aerial tram cars. Powered by 500-horsepower engines, they climb nearly $2^1/2$ miles in 12 minutes, offering jaw-dropping views across Jackson Hole. There are also five double chairs, a triple chair, a quad chair, and two Poma lifts spread over the rest of the terrain, and you can ski down 60 different named trails.

Services And Rates

Get to Teton Village from the town of Jackson by hopping on the START bus ($1 each way). This is the only inexpensive part of a visit to Jackson Hole Resort, with prices for lift tickets approaching the stratosphere. Single-day tickets are $35 for adults ($27/half-day) and $18 ($13/half-day) for kids under 14 and seniors. Tram tickets are an additional $2 each. Lifts are open 9-4 daily from early Dec. till early April. Skis and snowboards can be rented in Jackson or Teton Village. The ski school is headed by Pepi Stiegler—a 1964 Olympic gold medalist from Austria—and offers a special Kinderschule program for children. You can ski with Pepi Mon.-Fri. at 1:30 p.m.; meet him at the top of Casper lift. Every hour on the hour a ski host meets intermediate and advanced skiers at the top of Rendezvous Mountain, providing information and tours of the slopes. Racers and spectators will enjoy NASTAR events each Sun., Tues., and Thurs., along with various other events throughout the winter.

Teton Village, a Swiss-style resort at the base of the mountain, has lodges, condominiums, restaurants, bars, shops, a small grocery, ski rentals, lockers, a liquor store, car rentals, and even a travel agency for escapes to Hawaii. On-the-mountain facilities include a restaurant and ski shop in Casper Bowl and a snack bar at the top of the tram. For more information on Jackson Hole Ski Resort, contact them at Box 290, Teton Village, WY 83025, tel. 733-2292. For snow conditions (24 hours), call 733-2291. The messages are changed each morning before 5 a.m.

SNOW KING RESORT

Rising directly behind the town of Jackson, Snow King Resort's ski runs make up in difficulty what it lacks in size. From below, the mountain (7,871 feet tall) looks impossibly steep and narrow. High atop the big chair lift, the vista provides a panoramic tour of Jackson Hole. Jackson's "town hill," Snow King was the first ski area in Wyoming (opened in 1939), and one of the first in North America. The first chapter of the National Ski Patrol was established here in 1941.

There are more than 500 acres of skiable terrain at Snow King, with the longest run being nearly a mile in length. Two double chairs and a Poma lift climb up the mountainside. Lift tickets at Snow King are well below other Jackson Hole resorts: $20/day ($14/half-day) for adults and $14/day ($8/half day) for kids under 15 and seniors. Discount coupons worth $2 off are often available inside Snow King Resort. Hours of operation are 9:30-4:30, with **night skiing** (Wed.-Sat., 5:30-9:30 p.m.) available on the lower sections of Snow King for an additional $10/adults and $6/kids and seniors. The ski season is generally early Dec. to early April.

Hoback Sports rents skis at the foot of the mountain, and a ski school and guided Nordic tours down the back side of the mountain are also available. At the base of Snow King you'll discover an elaborate lodge, two restaurants, the Shady Lady Saloon, and a variety of other facilities. Jackson's town square is only seven blocks away and START buses (50¢) offer frequent service. For more info on Snow King Resort, call 733-5200 or (800) 522-5464 (outside Wyoming). Special package rates to Snow King Resort start around $230 pp (double occupancy) for three nights lodging and two days of skiing.

CROSS-COUNTRY SKIING

For many Jackson Hole residents the word "skiing" means heading across frozen Jenny Lake or telemarking down the bowls of Teton Pass rather than sliding down the slopes of the local resorts. Jackson Hole is becoming a national center for cross-country enthusiasts and offers an impressive range of conditions, from flat-tracking across summertime golf courses where a gourmet restaurant awaits you, to remote wilderness settings where a complete knowledge of snow crystal structure, avalanche hazards, and winter survival are essential. Beginners will probably want to start out at one of the five nearby Nordic centers, progressing to local paths and the more gentle lift-serviced ski runs with experience. More advanced skiers will quickly discover the incredible snow in the surrounding mountains.

Nordic Centers

Nordic skiing enthusiasts will find three different developed facilities near Jackson, along with ones at Grand Targhee and up on Togwotee Pass. Largest is **Jackson Hole Nordic Center**, tel. 733-2292, with 25 km of groomed trails—both set track and skating lanes—covering a wide range of conditions. Call 733-2291 for the snow report. Located right in Teton Village, this is the best place to try out cross-country skiing. Rates are $8/day for adults or $5/day for children and seniors. If you need equipment, the total cost is $11/day ($7/day for children and seniors), including trail fees and touring skis, boots, and poles, or $14/day ($9/day for children and seniors), for trail fees and telemarking equipment. Hours are daily 8:30-5. After 12:30 p.m., your alpine lift ticket at Jackson Hole Ski Resort is good at the Nordic center too. The center offers a wide range of lessons, along with naturalist-led tours of Grand Teton National Park ($40-65 pp), and trips to Teton Pass ($40 pp) for the more adventurous.

Teton Pines Cross Country Ski Center, three miles north on Teton Village Rd., tel. 733-1005, includes 13 km of machine-groomed track (both diagonal stride skiing and skating) on a summertime golf course. Rates are $5/day for adults, $3/day for children, and $15/day for a family. Ski rentals cost $10 ($7 children), and guided tours to Grand Teton National Park run $50 pp. Hours are 9 a.m. to dusk. The clubhouse here has a pricey restaurant for gourmet après-ski lunches and dinners.

Spring Creek Nordic Center, tel. 733-1004, is three miles north of U.S. 22 on Spring Gulch Rd., and is open 10-5 daily. If you're staying in town, you can catch the free shuttle bus at the Wort Hotel. (Call the Nordic center for specifics.) Guests of the Wort Hotel or Spring Creek Resort ski free. The center has 10 km of gentle groomed trails with skating lanes, perfect for beginners. Rates are $6/day for adults and $3/day for children and seniors, with ski rentals for $8/day.

Farther afield is **Togwotee Mountain Lodge**, 48 miles northeast of Jackson, tel. 543-2847 or (800) 543-2847; open daily 8:30-5. Just a couple of miles above the lodge, U.S. 26-287 heads over the Continental Divide at 9,658 feet, so expect to find luxuriously deep powder. Teton Wilderness lies just north of here, and when you face west the Teton Range offers up a jagged horizon line. Togwotee has over 25 km of groomed trails (single track) covering a wide variety of terrain. Rates are $6/day for adults and $4/day for children and seniors. Lessons are also available. Rent skis, boots, and poles for $8.50/day. The lodge itself is a pleasant, rustic place to stay for the night or to enjoy a dinner before returning to Jackson.

Drive another 10 miles over Togwotee Pass to **Brooks Lake Lodge**, tel. 455-2121, for some of the most incredible scenery and cross-country skiing in the West. (See "Wind River Mountains," p. 207 for lodging information.) Brooks Lake Lodge is five miles in on a machine-packed road, making a perfect destination for day trips. Once there, you'll find another five km of groomed trails (no charge) plus access to the nearby Teton Wilderness where skiers can escape the snowmobiles. At the lodge (closed Tues. and Wed.) you can relax and enjoy lunch or spend the night (advance reservations required).

The **Grand Targhee Everything Nordic Center**, tel. 353-2304, has 12 km of groomed cross-country ski trails covering rolling terrain. Trail passes are $5/day, and lessons and a variety of tours are also available. Rent skis,

BOB RACE

boots, and poles for $12.50/day or $8.50/day for children. Hours are daily 9-4:30. Guests with Targhee lodging packages can ski free on the cross-country tracks.

On Your Own

Nordic skiers who would rather explore Jackson Hole and the mountains that surround it on their own, discover an extraordinary range from beginner-level treks along old roads, to places where only the most advanced skiers dare venture. Because Jackson has so many cross-country fanatics (and visiting enthusiasts), trails are quickly broken along the more popular routes, making it easier for those who follow. For complete coverage of all these options, pick up a copy of the free *Cross Country Ski Guide to Jackson Hole* at Skinny Skis, 65 W. Deloney Ave., tel. 733-6094. If you're heading out on your own, be prepared for deep snow (four feet in the valley) and temperatures that often plummet far below zero at night. The **Teton County Parks and Recreation Department**, tel. 733-5056, leads a variety of cross-country ski outings every Tuesday (mid-Jan. to late-March) for $5. Bring your own skis. **Jackson Hole Mountain Guides**, tel. 733-4979, runs wintertime ski tours, ski mountaineering, rock and ice climbing classes, along with overnight trips into a ski hut on Teton Pass ($125 pp guided). Longer trips, such as a six-day Teton Crest tour, run around $550 pp.

Even rank beginners will enjoy exploring several local spots. Get to the **Moose-Wilson Rd.** by heading a mile north of Teton Village to where plowing ends. The nearly level road continues for two scenic miles across a creek and through groves of aspen. For more adventure, turn off at the Granite Canyon trailhead and follow the trail up toward the canyon. Conditions get more difficult as you progress, and avalanches are a potential hazard farther up.

The closest place to Jackson for on-your-own cross-country skiing is **Cache Creek Canyon** at the east end of Cache Creek Dr. where the plowing ends at a parking lot. Snowmobiles and other skiers have packed the route. For a longer trip, take the Rafferty ski lift at Snow King and then ski west through the trees and down to Cache Creek, returning via the road. Ask at Snow King for specifics. Another popular local place is along the **Snake River dikes**, where

U.S. 22 crosses the river (a mile east of Wilson). The dikes extend along both sides of the river for several miles, making for easy skiing. It's also a good place to watch ducks, moose, and other critters, or just to listen to the river rolling over the rocks.

A bit farther afield, but well worth the detour, are several trails in Grand Teton National Park. Orange markers denote the paths. Park at the Cottonwood Creek bridge (the road isn't plowed beyond this), and head out for **Jenny Lake** (nine miles RT) or **Taggart Lake** (three miles RT). Just three miles south of Moose on Moose-Wilson Rd., you may also want to try the trail to **Phelps Lake** (five miles RT). Or, if you have more ambition and skill, longer routes could take you far up into the canyons of the Tetons. Be sure to stop at the Moose Visitor Center for current conditions and a copy of their trail map. Ski mountaineers and overnight ski tourers must also register here.

For unsurpassed vistas of the Tetons, try skiing to the top of 8,252-foot **Shadow Mountain** near the town of Kelly, 14 miles northeast of Jackson. (The name comes from the shadows of the Tetons that fall across the mountain's face each evening.) From Kelly, drive another five miles north to a parking area (the road isn't plowed beyond this), and up the nearby Forest Service road that snakes up Shadow Mountain. It's fairly steep in places and 10 miles RT. Snowmobilers also use this road.

One of the most popular ski- and snowmobile-in sites is **Granite Hot Springs**, tel. 733-6318, a delightful 105° F hot spring-fed pool on Forest Service land. Get there by driving 25 miles southeast of Jackson into Hoback Canyon, and then skiing 10 miles in from the signed parking area. The route is not difficult, but due to the distance, it isn't recommended for beginners unless they are prepared for a 20-mile RT trek. The pool ($4) is open 10 a.m. to an hour before dark. Bring your swimsuit. Ask the attendant about places to snowcamp nearby.

Locals head to the 8,429-foot **Teton Pass** when they really want to test their ability. The summit parking area fills with cars on new-snow mornings, as everyone from advanced-beginners to beyond-advanced mountaineering skiers head out for a day in the powder or a week of wilderness trekking in the Tetons. Snow depths of eight feet or more are not uncommon in midwinter. (The snow once became so deep on the pass that it took snow plows two weeks to clear the road!)

Before heading out, check the above-mentioned Skinny Skis *Cross Country Ski Guide* for specifics on Teton Pass, or talk to folks at Skinny Skis or Teton Mountaineering. This is the backcountry, so there are no signs at the various bowls; ask other skiers if you aren't sure which is which. Avalanches do occur in some of these bowls, and it's possible to get lost up here during a storm; so be prepared. Skiers frequently continue down the old Teton Pass road, following it for five miles, to the Heidelberg Bed and Breakfast.

SAFETY IN AVALANCHE COUNTRY

❖ ❖ ❖ ❖ ❖ ❖

Backcountry skiing is becoming increasingly popular in the mountains surrounding Jackson Hole, but many skiers fail to take the necessary precautions. Given the enormous snowfalls that occur, the steep slopes the snow piles up on, and the high winds that accompany many storms, it should come as no surprise that avalanches are a real danger. If you really want to avoid avalanches, ski only on groomed ski trails or "bomb-proof" slopes that, because of aspect, shape, and slope angle, never seem to slide. Unfortunately, this isn't always possible, so an understanding of the conditions that lead to avalanches is imperative for backcountry skiers. The best way to learn this is from an avalanche class such as the four-day backcountry programs taught by the **American Avalanche Institute**, Box 308, Wilson, WY 83014, tel. 733-3315, or by **Jackson Community Education**, tel. 733-7425. Failing that, you can help protect yourself by following these precautions when you head into the backcountry:

❖ ❖ ❖ ❖ ❖   ❖ ❖ ❖ ❖ ❖

- Before heading out, get up-to-date avalanche information by calling the 24-hour **Forest Service Avalanche Forecast** at tel. 733-2664. If they say avalanche danger is high, try skiing on the flats instead.

- Be sure to carry extra warm clothes, water, high energy snacks, an avalanche transceiver (be sure you know how to use it!), a lightweight snow shovel (for digging snow pits, emergency snow shelters, or excavating avalanche victims), first-aid supplies, a topographic map, an extra plastic ski tip, a flashlight, matches, and compass. Many skiers also carry that cure-all, duct tape, wrapped around a ski pole. Let someone know exactly where you are going and when you expect to return.

- Check the angle of an area before you ski through it; slopes of 30-40 degrees are the most dangerous, while lesser slopes do not slide as frequently.

- Watch the weather; winds over 15 mph can pile snow much more deeply on lee slopes, causing dangerous loading on the snowpack.

- Be aware of gullies and bowls; they're more likely to slip than flat open slopes or ridgetops. Stay out of gullies at the bottom of wide bowls; these are natural avalanche chutes.

- Look at the trees. Smaller trees may indicate that avalanches rip through an area frequently, knocking over the larger trees. (Avalanches can, however, also run through forested areas.)

- Know how much new snow has fallen recently. Heavy new snow over older weak snow layers is a sure sign of extreme danger on potential avalanche slopes.

- Learn how to dig a snow pit and how to read the various snow layers. Particularly important are the very weak layers of depth hoar or surface hoar that have been buried under heavy new snow.

GRAND TETON NATIONAL PARK

Grand Teton National Park remains one of the preeminent symbols of American wilderness. The Tetons rise abruptly from the valley floor, their bare triangular ridges looking like broken shards of glass from some cosmic accident of creation. With six different summits topping 12,000 feet, plus some of the finest climbing and hiking in Wyoming, the Tetons are a paradise for lovers of the outdoors. They have long been a favorite of photographers and sightseers, and once even appeared in an ad promoting Colorado tourism! The Tetons change character with the seasons. In summer the sagebrush flats are a garden of flowers set against the mountain backdrop. When autumn falls on the land, the cottonwoods and aspens become swaths of yellow and orange. Winter turns everything a glorious, sparkling white, set against the fluorescent blue sky.

GEOLOGY

If ever there was a place to make you wish you'd paid more attention in that introductory geology class, it is the precipitous Teton range, with perhaps the most complex geologic history in North America.

Building A Mountain Range

Although the Tetons are ancient by any human scale, they are the youngest mountains in the Rockies, less than 10 million years old (versus 60 million years for the nearby Wind River Mountains). The Tetons are a fault-block range, formed when the earth's crust cracked along an angled fault. Forces within the earth have pushed the western side (the Tetons) up, while the eastern portion (Jackson Hole) dropped down like a trapdoor. Geologists believe the fault could slip up to 10 feet at a time, producing a violent earthquake. All this shifting has created one of the most dramatic and asymmetric mountain faces on earth.

Unlike typical mountain ranges, the highest parts are not at the center of the range, but along the eastern edge where uplifting continues. The western slope that drops gently into Idaho is much less dramatic, though the views are still very impressive. This tilting and subsidence process is still going on today. The town of Wilson in Jackson Hole now lies 10 feet below the level of the nearby Snake River; only riverside dikes protect the town from flooding.

As the mountains rose along this fault, millennia of overlying deposits were stripped away by erosion, leaving ancient three-million-year-old Precambrian rock jutting into the air above the more recent sedimentary deposits in the valley. Because of this shifting and erosion, sandstone deposits atop Mt. Moran match those 24,000 feet below Jackson Hole.

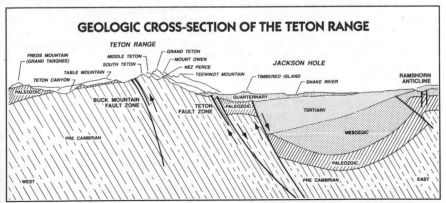

GEOLOGIC CROSS-SECTION OF THE TETON RANGE

REDRAWN FROM U.S.G.S. MAP OF GRAND TETON N.P.

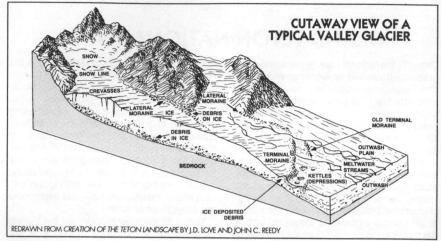

CUTAWAY VIEW OF A TYPICAL VALLEY GLACIER

SNOW
SNOW LINE
CREVASSES
LATERAL MORAINE
LATERAL MORAINE
ICE
DEBRIS ON ICE
DEBRIS IN ICE
BEDROCK
OLD TERMINAL MORAINE
OUTWASH PLAIN
TERMINAL MORAINE
MELTWATER STREAMS
KETTLES (DEPRESSIONS)
OUTWASH
ICE DEPOSITED DEBRIS

REDRAWN FROM *CREATION OF THE TETON LANDSCAPE* BY J.D. LOVE AND JOHN C. REEDY

Rivers Of Ice

In counterpoint to the uplifting actions that created the general outline of the Tetons, erosional processes have been wearing them down again. Glaciers—created when more snow falls than melts off—have proven one of the most important of these erosional processes. After a period of several years and under the weight of additional snow, the accumulated snow crystals change into ice. Gravity pulls this ice slowly downhill, creating what is essentially a frozen river that grinds against whatever lies in the way, plucking loose rocks and soil, and polishing hard bedrock. This debris moves slowly down the glacier as if on a conveyer belt, eventually reaching its terminus.

When a glacier remains the same size for a long period of time, large piles of glacial debris accumulate at its end, creating what glaciologists call a terminal moraine. One of these, Jackson Lake, was created when a huge glacier dumped tons of rock at its snout. After the glacier melted back, this terminal moraine became a natural dam for the waters of the Snake River. Similar mounds of glacial debris dammed the creeks that formed Jenny, Leigh, Bradley, Taggart, and Phelps lakes within Grand Teton National Park.

Streams flowed from the ends of the glaciers, carrying along gravel, sand, silt, and clay. The cobbles and sands from these glacial streams were dropped on the flat valley below, while the finer silts and clays continued downstream, leaving behind soils too rocky and nutrient-poor to support trees. Only sagebrush grows on this flat plain today, while the surrounding hills and mountain slopes (which were spared this rocky deposition) are covered with lodgepole and subalpine fir forests. Trees can also be found covering the silty terminal moraines that ring the lakes.

Other reminders of the glacial past are the "potholes" (more accurately termed "kettles") that dot the plain south of Signal Mountain. These depressions were created when large blocks of ice were buried under glacial outwash. Only a dozen or so small glaciers remain in the Tetons—largest is the 3,500-foot-long Teton Glacier, visible on the northeastern face of Grand Teton. For a more detailed picture of Teton geology, read *Creation of the Teton Landscape* by J. D. Love and John C. Reed, Jr. (Grand Teton Natural History Association, Moose).

WILDLIFE

Grand Teton National Park is an excellent place to look for wildlife. Moose are often seen in the willow meadows along Jackson Lake, south of the settlement of Moose, or along the Snake River. Herds of pronghorn antelope are common on the sagebrush flats near Kelly. Elk (park biologists prefer the term wapiti) are frequent sights in fall as they migrate down from the high country to the elk refuge near Jackson, but can

1↗   2↗

3↗   4↗   5↘   6↘

1. Rancher Tooter Rogers in the tiny settlement of Spotted Horse; **2.** writer Mardie Murie; **3.** Jackie and Eric Raymond at the Whiskey Mountain Rendezvous in Dubois; **4.** sheepherder Pedro Gonzalez in Flaming Gorge N.R.A.; **5.** Lee Kozell in his frontier town near Dubois; **6.** Victoria Napoleon at Eastern Shoshone Indian Days on the Wind River Reservation

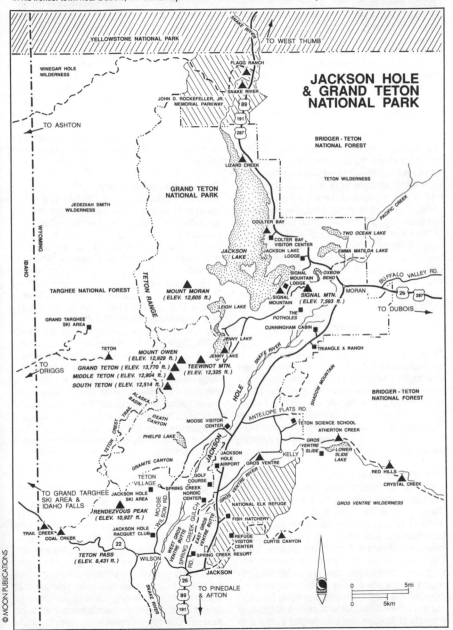

also be seen in the park during the summer. (Grand Teton is the only national park outside Alaska that allows hunting. The rules are pretty strange, however, requiring elk hunters to become temporarily deputized park rangers before they head out!) Grizzlies are currently found only on the park's northern margins, but black bears are present in wooded canyons and river bottoms.

Bison (buffalo) are commonly seen in the Moran Junction area. They were present historically (hence the name Buffalo River), but had been extinct for perhaps a century when eight bison were released into Grand Teton National Park in 1969. The population grew slowly for the first decade until they discovered the free alfalfa handout at the elk refuge north of Jackson. With this winter feed, the population has grown to 100 animals, much to the chagrin of the elk refuge managers. A public hunt has been instituted to control bison numbers. Other animals to look for are bald eagles and ospreys along the Snake River and trumpeter swans and Canada geese in ponds and lakes. The best times to see animals are in the early morning or at dusk.

HISTORY

Once the wonders of Yellowstone came to widespread public attention, it took only a few months for Congress to declare the area a national park, but the magnificent mountain range to the south proved an entirely different story. Early on, there were suggestions that Yellowstone be expanded to include the Tetons, but it would take decades of wrangling before Jackson Hole would finally be preserved.

Damning Jackson Lake

Jackson Lake represents one of the sadder chapters in the history of northwest Wyoming. Jackson Lake Dam was built in the winter of 1910-11 to supply water for Idaho potato and beet farmers. The town of Moran was built to house construction workers for Jackson Lake Dam, and at one time included more than a hundred ramshackle structures. Nothing remains of the town. The 70-foot-tall dam increased the size of the natural lake, flooding out more than 7,200 acres of trees and creating a tangle of floating and submerged trunks and stumps. To some, the dam seemed like the serpent in the Garden of Eden, a symbol of the developments that could destroy the valley if not stopped. The trees remained in Jackson Lake for many years, creating an eyesore until the Park Service and the CCC finally launched a massive cleanup project in the 1930s. The dam was completely rebuilt in 1988-89, and while the lake now looks quite attractive, it remains yet another example how Wyoming provides water for farmers in surrounding states. Fortunately, Idaho irrigators did not succeed in their planned dams on Jenny, Leigh, and Taggart lakes.

Dudes And Development

Because of the rocky soils and long winters, Jackson Hole has always been a marginal place for cattle ranching, and only in the southern end of the valley are the soils rich enough to support a decent crop of hay. It was this poor soil and harsh climate that saved Jackson Hole from early development, and forced the ranchers to bring in dudes to supplement their income. (One old timer noted, "Dudes winter better than cattle.")

The first Jackson Hole dude ranch, the JY, was established along Phelps Lake by Louis Joy. It was quickly followed by the Bar BC Ranch of Struthers Burt, an acclaimed East Coast author who had come west as a dude, but learned enough to go in the business for himself. The dude ranchers were some of the first to realize the value of Jackson Hole and to support its preservation. Burt proposed that the valley and mountains be saved not as a traditional park, but as a "museum on the hoof" where ranching and tourism would join hands to stave off commercial developments. The roads would remain unpaved, all homes would be log, and Jackson would stay a frontier town.

The movement to save Jackson Hole coalesced in a 1923 meeting at the cabin of Maude Noble. Horace Albright, superintendent of Yellowstone National Park was there, along with local dude ranchers, businessmen, and cattlemen anxious to save the remote valley from exploitation. To accomplish this goal, they proposed finding a wealthy philanthropist who might be willing to invest the two million dollars that would be needed to buy the land. Fortunately, one of Struthers Burt's friends happened to be Kenneth Chorley, an assistant to John D. Rockefeller, Jr. Burt used this contact to get Rockefeller interested in the project.

Rocky To The Rescue

In 1926, Rockefeller traveled west for a 12-day trip to Yellowstone. Horace Albright used the chance to take him on a side-trip into Jackson Hole, and to proselytize for protection of the valley. What they saw portended badly for the future: the Jenny Lake dance hall, roadside tourist camps and hot dog stands, rusting abandoned cars, and a place that billboards proclaimed "Home of the Hollywood Cowboy." Rockefeller was angered by the prospect of crass commercial developments blanketing Jackson Hole, and quickly signed on to the idea of purchasing the land and giving it to the Park Service.

To cover his tracks as he bought the land, Rockefeller formed the Snake River Land Company. (If ranchers had known the Rockefeller clan was behind the scheme, they would have either refused to sell or jacked up the price.) Only a few residents—mostly supporters—knew of the plan. The local banker, Robert Miller, served as land purchasing agent, although even he opposed letting the Park Service gain control of the valley. Miller used his position to buy out ranches with delinquent mortgages to his Jackson State Bank and then resigned, claiming the whole thing was part of a sinister plot to run the ranchers out and to halt "progress." In 1929, Congress voted to establish a small Grand Teton National Park that would encompass the mountains themselves—which stood little chance of development—but not much else. Conservationists knew that without preservation of the valley below, the wonderful vistas would be lost.

A National Battleground

Rockefeller and Albright finally went public with their land-purchasing scheme in 1930, releasing a tidal wave of outrage. Anti-park forces led by Sen. Milward Simpson (father of Sen. Alan Simpson) spent the next decade fighting the park tooth and nail, charging that it would destroy the economy of Jackson Hole, and that ranchers would lose their livelihood. Rockefeller's agents were falsely accused of trying to intimidate holdouts with strong-arm tactics. Congress refused to accept Rockefeller's gift, and local opposition blocked the bill for more than a decade.

Finally, in 1943, President Roosevelt made an end-run around the anti-park forces by accepting the 32,000-acres purchased by Rockefeller, adding 130,000 acres of Forest Service land, and declaring it the Jackson Hole National Monument. The move outraged those in the valley, prompting more hearings and bills to abolish the new national monument. Wyoming's politicians attacked Roosevelt's actions. A bill overturning the decision was pocket-vetoed by the president, but for the next several years, the Wyoming delegation kept reintroducing the measure. By 1947, however, the tide had turned as increasing post-war tourism revitalized the local economy. Finally, in 1950, a compromise was reached granting ranchers lifetime grazing rights and the right to trail their cattle across the park en route to summer grazing lands. The new-and-improved Grand Teton National Park had finally come to fruition.

Post-mortem

Some of the early fears that Rockefeller would use the new park for his own gain seem at least partly justified. His descendents still own the old JY Ranch and use Phelps Lake as something of a semi-private playground, while most of the other dude ranches have long since been taken over by the Park Service. Rockefeller also built the enormous Grand Teton Lodge along Jackson Lake plus facilities at Colter Bay and Jenny Lake, leading some to accuse the family of attempting to monopolize services within the park. The company—Rockresorts—was finally sold in 1986 to CSX Corporation.

Looking back on the controversial creation of Grand Teton National Park, it's easy to see how wrong park opponents were. Teton county has Wyoming's most vibrant economy, and millions of people arrive each year to enjoy the beauty of the undeveloped Tetons. As writer Nathaniel Burt noted, "The old enemies of the park are riding the profitable bandwagon of unlimited tourism with high hearts and open palms." Park opponents' claims that the Park Service would "lock up" the land ring as hollow as similar anti-wilderness claims today by the political descendents of the same politicians who opposed Grand Teton half a century ago. Without inclusion of the land purchased by Rockefeller, it is easy to imagine the valley covered with all sorts of summer home developments,

RV campgrounds, souvenir shops, motels, bill-boards, and neon signs. Take a look at the town of Jackson to see what might have been.

TOURING THE PARK

Grand Teton National Park has fewer "attractions" than Yellowstone—its big sister to the north—and an easy day's drive takes you past the road-accessible portions of Grand Teton. The real attraction is the mountains, and the incomparable views one gets of them from Jackson Hole. This is one backdrop you will never tire of seeing.

Roads
Grand Teton is bisected by the main north-south highway (U.S. 26-89-191), and by the road heading east over Togwotee Pass (U.S. 26-287). Both of these routes are kept open year-round, although wintertime plowing ends at Flagg Ranch, just south of the Yellowstone boundary. In addition, a paved park road cuts south from Jackson Lake Dam to Jenny Lake and Moose. Only the southern end of this is plowed in winter, with the remainder becoming a snowmobile and cross-country ski route. South of Moose, a narrow, winding road connects the park to Teton Village, nine miles away. It is rough dirt in places (no trailers or RVs) and is closed in winter. The following tour takes you past the points of interest along the main roads. The route follows a general clockwise direction beginning and ending at the Moose Visitor Center. Before heading out, step inside the center for an introduction to the park, and a look at the natural history videos, books, and oil paintings.

Menor's Ferry Area
Just inside the South Entrance to Grand Teton National Park, a side road leads to **Chapel of the Transfiguration** and **Menor's Ferry**. The rustic log church (built in 1925) is most notable for its dramatic setting. The back window faces directly toward the Tetons, providing ample distractions for worshippers. The bell out front was cast in 1842. Nearby Menor's Ferry is named for William D. Menor who first homesteaded here in 1894, and later built a cable ferry to make it easier to cross the river. His old whitewashed house still stands. A 1990 ferry reconstruction

floats in the river; check out the ingenious propulsion mechanism that uses the current to pull it across. For many years, Menor's ferry served as the primary means to cross the river in the central part of Jackson Hole. Wagons were charged 50¢, while those on horseback paid 25¢. (William Menor's brother, Holiday Menor, lived on the opposite side of the river, but the two often feuded, yelling insults across the water at each other and refusing to acknowledge the other for years at a time.)

Menor sold out to Maude Noble in 1918, and she ran the ferry until 1927 when a bridge was built near the present one in Moose. Her cabin now houses an excellent collection of historic photos from Jackson Hole. Maude Noble gained a measure of fame in 1923 when she hosted a gathering of residents to save Jackson Hole from development, a movement that would eventually lead to the creation of Grand Teton National Park.

Heading northwest beyond the Menor's Ferry area, the main road climbs up an old river bench (created by flooding from the rapid melting of the glaciers) and passes the trailhead to the turquoise waters of **Taggart Lake**. The land around here was burned in the 1,028-acre Beaver Creek lightning fire of 1985, and summers find a riot of wildflowers. A very popular day hike leads from the parking area here to Taggart Lake and then back via the Beaver Creek Trail, a distance of four miles round-trip. A side loop to **Bradley Lake** adds another two miles to this. These trails provide a fine way to see up close the glacial moraines that created the dams that formed these lakes.

Jenny Lake Area
The most loved of all the Grand Teton lakes is Jenny Lake, nestled at the foot of Cascade Canyon and surrounded by a luxuriant forest of Engelmann spruce, subalpine fir, and lodgepole pine. Jenny Lake is named for Jenny Leigh, the Shoshone wife of Beaver Dick Leigh (as in nearby Leigh Lake). A one-way loop road leads south past Jenny and String lakes, providing excellent views of the **Cathedral Group**: Teewinot, Grand Teton, and Mt. Owen. This is the most popular part of the park, and day hikers will find a plethora of trails to sample, along with crowds to contend with. Paths lead around both Jenny and String lakes, while another nearly

level trail follows the east shore of Leigh Lake to several pleasant sandy beaches. String Lake is narrow but very pretty, and makes a fine place for canoeing or swimming.

One of the most popular attractions in the area is **Inspiration Point**, located on the west side of Jenny Lake. It's two miles by trail from the Jenny Lake Ranger Station, or you can ride one of the summertime shuttle boats that cross the lake every 20 minutes or so for $3.50 RT ($1.75 for kids). Scenic boat cruises are also available.

From the boat dock, the trail climbs a half mile to **Hidden Falls**, and then another quarter mile to **Inspiration Point** which overlooks Jackson Hole. It is 400 feet above Jenny Lake. Many day-hikers continue up Cascade Canyon (see "Backcountry Trails," below).

Signal Mountain Area

As the road approaches Jackson Lake, a paved but narrow side road (no RVs or trailers) turns east and leads to the summit of Signal Mountain,

BEAVER DICK LEIGH

Around 1863, Richard "Beaver Dick" Leigh became the first white man to attempt a permanent life in Jackson Hole. An Englishman by birth, Beaver Dick lived in a log cabin with his Shoshone wife, Jenny, and their four children, scraping out the barest existence by hunting, trapping, and guiding. As guide for the 1872 Hayden Survey of the Jackson Hole area, Beaver Dick attained the respect of the surveyors who named Leigh Lake for him and Jenny Lake for his wife. Today a local bar denigrates this remarkable man by calling itself "Beaver Dick's" while using a cartoonish image of him in their ads. The real man was nothing like this, and reading his diaries and letters is a lesson in how difficult life was for early Wyoming settlers. On one terrible Christmas in 1876 he watched his entire family— Jenny, their newborn baby, and the four other children—all slowly die from smallpox. Their deaths left him badly shaken, as he related in a letter to a friend:

". . . Anne Jane died about 8 o clock about the time every year i used to give them a candy puling and thay menchond about the candy puling many times wile sick . . . William died on the 25 about 9 or 10 o clock in the evening . . . on the 26th Dick Juner died . . . Elizabeth [the last child] was over all danger but this, and she caught cold and sweled up agane and died on the 28 of Dec about 2 o clock in the morning. this was the hardist blow of all . . . i shall improve the place and live and die near my famley but i shall not be able to do enything for a few months for my mind is disturbed at the sights that i see around me and [the] work that my famley as done wile thay were liveing . . ."

But the human spirit is remarkably resiliant. Beaver Dick later married a Bannock girl, raised another family, and guided for others, even meeting Theodore Roosevelt on one of his hunting trips. Beaver Dick died in 1899 and was buried on a ridge overlooking Idaho's Teton Basin.

Beaver Dick and Jenny Leigh with their children

YELLOWSTONE NATIONAL PARK

800 feet above Jackson Hole. Fine panoramic views of the Tetons, Jackson Lake, the Snake River, and the long valley below. To the south are **The Potholes**, a hummocky area created when huge blocks of ice were left behind by retreating glaciers. The melting ice created depressions, some of which are still filled with water. Signal Mountain was burned by a massive 1879 fire and offers a good opportunity to see how Yellowstone may look in a century.

Signal Mountain Lodge hugs the southeast shore of Jackson Lake, and includes a full range of facilities, from campsites to a bar. Just east of the lodge is **Chapel of the Sacred Heart**, a small Roman Catholic church. The road then crosses **Jackson Lake Dam** which raises the water level by 39 feet, alters the river's natural flow, and inundates a large area upstream. Many conservationists fought to have Jackson Lake excluded from the park, concerned that it would establish a bad precedent for allowing reservoirs in other parks. Nevertheless, once you get away from the dam, the lake seems relatively natural today.

Along Jackson Lake

A pullout near Jackson Lake Junction provides views over the **Willow Flats** where moose are frequently seen, especially in the morning. Impressive **Jackson Lake Lodge** was built in the 1950s with the $5 million financial backing of John D. Rockefeller, Jr. The building tops a bluff overlooking the willow flats. Architects are not thrilled about the design (one author termed it "the ugliest building in Western Wyoming"), but the 60-foot-tall back windows frame an unbelievable view of the Tetons and Jackson Lake. A historic U.S.-Soviet diplomatic meeting was held here in 1989 between Soviet Foreign Minister Eduard Shevardnadze and Secretary of State James Baker. Immediately across from the lodge is a trail leading to **Emma Matilda** and **Two Ocean** lakes. It is 14 miles RT around both lakes, with lots of wildlife along the way, including moose, trumpeter swans, pelicans, and ducks. You may have to contend with large groups on horseback.

Colter Bay Village is one of the most developed parts of the park, with a full marina, stores, restaurants, and acres of parking. The main attraction here is the visitor center that houses the **Colter Bay Indian Arts Museum**, tel. 543-

2467. Open daily, 8-5 from mid-May through Sept. and till 7 p.m. in midsummer; no charge. Inside is the extraordinary David T. Vernon collection of Indian pieces, said to be the finest of its kind in any national park. The collection spreads through several rooms on two floors and includes beaded buckskin dresses, moccasins, kachina dolls, masks, ceremonial pipes, warbonnets, shields, bows, and other decorated items. Indian craft-making demonstrations are sometimes offered. An almost-level trail leads from the marina out to **Hermitage Point** and then back again, a distance of nine miles roundtrip. Along the way you pass beaver ponds and willow patches where trumpeter swans, moose, and ducks are commonly seen. Get a map of this trail from the visitor center. The **Colter Bay Nature Trail** (one mile) provides another nearby loop hike.

North To Yellowstone

North of Colter Bay, the highway cruises along the shore of Jackson Lake for the next nine miles, providing a number of fine vantage points across to the Tetons. The burned area on the opposite shore was ignited by lightning in the 1974 Waterfalls Canyon Fire that consumed 3,700 acres. By late fall each year, Idaho spud farmers have drawn down water in the lake, leaving a long, barren shoreline at the upper end.

Shortly after the road leaves the upper end of Yellowstone Lake, a signboard announces your entrance into **John D. Rockefeller, Jr. Memorial Parkway**. This 24,000-acre parcel of land was transferred to the National Park Service in 1972, in commemoration of Rockefeller's unstinting work in establishing Grand Teton National Park. The land forms a connection between Grand Teton and Yellowstone and is managed by Grand Teton National Park. Much of this area was severely burned by the 1988 Huck Fire that began when strong winds blew a tree into power lines. Despite immediate efforts to control the blaze, it consumed 4,000 acres in the first two hours, and later grew to cover nearly 200,000 acres, primarily within the Forest Service's Teton Wilderness. On the northern end of Rockefeller Parkway is **Flagg Ranch**, where facilities include a store, gas station, motel, restaurant, and campground. **Grassy Lake Road** takes off just north of Flagg Ranch and continues 52 miles to Ashton, Idaho. It's a scenic drive, but don't attempt this narrow and rough dirt road with a trailer or RV. This route provides a shortcut to the Bechler River area of Yellowstone, and is a popular wintertime snowmobile route.

Jackson Lake To Moran Junction

Heading east and south from Jackson Lake, the road immediately passes **Oxbow Bend**, where the pullout is almost always filled with folks looking for geese, ducks, moose, and other animals. The oxbow was formed when the meandering river cut off an old loop. The calm water here is a delightful place for canoes, though the mosquitoes can be a major annoyance in midsummer. Come fall, photographers line the shoulder of the road for classic shots of flaming aspen trees with Grand Teton and **Mt. Moran** in the background. Mt. Moran is the massive peak with a flattened summit, a skillet-shaped glacier across its front, and a distinctive black vertical diabase dike that looks like a scar from some ancient battle. It rises 12,605 feet above sea level. The peak is named for Thomas Moran, whose beautiful paintings of Yellowstone helped persuade Congress to set aside that area as the world's first national park.

At **Moran Junction** you pass the Buffalo Entrance Station and meet the road to Togwotee Pass and Dubois. A post office and school are the only developments here. The epic Western *The Big Trail* was filmed nearby in 1930, starring an actor named John Wayne doing his first speaking role. (John Wayne had never ridden a horse before this.) An interesting side trip is to head east from Moran on U.S. 26-287 for three miles to **Buffalo Valley Road**. This narrow, scenic road leads to Turpin Meadow, a major entryway into the Teton Wilderness (see p. 271). Very pretty—especially in early summer when the fields are carpeted with flowers. Beyond Turpin Meadow, it turns to gravel and climbs sharply uphill, rejoining the main highway a couple of miles below Togwotee Lodge.

Moran Junction To Moose

Heading south from Moran, U.S. 26-89-191 immediately crosses the Buffalo River (a.k.a. Buffalo Fork of the Snake River), where bison were once abundant. With a little help from humans, bison have been reestablished, and are now often seen just south of here along the road. The turnoff to the **Cunningham Cabin** is six miles south of Moran Junction. The structure actually consists of two sod-roofed log cabins connected by a covered walkway (a "dog-trot"). Built around 1890, it served first as living quarters and later as a barn and smithy. A park brochure describes the locations of other structures on the property.

Pierce Cunningham came here as a homesteader, and with his wife Margaret, settled to raise cattle. Although this was some of the better land in this part of the valley, the soil was still so rocky that they had a hard time digging fence-post holes. Instead, they opted to build the buck and rail fences that have become a hallmark of Jackson Hole ranches. Cunningham Ranch gained notoriety in 1893 when a posse surrounded two suspected horse thieves who were wintering at Cunningham's place while he was away. Vigilantes shot and killed George Spencer and Mike Burnett in an example of "mountain justice." Later, however, there was some suspicion that hired killers working for wealthy cattle barons had led the posse, and that the murdered men may have been innocent. **Spread Creek** is just north of the Cunningham cabin, gaining its name by having two mouths, separated by a distance of three miles.

The highway next rolls past **Triangle X Ranch**, one of the most famous dude ranches in Jackson Hole. Although on park land, the Turner family has managed Triangle X for over 60 years. (One of the owners, John Turner, is President Bush's director of the Fish and Wildlife Service.) Stop by just after sunup to watch wranglers driving 120 head of horses up from the lower pastures. It's a scene straight out of a Marlboro ad. Southwest from Triangle X, the road climbs along an ancient river terrace and passes the hidden **Hedrick Pond** where the 1963 movie *Spencer's Mountain* was filmed. Starring Henry Fonda, it was supposedly set in Virginial Trumpeter swans are sometimes seen on the pond. Several turnouts provide very popular photo-opportunity spots, the most famous being **Snake River Overlook**. Ansel Adams' famous shot of the Tetons was taken here, and has been repeated with less success by generations of photographers. Throughout the summer, a progression of different flowers bloom in the open sagebrush flats along the road, adding brilliant slashes of color. They are prettiest in late June. (In the high country, the peak comes a month or more later.)

Just north of Snake River Overlook is the turnoff to **Deadman's Bar**. An extremely steep dirt road (4WD recommended) drops down to one of the primary river access points used by river rafters. The river bar received its name from an incident in 1886. Four German prospectors entered the area, but only one—John Tonnar—emerged. Bodies of the other three were found along the Snake River, and Tonnar was charged with murder. The jury in Evanston believed his claim of self-defense, and he was set free, an act that so angered locals that they vowed to take care of future Jackson Hole criminals with a shotgun. A skull from one of the victims is on display in the Jackson Hole Museum. Another popular put-in for river runners is **Schwabacher Landing**, located at the end of a one-mile gravel road that splits off just north of the Glacier View Turnout. This is a pleasant place for riverside picnics.

A mile north of the turnoff to Moose, the Antelope Flats Rd. heads east along Ditch Creek. **Blacktail Butte** lies just south of here, a timbered knoll rising over the surrounding sagebrush plains. It's a favorite of rock climbers. Keep your eyes peeled for the much-photographed old farm buildings known as **Mormon Row**. The farmland here was homesteaded by Mormon (and non-Mormon) settlers in the early 1900s, but was later purchased by Rockefeller's Snake River Land Company and transferred to the Park Service. A few of the buildings are still occupied, but most are abandoned and gradually collapsing under the heavy winter snows.

Teton Science School

Hidden away in a valley along upper Ditch Creek is Teton Science School, a fine hands-on school for both young and old. Founded in 1967 as a summer field biology program for high school kids, it has grown into a year-round program with classes that run the gamut from elementary-school level all the way up to intensive college courses and adult seminars. Summertime visitors will enjoy their 3-5 day seminars on such subjects as bird songs, field botany, or even hydrology for river runners. Their excellent

month-long wilderness EMT course is one of the only programs of its kind in the nation. During the winter, TSS puts on a series of weekly lectures ($3) in Jackson, covering a spectrum of scientific, environmental, and social issues.

The school is based at the old Elbo dude ranch (started in 1932) which includes two small dormitories plus a central kitchen, dining area, and other structures. At the main building, visitors will find the large **Murie Collection** of birds, mammal skulls, and other natural history specimens, including casts of animal tracks used by famed wildlife biologist Olaus Murie in producing his *Peterson's Guide to Animal Tracks*. Check out the grizzly scat! Teton Science School achieved a measure of fame in 1989 when President Bush chose it as the site to announce his push for a new Clean Air bill. (At last count, nearly all the TSS staff were still registered Democrats, however.) Get a copy of the course catalog by contacting TSS at Box 68, Kelly, WY 83011, tel. 733-4765.

Kelly Vicinity

The small settlement of **Kelly** borders on the southeastern end of Grand Teton National Park, and has a small general store, some log homes plus a cluster of Mongolian-style yurts—certainly the most unusual dwellings in Wyoming. The Park Service's Gros Ventre Campground is three miles west of here. Gros Ventre Rd. leads east from the Kelly area, passing **Kelly Warm Spring** on the right. Its warm, clear waters are a favorite place for local kayakers to practice their rolls. A short distance up the road and off to the north are the collapsing remains of the **Shane cabin**, where a scene from this classic 1951 Western was filmed. Beyond this, the road enters Bridger-Teton National Forest and the Slide Lake area where there is a Forest Service campground.

Gros Ventre Slide

One of the most impressive geologic events in recent Wyoming history took place in the Gros Ventre (pronounced GROW-vont, "Big Belly" in French trapper lingo) Canyon, named for the Gros Ventre Indians in this area. Sheep Mountain, on the south side of the canyon, consists of of sandstone underlain by a layer of shale that becomes slippery when wet. Melting snow and heavy rains in the spring of 1925 lubricated this layer of shale, and on June 23, the entire north end of the mountain—a section 2,000 feet wide and a mile long—suddenly slid a mile and a half downslope, instantly damming the river below and creating Slide Lake. A rancher in the valley, Guil Huff, watched in amazement as the mountain began to move, galloping his horse out of the way as the slide roared within 30 feet of him. Huff's ranch floated away on the new lake several days later.

For two years folks kept a wary eye on the makeshift dam of rock and mud. Then, on May 18, 1927, the dam suddenly gave way, pushing an enormous wall of water through the downstream town of Kelly. Six people perished in the flood, and when the water reached Snake River Canyon nine hours later, it filled the canyon to the rim with boiling water, trees, houses, and debris. Today a smaller Slide Lake still exists, and the massive landslide that created it more than 65 years ago remains as an exposed gouge visible for miles around. Geologists say that, under the right conditions, more of Sheep Mountain could slide. Dead trees still stand in the upper end of Slide Lake.

Gros Ventre River

Above Slide Lake, the road turns to gravel (unplowed in winter), becoming quite rutted in spots. Surprising scenery makes the bone-jarring easier to take. The landscape here is far different from the Tetons, with the road passing colorful badlands hills rising sharply above the Gros Ventre River. Two more campgrounds (Red Hills and Crystal Creek) are four miles above Slide Lake. The road continues another 15 beautiful miles along the river, getting rougher at the upper end. The Gros Ventre Wilderness lies immediately south of the road, and there are quite a few trailheads along the way. On the way back down the Gros Ventre River valley you will discover some fine views across to the Tetons.

BACKCOUNTRY HIKING

The precipitous Tetons that look so dramatic from the roads are even more impressive up close and personal. Grand Teton National Park is laced with 200 miles of trails, and hikers can choose everything from simple day treks to week-long trips along the crest of the range. Unlike nearby Yellowstone where most of the country is forested, the Tetons contain extensive alpine scenery. This means, however, that many of the high passes won't be free of snow until late July, and may require ice axes before then. Check at the visitor centers or Jenny Lake Ranger Station for current conditions.

The most popular hiking area centers on the crest of the Tetons and the lakes that lie at their feet, most notably Jenny Lake. **Teton Crest Trail** stretches from Teton Pass north all the way to Cascade Canyon, with numerous connecting paths from both sides of the range. Three relatively short (two to three days) loop hikes are described below. For more complete descriptions of park trails, see *Teton Trails* by Bryan Harry (Grand Teton Natural History Association, Moose, WY), or *Hiking the Teton Backcountry* by Paul Lawrence (Sierra Club Books, San Francisco). Get topographic maps at the Moose Visitor Center or Teton Mountaineering in Jackson. Earthwalk Press, 2239 Union St., Eureka, CA 95501, produces an excellent topographic map of park trails (also available locally).

Regulations

The hiking trails of Grand Teton National Park are some of the most heavily used paths in Wyoming, and strict regulations are enforced. Backcountry use permits (free) are required of all overnight hikers, and you'll need to specify a particular camping zone or site for each night of your trip. Get permits at the visitor centers in Moose or Colter Bay, or at the Jenny Lake Ranger Station. Get there early in the morning during the summer for popular trails. A limited number of backcountry permits may be reserved in advance (Jan. 1-June 1 only) by writing to: Permits Office, Grand Teton National Park, P.O. Drawer 170, Moose, WY 83012. Any off-trail hiking requires special permission; see "Mountain Climbing" below for specifics. Grizzlies are only found in the northern end of Grand Teton, but you still need to hang all food since black bears roam throughout the park, particularly in the forested areas. Campfires are not allowed at higher elevations, so be sure to bring a cooking stove.

Cascade Canyon To Paintbrush Canyon

One of the most popular hikes in Grand Teton is this 19-mile loop trip up Cascade Canyon, over Paintbrush Divide, and down Paintbrush Canyon (or vice versa). The trip offers a little of everything: hiking through dense forests, magnificent views of Grand Teton, alpine lakes, and flower-covered meadows. This trip is best done in late summer, since a cornice of snow typically blocks Paintbrush Divide until late July. Begin at the String Lake trailhead and head south around Jenny Lake, stopping to enjoy the views (and crowds) at Inspiration Point before heading up along Cascade Creek. The trail splits at the upper end of this canyon; turning left takes you to Hurricane Pass and the Teton Crest Trail where you'll discover fine views of the back side of Grand Teton. Instead, turn right (north) and head up to beautiful Lake Solitude. Behind you, Teewinot, Mt. Owen, and Grand Teton are

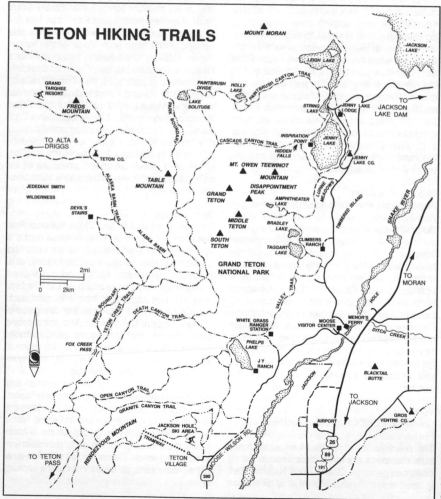

TETON HIKING TRAILS

© MOON PUBLICATIONS

framed by the glacially carved valley walls. Above Lake Solitude, the trail climbs sharply to Paintbrush Divide and then switchbacks even more quickly down into Paintbrush Canyon. The trail eventually leads back to String Lake. Be sure to stop at beautiful Holly Lake on the way down.

Amphitheater Lake

A relatively short but very steep hike begins at the Lupine Meadows trailhead just south of Jenny Lake. It is only five miles to the cirque of Amphitheater Lake, but 3,000 feet higher, making this the quickest climb to the Teton treeline. Many folks day-hike this trail to savor the wonderful vistas across Jackson Hole along the way. Camping is available at Surprise Lake, a half mile below Amphitheater. More adventurous folks may want to climb **Disappointment Peak**, the 11,618-foot summit directly in front of Grand Teton. (It was named by climbers who mistakenly thought they were on the east face of Grand Teton.) If you plan to do so, be sure to register at the Jenny Lake Ranger Station, and only attempt it if you're able to handle a few areas of Class 3 moves.

Rendezvous Mountain To Death Canyon

This 23-mile-long loop hike is different in that much of the way is downhill. Begin at the Jackson Hole tram in Teton Village where an $11 ticket takes you to the top of 10,450-foot Rendezvous Mountain. From the summit, the trail leads down to a saddle, across the South Fork of Granite Creek, and up to Teton Crest Trail. Head north on this trail to Marion Lake—a popular camping site—and then over Fox Creek Pass. The trail splits, with the right fork dropping sharply down into scenic Death Canyon, named for a member of a survey party who disappeared here in 1903. At the lower end of Death Canyon, cliffs rise nearly 3,000 feet on both sides. The trail forks at Phelps Lake, and from here you can either hike back to Teton Village via the Valley Trail, or head to the trailhead at White Grass Ranger Station, 1½ miles northeast of Phelps Lake. Note: If you reverse the direction of this hike, you can save your money since there is no charge for riding the tram down to Teton Village.

MOUNTAIN CLIMBING

The Tetons are considered some of the premier mountaineering country in the nation, with solid rock, good access, and a wide range of climbing conditions. Hundreds of climbing routes have been described for the main peaks, but the goal of many climbers is Grand Teton, better known as "the Grand." At 13,770 feet, this is Wyoming's second-highest summit, exceeded only by 13,804-foot Gannett Peak in the Wind River Mountains. In the climbing trade, first ascents always rate highly, but the first to scale Grand Teton has long been a matter of debate. The official record belongs to the party of William Owen (as in nearby Mt. Owen), Bishop Spalding (as in nearby Spalding Peak), John Shive, and Frank Petersen, who reached the summit in 1898. Today it appears that they were preceded by two members of the 1872 Hayden Expedition: Nathaniel P. Langford (first superintendent of Yellowstone National Park) and John Stevenson. In addition, another party made it to the top in 1893. Owen made a big deal out of his climb, and spent 30 years trying to work himself into the record books by claiming the Langford party never reached the top. The whole thing got quite nasty, with Owen even accusing Langford of bribing the author of a history book to gain top honors. In 1929, Owen convinced the Wyoming Legislature to declare his party the first on top. Few people believe it today, and the whole thing looks pretty foolish since even seven-year-old kids have made it to the top. Several thousand people climb the Grand each summer, many with only limited climbing experience (but excellent guides). And just to prove that it could be done, in 1971 one fanatic actually skied the Grand (he's the ski school director at Snow King Resort), followed in 1989 by a snowboarder. Both lived to tell the tale.

Most climbing takes place between mid-July and late Sept. when the snow has melted back. Mountain climbing or off-trail hiking requires a special permit available from the Jenny Lake Ranger Station (or the Moose Visitor Center during the winter). You'll also need to check in upon your return. The climbing rangers—one of the most prestigious jobs in the park—are all highly experienced mountaineers, and can provide specific route information for the various summits. Many climbers who scale Grand Teton follow the Amphitheater Lake Trail from Lupine Meadows to its junction with the Garnet Canyon Trail. This leads to a saddle separating Grand Teton and Middle Teton where both Exum and the Park Service have base camps. Other folks pitch tents behind boulders in this extraordinarily windy mountain gap. The final assault on the summit requires technical equipment and expertise. Mountaineers can stay at **Climbers' Ranch**, near Taggart Lake, for $5/night including bunk accommodations with showers and covered cooking areas. The ranch is open mid-June to mid-Sept. only. Call 733-7271 for reservations.

Climbing Schools

Jackson Hole is blessed with two of the finest climbing schools in North America, **Exum Mountain Guides**, tel. 733-2297, and **Jackson Hole Mountain Guides**, tel. 733-4979. Both are authorized concessions of the National Park Service and the U.S. Forest Service, and offer a wide range of classes, snow training, and climbs in the Tetons and elsewhere. Exum has been around since 1931 when Glenn Exum pioneered the first solo climb of what has become the most popular route to the top of the Grand, the Exum Route. (In 1981, a 70-year-old Glenn Exum led a 50th anniversary climb up this same route.) During midsummer, expect to pay around $400 (including food, gear, and shelter) for an ascent of Grand Teton that encompasses two days of basic and intermediate training followed by a two-day climb of the Grand and back. Rates are lower before mid-July and in September. Basic and intermediate climbing schools cost around $40-60/day. Also available are more advanced classes, a June snow school, and many climbs in the Tetons and the Wind River Mountains. If you're planning to climb the Grand, make reservations several months in advance during the peak summer season.

On Your Own

If you already have the experience and want to do your own climbing, the most accessible local spot is **Blacktail Butte**, just north of Moose near Ditch Creek. The parking lot here fills on warm summer afternoons as hang-dogging enthusiasts try their moves on the rock face. Get climbing gear at **Moosely Seconds Mountaineering** in Moose, tel. 733-7176, or in Jackson at **Teton Mountaineering**, 86 E. Broadway, tel. 733-3595. Both stores rent climbing boots. For more detailed info on local climbing, see Leigh N. Ortenburger's two-volume tome, *A Complete Guide to the Teton Range* (self-published, Palo Alto, CA).

GRAND TETON PRACTICALITIES

Entrance to Grand Teton National Park costs $10 per vehicle or $4 for individuals entering by bicycle, foot, motorcycle, snowmobile, or bus. The pass covers both Grand Teton and Yellowstone national parks, and is good for seven days. If you're planning to be here longer, or to make more visits, get an annual pass covering both parks for $15, or the Golden Eagle Passport which includes all national parks for $25 a year.

Lodging

Several places provide comfortable lodging in and around Grand Teton National Park. See the accommodations chart for specifics. A shuttle bus operates between Jackson Lake Lodge and Colter Bay Village during the summer. Togwotee Mountain Lodge, just below Togwotee Pass, is one of the most popular lodges in Wyoming. During the summer, it's a favorite place for horseback rides and other outings, while winter turns it into a center for snowmobiling and cross-country skiing. Flagg Ranch is a jumping off point for winter snowcoach or snowmobile trips into Yellowstone National Park.

Camping

Grand Teton National Park has six different campgrounds; largest is Gros Ventre Campground near the town of Kelly. The most scenic location (and the quickest to fill) is Jenny Lake Campground. All park campgrounds are on a first-come, first-served basis with no reservations. The Snake River Campground was closed in 1988 after it had been heavily impacted by its use as a firefighters' basecamp, but is expected to reopen in 1991. See the chart (p. 235) for a complete list of public campgrounds in the Jackson Hole area. In addition to these, private RV camps are available at both Colter Bay ($17) and Flagg Ranch ($17). Flagg Ranch also has tent sites (with showers) for $12. All these campgrounds are closed in winter, but campsites ($5; with restrooms and water) are available near the Colter Bay Visitor Center.

Food And Services

The little settlement called Moose has a couple of businesses. An old favorite is **Dornans'**, tel. 733-2415, offering very reasonable meals during the summer, including all-you-can-eat breakfasts ($4.50) and chuckwagon dinners ($9). Next door is **Mountain Bike Outfitters**, tel. 733-3314, where you can rent bikes, and **Moosely Seconds**, tel. 733-7176, offering good deals on hiking and climbing gear. Across the way is **Moose Village Store**, tel. 733-3471, with groceries, spirits (best selection of wine in Jackson Hole), and canoes for rent. **Colter Bay General Store**, tel. 733-2811, also has a good choice of groceries and supplies. In summer, smaller general stores can be found at Signal Mountain, Flagg Ranch, and Jenny Lake. The stores at Moose and Flagg Ranch are open year-round. Summertime restaurants are at Signal Mountain, Flagg Ranch, Jenny Lake, Jackson Lake Lodge, and Colter Bay. All of these locations except Jenny Lake also have gift shops. Horseback rides are available at Jackson Lake Lodge and Colter Bay. See p. 248 for info on transportation and tours of Grand Teton and Yellowstone. Post offices are located at Colter Bay (summer only), Moran, Moose Junction, and Kelly.

GRAND TETON NATIONAL PARK AREA ACCOMMODATIONS

Lodge	Location	Phone	Rates	Features
Colter Bay Village	Jackson Lake	543-2855	$45+ $17	AAA approved, cabins and tent cabins, open mid-May to late Sept.
Jackson Lake Lodge	Jackson Lake	543-2855	$64+ s or d	AAA approved, pool, open June to mid-Sept.
Jenny Lake Lodge	Jenny Lake	733-4647	$205 s or d	AAA approved, very nice cabins, includes breakfast and dinner, open June to mid-Sept.
Signal Mountain Lodge	Jackson Lake	543-2831	$55+ s or d	AAA approved, cottages with kitchenettes, open late May to mid-Oct.
Flagg Ranch	Rockefeller Parkway	733-8761 (800) 443-2311	$70 s or d	motel rooms and cabins, open mid-May to mid-Oct. and mid-Dec. to mid-March
Hatchet Motel	8 miles east of Moran Jct.	543-3413	$45 s, $49 d	AAA approved, rustic country motel
Togwotee Mountain Lodge	16 miles east of Moran Jct.	543-2847 (800) 543-2847	$45+ s, $50+ d	AAA approved, sauna, jacuzzi, horseback rides, open June-Sept. and Dec.-March

Boating

Canoeists will discover some excellent places to paddle within Grand Teton, particularly the Snake River Oxbow Bend along with String and Leigh lakes. Boaters within Grand Teton will need to purchase a permit ($10 for motorboats and $5 for other craft). Motorboats are only allowed on Jackson Lake, Jenny Lake (7 1/2 horsepower max), and Phelps Lake. Windsurfing, water-skiing, and sailing are permitted on Jackson Lake. For info on floating the Snake River through the park, see "River Rafting," p. 210. Marinas are located at Colter Bay, tel. 543-2811, and Signal Mountain, tel. 733-5470. Rent motorboats, rowboats, and canoes, or hire a guide to take you to the hot fishing spots. Scenic boat cruises ($7.50 and up) are available at Colter Bay Marina, including a variety of cruise-and-dine trips. For more on fishing and river rafting within the park, see appropriate sections under "Jackson."

Information And Services

Visitors receive a copy of *Teewinot,* the park newspaper, at the entrance stations. It lists park facilities and services, along with interpretive programs, nature walks, and other activities. Family favorites for generations have been the evening campfire programs at the outdoor amphitheaters. Grand Teton National Park headquarters are located in the settlement of Moose near the southern end of the park. **Moose Visitor Center,** tel. 733-2880, is open daily 8-4:30 year-round. **Colter Bay Visitor Center,** tel. 543-2467, is open daily 8-5 from mid-May through September. Both centers are open till 7 p.m. in midsummer. **Grand Teton Natural History Association** operates bookstores in the visitor centers and provides a mail order service for books about the park. For a catalog, contact them at: P.O. Drawer 170, Moose, WY 83012.

BRIDGER-TETON NATIONAL FOREST

Bridger-Teton National Forest is the second largest in the lower 48, stretching southward for 135 miles from the Yellowstone border, and covering 3.4 million acres. Portions of the forest are described elsewhere: the "Bridger Wilderness" (p. 270), and "Greys River Area" (p. 142). In Jackson Hole, the two areas of most interest for recreation are the Teton Wilderness and the Gros Ventre Wilderness. Because of its extensive wilderness areas, the B-T has more outfitters than any other national forest. Much of the remaining land managed by the Forest Service is multiple use, meaning lots of logging, cattle grazing, and oil and gas leasing. The latter has become one of the hottest political issues, since the Forest Service has attempted to open 95% of all non-wilderness lands to oil and gas exploration work, including areas around scenic Togwotee Pass. In 40 years of such exploration, only two commercially viable sites have been found on the B-T. Conservationists fear that if oil is found, the Forest Service will waive its no-surface-occupancy standards to allow development.

The **Bridger-Teton Supervisor's Office** is in Jackson at 340 N. Cache, tel. 733-2752. If you're planning a trip into surrounding Forest Service lands, be sure to stop by to pick up the forest map ($2) and to ask for other publications on camping and sights. Ranger stations are in Jackson, 140 E. Broadway, tel. 733-4755, and nine miles east of Moran Jct., tel. 543-2386.

TETON WILDERNESS

The Teton Wilderness covers 585,468 acres of mountain country, and is bordered to the north by Yellowstone National Park, to the west by Grand Teton National Park, and to the east by the Washakie Wilderness. Established as a primitive area in 1934, it was declared one of the nation's first wilderness areas upon passage of the 1964 Wilderness Act. The Teton Wilderness offers a diverse mixture of rolling lands carpeted with lodgepole pine, spacious grassy meadows, roaring rivers, and dramatic mountains. Elevations range from 7,500 feet to the 12,165-foot summit of Younts Peak. The Continental Divide slices across the wilderness, with headwaters of the Yellowstone River draining the eastern half and headwaters of the Buffalo and Snake rivers flowing down the western side. One of the most unusual places is **Two Ocean Creek**, where a creek abruptly splits at a rock, never to rejoin. One branch becomes Atlantic Creek, and its waters eventually reach the Atlantic Ocean, while the other becomes Pacific Creek and flows to the Snake River, the Columbia River, and thence into the Pacific Ocean!

Two natural events have had a major effect on the Teton Wilderness. On July 21, 1987, a world record high-elevation tornado created a massive blowdown of trees around the Enos Lake area. The blowdown covered 10,000 acres, and trails are only now being rebuilt through this incredible jackstraw pile. (Since this is a wilderness area, chainsaws cannot be used.) In 1988, extreme drought conditions led to a series of major fires in Yellowstone and surrounding areas. Within the Teton Wilderness, the Huck and Mink Creek fires burned (in varying degrees of severity) approximately 200,000 acres. Over half of the wilderness remained untouched. Don't let these incidents dissuade you from visiting; this is still a marvelous and little-used area. Herds of elk can be seen grazing in alpine areas, and the Thorofare country abutting Yellowstone National Park is considered the most remote place in the lower 48. This is prime grizzly habitat, so be very cautious at all times. Poles have been placed at most campsites to hang food.

Access

Three primary trailheads provide access to the Teton Wilderness: Pacific Creek on the southwestern end, Turpin Meadow on the Buffalo Fork River, and Brooks Lake just east of the Continental Divide. Campgrounds are at each of these trailheads. Teton Wilderness is a favorite of Wyoming people, particularly those with horses, and in the fall, elk hunters come here from across the nation. Distances are so great that few backpackers head into this wilderness area.

No permits are needed, but it's a good idea to stop in at the **Blackrock Ranger Station**, tel. 543-2386, nine miles east of Moran Junction on U.S. 26-287, for topographic maps and info on current trail conditions, bear problems, and regulations, along with a list of outfitters offering horse trips. Unfortunately, the Forest Service and USGS maps fail to show the many trails built and maintained (or not maintained) by private outfitters. They can make hiking confusing. A few of the many possible hikes are described below.

Whetstone Creek
Whetstone Creek Trail begins at the Pacific Creek Trailhead, located on the southwest side of Teton Wilderness. An enjoyable 20-mile (RT) hike leaves the trailhead and follows Pacific Creek for 1 1/2 miles before splitting left to follow Whetstone Creek. Bear left again when the trail splits another three miles upstream and continue through a series of small meadows to the junction with Pilgrim Creek Trail. Turn right here and follow this two more miles to Coulter Creek Trail, climbing up Coulter Creek to scenic Coulter Basin, and then dropping down along the East Fork of Whetstone Creek. This rejoins the Whetstone Creek Trail and returns you to the trailhead, passing many attractive small meadows along the way. The upper half of this loop hike was burned in 1988, and some areas were heavily scorched, while others are quite patchy. Flowers are abundant in the burned areas, and this is important elk habitat.

South Fork To Soda Fork
A fine loop hike leaves Turpin Meadow and follows South Buffalo Fork River to South Fork Falls. Just above this, a trail splits off and climbs to Nowlin Meadow (excellent views of Smokehouse Mountain) and then down to Soda Fork River where it joins the Soda Fork Trail. Follow this trail back downstream to huge Soda Fork Meadow (a good place to see moose and occasionally grizzlies) and then back to Turpin Meadow, a distance of approximately 23 miles roundtrip. A fascinating side trip from this route would be to head up the Soda Fork into the alpine at Crater Lake, a six-mile hike above the Nowlin Meadows-Soda Fork trail junction. The outlet stream at Crater Lake disappears into a gaping

hole, emerging as a large creek two miles below at Big Springs. It's an incredible sight.

Cub Creek Area
The Brooks Lake area just east of Togwotee Pass is a very popular summertime camping and fishing place with magnificent views. Brooks Lake Trail follows the western shore of Brooks Lake and continues past Upper Brooks Lakes to Bear Cub Pass. From here, the trail drops down to Cub Creek where several good campsites can be found. A long and very scenic loop can be made by following the trail up Cub Creek into the alpine country and then back down along the South Buffalo Fork River to Lower Pendergraft Meadow. From here, take Cub Creek Trail back up along Cub Creek to Bear Cub Pass and back out to Brooks Lake. Get a topographic map before heading into this remote country. Total distance is approximately 33 miles roundtrip.

GROS VENTRE WILDERNESS

The 287,000-acre Gros Ventre Wilderness was established in 1984 and covers the mountain country just east of Jackson Hole. This range trends mainly in a northwest-southeast direction and is probably best known for Sleeping Indian Mountain (maps now call it Sheep Mountain), the distinctive rocky summit visible from Jackson Hole. Although there are densely forested areas at lower elevations, the central portion of the wilderness lies above timberline, with many peaks topping 10,000 feet. Tallest is Doubletop Peak at 11,682 feet. The Tetons are visible from almost any high point in the Gros Ventre, and meadows line the lower-elevation streams. Elk, mule deer, bighorn sheep, moose, and black bears are found here, and a few grizzlies have been reported. The Forest Service office in Jackson has more info on the wilderness, including brief trail descriptions and maps.

Access And Trails
A number of roads provide good access to the Gros Ventre Wilderness: Gros Ventre River Rd. on the northern border, Flat Creek, Curtis Canyon, and Cache Creek roads on the western margin, and Granite Creek Rd. to the south.

Note that hikes beginning or ending in the Granite Creek area have the added advantage of nearby Granite Hot Springs, a great place to soak tired muscles.

An enjoyable two-day trip begins at **Jackpine Creek Trailhead** on Granite Creek Rd., 35 miles southeast of Jackson. Follow Jackpine Creek Trail up to Shoal Lake and then loop back down via the Swift Creek Trail. The distance is approximately 16 miles round-trip, but involves gaining and then losing 4,000 feet of elevation. Another good hike is to follow **Highline Trail** from the Granite Creek area across to Cache Creek, a distance of 16 miles. This route passes just below a row of high and rugged mountains, but since it isn't a loop route, you'll need to hitchhike or arrange a car shuttle. Plan on three days for this scenic hike. A third hike begins at the **Goosewing Ranger Station**, located 12 miles east of Slide Lake on Gros Ventre River Road. Take the trail from here to Two Echo Park, a fine camping spot, and then continue up to Six Lakes. You can return via the same trail or take the Crystal Creek Trail back to Red Rock Ranch and hitch back to Goosewing. The trail distance is approximately 23 miles round-trip.

TARGHEE NATIONAL FOREST

The 1.8 million-acre Targhee National Forest extends along the western face of the Tetons and then south and west into Idaho. Much of the forest is heavily logged, but two wilderness areas protect most of the Wyoming portion of the Targhee.

JEDEDIAH SMITH WILDERNESS

The 116,535-acre Jedediah Smith Wilderness lies on the west side of the Teton Range, facing Idaho, but lying entirely within Wyoming. Access is primarily from the Idaho side, although trails breach the mountain passes at various points, making it possible to enter from Grand Teton National Park. This area was not declared a wilderness until 1984. A second wilderness area, the 10,820-acre **Winegar Hole Wilderness** (pronounced WINE-a-gur) lies along the southern border of Yellowstone National Park. Grizzlies love this country, but hikers will find it uninteresting and without trails. In contrast, the Jedediah Smith Wilderness contains nearly 300 miles of paths, along with some incredible high mountain scenery.

A number of roads (most are gravel) lead up from the Driggs and Victor areas into the Tetons. Get a map showing wilderness trails and access points from Targhee National Forest ranger station in Driggs, Idaho, tel. (208) 354-2431. (Driggs is also home to the delightfully amusing Spud Drive-In, here since 1953.) Be sure to camp at least 200 feet from lakes and 50 feet away from streams. If you plan to cross into Grand Teton National Park from the west side, be sure you have a camping permit in advance.

Hidden Corral Basin

Located at the northern end of the wilderness, Hidden Corral Basin provides a fine loop hike. Locals (primarily horse parties) crowd this area on late summer weekends. Get to the trailhead by driving north from Tetonia on Idaho 32 to Lamont where you turn north on a gravel road. (The Tetonia area—Pierre's Hole—offers outstanding views of the Tetons, particularly at sunset. The three dominant peaks are more obvious from this side.) Follow it a mile and then turn right (east) onto Coyote Meadows Road. The trailhead is approximately 10 miles up, where the road dead-ends. An eight-mile trail parallels South Bitch Creek (the name Bitch Creek comes from the French word for female deer, biche) to Hidden Corral where you may see moose. Be sure to bring a fishing pole to try for the cutthroats. Above Hidden Corral, you can make a pleasant loop back by turning north onto the trail to Nord Pass and then dropping down along the Carrot Ridge and Conant Basin trails to Bitch Creek Trail and then on to Coyote Meadows, a distance of 21 miles round-trip. Note that this is grizzly country, so be sure to hang all food. By the way, Hidden Corral received its name from the outlaw days when rustlers would steal horses in Idaho, change the brands, and then hold them in this natural corral until the branding wounds healed. The horses were then sold to Wyoming ranchers. Owen Wister's *Virginian* describes a pursuit of horse thieves through Bitch Creek country.

Alaska Basin

The most popular hiking trail in the Jedediah Smith begins at Teton Canyon Campground ($5) and leads up into the flower-bedecked meadows of Alaska Basin. Great country, but don't expect a true wilderness experience with so many other hikers. Get to the campground by following the Grand Targhee Ski Area signs east from Driggs, Idaho. A gravel road splits off to the right approximately six miles beyond the little settlement of Alta. Follow it to the campground. (If you miss the turn, you'll end up at the ski area.) For an enjoyable loop, follow Alaska Basin Trail up the canyon to Basin Lakes, and then head southwest along the Teton Crest Trail to the Teton Shelf Trail. Follow this back to its junction with the Alaska Basin Trail, dropping down the Devils Stairs—a series of very steep switchbacks. You can then take the Alaska Basin Trail back to Teton Campground, a roundtrip distance of approximately 19 miles. You could also use these trails to access the high peaks of the Tetons or to cross the mountains into Death Canyon within Grand Teton National Park (permit required). Campfires and horse camping are not allowed in Alaska Basin.

Moose Meadows

For a somewhat less-crowded hiking experience, check out the Moose Meadows area on the southern end of the Jedediah Smith Wilderness. Get to the trailhead by going three miles southeast of Victor on State 22. Turn north to Moose Creek Rd. and follow it to the trailhead at Nordwall Campground. The trail parallels Moose Creek to Moose Meadows, a good place to camp. You'll need to ford the creek twice, so this is best hiked in late summer. At the meadows, the trail dead ends into Teton Crest Trail, providing access to Grand Teton National Park through some gorgeous alpine country. A nice loop can be made by heading south along the this trail to flower-covered Coal Creek Meadows. A trail leads from here past 10,068-foot Taylor Mountain (an easy side trip with magnificent views), down to Taylor Basin, through lodgepole forests, and then back to your starting point. The distance for this loop hike is 15 miles round-trip.

YELLOWSTONE NATIONAL PARK
THE SETTING

Mention the words "national park" and an almost Pavlovian response comes to mind: Yellowstone. The geysers, canyons, and bears of Yellowstone National Park are so intertwined in our collective conscience that even our cartoons use the park as a model: Jellystone Park where Yogi and Boo Boo are constantly out to thwart the rangers. Yellowstone brings out the child in everyone; something of a natural Disneyland.

On a map, Yellowstone appears as a gigantic box wedged so tightly against the northwest corner of Wyoming that it squeezes over into Montana and Idaho. The park reaches 63 by 54 miles across and covers 2.2 million acres, making it the largest national park in the lower 48. The UN has declared Yellowstone both a World Biosphere Reserve and a World Heritage Site.

Yellowstone evokes a torrent of emotions in anyone with a knowledge of and concern for the natural world. Here was the birthplace of the national park movement, a place so unusual that those who first wandered through were afraid to tell others lest they be labeled liars. In the Yellowstone backcountry, one can still walk for days without seeing more than a handful of other hardy hikers, and the wildlife, geysers, and canyons continue to bring smiles to the faces of young and old alike. Americans love Yellowstone, the nation's "crown jewel." One source estimates that 30% of the U.S. population have visited the park, and each year another 2 1/2 million roll through the gates.

More than any other national park, Yellowstone seems to provide the oddities of nature, creating, as historian Aubrey L. Haines noted, "a false impression that the park is only a colossal, steam-operated freak show." During midsummer, a trip into Yellowstone can be something less than a natural experience. Thousands of behemoth land yachts clog the potholed roads and crowd the parking lots. Throngs of visitors circle Old Faithful Geyser, waiting for an eruption, while dozens of others cluster around bewildered elk to get a photo for their scrapbook. Although less than three percent of the park is developed, Yellowstone contains more than 2,000 buildings of various types, ranging from graceful historic hotels to one-hour photo shops. In some spots, these developments have grown to the point that the natural world seems simply a backdrop to the human world that pulls visitors in to buy T-shirts or to watch a park slide show on geysers or wildlife.

From day one, Yellowstone National Park was set up for what Edward Abbey called "industrial tourism." The park came into being in part because of a railroad promoter who hoped to gain from its development, and grew to maturity on a diet of roads, hotels, and curio shops. Finally, in the 1960s and '70s, America began to take a second look at this heritage and to ask questions about what mattered more: providing a public playground or preserving an area that is unique on this planet. The inherent conflict between the need for public facilities and services in Yellowstone and the survival of a func-

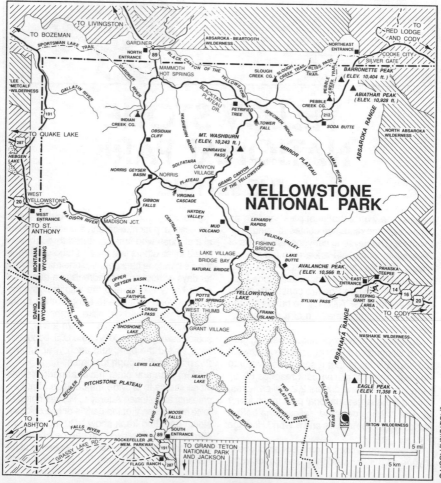

© MOON PUBLICATIONS

tioning ecosystem have come to the fore in recent years in such issues as wolf reintroduction, grizzly management, and fire suppression.

GEOLOGY

Yellowstone is perhaps the world's preeminent place to view geological processes, for here the forces that elsewhere lie deep within the earth seem close enough to touch. The forces are palpable not only in the geysers and hot springs, but also in the lake that fills part of an enormous caldera, the earthquakes that shake the land, the evidences of massive glaciation, and the deeply eroded Grand Canyon of the Yellowstone.

Volcanism

The geologic history of Yellowstone centers around volcanism. The Absaroka Mountains along the park's eastern border were created by volcanic activity some 50 million years ago, but the park itself was most influenced by three violent explosions. Molten lava pushing from below bulged the land upward into an enormous dome. Eventually, this pressure became too great, sending ash and rock blasting from fissures around the dome's margins. Afterward, the dome began to re-form as more magma was forced in. This process has been repeated three times over the last two million years, with the last eruption approximately 600,000 years ago. The magnitude of this most recent event is beyond the realm of imagination: 240 cubic miles of ash were blasted into the atmosphere! This eruption—perhaps the largest to ever occur on earth—ejected 20 times more material than the massive Krakatoa eruption of 1883, an explosion heard 3,000 miles away! Undoubtedly, ash from the eruption affected the global climate for years to follow.

After this eruption, the magma chamber collapsed into a gigantic, smouldering pit reaching 28 by 47 miles across, and perhaps several thousand feet deep. Over time, additional molten rock pushed up from underneath and flowed as thick lava over the land. Two resurgent domes—near Old Faithful and just north of Yellowstone Lake—are still rising at nearly an inch per year. The one north of Yellowstone Lake is raising the lake's outlet and causing the water level to increase at an inch a year, flooding trees along the margins. Yellowstone's volcanism is far from dead, and scientists believe another eruption is possible or even likely, though nobody knows just when it might occur.

Yellowstone is one of the hottest places on the planet; Firehole Basin has underground temperatures 700 times the global average. Geologists now believe that the source of this heat (and of the volcanism) is an enormous plume of superheated magma just below the surface. The earth's crust is gradually moving over this plume, sort of like pulling a piece of cloth across a candle. The plume has gradually shifted to the northeast over the millennia, leaving behind such places as Craters of the Moon in Idaho. (A similar situation is believed to exist in the chain of Hawaiian Islands.)

Geysers

Yellowstone is famous for geysers, and geyser-gazers will not be disappointed. At least 60% of the world's geysers are in the park, making it easily the largest and most diverse collection of geysers in existence! Yellowstone's more than 300 geysers are spread over nine different basins, the largest being Upper Geyser Basin.

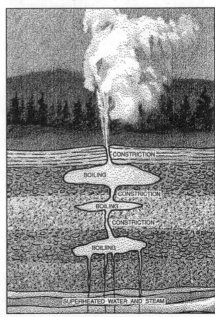

CONSTRICTION

BOILING

CONSTRICTION

BOILING

CONSTRICTION

BOILING

SUPERHEATED WATER AND STEAM

BOB RACE

Geysers need three essentials to exist: water, heat, and fractured rock. The water comes from snow and rain falling on this high plateau, while the heat comes from the molten rock close to the earth's surface. Massive pressures from below have created a ring of fractures around the edge of Yellowstone's caldera.

Geysers are based on the principle that cold, dense water sinks while less-dense hot water rises. The periodic eruption of geysers is due to constrictions in the underground channels that prevent an adequate heat exchange with the surface. Precipitation slowly moves into the earth, eventually contacting the molten rock. Because of high pressures at these depths, water can reach extreme temperatures without boiling (as in a pressure cooker). As this super-heated water rises back toward the surface, it emerges as hot springs, fumaroles, mudpots, or geysers. The most spectacular of these are geysers. Two general types of geysers exist in Yellowstone. Fountain geysers (such as Great Fountain Geyser) explode from a pool of water and tend to spray water more widely, while cone-type geysers (such as Old Faithful) jet out of a nozzle-like formation.

In a geyser, steam bubbles upward from this superheated source of water and expands as it rises. These bubbles block the plumbing system, keeping hot water from reaching the surface. Eventually, however, pressure from the bubbles begins to force the cooler water out of the vent. This initial release triggers a more violent reaction as the sudden lessening of pressure allows the entire column to begin boiling, sending up the quantities of steam and water for which geysers are known. Once the eruption has emptied the plumbing system, water gradually seeps back into the chambers to begin the process anew. Some of Yellowstone's geysers have enormous underground caverns that fill with water; in its rare eruptions, massive Steamboat Geyser can blast a million gallons of water into the air!

Unfortunately, some of Yellowstone's geysers have been lost because of human stupidity or vandalism. At one time, it was considered great sport to stuff logs, rocks, and even chairs into the geysers for a little added show. Others poured chemicals into them to make them play. As a result of such actions, some geysers have been severely damaged or destroyed, while a number of hot springs have become collection points for coins, rocks, sticks, and trash. It shouldn't be necessary to point out that such actions ruin these thermal areas for everyone.

Other Geothermal Activity

Although geysers are Yellowstone's best-known feature, they make up only a tiny fraction of perhaps 10,000 thermal features in the park. **Hot springs** appear where water can reach the ground surface relatively easily, allowing for a dissipation of the heat that builds up in the chambers of geysers. When less groundwater is present, you may find **mud pots** (also called paint pots), while the driest shoot only steam through **fumaroles** or steam vents. A note of warning: the surface around many of the hot springs and geysers is surprisingly thin, and people have been killed by falling through into the boiling water. Stay on the boardwalks in developed areas, and use extreme caution around back-country thermal features.

FLORA AND FAUNA

The Yellowstone Ecosystem

For most of its existence, Yellowstone has been regarded as an island of nature surrounded by a world of human development. Unfortunately, this attitude has led to all sorts of problems. Despite its size, Yellowstone alone is not large enough to support a viable population of all the animals that once existed within its borders. In recent years, there have been increasing calls to treat the park as part of the larger Greater Yellowstone Ecosystem—14 million acres of land at the juncture of Wyoming, Montana, and Idaho. Within surrounding lands, conflicts between development and preservation are even more obvious than within the park itself. Logging is one of the most obvious of these, and along the park's western border aerial photos reveal a perfectly straight line, with lodgepole trees on the park side and enormous clearcuts on the Forest Service side. One of these was the largest timber sale ever made outside of Alaska! Add to this encroachments in the form of housing developments, oil and gas drilling, and mining activities, and the future looks difficult for the Yellowstone ecosystem. Despite all these impacts, Yellowstone remains one of the largest intact temperate zone ecosystems on the planet.

Plants

Yellowstone National Park is primarily a series of high plateaus ranging from 7,500 to 8,500 feet in elevation. Surrounding this gently rolling expanse are the Absaroka Mountains along the east side and the Gallatin Range in the northeast corner. Elevations are lowest along the northern end of the park where the Yellowstone River and other streams cut through. Here one finds open country with sagebrush, grasses, and shrubs, along with patches of aspen and Douglas fir. Farther south on the central plateaus are found the extensive lodgepole pine forests that cover 60% of the park.

At higher and cooler elevations, lodgepole forests grade into Engelmann spruce and subalpine fir, and eventually into stands of whitebark pine—an important food source for grizzlies. At timberline (approximately 10,000 feet), even these trees give way, and only low-growing forbs, grasses, and shrubs survive. Not all areas follow this simple elevational gradient, however. The park contains extensive wet meadow areas in the Bechler and upper Yellowstone River areas. Other broad openings are found along the Gardner River, in Pelican Valley, and in Hayden Valley.

Wildlife

Yellowstone is world famous for its wildlife, and provides a marvelous natural setting to view bison, elk, moose, coyotes, antelope, bighorn sheep, and other animals. One of the easiest ways to find wildlife is by simply watching for the brake lights, the cars pulled half off the road, and the cameras all pointed in one direction. Inevitably, you'll find an elk or bison placidly munching away, oblivious to the chaos that surrounds it.

Because of the constant parade of visitors and the lack of hunting, many of Yellowstone's animals appear to almost ignore the presence of people, and it isn't uncommon to see visitors approach them without respecting the animal's need for space. Although they may appear "tame," these really are wild animals, and attacks are not uncommon. Those quiet bison can suddenly erupt with an enormous ferocity if provoked by photographers who come too close. Stay at least 25 yards away from bison and elk, and at least 100 yards away from bears. The Park Service has a free brochure showing where

you're most likely to see wildlife in Yellowstone. Get it at any visitor center. Mosquitoes are a special treat, and can be found almost anywhere in Yellowstone before mid-August. Fall is the best time to avoid these friendly critters.

Trumpeter swans—beautiful white birds with eight-foot wingspans—are a fairly common sight in Yellowstone, particularly on the Madison and Yellowstone rivers. Many trumpeter swans winter in the hot springs area. Another large white bird is the awkward-looking and bulbous-billed white pelican, common on Yellowstone Lake. Bald eagles and osprey have also managed a comeback in recent years, and are seen along the Yellowstone River.

Killing The Predators

Wildlife have always been one of the big drawing cards at Yellowstone, and early on there were constant charges of mass slaughter by poachers and market hunters. It was not until 1894 that Congress passed the Lacey Act, finally making it illegal to hunt within the park. Unfortunately, predators such as wolves, coyotes, mountain lions, and wolverines were regarded as despoilers of the elk, deer, and moose, and became fair targets for poisoning and shooting by early park managers. The campaign proved all too successful, decimating the wolf and mountain lion populations.

Bears

During its early years as a park, bears seem to have been viewed as either pets or nuisances. Cubs were tethered to poles out front of the hotels, while other bears fed on the garbage piles that grew up around the hotels and camps. Older folks still recall the bear feeding grounds at the garbage dumps, where visitors might see 50 bears pawing through the garbage. The feeding shows continued until 1941, but it wasn't until 1970 that the park's open-pit dumps were finally sealed off and the garbage cans bearproofed. Unfortunately, rather than gradually reducing the food available at the dumps to wean bears from the sites, they were abruptly shut down. The dumps had artificially maintained bear populations above their natural levels, and their closure brought almost immediate consequences. Over the next few years, at least 50 grizzlies died in confrontations with humans in the park or surrounding areas. Fortunately, the population appears to have finally begun to recover.

There are believed to be 200 grizzlies in the greater Yellowstone ecosystem, fewer than in the 1960s when many lived on garbage dumps and campers' coolers, but more than in the early '80s. Both black and grizzly bears are found throughout Yellowstone, but the days of bear-jams along the park roads are past, since rangers actively work to prevent bears from becoming habituated to people. Most bears have returned to their more natural ways of living, although problems still crop up with bears wandering through campgrounds in search of food. You're more likely to encounter a bear in the backcountry areas. Some places—especially around the north end of Yellowstone Lake in Pelican Valley—are off limits to hiking much of the year for this reason.

Bison
When Yellowstone was established in 1872, perhaps 1,000 mountain (wood) bison ranged across this high plateau. Sport and meat hunting—legal until 1894—along with later poaching reduced the population, and by 1902, perhaps only 25 remained. That year, plains bison were brought in from private ranches in Montana and Texas to help restore the Yellowstone herd, and today there are around 2,600 buffalo in the park. Unfortunately, interbreeding between the mountain and plains bison means that the animals in Yellowstone today are genetically different from the original inhabitants.

In 1985, Yellowstone's bison began wandering north into the Gardiner area for the winter. Ranchers feared that the bison could spread the disease brucellosis to their cattle, causing cows to abort calves. A highly controversial "hunt" during the late 1980s let Montana hunters shoot bison when they wandered outside the park. The policy is currently under review. (Ironically, the more numerous elk also carry brucellosis. Although they are hunted, nobody seems anxious to kill all the elk that wander across Yellowstone's borders.)

Wolves
One of the easiest ways to start a bar fight at a town adjoining Yellowstone is to bring up the subject of wolves. Despite their reputation, wolves do not attack humans. They can, however, have an effect on elk, deer, and other ungulates by thinning out their populations. Many of the animals taken are the weak, sick, or old—the easiest to chase down. Without wolves and other predators in Yellowstone, the elk population has grown well above its natural level, throwing the entire system out of balance.

Wolves once ranged across North America, but are now found only in Canada, Alaska, northern Minnesota, Isle Royale, and Glacier National Park. For many years, wolves (along with mountain lions and coyotes) were regarded as unwanted predators in Yellowstone, and both the Army and the Park Service did their best to poison or shoot any that could be found. By 1940, the wolf was probably gone from Yellowstone, though a few turned up briefly again in the early 1970s. With a more enlightened attitude in recent years, ecologists and conservationists began pushing for the reintroduction of wolves to Yellowstone, considered one of the few remaining areas in the lower 48 that could support a viable wolf population.

Opponents of wolf reintroduction (especially Wyoming's senators, Malcolm Wallop and Alan Simpson) have fought these efforts, despite support from a majority of people in Wyoming, Montana, and Idaho. Opponents of wolf reintroduction even succeeded in muzzling the Park Service's educational programs on wolves and blocking them from even mentioning wolf reintroduction in park newsletters! Despite studies that point to negligible economic losses in Minnesota where wolves and cattle coexist, Yellowstone area ranchers are nervous. Yet another study was commissioned in 1990, and there are now hopes that the cry of the wolf will again be heard within the Yellowstone wilderness.

PARK HISTORY

Yellowstone National Park has a rich and fascinating history that reaches back for thousands of years of settlement. The most thorough source for history is *The Yellowstone Story,* an excellent two-volume set by former park historian Aubrey L. Haines.

Sheepeater Indians
Yellowstone has been inhabited by people for at least 11,000 years, although the tribes changed

Sheepeater Indian in wickiup

over the centuries. By the mid-19th century, the country was surrounded by Blackfeet to the north, Crow to the east, and Shoshone and Bannock to the south and west. These tribes all traveled through Yellowstone and hunted here periodically, but only the Sheepeater Indians actually lived on this high plateau. The Sheepeater were of Shoshone stock, a simple and timid people who hunted bighorn sheep (hence the name), but also depended on other animals, fish, roots, and berries. They built temporary shelters called wickiups made of aspen poles covered with pine boughs, a few of which still exist in Yellowstone. Because they did not have horses, the Sheepeaters used dog travois to carry their few possessions from camp to camp. Summers were spent in high alpine meadows and along passes where they hunted migrating game animals or gathered roots and berries. They wintered in protected canyons.

The Sheepeaters were smaller than other Indians, and have achieved an aura of mystery since so little is known of their way of living. Yellowstone was at the heart of their territory, but with the arrival of whites came devastating diseases, particularly smallpox. The survivors joined their Shoshone brothers on the Wind River Reservation or the Bannock Reservation in Idaho. The last of the tribe left Yellowstone in the 1870s.

Fur Trappers

The word "Yellowstone" appears to have come from the Sioux Indians who called the river "Mi tse a-da-zi," a word French-Canadian trappers translated into "Rive des Roche Jaune"—literally, "Yellow Rock River." The Indians called it this because of the yellowish bluffs along the river mouth (not, as some claim, because of the colorful Grand Canyon of the Yellowstone). The term "Yellow Stone" was first used on a map made in 1798. When the William and Clark Expedition traveled through the country north of Yellowstone in 1804, the Indians told them tales of this mysterious place where, "There is frequently heard a loud noise like thunder, which makes the earth tremble, they state that they seldom go there because children Cannot sleep —and Conceive it possessed of spirits, who were adverse that men Should be near them." (This certainly was not the attitude of all the Native peoples, for the park had long been inhabited.) The first white man to come through Yellowstone was John Colter, a former member of the Lewis and Clark Expedition who wandered through the region in the winter of 1807-08. A map based on Colter's recollections shows Yellowstone Lake ("Eustis Lake"), along with an area of "Hot Spring Brimstone."

As fur trappers spread through the Rockies in the 1820s and '30s, many discovered the geysers and hot springs of Yellowstone, and stories quickly spread around the rendezvous fires. The word of the trappers was passed on to later settlers and explorers, but not entirely believed. After all, mountain man Jim Bridger described not just petrified trees, but petrified birds singing petrified songs! His tales of a river that "ran so fast that it became hot on the bottom" could well have referred to the Firehole River. When Bridger tried to lead a party of military explorers into Yellowstone, they were stymied by deep snows. Still, the word gradually got out that something very strange could be found in this part of the mountains.

Expeditions

National attention finally came to Yellowstone with a series of three expeditions to check out the wild claims of local prospectors. In 1869, David E. Folsom, Charles W. Cook, and William Peterson headed south from Bozeman, finding the Grand Canyon, Lake Yellowstone, and the geyser basins. When a friend pressured them to submit a description of their travels for publication, the *New York Tribune* refused, noting that it "had a reputation that they could not risk with such unreliable material."

Their adventures led another group of explorers into Yellowstone the following year, but this time money was the motive. Jay Cooke's Northern Pacific Railroad needed investors for a planned route across Montana. A good public relations campaign was the first step, and it happened to coincide with the visit of a former Montana tax collector named Nathaniel P. Langford who had heard of the discoveries of Folsom, Cook, and Peterson. The collection of 19 soldiers and civilians headed out in August of 1870 under Gen. Henry D. Washburn. They were thrilled by what they discovered, and proceeded to name the geysers—Old Faithful, Castle, Giant, Grotto, Giantess—names that became permanently attached to them.

With the return of the Washburn Expedition,

THE NEZ PERCE WAR

One of the saddest episodes in the history of Yellowstone took place in 1877 and involved the Nez Perce (pronounced nez-PURS) Indians of Oregon's Wallowa Valley. When the government tried to force the people of Chief White Bird and Chief Joseph onto an Idaho reservation so that white ranchers could have their lands, they stubbornly refused. A few drunk young men killed four whites, and subsequent raids led to the deaths of at least 14 more. The Army retaliated, but were turned back by the Nez Perce. Rather than face government reinforcements, more than 1,000 Nez Perce began an 1,800-mile flight in a desperate bid to reach Canada. A series of running battles followed as the Indians used their geographic knowledge and battle skills to confound the inept army. The Nez Perce entered Yellowstone from the west, and a few hotheads immediately attacked vacationing tourists and prospectors. Only two whites were killed in the park, but others were kidnapped and one man nearly died from his wounds.

The Nez Perce exited Yellowstone two weeks after they arrived, narrowly missing an encounter with their implacable foe, Gen. William T. Sherman, who just happened to be vacationing in Yellowstone at the time. East of the park, the Indians plotted a masterful escape from two columns of Army forces, feinting a move down the Shoshone River and then heading north along a route that left their pursuers gasping in amazement—straight up the narrow Clarks Fork Canyon, "where rocks on each side came so near together that two horses abreast could hardly pass." Finally, less than 40 miles from the international border with Canada, the Army caught up with the Nez Perce, and after a fierce battle, they were forced to surrender (although 300 did make good their escape).

Chief Joseph's haunting words still echo through the years: "Hear me, my chiefs, I am tired; my heart is sick and sad. From where the sun now stands, I will fight no more forever." Despite promises that they would be allowed to return home, the Nez Perce were hustled onto a reservation in Oklahoma, while whites remained on their ancestral lands. Chief Joseph died in 1904, reportedly of a broken heart. Yellowstone's Nez Perce Creek which feeds the Firehole River is named for this desperate bid for freedom.

Chief Joseph in October 1887 immediately after his surrender at Bear Paw Mountain, Montana

national newspapers and magazines finally began to pay attention to Yellowstone, and Langford began lecturing in the East on what they had found. One of those listening was Dr. Ferdinand V. Hayden, director of the U.S. Geological Survey. Hayden asked Congress to fund an official investigation. With the help of Representatives James G. Blaine (coincidentally a supporter of the Northern Pacific Railroad) and conservationist Henry M. Dawes, Congress appropriated $40,000 for an exploration of "The sources of the Missouri and Yellowstone Rivers." Thus began the most famous and influential trip into Yellowstone, the 1871 Hayden Expedition. The troop included 34 men, an escort of cavalry, plus painter Thomas Moran and photographer William H. Jackson.

Establishing The Park

When Hayden returned to Washington to prepare his report, he found a letter from railroad promoter Jay Cooke. In the letter, Cooke proposed that "Congress pass a bill reserving the Great Geyser Basin as a public park forever—just as it has reserved that far inferior wonder the Yosemite valley and big trees." In an amazingly short time, a bill was introduced to set aside the land, and Hayden rushed to arrange a display in the Capitol rotunda of geological specimens, sketches by Moran, and the photos by Jackson. The bill easily passed both houses of Congress and was signed into law on March 1, 1872 by President Ulysses S. Grant. The first national park had come into existence, a culmination not just of the discoveries in Yellowstone, but also of a growing appreciation for preserving the wonders of the natural world. (Yosemite had actually been established earlier, but as a state park.)

Congress saw no need to set aside money for this new creation since it seemed to be doing fine already. Besides, it was thought that Jay Cooke's new railroad would soon arrive, making it easy for thousands of vacationers to explore Yellowstone. In turn, concessioners would build roads and hotels and pay the government franchise fees. The park was placed under the control of the Secretary of the Interior, with Nathaniel P. Langford as its unpaid superintendent. Meanwhile, the planned railroad fizzled when Jay Cooke & Co. declared bankruptcy, precipitating the Panic of 1873.

Roads And Railroads

Because of the difficult access, fewer than 500 people came in each of the first few years as a park, most to soak in tubs at Mammoth Hot Springs. Not a few decided to take home souvenirs, bringing pick axe and shovel for that purpose. Meanwhile, hunters—including some working for the Mammoth Hotel—began shooting the park's abundant game. Two brothers who had a ranch just north of the park killed 2,000 elk in a single year. Superintendent Langford did little to stop the slaughter, only bothering to visit the park twice. Finally, in 1877, the Secretary of the Interior fired him, putting Philetus W. Norris in charge instead. Norris proved a good choice, despite a knack for applying his name to everything in sight. (Most of his attempts at immortality have been replaced by other titles, but Norris Geyser Basin, Norris Road, and even the town of Norris, Michigan remain.)

Norris oversaw construction of the first major road in Yellowstone, a rough 60-mile route built in just 30 days to connect Upper Geyser Basin with Mammoth and the western entrance. All of this was precipitated by the raids of the Nez Perce Indians earlier that summer and threats that the Bannock Indians would be next. In addition, Norris began, but never completed, the "Queen's Laundry," a bathhouse that is considered the first government building built for the public in any national park. The log walls are still visible in a meadow near Lower Geyser Basin.

By 1882, Norris had managed to alienate the company that helped found the park: the Northern Pacific Railroad. The company announced plans to build a railroad line to the geysers and construct a large hotel, "being assured by the Government of a monopoly therein." Norris' opposition led to his being fired and replaced by railroad man Patrick H. Conger. Soon, however, the scheme began to unravel. The Yellowstone Park Improvement Company—whose vice-president happened to be construction superintendent for the Northern Pacific's branch line into Gardiner—had planned not just a lodging monopoly, but also a monopoly on all transportation, timber rights, and ranching privileges in the park. Later it was discovered that the company had let a contract for 20,000 pounds of venison (killed in the park) to feed the construction crews. As one newspaper writer commented, "It is a 'Park Improvement Company' doing this, and I suppose they consider it an improvement to rid the park, as far as possible of game."

Superintendent Conger was later replaced by Robert E. Carpenter, a man about whom historian Hiram Chittenden noted, "In his opinion, the Park was created to be an instrument of profit to those who were shrewd enough to grasp the opportunity." Carpenter lobbied Congress to remove lands from the park so that the Northern Pacific could construct a railroad along the Yellowstone River to Cooke City. In return, friends promised to locate claims in his name along the route so that he too might profit from the venture. The land grab fell apart when the Senate vetoed the move, and Carpenter was summarily removed from office. Not long thereafter, Congress flatly refused to fund the civilian administration of Yellowstone, and the secretary of the interior was forced to call in the military beginning in 1886. It proved a fortuitous step.

The Army Years

The Army finally brought a semblance of order, eliminating the political appointees who viewed Yellowstone as a place to get rich. That first year, a temporary fort—Camp Sheridan—was thrown up and a troop of soldiers arrived, but it wasn't until 1891 that work began on a permanent Fort Yellowstone at Mammoth. By 1904, the fort consisted of some 26 buildings, housing 120 men. The soldiers had clear objectives— protecting wildlife (or at least bison and elk) from poachers, fighting fires, stopping vandalism, and generally achieving order out of chaos. These goals were accomplished with a fervor that gained widespread respect, and in a way that would later influence the organization of the National Park Service. One of the major accomplishments of the soldiers was completion of the "Grand Loop Road" that passes most of Yellowstone's attractions. The basic pattern was completed by 1905.

Before the arrival of cars, many visitors to Yellowstone were wealthy people from the East

THE YELLOWSTONE FIRES OF 1988

The summer of 1988 will long be remembered as the year when Yellowstone National Park was "destroyed" by fire. TV reporters flocked to the park, pronouncing the death of America's most famous national wonder as they stood in front of trees turned into towering torches and 30,000-foot clouds of black smoke. Newspaper headlines screamed, "Park Sizzles," "Winds Whip Fiery Frenzy Out of Control," and "Firestorms Blacken Yellowstone." Residents of nearby towns complained of lost tourism dollars, choking smoke, and intentionally lit backfires that threatened their homes and businesses; Wyoming politicians berated the Park Service's "Let Burn" policy; President Reagan expressed astonishment that fires were ever allowed to burn in the national parks (a policy that had been in place for two decades). Perhaps the most enduring image is from a forest that had been blown down by tornado-force winds in 1984 and then burned by the wind-whipped fires of 1988. The media ate it up, with one headline reading, "Total Destruction: Intense Heat and Flames from the Fires in Yellowstone Left Nothing but Powdered Ash and Charcoal Near Norris Junction." Unfortunately, the real story behind the fires of '88 was lost in this media feeding frenzy.

A Century Of Change

In reality, these fires were not unprecedented; we were just fortunate enough to witness one of the incredible spectacles of nature that may not occur again for another 300 years. When Yellowstone National Park was established in 1872, most of the land was carpeted with a mixture of variously aged lodgepole pine stands established following a series of large fires. Fewer large fires, partly due to unusually moist summer weather conditions, and partly because of a fire suppression policy that was in effect until 1972, meant that by the 1980s, a third of the park's lodgepole stands were more than 200 years old. Yellowstone was "ripe to burn."

Since the early 1950s, Smokey the Bear drummed in an incessant message: "Only You Can Prevent Forest Fires." Forest fires were viewed as dangerous, destructive forces that had to be stopped to protect our valuable public lands. Unfortunately, this immensely effective and generally valid ad campaign convinced the public that all fires were bad. Ecological research has shown that this is not only wrong, but that putting out all fires can sometimes create conditions far more dangerous than if fires had been allowed to burn in the first place. Fire, like the other processes that have affected Yellow-

Coast or Europe intent upon doing the grand tour of Western sights. The railroads (Northern Pacific to the north, Union Pacific to the west, and the Burlington to the east) deposited them near park borders where they were met by carriages, Tallyhos (26-passenger stagecoaches), and surreys. In 1915, there were some 3,000 horses in use within the park! Most "dudes" paid approximately $50 for a six-day tour that included transportation, meals, and lodging at the hotels. They paid another $2.50 for the privilege of sailing across Lake Yellowstone on the steamship *Zillah*. By contrast, another group, the "sagebrushers" came to Yellowstone in fewer numbers, arriving in their own wagons or hiring a coach to transport them between the "Wylie Way" campgrounds. These seasonal tent camps were scattered around the park, providing an inexpensive ($35 for a seven-day tour) way to see the sights. Even as early as 1908, Yellowstone was being seen by 18,000 visitors a year.

The Northern Pacific was still intent upon carving up Yellowstone into a money-making resort, even going so far as to propose an electric railroad, to be powered by a dam at the falls of the Yellowstone River. Fortunately, equally powerful forces—notably Gen. Phillip Sheridan and naturalist Joseph Bird Grinnell—saw through their designs and thwarted each attempt to bring railroads into Yellowstone. Still the Northern Pacific's interests were represented by its indirect control of many of Yellowstone's hotels, stagecoaches, wagons, and other vehicles used to transport tourists.

All this changed when the first car was allowed through the gate on Aug. 1, 1915. (Entrance fees were a surprisingly stiff $5 for single-seat vehicles and $7.50 for five-passenger cars.) Almost immediately, it became clear that horses and cars could not mix, and motor busses replaced the old coaches. From then on, the park would be increasingly a place for "autoists." Interestingly, within a year the park would come under the jurisdiction of the newly created National Park Service.

---

stone—cataclysmic volcanic explosions, geothermal activity, and massive glaciation—is neither good nor evil. It is simply a part of the natural world that national parks are attempting to preserve. Unfortunately, national parks are no longer surrounded by similarly undeveloped land, so when fires burned in Yellowstone and surrounding Forest Service lands they also affected the nearby towns and the people who make a living from tourism or logging.

Fire In Lodgepole Forests

Fire has played an important role in lodgepole pine forests for thousands if not millions of years, and as a result, the trees have evolved an unusual adaptation. Some of the cones are serotinous, having a resin that melts under the heat of forest fires. The parent trees are killed, but a new generation is guaranteed by the thousands of pine seeds (20 seeds per square foot) that are released to the bare, nutrient-rich soil underneath the blackened overstory. Within five years the landscape is dotted with thousands of young pines, competing with a verdant cover of grasses and flowers.

Although some animals are killed in the fires (including, in 1988, 257 elk out of a Yellowstone population of 30,000), and others die from a lack of food immediately after a fire, the early decades following a fire create conditions that are unusually rich for many animals. Wildlife diversity in lodgepole forests reaches a peak within the first 25 years as woodpeckers, mountain bluebirds, and other birds feed on insects in the dead trees, while elk and bears graze on the lush grasses.

As the forest ages, a dense stand of trees forms, keeping light from reaching the forest floor and making it difficult for understory plants to survive. These trees eventually thin themselves out, creating openings in the forest, but after 200-300 years without fire the lodgepole forests become a tangle of fallen trees that are difficult to walk through, are of limited value to many animals, and burn easily. They also become susceptible to attacks by bark beetles such as those that killed thousands of acres of trees in Yellowstone during the 1980s, creating even more potential fire fuel.

Yellowstone In 1988

The cause of Yellowstone's 1988 fires is not just the heavy fuel loading from aging forests, but weather conditions that were the driest and windiest on record. The winter of 1987-88 had been a mild one, and by spring there was a moderate to severe drought in the park, lessened only by above normal rainfall in April and May. Since 1972, when Yel-

continued on next page

The Park Service Takes Over

After years of Army control, supporters of a separate National Park Service finally had their way in 1916. The congressional act created a dual role for the new park system: to "conserve the scenery" and to "provide for the enjoyment of the same," a contradictory mandate that would later lead to all sorts of conflicts. The first couple of years were tenuous, as management flip-flopped between the Army and civilians, with the final changeover coming in 1918, thus ending three decades of military supervision. The management of Yellowstone fell on the shoulders of two men, Horace M. Albright, and his mentor, Stephen Mather, both of whom had been heavily involved in lobbying to create the new agen-

lowstone Park officials first began allowing certain lightning fires to burn in backcountry areas, the total acreage burned totaled less than two percent of the park. (Mistakenly called a "let burn" policy, the natural fire program actually involved close monitoring of these lightning-ignited fires to determine when and if a fire should be suppressed. All human-caused fires were immediately suppressed, along with any that threatened property or life.)

When the first lightning fires of the 1988 season began in late May, those in the backcountry areas were allowed to burn, as fire management officials anticipated normal summer weather conditions. Many went out on their own, but when June and July came and the rains failed to materialize, the fires began to spread rapidly. Alarmed park officials declared them wildfires and sent crews to attempt to put them out. (Ironically, the largest fire, the North Fork/Wolf Lake Complex was started by humans and although firefighters immediately attacked the blaze, it consumed more than 500,000 acres.) As the summer progressed, more and more firefighters were called in, eventually totaling over 25,000 personnel at a cost exceeding $120 million. Firefighters managed to protect many of park buildings, but had little effect on the forest fires themselves. Experts say that conditions in the summer of 1988 were so severe that even if all the natural fires had been immediately fought, it may have made little difference. Yellowstone has experienced these massive fires in the past and will again in the future, no matter what humans do.

Out Of Control

Firefighters found the weather worsening with each passing hour. Winds blew steadily at 20-40 miles an hour, and gusts to 70 mph threw firebrands two miles in front of the firefront, across firelines, roads, and even the Lewis River Canyon. Fuel moisture in the large logs approached that of kiln-dried wood. By mid-August, more than 25 fires were burning simultaneously all over the park and surrounding na-tional forests, with many joining together to create massive complexes such as the Clover-Mist Fire, the Snake River Complex, and the North Fork/Wolf Lake Fire Complex. On a single day—September 7 —more than 100,000 acres burned, and 20 buildings in Old Faithful were torched (out of more than 400). The fires seemed poised to consume the remainder of Yellowstone, but four days later the season's first snow carpeted the park. Within a few days firefighters had the upper hand.

A Transformed Landscape

More than 793,000 acres (36% of the park) had been burned by the fires, along with another 600,000 acres on adjacent Forest Service lands. Of the park total, 41% were canopy fires in which all the trees were killed, and another 35% were a mixture of ground fires and canopy fires. The remainder were lighter burns. The fires are out and the land is slowly recovering, but there continue to be many questions asked about what-ifs and what-might-have-beens. The park's natural fire program was temporarily scrapped, replaced by a revised plan that should be in effect for the summer of 1991. Visitors to Yellowstone today see enormous expanses of blackened trees in some parts of the park, while in other areas they find a complex mosaic of burned and unburned forest land. Once you grow accustomed to the burned areas and understand that they are a part of the natural process, they actually add interest to the park. Get out of your car and walk through a blackened area and you'll discover thousands of lodgepole and aspen seedlings, along with impressive displays of wildflowers (particularly fireweed—the pink flower so common after fires), forbs, and grasses. Vistas that were long blocked by dense forests are now more open. The Park Service has placed informative signboards at seven sites around Yellowstone, describing the fires and the changes they brought about, and has a special display on the fires at the Grant Village Visitor Center.

cy. Mather became the Park Service's first director, while Albright served as superintendent at Yellowstone and later stepped into Mather's shoes to head the agency.

Albright quickly upgraded facilities to meet the influx of autoists who demanded more rustic camping facilities, but also cabins, lodges, cafeterias, and bathhouses. Forty-six camps were constructed (only 12 survive today), fulfilling Albright's dream of "a motorist's paradise." The focus of the new Park Service was clearly on visitation rather than preservation. Albright assembled a first-rate force of park rangers, and instituted the environmental education programs that have been the agency's hallmark ever since.

As the automobile took over Yellowstone, the railroads gradually lost their sway. The last passenger train to the park's gateway towns stopped in 1961. In the 1950s, the Park Service initiated "Mission 66," a decade-long project to upgrade facilities and add more lodging. By the late '60s, a growing appreciation for the natural world was shifting public opinion away from such developments, and the 1973 master plan scaled back proposed developments. In recent years such issues as wolf reintroduction, grizzly management, winter use, and the fires of 1988 have attracted widespread attention.

TOURING YELLOWSTONE

Yellowstone is perhaps the most accessible of any national park. Nearly all the famous sights are within a couple hundred feet of the Grand Loop Rd., a 142-mile figure-8 through the middle of the park. For all too many visitors, Yellowstone becomes a checklist of places to visit, geysers to watch, and animals to see. The Park Service has done its part by putting signs and labels on everything, right down to the smallest hot springs. All this tends to inspire an attitude that treats this great national park as a drive-thru zoo where the animals come out to perform and the geyser eruptions are predicted so everyone can be there on time. If you're one of this crowd, give yourself a giant kick in the rear and take a walk, even if it is just around Upper Geyser Basin where you see something beyond Old Faithful. Whatever you do, *don't* see Yellowstone at 45 miles an hour; that's like seeing the Louvre from a passing train.

The following loop tour of Yellowstone begins in the south and traces a clockwise path around the Grand Loop (with side trips). Although it is possible to follow this sequence (or some variation) the entire distance, a far better way to learn about Yellowstone is to stop for a while in the places that are the most interesting to you and really explore them, rather than trying to see everything in a cursory way. If you have the time, the entire park is well worth visiting, but if you have only a day or two, pick a couple of spots and see them right. Be sure to at least spend time at Grand Canyon of the Yellowstone and Norris Geyser Basin. And don't just check out the views everyone else sees; find a nearby trail and do a little exploring on your own. If you are planning a trip to the area, try to set aside a bare minimum of three days in Yellowstone.

SOUTH ENTRANCE ROAD

The South Entrance Station consists of several new log structures, right along the Snake River. Just 1 1/2 miles beyond the entrance is an easily missed turnout where you can walk down to 30-foot-high **Moose Falls**. Beyond this, the road climbs up a long, gentle ramp to Pitchstone Plateau, passing green forests of lodgepole pine. Stop at a turnout to look back at the majestic Tetons. Abruptly, this gentle country is broken by the edge of **Lewis River Canyon** whose rhyolite walls drop 600 feet on either side. Anyone who has not been to Yellowstone since the fires of 1988 will be shocked by the scene here—blackened remains of trees seem to extend in all directions. The Snake River Complex of fires joined together to leap a quarter mile across this canyon, revealing the futility of bulldozer-cut firebreaks in trying to halt an inferno under the high wind conditions and severe drought that existed.

The road parallels the river for the next seven miles. Nearly everyone stops at the 37-foot-high **Lewis Falls**. Camping is available at the south end of **Lewis Lake**. (The lake, falls, river, and canyon are all named for the Lewis and Clark Expedition's Meriwether Lewis.) Lewis Lake is

1. Nighttime turns Devils Tower into an otherworldly apparition;
2. the bleak, arid landscape west of Crowheart

the park's third-largest body of water (after Yellowstone and Shoshone lakes) and is popular with boaters and anglers. The clear waters contain brown trout and Mackinaw. Approximately four miles north of Lewis Lake, the highway tops the Continental Divide, but the point (7,988 feet above sea level) is not particularly noticeable. This is one of three such traverse roads make within Yellowstone.

Lewis Lake Hikes

Two trailheads are a mile north of Lewis Lake, providing access east to Heart Lake and west to Shoshone Lake through country burned in the fires of 1988. The four-mile-long **Dogshead Trail** offers a direct route to Shoshone Lake, while the **Lewis Channel Trail** takes the scenic trek via the Lewis River channel that connects Shoshone and Lewis lakes. It's seven miles to Shoshone Lake on this path. The path is popular with anglers who come to the channel for brown and cutthroat trout during the fall spawning season. The trail to Heart Lake begins on the opposite side of the road and south a few hundred feet. See "Into the Backcountry" (p. 306) for hikes in the Heart Lake and Shoshone Lake areas. Canoeists sometimes paddle across Lewis Lake and then portage to Shoshone Lake.

Grant Village

The newest Yellowstone development is Grant Village, built to replace facilities at Fishing Bridge, an area of vital grizzly habitat. Unfortunately, instead of one bad development, Yellowstone now has two; Fishing Bridge still exists (although some of the buildings are gone). Grant Village was completed in the 1980s, but unlike some of the more historic places where a natural rusticity prevailed, Grant Village has less charm than most K marts and absolutely no sense of organization. A steakhouse restaurant juts out along the shore of Yellowstone Lake, and the Grant Village Hotel forms a chintzy condo backdrop. Other facilities include a campground, store, gas station, and post office. Much of the area around here was consumed in the 1988 Snake River Fire; it unfortunately missed this scar on the Yellowstone landscape. **Grant Village Visitor Center** is open 8:30-5 from late May to late Sept., and 8-8 mid-June to late August. Inside, find a fine exhibit on the fires of 1988, along with films and slide shows on the

fires. (The exhibit will move to Canyon Visitor Center in 1992.)

West Thumb

If you look at a map of Yellowstone Lake, it's possible to imagine the lake as a giant hand with three mangled fingers heading south, and a gnarled thumb extending west. Thus the name, West Thumb. This portion of Yellowstone Lake is the deepest (to 390 feet), and is actually a caldera that filled with water after erupting 200,000 years ago. Because of this, there is still considerable heat just below the surface, as revealed by **West Thumb Geyser Basin**. A short loop trail leads through the steaming hot springs and pools. Just offshore is **Fishing Cone Geyser** where tourists once caught fish and then plopped them in the cone to be cooked. The water is no longer hot enough for this stunt, and besides, it's illegal.

WEST THUMB TO UPPER GEYSER BASIN

Heading west from West Thumb, the highway climbs over the Continental Divide twice. (It makes a big U-turn just north of the road.) Most of these forests escaped the 1988 fires. A couple miles beyond the unmarked eastern crossing is a turnout at **Shoshone Point** where you catch glimpses of Shoshone Lake and the Tetons. In 1914, highwayman Ed Trafton held up 15 stagecoaches as they passed by this point carrying tourists. He got away with $915.35 in cash and $130 in jewelry, but made the mistake of allowing his photo to be taken in the process. He was caught the following year and spent five years in Leavenworth. When he died, a letter in his pocket claimed that he had been Owen Wister's model for the Virginian. Others suspected that he was more likely to have been Wister's model for the villain, Trampas.

DeLacy Creek Trail provides access to Shoshone Lake, and begins at the picnic area between the two passes. It's three miles to the lake, which is circled by more trails. The western crossing of the Continental Divide is at **Isa Lake**, a tiny pond that empties into both the Atlantic and Pacific oceans through its two outlet streams. This is Craig Pass.

1↗   2↗   3↘

1. U.S. 85 cuts straight across the short-grass plains south of Newcastle; **2.** cattle country in the Powder River Basin near the tiny settlement of Recluse; **3.** Cowboys move cattle between pastures on the PK Ranch west of Sheridan.

Approximately 14 miles beyond West Thumb, pull off to see the Firehole River as it drops over **Kepler Cascades**. Just to the east, a wide and partly paved trail (actually an old road) leads 2¹/₂ miles to **Lone Star Geyser**. This is a popular route for bikes in the summer and skiers in the winter. (No bike traffic beyond the geyser, however.) Lone Star Geyser erupts every three hours from a distinctive nine-foot-high cone, with eruptions generally reaching 45 feet and lasting for 30 minutes. Hikers can also get to Lone Star via the Howard Eaton Trail out of Old Faithful. For a longer hike, you can continue

south from Lone Star on **Shoshone Lake Trail** to Shoshone Lake, eight fairly easy miles from the main road. See "Into the Backcountry," p. 307, for other Shoshone Lake hikes.

UPPER GEYSER BASIN

As you approach Old Faithful from either direction, the two-lane road suddenly widens into four, and you are confronted with what has to be one of the only cloverleafs in the entire national park system. Welcome to Upper Geyser Basin,

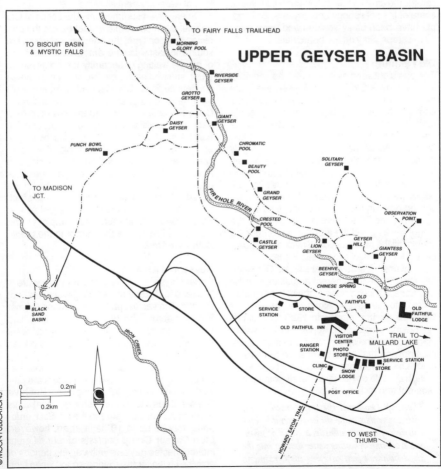

home of Old Faithful, some 400 buildings of all sizes, and a small town's worth of people. For many folks, this is the heart of Yellowstone, and a visit to the park without seeing Old Faithful is like starting a baseball game without singing the national anthem. If you came to Yellowstone to see the wonders of nature, you're going to see more than your share here, but you'll probably have to share your share with hundreds of other folks. Fortunately, this area contains the largest concentration of geysers in the world, and the adventurous will even discover places where almost nobody ever visits. But be very careful, the crust can be dangerously thin around some of the hot springs and geysers, and people have been badly scalded and even killed by missteps. Stay on the boardwalks.

Old Faithful

The one sight seen by everyone who comes to Yellowstone is Old Faithful Geyser, easily the most visited geyser in the world. Its fame is second only to Iceland's Geysir (meaning "gusher" in Icelandic). Old Faithful is neither the tallest nor the most frequent geyser in Yellowstone, but it always provides a good show, is highly accessible, and relatively predictable. Contrary to the rumors, Old Faithful never erupted "every hour on the hour," but for many years its periodicity was around 64 minutes. It seems to have slowed down in recent years, and is now averaging around 75-90 minutes. In general, the longer the length of the eruption, the longer the interval till the next eruption. Check at the visitor center for the latest prognostications.

An almost level paved path circles Old Faithful, providing many different angles to view the eruptions, although none of these is particularly close to the geyser. Along the north side is **Chinese Spring**, named in 1885 for a short-lived laundry operation. Apparently, the washman had filled the spring with clothes and soap, not knowing that soap can cause geysers to erupt. One newspaper correspondent claimed—though the tale obviously suffered from embellishment and racism—that,

The soap awakened the imprisoned giant; with a roar that made the earth tremble, and a shriek of a steam whistle, a cloud of steam and a column of boiling water shot up into the air a hundred feet, carrying soap, raiment,

tent and Chinaman along with the rush, and dropping them at various intervals along the way.

Old Faithful provides a textbook example of geyser activity. The first signs of life are when water begins to splash out of the vent in what is called "preplay." This splashing can last up to 20 minutes, but generally only a couple minutes before the real thing. The water quickly spears into the sky, reaching 100-180 feet and lasting two to five minutes before rapidly dropping down. During a typical eruption, more than 11,000 gallons of water are sent skyward.

On any given summer day, the scene at Old Faithful is almost comical. Just before the predicted eruption time, the benches encircling the south and east sides are jammed with hundreds of people waiting expectantly for the geyser to erupt, and with each tentative spray the camera shutters begin to click. Listen closely, and you'll hear half the languages of Europe and Asia. Once the action is over, there is a mad rush back into the visitor center, the stores, and Old Faithful Inn, and within a few minutes the benches are again empty. A story is told of two concessionaire employees who once decided to have fun at Old Faithful by placing a large crank atop a box and putting the contraption near the geyser. When they knew it was ready to erupt, they ran out and turned the crank just as Old Faithful shot into the air. Their employer and the park failed to see the humor in the prank. Both were fired.

Geyser Hill Area

Upper Geyser Basin is laced with paved trails that lead to dozens of nearby geysers and hot springs. The easiest path loops around Geyser Hill, just across the Firehole River from Old Faithful (see map, p. 289). Here are 40 different geysers. Check at the visitor center to get an idea of current activity, and while there, pick up the Upper Geyser Basin map (25¢) that describes most of them. Several geysers are particularly noteworthy. When it plays, **Beehive Geyser** (it has a tall beehive-shaped cone) vents water as high as 200 feet into the air. Such eruptions may be up to 10 days apart, however. **Lion Geyser Group** consists of four different interconnected geysers with varying periods of activity. Listen for the roaring sound when Lion is ready to erupt. **Giantess Geyser** is active only a few times a year, but the eruptions are spectacularly powerful, sending water 100-200 feet skyward. **Doublet Pool** is a strikingly beautiful deep blue pool that is a favorite of photographers. Not far away is **Sponge Geyser** which rockets water up to 229 millimeters into the air (nine inches). It's considered the smallest named geyser in Yellowstone, a title achieved by sending up a spurt of water big enough to be mopped up by a sponge.

The two-mile-long **Observation Point Loop Trail** splits off shortly after you cross the bridge on the way to Geyser Hill, and climbs to an excellent overlook where you can watch eruptions of Old Faithful. This is also a good place to view the effects of the 1988 North Fork Fire. Another easy trail splits off from this path to **Solitary Geyser**—actually just a pool that periodically burps four-foot splashes of hot water. This is not a natural geyser. In 1915, the hot spring here was tapped to provide water for Old Faithful Geyser Bath, a concession that lasted until 1950. The lowering of the water level in the pool completely changed the plumbing system of the hot springs and turned it into a geyser that at one time shot 25 feet in the air. The system still hasn't recovered, although water levels have been restored for more than 40 years.

More Geyser Gazin'

Another easy, paved path follows the Firehole River downstream, looping back along the other side for a total distance of three miles (see map, p. 289). Other trails head off from this loop to the Fairy Falls Trailhead, Biscuit Basin, and Black Sand Basin. The loop is a very popular wintertime ski path, and portions are open to bikes in the summer. Twelve-foot-high **Castle Geyser** does indeed resemble a ruined old castle. Because of its size and the slow accretion of sinter (silica) to form this cone, it is believed to be somewhere between 5,000 and 50,000 years old. Castle sends up a column of water and steam 90 feet into the air, and often erupts every 11 hours or so. Check at the visitor center for current activity.

Daisy Geyser is farther down the path and off to the left. It is usually one of the most predictable of the geysers, erupting to 75 feet approximately every 90 minutes. The water shoots out at a sharp angle, and is visible all over the basin, making this a real crowd pleaser. Just east of Daisy is **Radiator Geyser** which isn't much to look at (eruptions to two feet), but was named when this area was a parking lot and the sudden eruption under a car led people to think its radiator was overheating. **Grotto Geyser** is certainly the weirdest of all the geysers, having formed around a tangle of long-petrified tree stumps. It is in eruption almost half of the time, but most eruptions only reach 10-15 feet.

Look for **Riverside Geyser** across the Firehole from the path and not far below Grotto. This beautiful geyser arches its spray 75 feet over the river, and is one of the most predictable, with eruptions approximately every seven hours. The paved trail crosses the river and ends at **Morning Glory Pool**. For many years, the main road passed this colorful pool, and it became something of a wishing well for not just coins, but trash, rocks, logs, and other debris. Because of this junk, the pool began to cool, and the beautiful blue color is now tinged by brown and green algae, despite efforts to remove the debris.

Turning back at Morning Glory, recross the bridge and head left where the paths split at Grotto Geyser. **Giant Geyser** is on the left along the river. Years may pass between eruptions of Giant—but when it does go, the name rings true since the water often reaches 200 feet. Cross the river again and pass **Beauty Pool** and **Chromatic Pool** which are connected below the ground so that one declines as the other rises. Very pretty. **Grand Geyser** is a wonderful sight. The water column erupts in a towering burst of power every 8-10 hours, with a series of bursts lasting 9-16 minutes and reaching up to 200 feet. When Grand isn't playing, watch for eruptions of nearby **Turban** and **Sawmill** geysers. Cross the river again just beyond Grand Geyser and pass **Crested Pool** on your way back to Castle Geyser. The pool contains deep blue water that is constantly boiling, preventing the survival of algae.

Black Sand Basin

Just a mile west of Old Faithful is Black Sand Basin, a small cluster of geysers and hot springs. Most enjoyable is unpredictable **Cliff Geyser**, which often sends a spray of hot water 15-30 feet over Iron Creek. Three colorful pools are quite interesting in the basin: **Emerald Pool, Rainbow Pool,** and **Sunset Lake. Handkerchief Pool** is now just a small spouter, but was famous for many years as a place where visitors could drop a handkerchief in one end and then recover it later at another vent. In 1929, vandals jammed logs in the pool, destroying this little game. The pool was covered by gravel in subsequent eruptions of Rainbow Pool.

Biscuit Basin And Mystic Falls

This basin is named for biscuit-like formations that were found in one of the pools, but were destroyed in an eruption following the 1959 Hebgen Lake earthquake. From the parking lot, the trail leads across Firehole River to **Sapphire Pool** and then past **Jewel Geyser** which typically erupts every 10 minutes to a height of 15-20 feet. The boardwalk follows a short loop through the other sights of Bisquit Basin. From the west end of the boardwalk, a one-mile trail leads to where the Little Firehole River cascades 70 feet over **Mystic Falls.** You can switchback farther up the trail to the top of the falls and then connect with another trail for the loop back to Biscuit Basin (3 1/2 miles RT). This is a very nice short hike, and can be lengthened into a trip to **Little Firehole Meadows** and back via the Fairy Creek Trail to Midway Geyser Basin (14 miles RT). Bison are often seen in the meadows.

Old Faithful Inn

Despite its proximity to one of the great sights of the natural world, it is impossible not to love Old Faithful Inn, a place that contains perhaps the most winsome interior of any American building. It is said to be the largest log structure of its kind in existence. Designed by Robert Reamer and built in the winter of 1903-04, the inn has a steeply angled roofline reaching seven stories high, with gables jutting out from the sides and flags flying from the roof. Open the rustic old front door and you enter a world of the past dominated by a massive four-sided stone fireplace (500 tons of native stone were used) and a central space that arches 85 feet overhead. Four overhanging balconies extend above, each bordered by posts made from gnarled lodgepole burls found within the park. Above the fireplace is an enormous clock designed by Reamer and built on the site by a blacksmith. Reamer also designed the two wings that were added in 1913 and 1928.

On warm summer evenings, visitors stand out on the porch where they can watch Old Faithful erupting, while others sit at the old handcrafted tables to write letters as someone plays the piano in the corner. It's enough to warm even the most cynical visitor. A good restaurant is on the premises, along with a rustic but comfortable bar, a gift shop, and fast food eatery. **Chambermaid tours** of Old Faithful Inn are given Thurs.-Mon. between 9:30 a.m. and 3 p.m. Check at the front desk for specifics. Old Faithful Inn closes during the winter months; it would be hard to imagine trying to heat such a chasm when it's 40° below zero outside! Another building of interest is **Old Faithful Lodge**. Built in 1928, this is the large stone and log building just south of the geyser of the same name. The giant fireplace inside is a joy on frosty evenings.

Old Faithful Services

The Park Service's **Old Faithful Visitor Center** is open mid-April through Oct., and mid-Dec. to mid-March. Hours vary throughout the year, but it's generally open daily 9-4:30 (8-8 in midsummer). Films about Yellowstone are shown throughout the day. The center has a good selection of books, maps, and other publications, and posts predictions for six of the major geysers (including Old Faithful) during the summer. The staff can provide you with all sorts of other info, from where to see bighorn sheep to where to find the restroom.

Backcountry permits are available from the ranger station, while food, supplies, and postcards can be purchased at either of the two Hamilton Stores. Old Faithful Inn has a gift shop, restaurant, snack bar, lounge, and ATM machine, while cafeteria meals are available at Old Faithful Lodge. Other facilities include two gas stations, a post office, photo shop, and clinic. See "Yellowstone Practicalities," p. 312 for lodging details. Note that camping is *not* available in the Old Faithful area, and it's illegal to "camp" in the parking lots. The closest campgrounds are Madison (16 miles north) and Grant Village (19 miles southeast).

MIDWAY AND LOWER GEYSER BASINS

Heading north from Upper Geyser Basin, the road follows the Firehole River past Midway and Lower geyser basins, both of which are quite interesting. The river is very popular with fly-fishing enthusiasts, and several side roads provide access to a variety of hot springs.

Midway Geyser Basin

Midway is a large and readily accessible geyser basin, with a loop path leading to most of the sights. Climb the hill across the road for fine views of the basin and its colorful pools. **Excelsior Geyser** is actually an enormous hot springs that pours 4,000 gallons per minute of steaming water into the Firehole River. The water is a deep turquoise blue. During the 1880s, this was a truly spectacular geyser with explosions that reached 380 feet in the air and were almost as wide. These violent eruptions apparently damaged the plumbing system that fed them and it was dormant for nearly a century, although smaller eruptions took place in 1985. At 370 feet across, **Grand Prismatic Spring** is Yellowstone's largest hot spring. The brilliant reds and yellows around the edges of the blue pool are from algae and bacteria that can tolerate temperatures of 170° F. There are additional geysers just south of here near a trailhead to Fairy Falls. The first mile of this trail is part of the old Fountain Flat Dr. and is open to bikes.

Firehole Lake Drive

This road (one-way heading north) goes three miles through Lower Geyser Basin, the park's most extensive geyser basin. **Great Fountain Geyser** is truly one of the most spectacular geysers in Yellowstone. Charles Cook of the 1869 Cook-Folsom-Peterson Expedition recalled being so impressed, that "we could not contain our enthusiasm; with one accord we all took off our hats and yelled with all our might." Modern-day visitors would not be faulted for reacting similarly.

Great Fountain erupts every 8-12 hours (although it can be irregular) and usually reaches 100 feet. It has been known to blast as high as 230 feet! Eruptions begin approximately an hour

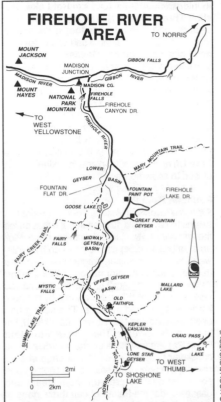

FIREHOLE RIVER AREA

after water starts to overflow from the crater, and last for 45-60 minutes, consisting of a series of eruptive cycles. Eruption predictions are posted at the geyser. While you're waiting, watch the periodic eruptions of **White Dome Geyser**, just a hundred yards down the road. Because of its massive 30-foot cone, this is apparently one of the oldest geysers in the park. Eruptions generally occur every 15-30 minutes and spray 30 feet into the air.

Another mile down, the road literally cuts into the mound of **Pink Cone Geyser** which now erupts every 6-15 hours and reaches a height of 30 feet. The pink color comes from manganese oxide. Just up from here at the bend in the road is **Firehole Lake** which discharges 3,500 gallons of water per minute into Tangled Creek which then drains across the road into **Hot Lake**. The short **Three Senses Nature Trail** gives blind visitors (and sighted ones too) a chance to touch, smell, and hear the world of the geysers and hot springs. **Steady Geyser** is unusual in that it forms both sinter (silica) deposits as well as travertine (calcium carbonate) deposits. It is located along the edge of Hot Lake and, true to its name, erupts almost continuously, though the height is only five feet. Firehole Lake Dr. continues another mile to its junction with the main road right across from the parking area for Fountain Paint Pot. (In the winter, Firehole Lake Drive is a popular place for skiers, but is closed to snowmobiles.)

Fountain Paint Pot

Always a favorite of visitors, Fountain Paint Pot seems to have a playfulness about it that belies the immense power just below the surface. Pick up a trail guide (25¢) as you head up the walkway. During the summer, rangers are often here to offer additional information. **Silex Spring** ("silex" is Latin for "silica") is off to the right as you walk up the small hill, and is colored by different kinds of algae and bacteria. The spring has been known to erupt as a geyser (to 20 feet), but is currently dormant. The famous **Fountain Paint Pot** is a few steps up the boardwalk and consists of colorful muds that change in consistency throughout the season depending upon soil moisture. The pressure from steam and gasses under the Paint Pot can throw gobs of mud up to 20 feet into the air. Just north of here are fumaroles that spray steam, carbon dioxide, and hydrogen sulfide into the air. Continuing down the boardwalk, you come upon an impressive overlook to a multitude of geysers that change constantly in activity. Some of the largest geysers in the park are here—including Morning Geyser which erupts to over 150 feet. The most active is **Clepsydra Geyser**, in eruption much of the time. **Fountain Geyser** is usually active every 11 hours or so, and can occasionally reach 80 feet. The rest of the loop trail passes dead lodgepole pines that are being petrified as the silica is absorbed, creating a "bobby socks" appearance.

Fountain Flat Drive

Fountain Flat Dr. is an interesting side road that passes through meadows along the Firehole River, and provides a good place to see bison and elk. Look for **Ojo Caliente**—a small hot springs with a big odor—right along the edge of the river and just before the bridge. Several more are upstream from here. The paved road ends after three miles at a barricade, but bikes (or skiers and snowmobiles in winter) can continue another two miles to its junction with the main road again. Beautiful 200-foot-high **Fairy Falls** can be reached by hiking the road a mile beyond the barricade, to a junction at the end of the meadow. Here it's another 1 1/2 miles to the falls. This makes a pleasant afternoon walk, and can be combined with a scenic loop back along the west edge of the meadow (see map, p. 293) for a RT distance of 6 1/2 miles. A side trip takes you to **Imperial Geyser**, which now shoots water approximately six feet in the air almost continuously.

Firehole Canyon Drive

This one-way road (south only) curves for two miles through Firehole Canyon where dark rhyolite cliffs rise 800 feet above the river. The road begins just south of Madison Junction, and was intensely burned in the 1988 North Fork Fire, giving the canyon's name a dual meaning. **Firehole Falls** is a 40-foot drop that is worth stopping to see, as is **Firehole Cascades** a bit farther up. Kids of all ages enjoy the swimming hole (warmed by hot springs) a short distance up the road.

TO WEST YELLOWSTONE

At Madison Junction, the Gibbon and Firehole rivers join to form the Madison River, a major tributary of the Missouri River. The 14-mile drive from Madison Junction to the West Entrance closely parallels this scenic river where geese, ducks, and trumpeter swans are almost always present. Bison and elk are other critters to watch for in the open meadows. The 406,359-acre North Fork Fire of 1988 ripped through most of the Madison River country, so be ready for many blackened trees, but also expect to see many flowers in midsummer. The river is open only to fly-fishing, and is considered one of the finest places to catch trout anywhere in the nation (though they can be a real challenge to fool). On warm summer evenings, you're likely to see dozens of anglers casting for wily rainbow and brown trout and mountain whitefish. **West Entrance** is the busiest of all the park entry stations, handling roughly half of the 2¹/2 million people who enter Yellowstone each year. The tourist town of West Yellowstone, Montana (see p. 316) is right outside the boundary.

MADISON JUNCTION TO NORRIS

The small **Madison Explorers Museum** at Madison Junction contains displays on the establishment of Yellowstone National Park. It's open dawn to dusk Memorial Day–Oct., but is unstaffed. Directly behind the very popular Madison Junction campground is 7,560-foot **National Park Mountain**, named in honor of a fabled incident in 1870. Three explorers were gathered around the campfire, discussing the wonders that they had found in this area, when one suggested that rather than letting all these wonders pass into private hands, they should be set aside as a national park. Thus was born the concept that led to the world's first national park. The tale was passed on as the gospel truth for so long that the mountain was named in honor of this evening. Unfortunately, the story was a fabrication. Cynics may read something into the fact that National Park Mountain was torched by the fires of 1988.

North of Madison Junction, the road follows the Gibbon River nearly all of the 14 miles to Norris. It crosses the river five times, and hangs right on the edge through Gibbon Canyon. The pretty 84-foot-high **Gibbon Falls** are approximately five miles up the road, and are situated right at the edge of the enormous caldera that fills the center of Yellowstone. The 1988 fires consumed most of the trees around the falls. Another five miles beyond this, the road emerges from the canyon into grassy **Gibbon Meadows** where elk and bison are commonly seen. The prominent peak visible to the north is 10,336-foot Mount Holmes.

An easy half-mile trail leads to **Artist Paint Pots**, filled with colorful plopping and steaming mud pots and hot springs. This is a nice place to escape the crowds. The forest was burned in the North Fork Fire, so it's also a good place to see how the lodgepole pine trees are regenerating. Just south of the parking area for Artist Paint Pots is a trail to **Monument Geyser Basin** where there isn't much activity, but the tall sinter cones form all sorts of bizarre shapes, including Thermos Bottle Geyser. The mile-long hike climbs 500 feet, and provides good views of the surrounding country. Another attraction is **Chocolate Pots**, found along the highway just north of Gibbon Meadows. The reddish-brown color comes from iron, aluminum, and manganese oxides. Just before you reach Norris, the road crosses through the appropriately named **Elk Park**.

NORRIS GEYSER BASIN

Although Old Faithful is more famous, many visitors to Yellowstone find Norris Geyser Basin more interesting. Norris sits atop the junction of several major fault lines, providing conduits for heat from the molten lava below. Because of this, Norris is considered the hottest geyser basin in North America, if not the world; a scientific team found temperatures of 401° F at just 265 feet underground, and were forced to quit drilling when the pressure threatened to destroy their drilling rig! Because of considerable sulphur (and hence sulfuric acid) in the springs and geysers, the water at Norris is quite acidic; a majority of the world's acid geysers are here. The acidic water kills lodgepole trees in the basin, creating an open, nearly barren place. Norris Basin has been around at least 115,000 years, making it the oldest of any of Yellowstone's active geyser basins. It is a constantly changing place, with small geysers seeming to come and go on an almost daily basis.

The paved trail from the oft-crowded parking area leads to **Norris Museum**, built of stone in 1929-30. The small museum houses exhibit panels on hot springs and geothermal activity, and is generally open daily 9-4:30 (8-6 in midsummer) mid-May through September. Pick up a brochure (25¢) describing the various features at Norris. Ranger-led walks are given most days. From the museum, the Norris Basin spreads both north and south, with two rather different trails to hike. Take the time to walk along both; you won't regret it. The Norris Campground is only a quarter mile from the geyser basin.

Porcelain Basin

Just behind the museum is an overlook that provides a fascinating view of Porcelain Basin. The path drops down into the basin, passing steam vents, hot pools, and small geysers along the way, including **Dark Cavern Geyser** which erupts several times an hour to 20 feet. **Whirligig Geyser** is another one that is often active, spraying a fan of water. (Watch your glasses and camera lenses in the steam, since silica deposits can be very hard to remove.) For an enjoyable short walk, follow the boardwalk around the mile-long loop. Stop to admire the bright colors in the steaming water, indicators of iron, arsenic, and other elements, along with algae and cyanobacteria.

Back Basin

A mile-long loop trail takes you to the sights within the Back Basin, south of the museum. Before heading out, check at the museum for the latest on geyser activity. Most people follow the path in a clockwise direction, coming first to **Emerald Spring**, a beautiful green pool with acidic water just below boiling. A little ways farther down the path is **Steamboat Geyser**. Wait a few minutes, and you're likely to see one of its minor eruptions that may reach 40 feet. But on occasion, Steamboat erupts with a fury that is hard to believe, blasting 380 feet into the air—three times the height of Old Faithful—making this the world's tallest geyser. Eruptions can last up to 20 minutes, enough time to pour out a million gallons of water! They have been heard up to 14 miles away. Steamboat's unforgettable eruptions cannot be predicted; a 50-year span once passed, while at other times they may occur several times a year.

The path splits just below Steamboat, and on the right is **Cistern Spring** whose deep blue waters are constantly building deposits of sinter (a grey silica deposit), and have flooded the nearby lodgepole pine forests, killing the trees. If you turn left where the trail splits, you come next to **Echinus Geyser**, a personal favorite. (The name—Greek for "spiny"—comes from the sea urchin-like pebbles around the geyser; they are a result of sinter accumulation.) Echinus erupts every 35-75 minutes, so be sure to check at the museum to see when it last played. Watch the pool closely, since explosions of steam and water generally begin once it has filled, with

acidic water (pH 3.5) reaching 60-125 feet. Unlike Old Faithful, this is one geyser where you can get up close and personal. Bench-sitters are likely to get wet, although the water is not hot enough to burn. Continue along this trail to see many more hot springs and steam vents. **Porkchop Geyser** was in continuous eruption for several years, but in 1989 it self-destructed in an explosion, leaving behind a bubbling hot spring.

NORRIS JUNCTION TO CANYON

The dozen miles from Norris Geyser Basin to Canyon cut across the center of the park on the high Solfatara Plateau. This stretch of road is best known for what looks like a scene from an atomic blast, with the blackened remains of a forest seemingly blown down by the ferocity of the 1988 North Fork Fire. This is the place the news media focused on after the fires, making it appear as if it were typical of the park as a whole. In reality, the lodgepole pines were all uprooted in a wild 1984 windstorm that flattened many miles of forest both here and farther south in the Teton Wilderness. The dead trees dried out over the next four years, and when the wind-whipped fires arrived, they went up in a holocaust. In 50 years, this may well be a meadow. The **Virginia Cascades Rd.** is a 2½-mile-long, one-way road that circles around this blow-down area and provides a view of the 60-foot-tall Virginia Cascade of the Gibbon River. Back on the main highway heading east, keep your eyes open for elk and bison as the road approaches Canyon. Also note the thick, young forest of lodgepole pines that was established after a fire burned through in 1955.

NORRIS JUNCTION TO MAMMOTH

The park road between Norris and Mammoth Hot Springs provides a number of interesting sights, although much of this country burned in the 1988 North Fork Fire. Just beyond the highway junction is the **Log Soldier Station** built by the Army in 1908, one of just three still standing in the park. Just up the road is **Frying Pan Spring** (named for its shape) where the water is actually not that hot. The bubbles are from pungent-smelling hydrogen sulfide gas. **Roaring Mountain** is a bleak, steaming mountainside four miles north of Norris. In 1902, the mountain erupted into activity with fumaroles that made a roar audible at great distances. It is far less active today.

Stop at **Obsidian Cliff** to see the black glassy rocks formed when lava cooled very rapidly. One mountain man (not, as many sources claim, Jim Bridger) told tales of an elk kept missing. When he got closer, he found he had actually been firing at a clear mountain of glass. The elk was 25 miles away, but the mountain was acting as a telescope to make the animal appear close. Obsidian Cliff was an important source of rock that Indians used in making arrowheads and other tools. Obsidian points made from this rock have even been found in the Ohio River Valley. North of here the countryside opens up along Obsidian Creek at **Willow Park**, one of the best places to see moose, especially in the fall.

Approximately 13 miles north of Norris, the road passes Indian Creek Campground and the basalt columns of **Sheepeater Cliffs**, named for the Indian inhabitants of these mountains. North of this, the country opens into Gardners Hole, where you get a fine gander at 10,992-foot Electric Peak, nine miles to the northwest. At **Golden Gate** the road suddenly enters a narrow defile through which flows Glen Creek. Stop to look over the edge of **Rustic Falls** and to note how the road is cantilevered over the cliff edge. Acrophobics should *not* stop here. Instead, have someone else drive, close your eyes, and say three Hail Marys.

Bunsen Peak is the 8,564-foot volcanic cone that is visible just south of Mammoth. Any chemistry student will recognize the name, for Robert W. Bunsen not only first explained the action of geysers, but he also invented the Bunsen burner. Bunsen Peak looks like a chemistry experiment run amuck. The North Fork Fire of 1988 swept through this area in a patchy mosaic, leaving long strips of unburned trees next to those that are now just a forest of telephone poles. Trails lead up to the top of Bunsen Peak from both the east and west sides. The west trail (two miles) begins at the entrance to **Bunsen Peak Rd.**, located just south of Rustic Falls. This rough one-way dirt road (six miles) circles

around the east side of the mountain, and is closed to trailers and RVs. The road begins a quarter mile south of the Golden Gate (see map, p. 298). Another interesting side trail leads from Bunsen Peak Rd. to the base of 150-foot-high **Osprey Falls**, two miles and 800 feet lower. Well off the beaten track, but beautiful. Watch your footing around the falls.

If you take the steep main road rather than the Bunsen Peak Rd., you will soon come to the **Hoodoos**, a fascinating jumble of travertine boulders leaning in all directions. The rocks were created by hot springs thousands of years ago and toppled from the east face of Terrace Mountain. Just before Mammoth, you'll see the turnoff for Upper Terrace Dr. on the left. This half-mile loop road provides access to the upper end of Mammoth Hot Springs.

MAMMOTH HOT SPRINGS VICINITY

Mammoth Hot Springs lies near the northern border of Yellowstone, and contains park headquarters, a variety of other facilities, and colorful hot springs. The Mammoth area is an important wintering area for elk, antelope, deer, and bison. During the fall, a bull elk and his harem can be seen wandering across the green lawns while lesser males bugle challenges from behind the buildings. The bugling can keep you awake at night if you're staying in the Mammoth Hotel. The town of Gardiner, Montana is just five miles away.

Mammoth Hot Springs

Mammoth Hot Springs consists of a series of multi-hued terraces down which hot, mineral-laden water trickles. The source of this water is snow and rain that falls on the surrounding country, although some is believed to come from the Norris area, 20 miles to the south. As it passes through the earth, the water comes in contact with volcanic magma containing massive amounts of carbon dioxide which is absorbed by the water to form carbonic acid. The now-acidic water passes through and dissolves the region's sedimentary limestone, and the calcium carbonate remains in solution until it reaches the surface at Mammoth. Once at the surface, the carbon dioxide begins to escape into the atmosphere, reducing the acidity, and causing the lime to precipitate out, forming the travertine terraces that are so prominent here. As the water flows over small obstructions, more carbon dioxide is released, causing accumulations that eventually grow into the lips that surround the terrace pools. The accumulation of travertine (calcium carbonate) is astounding: more than two tons a day at Mammoth Hot Springs. Some terraces grow by eight inches a year.

Mammoth Hot Springs covers a steep hillside, and consists of a series of colorful springs in various stages of development or decay. Road access is either from below or above (Upper Terrace Dr.), with a boardwalk/staircase connecting the two. Pick up a Park Service brochure (25¢) for more on the springs. The most interesting of the springs are **Minerva Terrace** and **Canary Spring**. Cleopatra and Angel terraces which were active in the 1930s are now simply a bland mass of gray rock. At the bottom of Mammoth Hot Springs and off to the right side is a 37-foot-tall mass of travertine that is known as **Liberty Cap** for its faint resemblance to the caps worn by Revolutionary War soldiers. The spring that created this no longer flows.

Directly across the road is **Opal Terrace**, one of the most active of all the springs. It began flowing in 1926, and has continued to expand over the years until it now threatens the lush lawns of a house built in 1908 and designed by Robert Reamer (of Old Faithful Inn fame). All the water flowing out of Mammoth terraces quickly disappears into underground caverns. In front of the Mammoth Hotel are two sinkholes from which steam can often be seen rising. Caverns above the terraces were once open to the public, but later closed when it became apparent that they contained poisonous gasses. Dead birds are sometimes found around one of the small pools in this area, appropriately named Poison Spring.

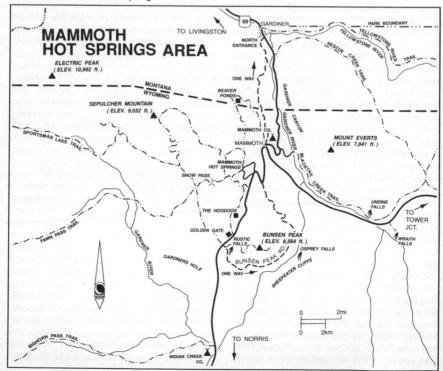

MAMMOTH HOT SPRINGS AREA

Buildings

Albright Visitor Center is named for the first National Park Service superintendent at Yellowstone, Horace Albright, and is housed in the Army's old Bachelor Officers' Quarters. Open daily 8:30-5 year-round, with extended hours in midsummer. Inside, find an information desk, racks of books, films and slide shows about the park, and frequent ranger-led walks to surrounding sights. Spread over the two floors are various exhibits, but the real treats are the works of two artists who had a major hand in bringing Yellowstone's magnificent scenery to public attention. Twenty-three of painter Thomas Moran's famous Yellowstone watercolors line the walls. Equally impressive are 26 classic photographs taken by William H. Jackson in the 1871 Hayden Survey, including one of Thomas Moran at Mammoth Hot Springs.

Mammoth contains a number of other historic structures constructed during the Army's tenure at Fort Yellowstone. The most distinctive are a row of six buildings built between 1891 and 1909 that were quarters for the officers and captains. Most of the grunt soldiers lived in barracks just behind here, one of which is now the park administration building. The U.S. Engineers Department was housed in an odd stone building (across from the visitor center) with obvious Asian influences.

Most of the **Mammoth Hot Springs Hotel** was built in 1937, although one wing survives from a hotel built in 1911. Step inside to see the large wooden map of the United States. Other facilities at Mammoth include a Hamilton Store, post office, gas station, restaurant, fast food eatery, and horseback rides. Mammoth Campground is just down the road. The main road north follows the Gardner River. (Both this and the misspelled town of Gardiner are named for a ruthless trapper from the 1820s, Johnson Gardner.) The river is a favorite of fly-fishing enthusiasts. Just before the town of Gardiner (see p. 319), look for a herd of pronghorn antelope. Bighorn sheep are sometimes seen during the winter.

Day Hikes

For a relatively easy loop hike, try the five-mile-long **Beaver Ponds Trail** that begins between Liberty Cap and the stone house. It gains 500 feet in elevation, passing through spruce and fir forests along the way, and ending at several small ponds. The path then drops down to join the old Gardiner Rd. which you can follow back to Mammoth. This trail provides a good opportunity to see mule deer, antelope, and moose, but is best hiked in the spring or fall when temperatures are cooler. Black bears are sometimes seen along the way, so be sure to make noise while you walk.

A longer (12 miles RT) hike is the **Sepulcher Mountain Trail** that climbs to the top of this 9,652-foot peak just northwest of Mammoth. There are several possible routes to the top, and any of these can be combined into a very nice loop hike. One of these begins at the same place as the Beaver Ponds Trail. You'll find many flowers in the expansive meadows on the south side of Sepulcher Mountain (named for several strange rocks at its summit). From Mammoth, it is a 3,400-foot elevation gain, so be ready to sweat. Before heading out, check at the visitor center to see if there are any major bear problems in the area.

MAMMOTH TO TOWER JUNCTION

The 18-mile drive from Mammoth to Tower Junction takes visitors through some of the driest and most open country in Yellowstone. Two waterfalls provide stopping places along the way. Beautiful **Undine Falls** is a 60-foot-high double falls located just north of the road. Just up the road is a gentle half-mile path to **Wraith Falls**, where Lupine Creek cascades 90 feet. Look for ducks and trumpeter swans in **Blacktail Pond**, a couple of miles farther east. **Blacktail Plateau Dr.**, approximately nine miles east of Mammoth, turns off from the main road. The rough seven-mile dirt road is a one-way route that loosely follows the Bannock Trail, a path used from 1838 to 1878 by the Bannock tribe on their way to buffalo hunting grounds east of here. Their travois trails are still visible. Much of the road is through open sagebrush, grass, and aspen country where you're likely to see deer and antelope. The trees are very pretty in the fall. On the east end, it drops back into a forest burned by a severe crown fire in 1988. Look for aspen and lodgepole seedlings among the abundant summertime flowers.

A half mile beyond where Blacktail Plateau Dr.

re-enters the main road is the turnoff to the **pet-rified tree**. The 20-foot-tall stump of an ancient redwood tree (50 million years old) stands behind iron bars. A second petrified tree that used to stand nearby was stolen piece by piece over the years by thoughtless tourists. The **Tower Ranger Station**, originally occupied by the U.S. Army, is just before Tower Junction where the road splits, leading to either Northeast Entrance Road or Canyon.

NORTHEAST ENTRANCE ROAD

Of the five primary entryways into Yellowstone, Northeast Entrance is the least traveled, making this a nice place to escape the hordes in midsummer. It is also one of the few places in Yellowstone where one sees tall mountains. The road heads east from Tower Junction, and immediately enters **Lamar Valley**, an area of grass and sage along the sinuous Lamar River. Osborne Russell, who trapped this country in the 1830s, described it with affection:

There is something in the wild romantic scenery of this valley which I cannot . . . describe; but the impressions made upon my mind while gazing from a high eminence on the surrounding landscape one evening as the sun was gently gliding behind the western mountain and casting its gigantic shadows across the vale were such as time can never efface from my memory.

This is still one of the best places in Yellowstone to view bison. Elk and mule deer are also commonly seen. The valley contains a number of small ponds created when the retreating glaciers left large blocks of ice that formed "kettles." Erratic glacial boulders are scattered along the way. There are campgrounds at Slough Creek and Pebble Creek. They are the last to fill in the park, but even these fill quickly in July and August. Very good fishing in Slough Creek.

Yellowstone Institute

The nonprofit Yellowstone Institute is housed within Lamar Valley's historic Buffalo Ranch, where turn-of-the-century efforts were made to protect and breed bison. Plains bison were brought here and kept in pens at night and herded during the day. After 1915, they were allowed to roam freely during the summer, although all the park's bison were rounded up and driven here for the winters. After 1938, the roundups ended, but hay was fed every winter in Lamar Valley. Finally in 1952, even this was halted.

Yellowstone Institute offers more than 80 different environmental classes between May and mid-Sept., with most running around $35 a day and lasting two to five days. The courses cover the spectrum from grizzly bear ecology to fly-fishing. Participants stay in primitive cabins at the ranch ($7/night) and cook meals in the kitchen. The Institute is funded in part by the Yellowstone Association, and discounts are available to association members. For a brochure, write Yellowstone Institute, Box 117, Yellowstone National Park, WY 82190; tel. 344-7381.

Specimen Ridge

Just east of Yellowstone Institute is a turnout across from Specimen Ridge, where explorers discovered the standing trunks of petrified trees that had been buried in volcanic ash and mudflows some 50 million years ago. Over the centuries, the trunks literally turned to stone as silica entered the wood. The process was repeated again and again over the centuries as new forests gradually developed atop the volcanic deposits, only to be buried by later flows. Scientists have found 27 different forests on top of each other, containing walnut, magnolia, oaks, redwood, and maple—evidence that the climate was once more like that of today's central states. Erosion eventually revealed the trees, many of which are still standing. This is one of the largest areas of petrified trees known to exist.

There is no trail to the petrified forest, but during the summer, rangers lead hikes into the area. Check at the Mammoth Visitor Center for upcoming treks. Mark Marschall's *Yellowstone Trails* provides a description of the 1¹/₂-mile route if you want to try it on your own. A lesser known petrified forest in the northwest corner of Yellowstone is accessible via U.S. 191.

Northeast Entrance

At the east end of Lamar Valley, U.S. 212 continues northeast up Soda Butte Creek and between the steep rocky cliffs of Barronette Peak (10,404 feet) and Abiathar Peak (10,928 feet). Stop at **Soda Butte** where you'll find a small travertine mound similar to those at Mammoth. Although the springs are no longer very active, the air still reeks of hydrogen sulfide, the "rotten egg" gas. South of Soda Butte, and several miles up a backcountry trail is **Wahb Springs**, found within Death Gulch. Here poisonous gases are emitted from the ground, killing animals in the vicinity. Early explorers reported finding dead bears who had wandered into the area and had been overcome by the fumes.

Above Pebble Creek Campground, the road squeezes through chilly **Icebox Canyon** and into the lodgepole pine forests. It follows the creek all the way to the edge of the park, crossing into Montana two miles before the park border. The **Northeast Entrance Station** is a classic log building built in 1935, and designated a National Historic Landmark. The twin towns of Silver Gate and Cooke City (see p. 320) are just up the road.

TOWER JUNCTION TO CANYON

Right at the junction of the roads to Canyon, Mammoth, and Lamar Valley, is **Roosevelt Lodge**, built in 1920 and named for President Theodore Roosevelt who camped a few miles south of here when he visited in 1903. President Roosevelt remained a lifelong supporter of Yellowstone, and helped push through legislation that clamped down upon the rampant destruction of its wildlife. Inside the lodge are two giant stone fireplaces. Lodging, food, and horseback rides are available. Stop at the overlook to **Calcite Springs**, two miles southeast of the junction, where a walkway provides dramatic views into the canyon, with steaming geothermal activity far below. The cliff faces contain a wide strip of columnar basalt, some of which overhangs the highway just south of here.

At **Tower Fall**, Tower Creek plummets 132 feet before joining the Yellowstone River. The tower-like black rocks of the area are made of basalt, a volcanic material. Nearby are a campground and a Hamilton Store. Tower Fall overlook is just a couple hundred paved feet from the parking area, or you can follow the path a half mile down the switchbacks to the canyon bottom where the vista is far more impressive, and a rainbow is sometimes visible. Be prepared to get wet in the spray. A ford of the Yellowstone

River—used by Bannock Indians in the 19th century—is just a quarter mile away. For more than a hundred years, a huge boulder stood atop Tower Fall; the water and gravity finally won in 1986.

Continuing south, the road climbs along Antelope Creek, and eventually switchbacks up the aptly named Mae West Curve. The North Fork fire swept through this country in 1988, leaving a blackened forest but abundant summertime flowers and verdant grasses. A popular trail to **Mt. Washburn** splits off just above Mae's curves, and you can drive up the first mile on old Chittenden Road. Park your car and hike the remaining three miles to the top. This is one of the nicest day-hikes in the park, providing a fine opportunity to see and photograph bighorn sheep. Many wildflowers bloom in midsummer, and hikers discover fantastic vistas from the lookout tower on top. Another popular three-mile trail up Mt. Washburn begins at the Dunraven Pass Picnic Area.

Dunraven Pass (8,859 feet) is named for the Earl of Dunraven, who visited the park in 1874, and whose widely read book *The Great Divide* brought Yellowstone to the attention of wealthy European travelers. This is the highest point along any park road. Look for whitebark pines near the road, and be sure to stop just south of here for a view across to the distant Grand Canyon of the Yellowstone.

GRAND CANYON OF THE YELLOWSTONE

Yellowstone is best known for its geysers and animals, but for many, the Grand Canyon is its most memorable feature. The 20-mile-long canyon is 4,000 feet across, with colorful yellow, pink, orange, and buff cliffs that drop as much as 1,200 feet on either side. The river itself tumbles abruptly over two massive waterfalls, sending up a roar audible for miles along the rims. Grand Canyon is accessible by road from both the north and south sides, with equally amazing views. None of the lodgepole forests around here were burned in the fires of 1988.

Carving A Canyon
After the massive volcanic eruptions some 600,000 years ago, rhyolite lava flows came

GRAND CANYON OF THE YELLOWSTONE

through what is now the Grand Canyon. The flows eventually cooled, but geothermal activity within the rhyolite weakened the rock with hot steam and gasses, making it susceptible to erosion. Over the centuries, a series of glaciers blocked water upstream, and then allowed the water in this lake to empty suddenly when they retreated. The weakened rhyolite was easily eroded by these floods of water and glacial debris, thus revealing pastel yellow and red canyon walls colored by the thermal activities. The **Lower Falls** are at the edge of the thermal basin, above rock that was not weakened by geothermal activity. The **Upper Falls** are at a contact point between hard rhyolite that does not erode easily, and a band of rhyolite that contains more easily eroded volcanic glass. Today, the canyon is eroding more slowly, having increased in depth only 50 feet over the last 10,000 years.

Canyon Village
Canyon Village on the north rim is a forgettable shopping mall in the wilderness, complete with various stores and eating places, a post office,

gas station, cabins, and campground (RVs only). Horseback rides are available nearby. **Canyon Visitor Center** includes exhibits on the geology and natural history of the area, along with films and slide shows. Hours are generally 9-5 from mid-May through September.

North Rim Vistas
A one-way road takes visitors to a series of extremely popular overlooks along the north rim. Farthest east is **Inspiration Point**, where the views of the Canyon and Lower Falls are, well, inspirational. **North Rim Trail** leads along the rim, from Inspiration Point up to Chittenden Bridge, three miles away. Some sections of this scenic and nearly level path are paved. Just a couple hundred feet up from Inspiration Point, be sure to look for the 500-ton boulder left behind 15,000 years ago by the retreating glaciers. It originated at least 15 miles north of here and was carried south atop the moving river of ice. The five-mile-long **Seven Mile Hole Trail** takes off near this boulder, providing fantastic views for the first mile or so, minus the crowds at Inspiration Point. Look for **Silver Cord Cascade**, a

thin ribbon of water dropping over the opposite wall of the canyon, but be careful not to go too close to the very loose edge. It's a long way down! The trail switchbacks steeply down to the Yellowstone River, passing odoriferous thermal areas en route. Many anglers come to Seven Mile Hole (it's seven miles downriver from Lower Falls), while others come to relax along the river. Save your energy for the strenuous 1,400-foot climb back up.

The one-way road continues westward to overlooks at **Grandview** and **Lookout Point**. From Lookout Point, a half-mile trail drops several hundred feet to **Red Rock Point** for a closer view of Lower Falls. Farthest west along the one-way North Rim Rd. is the trail to the **Brink of the Lower Falls**. It's half a mile long and paved, descending 600 feet to a viewing area where you can peer over the 308-foot precipice (twice the height of Niagara Falls). Not recommended for anyone suffering from vertigo. Just south of where the one-way road rejoins the main highway, is a turnoff to the **Brink of the Upper Falls**, where a short walk takes you to an over-the-edge view of the 109-foot-high Upper Falls.

A party of prospectors wandered north into this country in 1867, following the Yellowstone downriver without suspecting the canyon below. A. Bart Henderson wrote in his diary of strolling down the river and being

> *very much surprised to see the water disappear from my sight. I walked out on a rock & made two steps at the same time, one forward, the other backward, for I had unawares as it were, looked down into the depth or bowels of the earth, into which the Yellow plunged as if to cool the infernal region that lay under all this wonderful country of lava and boiling springs.*

South Rim Vistas

The south rim is lined with more dramatic views into Grand Canyon. Cross the Chittenden Bridge over the Yellowstone River (otters are sometimes seen playing in the river below) and continue a half mile to Uncle Tom's parking area, where a short trail leads to views of the Upper Falls and Crystal Falls. More unusual is **Uncle Tom's Trail** which descends 500 feet to Lower Falls. The trail is partly paved, but steep, and includes 328 metal steps before you get to the

bottom. Good exercise if you're in shape. It was named for "Uncle" Tom Richardson who, with the help of wooden ladders and ropes, led paying tourists to the base of the falls around the turn of the century. Because there was no bridge, Uncle Tom also rowed his guests across the river near the present Chittenden Bridge. After his permit was revoked in 1903, visitors had to make do on their own.

A mile beyond the Uncle Tom parking area, the road ends at the parking area for **Artist Point**, the most famous of all Grand Canyon viewpoints. A short paved path leads to an astounding point where one can look upriver to the Lower Falls or down the opposite direction into the canyon. Look for thermal activity far below. The point is apparently where artist Thomas Moran painted a number of his famous watercolors. **South Rim Trail** begins at the Chittenden Bridge, and follows along the rim to Artist Point (two miles), providing more viewpoints along the way. The least-traveled part of this trail continues eastward another 1¼ miles to Sublime Point, with many fine looks into the canyon. Watch for loose rocks on the edge.

CANYON TO LAKE JUNCTION

Hayden Valley

Just a few miles south of Canyon, the country abruptly opens into beautiful Hayden Valley, named for Ferdinand V. Hayden, leader of the 1871 expedition into Yellowstone. Reaching eight miles across, this relatively level part of the park was once occupied by an arm of Yellowstone Lake. The sediments left behind by the lake, along with glacial till, do not hold sufficient water to support trees. As a result, the area is occupied primarily by grasses, forbs, and sage. This is one of the best areas in the park to see wildlife, especially bison and elk. The Yellowstone River wanders across Hayden Valley, while streams enter from various sides. The waterways are excellent places to look for Canada geese, trumpeter swans, pelicans, and many kinds of ducks. Although they are less common, grizzly bears sometimes can be found feeding in the eastern end of the valley. Because of the bears, hikers need to be especially cautious when tramping through the grasses and shrubs, where it is easy to surprise a bear or to be likewise surprised. On the north end of Hayden Valley, the road crosses **Alum Creek**, named for the highly alkaline water that could make anything shrink. In the horse-and-buggy days, Yellowstone wags claimed that a man had forded the creek with a team of horses and a wagon, but came out the other side with four Shetland ponies pulling a basket!

Mud Volcano Area

Shortly after the road climbs south out of Hayden Valley, it passes one of the most interesting of Yellowstone's many thermal basins. On the east side of the road, a turnout overlooks **Sulphur Caldron** where a highly acidic pool is filled with sulfur-tinted waters, and the air is filled with the odor of hydrogen sulphide gas. Directly across the road is the Mud Volcano area, where a two-thirds of a mile loop trail provides what could be a tour through a very bad case of heartburn. Pick up a Park Service brochure (25¢) from the box for descriptions of all the bizarre features. The area is in a constant state of flux as springs dry up or begin overflowing, killing trees in their path. One of the most interesting features is **Black Dragons Caldron** where an explosive spring blasts constantly through a mass of seething black mud. The wildest place at Mud Volcano is **Dragon's Mouth**, which the Park Service notes is named for "the rhythmic belching of steam and the flashing tongue of water as it strikes out from the cavernous opening." Easy to imagine the fires of hell not far below this. The waters are 180° F. During the winter months, the Mud Volcano area is a good place to see elk or bison.

Along The Yellowstone

South of Mud Volcano, the road parallels the Yellowstone River. At **LeHardy Rapids** a board-walk provides an overlook where early summer visitors see blush-red spawning cutthroats. In late summer, this part of the Yellowstone River is a very popular fly-fishing spot—some call it the finest stream cutthroat fishing in the world—and a good place to view ducks and swans. Earlier in the year, it's open only to the bears that gorge on the cutthroats. By the way, the Yellowstone River is the longest free-flowing (undammed) river in the lower 48 states.

YELLOWSTONE LAKE

When first-time visitors see Yellowstone Lake, they are stunned by its magnitude. The statistics are impressive: 110 miles of shoreline, 20 miles north to south and 14 miles east to west, with an average depth of 139 feet and a maximum depth of 390 feet. This is North America's largest mountain lake. Yellowstone can seem a sheet of glass laid to the horizon, and then just a half-hour later, a roiling ocean of whitecaps and wind-whipped waves. The changeable waters can be dangerous to those in canoes or small boats; a number of people have drowned. The water is covered by ice at least half of the year, and breakup does not come until late May or early June. Even in summer, water temperatures are often only in the 40s.

Fishing Bridge

The area around famous Fishing Bridge (built in 1937) was for many years a favorite place to catch cutthroat trout. Unfortunately, these same fish are a major food source for grizzlies, and this area is considered some of the most important bear habitat in Yellowstone. Conflicts between bears and humans led to the death of 16 grizzlies here. To help restore grizzly populations, the Park Service banned fishing from Fishing Bridge in 1973 and tried to move the developments to the Grant Village area. Lobbying by folks from Cody (worried lest they lose some of the tourist traffic) has kept some of the facilities at Fishing Bridge from closing. Remaining facilities include an RV park run by TWR Services, a Hamilton Store, and a gas station. **Fishing Bridge Visitor Center** has exhibits of Yellowstone birds and animals, plus nature films, and is open daily 8:30-5 Memorial Day-Labor Day, with extended hours in midsummer. A nice loop path is the **Elephant Back Mountain Trail**, which begins a mile south of Fishing Bridge Junction. The four-mile (RT) trail climbs 800 feet, providing panoramic views across Yellowstone Lake and into Pelican Valley.

Lake Yellowstone Hotel

Lake Hotel, the oldest extant park hostelry, was built in 1889-91 by the Northern Pacific Railroad, and consisted of a simple box-like structure facing onto Yellowstone Lake. The hotel was sold to Harry Child in 1901, and two years later Robert Reamer—the architect who designed Old Faithful Inn—was given free reign to transform this into a more attractive place, with distinctive Ionic columns added out front. During the 1960s and '70s the hotel fell into disrepair under the management of General Host Corporation. Finally, in disgust, the Park Service bought out the concession and leased it to TWR Services which has managed it since. Major renovations in the 1980s transformed the dowdy old structure into a luxurious grand hotel with much of the charm it had in the 1920s when President Calvin Coolidge stayed here. Today, Lake Hotel is one of the nicest lodging places in the park, with fine vistas out over the lake. Relax with a drink in the Sun Room.

Be sure to take a walk along the lakeshore out front of the hotel, where the Absaroka Range forms a backdrop far to the east. The highest mountain is Avalanche Peak (10,566 feet). Almost due south is the 10,308-foot summit of Mt. Sheridan, named for Gen. Philip Sheridan, a longtime supporter of expanding the park to include the Tetons. Watch for the big white pelicans catching fish on the lake. Just east of Yellowstone Hotel is the **Lake Ranger Station**, built in 1922, and on the National Register of Historic Places. Inside the octagonal main room is a massive fireplace, exposed log rafters, and rustic light fixtures. Not far away is **Lake Lodge**, another rustic log structure. Inside is a reasonably priced cafeteria, while out back are row upon row of simple cabins. A Hamilton Store stands nearby.

To West Thumb

The highway south from Lake Junction to West Thumb follows closely along the lake shore nearly the entire distance. A campground and boat harbor are at **Bridge Bay**, along with a ranger station and marina store. Immediately south of Bridge Bay is a turnoff to **Natural Bridge**. The mile-long road ends at a 59-foot-high natural span carved by the waters of Bridge Creek. Hikers will discover a three-mile trail that leaves from the campground and climbs to the rock bridge. Back on the main road, keep your eyes open for Canada geese and trumpeter swans as you drive south. **Gull Point Drive**, a two-mile-long side road, offers views of **Stevenson Island** just offshore, while farther south,

Frank Island and tiny **Dot Island** become visible. The small **Potts Hot Springs Basin** just north of West Thumb is named for fur trapper Daniel T. Potts, one of the first white men to explore the Yellowstone country.

EAST ENTRANCE ROAD

Heading east from Fishing Bridge, the road follows the shore of Yellowstone Lake, passing country that escaped the fires of 1988. Three miles east of the bridge are Indian Pond and the trailhead for **Storm Point Trail**, a pleasant three-mile hike (RT). This loop trail is essentially level, and goes past a large colony of yellow-bellied marmots before reaching Storm Point where waves pound against the rocks. The trail is often closed because of grizzlies. North of here, the Pelican Valley is considered even more important grizzly habitat, and is closed to all overnight camping or travel between 7 p.m. and 9 a.m. Even daytime use is not allowed during early summer. Before venturing out on the Storm Point Trail or in Pelican Valley, check at the Lake Ranger Station for bear info.

At **Steamboat Point** the road swings out along the shore, providing excellent views across the lake, along with a noisy fumarole. For an even better view (don't miss this one!), take the **Lake Butte Overlook** road which continues one mile to a small parking area a thousand feet above the lake. This is a fine place to watch sunsets and to get a feeling for the enormity of Yellowstone Lake. Back on the main highway and heading east, Yellowstone Lake is soon behind you, and visible in only a few spots as the road climbs gradually, passing scenic **Sylvan Lake**, a nice place for picnics. Just up the road is tiny Eleanor Lake (little more than a puddle) and the trail to 10,566-foot **Avalanche Peak**. This two-mile-long unmarked trail begins across the road on the east side of the creek, and climbs steeply. It emerges from the forest halfway up, with the top gained via a scree slope. At the summit, you can see most of the peaks in the Absarokas, along with the Tetons, 70 miles away.

Immediately east of Eleanor Lake, the main road climbs to 8,541-foot **Sylvan Pass**, flanked by Hoyt Peak on the north and Top Notch Peak to the south. Steep scree slopes drop down both sides. East of Sylvan Pass, the road drops quickly along Middle Creek (a tributary of the Shoshone River), providing good views to the south of Mounts Langford and Doane. **East Entrance Ranger Station** was built by the Army in 1904. For many years, the road leading up to

Sylvan Pass from the east took drivers across Corkscrew Bridge, a bridge that literally looped over itself as the road climbed steeply up the narrow valley. For more on the country east of here, see "Wapiti Valley" in the "Bighorn Basin" chapter. The road leads to Cody.

INTO THE BACKCOUNTRY

The vast majority (over 98%) of Yellowstone's visitors do not venture farther than a few feet off the main roads, but those who do, discover another world beyond the spectacular geysers and canyons. Many parts of the Yellowstone backcountry are heavily visited, but regulations keep the sense of wildness intact by separating campsites and limiting the number of hikers.

Much of Yellowstone consists of rolling lodgepole pine (or burned lodgepole) forests. With a few exceptions, anyone looking for dramatic alpine scenery would probably be better off heading to Grand Teton National Park or the Wind River Mountains. Despite this, the backcountry is enjoyable to walk through, and many trails lead to waterfalls, geysers, and hot springs. Besides, this is one of the finest places in America to view wildlife—including grizzlies—in a natural setting. Before August when they start to die down, you should also be ready for the ubiquitous mosquitoes.

Rules And Regulations
A backcountry use permit (free) is required of each overnight party, and is available only in person at the various ranger stations within 48 hours of your hike. You'll need to specify exactly where you plan to camp each night, and will be given a lengthy rundown of what to expect and precautions to take. In many parts of the park, hikers stay at campsites with pit toilets, fire rings, and bear poles. Bear management areas have special regulations that may include seasonal restrictions, day-use only, or minimum group sizes. Wood fires are not allowed in many areas, so be sure to have a gas stove for cooking. Pets are not allowed on the trails within Yellowstone, and special rules apply for those coming in with horses. For a description of backcountry rules and suggestions for hiking and horsepacking, pick up a copy of the free park brochure *Beyond Road's End* at any ranger station.

More Info
I have selected a few two- to four-day backcountry hikes covering various parts of Yellowstone. The park has over 1,200 miles of trails, so this is obviously a tiny sampling of the various hiking options. In addition, a number of day hikes are described above in conjunction with adjacent sights (such as Mt. Washburn trails in the "Tower Junction to Canyon" section and Mystic Falls in the "Upper Geyser Basin" section). A fine small guide to park trails is *Hiking the Yellowstone Backcountry,* by Orville E. Bach, Jr. (Sierra Club Books, San Francisco), but your best bet (extensively updated since the 1988 fires) is Mark C. Marschall's excellent *Yellowstone Trails,* published by the Yellowstone Association. The best topographic park map is produced by **Earthwalk Press**, 2239 Union St., Eureka, CA 95501. It includes all the major trails, and shows the severity of burn from the 1988 fires, a considerable help when planning hiking trips. Detailed topographic maps are available from the Mammoth and Old Faithful visitor centers.

NORTH YELLOWSTONE TRAILS

Sportsman Lake Trail
The land west of Mammoth is some of the most rugged in Yellowstone, with a number of peaks topping 10,000 feet. Several trails cut westward across this country, one of the most interesting being the Sportsman Lake Trail(see maps p. 276 and p. 298). It begins at Glen Creek Trailhead, five miles south of Mammoth, and follows Glen Creek for the first four miles before dropping into the Gardner River drainage. You'll need to ford the river twice, and before late summer it can be dangerously deep, so do this hike later. A spur trail makes it possible to climb **Electric Peak**, the 10,992-foot rocky summit just north of

here; see Marschall's *Yellowstone Trails* for specifics. Beyond the river fords, the main trail climbs to Electric Divide, and then drops to Sportsman Lake. West of here the trail splits, and you can either continue to the right and reach U.S. 191 (total distance of 24 miles), or follow the Fan Creek and Fawn Pass trails back to the Mammoth area (approximately 40 miles RT). Warning: This country overflows with grizzly activity, and parties of four or more are required for travel here. Off-trail travel is prohibited.

Pebble Creek Trail

This 12-mile-long path cuts through a part of Yellowstone that is far away from the geysers and canyons for which the park is famous. The crowds don't come here, but the country is some of the nicest mountain scenery in the park. Pebble Creek Trail connects with the Northeast Entrance road at both ends, making access easy (see map, p. 276). You can start from either end, but beginning from the Warm Creek Picnic area (1½ miles west of the entrance station) makes it all downhill after the first steep climb. Best time to hike this trail is in late summer when the water levels are down (there are two fords) and the mosquitoes have abated. Lots of alpine flowers and grand mountain scenery along the way. Halfway down the valley, **Bliss**

Pass Trail splits westward and crosses Pebble Creek (quite deep till late summer) before climbing 1,400 feet to the pass and then dropping down 2,700 feet to **Slough Creek Trail**. The latter takes you into Slough Creek Campground.

SOUTH YELLOWSTONE TRAILS

Shoshone Lake

Shoshone Lake—the largest lake in the lower 48 without direct road access—is probably the most visited part of Yellowstone's backcountry. Although its shoreline is dotted with more than 20 campsites, nearly every site fills up on midsummer nights. Access to Shoshone Lake is primarily from trailheads along the South Entrance Rd. and the road between West Thumb and Old Faithful. Paths circle Shoshone Lake, although they are away from the shoreline much of the distance. You may see moose or elk along the way. On the west end of the lake, hikers are delighted to find **Shoshone Geyser Basin**, an area filled with small geysers, beautiful pools, and bubbling mudpots. **Minute Man Geyser** is the most notable one here, with a distinctive five-foot-tall cone and eruptions 10-40 feet into the air. Befitting its name, it often erupts every one to three minutes.

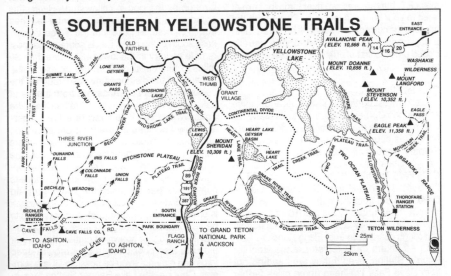

Heart Lake

The Heart Lake area is another extremely popular backcountry (and day hiking) area, offering easy access along with all sorts or sights: a pretty lake, hot springs, and impressive mountain vistas. **Heart Lake Trail** begins just north of Lewis Lake and six miles south of Grant Village. The trail is fairly easy, climbing slowly for the first 5 1/2 miles and then dropping down the other side to Heart Lake (2 1/2 more miles), along the severely burned Witch Creek drainage. This creek is fed almost entirely by the hot springs and geysers scattered along it.

At Heart Lake Ranger Station the trail splits. Turning right, hike a half mile to the **Mt. Sheridan Trail** which heads west, climbing 2,850 vertical feet in a distance of 3 1/2 miles. A fire lookout at the summit provides views across Yellowstone Lake and south to the Tetons. At the base of Mt. Sheridan and just to the north is another small thermal area that contains **Rustic Geyser** (eruptions to 50 feet every half-hour or so, but irregular) and **Columbia Pool** among other attractions. Be very careful when walking here due to the overhanging rim at the pool edge. Although many people simply hike to Heart Lake for an overnight trip, there are many longer hikes one could take out of here. A complete loop around the lake is approximately 33 miles RT, but requires two river fords that are at least to your knees in late July. Check with the rangers for current conditions. The Heart Lake area is prime grizzly habitat, and is usually closed until the first of July. Do not take chances in this country.

Bechler River

The southwest portion of Yellowstone is known as Cascade Corner, a reference to its many tall waterfalls; more than half of the park's falls are here. This country escaped the fires of 1988. Primary access is from either the Bechler Ranger Station (pronounced BECK-ler) or the Cave Falls Trailhead, both of which are well off the beaten path and must be reached via the Cave Falls Rd. from the Idaho side. It's 26 miles in from Ashton, Idaho, the last 10 of this on a gravel road. (Grassy Lake Rd. provides a narrow and rough connection from Flagg Ranch to Ashton.) All hikers must register at the Bechler Ranger Station, even if they are heading out from Cave Falls Trailhead (three miles farther

down the road). Cave Falls itself is a very wide, but not particularly tall, drop along the Falls River. It's named for a cave on the west end of the waterfall. The Forest Service has a campground ($5) here.

A maze of trails cuts across the Bechler country, leading to the many waterfalls and other attractions. One very popular hike goes from Bechler Ranger Station to the Old Faithful area (or vice versa), a distance of 32 miles. From Bechler, the trail cuts across the expansive Bechler Meadows and then up narrow Bechler Canyon, passing Colonnade, Ouzel, and Iris falls along the way. Many people stop overnight in Three River Junction before punching on up to the Continental Divide. Beyond this, the trail cuts above Shoshone Lake and on to Lone Star Geyser and the trailhead at Kepler Cascades. It's best to hike this route in late summer or early fall after the meadows have dried out a bit and the mosquitoes are down to a dull roar. Midsummer finds standing water and the ever-friendly leaches, although it is possible to skirt around the meadows.

The Thorofare

If any part of Yellowstone deserves the title untamed wilderness, it has to be the Thorofare. Situated along Two Ocean Plateau and cut through by the upper Yellowstone River, this broad expanse of unroaded country reaches from Yellowstone Lake into the Teton Wilderness south of the park. This is some of the most remote country in the lower 48—more than 30 miles in any direction from the nearest road. Because of the distances involved, much of the use is via horseback. Access is from the Heart Lake area, via the Thorofare Trail, or from the Teton Wilderness. The **Thorofare Trail** begins at 9-Mile Trailhead on the East Entrance Rd., and hugs the shore of Yellowstone Lake for the first 17 miles. This stretch was spared from the fires of 1988, and provides some incredible opportunities for sunsets over the lake. Canoeists sometimes paddle along the lakeshore and camp. Because of grizzly activity, off-trail travel is prohibited until mid-August, and you need to be very cautious along streams where bears may be fishing for spawning cutthroats. Longer trips are also possible, but they require deep fords and may not even be possible till late summer. Check at the Lake Ranger Station for current conditions.

WINTER IN YELLOWSTONE

During Yellowstone's first 75 years as a park, winter visitation was almost unknown. The only people in the park were winterkeepers who spent months at a time with no contact with the world outside. This began to change in 1949 when snow plane tours were first offered from the West Entrance. The planes could only hold two people—the driver and a passenger—so visitation barely topped 30 people that winter. In 1955, snowcoaches were permitted to come into Yellowstone, and more than 500 people arrived that winter, though few stayed overnight. The first snowmobiles arrived in 1964 when they were a novelty. With the increasing interest in cross-country skiing and snowmobiling, the park opened Old Faithful Snow Lodge in the winter of 1971-72, and since then, winter use has rocketed five-fold to over 100,000 people. On busy days, over a thousand snowmobiles roar into the park through the West Yellowstone gate. While these numbers pale in comparison to those in summer, there is growing concern that skiers and snowmobilers could adversely affect the park's wildlife at a time when they are already under great stress.

Approximately 60% of Yellowstone's winter use consists of people who come in on a quick day-tour of the park via snowmobile, and then spend the night back in one of the gateway towns. To see Yellowstone right, however, it's best to spend more time, either snow camping or staying at Mammoth or Old Faithful. Winter transforms Yellowstone into an extraordinarily beautiful place where the fires and brimstone of hell meet the bitter cold and snow of winter. The snow often averages four feet in depth, but can exceed 10 feet on the mountain passes. The snow is usually quite dry, although late in the season, conditions deteriorate as temperatures rise. Early in the winter or after major storms, backcountry skiing can be very difficult due to the deep powder. Temperatures generally fall in the 10-30° F range during the day, while nights frequently dip well below zero. (The record is -66° F, recorded on Feb. 9, 1933.) Winds can make these temperatures feel even colder, so visitors should come prepared for extreme conditions.

The thermal basins are a real winter treat. Hot springs that are simply colorful pools in summer send up billows of steam in the winter, coating the nearby trees with a thick layer of ice and turning them into "ghost trees." The geysers put on an astounding display as boiling water meets frigid air; steam from Old Faithful can tower 1,000 feet into the air! Bison and elk gather around the hot springs, soaking up the heat and searching for dried grasses, while eagles are often seen flying over the heated waters of Firehole River. The bison are perhaps the most interesting to watch as they swing their

The Schwatcha Winter Expedition (U.S. Army) of 1887 at Obsidian Cliff

enormous heads from side to side to shovel snow off the grass. Grand Canyon of the Yellowstone is another place transformed by the snow and cold. Although the water still flows, the falls are surrounded by a tall cone of ice, while the canyon walls lie under deep snow.

BOB RACE

Roads

Most of Yellowstone's roads officially close to cars when the first heavy snows block the passes, and by the first of November things are generally shut down all over, except for the 56 miles between Mammoth and Cooke City. Roads don't open for cars again until May, and sometimes not until early June. The roads are open to snowmobiles and snowcoaches from mid-Dec. to mid-March. The rest of the winter you'll only find skiers and park personnel on the snow-covered roads. During the winter, the most popular (and crowded) times to visit Yellowstone are around Christmas and New Year's, and over the Presidents' Day weekend in February. If you plan to arrive at these times, make reservations six months to a year in advance. The rest of the winter, you should probably do so at least three months ahead.

Accommodations And Services

During the winter, only two places offer lodging in the park. **Mammoth Hotel** is the only one accessible by road, while the **Old Faithful Snow Lodge** and cabins provide accommodations and a proximity to many miles of skiing trails. Same rates as during the summer (see chart, p. 313). Both places have a restaurant, lounge, and gift shop, and for a fee, Mammoth also offers a variety of special events, along with ice skating and hot tubs. Warming huts are located at Madison, Canyon, West Thumb, Fishing Bridge, and Mammoth Terraces. All are open 24 hours, and contain restrooms and snacks. Those at Mammoth and Canyon also have snack bars offering hot chili or soup. The Mammoth general store is open for groceries and supplies, but supplies are not available at Old Faithful.

Only the Mammoth and Old Faithful visitor centers are open during the winter. Free ranger-led activities include ski tours, snowshoe hikes, snowmobile tours, films, slide shows, and walks. Check the winter edition of *Yellowstone Today* for details. The only wintertime campground is at Mammoth, where temperatures are milder and there is less snow. **Karst Stage**, tel. (406) 586-

8567, has daily bus service from Bozeman to Mammoth and West Yellowstone in the winter.

Snowcoaches

The easiest and most fun way to get into Yellowstone in the winter is on the ungainly snowcoaches, machines that look like something the Norwegian Army might have used during WW II. Most were actually made by a Canadian company, Bombidier. The windows fog up (hence the spray bottles of antifreeze) and they can be noisy. Despite their ancient condition and spartan interior, these beasts still work well, and can carry 10 passengers along with gear (two suitcases pp) and skis. The more modern ones (Hagglunds) based at Mammoth are actually not nearly as comfortable on the bumpy snow-packed roads, and the separate back compartment makes communication with the driver/guide difficult.

A variety of snowcoach tours are available through **TWR Services**, Yellowstone National Park, WY 82190, tel. 344-7311. Roundtrip rates to Old Faithful Snow Lodge are: $58 from Flagg Ranch (where the plowing ends just south of Yellowstone), $48 from West Yellowstone, and $59 from Mammoth. An excellent all-day tour of the south loop is $58 from Old Faithful. See the following pages for combination snowcoach-and-ski trips. For any of these trips, be sure to make reservations well in advance. **Yellowstone Alpen Guides**, Box 518, West Yellowstone, MT 59758, tel. (406) 646-9591, offers a variety of snowcoach tours from West Yellowstone to the park, including a short ski tour of Upper Geyser Basin for $49 pp. All-day guided ski tours are $59 pp. **Yellowstone Expeditions**, tel. (406) 646-9333, in West Yellowstone runs some of the strangest vehicles in the park, converted vans jacked up above tracks and skis. Five-day tours ($485) include housing in yurts at Canyon, plus transportation, food, lodging, and a ski guide. Recommended.

Cross-country Skiing

Skis provide the finest way to see Yellowstone in the winter. Rent them at shops in Jackson, Cody, West Yellowstone, Gardiner, and Pahaska, or in the park at Old Faithful and Mammoth. (Snowshoes can also be rented at Mammoth and Old Faithful.) The Old Faithful area is the center for skiing within Yellowstone, with trails circling the Upper Geyser Basin and leading to nearby sights. Similar ski trails (marked but not groomed) can be found in the Tower Fall, Canyon, and Mammoth areas. Get free ski trail maps at the visitor centers.

Skiers sometimes assume that they can't possibly cause problems for Yellowstone's wildlife, but studies show that elk and bison often move away from skiers, forcing them to expend energy the animals need to survive through the bitterly cold winters. It's best to stay on the trails and to keep from skiing into areas where elk or bison may be disturbed by your presence.

TWR Services (tel. 344-7311) maintains skier shuttles ($7 RT) from Mammoth to Tower Junction, Blacktail Plateau, and the Swan Lake Flats and Indian Creek areas. A similar skier shuttle (via snowcoach) is available from Old Faithful to Fairy Falls or the Continental Divide area for $6.50. The latter is a one-way service that allows you to ski back to the lodge. A variety of other snowcoach-and-ski trips are also available, including a Canyon ski tour ($79 RT) and a Fountain Flat afternoon ski tour ($22). Park naturalists sometimes lead ski trips from Old Faithful to nearby sights.

Yellowstone's roads are heavily traveled by snowmobiles and snowcoaches, making for all sorts of potential conflicts. Be sure to keep to the right while skiing. If you're planning a longer backcountry trip, pick up a use permit at one of the ranger stations. A thorough understanding of winter camping and survival is imperative before you head out on any overnight trip. For more on skiing and winter visitation in the park, get the small booklet *Winter at Old Faithful* by Frank Balthis, Steve Bogen, and Fred Hirschmann (Firehole Press, Yellowstone). It's available in the Old Faithful Visitor Center.

Snowmobiles

Winter snowmobile use in Yellowstone has risen in recent years, and it isn't uncommon to meet long lines of machines ripping down the roads at any time of the day, disrupting Yellowstone's pristine winter silence with their noise and smoke. Despite the fact that the five national forests that surround Yellowstone have many hundreds of miles of groomed trails, along with thousands of square miles of terrain open to the machines, Yellowstone's 180 miles of roads have become the focus of this mechanized winter onslaught. Environmentalists fear that the problems will worsen if the proposed Continental Divide Snowmobile Trail is opened through Grand Teton National Park, thus attracting even more 'bilers.

If you really must come into Yellowstone by snowmobile, please show a few courtesies and precautions. In particular, stay on the roads, and stay well away from the bison and elk that are commonly found along or on the roads. This is a stressful time of the year for them already, without being harassed by a steady stream of machines. If skiers are on the road, slow down and give them a wide berth as you pass. The speed limit (45 mph) is enforced, and one of the most bizarre Yellowstone sights is a park ranger waiting in a speed trap with his radar gun, ready to catch speeding sleds. Park rangers lead 1¹/₂-hour snowmobile tours from the Canyon Warming Hut on weekends.

Snowmobiles are available for rent from all four sides of the park, with West Yellowstone being the most popular entry point. Contact the chambers of commerce in West Yellowstone, Jackson, Cody, or Gardiner for a listing of companies. Snowmobiles cost $65-115/day, with the lowest rates generally out of West Yellowstone. Snowmobile suits run another $10-12/day. Most 'bilers join a guided tour through the park. Gas can be purchased at Mammoth, Canyon, and Old Faithful.

YELLOWSTONE PRACTICALITIES

Entrance to Yellowstone costs $10 per vehicle or $4 for individuals entering by bicycle, foot, motorcycle, snowmobile, or bus. The pass covers both Yellowstone and Grand Teton national parks, and is good for seven days. If you're planning to be here longer, or to make more visits, get an annual pass covering both parks for $15, or the Golden Eagle Passport that includes all national parks for $25 a year. The Golden Age Passport is free to anyone over 62, as is the Golden Access Passport for disabled individuals. Both of these also give you a 50% reduction in camping fees.

Upon entering the park, you'll receive a Yellowstone map, along with a copy of *Yellowstone Today,* a quarterly newspaper that describes current activities. This is the best source for up-to-date park information. If you're planning a trip to Yellowstone, write the park and request a copy of another free publication, *Yellowstone Guide.* The address is: Yellowstone National Park, WY 82190, tel. 344-7381.

Founded in 1933, the **Yellowstone Association** is a nonprofit organization that serves an educational and scientific role in the park by producing books and pamphlets, helping fund the Yellowstone Institute, and assisting in the visitor centers. Members receive a 15% discount on books. Contact them for membership information ($25 and up) along with a listing of Yellowstone books at: Box 117, Yellowstone National Park, WY 82190, tel. 344-7381.

Getting Around

The speed limit on all park roads is 45 mph, and it enforced, although during the summer you're not likely to approach this speed since long lines of traffic form behind monstrous RVs. Most roads in Yellowstone close with the first heavy snows, generally around Nov. 1, and open again around May 1. They open in sections, with the roads connecting Mammoth to West Yellowstone opening first, and Dunraven Pass being plowed last. Only the road between Mammoth and Cooke City is kept plowed through the winter. If you're planning a trip early or late in the season, call the park (tel. 344-7381) for current road conditions.

During the summer, most people come into Yellowstone in private cars or RVs, but there *are* other ways of getting around. **TWR Services**, tel. 344-7311, offers full-day bus tours from Canyon, Lake, Old Faithful, Fishing Bridge, Grant Village, and West Yellowstone. Tours of either the upper or lower loops run around $22 adults or $11 for kids. **Gray Line Tours**, tel. (406) 646-9374, has similar tours from West Yellowstone for around $24, cheaper for seniors and children.

Powder River Transportation, tel. (800) 442-3682, offers full-day summertime tours ($38 including park entrance fee) of Yellowstone from Cody or Jackson. Powder River lets you stop off in Yellowstone for a few days and then get back on the bus at a later date at no extra charge, making it possible to come in from Cody, spend several days in the park, and then hop back on the bus for Jackson (also true for an opposite routing). There are also bus connections to West Yellowstone via Greyhound and Karst Stage, plus Mammoth via Karst Stage (winter only).

Interpretive Programs

The Park Service maintains visitor centers in five different places: Mammoth Hot Springs, Old Faithful, Canyon, Fishing Bridge, and Grant Village. All of these places sell maps and natural history books covering the park and surrounding areas. See "Touring Yellowstone" (p. 287) for hours and seasons. Park interpreters provide slide programs, films, hikes, kids programs, campfire talks, and other activities at the various campgrounds and visitor centers. These are always a favorite of visitors, and on summer days you can choose from any one of more than two dozen different Yellowstone activities. For a complete listing of the many daily events, stop by a visitor center to pick up a copy of *Discover Yellowstone* (50¢).

CAMPGROUNDS

Camping is available at a dozen sites scattered along the road network. Bridge Bay RV Park can be reserved up to eight weeks in advance

YELLOWSTONE CAMPGROUNDS

Campground	Approximate Season	Fee	Features
Bridge Bay	5/25-9/15	$9	fills early, Ticketron
Canyon Village	6/10-9/10	$7	fills early, RVs only, showers
Fishing Bridge	5/25-9/10	$16	fills early, RVs only
Grant Village	6/20-10/15	$7	fills early, showers
Indian Creek	6/10-9/15	$5	
Lewis Lake	6/15-10/31	$5	fills early
Madison	5/1-10/31	$7	fills early, dump station
Mammoth	year-round	$7	
Norris	5/15-9/25	$7	fills early
Pebble Creek	6/15-9/10	$5	
Slough Creek	5/25-10/31	$5	
Tower Fall	5/25-9/15	$7	fills early

between mid-June and Labor Day through Ticketron (tel. 900-370-5566). All other campgrounds in Yellowstone are on a first-come basis. Roadside or parking lot camping is not allowed. During peak season, all campsites in Yellowstone fill *before noon,* so get there early! The most popular campgrounds fill up even in late fall and early summer. Only the Mammoth Campground remains open year-round. When everything else is full, folks head to campgrounds on surrounding Forest Service lands or to motels in the gateway towns. See "Shoshone National Forest" (p. 323) for areas east of Yellowstone and "Jackson Hole Campgrounds" (p.238) for areas to the south. Other campgrounds (both public and private) are described under the various park gateways—Cody, Jackson, Dubois, West Yellowstone, Gardiner, Silver Gate, and Cooke City. The farther you get from Yellowstone, the more likely you are to find space. Campers will be happy to know that showers are available at Old Faithful Lodge, Grant Village Campground, Lake Lodge, Fishing Bridge RV Park, and Canyon Village Campground.

YELLOWSTONE LODGING

Note: These rates are for one or two people. Children under 12 stay free. Extra persons are $6 each, or $2.25 each if they sleep on the floor in a sleeping bag. The less expensive rooms and cabins have bathrooms nearby, but not in the rooms.

Location	Hotel Rooms	Cabins
Canyon Lodge Cabins		$46-61
Grant Village	$48-49	
Lake Lodge Cabins		$39-61
Lake Yellowstone Hotel and Cabins	$61-93	$46
Mammoth Hot Springs Hotel and Cabins	$32-48	$21-46
Old Faithful Inn	$32-61	
Old Faithful Lodge Cabins	$17-30	
Old Faithful Snow Lodge and Cabins	$32	$46-61
Roosevelt Lodge Cabins		$16-46

HOTELS AND CABINS

At the turn of the century, most visitors to Yellowstone stayed in park hotels rather than roughing it on the ground. Three of these wonderful old lodging places remain: Old Faithful Inn, Lake

Yellowstone Hotel, and Mammoth Hot Springs Hotel. **TWR Services** (Yellowstone National Park, WY 82190, tel. 344-7311) is the official concessionaire for lodging. In addition to the hotels, they operate everything from very plain cabins to modern motel rooms. Most of these are open early June to mid-Sept., but this varies from year to year. During the winter, only Mammoth Hot Springs Hotel and the Old Faithful Snow Lodge are open. Try to book rooms at least six months ahead. Note that, following a fine old Yellowstone tradition, none of these rooms have phones, radios, or TVs. Many more motel rooms are available in the towns that surround the park.

FISHING

In the early years of the park, fish from Yellowstone Lake were a specialty at the various hotels, and because there was no limit on the take, up to 7,500 pounds of fish were caught each year. By the 1970s, Yellowstone Lake had been devastated by overfishing, and new regulations were needed. Beginning in 1973, bait fishing was banned, Fishing Bridge was closed to anglers, and catch and release rules were put into place. Because of these regulations, Yellowstone National Park has achieved an almost mythical status when it comes to fishing—the average cutthroat caught in Yellowstone Lake measures 18 inches. Increased fish populations have also been a boon for wildlife, especially grizzlies, bald eagles, and osprey. The most commonly caught fish in Yellowstone are cutthroat, rainbow, brown, and brook trout, and mountain whitefish. Grayling are found in the Madison, Firehole, and Gallatin rivers, while lake trout swim in Shoshone, Lewis, Heart, and Grebe lakes. Above the falls on the Yellowstone River (and in Yellowstone Lake), the only trout is the native cutthroat. The best Yellowstone Lake fishing is from boats rather than from the shoreline.

Fishing Regs
In most parts of Yellowstone, the fishing season extends Memorial Day through Oct., but check the regulations for specifics. Anglers don't need a state fishing license, but must obtain a free permit from Yellowstone, available from any visitor center or ranger station. Note that some

waters are closed entirely to fishing, often to prevent conflicts with bears. Only artificial lures are allowed, and a catch-and-release policy (with exceptions) is in effect for cutthroat and rainbow trout, and grayling. Many of the fish are caught over and over again; a typical fish may be caught 45 times in its life! Barbless hooks are preferable for catch-and-release fishing since they cause less damage and are easier to remove.

BICYCLING

One of the finest ways to see Yellowstone is by bicycle. Unfortunately, Yellowstone's roads tend to be narrow and with little or no shoulders, making for dangerous conditions. These problems are exacerbated early in the year by high snowbanks, leading to bikes not being allowed on some roads. Call 344-7381 for current road conditions. Some stretches—especially the road over Dunraven Pass and between Madison and Norris—are filled with potholes. If you're planning a cycling trip through Yellowstone, be sure to wear a helmet and high-visibility clothing. A bike mirror also helps.

The best times to ride are before 10 a.m. when the traffic thickens, or late in the afternoon before the light begins to fade. The best roads to ride (less traffic and better visibility and shoulders) are the Northeast Entrance Rd. (Tower to Cooke City), Canyon to Lake, and Lake to Grant Village. There are a couple of short bike/hiking trails in the Old Faithful and Midway Geyser Basin areas, but the other roads are all open to cars. Bikes are not allowed on backcountry trails. For more on cycling in the park, get Gene Colling's *The Bicyclist's Guide to Yellowstone National Park,* (Falcon Press, Helena, Montana). **Off the Deep End Travels,** tel. (800) 223-6833, offers week-long cycling tours of Yellowstone for $475 pp.

OTHER RECREATION

During the summer months **TWR Services**, tel. 344-7311, offers a variety of other recreation in Yellowstone. Horseback rides are available at Mammoth Hot Springs, Canyon Lodge, and Roosevelt Lodge for $10/hour. Roosevelt also has daily stagecoach rides ($5 adults or $4 kids) and Old West dinner cookouts combined with a stage or horseback ride for $25-$36 adults or $17-28 kids. Get tickets from any hotel or lodge in the park. Bridge Bay Marina runs scenic boat tours of Yellowstone Lake ($6 adults or $3 children), motorboat rentals ($14-19/hour), as well as guided fishing trips ($33-48/hour for up to six people). Rent rowboats for $3.50/hour. If you're bringing your own boat or canoe to Yellowstone, pick up a park permit ($10) at the Lake Ranger Station or Grant Village Visitor Center. All streams are closed to watercraft with the exception of the Lewis River between Shoshone and Lewis lakes. Motorboats are allowed only on Lewis Lake and parts of Yellowstone Lake.

Many people are disappointed to discover that there are no places in Yellowstone where you can soak in the hot springs. Not only is this illegal, but it can be dangerous since temperatures often approach boiling, and batherscan cause severe damage to these surprisingly fragile natural wonders. Legal bathing pools are found in cold-water streams that have hot springs feeding into them. You're not allowed to enter the source pool or stream itself. Locations of these legal bathing streams are not publicized.

FACILITIES AND SERVICES

Nearly every road junction in Yellowstone has some sort of general store, gas station, gift shop, or other facility. Hamilton Stores are the most interesting, since they tend to be located in rustic old log structures and staffed by friendly retired folks and fresh college kids. All the standard tourist supplies and paraphernalia can be found, along with groceries, camping equipment, books, and fishing supplies. Restaurants are located at Mammoth Hot Springs, Lake Hotel, Old Faithful Inn, Old Faithful Snow Lodge, Grant Village, and Canyon Lodge, offering reasonably priced and surprisingly good meals. Dinner reservations are required at all of these except Canyon Lodge. Roosevelt Lodge offers an "Old West" barbecue dinner, while cafeteria food can be found at Lake Lodge, Old Faithful Lodge, and Canyon Lodge. Get box lunches from any of these places. In addition, fast food eateries (not the chains) are found at Mammoth, Old Faithful, Lake, and Canyon.

Medical facilities include clinics at Old Faithful and Mammoth Hot Springs, and a small hospital at Lake. Check at any visitor center for a schedule of church services. Foreign currency can be exchanged at front desks in the various park hotels. For a complete directory of the many other Yellowstone visitor services—including an ATM machine and one-hour film processing—see the *Yellowstone Today* which you get upon entering the park.

Greater Yellowstone Coalition

The most important environmental group involved with protecting Yellowstone and the surrounding public lands from development is the Greater Yellowstone Coalition. This private, nonprofit organization is involved in all sorts of controversies within the 10-million-acre Greater Yellowstone Ecosystem—from wolf reintroduction to timber harvesting and mineral development. It represents some 4,000 members, and publishes a quarterly newsletter detailing various issues. Membership costs $25 and up; write GYC, Box 1874, Bozeman, MT 59771, tel. (406) 586-1593.

WORKING IN YELLOWSTONE

During the summer months, Yellowstone National Park provides several thousand jobs for both young and old. Most of these are with the concessionaires, but the Park Service also hires a cadre of park rangers, interpretive staff, maintenance workers, and backcountry rangers. Get applications from: National Park Service, Seasonal Employment Unit, 18th and C St. NW, Room 2229, Washington, D.C. 20240. In addition, volunteer jobs are available in Yellowstone through the **Student Conservation Association** at Box 550C, Charlestown, NH 03603. For both paid and volunteer positions, you need to apply early, before mid-January. Paid Park Service positions require U.S. citizenship.

Hamilton Stores is the oldest privately owned concession in the entire national park system, having been around since 1915. Contact the company in the winter months at: Personnel Dept., Hamilton Stores Inc., Box 2700, Santa Barbara, CA 93120, tel. (805) 963-0701, or in summer at Box 250, West Yellowstone, MT 59758, tel. (406) 646-7325. **TWR Services** (once a division of TWA, but now owned by Canteen Corporation) is in charge of lodging, restaurants, bus tours, boat rentals, horse rides, and similar services. It hires more than 2,200 people each summer. For more info, write TWR Services, Human Resources Dept., Yellowstone National Park, WY 82190, tel. 344-7901. Many of the employees of these companies are either college students (who live in dorm-style accommodations) or retired folks (who live in their RVs). Don't expect high pay; entry positions start around $4.25 an hour, with meals and lodging deducted from this. It's best to apply early in the year for summer jobs. The more-competitive winter positions often go to those with previous work experience in the park.

GATEWAY TOWNS

Yellowstone National Park is most commonly entered via one of several Wyoming or Montana towns. The Wyoming entry points—Cody, Dubois, and Jackson—are described in other chapters. The four towns listed below are in Montana, but lie just across the border and are important gateways into the park. Note that the area code for all these Montana towns is 406.

WEST YELLOWSTONE

West Yellowstone, Montana is the definitive Western tourist town. With a year-round population of around 800 (twice that in the summer), and more than 45 motels, it's pretty easy to see what makes the cash registers ring here. The West Entrance gate—most popular of all Yellowstone entrances—lies just a couple hundred feet away. The town itself isn't particularly noteworthy, unless you like rows of motels, restaurants, T-shirt stores, and tacky gift shops. West Yellowstone is surrounded by the Gallatin (GAL-a-tin) National Forest, with Targhee National Forest only a few miles to the south. "West," as the town is known locally, began in 1908 when the first Union Pacific Yellowstone Special rolled into town from Salt Lake City. From here, stagecoaches took tourists into the park. The historic stone depot, and a neighboring dining hall still stand, although the last passengers stopped coming in 1959. Hamilton Stores—one of the primary Yellowstone concessionaires—has its offices in West Yellowstone.

Sights
Museum of the Yellowstone, tel. 646-7814, is a stone and log structure located right along the main highway into the park. Entrance is $3.75 for adults, $3.25 for seniors, $2.50 for ages 9-12, and $8.50 for families. Kids under nine are free. It is open daily 8 a.m.-10 p.m. May-Oct., and has a good collection of regional books for sale. The museum houses excellent displays on black and grizzly bears, an extensive Plains Indian collection, mountain men and U.S. cavalry artifacts, and an exhibit on the Yellowstone fires of 1988. The grand old park bus parked out front was last used in 1959.

Right next door is another wonderful stone structure (built in 1925) that served until the late 1950s as an elegant Union Pacific Dining Lodge. It now houses the **International Fly Fishing Center**, tel. 646-9541, a free museum run by the Federation of Fly Fishers. Open summers only, daily 11-8. The building has a spacious dining hall containing an enormous fireplace, a 45-foot-tall vaulted ceiling, and handmade light fixtures. Displays cover the art of fly-tying and aquatic insects. An aquarium has baby trout and an art gallery contains paintings of fish and fishing (of course). Out back, find a fly-casting pond where you can practice. Local fly-fishing shops offer classes, and free casting lessons are given on Saturday and Sunday evenings. They even supply the rods. For $20 a year, you can join the organization that sponsors this.

There are five different **fly-fishing shops** in town, a reflection of the sport's importance in Yellowstone. The family-run **Eagle's Store**, on the corner of Canyon and Yellowstone, tel. 646-9300, is well worth a stop. Built in the 1920s, this historic log building contains all the standard tourist knickknacks, along with quality Western clothing and a delightful old-fashioned soda fountain (summer only).

Accommodations

The proximity to Yellowstone makes the town of West Yellowstone an exceptionally popular stopping place for vacationers in both summer and winter. Every street is lined with motels, so I won't try to list all of them. If you're a member of AAA, check their *TourBook* which lists at least 18 of the best. Be aware that in midsummer, everything fills up by 2 p.m., so get there early or make advance reservations. The chamber of commerce's brochure lists the West Yellowstone motels, and reservations can be made for any of them by calling (800) 521-5241.

Travelers on a budget will be happy to find the **West Yellowstone International Hostel** (not affiliated with AYH) in the historic Madison Hotel, 139 Yellowstone Ave., tel. 646-7745. Built in 1912, and on the National Register of Historic Places, the hotel has a rustic downstairs lobby, but no kitchen. Very friendly owner. Rates are $12 pp ($14 for non-hostel members) in dorm rooms or $24 d and up for a private motel room. It's open summers only, but almost always has space. No smoking.

Two recommended budget-end places are **Al's Westward Ho Motel**, 16 Boundary St., tel. 646-7331, where rooms are $26 s or d and up, (kitchenettes $3 more), and **Alpine Motel**, 120 Madison Ave., tel. 646-7544, where rooms start at $27 s or d. Both these are open May-Oct. only. For inexpensive year-round lodging, head to **Lazy G Motel**, 123 Hayden, tel. 646-7586, where nice rooms start for $28 s or d. Beyond these places, you'll find many motels in the $30-45 price range. Excellent new accommodations can be found at **Brandin' Iron Motel**, 201 Canyon St., tel. 646-9411 or (800) 231-5991. Rooms are $37 s or $41 d, with access to hot tubs. Families may prefer renting a furnished condo from **Yellowstone Townhouses** on Horse Rd., tel. 646-9331, or **Geyser Apartments**, 318 Geyser St., tel. 646-7518. Two-bedroom units go for around $105 per night (two-night minimum stay).

If you're willing to drive the extra seven miles west of town, **Lionshead Super 8 Lodge**, tel. 646-9584 or (800) 843-1991, has quality rooms, a very nice country setting, and a sauna and hot tub. Rooms are $37 s or $44 d. It's very popular with the retirement crowd who park RVs in their "campground" for $10. The fanciest lodging in West Yellowstone is the block-long **Stage Coach Inn**, 209 Madison Ave., tel. 646-7381 or (800) 842-2882, owned by Hamilton Stores. Rooms start for $56 s or $63 d in the old wing, and include access to a sauna and hot tubs. The impressive lobby is a treat. **Sportsman's High Bed & Breakfast**, 750 Deer St., tel. 646-7865, is in an attractive home eight miles west of town, and costs $45 s or $50 d.

Camping

The closest public camping (RVs only) is at **Baker's Hole** ($7; open late May to mid-Sept.), three miles north of West Yellowstone. Tent campers will need to go to **Hebgen Lake**, eight miles north of town, where five different camping areas are strung westward along the lake; farthest is 23 miles from West Yellowstone. Rates range from free at the undeveloped sites to $7 a night, and reservations (additional $6) can be made by calling (800) 282-2267. The Forest Service also maintains three public use cabins ($20/night) in the country around here; check at the ranger station for details. West Yellowstone has a dozen different private campgrounds, but most of these are just RV parking lots. The nicest are **Rustic RV Campground**, 634 U.S. 20, tel. 646-7387, and **Wagon Wheel RV Park**, 408 Gibbon Ave., tel. 646-7872. Rates at both are $12.50 for tents or $15 for RVs. Noncampers can shower for $3. Open mid-April to mid-October.

Food

West Yellowstone has quite a number of good eateries. For breakfast, both **Running Bear Pancake House**, 538 Madison Ave., tel. 646-7703, and **Jedediah's House of Sourdough**, 315 Madison, tel. 646-7656, are good. **B.J.'s Bighorn Deli**, 406 Highway Ave., tel. 646-9467, makes unbeatable sandwiches. **Coachman Restaurant** in the Stage Coach Inn, 209 Madison Ave., tel. 646-7381, has a good salad bar and is popular with families. Get pizza at **Yellowstone Pizza Co.**, 111 Yellowstone Ave., tel. 646-7820, or **Gusher Pizza and Sandwich Shoppe**, Madison and Dunraven, tel. 646-9050. Gusher has an all-you-can-eat spaghetti dinner on Wednesday nights. Pig out cheaply at the tiny **Thiem's Cafe**, 38 Canyon, tel. 646-9462, where the chicken soup and homemade biscuits are local favorites. For a treat, head to **Arrowleaf Ice Cream Parlor**, 29 Canyon St., tel.

646-9776, home of "2001 flavors." **Dude Dining Room**, 14 Madison Ave., tel. 646-7573, serves prime rib and steak. Fine German cooking at **Alice's Restaurant**, seven miles west of town, tel. 646-7296, where the fresh rainbow trout is a specialty. Get delicious fresh baked goods—including great cinnamon rolls—at **Sunflour Bakery**, 29 Canyon St., tel. 646-9737. Open summers only.

Entertainment

During the summer, two places in town offer melodramas: **Musical Moose Playhouse**, 124 Madison Ave., tel. 646-9710, and **Playmill Theatre**, 29 Madison Ave., tel. 646-7757. Several places have live music in West. For C&W and light rock, try **Stage Coach Inn**, 209 Madison Ave., tel. 646-7381, or **The Ranch Lounge**, 235 Canyon, tel. 646-7388. Rock music at **Dude Lounge**, 14 Madison Ave., tel. 646-7573. For something different, **Lionshead Super 8 Lodge**, seven miles west of town, tel. 646-9584, offers square dancing with callers from all over the nation, and even provides the outfits. Entrance is $5.50 per couple.

Summer Recreation

Llamas of West Yellowstone, tel. 646-9605, has guided day treks into Yellowstone for $45/day. Horseback trail rides and Western cookouts are available at **Parade Rest Guest Ranch**, eight miles north of town, tel. 646-7217. Rent mountain bikes for $20 a day from **Gallatin Fats Cyclery**, 504 U.S. 20, tel. 646-9318. They also offer guided five-day tours of Yellowstone and adjacent Forest Service lands for $595, complete with food, lodging, and sag wagon.

Winter Sports

West Yellowstone is infamous for its bitterly cold winters when the thermometer can drop to 50 below zero. Fortunately, it doesn't always stay there, and by March the days have often warmed to a balmy 20 above. In November, West becomes a national center for cross-country skiers, with the U.S. Nordic and Biathlon ski teams training here. Both the 25-km Rendezvous Trail and the 10-km Riverside Trail take off right from town. The streets are snow-packed and can be skied down in winter. In mid-March the **Yellowstone Rendezvous**, a nationally known Nordic ski race, attracts hun-

dreds of participants. There are many more places for flat tracking or telemarking in adjacent Yellowstone National Park and the Gallatin and Targhee national forests. Rent skinny skis at **Bud Lilly's Trout Shop**, 39 Madison Ave., tel. 646-7801, or **Rendezvous Ski Shop**, Madison and Electric, tel. 646-9332.

The chamber of commerce trumpets West as "snowmobile capital of the world," and each day between Nov. and late March, hundreds of 'bilers show up to roar through Yellowstone's entrance or across thousands of acres of adjacent Forest Service lands. At least half-a-dozen different tour and snowmobile rental companies operate out of West Yellowstone. (See the chamber of commerce for a list.) Hundreds more folks bring in their own "crotch rockets" to ride on Yellowstone National Park roads and across Gallatin and Targhee national forest lands. The chamber has a map of trails.

Information And Services

The **West Yellowstone Chamber of Commerce office** is at the corner of Canyon St. and Yellowstone Ave., tel. 646-7701. Open daily 9-9 in summer, and Mon.-Fri. 8-5 in winter. The **Hebgen Lake Ranger District Office** is just north of town on U.S. 191-287, tel. 646-7369. Get maps of Gallatin forest and info on the **Madison River Canyon** where a magnitude 7.1 earthquake hit the area in 1959. It caused a massive landslide that killed 28 people, created Quake Lake, and caused cracks in Hebgen Dam. The quake also dramatically affected Yellowstone's geysers and hot springs. The site of the slide is approximately 20 miles north and west of West Yellowstone on U.S. 287. It is marked with various signs.

Canyon Street Laundromat, 312 Canyon, tel. 646-9649, has hot showers for $1. **The Book Peddler**, 106 Canyon St., tel. 646-9358, is an attractive bookstore with many Montana, Wyoming, and Yellowstone titles. Sip a cup of espresso while you read. **Bookworm Books**, 14 Canyon, tel. 646-9736, is another large bookshop with both new and used titles. Open till midnight in the summer!

Transportation

Greyhound Bus, 127 Yellowstone Ave., tel. 646-7666, has daily runs between Bozeman and Salt Lake City with a stop in West Yellowstone. You can also get tickets here for **Karst Stage,** tel. 586-8567, which provides bus service between Bozeman and West Yellowstone. This is primarily a winter service, though there are once-a-week summer runs. See p. 312 for park tours from West Yellowstone. **Sky West Airlines,** tel. (800) 453-9417, has summer-only service to West Yellowstone airport from Salt Lake City. During the winter, the closest airports are in Bozeman or Jackson Hole. Rental cars are available through **Budget,** tel. (800) 527-0700; **Hertz,** tel. (800) 654-3131; and **Payless,** tel. (800) 729-5377.

GARDINER

The little tourism town of Gardiner, Montana (pop. 600) lies barely outside Yellowstone's northwest entrance, and three miles from the Wyoming line. The Yellowstone River slices right through Gardiner. Park headquarters at Mammoth Hot Springs is just five miles away, and the large warehouses of TWR Services (a park concessionaire) dominate the vicinity. Gardiner is the only year-round entrance to Yellowstone, and the Absaroka-Beartooth Wilderness lies just north of here. Also nearby is the 33,000-acre ranch of the Church Universal and Triumphant (CUT). Led by Elizabeth Clare Prophet, CUT has been involved in all sorts of end-of-the-world fantasies, including bomb shelter developments within grizzly bear habitat (one can house 756 people), weapons stockpiles, fences that block elk migrations, and proposals for geothermal projects that could affect Yellowstone's hot springs. CUT is not exactly popular with the townsfolk of Gardiner.

Completion of a Northern Pacific Railroad depot in Gardiner in 1903 led to it becoming the first major entryway into Yellowstone. The most distinctive structure in town is the monumental stone park entryway—similar to France's Arc de Triomphe—that was for many years the primary entry point into Yellowstone. Built in 1903, **Roosevelt Arch** was dedicated by President Theodore Roosevelt, a man regarded by many as Yellowstone's patron saint. A tablet above the keystone is inscribed, "For the Benefit and Enjoyment of the People." (The arch was actually built to offset the park visitors' initial disappointment at finding the rather uninteresting country in this part of Yellowstone!)

Accommodations
Gardiner has nine different motels; see the chart for specifics. Public camping is available within Yellowstone at **Mammoth Campground,** ($7) or on Gallatin National Forest in the undeveloped **Eagle Creek Recreation Area** (free), two miles northeast of Gardiner on Jardine Road. Park RVs at **Yellowstone Village North Motel,** tel. 848-7417, or at **Rocky Mountain Campground,** tel. 848-7251, for $14 ($10 for tents). Showers for non-campers cost $4.

Food
K Bar Club, tel. 848-9995, doesn't look like much either outside or inside, but the from-scratch pizzas are very good in this locals' hangout. **Town Cafe,** tel. 848-7322, has sandwiches, burgers, and a big salad bar. Better food upstairs in the Loft (summer only) where you can enjoy the vistas while you eat. **Yellowstone Mine Restaurant** in the Best Western, tel. 848-7336, offers very good, but overpriced meals. For lighter fare, **Frontier Fun,** tel. 848-7721, has burgers, tacos, and ice cream. The most distinctive food in town is, surprisingly, **Corral Drive Inn,** tel. 848-7627, where Helen and her sons serve up the biggest and juiciest hamburgers anywhere around.

Other Practicalities
Look for live bands in the Two Bit Saloon or the Blue Goose Tavern. The big annual event in town is the **Gardiner Rodeo** which comes around in late June. During the summer, **Yellowstone Raft Company,** tel. 848-7777, offers half-day ($25) and full-day ($48) whitewater rafting trips down the Yellowstone beginning in Gardiner. Guided fishing trips are also available. **Wilderness Connection,** tel. 848-7287, has horseback trips into Yellowstone. During the winter, rent cross-country skis at **Trailhead Sporting Goods,** tel. 848-7712, or **Park's Fly Shop,** tel. 848-7314.

No chamber of commerce office in Gardiner, but local info is available at a bulletin board in the center of town. The **Gardiner District Office** of Gallatin National Forest, tel. 848-7375, has maps and info on the 930,584-acre **Absaroka-Beartooth Wilderness.** The portion around Gardiner is lower in elevation and covered with forests, while farther east are the alpine peaks of the Beartooth Mountains. **Karst Stage,** tel. 586-8567, has daily bus service from Bozeman to

Gardiner in the winter, and may also offer limited summertime service.

SILVER GATE AND COOKE CITY

A couple of miles after you exit Yellowstone's northeast corner along U.S. 212, the road widens slightly to pass through the historic gold-mining towns of Silver Gate and Cooke City (originally called Shoofly), Montana, located just a couple miles apart and almost within spitting distance of the Wyoming line. The area code (406) for Silver Gate and Cooke City is larger than the total population of both settlements! Most establishments are built of log, befitting

GARDINER, COOKE CITY, AND SILVER GATE ACCOMMODATIONS

Motel	Telephone	Rates	Features
Gardiner			
Hillcrest Motel	848-7353	$22 s, $28 d	kitchenettes, recommended
Mile Hi Motel	848-7544	$25+ s or d	
Town Motel	848-7322	$25 s, $29 d	
Blue Haven Motel	848-7719	$30/cabin	kitchenettes
Yellowstone River Motel	848-7303	$35 s or d	AAA approved
Jim Bridger Court	848-7371	$35/cabin	comfortable
Flamingo Motor Lodge	848-7536	$35 s or d	AAA approved
Super 8 Motel	848-7401 (800) 848-8000	$35 s, $40 d	
Westernaire Motel	848-7397	$45 s, $50 d	very nice
Yellowstone Village North Motel	848-7417	$52 s or d	AAA approved, pool, sauna
Absaroka Lodge	848-7414	$60 s or d	immaculate, continental breakfast, overlooks Yellowstone River
Best Western	848-7311 (800) 528-1234	$62 s or d	AAA approved, sauna, hot tub by Mammoth Hot Springs
Cooke City and Silver Gate			
Parkview Cabins	838-2371	$27/cabin	kitchenettes $35
Alpine Motel	838-2262	$28 s, $30 d	
Elk Horn Lodge	838-2332	$30 s or d	kitchenettes $35, continental breakfast
High Country Motel	838-2272	$32+ s or d	
Hoosier's Motel	838-2241	$32+ s or d	AAA approved
Bearclaw Cabins	838-2336	$32+/cabin	
Grizzly Lodge	838-2219	$35 s or d	kitchenettes available
All Seasons Inn	838-2251	$40 s, $45 d	pool, hot tub
Anvil Inn	838-2261	$50/cabin	kitchenettes, sauna

the mining heritage, and evidence of the old mines abound. The towns now depend almost entirely on tourism, and are crowded during the peak summer season. Because the road is plowed all the way into Cooke City, this is also a popular winter staging area for snowmobilers heading into the Beartooth Mountains. The Beartooth Hwy. across 10,947-foot Beartooth Pass is closed by November 1 (often earlier), and doesn't open again until June.

The country around both Silver Gate and Cooke City was torched in the Storm Creek Fire in 1988, leaving charred hills just a couple hundred feet to the north, and prompting alterations in the road signs to read "Cooked City." The **Absaroka-Beartooth Wilderness** is accessible directly north of Cooke City or from various other points to the east along the gorgeous Beartooth Highway. One of the more unusual sights is **Grasshopper Glacier**, eight miles north of Cooke City by car and foot, and four thousand feet higher. The glacier contains the remains of a swarm of locusts that were apparently caught in a snowstorm while flying over the mountains. (See "Bighorn Basin," p. 179 for more on the wilderness.) Pilot and Index Peaks are the prominent rocky spires visible along the highway east of Cooke City. Dramatic Abiathar Peak juts out just south of Silver Gate.

Practicalities

See the chart for cabins and motel rooms in Cooke City and Silver Gate. Two Forest Service campgrounds ($5; open July-early Sept.) are just east of Cooke City. Good breakfasts at **Ma Perkin's Cafe**, tel. 838-2268. **Joan and Bill's Restaurant**, tel. 838-2280, serves excellent family-style food, along with justly famous homemade pies and huge cinnamon rolls. **Beartooth Cafe** makes good sandwiches and all-American dinners. Get groceries in the old red **Cooke City General Store**, tel. 838-2234, built in 1886 (open summers only), or in Silver Gate at **Summit Provisions**, tel. 838-2248. The saloon at **Alpine Motel**, tel. 838-2262, sometimes has live tunes. **All Seasons Inn**, tel. 838-2251, rents snowmobiles in the winter.

BIGHORN BASIN

Bighorn Basin is an enormous intermountain desertscape, reaching almost 100 miles north to south and 50 miles east to west. Mountain ranges rim the basin—the Absarokas rise as a western border, the Owl Creek Mountains line the southern horizon, and the snowcapped Big Horns gleam in the east. The basin's rolling desert hills are topped with oil pumpjacks, and the wind blows incessantly. Cactus and sagebrush struggle up through a hardened surface of small rocks, while rugged badland buttes rise above dry creekbeds. The countryside looks like southern Nevada.

Much of the basin gets less than 10 inches of precipitation per year; in some places just half that, and even in midwinter, there isn't much snow on the ground. Three lazy rivers—Bighorn, Greybull, and Shoshone—create long green corridors through this desolation, offering an oasis in the dry desert country. Because of the lack of water, this was one of the last parts of Wyoming to be settled, and most of the towns did not spring up until the 1890s when passage of the Carey Act brought a flood of irrigation speculators, investors, and farmers. Canals

have created wide swatches of irrigated green around the towns and along the rivers. Much of this water comes from the Buffalo Bill Reservoir just west of Cody and a series of canals supplying water to sugar beet and barley farms along the Bighorn and Greybull rivers.

In the early part of this century boomtimes came to the basin with discoveries of oil and natural gas at Grass Creek and Byron. Along with cattle and sheep ranching (important since the 1880s), these industries still dominate the economy of Bighorn Basin. To most tourists, the basin (with the exception of Cody) is a place to get through on the way to Yellowstone or the Black Hills. Locals, however, call it a retirement haven, offering as proof the dry, sunny climate (more than 300 days of sun per year), relatively mild winters, cheap housing, low crime rate, and proximity to the recreational wonderlands of Yellowstone and the Absaroka and Big Horn mountains. (In case you're confused, the word "Bighorn" is used for the the national forest, river, canyon, and the basin, while "Big Horn" is the correct spelling for the mountain range, town, and county.)

SHOSHONE NATIONAL FOREST

Shoshone National Forest encompasses 2.4 million acres, and extends along a 180-mile strip from the Montana border to the Wind River Mountains. Sagebrush dominates at the lowest elevations, but as you climb, lodgepole, Douglas fir, Engelmann spruce, and subalpine fir cover the slopes. Above 10,000 feet, the land opens into alpine vegetation and barren rocky peaks. The supervisor's office is in Cody at 225 W. Yel-lowstone Ave., tel. 527-6241, with ranger stations in Dubois, Powell, Meeteetse, and Lander. Forest maps ($2) are available at any of these.

More than half the forest lies inside wilderness boundaries; the Absaroka-Beartooth, North Absaroka, and Washakie wilderness areas cover much of the country east of Yellowstone National Park, while the Wind River Mountains

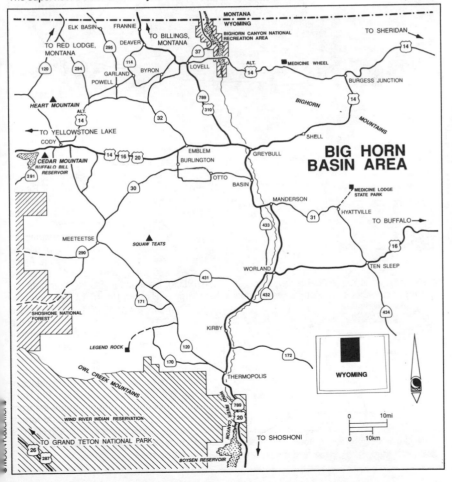

NORTHERN SHOSHONE NATIONAL FOREST

WAPITI VALLEY LODGES

The lodges are arranged by their distance from Yellowstone's East Entrance. (Subtract these numbers from 52 to determine the mileage from Cody.) All of these offer horseback rides.

Lodge	Phone	Miles from Yellowstone	Rates	Features
Pahaska Tepee	527-7701 (800) 628-7791	2	$36+ s, $40+ d	cabins, historic place, open year-round
Shoshone Lodge	587-4044	4	$40 s, $46+ d	AAA approved, cabins, open year-round
Goff Creek Lodge	587-3753	11	$40+ s or d	AAA approved, cabins
Elephant Head Lodge	587-3980	12	$42 s, $48 d	cabins
Absaroka Mountain Lodge	587-3963	13	$35+ s, $39+ d	AAA approved, cabins, open year-round
Bill Cody's Ranch Resort	587-6271	27	$80+ s or d	AAA approved, cabins, jacuzzi, open year-round
Lodge at June Creek	587-2143	28	$50+ s or d	cabins
Mountain View Lodge	587-2081	29	$38 s, $40 d $35 s or d	cabins motel
Wise Choice Inn	587-5004	30	$32 s, $36 d	AAA approved, motel, jacuzzi, continental breakfast
Yellowstone Valley Inn	587-3961 (800) 234-2902	34	$34+ s or d	AAA approved, motel, pool
Trout Creek Inn	587-6288 (800) 341-8000	37	$36 s, $38 d	AAA approved, motel, pool

contain the Fitzpatrick and Popo Agie wildernesses. (See p. 214 for the latter two.) More than 1,500 miles of trails offer hiking and horseback access to much of this country. Shoshone has more than 50 campgrounds, with most costing $5 per night during the summer. Once the water has been shut off for the winter months (generally Oct.-April) you can camp for free, but will have to haul out your own trash. Space is generally available even at the busiest times of year. In addition, dispersed camping is possible throughout the forest, with the exception of heavily traveled U.S. 14-16-20 where you must be a half mile off the road.

Black bears roam throughout the forest (though uncommon), and grizzlies are found within the northern portions, including the North Absaroka and Washakie wilderness areas. Be sure to take the necessary bear precautions anywhere in the backcountry. Bears also sometimes wander into campgrounds along U.S. 14-16-20 near Yellowstone National Park. Actually, you are more likely to encounter mosquitoes, deer flies, and horse flies in midsummer; be sure to bring insect repellent.

History

Shoshone National Forest is America's oldest. On March 30, 1891, President Benjamin Harrison signed a proclamation creating Yellowstone Timber Reserve adjacent to Yellowstone National Park. At first this title meant very little, but in 1902, President Theodore Roosevelt appointed rancher and artist A.A. Anderson to control grazing and logging, and catch poachers. His strong management almost got him lynched. Three years later under Gifford Pinchot, the forest reserves were transferred to the Department of Agriculture and renamed national forests. Part of the credit for the surprising expanse of wilderness areas on the Shoshone goes to Buffalo Bill. By bringing people into the area to hunt, fish, and explore, he helped create what one author called a "dude's forest." In addition, the Buffalo Bill Dam (which he vociferously supported) prevented logs from being sent down the North Fork of the Shoshone River, and thus made logging less important.

WAPITI VALLEY

Wapiti Valley provides one of the most popular and scenic routes into or out of Yellowstone National Park. Along the way are numerous lodges and resorts, private summer homes, Forest Service campgrounds, and hiking trails. The fishing is great in the North Fork of the Shoshone River which the road parallels for the entire 52 miles from Yellowstone to Cody. After Sylvan Pass, the highway drops through high forests and past an array of volcanic pinnacles and cliffs as the country becomes drier and more open. Cottonwoods line the gradually widening river, and Douglas firs intermix with sage, grass, and rock at lower elevations. Two wilderness areas border the highway, North Absaroka and Washakie (see below), with trailheads scattered all along the valley. Many mountain resorts and dude ranches line the road between Yellowstone and Cody; most offer both food and lodging in a rustic but scenic setting, and all have horseback rides. Eleven different Forest Service campgrounds ($5) provide more rustic living along the North Fork.

Pahaska Tepee
Pahaska Tepee (pronounced pa-HAZ-ka) is just 2¹/₂ miles from Yellowstone's East Entrance, and was built around the turn of the century to house Buffalo Bill's guests and others on their way to the park. (Pahaska was Buffalo Bill's nickname, a Crow Indian word meaning "Long Hair.") Come winter, Pahaska Tepee is a very popular place to rent snowmobiles and cross-country skis for trips into Yellowstone. The road is not plowed beyond Pahaska. The ski center here has 12 km of groomed ski trails ($2), covering a widely varied terrain. Buffalo Bill's original lodge is a two-story log building with many of the original furnishings, including an old buffalo skull over the stone fireplace. It's no longer used and is in need of repairs, but is open for tours

during the summer. On one of Buffalo Bill's many hunting treks with European royalty, he led the Prince of Monaco into the North Fork country. **Camp Monaco**, 15 miles up the Pahaska-Sunlight Trail from Pahaska Tepee, was named in his honor. Unfortunately, the old aspen tree inscribed with the words "Camp Monoco," was killed when the Clover-Mist Fire burned through here in 1988.

Sleeping Giant
Sleeping Giant Ski Area, a small family area four miles from Yellowstone's East Gate, is open Fri.-Sun., ski from mid-Dec. to mid-April. Two surface lifts provide 500 feet of vertical rise above a 6,700-foot base. Lift tickets cost $9 for adults, $8 for kids, and $6 for children. Ski rentals are available for $8. For more info, call 587-4044, or 527-7669 for snow conditions. You can also rent cross-country skis here and ski on 20 km of nearby groomed trails. Kids of all ages will enjoy the tubing hill near the parking lot.

Down The Road
Below Sleeping Giant, the road passes by a whole series of delightfully weird volcanic rock formations. Signs point out several of the most obvious. Stop at a rock memorial to 15 firefighters who were killed in the Blackwater Fire of 1937. The picnic area here has a special pond for handicapped anglers. Eight miles farther is the historic **Wapiti Ranger Station**. Built in 1903, it was the nation's first Forest Service ranger station. A summer-only **visitor center** has a short video on grizzlies. Three campgrounds are nearby.

Next up is a parking area at **Holy City**, an impressive group of dark red volcanic rocks with the Shoshone River cutting away at their base. Try to pick out Anvil Rock, Goose Rock, and Slipper Rock here. The highway leaves Shoshone National Forest and then passes the scattered settlement called **Wapiti**—an Indian word meaning "elk"—20 miles east of Cody. As you might guess, a large elk herd winters in this valley. An unusual volcanic rock ridge near here is locally called Chinese Wall. The eastern half of the road between Cody and Yellowstone passes the northern shore of Buffalo Bill Reservoir, cutting through three tunnels along the way.

SUNLIGHT BASIN

State 296, popularly known as Sunlight Basin Road, is now officially called Chief Joseph Scenic Highway. The road has approximately 20 miles of gravel, but the paved portions get longer every year. It remains open year-round, providing access for snowmobilers to Beartooth Pass. The road begins 17 miles north of Cody along State 120, with Heart Mountain prominent to the southeast, and climbs sharply up from the dry east side, passing a red butte en route to **Dead Indian Pass**, named for an incident during an 1878 fight between Bannocks and the U.S. Army. After the battle, Crow scouts found a wounded Bannock here and killed him, burying the body under a pile of rocks. Other tales claim that the name came from the body of an Indian propped up as a ruse to trick the Army during Chief Joseph's attempted escape to Canada in 1877. Chief Joseph *did* lead the Nez Perce through this country, avoiding the cavalry by heading up Clarks Fork Canyon, a route the Army had considered impassable. An overlook on top of Dead Indian Pass provides panoramic vistas of the rugged mountains and valleys. The river forms a boundary between the volcanic Absarokas to the south and the granitic Beartooth Mountains to the north.

West of the overlook, the road switchbacks down hairpin turns into Sunlight Basin where it turns to pavement again. A gravel side road leads seven miles to **Sunlight Ranger Station**, built in 1936 by the CCC. This is some of the finest elk winter range anywhere and the home for a number of scenic old ranches. Back on the main road, a bridge (highest in Wyoming) spans deep, cliff-walled **Sunlight Gorge**. The highway then continues northwest past Cathedral Cliffs and through the scenic ranching and timbering valley of the Clarks Fork, with views into the 1,200-foot-deep gorge. Part of the area burned by the 1988 Clover-Mist Fire is visible near Crandall Guard Station. Eventually you reach the junction with U.S. 212, the Beartooth Highway.

Three campgrounds ($5) are found along Chief Joseph Scenic Highway. **Dead Indian Trail** (just uphill from Dead Indian Campground) goes two miles to a fine overlook into Clarks Fork Canyon. Also of interest is **Windy Mountain Trail** which climbs 10,262-foot Windy Mountain. It starts at Reef Creek Campground and is approximately seven miles one way, gaining 3,700 feet in elevation. Windy Mountain can also be climbed from the other side near the Sunlight Ranger Station. Trailheads to the North Absaroka Wilderness are at the Crandall Guard Station (interesting old log buildings) and beyond the Sunlight Ranger Station on Forest Rd. 101.

Clarks Fork of the Yellowstone River (named for William Clark of the Lewis and Clark expedition) has been proposed as a Wild and Scenic River. Experienced kayakers will find a couple of great stretches of Class IV-V whitewater in the upper Clarks Fork, but use considerable caution since there are several big drops. Be sure to pull out before dangerous Box Canyon, considered unrunnable. More Class IV waters farther down the river. Check with the Forest Service for specifics.

BEARTOOTH MOUNTAINS

Spectacular Beartooth Scenic Byway (U.S. 212) connects Cooke City and Yellowstone National Park with the historic mining town of Red Lodge, Montana. Along the way, it passes through the Beartooth Mountains on a road built by the CCC in the 1930s. A small corner (23,750 out of a total of 945,334 acres) of the **Absaroka-Beartooth Wilderness** lies in Wyoming north of the highway, with the rest right across the Montana border. Some have called this the most scenic route in America. If you like alpine country, hundreds of small lakes, and towering rocky spires, you're gonna love this drive. Be sure to take a few casts for the brook, cutthroat, and rainbow trout in the lakes and streams.

The road sails across a high plateau and then over Beartooth Pass, 10,947 feet above the sea, the highest highway pass in Wyoming and one of the highest in America. As the road crosses into Montana, it passes the Beartooth Mt. and begins a rapid elevator ride down folded ribbon curves into Red Lodge. On top, keep your eyes open for moose, mule deer, mountain goats, bighorn sheep, marmots, and pikas. Be ready for strange weather at this elevation, including snow at any time of year. The highway is closed with the first heavy snows (generally in September) and doesn't open till June.

Recreation

Lots to see and do in the Beartooths. Majestic rock faces rise in all directions, the most obvious being Beartooth Mt., Pilot Peak, and Index Peak. Twenty-three miles east from Cooke City is the turnoff to an old fire lookout tower at **Clay Butte** (three miles off the main road). Although no longer used, the tower offers a chance to see even more of the surrounding countryside. There are four developed campgrounds ($5) along this stretch of State 212, with more once you drop into Montana. **Beartooth Lake** and **Island Lake campgrounds** border on alpine lakes with marvelous cross-country hiking opportunities all around. (Be sure to bring a compass and topo map, plus warm clothes.) The trees are whitebark pine and Engelmann spruce. **Top-of-the-World Store** (gas, food, and limited accommodations) lies between the two campgrounds along the highway. A nice 11-mile loop hike leaves Island Lake and climbs up past several lakes before circling back. **Beartooth Loop National Recreation Trail** is a popular hiking path just two miles east of Beartooth Pass. This 15-mile loop traverses alpine tundra and passes several lakes and a century-old log stockade of unknown origins.

NORTH ABSAROKA WILDERNESS

The 350,488-acre North Absaroka Wilderness is one of the lesser-known wild places in Wyoming. The wilderness abuts Yellowstone National Park to the west, and is bordered by the Sunlight Basin and Beartooth highways to the north and U.S. 14-16-20 to the south. North Absaroka Wilderness is primarily used by hunters who arrive on horseback. The few hikers tend to be quite experienced with backcountry travel and willing to tolerate the lack of trail signs and the steep and frequently washed-out paths. Much of the wilderness is relatively inaccessible, and snow may be present on passes until mid-July. Ask at the ranger stations for current trail conditions, and be sure to get topographic maps before heading out. Large populations of grizzly and black bears, bighorn sheep, moose, and elk are found in the Absaroka Mountains, and golden eagles are a common sight. The tough landscape is of volcanic origin, and the topsoil erodes easily, turning mountain creeks into churning rivers of mud after heavy summer rainstorms.

Hikes

The enormous 1988 Clover-Mist Fire that began in Yellowstone, burned through a large portion of the North Absaroka Wilderness, so be prepared for blackened forests. Pick up a map of burned areas from the Forest Service in Cody if you want to avoid these areas. Probably the most popular wilderness path is **Pahaska-Sunlight Trail**, an 18-mile-long trek that begins at Pahaska Campground on U.S. 14-16-20 and heads north through historic Camp Monaco to Sunlight Basin. Another popular path is the 25-mile-long **Big Creek-Dead Indian Trail** across the eastern (unburned) portion of the wilderness. At opposite ends are the Dead Indian trailhead and the Big Creek trailhead. This is not a loop route, so you'll need to either hike out and back the same route or arrange transportation to and from the trailheads.

WASHAKIE WILDERNESS

Covering 704,529 acres, Washakie Wilderness is one of the largest chunks of wild land in Wyoming. Named for Shoshone Chief Washakie, it lies between U.S. 14-16-20 (the road connecting Yellowstone and Cody) and U.S. 26-287 (Dubois area). To the west are Yellowstone National Park and Teton Wilderness. The Washakie is a land of deep narrow valleys, mountains of highly erodible volcanic material, and step-like buttes. The mountains—a few top 13,000 feet—are part of the Absaroka Range. About half of the land is forested. One of the unique features of Washakie Wilderness is a petrified forest, a reminder of the region's volcanic past.

Hikes

There are numerous trails through the Washakie Wilderness, but most require that you either return the same way or end at a location far from your starting point. Several trails extend into Yellowstone National Park and are popular with extended horsepacking trips. The most popular Washakie Wilderness hikes are from U.S. 14-16-20 in Wapiti Valley. Most folks use them for short day-hikes or horseback rides rather than attempting longer backcountry treks.

Kitty Creek Trail leaves from the Kitty Creek summer home area, nine miles east of Yellowstone. Low clearance vehicles will need to park along the highway. The trail follows the creek past two large scenic meadows to Flora Lake, 6½ miles and 2,500 feet higher. This is the shortest hike in the area, and one of the most popular.

The 21-mile-long Elk Fork Trail starts at Elk Fork Campground and crosses Elk Creek several times en route to remote Rampart Pass at nearly 11,000 feet. It is steep and rocky in the higher elevations. West of the Continental Divide you enter the Teton Wilderness. For the really ambitious, the Open Creek and Thorofare trails continue on into Yellowstone National Park.

Deer Creek Trail departs from the free Deer Creek Campground, 42 miles southwest of Cody on State 291 (South Fork Road). The trail switchbacks very steeply uphill at first and after two miles reaches an attractive waterfall. Continue another eight miles from here to the Continental Divide and the Thorofare portion of the Teton Wilderness. This is probably the quickest route into this remote country and is popular with both horsepackers and hikers.

South Fork Trail takes off from the South Fork Guard Station across the creek from Deer Creek Campground. (Take a signed spur road to get there.) It climbs up along South Fork Creek to Shoshone Pass on the Continental Divide (9,858 feet). From here you can continue on a number of trails to the south, rambling over three more passes to eventually reach Double Cabin Campground, 27 miles north of Dubois. Another long hike into Washakie Wilderness leaves from this campground and follows the Wiggins Fork Trail up into a connecting series of paths: Absaroka, Nine Mile, East Fork, and Bug Creek trails. It ends back at Double Cabin Campground. Total length is 60 miles. Along the way you're likely to see hundreds of elk in the high country as well as bighorn sheep. You won't see many other hikers.

CODY

The city of Cody (pop. 8,000) marks the transition point between the forested mountains of northwest Wyoming and the barren deserts of Bighorn Basin. It's a favorite stopping place for Yellowstone tourists. The park is just 52 miles due west, and other magnificent country spreads in all directions—the Beartooth Mountains and Sunlight Basin to the north, and the Absaroka Range and Wapiti Valley to the west and south. Established as an agricultural and tourism center, Cody retains both roles today, though tourism seems to be gaining in importance with each passing year. The town is one of the few places in Wyoming that continued to grow through the 1980s; only Jackson Hole exceeds Cody as a center for tourism. Not surprisingly, both are gateways to the two national parks that dominate northwest Wyoming.

Cody itself has a number of attractions, including the justly famous Buffalo Bill Historical Center, Trail Town, and other local sights. The Shoshone River flows right through town, providing scenic float trips. Lots of events crowd the summer calendar, from nightly rodeos to parades and powwows; biggest of all is the annual Cody Stampede in July. The town also takes pride in a long list of artists that includes Charles Cary Rumsey and Harry Jackson. Famed abstract expressionist Jackson Pollock was born here, but achieved his fame in New York and never returned to his birthplace.

History

Just west of Cody are the Absaroka Mountains (pronounced ab-SOR-ka), named for the Native Americans who first lived here. They called themselves the Absaroka, or "Children of the Large Beaked Bird." Whites interpreted this as crow, and they have been called Crow Indians ever since. Explorer John Colter passed through this region in 1808 while recruiting Indians to supply beaver furs. When Colter returned to the semblance of civilization called Fort Manual Lisa, everyone laughed at his tales of a spectacular geothermal area along the "Stinkingwater River." Soon everyone was calling it "Colter's Hell." But the geysers were real; they still steam along the Shoshone (formerly the Stinkingwater) just west of present-day Cody. Other mountain men came later, followed by miners who found copper and sulfur in Sunlight Basin. The first real settler in the area was a Prussian, Otto

Franc, who developed a large cattle spread.

In 1895, William F. "Buffalo Bill" Cody and two partners began plans for the Shoshone Land and Irrigation Company, with headquarters along the Shoshone River just west of the present city of Cody. Cody had spent much time in the Bighorn Basin, guiding parties of wealthy sportsmen and exploring the country, and was convinced that a combination of tourism and irrigated farming could transform this desert land. At the urging of Buffalo Bill, the Chicago, Burlington, & Quincy Railroad arrived in 1901, bringing in thousands of tourists who continued west up Shoshone Canyon to Yellowstone by stagecoach. Oil was first discovered near Cody in 1904, and Park County is now the second-largest oil producer in the state. Marathon Oil Company has its Rocky Mountain headquarters in Cody and is one of the town's largest employers.

BUFFALO BILL HISTORICAL CENTER

Each year, a quarter of a million people visit Cody's main attraction, the Buffalo Bill Historical Center. This is the largest and most impressive museum in Wyoming; author James Michener called it "one of the top four museums in America." The collection focuses on the Western frontier, and includes thousands of artifacts and works of art spread through more than 200,000 square feet of space. The center actually houses four separate museums, a research library, the boyhood home of Buffalo Bill, and two sculpture gardens. The original Buffalo Bill Museum opened in 1927 in what is now the chamber of commerce log cabin. The Whitney Gallery of Western Art formed a nucleus for the current museum location, opening in 1959. Later additions included the Buffalo Bill Museum, the Plains Indian Museum, and a new Cody Firearms Museum (completed in 1991).

Other facilities at the Buffalo Bill Historical Center include a large gift shop/bookstore, a snack bar, and a downstairs exhibition space. The Harold McCracken Research Library has thousands of historical photos and books, including more than 300 volumes about Buffalo Bill, mostly dime novels and comic books. Check the calendar of events at the historical center for activities ranging from historical talks to cowboy singing. The complex is open daily 7 a.m.-10 p.m. in June-Aug., and daily 8-8 in May and September. April and Oct. hours are daily 8-5, while March and Nov. hours are Tues.-Sun. 10-3. The museum is closed Dec.-February. Call 587-4771 for more information. A two-day admission pass costs $7 for adults, $2 for children ages 6-12, $4 for students, $6 for seniors, and $18 for families. Children under 6 are free. Excellent recorded audio tours of the museum are just $2.

Outside

Before heading inside, stop to view Buffalo Bill's **boyhood home**, a tiny yellow building built in 1841 by Isaac Cody. The house stood in LaClarie, Iowa for almost a century. In 1933 it was sawn in half, loaded on two railcars, and hauled to Cody to be reassembled and refurbished. The house is on your left as you·face the museum. Flanking the museum on the opposite side is *The Scout,* a dramatic larger-than-life statue of a larger-than-life character, Buffalo Bill. This huge bronze piece was created by New York sculptress Gertrude Vanderbilt Whitney, and was unveiled in 1924. Her family later donated 40 acres of surrounding land to the Buffalo Bill Museum. Directly in front of the historical center are three colorfully painted **tipis**, a treat for kids.

Buffalo Bill Museum

The Buffalo Bill Museum is a real joy. In it, the life of Buffalo Bill Cody is briefly sketched, with all sorts of memorabilia from his Wild West Show, including the famous Deadwood Stage, silver-laden saddles, enormous posters, furniture, guns, wagons, and clothing. Be sure to look for "Lucretia Borgia," the Springfield rifle that gave William Cody his nickname. Also here are some of the gifts given to Buffalo Bill by European heads of state (including a fur carriage robe given him by Czar Alexander II), and by Wild Bill Hickok and Sitting Bull. Original film footage from the Wild West Show runs continuously, offering a fascinating and sometimes unintentionally comical glimpse into the past. Amazingly choreographed marching soldiers, fake Indian battles, and bucking broncos make it easy to see how the Wild West Show could have inspired Western movies. Downstairs from the Buffalo Bill Museum are changing exhibits.

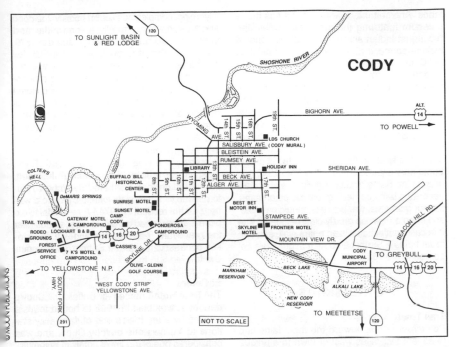

CODY

TO SUNLIGHT BASIN & RED LODGE

SHOSHONE RIVER

TO POWELL

BIGHORN AVE.

COLTER'S HELL

DeMARIS SPRINGS

BUFFALO BILL HISTORICAL CENTER

LDS CHURCH (CODY MURAL)

SALISBURY AVE.

BLEISTEIN AVE.

RUMSEY AVE.

LIBRARY

BECK AVE.

ALGER AVE.

HOLIDAY INN

SHERIDAN AVE.

SUNRISE MOTEL

SUNSET MOTEL

CAMP CODY

BEST BET MOTOR INN

STAMPEDE AVE.

TRAIL TOWN

GATEWAY MOTEL & CAMPGROUND

RODEO GROUNDS

LOCKHART B & B

PONDEROSA CAMPGROUND

SKYLINE MOTEL

FRONTIER MOTEL

MOUNTAIN VIEW DR.

BEACON HILL RD.

FOREST SERVICE OFFICE

7 K'S MOTEL & CAMPGROUND

CASSIE'S

CODY MUNICIPAL AIRPORT

TO GREYBULL

TO YELLOWSTONE N.P.

OLIVE-GLENN GOLF COURSE

SKYLINE DR.

MARKHAM RESERVOIR

BECK LAKE

ALKALI LAKE

"WEST CODY STRIP" YELLOWSTONE AVE.

SOUTH FORK HWY.

NEW CODY RESERVOIR

TO MEETEETSE

NOT TO SCALE

© MOON PUBLICATIONS

Whitney Gallery Of Western Art

The Whitney Gallery contains a memorable collection of masterworks by such Western artists and sculptors as Charles Russell, Frederic Remington, Carl Bodmer, George Catlin, Thomas Moran, Albert Bierstadt, Alfred Jacob Miller, Edgar Paxson, N.C. Wyeth, and others. The studios of Frederic Remington and W.H.D. Koerner have been re-created, and Gertrude Vanderbilt Whitney's *The Scout* is visible from a large window on the north end. The collections of both "cowboy artist" Charles Russell, and Frederic Remington—best known for his paintings of battles during the Indian wars—are the most complete here; the museum has more than a hundred of each man's paintings. There are even a few contemporary works on display.

Cody Firearms Museum

The brand-new 45,000-square-foot Cody Firearms Museum contains one of the most comprehensive collections of American firearms in the world, including everything from early matchlocks to self-loading semi-automatic pis-

tols. The museum grew out of a donation of arms owned by the Winchester Company, and now totals more than 7,500 weapons. It houses chronologically arranged displays, along with a reconstructed Colonial gunsmith shop, and the Boone and Crockett Club's collection of trophy animal heads. Some of the more unusual weapons include a 10-shot repeating flintlock rifle made for the New York Militia around 1825, and a double-barrel knife-pistol. One of the most lavish is an intricately carved flintlock sporting carbine presented by Empress Elizabeth I of Russia to King Louis XV of France. A 10-minute slide program describes how guns work and their history; interesting even for those who are not gun fanatics. In fact, the entire firearms collection is remarkably informative and well worth taking time to view.

Plains Indian Museum

The largest exhibition space in the historical center encloses the Plains Indian Museum, with items from the Sioux, Cheyenne, Blackfeet, Crow, Arapaho, Shoshone, and Gros Ventre tribes. At first it may seem incongruous that a museum featuring the man once called the "youngest Indian slayer of the plains," should include so much about the culture of Indians, but Cody's later maturity forced him to the realization that Indians had been severely mistreated and that their culture was of great value. His Wild West Shows re-created some semblance of that lost society, if only for show. Some of the more important items here were given to Buffalo Bill by various Indian performers over the years, and the collection of artifacts is now one of the finest in America. Included is an extraordinary painted buffalo robe from 1890 that depicts the Battle of Little Big Horn, elaborately decorated baby carriers, ghost dance dresses, leather garments, war bonnets, medicine pipes, and even a Pawnee grizzly claw necklace. The moccasin collection fills an entire wall, and one room holds a Sioux camp as it might have appeared in the 1880s.

OTHER SIGHTS

Trail Town

Point your horses toward the mountains and head 'em two miles west of town to a unique collection of historic buildings at Trail Town, tel. 587-5302. The site is open daily 8 a.m.-8 p.m., mid-May to mid-Sept. only; $3 entrance. This was the original location of "Cody City" in 1895. Trail Town is the creation of archaeologist Bob Edgar, the man who in 1957 discovered Mummy Cave—one of the most important archaeological finds in the West. In 1965, he and his wife Terry bought the old Arland and Corbett trading post that had stood here since the 1880s, and began to drag in other historic Wyoming cabins. Some were transported whole, while others were disassembled and then put back together at Trail Town. Twenty-two buildings, dating from 1879 to 1901, and 100 wagons are currently on the site.

For those who love history, Trail Town is an incredible treasure trove without the fancy gift shops and commercial junk that tag along with most such endeavors. This is the real thing, low key, but genuine. Probably the most famous building here is a cabin from the Hole-in-the-Wall country that Butch Cassidy and the Sundance Kid used as a rendezvous spot. Also at Trail Town is the oldest saloon from this part of Wyoming, complete with bullet holes in the door, and a cabin where Jim White—one of the most famous buffalo hunters—was murdered in 1879. The log home of Crow Indian scout Curley stands along main street too. (Curley was the only one of Gen. Custer's command that escaped alive from the Battle of the Little Big Horn.) Inside the old Burlington Store are a black hearse, arrowheads, a cradleboard, and items from fur traders. The bodies of buffalo hunter Jim White, Belle Drewry ("The Woman in Blue"), and several other historic figures have been reinterred in a small graveyard at Trail Town. Most famous is **John "Liver Eating" Johnson**, the mountain man portrayed by Robert Redford in the film *Jeremiah Johnson*. (Redford was here for the reburial in 1974.) A memorial to explorers John Colter and Jim Bridger stands near the graveyard. Trail Town provides a fine low-key contrast to the glitzier Buffalo Bill Historical Center.

Et Cetera

The **Irma Hotel**, named for Buffalo Bill Cody's daughter, was built in 1902 to house tourists arriving by train. It was one of three way stations to Yellowstone built by Cody, and was considered one of the finest hotels in Wyoming. The luxurious saloon still has a French-made $100,000 cherrywood bar given to Buffalo Bill by Queen Victoria. Many famous people have gathered here over the years. Another place of lodging with a famous past is the **Lockhart Bed & Breakfast Inn**, 109 W. Yellowstone, tel. 587-6074, once the home of novelist and flamboyant newspaper editor Caroline Lockhart (see p. 350). The **Cody Wildlife Exhibit**, 433 Yellowstone Hwy., tel. 587-2804, has a rather nice display of more than 400 mounted American and African wildlife in their natural settings. All sorts of record-sized critters, from a 17-foot-tall giraffe to a 2,800-pound buffalo. Admission costs $2.50 ($1 for kids). The **Foundation for North American Wild Sheep** has its national headquarters at 720 Allen Ave., tel. 527-6261 (across from Buffalo Bill Historical Center). Open Mon.-Fri. 8-5. This nonprofit group works to preserve and re-establish wild sheep. The films and sculpture garden here are worth a look.

East of Cody near Beck Lane is the **Wyoming Vietnam Veterans Memorial**, a black granite memorial modelled after the one in

Washington. It contains the names of 137 Wyoming men who were killed or missing in action. **Cedar Mountain**, the 7,889-foot-tall summit overlooking Cody from the west, is where Buffalo Bill had wanted to be buried. A winding 4WD trail climbs to the top, making a fine mountain bike ride if you don't mind the 2,800-foot elevation gain. Also here is **Spirit Mountain Cave**, one of the first national monuments ever designated (1909). A lack of interest caused the designation to be withdrawn, but the caverns are still on public land. Get permission to enter from the BLM office in Cody. If you're really desperate for something to do, visit the **Cody Mural** on the domed ceiling of the LDS church at 1719 Wyoming Ave., tel. 587-3290, open Mon.-Fri. 9-9. No, it isn't the Sistine Chapel. The mural (painted in 1951) offers a rosy-tinted version of Mormon Church history.

Buffalo Bill Reservoir

Located six miles west of Cody, Buffalo Bill Reservoir is a very popular place for local boaters and fishermen. **Buffalo Bill State Park** encompasses the reservoir of the same name, and includes two campgrounds ($4). A new visitor center is in the works to sit atop Buffalo Bill Dam. Fishing is good for rainbow, cutthroat, brown, and Mackinaw trout. The lake also offers some of the finest windsurfing conditions anywhere. (*Outside Magazine* rated it one of the country's 10 best spots.)

History: In 1899, Buffalo Bill Cody acquired the rights to build canals and irrigate some 60,000 acres of land near the new town of Cody. With passage of the Reclamation Act of 1902, the project was taken over by the Reclamation Service and an enormous concrete-arch dam was added to provide water. The 328-foot-high dam was begun in 1904, and required five long years to finish. It cost nearly $1 million. When finally completed, it was the tallest dam in the world. Seven men died along the way—including a chief engineer—and the first two contractors were forced into bankruptcy as a result of bad weather, floods, engineering difficulties, and labor strife. A lack of sand and crushed gravel forced them to manufacture it from granite, and 200-pound boulders were hand-placed into the concrete to save having to crush more gravel.

Originally named Shoshone Dam, the im-

CODY ACCOMMODATIONS

Motel	Address	Telephone	Rates	Features
4 Bar Motel	1213 17th St.	587-2084	$21 s, $27 d	kitchenettes, very plain
7 K's Motel	232 Yellowstone	587-5890	$24 s, $26 d	pool, kitchenettes, open May-Sept.
Gateway Motel	203 Yellowstone	587-2561	$25+ s or d	kitchenettes, cabins, open April-Oct.
Holiday Motel	1807 Sheridan Ave.	587-4258	$33 s, $36 d	AAA approved
Rainbow Park Motel	1136 17th St.	587-6251	$33+ s or d	AAA approved, kitchenettes
Skyline Motor Inn	1919 17th St. (800) 843-8809	587-4201	$34 s or d	AAA approved, pool, kitchenettes
Buckaroo Motel	1701 Central Ave.	587-4295	$35 s or d	kitchenettes
Covered Wagon Motel	1816 8th St.	587-2572	$35 s, $38 d	kitchenettes, open April.-Nov.
Uptown Motel	1562 Sheridan Ave.	587-4245	$35 s, $40 d	kitchenettes
Super 8 Motel	730 Yellowstone	527-6214 (800) 843-1991	$35 s, $48 d	AAA approved

continued on next page

poundment was renamed in honor of Buffalo Bill in 1946. Other changes included a hydroelectric plant and a 25-foot addition to the top, completed in 1990, bringing the total dam height to 353 feet. The dam irrigates more than 93,000 downstream acres through the Shoshone Reclamation Project, making it one of the only Wyoming irrigation schemes that really benefitted the state's farmers to a large extent.

ACCOMMODATIONS

Motels And Hotels
The tourist town of Cody is jam-packed with lodging facilities, but be ready to pay more than just about anyplace in Wyoming except Jackson Hole. Budget accommodations are nonexistent during the summer, though rates plummet with the first cold nights of fall. A youth hostel is definitely needed! Most of the year, lodging in Cody is not a problem as long as you check in before 4 p.m., but during the Cody Stampede (early July), you're advised to book well in advance. See the chart for rates at Cody's motels and hotels. Mountain lodges are listed in the section on Shoshone National Forest (p. 325), and the chamber of commerce has a listing of more than 20 guest ranches in the area.

Campgrounds
The closest public campground ($4) is 11 miles west in Buffalo Bill State Park. Many more campgrounds ($5) in Shoshone National Forest, but the nearest is 28 miles west of town. There are six different private RV park/campgrounds in Cody. The best are: **Ponderosa Campground**, 1815 8th St., tel. 587-9203, where tent sites are $11 and RVs cost $16; and **7 K's RV Park**, 232 Yellowstone Ave., tel. 587-2532, where tent sites cost $10, and RVs sites run $12. Both of these have shade trees. The **Cody KOA**, two miles east of Cody on U.S. 14-16-20, tel. 587-2369, was the first franchised KOA in the nation, opening in 1964. Tent sites cost $12, RVs $15. Other places are: **Buffalo Bill Village**, 1701 Sheridan Ave., tel. 587-5544; **Gateway Campground**, 203 Yellowstone Ave., tel. 587-2561; and **Cody Campground**, 415 Yellowstone Ave., tel. 587-9730. Cody Campground is open year-

CODY ACCOMMODATIONS (CONT.)

Motel	Address	Telephone	Rates	Notes
Wigwam Motel	1701 Alger Ave.	587-3861	$37 s or d	kitchenettes
Big Bear Motel	139 Yellowstone	587-3117	$38 s or d	pool
Colonial Inn	720 Yellowstone	587-4208	$42 s, $57 d	pool
Frontier Motel	U.S. 14-16-20 E	527-7119	$44 s or d	kitchenettes
Buffalo Bill Village	1701 Sheridan Ave.	587-5544	$45 s or d	pool, kitchenettes, cabins, open May-Sept.
Irma Hotel	1192 Sheridan Ave.	587-4221	$47+ s, $52+ d	historic hotel
Best Western Sunrise	1407 8th St.	587-5566 (800) 528-1234	$51 s or d	pool, open May-Sept.
Cody Motor Lodge	1455 Sheridan Ave.	527-6291	$52 s, $56 d	
Mountaineer Court	1015 Sheridan Ave.	587-2221	$54 s, $60 d	pool, open May-Nov.
Best Western Sunset	1601 8th St.	587-4265 (800) 528-1234	$59 s, $64 d	pool, very nice
Lockhart B&B Inn	109 Yellowstone	587-6074	$70 s or d	AAA approved, kitchenettes, historic
Holiday Inn	1701 Sheridan Ave.	587-5555 (800) 465-4329	$80 s, $86 d	AAA approved, pool, overpriced

round; others are generally open May-September. Non-campers can take showers ($3) at Cody Campground or Ponderosa Campground.

FOOD

Because Cody is a tourist town, it comes as no surprise to find many fine places to eat, covering the spectrum from burgers to gourmet dining. Two good spots for breakfast are **Cody Country Kitchen**, 1550 Sheridan Ave., tel. 587-4829, and **Maxwell's**, 1256 Sheridan Ave., tel. 527-7749. Maxwell's also has homemade lunches, including pizzas and salads. **Pizza on the Run**, 1453 Sheridan Ave., tel. 587-5550, sells hot slices for $1.50, and **Pat's Homestyle Deli**, 1125 16th St., tel. 527-7109, is a great place for sandwiches and salads. **Silver Dollar Bar & Grill**, 1313 Sheridan Ave., tel. 587-3554, makes the best hamburgers and other cowboy grub in town, served in a "kick-ass" Western atmosphere. Guaranteed to fill you up. **Proud Cut Saloon**, 1227 Sheridan Ave., tel. 587-7343, is an old-time Wyoming bar offering unusual sandwiches, including diced chicken and grapes! It's also popular for dinners.

Dinners
The nightly smorgasbord at **Eugene's**, 875 Sheridan Ave., tel. 587-2989, is a good deal. **Tags on 10th**, 937 Sheridan Ave., tel. 587-4971, offers homestyle American cooking, reasonable prices, and a pleasant atmosphere. **Shannon's Place**, 1102 Beck Ave., tel. 587-2101, also has a wide range of American favorites. The **Irma Hotel**, 1192 Sheridan Ave., tel. 587-4221, is a longtime favorite for lunch and dinner, and has a big salad bar. **QT's Restaurant** at the Holiday Inn, 1701 Sheridan Ave., tel. 587-5555, offers a chuckwagon buffet each evening for $7.50, including C&W entertainment. Be sure to try their oatmeal pie for dessert. Two other places for all-American family food are: **White Buffalo Restaurant**, 610 Yellowstone Ave., tel. 587-2571 (summer only), and **Sunset House Restaurant**, 1651 8th St., tel. 587-2257. The latter features a low-fat menu.

Outstanding Northern Italian cuisine at **Franca's**, 1374 Rumsey Ave., tel. 587-5354. The menu changes through the week, with a fixed-price dinner each evening ($16-23). Completely authentic, right down to the chef. **La Comida**, 1385 Sheridan Ave., tel. 587-9556, has very good Mexican food for reasonable prices. For Chinese food, visit **Hong Kong Restaurant**, 1244 Sheridan Ave., tel. 587-6420.

Grocers
Cody's grocers include an **IGA** at 1526 Rumsey, tel. 587-6289; **Wea Market**, 1543 Depot Dr., tel. 587-5384; and **Blair's Market** at 1825 17th, tel. 587-6721. For natural foods, head to **Whole Foods Trading Co.**, 1243 Rumsey, tel. 587-3213.

EVENTS AND ENTERTAINMENT

Cody calls itself "Rodeo Capital of the World," and packs the calendar with nightly summertime rodeos, plus the famous Cody Stampede. The rodeo grounds are a mile west of town on U.S. 14-16-20.

Cody Nite Rodeo
Almost everyone who passes through Cody during June, July, and August, makes sure to attend one of the evening rodeos. After more than 50 years of operation, the Cody Nite Rodeo is still one of the best in a state filled with rodeos. A favorite is always the calf scramble, starring kids from the stands. Performances begin at 8:30 p.m., and cost $6 ($4 for children). The best performances are on Friday and Saturday nights when you'll see events sanctioned by the Professional Rodeo Cowboys Association (PRCA).

Cody Stampede
Independence Day sets the stage for Cody's main event, the Cody Stampede, held July 2-4. Established in 1922, the Stampede attracts thousands of folks. Parade fans are treated to one each morning (including a kiddies parade), with dozens of marching bands, mountain men, vintage autos, floats, cowboys, and tons of free candy. Special PRCA rodeo performances, a street dance, art shows, running events, fireworks, and a carnival complete the schedule.

More Events
Frontier Festival, held each June at the Buffalo Bill Historical Center, is a celebration of the

many turn-of-the-century skills that were needed to survive on the frontier. Included are demonstrations of horsepacking, hide tanning, gunsmithing, rawhide braiding, weaving, and other homegrown talents. Various contests, musical performances, and booths make this an enjoyable and popular event. The **Cookie Lovers Festival**, held at the same time, is a treat for anyone with a sweet tooth. **Wild West Classic** in late June is a popular windsurfing event at Buffalo Bill Reservoir. Held in front of the Buffalo Bill Historical Center in late June, the **Plains Indian Powwow** attracts participants from all over the Rockies and Canada. It in-cludes day-long singing and dancing in tribal regalia, along with various dance competitions. The **Yellowstone Jazz Festival** in mid-July attracts both regional and national jazz groups, and **Roamin' Wyoming Rally** in late August draws some 3,000 motorcycle riders.

Nightlife

Silver Dollar Bar, 1313 Sheridan Ave., tel. 587-3554, is the place to go for rock music. Bands sometimes play outside on the "beach" next door. The **Sarsaparilla Saloon and Stage**, tel. 587-5544, at Buffalo Bill Village (Holiday Inn) has summertime evening performances of songs and yarns.

BUFFALO BILL CODY

For many people today, the name "Buffalo Bill" brings to mind a man who helped slaughter the vast herds of wild bison. But William F. Cody cannot be so easily pigeon-holed, for here was one of the most remarkable men of his or any other era, a man who almost single-handedly established the aura of the Wild West. More than 800 books—many of them the dimestore novels that thrilled generations of youngsters—have been written about Cody. In many of these, the truth was stretched far beyond any semblance of reality, but the real life of William Cody contains so many adventures and plot twists that it seems hard to believe one person could have done so much.

Young Cody

Born to an Iowa farm family in 1846, William Cody started life like many others of his era. His parents moved to Kansas when he was six, but soon his abolitionist father, Isaac Cody, became embroiled in arguments with the many slaveholders. While defending his views at a public meeting, Isaac Cody was stabbed in the back and fled for his life. When a mob learned of his father's whereabouts, the eight-year-old Will Cody rode on his first venture through enemy lines, galloping 35 miles to warn of the impending attack. Three years later, when Isaac Cody died from complications of the stabbing, 11-year-old Will Cody became the family's breadwinner. There were four other children to feed. Will quickly joined the company of Alexander Majors, running dispatches between his Army supply wagons, with his $40/month wages going to his mother. In Cody's autobiography, he claimed to have killed his first Indian on this trip, an action that gave him the then-enviable title "Youngest Indian Slayer of the Plains."

On his first long wagon trek west, the Army supply wagons were attacked by Mormon zealots who took all the weapons and horses, forcing Cody to walk much of the thousand miles back to his Kansas home. It was apparently on this walk that Cody met Wild Bill Hickok. At Wyoming's Fort Laramie, young Will sat in awe as famed scouts Jim Bridger and Kit Carson reminisced about their adventures. The experience was a turning point in Cody's life; he resolved to one day become a scout. Cody's next job offered excellent training: a rider for the Pony Express. At just 15 years of age he already was one of the finest riders in the West and a crack shot with a rifle. On one of his Pony Express rides Cody covered a total of 320 miles in just 21 hours and 40 minutes, the longest Pony Express ride ever. The Civil War had begun, and at age 18 Cody joined the Seventh Kansas Regiment, serving as a scout and spy for the Union Army.

Buffalo Hunter And Scout

In 1867, Cody found work hunting buffalo to supply fresh meat for the railroad construction crews, a job that soon made him famous as "Buffalo Bill," and that paid a hefty $500 per month. With 75 million bison spread from northern Canada to Mexico, and herds so vast that they took many days to pass one point, it seemed impossible that they could ever be killed off. Cody was one of the best hunters in the West; in just eight months, he slaughtered 4,280 buffalo, often saving transportation by driving the herd toward the camp, and dropping them within sight of the workers. Cody's name lives on in the jingle: "Buffalo Bill, Buffalo Bill; never missed and never will; always aims and shoots to kill; and the company pays his buffalo bill . . ."

RECREATION

River Rafting

One of the most popular summertime activities in Cody is floating down the Class I and II Shoshone River. Beware, however, that even with these mild conditions, you should plan on getting soaked in the rapids. Prices vary depending upon the trip length and whether it includes lunch, but expect around $15 for a six-mile run (1 1/2 hours) or $21 for a 13-mile (three-hour) float. Longer half-day whitewater trips down the North Fork cost $30-35 pp. For details, contact

Cody Rapid Transit, 1370 Sheridan Ave., tel. 587-3535 or (800) 227-8483; **Wyoming River Trips**, 1701 Sheridan Ave., tel. 587-6661; or **River Runners**, 1491 Sheridan Ave., tel. 527-7238.

If you want to try rafting or kayaking on your own, there are several miles of very technical Class IV water with some Class V drops below the dam and above DeMaris Springs. Above the dam are stretches of Class I and II water with good access from the main highway. Ask around for flow conditions before heading out since snow melt and dam releases can dramatically affect water levels. The most popular put-in spot for rafting companies is across the

BUFFALO BILL HISTORICAL CENTER

Buffalo Bill with Indian children, 1913—this photo was probably taken during the filming of The Indian Wars.

After this stint, Cody finally got the job he wanted, chief scout for the U.S. Army in the West, a job packed with excitement and danger. Conflicts with Indians had reached a fever pitch as more and more whites moved into the last Indian strongholds. Cody worked as scout for Gen. Philip Sheridan, providing information on movements of the Indians, leading troops in pursuit of the warriors, and joining in the battles, including one in which he supposedly killed Chief Tall Bull. His men considered Buffalo Bill good luck, since he managed to keep them out of ambushes.

During the Indian campaigns, the writer/preacher/scoundrel Ned Buntline, began writing of Cody's exploits for various New York papers, giving Buffalo Bill his first taste of national acclaim. Soon Bunt-

line had cranked out several romantic novels loosely based on Cody's adventures. America had a new national hero. European and Eastern gentry began asking Cody to guide them on buffalo hunts. On the trips, Cody referred to them as "dudes" and to his camps as "dude ranches," perhaps the first time anyone had used the terms for the hunters. One of Wyoming's most unusual businesses had begun. Cody's incredible knowledge of the land and hunting impressed the men, but they were stunned to also discover in him a natural showman. In 1872, the Grand Duke Alexis of Russia came to the U.S. and was guided by Cody on a hunt that made national headlines and brought even more fame to the 26-year-old Buffalo Bill. On a trip to New York in 1872, Cody met Buntline again and watched a wildly dis-

continued on following pages

rickety old bridge near **DeMaris Springs**, three miles west of Cody. The hot springs were once the site of a spa and resort hotel owned by C.C. "Charley" DeMaris. The buildings burned, and a later supper club also burned in the 1960s. Not much remains, but locals still play in the warm mineral water of the old pool. This was a part of Colter's Hell, and was once far more active, with hot springs bubbling out of the river and sulphurous smoke rising all around. People actually died from the poisonous gas. Today the geothermal activity has lessened, but the air still smells of sulfur and small hot springs color the cliff faces. Miners worked over nearby hillsides in search of sulphur; the diggings are still apparent. Pretty obvious why they first called this the Stinkingwater River.

Trail Rides

Hidden Valley Ranch at the Holiday Inn, tel. 587-2150, offers wagon rides around Cody ($3.50 and up), trail rides on Cedar Mountain ($35 for a half day), and a variety of longer horsepacking trips. More horseback rides at **Gateway Motel and Campground**, 203 Yellowstone, tel. 587-2561. The chamber of commerce office has a complete listing of the many outfitters and guides in the Cody area.

More Recreation

Windsurfing lessons and rentals are available through **Alpine Windsurfing**, 435 Yellowstone, tel. 587-4460. **Sunlight Sports**, 1251 Sheridan Ave., tel. 587-9517, also rents boards. The 18-hole **Olive-Glenn Golf and Country Club**, 802 Meadow Lane, tel. 587-5688, is a PGA championship course. Weekday rates are $14 for 18

---

torted theater production called *Buffalo Bill*. Amazingly, Cody adjusted quickly to the new surroundings. Dressed in the finest silk clothes, but with his long scout's hair under a Western hat, Cody suddenly entered the world of high society.

In a short while, Cody was on the stage himself, performing with Ned Buntline and fellow scout Texas Jack in a play called *Scouts of the Plains*. Although meant to be serious, the acting of all three proved so atrocious that the play had audiences rolling in the aisles with laughter. A New York reviewer called the play "so wonderfully bad it was almost good. The whole performance was so far aside of human experience, so wonderful in its daring feebleness, that no ordinary intellect is capable of comprehending it." Audiences packed the theaters for weeks on end. But then, suddenly Cody was called back to the West, for the Sioux were again on the warpath.

Shortly after Cody had returned to guide Gen. Eugene Carr's forces, they learned of the massacre of Custer's men at the Battle of the Little Big Horn. In revenge, Carr's men set out to pursue Indians along the border between Nebraska and Wyoming. Under Cody's guidance, they surprised a group of warriors at War Bonnet Creek. Cody shot the chief, Yellow Hand, and immediately scalped him, raising the scalp above his head with the cry "first scalp for Custer!" (Cody later claimed that he scalped the chief because he was wearing an American flag as a loincloth and had a lock of yellow hair from a white

woman's scalp pinned to his clothing.) The Sioux immediately fled. If Cody had been famous before, this event propelled him to even more acclaim. It became the grist for countless dimestore novels, and was embellished in so many ways over the years that the true story will never be known.

The Wild West Show

Buffalo Bill's days in the real Wild West were over, and he returned to staging shows, eventually starting his famed Wild West extravaganza. This was unlike anything ever done before, an outdoor circus that seemed to transport all who watched to the frontier. One newspaper remarked that Cody had "out-Barnumed Barnum." There were buffalo stampedes, cowboy bronc riding, Indians camps, a Deadwood stage and outlaws, crack shooting by Annie Oakley, and of course, Buffalo Bill. At its peak in the late 1890s, the show made Cody more than a million dollars in profit each year.

Amazingly, Sitting Bull and Buffalo Bill became good friends. Cody, who had earlier bragged of his many Indian killings, changed his attitude, eventually saying, "In nine cases out of 10 when there is trouble between white men and Indians, it will be found that the white man is responsible." Meanwhile, Cody's other attitudes continued to evolve. He criticized the buffalo hidehunters of the 1870s and 1880s for their reckless slaughter, and later became an ardent supporter of game preserves and limitations on hunting seasons.

holes. Rent mountain bikes from **Alpine Style Outdoor Shoppe**, 1234 Sheridan, tel. 527-6805. They also have good maps showing local mountain bike routes. **Swim** at the outdoor pool, 1240 Beck Ave., for 75¢ (kids 50¢), or the **Stock Natorium**, 9th St. and Beck Ave., for 50¢.

OTHER PRACTICALITIES

Shopping

Big Horn Gallery, 1167 Sheridan Ave., tel. 587-6762, contains a wide selection of Western and wildlife art prints and paintings. If you're a serious art patron, make an appointment to view the bronze pieces of nationally known sculptor **Harry Jackson** at his private studio. Call 587-5508 for details, but be ready to part with a hundred thou or so. Next to the chamber of commerce office is the **Cody Country Art League**, tel. 587-3597, with a variety of paintings, sculptures, and crafts for sale, plus workshops and judged art shows.

Corral West Ranchwear, 1202 Sheridan Ave., tel. 587-2122, has a large collection of big game heads and a couple of stuffed nine-foot-tall bears. Books are available at **The Thistle**, 1243 Rumsey, tel. 587-6635; **Wyoming Well Book Exchange**, 2220 Big Horn Ave., tel. 587-4249; and **Cody Newstand**, 1121 13th St., tel. 587-2843. **North Fork Fly & Tackle**, 937 Sheridan ave., tel. 527-7274, has anything you might need for fly-fishing, including professional fishing guides. Get camping and hiking supplies at **War Surplus** (there always does seem to be a surplus of wars, so you might as well buy a couple while you're in town), 130 N. Bent, tel. 754-2694. **Wilderness Canvas & Leather**, 1220 Sheridan, tel. 587-4580, does repairs on tents and packs.

Information And Services

The **Cody Country Chamber of Commerce**, 836 Sheridan Ave., tel. 587-2297, is open Mon.-

---

The Wild West Show became one of the most popular events anywhere in America and Europe, attracting crowds of up to 40,000 people. Queen Victoria was a special fan (although rumors of an affair are probably false). At the peak of his fame around the turn of the century, Buffalo Bill was arguably the world's best-known man. For the next decade the show continued to tour, gradually losing its originality as other forms of entertainment came along, especially movies. Cody used his money to buy the 40,000-acre TE Ranch in northwestern Wyoming near Yellowstone National Park. For him the Bighorn Basin was paradise. The town that he helped establish here was named Cody in his honor, and he backed the massive Shoshone irrigation project.

The End

Unfortunately, Buffalo Bill seemed to have no comprehension of how to save money. He was a notoriously soft touch, and would give money to almost anyone who asked. As his fortune slipped away and his show became more dated, Cody was finally forced to join up with the crooked owner of the *Denver Post*, H. H. Tammen. Tammen used the aging Cody's fame to attract people to his own circus. He forced Cody's Wild West Show into bankruptcy in 1913, selling off all the incredible collection of historical artifacts that had been amassed over the years, and leaving workers to find their own way home. Buffalo Bill was heartbroken, but still trusting Tammen, agreed to join his circus almost as a sideshow act.

Three years later, Cody died while visiting his sister in Denver and was buried on Lookout Mountain near Denver. Cody had wanted to be buried on Cedar Mountain above the town of Cody, but even this wish was denied by Tammen, who apparently paid Cody's widow Louisa $10,000 for the privilege of choosing the burial site (and to use the funeral parade to the burial site as an advertisement for his circus troop). When rumors came that folks from Wyoming intended to dig up Cody's body and take it back to its rightful burial place, Tammen had tons of concrete dumped on top of the grave.

Despite the tragic ending to Buffalo Bill's life, there are few individuals who lived such a diverse and adventure-filled life, and who could count so many people as his friends, from the lowliest beggar to the richest king. Cody's life spanned one of the most remarkable eras in American history, and his impact on American culture is still felt today, not just in the image of the West that he created and that lives on in hundreds of Western movies, but also in the Boy Scouts (an organization inspired partly by his exploits), the city of Cody, and even in the dude ranches that dot Wyoming.

Sat. 8-7, and Sun. 10-3 during the summer and Mon.-Fri. 8-5 the rest of the year. This log building housed the original Buffalo Bill Museum from 1927 to 1969, and was built as a replica of Cody's TE Ranch. It is on the National Register of Historic Places. For a list of other historic buildings in town, pick up a walking-tour map from the chamber. Be sure to also get the free *Cody Country Summer Guide* here for up-to-date regional information. The **Park County Library**, 1057 Sheridan Ave., tel. 587-6204, is open Mon.-Fri. 10-5:30, Sat. 10-1, and Mon. 7-9 p.m. The BLM's **Cody Resources Office** is at 1714 Stampede Ave., tel. 587-2216, while the Forest Service's **Shoshone National Forest Supervisor's Office** is at 225 W. Yellowstone Ave., tel. 527-6241.

Transportation

Yellowstone Regional Airport is just east of town on U.S. 14-16-20. **Mesa Airlines**, tel. (800) 637-2247, has daily flights to Denver via Laramie and Worland. **Continental Express**, tel. (800) 525-0280, and **United Express**, tel. (800) 241-6522, fly directly to Denver. Rent cars at the airport from **Avis**, (800) 331-1212, or **Hertz**, tel. (800) 654-3131. Daily summertime tours of Yellowstone National Park ($38) are available through **Powder River Transportation** at Buffalo Bill Village, 1701 Sheridan Ave., tel. 344-5555, or (800) 442-3682. This can also be used to transfer to buses en route to Jackson. Unfortunately, there is no direct service to the rest of Wyoming, although **Cody Bus Lines**, 1734 17th St., tel. 587-4181, has daily bus service to Billings, Montana..

MEETEETSE

Along the western edge of Bighorn Basin is a charming little ranching center called Meeteetse (pop. 570). The name is a Crow Indian word meaning "Meeting Place of the Chiefs." The Absarokas rise gently to the south and west, and the Greybull River flows right through town, cottonwood trees on either side. To the north, the highway crosses a rolling land of sage and greasewood, while to the south are rugged badlands. The town has wooden sidewalks and hitching rails; cattle drives right down Main St.; and not just one, but two free museums. The last wild black-footed ferrets (see p. 68) were discovered just a dozen miles to the west at the famed Pitchfork Ranch. They were captured in 1987 after an outbreak of canine distemper threatened to kill all the remaining wild ferrets.

One of the oldest towns in Bighorn Basin, Meeteetse was first settled in the early 1880s by homesteaders and wealthy European cattle barons. By 1890 it was the largest town in the basin. Several original buildings are still standing, including the **Meeteetse Mercantile**, built in 1899, and still stocked with everything you might need to survive. Come to Meeteetse on **Labor Day weekend** for a small town parade, country rodeo, barbecue, street dance, and crafts fair. The two local museums are: the **Meeteetse Archives**, located in the old Hogg, Cheeseman, and MacDonald's Bank (1901), and the larger **Town Hall Museum**, built in 1900. They contain antiques, guns, old bottles, historic photographs, and other items. Both are open Sun. 1-4 and Mon.-Sat. 11-5 during the summer, or by appointment at other times, tel. 868-2423. The **Forest Service District Office** is at 2044 State St., tel. 868-2379.

Oasis Motel, 1702 State St., tel. 868-2551, has cabins for $25 s or $30 d, along with campsites for $7 and RV spots for $10. Open June-October. **Vision Quest Motel**, 2207 State St., tel. 868-2512, charges $25 s or d. **Lucille's Cafe**, 1906 State St., tel. 868-9909, is the place to go for meals, and the adjacent **Elkhorn Bar** is a meeting spot for local folks, especially on weekend evenings when country bands play. Check out the old photos from early-day Meeteetse. **High Island Guest Ranch** in Hamilton Dome, tel. 867-2374, provides a chance to take part in cattle drives and other cowpoke adventures on a working ranch. Visits by the week only.

MEETEETSE AREA

The excellent **Wood River Valley Ski Touring Park** (free) is 22 miles southwest of town on Wood River Road. Meeteetse Recreation District, tel. 868-2603, runs the park and provides ski rentals in town. The cross-country skiing area includes 25 km of groomed trails, wonderful mountain scenery, a warming hut, and an overnight tent with wood stove ($15 per group per night; reserve ahead). It's open daily through the winter. The drive up Wood River Rd. is also enjoyable at other times of the year, offering the chance to see moose and elk in the bottomlands. Two free Forest Service **campgrounds** are available near the end of the road. From here you can hike into the Washakie Wilderness along any of several different trails, or from Jack Creek Trailhead at the end of the road up the Greybull River. The latter road passes historic Palatte Ranch, once owned by A.A. Anderson, first superintendent of the Yellowstone Timber Reserve (now Shoshone National Forest).

Legend Rock Petroglyph Site

One of the finest sites for Indian rock art in all Wyoming lies between Meeteetse and Thermopolis in the foothills of the Owl Creek Mountains. Head 31 miles southeast of Meeteetse on U.S. 120, and turn left at the Hamilton Dome road (signed). After five miles, turn right onto the gravel Cottonwood Creek Road. Immediately after the second cattle guard, turn left and follow the road to a Y, staying to the left. Continue through a gate (be sure to close it behind you), and park your car at the hairpin curve. If the road is wet, park just beyond the gate and walk down to the site. The total distance from Hwy. 120 to the petroglyph site is eight miles.

At least 283 petroglyphs have been found on the nearby sandstone cliffs, covering a variety of styles, including some that resemble X-ray vision. The most unusual is a huge flying rabbit. The rock art is believed to have been associated with shamanism and ritual healing, and may date back for 2,000 years. The area is currently being developed as a state park with interpretive signs and trails. Shoshone or Arapaho guides are sometimes here. Northwest of Meeteetse is another important Indian site, the **Great Arrow**, a 58-foot-long arrow made from rocks and placed atop a long hogback ridge. It points toward the Medicine Wheel (see p. 368) in the Big Horn Mountains, 70 miles to the northeast. Its age is unknown. Ask locally for directions.

HEART MOUNTAIN RELOCATION CENTER

Halfway between Cody and Powell is Heart Mountain, so named because it faintly resembles the traditional valentine shape. The mountain is visible for many miles in all directions. Geologists scratch their heads over this seemingly upside-down mountain. The Heart Mountain detachment fault stretches for over a hundred miles, cutting southwest from near Cooke City, Montana. To the east are enormous blocks of land that have slid onto the top of more recent deposits, reversing the normal situation in which older rocks lie beneath more recent ones. Scientists know that these limestone and dolomite blocks moved around 45 to 50 million years ago, but none have been able to adequately explain how entire mountains, including Heart Mountain, could have slid for dozens of miles.

History

For Americans of Japanese ancestry, Heart Mountain might as well have been called Broken Heart Mountain. After the Japanese attack on Pearl Harbor in 1941, Japanese-Americans found their patriotism under increasing suspicion, and the following spring, President Roosevelt signed an executive order establishing the War Relocation Authority to move them away from the coasts. The authority built 10 remote "relocation centers" to imprison anyone of Japanese ancestry, including one just east of Heart Mountain that housed nearly 11,000 Japanese-Americans (two-thirds of them born in America). The camp became Wyoming's third-largest settlement. It took just 62 days to complete the 468 barracks, 40 laundry-toilet buildings, Buddhist and Christian churches, high school, fire station, recreation hall, power station, mess hall, hospital, sewage plant, administrative offices, and numerous other structures. (No environmental impact reports on this baby!) Barbed wire surrounded the perimeter, and military police manned nine guard towers with high-beam searchlights.

Most of the Japanese-Americans took the forced relocation with remarkable aplomb, realizing the futility of any escape attempt. It almost seemed the patriotic thing to do; "shikata-ga-nai" (or "I guess it cannot be helped") became the accepted phrase. Although life in the camp maintained a sense of normalcy—some kids came to enjoy their peaceful high school years and the picnics in Yellowstone—the camp was far from idyllic. Three or four people were jammed into each room, furniture was minimal, people had to share communal bathhouses, and the winter winds blew through the uninsulated tar paper buildings. Wyoming folks resented the Japanese-Americans, but appreciated the cheap farm labor that they supplied while their sons were off fighting the Germans and Japanese.

With the war's end in 1945, the camp was closed and the internees were allowed to return home (or rather to what remained; many found their homes ransacked). Over the next four years the 740 acres of land was opened to homesteading, with the barracks being sold at two for $1. Most ended up as temporary homes for the new settlers. None of the Japanese-American interns remained in the area, and most have little desire to even visit what seemed such a desolate, god-forsaken place. They would rather try to forget. Today the only reminders of the camp are the old hospital heating plant with its tall brick chimney, some root cellars, and a couple of plaques, one noting the more than 600 men who left the camp to join the U.S. Army in Europe. Twenty-one internees and a camp teacher did not return. The never-ending wind is rapidly erasing the names of those who fought.

There are plans to return an old barracks to the site as a lasting monument to one of the more trying chapters in American race relations. The site is 11 miles east of Cody on U.S. 14A. Barley fields now surround the former camp, while Heart Mountain guards the western flank. The nonprofit **Heart Mountain Relocation Center Memorial Association**, Box 774, Ralston, WY 82440, works to preserve the memory of this era.

POWELL

One of the nicest settlements in Bighorn Basin is Powell (pop. 5,800), a farming, oil, and college town halfway between Cody and Lovell. Sugar beets, malting barley (grown for Coors and Anheuser-Busch), and dry beans are the primary crops grown here. Because they are harvested at different times of the year, many farmers grow all three. The big elevators of Powell Bean Growers Association and Baker Bean & Feed border the railroad tracks on the south edge of town. A dozen miles to the north is the giant Elk Basin oil field. First discovered in 1915, it had 150 wells pumping more than 4,200 barrels a day within five years. The field has proven a major factor in the growth of the northern Bighorn Basin. Although production is gradually declining as the supply is exhausted, modern recovery techniques pushed pumping over 11,000 barrels per day in the 1980s. The U.S. Air Force also maintains a radar installation just west of Powell.

History

Powell was named for Maj. John Wesley Powell (1834-1902), the famed one-armed explorer of the Colorado River, and an early director of the U.S. Geological Survey. His 1889 report on the agricultural potential of western desert lands had declared the value of irrigation in "reclaiming" these areas through dams and canal systems funded by the government. One of the earliest of these was the mammoth Shoshone Project, involving Buffalo Bill Dam and a series of canals to feed water to the fields along the Shoshone River. Powell is right at the center of all this irrigation, and homesteaders flocked here in the first two decades of this century. (Because of the abundance of water from the project, there are no water meters in Powell.) The town sprang up at a campsite used by workers on the Shoshone Project. With the arrival of the Chicago, Burlington and Quincy Railroad (now Burlington Northern), Powell became an agricultural shipping point.

Folks still talk about "Tarzan of the Tetons," a local kid gone bad. **Earl Durand** was a crack shot and a mountain man of sorts. He had once traveled by horse and foot to Mexico, and could live on anything, even raw bobcat meat. Durand hated being cooped up inside buildings, so when he was arrested for poaching in 1939, he escaped the Cody jail by striking an undersheriff on the head with a milk bottle and forcing him to drive to his parents' place. Five people died in the shooting rampage that followed, and the murders attracted intense national attention. The climax came when Durand robbed a Powell bank and suddenly found himself surrounded. A 17-year-old kid shot, but didn't kill, Durand as he came out of the bank with a screen of hostages. Sensing the futility of the situation, he went back inside and committed suicide. Powell's Homesteader Museum has lots of old newspaper clippings on this sad story, and the incident inspired a minor 1974 movie that starred Slim Pickens, Peter Haskell, and Martin Sheen, *The Legend of Earl Durand*.

Sights

The free **Homesteader Museum**, on the corner of 1st and Clark streets, tel. 754-9481, is open Tues.-Fri. 1-5 May-Sept., and Fri. and Sat. 10-5 the rest of the year. The museum captures the hardscrabble life of turn-of-the-century homesteaders in the northern Bighorn Basin. You'll find interesting old photographs, a beautiful collection of dryhead agate, and some Indian artifacts. The grotesque elk chairs and furniture in the back corner are unique, to say the least. Lots more junk to check out. Be sure to take the time to watch the videotape detailing the history of the nearby Heart Mountain Relocation Center (see above). An adjacent building is

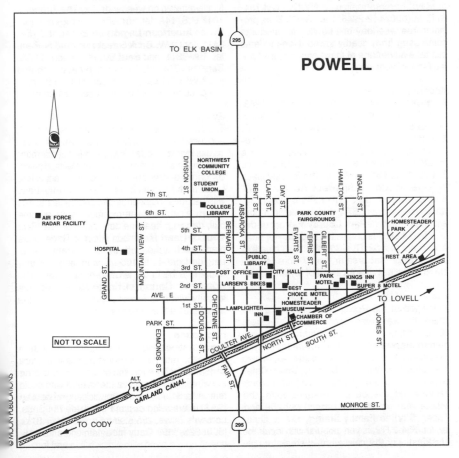

POWELL

NOT TO SCALE

TO ELK BASIN

TO LOVELL

TO CODY

AIR FORCE RADAR FACILITY

HOSPITAL

NORTHWEST COMMUNITY COLLEGE

STUDENT UNION

COLLEGE LIBRARY

PARK COUNTY FAIRGROUNDS

HOMESTEADER PARK

REST AREA

PUBLIC LIBRARY

POST OFFICE

CITY HALL

LARSEN'S BIKES

PARK MOTEL

KINGS INN

SUPER 8 MOTEL

BEST CHOICE MOTEL

HOMESTEADER MUSEUM

LAMPLIGHTER INN

CHAMBER OF COMMERCE

DIVISION ST.

7th ST.

6th ST.

5th ST.

4th ST.

3rd ST.

2nd ST.

AVE. E

1st ST.

PARK ST.

MOUNTAIN VIEW ST.

GRAND ST.

BERNARD ST.

ABSAROKA ST.

BENT ST.

CLARK ST.

DAY ST.

EVARTS ST.

FERRIS ST.

GILBERT ST.

HAMILTON ST.

INGALLS ST.

CHEYENNE ST.

DOUGLAS ST.

EDMONDS ST.

COULTER AVE.

FAIR ST.

NORTH ST.

SOUTH ST.

JONES ST.

MONROE ST.

ALT. 14

GARLAND CANAL

© MOON PUBLICATIONS

filled with horse-drawn machines and old tractors, while outside are a caboose and various pieces of old farm equipment.

Founded in 1946, **Northwest Wyoming Community College** (NWCC) is one of the state's top junior colleges. The 95-acre campus is quite attractive, with modern brick buildings and fluorescent green lawns (at least in the summer). Two-thirds of the students live on campus, but the school does offer evening classes in the surrounding towns. NWCC is a cultural and social center for Powell and the area, bringing a variety of theater productions and entertainment, plus art exhibits at the **Northwest Gallery**. (open Mon.-Fri. 8 to 5 from Sept. to May). For information on NWCC, call 754-6111 or (800) 442-2946. The **NWCC Bus**, provides free weekday bus service for students commuting from nearby towns. Non-students can take advantage of these connections for a fee (school year only).

Accommodations
Best Choice Motel, 337 E. 2nd, tel. 754-2243, offers budget motel accommodations for $23 s or $25 d. A bit nicer are **Park Motel**, 737 E. 2nd, tel. 754-2233, for $28 s or $32 d; **Lamplighter Inn**, 234 1st St., tel. 754-2226, for $26 s or $28 d; and **Super 8 Motel**, 845 E. Coulter, tel. 754-7231, for $31 s or $37 d. The fanciest place in Powell is **King's Inn (Best Western)**, 777 E. 2nd St., tel. 754-5117 or (800) 528-1234, where rooms cost $57 s or d, including a pool and steam baths. **Park County Fairgrounds**, tel. 754-5421, has campsites and shower facilities. Tents cost $2; RVs, $6. RVers often park at the highway rest area in the 57-acre **Homesteader Park** on the east end of town.

Food
At the top of the Powell food chain is a little hole-in-the-wall greasy spoon called **Munchies**, 333 E. 2nd, tel. 754-2683. Good breakfasts, authentic Mexican food, and homemade pies. Highly recommended. Easily the least expensive meal deal in Powell is the **Student Union Cafeteria** on the college campus. It's just a snack bar on weekdays, but on weekends during the school year, is open for brunch ($2.25!) and dinner. **Skyline Family Dining**, 141 E. Coulter, tel. 754-2772, is very popular with locals for breakfast. Try the chicken-fried steak for din-

ner. **Hansel & Gretel's**, 113 S. Bent, tel. 754-2191, makes good spaghetti, soups, and sandwiches. For more elegant dining, and a juicy steak, visit **The Lamplighter Inn**, 234 E. 1st, tel. 754-2226. There is a nice salad bar at **The Burgher Haus**, 749 E. 2nd, tel. 754-5721, and **Powell Drug**, 140 N. Bent, tel. 754-2031, has an old-fashioned soda fountain. **Candy World**, 112 N. Bent, tel. 754-9236, is two doors down from the Diet Center. Coincidence? Get groceries at **Blairs Market**, 210 S. Douglas, tel. 754-3122, or **Food Basket IGA**, 421 E. 1st, tel. 754-3602.

Entertainment
Since this is a college town, you can always find live music on weekends. Try **The Timbers**, 1017 U.S. 14A, tel. 754-9581, for rock or country, or **American Legion** on E. 1st, tel. 754-3411, for C&W. **Back Street Pub**, 146 S. Bent, tel. 754-9811, and **Bent Street Station**, 117 S. Bent, tel. 754-3384, may also have rock and roll. NWCC's **Pub** in the Student Union Building is a popular student hangout before 10 p.m.

Events
The two main events in Powell follow in quick succession in late July and early August. First comes **Homesteader Days**, with frontier demonstrations, crafts for sale, races, contests, picnics, concerts, a street dance, and other activities. Later in the month is the **Park County Fair**, with parades, horseshoe pitching contests, 4-H shows, a demolition derby, tractor pulls, a horse pull, dancing, headline acts, and carnival. The **Tour of Heart Mountain Bicycle Race** takes place each June, with three different events ranging from 40 to 100 miles in length. If you happen to be in the area in early December, stop by for **Country Christmas**, a three-day festivity with a variety of activities and craft exhibits, plus a live nativity scene.

Recreation
Homesteader Park has a number of modern recreation facilities, including a pool where you can swim for $1 (kids and seniors 75¢). During the winter, there is an ice arena here with skate rentals for $1. A nine-hole municipal **golf course** ($5-8) is five miles east of Powell, tel. 754-3039. **Larsen's Bikes**, 255 E. 2nd St., tel. 754-5481 or (800) 325-7653, rents mountain bikes for $15/day.

Information And Services

The **Powell Valley Chamber of Commerce**, 111 S. Day, tel. 754-3494 or (800) 325-4278 (outside Wyoming), is open Mon.-Fri. 8:30-4:30. The new **Powell Public Library**, 217 E. 3rd, tel. 754-2261, is open Mon.-Fri. 10-5:30, Mon. and Thurs. 7-9 p.m., and Sat. 10-1. **John Hinckley Memorial Library**, on the NWCC campus, tel. 754-6207, is open Sun. 2-10, Mon.-Thurs. 7:45 a.m.-10 p.m., Fri. 7:45-4, and Sat. 11-4. (No, it isn't named for the man who shot former President Reagan.) Get books at the **College Bookstore** at the NWCC Student Union, tel. 754-6308. The **Shoshone National Forest District Office** is 2¹/₂ miles west of town, tel. 754-2407.

EAST TO LOVELL

A tangle of roads wanders through the country between Lovell and Powell, tying together a cluster of small agriculture and oil settlements established by Mormon emigrants. **Byron** (pop. 600) has quite a few old log buildings and is surrounded by dairy farms. Just two miles south of the Montana border on U.S. 310 lies **Frannie** (pop. 100), straddling the line between Park and Big Horn counties. Residents say it's "The Biggest Little Town in Wyoming because it takes two counties to hold the people." Stop by **Frannie Tack Shop**, tel. 548-2344, to see the saddles or to get repairs on canvas or leather items. In **Deaver** (pop. 170) be sure to drop in at the unusual **Showboat Dinner Theatre**, tel. 664-2504, for live music and dramas with your dinner. The dot of a place called **Garland** (pop. 50) has a wonderful old schoolhouse (now used as a church) built in the early 1900s.

Just east of Lovell, the pungent odors of sulfur and oil hang in the air, and the dry badlands are punctuated by oil pumpjacks. More than 117 million barrels of oil and 13 million cubic feet of gas have been produced in the Byron Oil Field since it's discovery in 1918. The other business here is farming. Much of this desert land is now under irrigation, and the lush green farmlands are filled with sugar beets, beans, malting barley, alfalfa, and corn. A sign along Hwy. 14A notes the **Sidon Canal**, built in 1900 by Mormon settlers of the Bighorn Basin. The 37-mile-long canal was entirely self-financed with land donated by the government, and transports water from the Shoshone River to 20,000 acres of farm land. Mormons claim that "Prayer Rock," a large impediment to the canal's construction, was miraculously split as a result of their supplications.

LOVELL

The sleepy little burg of Lovell (pop. 2,300; pronounced LOVE-ul) calls itself the "City of Roses," a title that comes from Dr. William Horsley, who lived here from 1924 till his death in 1971. Horsley loved roses, and in the course of a lifetime of cultivating them, became one of the nation's foremost authorities. The "Rose Doctor's" enthusiasm rubbed off on others, and today gardens all over town are packed with roses. Oil fields crowd around Lovell, and a Georgia Pacific wallboard plant and two bentonite plants are substantial local employers, but farming is king. The Western Sugar factory stands on the edge of town, providing jobs for workers and a market for local farmers who contract with the plant to grow sugar beets. In late fall, huge mounds of straw-covered beets pile up beside the factory and the odor of cooking beets fills the air with a slightly sweet, slightly rancid smell. Stray beets, spilled from overloaded farm trucks, lie along the highway for miles. Lovell doesn't offer much for tourists, but the surrounding country includes Bighorn National Recreation Area and the Big Horn Mountains. A state-run fish rearing station at Tillett Springs, 17 miles north of Lovell, raises cutthroat and rainbow trout.

Like most towns in the northern Bighorn Basin, Lovell is dominated by Mormons. An enormous brick LDS church fills an entire block along the main drag, but the decaying town that surrounds the church is a real let down. It's easy to see analogies between Lovell and the European villages with their magnificent Catholic churches surrounded by poor peasants. Something like half of downtown has boarded-up windows, a reflection of the depressed oil and ranching economy, and of a community torn apart by one of the most ignominious crimes in recent Wyoming history.

History

The town of Lovell has its roots in the great ML Ranch, founded in 1880 by Anthony L. Mason and Henry Clay Lovell. Lovell trailed herds of cattle up from Kansas to this newly opened country, building his main headquarters along the Bighorn River, just east of the community that was later named for him. The vast unfenced ranch became known as the "Big Outfit," and employed hundreds of cowhands. Grazed by 25,000 cattle, it stretched from Thermopolis all the way to the Crow Reservation in Montana, 90 miles away.

In 1900, Mormon settlers moved to the remote Bighorn Basin (partly to escape prosecution for polygamy), working on the Burlington Railroad and developing irrigation projects. The area boomed with the discovery of natural gas and the opening of various factories. A few years later, German emigrants provided labor for the farm fields and then settled down to acquire their own land. With completion of U.S. 14A through the Big Horn Mountains in 1925, Lovell found itself along one of the main routes to Yellowstone. Yellowtail Dam on the Bighorn River was built in 1965, and the surrounding land became a national recreation area the following year.

Lovell claims to have the lowest crime rate in Wyoming, but nowhere in the tourist brochures do they mention the history of two of its most prominent doctors. A few years before his 1971 death, Dr. William Horsley, the famed "Rose Doctor," was forced to resign from the local hospital following a series of homosexual incidents with boys. But another respected physician, Dr. John Story, gained considerably more notoriety for his actions. Story arrived in 1958 to practice general medicine, joining the local Baptist church, and becoming a strong conservative community leader. Unfortunately, over the next 25 years he also raped or molested dozens (some say hundreds) of women and girls in his office. A combination of strict Mormon upbringing, sexual ignorance, shame, and fear prevented them from talking, and the few who did speak up were called liars. Finally, in 1983, the charges began to surface. The trial turned Lovell inside out. Despite intense pressure from local and state politicians (then-Governor Herschler called the victims' testimony "hogwash"), Story was convicted in April 1985 of several rape charges and is currently serving a 20-year sentence in the Wyoming State Penitentiary. Jack Olson's harrowing book, *Doc*, describes this sorry chapter in recent Wyoming history. It is perhaps fitting that Lovell will be the site of a new state prison currently under construction.

Accommodations

Western Motel, 180 W. Main St., tel. 548-2231, offers basic accommodations for $21 s or $25 d. **Horseshoe Bend Motel**, 375 E. Main St., tel. 548-2221, charges $22 s or $25 d, including kitchenettes and a pool; while **Cattleman Motel**, 470 Montana Ave., tel. 548-2296, provides comfortable rooms for $25 s or $28 d. **Super 8 Motel**, 595 E. Main St., tel. 548-2725 or (800) 843-1991, costs $27 s or $30 d. The **TX Ranch**, a 10,000-acre cattle ranch, offers a unique chance to take part in ranch life. It isn't a dude ranch, and visitors end up joining in cattle drives, branding calves, and doing roundups. The living conditions are not luxurious (tents), but the country is. Call (406) 484-2583 for details. The best campsites in the Lovell area lie within nearby Bighorn Canyon National Recreation Area (see below). In town, camp for free (including showers!) at **Lovell Camper Park** on Quebec Ave. north of Main St., or pay to stay at **Camp Big Horn RV Park**, 595 E. Main St., tel. 548-2725.

Food

Rose Bowl Cafe, 483 Shoshone Ave., tel. 548-7121, is popular for breakfast and lunch; try one of their big cinnamon rolls. **Juan's Restaurant** on Main St. near Montana Ave. has authentic Mexican food for very reasonable prices. Recommended. For pizzas, try **Pizza on the Run**, 214 Main St., tel. 548-2206. **Grandma's**, 443 E. Main, tel. 548-7134, offers fast food. The nicest local eatery is **Big Horn Restaurant**, 605 E. Main St., tel. 548-6811, where locals and visitors come for a dinner out or to enjoy a leisurely breakfast. Get groceries at **Big Horn IGA**, 9 E. Main St., tel. 548-9907. While there, take a gander at the War Memorial.

Information And Services

For local info, head to the **Town Hall**, 336 Nevada Ave., tel. 548-7552. Rent cars from **Murphey Ford**, 80 E. Main, tel. 548-6546. There's a big indoor **pool**, along with other recreation facilities on the southwest end of town. The big annual event in Lovell is **Mustang Days**, held the third week in June. Activities include parades (look for the cancan dancers), fireworks, barbecues, and a rodeo. Since the town has a bentonite plant, it is also home to **American Colloid Days**, in early August.

BIGHORN CANYON NATIONAL RECREATION AREA

Just east of Lovell is one of America's lesser-known but most stunning sights, Bighorn Canyon. Over the eons, the Bighorn River has slowly carved out a 2,200-foot-deep chasm through the desert country. Since 1965, when the 525-foot-tall Yellowtail Dam was completed, the canyon has lain under a deep blanket of water, water that provides 250,000 kilowatts of electricity for the western U.S, and that irrigates thousands of acres of Montana farmland. The dam itself is—as the raven flies—more than 20 miles north of the Wyoming-Montana border, but its impact reaches 70 river miles upstream, creating Bighorn Lake. The upper parts of the lake are shallow, and by late summer when the reservoir has been drawn down, the stretch of water that maps show Hwy. 14A crossing east of Lovell is actually just the river surrounded by marshland.

The 120,000-acre Bighorn Canyon National Recreation Area (no charge) is managed by the National Park Service. Separate facilities on both ends of the recreation area are linked by a circuitous 180-mile route that takes you through Billings. For this reason, most road-bound visitors come to either the Montana side or the Wyoming side, but not both. Boaters can traverse the entire reach of the canyon. Attractions accessible only from Montana include the dam itself (daily tours available through the summer), tel. (406) 666-2358, the nearby **Ft. Smith Visitor Center**, tel. (406) 666-2339, a short nature trail, and the site of two Bozeman Trail features: Fort C. F. Smith and the Hayfield Fight (both on private land).

From the Wyoming side, things are considerably more interesting, even though some of the sights actually lie across the Montana border. A paved road extends for 27 miles along the western side of the recreation area, with a rough dirt road continuing 15 more miles to the Crow Indian Reservation. Along the way are a couple of campgrounds, the historic Bad Pass Trail, two old ranches, magnificent Devil Canyon, and a good chance to see bighorn sheep and wild horses. The road cuts through impressive red and gray badlands carpeted by juniper and sagebrush.

For a good orientation to the area, stop by **Bighorn Canyon Visitor Center**, tel. 548-2251, just east of Lovell along U.S. 14A. It's open daily 8-6 in the summer, or Sat. and Sun. 8-5 the rest of the year. Opened in 1977, this solar-heated center is an attraction in itself; 70% of its heat comes directly from the sun. Inside are a relief map of the canyon, displays on local animals, books and topo maps for sale, plus slide shows and films. Check the notice board for other talks or hikes in the recreation area, including the weekend **campfire programs** at Horseshoe Bend Campground (summer only). Be sure to pick up a copy of *Canyon Echoes,* the free visitor guide with current information. Ranger stations are found at Horseshoe Bend and in an old log house at Hough Creek.

Camping

There are three campgrounds in the southern half of Bighorn Canyon. Folks in RVs park at **Horseshoe Bend** ($3). It has water and toilets, but just one lone tree for shade, making this a rather bleak place for anyone in a tent. The drive in to Horseshoe Bend passes lovely red sandstone badlands. **Barry's Landing Campground** is much nicer (and also much smaller). No charge, but bring your own water. In addition, you can pitch a tent at the free **Medicine Creek Campground**, though you'll need to hike in on a two-mile dirt road or come in by boat. Backcountry camping is available throughout the southern end of the recreation area, but be sure to get a permit at the visitor center first. Also be sure to avoid trespassing on the nearby Crow Indian Reservation.

BIGHORN CANYON NATIONAL RECREATION AREA

FORT SMITH VISITOR CENTER

AFTERBAY
YELLOWTAIL DAM
PARK HEADQUARTERS
OK - A - BEH'

313

CROW INDIAN RESERVATION BOUNDARY

CROW INDIAN RESERVATION

LOCKHART RANCH
MEDICINE CREEK CAMPGROUND
HILLSBORO
BARRY'S LANDING
HOUGH CR. RANGER STATION

BIGHORN CANYON

PRYOR MOUNTAIN WILD HORSE RANGE

DEVIL CANYON OVERLOOK
DEVIL CANYON

MONTANA
WYOMING

MONTANA
WYOMING

HORSESHOE BEND

37

BIGHORN LAKE

TO COWLEY

SHOSHONE RIVER

310

LOVELL

ALT.
14

BIGHORN CANYON VISITOR CENTER

TO POWELL

310
789

TO GREYBULL

MASON - LOVELL RANCH

ALT.
14

TO BIGHORN NAT'L. FOREST & SHERIDAN

BIG HORN RIVER

Inset map:

87

94

BIG HORN RIVER

BILLINGS
I-90

HARDIN

212

CUSTER BATTLEFIELD NATIONAL MONUMENT

212
310

CROW INDIAN RESERVATION

313

FORT SMITH

BIGHORN CANYON NATIONAL RECREATION AREA

MONTANA
WYOMING

COWLEY

ALT.
14

114

LOVELL

ALT.
14

87

90

SHERIDAN

CODY
POWELL

SHOSHONE RIVER

310

16
20

14

GREYBULL

16
20

BIGHORN NATIONAL FOREST

120

0   5mi

0   5km

Recreation

Most visitors come to Bighorn Canyon to play on the water. You'll see lots of people tooling around in powerful boats, towing water-skiers, trolling for fish, or windsurfing. Fishing is the biggest attraction, with walleye, rainbow, and brown trout, yellow perch, ling, crappie, and catfish commonly caught. Note that because the lake straddles the state line, you need to purchase fishing licenses for both Wyoming and Montana if you plan on cruising around the lake. Launch ramps are at Barry's Landing and Horseshoe Bend, plus several other sites at the north end of the lake. Swimmers hang out at the Horseshoe Bend swim beach, the only place with a lifeguard (Fri.-Tuesday).

The Park Service provides free two-hour **canoe tours** of the canyon several times a week during the summer. See the visitor center for specifics. **Horseshoe Bend Marina**, tel. 548-7766, is open daily in summer and rents boats, inner tubes, air mattresses, water-skis, and sells food and beer. Ok-A-Beh Boater Service on the northern end has more limited supplies. For something different, try a **boat tour** of the canyon by S-S Enterprises, tel. 548-6418. Available mid-June to mid-Sept. only, these 1 1/2-hour trips provide a good chance to glimpse the magnificent canyon walls from below. Led by experienced guides, they cost $12.50 for adults, $10 for seniors, $8.50 for students, and $5 for children under 5. Bring your camera!

Hiking is almost unheard of in Bighorn Canyon, but the open badland country makes it relatively easy, even when there are few real trails. Best times are in the fall or in February or March when temperatures are milder and you're less likely to meet a rattler. Prairie rattlesnakes and black widow spiders are both common in this desert country, so be aware, especially when exploring old buildings. **Crooked Creek Nature Trail**, a short path with self-guiding brochures, takes off from the Horseshoe Bend campground. You can also hike the mile-long dirt path to **Hillsboro** and the 2 1/2-mile road to the **Lockhart Ranch**.

Sights

The visitor center loans out free 45-minute cassette tapes (and recorders) that provide an informative tour of Bighorn Canyon. The pièce de résistance of the National Recreation Area is **Devil Canyon**, at the confluence of the Bighorn River and Porcupine Creek. From the overlook, the earth drops suddenly away. More than a thousand feet below, motorboats look like miniature toys in a bathtub. A real treat in the canyon is the chance to see **bighorn sheep** up close. Although the more impressive rams tend to hang out in remote parts of the Pryor Mountains most of the year, ewes and lambs can be seen along the road between Horseshoe Bend and Devil Canyon Overlook. The rams are more likely to be seen during the Nov.-Dec. rutting season.

The ghost settlement of **Hillsboro** is about a mile above Barry's Landing, and is accessible only by foot. Established around the turn of the century by a self-proclaimed physician, Grosverner William Barry, the site was originally a goldmining center. When that didn't "pan out," he turned to dude ranching, promoting his ranch as a place where guests could cruise through Bighorn Canyon on motorboats or ride the English Hackney horses. The dude ranch flourished until the 1930s, but the collection of antique furniture and paintings was destroyed by a fire in the winter of 1947-48. Still standing are the old post office and various cabins.

Precipitous Bighorn Canyon was known as **Bad Pass** by the Indians. The trail they used to reach the buffalo herds followed the canyon rim for many miles, marked by rock cairns. Some of these cairns are still visible between Devil Canyon Overlook and Barry's Landing, as are some of the caves where they wintered near the canyon bottoms. The river offered a torrent of rushing rapids and falls, with jagged rocks waiting to punch holes in any boat, and a canyon so deep that the sun only reached the bottom for a brief period each day. In 1825, the famed mountain man and guide Jim Bridger decided to take a wooden raft down the canyon to see if it could provide a way to ship furs back east. It was a feat that was not matched for over a century, when a motorboat finally ran the wild currents.

Most of the buildings from the old **ML Ranch** of Henry Clay Lovell are now gone, but you can still visit the restored bunkhouse, blacksmith shop, and two cabins. Most interesting is the bunkhouse, actually three cabins connected by dogtrots (covered breezeways). The end cabins acted as sleeping quarters, while the middle one was a cook shack and mess hall. Get here by heading east from Lovell across the bridge over Bighorn Reservoir. A sign points out the ranch. Check at the visitor center for tours.

Adjacent to the recreation area is the 19,424-acre **Yellowtail Wildlife Habitat Management Unit**, a popular place for hunters and bird-watchers. Lots of dirt roads and trails crisscross the area, and wildlife of all types abound. During fall migration, the wetlands here are jammed with up to 10,000 ducks. Get a map of the roads and trails of Yellowtail at the Bighorn Visitor Center.

Caves create a latticework under portions of the recreation area. On the east side of Bighorn Lake is **Bighorn Caverns**. Access is limited to experienced spelunkers and requires 4WD vehicles; get the gate key and directions at the Bighorn Visitor Center. This cave is also linked with **Horsethief Cave** several miles north. Although closed to the public, **Natural Trap Cave** is of biological value. Located 35 miles northeast of Lovell, a 12- by 15-foot opening drops into the 65-foot-deep cavern. Over the centuries many animals—from prehistoric horses to rabbits—have fallen in.

Pryor Mountain Wild Horse Range

Bordering on the western side of Bighorn Canyon is 47,000 acres of rugged country set aside in 1968 as the nation's first wild horse preserve. (Two other wild horse ranges now exist in Nevada and Colorado, and there are another 3,000 wild horses in the Red Desert of southwestern Wyoming.) Managed by the BLM, Pryor Mountain's desert country contains three herds to-

talling approximately 120 wild horses. Many of them remain out of sight in remote box canyons, but you're likely to see some relatively tame ones along the road between Horseshoe Bend and Hough Creek Ranger Station, especially during cooler parts of the year.

The "wild horses" of the West are probably of mixed origins. Some folks claim that the Pryor Mountain horses originated from Spanish mustangs that escaped Hernando Cortes' 1519 expedition into Mexico. They note that some of the horses lack the sixth vertebra or have the fifth and sixth vertebrae fused—as did the Spanish horses. But others note that many of the truly wild horses were killed by ranchers in the 1920s and '30s, and that during WW II domestic horses were released into the wild since local ranchers had lost their cowhands to the war effort. Critics also note that it isn't just the Spanish horses that have fused or missing vertebrae; so do some quarter horses. Take your pick on whom to believe.

Prior to protection of the wild horses, many were rounded up for use on ranches or for the glue factory, but with their protection in 1971 (it's now illegal to harass or kill a wild horse), the numbers began to grow rapidly. Each year's colt crop increases the herd by 20%, creating conflicts with deer, elk, and antelope. Today, the BLM controls numbers through its adopt-a-horse program, removing 20 to 30 horses a year from Pryor Mountain and offering them to the public. For details on acquiring a wild horse, contact the BLM at 810 E. Main St. Billings, MT 59105, tel. (406) 657-6262.

Winter looks like a fictional place, an elaborate simplicity, a Nabokovian invention of rarefied detail. Winds howl all night and day, pushing litters of storm fronts from the Beartooth to the Big Horn Mountains. When it lets up, the mountains disappear. The hayfield that runs east from my house ends in a curl of clouds that have fallen like sails luffing from sky to ground. Snow returns across the field to me, and the cows, dusted with white, look like snow-capped continents drifting.

—Gretel Ehrlich in *The Solace of Open Spaces*

GREYBULL

To travelers on their way to Yellowstone, the crossroads town of Greybull (pop. 2,200) is a splotch of irrigated green that sets off the desert lands on either side. Greybull lies at the junction of Shell Creek and the Bighorn River, and at the intersection of U.S. highways 14 and 16-20. As such, it is both an agricultural center, and a commercial center for tourists and oil workers. Most of Greybull lies along the western shore of the river, behind a long levee; barren rocky bluffs line the opposite bank. There are bentonite processing plants just north of town, oil pumpjacks farther afield, and irrigated farms along the river.

History

The land around Greybull was first settled in the 1880s by stockmen, with several hundred Mormon homesteaders moving in a decade later to dig irrigation ditches and establish the miniscule farming settlements of **Burlington** and **Otto** north of the Greybull River. Nearby **Emblem** was established by 600 German farmers in the late 1890s. A diversion of the Greybull River was begun in 1895, the first reclamation project under the Carey Act. Originally called Germania, the name was changed to Emblem (a reference to the American flag) during the anti-German hysteria of WW I.

The word Greybull comes from a huge albino buffalo that once roamed this country. The animal was sacred to the Indians, who noted it by pictographs that are still present on the sandstone bluffs along the river. The town is a creation of the Burlington Railroad in 1909-10, but much of its growth has been fueled by oil and gas developments in the surrounding country. Completion of U.S. 14 across the Big Horn Mountains in the 1930s brought tourists and led to Greybull's development as a way station for folks heading east to the Black Hills or west to Yellowstone.

Sights

The free **Greybull Museum** is in the same building as the library (325 Greybull Ave., tel. 765-2444), and is open Mon.-Sat. 9 a.m. to 9:30 p.m. during the summer and Mon.-Sat. 1-5 in the winter. It houses agate collections and polished petrified wood pieces, plus a fine fossil collection that includes one of the largest fossil ammonites ever found. Also here are various Indian items, guns, and historical artifacts. **Sheep Mountain**, a long hogback of eroded land just north of Greybull, is a favorite of geologists, who marvel at this eroded anticline. Photographers love the vivid reds, browns, and yellows of this desert landscape. Greybull **airport** is just north of town. No commercial service, but this is an interesting place to see a couple dozen aging military planes, some dating back to WW II. Several of the Royal Canadian Air Force's old B-29s are being cannibalized for parts by Hawkins & Powers Aviation, a charter company that uses them to drop fire retardant on forest fires.

PRACTICALITIES

Motels

Wheels Motel, 1324 N. 6th Ave., tel. 765-2105, has some of the cheapest rooms in town: $16 s or $19 d. Also inexpensive are: **Sage Motel**, 1135 N. 6th Ave., tel. 765-4443, for $25 s or d; **Greybull Motel**, 300 N. 6th Ave., tel. 765-2628, for $25 s or d; and **Antler Motel**, 1116 N. 6th Ave., tel. 765-4404, for $25 s or $27 d. (Antler is open April-Sept. only.) **K-Bar Motel**, 300 Greybull Ave., tel. 765-4426, costs $28-30 s or d. Open late May to mid-September. The nicest place in Greybull is **Yellowstone Motel**, 247 Greybull Ave., tel. 765-4456 or (800) 456-4155, with rates starting at $30 s or $34 d.

Camping

Green Oasis RV Park, 540 N. 12th Ave., tel. 765-2524, has tent sites for $9 and RV sites for $11. Showers for non-campers cost $2. Open May-October. **Greybull KOA**, 333 N. 2nd Ave., tel. 765-2555, charges $12 for tent sites and $13 for RVs. Showers cost $2 for non-campers. Open all year, with trees and a pool.

Restaurants And Bars

MJ's Cafe in the KOA, 333 N. 2nd Ave., tel. 765-2555, is one of the better local eateries. Locals drop in for a breakfast, or for burgers and steaks later. **Pizza on the Run**, 427 Greybull Ave., tel. 765-4454, is the place to go for pizza by the slice or pie. Drive up to the **Dairy Freez**, 601 N. 6th Ave., tel. 765-4718, for fast food. **Parker Cafe**, 536 Greybull Ave., tel. 765-2152, has working-class food at reasonable prices, while **Wheels Inn Restaurant**, 1336 N. 6th Ave., tel. 765-2456, is open 24 hours a day, and serves up standard American fare. Get groceries at **Ron's Thriftway**, 909 N. 6th, tel. 765-2890.

Entertainment And Events

For live music, head to **Hanging Tree Lounge**, 1040 N 6th Ave., tel. 765-9986 (rock), or **Silver Spur**, 445 Greybull Ave., tel. 765-2300 (C&W). Greybull's big annual event is **Days of '49** (1949 that is), held the second weekend in June. There's a top-notch rodeo, plus a parade, barbecue, dancing, and demolition derby.

Information And Services

The **Greybull Chamber of Commerce** office, 527 S. 1st Ave., tel. 765-2100, is open Mon.-Fri. 9-2. Ask here for directions to the Indian pictograph of an albino bison, after which the town is named. Two other places may be of interest: **Greybull Wildlife Museum**, 420 Greybull Ave., has a small collection of stuffed critters, while the big **Probst Western Store**, 547 Greybull Ave., tel. 765-2171, has a fine selection of cowboy hats, boots, and Western clothes. The Forest Service's **Paintrock Ranger Station** is at 1220 N. 8th Ave., tel. 765-4435. The **Greybull Public Library**, 325 Greybull Ave., tel. 765-2551, is open Mon. 12-8, Tues., Thurs., and Fri. 12-6, and Wed. 10-8. **Powder River Transportation**, tel. (800) 442-3682, has daily bus service from Greybull to Billings, Montana and parts of northern Wyoming. A marvelous old log building, built in the 1920s, houses the **Greybull Roller Rink**. Located at 527 S. 1st Ave., tel. 765-2761, the cost is $2 per skate. Swim at the **pool** across from the high school for $1.25 (children 50¢).

GREYBULL VICINITY

Basin

South of Greybull, the highway follows the Bighorn River. Sharp bluffs rise along the eastern side of the river, while cottonwoods and willows crowd the banks. Heading away from the broad river valley, the endless hills are covered with dry grass, sage, and greasewood. It's a plain-Jane, arid landscape. Eight miles away lies the pleasant, but quietly dying town of Basin (pop. 1,300). Half the businesses are boarded up with "For Sale" signs out front. It seems the only things keeping Basin sputtering along are its title as Big Horn County seat and an impressive state retirement center. Basin is a relaxing place to retire after a long day of driving. Established in 1896, the town has always been an agricultural center, with both farming and ranching in the surrounding land. In 1897, a bitter custody battle for the county seat split voters between Basin City, as it was then known, and the older town of Otto. Basin City won by 38 votes.

Practicalities: Free **camping** in the town park, but you'll have to pitch tents on the dirt. The **Lilac Motel**, 710 W. C St., tel. 568-3355, has a quiet location and kindly owner. Rates are just $19 s or $21 d. Decent breakfasts at **Big B Restaurant**, 602 S. 4th St., tel. 568-2246, and very good steak and seafood at **Outpost Lounge**, 151 N. 4th St., tel. 568-2134. Also try **Mom's Cafe**, 257 N. 4th, tel. 568-3301. The **Big Horn County Library**, 103 W. C St., tel. 568-2388, is open Mon.-Fri. 10-5 and Sat. 9-12. There is a public **pool** at the high school. **Stockman's Bar**, 105 S. 4th St., tel. 568-9942, has live country music a couple of times a month. For other entertainment, head to **Kar-Vu Drive In**, 725 S. U.S. 20, tel. 568-2771, one of the last drive-in theaters in Wyoming. Each August, Basin hosts the **Big Horn County Fair and Bean Festival** (pretty funny combination!) with livestock judging, a barbecue, and other activities.

Shell, Manderson, And Hyattville

The Shell Valley is farming and ranching country, its lush irrigated hay fields contrasting sharply with the arid landscape to the west. Tiny **Shell** has a country store/bar. Be sure to stop at the **Old Stone School** here, built in 1903, and used as a one-room school until the early 1950s. It is now run as an excellent little art gallery and bookstore, tel. 765-4384. **Kedesh Ranch**, three miles east of Shell on U.S. 14, tel. 765-2791, has log cabins with fine views for $30 s or $35 d, open only June-October.

State 789 heads south from Basin to **Manderson** (pop. 170), where you'll find a small country store and cafe. South of Manderson the road splits and continues on both sides of Bighorn River to Worland. The main road (on the east side of the river) plays tag with the irrigation ditch much of the way, passing eroded desert bluffs to the east and flat farm country closer to the river. A thin strip of trees runs right down the middle; in fall they look like skeletons against the skyline. Lots of barley, sugar beet, and hay fields.

Twenty-one miles east of Manderson on State 31 is the ranching center called **Hyattville**, really not much more than a crossroads. Get to **Medicine Lodge State Park** by turning north on Cold Springs Rd. (just west of Hyattville). After four miles, turn left again at the "Medicine Lodge Habitat Unit" sign, and follow the gravel road

1 1/2 miles to the park. One of the lesser-known state parks, Medicine Lodge has a visitor center (tel. 469-2234), plus a free campground with restrooms and water. This is one of the most distinctive archaeological sites in Wyoming; a 750-foot-long ledge here served as the backdrop for Indian settlements that lasted for 10,000 years. Dozens of unusual petroglyphs on the cliff face, and good fishing for brown trout in the creek. You can also continue on up the dirt road another 15 miles to Paint Rock Lakes, a jumping off point for Cloud Peak Wilderness (see p. 369). North of Hyattville is another place of interest to folks willing to do a bit of adventuring, **Trapper Canyon**. Located on BLM land, the canyon has colorful walls rising 1,200 feet above Trapper Creek. Check with the BLM office in Worland for details.

WORLAND

The prosperous farming town of Worland (pop. 6,700) depends upon a mixture of agriculture (primarily malt barley and sugar beets), sheep and cattle ranching, oil production, and manufacturing. Sheep glean plowed fields near town, and the Holly Sugar Company's plant on the southwest edge of Worland provides economic stability, keeping more than 15,000 acres in beets. The town itself has a pleasant Midwestern feel, with nightly baseball games through the summer, tree-bordered streets and simple homes in the center, and suburban ranchstyle homes spreading across the surrounding countryside. The slow Bighorn River twists its way along the edge of Worland, but just a few miles farther west is desert country with dry rocky buttes, sagebrush, and sheep.

History

Worland is named for Charlie "Dad" Worland, one of the first homesteaders in this part of the Bighorn Basin, and the manager of a stage station and saloon built along the old Bridger Trail in 1900. It wasn't much to look at—a cave dug into the riverbank, with log walls out front. His bar quickly acquired the title, "The Hole-in-the-Wall." A cigar box just behind the bar served as the local bank, and anyone needing money could borrow it and leave behind an I.O.U. Other folks

settled around Dad Worland, and A.G. Rupp added a general store nearby, also built into the side of the bank to save precious timber. Ray Pendergraft in *Washakie: A Wyoming County History,* relates the following story about early-day Worland:

> *Once a compactly-built man rode into the settlement, refreshed himself at Worland's saloon, then went on to Rupps for some supplies. On one wall of the store was a poster, complete with a picture. It read, "$5,000 Reward, Dead or Alive Robert Leroy Parker, alias Butch Cassidy." The visitor examined it. "It's not a very good likeness," he told Rupp. Rupp examined the poster, looked at the man, and readily agreed. "You don't want it up there do you, Mr. Rupp?" the man politely asked. "No, I don't," replied Mr. Rupp. "I'll take it down for you," the man said, did so and went on about his selection of supplies.*

Originally located on the western side of the Bighorn River, Worland moved to the other side after the Chicago, Burlington, and Quincy Railroad announced plans to build along the east bank. The nucleus of Worland, 10 buildings, was slid across the river on the ice during the winter of 1905-06. The following year, construction was finished on the 54-mile-long Big Horn irrigation canal, opening some 30,000 acres to agriculture. It had been begun almost 20 years earlier. A new sugar beet-processing plant in 1917 attracted more farmers and workers from the Midwest, along with many Germans and Ukrainians. The discovery of oil in the Hidden Dome field in that same year brought boom times as speculators flooded the area. Oil and agriculture, especially sugar beets, have remained important ever since, although oil production has declined since the 1950s as the fields are pumped out.

Sights

The **Washakie County Museum and Cultural Center**, 1115 Obie Sue Ave., tel. 347-4102, is housed in an old LDS church and is open Sun. 1-4 and Tues.-Fri. 10-5. Inside is a re-creation of the A.G. Rupp Store, an array of cowboy and ranch equipment, and other historical items, plus a fine geology and fossil collection. Next to the County Court House at the corner of Big Horn Ave. and 10th St. is a fountain fed by a 4,330-foot-deep **artesian well** located 23 miles north of Worland. The well flows at an impressive 14,000 gallons per minute, and with sufficient pressure to push water all the way to Worland. Also on the courthouse grounds is an incredibly ugly 15-foot-tall **Indian statue** carved out of wood by Peter Toth, and placed here in 1980. West of Worland in the Painted Desert, you'll find some of the most interesting badland country in Wyoming. Of particular note is **Bobcat Draw** on BLM land near Squaw Teats and off State 431. Plenty of eroded country to explore, including arches and a variety of bizarrely carved shapes. Stop by the BLM office in Worland for directions.

Accommodations And Camping

Check out the tropical fish at **Pawnee Motel**,

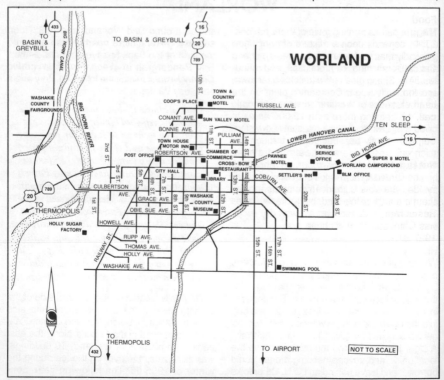

1735 Big Horn Ave., tel. 347-3206, where you'll also find the least expensive rooms in town: $20 s or $26 d. **Town House Motor Inn**, 119 N. 10th St., tel. 347-2426, costs $25 s or $27 d, including a pool. The AAA-rated **Sun Valley Motel**, 500 N. 10th St., tel. 347-4251, charges $26 s or $30 d, while **Town & Country Motel**, 1021 Russell St., tel. 347-3249, runs $30 s or d. For the nicest lodging in Worland, head to **Settler's Inn (Best Western)**, 2200 Big Horn Ave., tel. 347-8201 or (800) 528-1234, where $32 s or $38 d includes a continental breakfast. The priciest spot to knock off for a night ($35 s or $43 d) is **Super 8 Motel**, 2500 Big Horn Ave., tel. 347-9236 or (800) 848-8888. No public campgrounds near Worland (although you can pitch a tent on nearby BLM lands), but the private **Worland Campground**, 2401 Big Horn Ave., tel. 347-2329, has shady tent sites for $10, RV spaces for $13. Showers for non-campers cost $4. Open April-October.

Food
Maggie's Cafe, 541 Big Horn Ave., tel. 347-3354, has very reasonable breakfasts and lunches, including homemade soups and breads. **Cross-Bow Restaurant**, 1110 Big Horn Ave., tel. 347-8296, is one of the best local spots for breakfast. Their lunchtime salad bar is fine, but head elsewhere for dinner. **Someplace Special**, 1735 Big Horn Ave., tel. 347-3206, has good sandwiches, tacos, and salads. Try their Surprise Sundae on a hot afternoon. For something on the organic side, head to the **Health Nut Hut**, 635 Big Horn Ave., tel. 347-8392.

The **Coffee Cup Shop**, 1010 Big Horn Ave., tel. 347-8501, is a Mexican cafe serving authentic south-of-the-border fare. **New China Restaurant**, 1620 Big Horn Ave., tel. 347-4575, has Chinese/American food, and **Pizza Hut**, 1927 Big Horn Ave., tel. 347-2434, makes the best local pizzas. The Friday night seafood buffets, Sunday brunches, and lunch specials at **Ram's Horn Cafe**, 629 Big Horn Ave., tel. 347-6351, make this a local favorite. **Antone's Supper Club**, three miles east of town on U.S. 16, tel. 347-2301, has great deals on top sirloin steaks, and a Wednesday night smorgasbord for around $6. **Landerson's** at the Worland Country Club, tel. 347-2695, has excellent seafood, steaks, and veal.

Stop by **Rolling Pin Bakery**, 105 N. 15th St., tel. 347-2763, for fresh breads, cookies, and donuts. **Jon's IGA Foodliner**, 221 N. 10th St., tel. 347-3628, or the **Worland Thriftway**, 420 N. 10th St., tel. 347-9820, are the places to go for groceries. Jon's also has a deli.

Other Practicalities
The big annual events in town are the **Washakie County Fair** in mid-August, and **Dad Worland Day** in mid-September. The **Worland Chamber of Commerce** office, tel. 3476-3226, sits in front of the county courthouse at 120 N. 10th St., and stays open Mon.-Fri. 8-5. **Washakie County Library**, 1019 Coburn Ave., tel. 347-2231, is open Mon-Fri. 8-5 with evening hours (7-9 p.m.) on Tuesday and Thursday. **Pages Bookstore**, 724 Big Horn Ave., tel. 347-9365, has a good choice of both new and used titles. The **Bighorn National Forest Tensleep Ranger Station** is at 2009 Big Horn Ave., tel. 347-8291, and the **BLM Worland District Office** is at 101 S. 23rd St., tel. 347-9871. There is a public swimming **pool** at the high school, 1706 Washakie Ave., tel. 347-4113, and an 18-hole **Municipal Golf Course**, tel. 347-2695, next to the airport. The airport is two miles south of town, and is served by **Mesa Airlines**, tel. (800) 637-2247, with daily flights to Cody or Laramie. Rent cars from **Big Horn Chevrolet**, 545 N. 10th Ave., tel. 347-4229.

TEN SLEEP

Ten Sleep (pop. 440) has one of the most picturesque settings in all Wyoming. The drive in from Worland offers a traipse across dry desert badlands crowded with oil pumpjacks and then up into rolling grass and sagebrush country with the tree-covered Big Horn Mountains marking the distant horizon. Great views from atop the long hills, before the road descends sharply into a lush green valley cut through by Nowood and Tensleep creeks. Because of its mountain valley location, the town of Ten Sleep offers an escape from the oppressive summer heat of Bighorn Basin. This verdant valley is one of the few places in Wyoming where apple, peach, and pear trees grow. Rustic log buildings fill this tiny ranching and tourism center. Take away the cars and the asphalt, and its easy to imagine Ten Sleep as the location for some Hollywood film about the Green Valley. It is especially a treat given the surrounding badlands topography.

The name Ten Sleep comes from the Sioux Indians who frequently stopped in this valley during their travels between a permanent camp along the Clarks Fork River in Montana and another one along the Platte River. Halfway between the two was Ten Sleeps, so-named because they measured distances in the number of nights it took to get to a place. The town of Ten Sleep was established as a trading center for the Scottish and Irish sheepmen who came here in the 1890s.

Accommodations

Pitch your tent at **Flagstaff Camp**, tel. 366-2250, for $6 ($10 for RVs); open June-October. **Flagstaff Motel**, tel. 366-2330, on the other end of town, charges $20 s or $25 d, but is open

THE TEN SLEEP RAID

Cattlemen have always viewed sheep with disdain, regarding them as despoilers of the range, "a locust with hooves," or "range maggots." Cattle reached Wyoming's grazing lands first, and when sheep began to arrive in large numbers around the turn of the century, the cattle owners fought back with intimidation and violence. In many places, the cattlemen declared a "dead line," and any sheep or sheepherder that came into that area risked being killed. (One such line existed in Jackson Hole; even today the county has just 300 sheep versus 12,000 cattle.) Despite these threats, sheep ranching was simply too lucrative to pass up; by 1889 Bighorn Basin was overrun with more than 387,000 sheep versus fewer than 22,000 cattle.

Perhaps 10,000 sheep throughout the state were killed by cattlemen; some flocks were driven over cliffs, others were dynamited or attacked by dogs, while thousands more died from gunshots. Many of Wyoming's sheepherders were viciously attacked, and at least 16 were murdered. The most notorious of all these incidents took place along Spring Creek near Ten Sleep in 1909. Joe Emge, a hot-headed cattleman turned sheepman, announced plans to trail his sheep across the dead line set up in the Nowater Creek area. One April night just after they had reached the grazing grounds, at least half a dozen masked men burst into the sheep camp, murdering Emge, his partner, and a herder. Their wagons were then set afire and many sheep were shot. The attackers disappeared into the night, leaving a grisly scene to be discovered the next morning.

The investigation pointed directly at local cattleman, and after testifying before a grand jury, one of the suspected raiders was found dead; officially it was called suicide, but it appeared he had been waylaid by others seeking to silence anyone who might tell the truth. Eventually, two men broke the silence and fingered five others, including several prominent ranchers. All five were convicted, spending from three years to life in prison for the murders. Like the Johnson County War two decades earlier, this incident helped turn many people against the cattlemen. Sheep continued to grow in importance for a while, with Wyoming becoming the largest wool-producing state, but overgrazing, the severe winter of 1911-12, and the removal of a wool tariff the following year led to a long decline. Wyoming is still the third-largest wool producer in America.

summers only. **Circle S Motel**, tel. 366-2320, has rooms for $18 s or $20 d and an overnight camping area. If you're camping elsewhere, take showers at the laundromat here for $2. Rooms at **Valley Motel**, tel. 366-2321, are $27 s or d. You can also stay at any of a dozen campgrounds ($5) in Bighorn National Forest east of town.

Other Practicalities
For meals, head to **Flagstaff Cafe**, tel. 366-2330, or **Basque Cafe**, tel. 366-2212. Basque Cafe is the only place open year-round. American, not Basque food, alas. **Dirty Sally's**, tel. 366-2319, has a soda fountain and gift shop. Drop into the **Ten Sleep Saloon** or the **Big Horn Bar** for a cold beer with local ranchers. **Ten Sleep Merchantile** sells groceries. The tiny **Vista Park Museum** in the town park has local artifacts, and is open daily during the summer. A summer-only information booth provides local specifics. **Ten Sleep Celebration Days** in July brings a rootin'-tootin' rodeo, arts and crafts exhibits, chili cookoff, dancing, fiddling, a parade, and other festivities. Evening **rodeos** are also held in Ten Sleep throughout the summer.

Tensleep Canyon
Five miles east of Ten Sleep, the highway climbs up spectacular Tensleep Canyon toward 9,666-foot Powder River Pass in the Big Horn Mountains. **Wigwam Fish Rearing Station**, run by the Wyoming Game and Fish Dept., is five miles east of town. Another five miles up is the turnoff to **Ten Sleep Fish Hatchery**. Both of these are open daily. See p. 365 for more on this route.

THERMOPOLIS

The town of Thermopolis (pop. 4,500) lies on the southern edge of the Bighorn Basin, where the Owl Creek Mountains gradually close in around the desert country. It's one of two towns in Wyoming established because of the presence of a hot springs; the other is Saratoga. The name comes from the words *thermae* (Latin for "hot springs") and *polis* (Greek for "city"). It is a fitting title, since the world's largest hot springs are the centerpiece of Thermopolis. Hot Springs State Park is right in town, encompassing both a wonderful public bath house and several commercial endeavors. The economy of Thermopolis was for a long while dependant upon oil and ranching, but tourism has become increasingly important. There are ample reasons for travelers to stop here.

Thermopolis came into existence with the 1896 purchase of Big Springs from the Shoshones and Arapahos. Streets were laid out wide enough for a 16-mule team to turn around in the middle of the block, something still obvious today, though you don't often see mule teams on the streets. Because of their medicinal value, the hot springs attracted many people, and the town became a health center, particularly for those suffering from arthritis and polio. Not much timber around here, so the first lodging place was the Sage Brush Hotel, made from a wooden frame laced with sagebrush and covered with a thatched roof of more sage.

SIGHTS

Hot Springs State Park
Shoshone legends tell of a young warrior and his true love who were standing in the Wind River Canyon when an eagle feather—earned in battles with the enemy—blew out of his hair and wafted down the canyon. They raced after it, finding it floating in an enormous hot spring with steam gushing from its mouth. The springs were a gift from the Great Spirit.

Originally a part of Wind River Reservation, Big Springs and 10 square miles of surrounding land were sold to the United States government in 1896 for the bargain-basement price of $60,000. The treaty was signed by Shoshone Chief Washakie and Arapaho Chief Sharp Nose. In it, Washakie stipulated that some of the water must remain free to all people, and that a campground be set aside for Indians. Thus was established Wyoming's first state park. Today the park is the third most popular attraction in Wyoming; only Yellowstone and Grand Teton national parks attract more visitors. The park includes a variety of facilities: a state-run bath house, two commercial establishments, a senior center, rehabilitation center, and even a herd of buffalo. Adjacent are the Plaza Inn and Holiday Inn spa facilities.

Big Springs flows approximately 2,575 gallons per minute at 135° F, and is considered the largest hot springs in the world. The springs are located located at the base of a small butte; just in case there might be some confusion, someone has placed white rocks along the hillside, spelling out "World's Largest Mineral Hot Spring." A number of cooling ponds spread out in front of the springs, dropping water over terraces of lime and gypsum to the Bighorn River.

(Because of the hot water, this stretch of the Bighorn River remains open through the winter, attracting ducks and other birds.) The cooling ponds are very colorful, with algae and minerals (particularly calcium carbonate, bicarbonate, sulfate, and sodium) adding splashes of reds, greens, browns, and yellows. A concrete path winds around them and along the river. Many people drink the mineral-rich water, claiming all sorts of medicinal benefits.

For an incredibly relaxing soak, be sure to visit the very nice **State Bath House**, tel. 864-3765, open Mon.-Sat. 8-6, and Sun. noon-6. No entry charge, and the facilities are always ex-

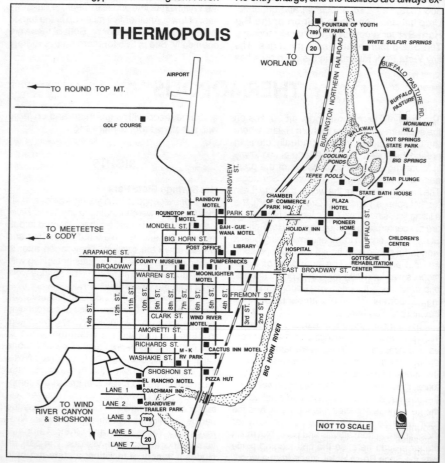

ceptionally clean, with lockers to store your clothes. Rent towels and swimsuits for 30¢. There are private tubs in the locker rooms (where you can temper the 104° F mineral water with cooler water), a central indoor pool, and an outdoor soaking pool (open May-Sept. only). The pools are wheelchair accessible. Attendants generally try to make sure folks don't stay in the hot water for more than 20 minutes, since the heat can be weakening. This is not a place to clean up, and no soap is allowed, even in the showers.

Tepee Pools, tel. 864-9250, in the white dome building next to the state bath house, has two pools, a 160-foot-long indoor water slide, a steam room, sauna, and mineral spa. Adults pay $4, kids $1-3, seniors $3.

Even bigger is **Star Plunge**, tel. 864-3771, also in the state park, with two long water slides and two spacious pools (one outdoor), a steam room, jacuzzi, and tanning booths. The 500-foot-long outdoor slide is one of the three longest in the nation. Entrance to Star Plunge costs $5 for adults, $4 for kids. Towels and swimsuits rent for $1.50.

Also on the grounds of the state park is **Gottsche Rehabilitation Center**, an outpatient treatment facility established in 1959 to make use of the medicinal properties of the hot springs, **Bighorn Children's Center** for handicapped kids, and a **Wyoming Pioneer Home** for the elderly. A statue commemorating Chief Washakie's "gift of the smoking waters" stands in front of the home. Washakie would be proud of all the good his gift has done.

In addition to facilities associated with the hot springs, the park includes shady picnic tables and playgrounds. A rough trail cuts to the top of **Monument Hill**, right behind Big Springs. The northeast portion of Hot Springs State Park includes a pasture where a herd of 30-50 **buffalo** roam. A loop road through the pasture gives you a chance to drive by. They are fed daily at 8:30 a.m.

Museum

The free **Hot Springs Historical Museum** calls itself "one of the best small museums in the country," and lives up to this billing with an impressive collection of old photos, wagons, Indian artifacts, and much more. Located at 700 Broadway, tel. 864-5183, the museum is open

Mon.-Sat. 8-6, and Sun. 1-5 June-Aug., and Mon.-Sat. 8-5 and Sun. 1-5 the rest of the year. It sprawls through two floors of the main building and across the street to include an agriculture building, an old schoolhouse, a petroleum building, and a caboose. The main museum houses various displays of frontier life: a newspaper shop, dentist's office (complete with frightening tools), blacksmith shop, and general store. The cherrywood bar from the Hole-in-the-Wall Saloon is particularly popular; here members of the famous outlaw gang tipped their glasses with sympathetic locals. The Indian artifact collection downstairs is very impressive, not just because of the thousands of arrowheads, but also because it includes an elk hide painted by Shoshone Chief Washakie. Outside, the 1920 Middleton Schoolhouse comes complete with old desks; check out the amusing letters from present-day school children. Kids of all ages love traipsing through the old Burlington Northern caboose and trying to figure how the agriculture building's amazing 1926 Case threshing machine worked. The petroleum building houses exhibits on drilling and refining oil, including old gusher photos and a gigantic power unit once used to pump oil before the arrival of electric pumps. Also of interest in Thermopolis is **Conrad Memorial Art Museum**, 315 N. 5th, tel. 864-3262, where the paintings of the late Rupert Conrad are on display. The building once served as a stagecoach station.

PRACTICALITIES

Motels And Hotels

Because of the popularity of Thermopolis during the summer, it's a good idea to reserve ahead (or check in before 6 p.m.) to be assured of having a place to stay. See the chart for specific motel and hotel rates. The fanciest place in town is **Holiday Inn**, located right in Hot Springs State Park. It is very popular with busloads of blue-haired Grey Line tourists, and includes racquetball courts, a weightroom, swimming pool, hot mineral jacuzzi, soaking tubs, saunas, massages, and more. Most of these cost extra. Hunters will enjoy the dozens of photos of the great white predators and their deceased quarry lining the walls. Big-game trophy mounts and skins from all over the world hang around the

THERMOPOLIS ACCOMMODATIONS

Motel	Address	Telephone	Rates	Features
Plaza Inn	Hot Springs Park	864-2251	$14+ s, $22+ d $10 pp	massage, mineral bath youth hostel
Cactus Inn	U.S. 20 South	864-3155	$22 s, $24 d	kitchenettes
Bah-Gue-Wana Motel	401 Park St.	864-3119	$23 s, $26 d	
El Rancho Motel	924 Shoshoni Rd.	864-2341	$25+ s, $34+ d	AAA approved
Coachman Inn	U.S. 20 South	864-3141	$28 s, $32 d	
Roundtop Mt. Motel	412 N. 6th	864-3126	$30 s, $32 d	
Rainbow Motel	408 Park St.	864-2129	$30 s, $32 d	
Wind River Motel	501 S. 6th	864-2325	$33 s, $35 d	
Moonlighter Motel (Best Western)	600 Broadway	864-2321 (800) 528-1234	$40+ s, $43+ d	AAA approved, pool
Holiday Inn	Hot Springs Park	864-3131 (800) 465-4329	$46+ s, $49+ d	AAA approved, pool, jacuzzi, sauna, exercise facility

restaurant and bar.

Directly across from the elaborate Holiday Inn is **Plaza Inn**, a funky old hotel with very friendly owners and some surprising amenities. Built in 1918, the hotel is currently being re-modelled, so some of the rooms are extremely plain and don't have TVs or phones. Plaza Inn also houses an **International Youth Hostel** ($10 pp) with a communal kitchen and no cur-few. Try an hour-long steam bath, mineral soak, and blanket wrap for just $5, or a 1 1/2-hour mas-sage with acupressure for an incredibly rea-sonable $20.

Campgrounds

The closest public camping is a dozen miles south in Wind River Canyon (see p. 362). **Foun-tain of Youth RV Park**, two miles north of Ther-mopolis on U.S. 20, tel. 864-9977, boasts Wyo-ming's largest mineral swimming pool, fed by what was intended to be an oil well. In 1918, C.F. Cross began drilling, but instead of hitting oil, he struck hot mineral water, blowing the pipe casing out of the ground. Eventually a small travertine cone formed around the old casing. The "Sacajawea" well still flows 1.3 million gal-lons per day. Not surprisingly, this is a very pop-ular place with the "snowbird" RV crowd. Open

year-round, it costs $11 for RVs. **Grandview RV Park**, 122 U.S. 20 S, tel. 864-3463, has RV sites for $10. Showers for non-campers cost $3. Open May to mid-October. **M-K RV Park**, 720 Shoshoni, tel. 864-2778, has RV sites for $8. Showers for non-campers cost $2. Right by the road and noisy; not a good place for campers; open May-September. **Latchstring Campground**, on the south edge of town, tel. 864-5262, charges $10 for tents and $13 for RVs, showers cost $3 for non-campers; open May-early October. More RV spots are avail-able at **Camper/Motor Home Park** at 2nd and Arapahoe, tel. 864-3926, for $7.

Food

Granny's, 200 N. 6th, tel. 864-2809, makes very good sandwiches and soups. The finest lunches and dinners in Thermop can be found at **Pumpernick's**, 512 Broadway, tel. 864-5151. Try their pita-pocket sandwiches for lunch, or the homemade desserts. **The Sideboard Cafe**, 109 S. 6th, tel. 864-5335, is the best local place for breakfast. **Manhattan Cafe**, 526 Broadway, tel. 864-2501, has BBQ beef ribs for just $4. Excellent malts too. **County Seat Restaurant**, 530 Arapahoe, tel. 864-2632, features BBQ pork ribs, salads, and pizzas. Stop by **Pizza**

Hut, 545 Shoshoni, tel. 864-2345, for the best pizzas in town. **Legion Supper Club,** at the golf course on Airport Hill, tel. 864-3918, is the local steak and seafood spot. Pricey, but good. **The Safari Club,** in the Holiday Inn, tel. 864-3131, has a buffet every day except Saturday. Interesting atmosphere, but variable food. Get groceries at **Consumers' Thriftway,** 600 S. 6th, tel. 864-3112, or **Don's IGA,** 225 S. 4th, tel. 864-5576. Don's also has a good deli and bakery.

Entertainment And Events

Come to the **Safari Club** at the Holiday Inn on weekends for a mixture of country, rock, and pop dance tunes, or head to **Mac's Bar,** 506 Broadway, tel. 864-3763, for twangy country sounds. The **Gift of the Waters Pageant** each August at Hot Springs State Park, commemorates the transfer of Big Springs to the federal government in 1896. The pageant has been presented every summer since 1950, with a cast that includes both local residents and Shoshones from the Wind River Reservation in full regalia. A tipi camp is set up near the hot springs for the festivities. Other events during Gift of the Waters include Indian dancing and parades. **Hot Springs County Fair** is also held in August, with rodeos and various agricultural and ranching shows. **Railroad Days** in mid-June commemorates arrival of the railroad in 1919, and includes train displays, a craft show, a street dance, and more.

Recreation

Most of the playing takes place around the many pools in Thermopolis, including those in the state park, but there are other things to do as well. Rent clunker **bikes** from the Holiday Inn, tel. 864-3131, for $3/hour. The nine-hole **Legion Golf Course,** tel. 864-5294, costs $8 and is on Airport Hill north of town. **Roundtop Mountain,** the distinctive butte that dominates the Thermopolis area, is an enjoyable but fairly steep hike. Take 7th St. to Airport Hill, and turn on the first left. After the cemetery, turn right onto a gravel road that takes you to the trailhead.

Shopping

For a good selection of books and tapes, stop by **The Wherehouse,** 107 N. 5th St., tel. 864-5702.

CAROLINE LOCKHART

One of the most interesting Westerners was Caroline Lockhart (1871-1962), a woman who began her career as an actress, but turned quickly to journalism. Using the pen name "Suzette," she became one of the country's first woman newspaper reporters, a job that led her into all sorts of adventures, from entering a circus cage with a lion that had killed his trainer the previous day, to testing the Boston Fire Department's new fire nets by jumping out of a fourth-story hotel window. When she heard of a "Home for Intemperate Women" where the women were being severely mistreated, Caroline decided to investigate by posing as a derelict. She got her story alright, but it took considerable convincing from her editor to get her out. "Release!" shouted the matron running the house, "We can't! She's not cured yet." One of her most lasting impacts was the creation of Mother's Day. Although the idea was that of Anna Jarvis, it was Caroline Lockhart who made it a reality by tirelessly pushing the idea in the newspapers.

In 1904, after an interview with Buffalo Bill Cody in the town named for him, she decided to move to Wyoming. She purchased the local newspaper, the *Cody Enterprise,* and quickly made a name for herself as a crusader against prohibition and "game hogs." She founded the Cody Stampede, the big annual event in Bighorn Basin, and later wrote several novels about the West, including *The Lady Doc,* a book that managed to ruffle local feathers with its too-close-to-the-truth descriptions of real-life Cody people. Lockhart's witty, humorous, and insightful writing gained her a national reputation.

In 1924, she bought a 7,000-acre ranch in the country along the Bighorn River north of Lovell, dividing her time between her Cody home (now the Lockhart Bed and Breakfast) and her ranch. Today her old ranch lies within Bighorn Canyon National Recreation Area.

Hole-in-the-Wall Gallery, 105 N. 5th St., tel. 864-2208, sells limited-edition prints and original paintings, and Domhoff's Potter Studio, north of Thermopolis, tel. 864-3710, offers some of the finest pottery in Bighorn Basin.

Information And Services

The Thermopolis Chamber of Commerce office, 220 Park St., tel. 864-3192 or (800) 433-6235, is right at the entrance to Hot Springs State Park. Hours are daily 8-5 in the summer, and Mon.-Fri. 9-5 in the winter. Just behind the chamber office is an impressive travertine cone, created when workers put in a vent pipe. Big Horn County Library, 344 Arapahoe St., tel. 864-3104, is open Mon., Wed., and Fri. 9-5, Tues. and Thurs. 9-8, and Sat. 12-5. Laundromats don't normally merit mention, but it is hard to omit a place with a name like Wishy Washy Laundromat on 630 Shoshoni. Rent cars from Chopping Chevrolet, 160 U.S. 20 S, tel. 864-2339.

WIND RIVER CANYON

South of Thermopolis, the highway cuts across lush irrigated farm fields. Turn around and you'll see the steep slopes of Roundtop Mountain dominating the vistas. The highway bridges the Bighorn River, and then, four miles south of town, abruptly enters magnificent Wind River Canyon. At this point the river's name changes just as abruptly. Lewis and Clark had named the Bighorn River; Crow Indians the Wind River. Early explorers somehow concluded that they were two separate waterways, and in the confusion Wind River Canyon became the "Wedding of the Waters." Above this point the river is called Wind River, while below, it is the Bighorn River. A bit confusing. Many people float the Bighorn River, putting in at the Wedding of the Waters and taking out in Thermopolis. It's an enjoyable, leisurely drift with nice scenery and excellent fishing for rainbow trout (average size 15 inches) along the way. A special permit (call 332-7207 for specifics) is required to fish in the canyon above Wedding of the Waters since it is part of the Wind River Indian Reservation. Fishing and float trips down the Bighorn are offered by Wind River Canyon Outfitters, 6th and Richards, tel. 864-3617. They also provide horseback and 4WD tours of the high country.

The drive through Wind River Canyon is one of the most dramatic in Wyoming, with U.S. 20 clinging to the eastern bank of the river, and canyon walls rising up to 2,500 feet overhead. Tracks of the Burlington Northern Railroad (built in 1913) parallel the river on the other side, threading in and out of several tunnels. This place is a geologist's wet dream, slicing through rocks that grow progressively older as you continue south, with the oldest dating back to the Precambrian era, 2.7 billion years ago. A succession of roadside signs notes the various geologic formations, and the Thermopolis Chamber of Commerce can provide you with a descriptive log of the canyon's complex geology. At the upper end, the road quickly climbs past Boysen Dam and into the open country of Boysen State Park (see p. 184). Within the canyon are two attractive campgrounds, Upper and Lower Wind River State Parks ($4). The river flows right alongside, and there are many big old cottonwoods, but highway noise may keep you awake. Tours of Boysen Powerplant, tel. 864-3772, are available Mon.-Fri. 8-4.

POWDER RIVER COUNTRY

Powder River country is the most historically interesting part of a state overflowing with history. For the Indians who made this their home, the basin was paradise, a place of massive bison herds and abundant forage for horses. Because of this richness, the area became a confrontation point between various Indian tribes and later between Indians and invading whites along the Bozeman Trail. Still later, the clashes were among the whites: cattlemen versus homesteaders, and outlaws against lawmen. Today, the clashes have faded into memory, but the rich country remains. Coal, cattle, and sheep rule.

The Powder River Basin stretches from the crest of the Big Horn Mountains to the Black Hills and then south to Casper. The three largest settlements—Gillette, Sheridan, and Buffalo—dominate the region's economy. Sheridan and Buffalo provide gateways to the magnificent Big Horn Mountains, a recreation paradise capped by barren alpine peaks. Rolling grassland predominates across Powder River Basin, accented by steep-sided buttes and lush river bottoms. The land is grazed extensively by cattle and sheep, though alfalfa and wheat are grown in many places. Oil and coal resources are vital to the economy of the Powder River Basin, especially around Gillette, making this the most important energy region in Wyoming. Despite the many large coal mines, the land remains relatively untouched. Nearly everyone chooses to live in the cities and smaller settlements, leaving enormous open expanses of land.

BIG HORN MOUNTAINS

Sandwiched between two broad basins—Big Horn to the west and Powder River to the east—are the majestic Big Horn Mountains. To the early explorers this 70-mile-long range was "The Shining Mountains," a name inspired by its snowcapped peaks, some topping 13,000 feet.

The Indians called it "Ahsahta," meaning "The Big Horns," after the Rocky Mountain bighorn sheep found here. Eventually, whites applied the name to all sorts of places in the region. The mountain country here is carpeted primarily with lodgepole and ponderosa pine, along

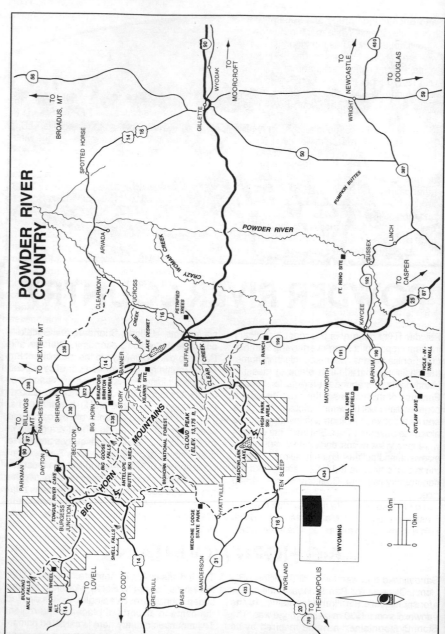

POWDER RIVER COUNTRY

with Engelmann spruce and subalpine fir at higher elevations. While much of the country here is not as rugged as the mountains on the western border of Wyoming, the Big Horns do contain many rocky peaks above 9,000 feet, with 13,175-foot Cloud Peak crowning the skyline. Hundreds of small lakes reflect this dramatic scenery within the Cloud Peak Wilderness.

Nearly all of these mountains lie within **Bighorn National Forest**, a million-acre chunk of public land set aside by President Grover Cleveland in 1897. Forest headquarters is in Sheridan at 1969 S. Sheridan Ave., tel. 672-0751, with other district offices in Lovell (tel. 548-6514), Worland (tel. 347-8291), Buffalo (tel. 684-7981), and Greybull (tel. 765-4435). Any of these can provide detailed forest maps ($2) and a listing of local outfitters.

This is multiple-use country, with logging, grazing, and recreation the primary attractions. Commercial logging has gone on within the forest for almost a century, and old tie flumes are still visible near Dayton. At one time, vast numbers of sheep grazed the Big Horns, totalling perhaps half a million. More than 50,000 sheep and 30,000 cattle still graze in these mountains, and sheepherder camps are a common sight in the high meadows.

Most visitors simply drive through the Big Horns on one of the three scenic highways, but the country is well worth stopping to savor, especially if you're a fan of waterfalls. There are many campgrounds, over 630 miles of hiking trails, and good fishing for rainbow, cutthroat, brook, and brown trout. Come winter, this is a popular destination for snowmobilers as well as cross-country and downhill skiers. Quite a bit of wildlife to see here, too. Bighorn sheep have been re-introduced and now number around seventy. No grizzlies,

The Crow country is a good country; the Great Spirit has put it in exactly the right place. It is good for horses—and what is a country without horses? On the Columbia, the people are poor and dirty; they paddle about in canoes and eat fish. On the Missouri the water is muddy and bad. To the north of the Crow country it is too cold, and to the south it is too hot. The Crow country is just right. The water is clear and sweet. There are plenty of buffalo, elk, deer, antelope, and mountain sheep. It is the best wintering place in the world and has plenty of game. Is it any wonder that the Crows have fought long and hard to defend this country, which we love so much?

—*Crow Chief Arapooish, describing the Powder River Basin*

but quite a few black bears in these mountains. Also look for mule and white-tailed deer, elk, and moose.

CRUISIN' THROUGH

Three paved highways cut across the Big Horn Mountains, providing popular connections between Yellowstone and the Black Hills. U.S. 14 and 16 are both kept plowed through the winter, while U.S. 14A generally closes Nov.-May. All three are National Scenic Byways, a status that becomes more obvious with each mile traveled. **Off the Deep End Travels**, tel. (800) 223-6833, offers six-day cycling tours of the Big Horns for $440 pp.

Highway 16

U.S. 16 climbs across the southern end of the range from Ten Sleep to Buffalo. More than a dozen Forest Service campgrounds line the route. This was the original "Black and Yellow Trail," first proposed in 1912 as a link between Chicago, the Black Hills, and Yellowstone. The first caravan of automobiles made it over the old sheepwagon track in the following year, reaching Yellowstone after 18 hard days on the road. By the 1920s, the highway was marked by poles with alternating black and yellow bands, and remained for many years, the main route to Yellowstone. East from Ten Sleep, U.S. 16 parallels the cottonwood-lined Tensleep Creek, climbing past impressive red and yellow cliffs. A cross and marker commemorate Gilbert Leigh, an English nobleman who fell to his death while hunting here in 1884. Eventually the switchbacks take you up to **Meadowlark Lake**, a popular winter destination for both cross-country skiers and 'bilers. The dirt road to **High Park**

Lookout Tower, is two miles east of here. Look for the flower bedecked St. Christopher's Chapel of the Big Horns as this side road climbs to the fire tower (not in use). Great views from the top. East of here, the road winds over Powder River Pass, providing breathtaking views into Cloud Peak Wilderness.

Highway 14

U.S. 14 offers an equally impressive passage over the Big Horns between Greybull and Dayton. Above the dot of a town called Shell, the road passes a remarkably phallic rocky butte, then catches Shell Creek, winding with it through the deep red rocks of Shell Canyon, past Shell Falls and the Antelope Butte Ski Area before topping out at Granite Pass. At the 120-foot-high Shell Falls, approximately eight miles east of Shell on U.S. 14, you'll find a visitor center and several short walking trails with interpretive signs. Douglas fir and limber pine grow nearby. After joining up with U.S. 14A at Burgess Junction, the road continues to Twin Buttes, Sibley Lake, and the amusing jumble of rocks called Fallen City before zig-zagging sharply down to Tongue River Canyon and the town of Dayton.

Highway 14A

U.S. 14A (officially this is Alternate U.S. 14) was completely rebuilt in the 1980s. Engineers like this road, modelled after similar routes in the Alps. This is said to be the most expensive stretch of road built in America. Locals say the "A" in U.S. 14A stands for adventure. With three different runaway truck ramps and 10% grades on some stretches, it's easy to see why. A cold clear spring gushes from a pipe next to a turnout on the forest boundary, and the view makes the long, tough climb worthwhile. U.S. 14A rises over the Big Horns from Lovell to Burgess Junction, where it meets up with U.S. 14. Along the way you're treated to miles of open sage and grass country with timbered islands on Bald and Little Bald mountains, spectacular Bucking Mule Falls, and the famous Medicine Wheel. Look for moose and deer in the meadows near Burgess Junction.

PRACTICALITIES

Camping

With 35 different campgrounds ($5), you should have no trouble finding a place to commune with nature. Most are above 5,000 feet in elevation, making for a welcome escape from summertime heat. Reservations ($7 extra) are available for the most popular ones through MISTIX, tel. (800) 283-2267. During weekends in July and August, campgrounds along the main roads are frequently filled (get there before 2 p.m.), but harder-to-reach campgrounds usually have space. The BLM's Five Springs Campground (free) is just off U.S. 14A on the western border of the National Forest. Scenic Five Springs Falls is nearby. In addition to the official campgrounds, you can camp anywhere in the forest for free, as long as you are a half mile off the main highways.

Lodging And Food

Scattered throughout the Big Horns are six mountain lodges, all of which have a bar and restaurant. Bear Lodge, at Burgess Junction, tel. 655-2444, has live music on some weekends, plus motel rooms ($33 s or d) and bring-your-own-linen rustic cabins ($18). Arrowhead Lodge, tel. 655-2388, four miles east of Burgess Junction on U.S. 14, has rustic cabins for $24 s or d and up, with motel rooms for $33 s or d. Be sure to check out the ceiling in their bar.

Deer Haven Lodge, 18 miles east of Ten Sleep on U.S. 16, tel. 366-2449, has rustic cabins starting for $17 s or $20 d, and motel rooms for $32 s or d. Meadowlark Resort, 30 miles east of Ten Sleep along U.S. 16, tel. 366-2449, has rustic cabins ($24), cottages ($38 and up), and motel rooms ($34). Their Sunday all-you-can-eat buffet is a real bargain at just $7. Meadowlark also rents boats for the lake, and offers snowmobile tours in winter. Rent horses at nearby Willow Park. Lodge in the Pines, 14 miles west of Buffalo on U.S. 16, tel. 686-4620, has cabins of all types for $22-50. Kids and seniors can throw in a line at the fishing pond. South Fork Inn, 16 miles west of Buffalo on U.S. 16, tel. 684-9609, also has a wide variety of cabins for $28-65. They also rents bikes. Open mid-May to mid-Sept. only.

Skiing And Snowmobiling

The Big Horns provide some of the finest snow in Wyoming, with cross-country ski trails at Sibley Lake, Willow Park, and Pole Creek. The rest of the forest makes for outstanding skiing most of the winter, but you'll need to break your own trail. Snowmobilers will find trails all over the forest; get a route map from Forest Service offices. **Meadowlark Resort**, tel. 366-2424, offers guided snowmobile tours. **High Country Adventures**, tel. 664-2241, has rustic winter cabins with ski-in or snowmobile-in access.

Antelope Butte Ski Area, tel. 672-0369, is a small family ski area located 60 miles west of Sheridan and 35 miles east of Greybull on U.S. 16, with a chair lift and platter. The vertical rise is 1,000 feet. Open Fri., Sat., Sun., and holidays 9:30-4, mid-Nov. through March. Lift tickets cost $15 for adults, $12 for ages 6-15, and free for young-uns. Rent skis, boots, and poles here for just $12, or take lessons from the ski school. The lodge has light meals.

High Park Ski Area, 35 miles east of Ten Sleep on U.S. 16, tel. 347-4480, is another small ski area with two platter lifts covering a 620-foot vertical rise. Open mid-Dec. to early April, with lifts running Fri., Sat., and Sun. 10-4. Get food, drinks, and ski rentals at the base lodge. Tickets cost $12 adults, $9 students, and $6 under age 12. Half-day prices are $2 less.

Hikes And Sights

Plenty to see and do in the Big Horns, including Medicine Wheel and the Cloud Peak Wilderness (described separately below). Several trails take off from Sheep Mountain Rd., on U.S. 14A, approximately 30 miles east of Lovell and three miles east of the turnoff to Medicine Wheel. **Littlehorn Trail** parallels the Little Bighorn River for 18 miles. Along the way you'll see 1,600-foot canyon faces, and water fountaining off the limestone cliffs of Leaky Mountain. The trailhead is two miles up Sheep Mountain Road (see map, p. 368). A half mile farther up the road is the trailhead for **Porcupine Falls**, a 200-foot-tall cascade accessed by a half-mile path. Along the way the trail passes a 1930s-era gold mine. One of the not-to-be-missed places in the Big Horns is spectacular **Bucking Mule Falls**, a 600-foot cascade dropping into Devil Canyon. The trailhead for Bucking Mule Falls is 11 miles off U.S. 14A on Sheep Mountain Rd., and the waterfall is a three-mile RT hike. You can also do an 11-mile loop hike by following the trail to the falls and then continuing south to Porcupine Campground.

The trailhead for **Tongue River Canyon** is 3 1/2 miles southwest of Dayton to the end of Tongue Canyon Road. This loop trail climbs up the canyon and then back again for a total of 14 miles, offering glimpses of the old McShane brothers' tie flume (1894), the fast-flowing "blue ribbon" fishing stream (cutthroat, rainbow, brook, and German brown trout), and canyon walls reaching a thousand feet into the air. Ambitious hikers may want to continue all the way to Burgess Junction. Locals float down parts of the river during the spring when water levels are high. **Tongue River Cave** is near the trailhead. With well over a mile of passages, it's one of the most popular caves in Wyoming, but has been considerably vandalized. More than 100 other caves honeycomb this country; see the Forest Service for locations and precautions. Their Sheridan office also has a helpful brochure listing other local hikes.

An enjoyable waterfall is **Big Goose Falls**. Follow Forest Rd. 26 (it starts approximately five miles south of Burgess Junction on U.S. 14) to Big Goose Ranger Station, continuing on from there via Forest Rd. 296 to the end. The falls are about five miles below the ranger station, along the East Fork of Big Goose Creek. They include plunge pools and water-sculptured rocks.

One of the most interesting drives in the Big Horns slices through **Crazy Woman Canyon**. The name comes from either (take your pick) an Indian squaw who went insane while living alone in her tipi here, or a white woman who, after her wagon train had been brutally attacked by Indians, became demented and wandered away, never to be seen again. Not exactly a soothing name for migrants on the old Bozeman Trail! Nevertheless, the canyon cut by cascading Crazy Woman Creek is a stunning one, with steep cliffs on both sides. A rough dirt road heads down-canyon from Crazy Woman Campground (25 miles west of Buffalo on U.S. 16). You can follow the road all the way to the mouth of the canyon and then on to State 196. **Crazy Woman Canyon Tours**, tel. 684-5446, offers 4WD trips through this scenic canyon.

MEDICINE WHEEL

High atop a windswept mountain plateau sits one of the best-known and least-understood archaeological sites in America, the Medicine Wheel. Measuring 80 feet across, this uneven "wagon wheel" of stones seems ready to roll over the nearby slopes. Twenty-eight rock spokes radiate out from a central hub that is 13 feet in diameter, with six smaller rock cairns scattered around the rim. A variety of lesser-known rock structures surround the Medicine Wheel on nearby slopes, including an arrow that points southwest to another "wheel" near Meeteetse (70 miles away), a large rectangle of stones, and more than 50 tipi rings. An ancient cairn-marked travois trail continues northwest from Medicine Wheel over the Big Horn Mountains.

What Is It?

The Medicine Wheel has been variously interpreted and attributed to all sorts of folks—Aztecs, Celtics, Pueblo Indians, Egyptians, Babyloni-ans, and even Masons. None of these is the least bit likely, but nobody has come up with an adequate explanation for the wheel. Prospectors from the nearby gold-mining camp of Bald Mountain City (now entirely gone) discovered the Medicine Wheel around 1885. Various reports have attributed it to the Crow, Sheepeater, Arapaho, or Cheyenne tribes. In 1958, an archaeologist dated bits of wood found in one of the cairns to approximately 1760. The rocks have probably been here for at least that long.

Prevailing theories about the purpose behind the Medicine Wheel seem to fall into two schools: that it was an astronomical observatory, or that it was a site for sacred ceremonies. One of the most interesting theories was suggested by astronomer John Eddy in a 1977 *National Geographic* article. He noted that the 28 spokes are equal to the number of days in the lunar calendar and that two of the cairns served as horizon markers for sunrise and sunset, with the other four cairns marking the rising of three of the brightest stars. These could have signaled the summer solstice. Interestingly, similar alignments occur on a stone wheel in Saskatch-

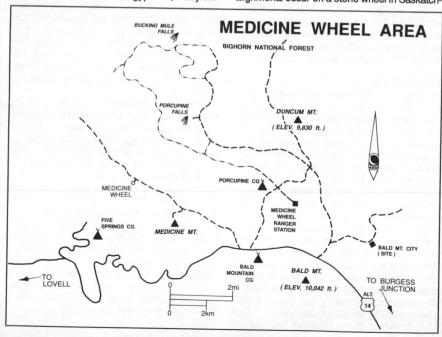

MEDICINE WHEEL AREA

BUCKING MULE FALLS

BIGHORN NATIONAL FOREST

PORCUPINE FALLS

DUNCUM MT. (ELEV. 9,830 ft.)

MEDICINE WHEEL

PORCUPINE CG

MEDICINE WHEEL RANGER STATION

FIVE SPRINGS CG

MEDICINE MT.

BALD MT. CITY (SITE)

BALD MOUNTAIN CG

BALD MT. (ELEV. 10,042 ft.)

TO LOVELL

TO BURGESS JUNCTION

0   2mi

0   2km

ALT. 14

© MOON PUBLICATIONS

ewan, Canada. Other scientists counter that the Indians would have little reason to care exactly when summer solstice occurred since they were not farmers, and that the rocks probably served some religious function. Given the Medicine Wheel's location and the importance of ceremony in Native American life, it is likely that this was a sacred site, whether or not it served any astronomical function. The Medicine Wheel remains an enigma wrapped in a mystery.

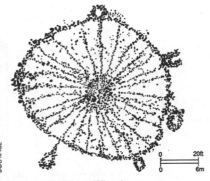

Visiting Medicine Wheel

Get to Medicine Wheel by turning onto a well-marked gravel road that heads north from U.S. 14A, approximately 27 miles east of Lovell. The wheel is three miles in. The road passes an FAA radar dome built on nearby Medicine Mountain, an incredibly disturbing structure to find in such a significant Native American site. A wire fence surrounding the wheel is frequently festooned with strips of cloth, feathers, bells, herbs, flowers, and other offerings left behind by Indians who come here on various sacred ceremonies and celebrations. They are particularly evident following solstices and equinoxes. Respect the importance of this religious site by not disturbing these items.

It is obvious why this mountain was chosen for the Medicine Wheel. The surrounding open country has scattered pine, juniper, and spruce, and the ridge drops off a 150-foot precipice just 50 feet away. From its 9,956-foot elevation, a vast panorama stretches to include the Bighorn Basin, the Wind River, the Absaroka Range, and the Pryor Mountains. Medicine Wheel is also a good place to look for hawks wheeling through the sky, especially red tails and kestrels.

CLOUD PEAK WILDERNESS

Although maintained as a primitive area since 1932, the 195,500-acre Cloud Peak Wilderness did not receive official wilderness status until 1984. It's named for 13,175-foot **Cloud Peak**, a rocky mountain visible for a hundred miles in all directions. At one time this entire range was glaciated, and reminders abound in the sharpened peaks, broad U-shaped valleys, and a multitude of lakes in glacial tarns. There are even a few small patches of glacial ice. The Big Horns still get plenty of snow, leaving many hiking trails in the high country blocked until July. One oddly named mountain in the wilderness is **Bomber Peak**, just south of Cloud Peak. An Air Force B-17 bomber crashed here in 1943, killing all 10 men on board. It was not found for two years.

With more than 100 miles of trails and thousands of acres more above timberline, there are abundant hiking and horsepacking opportunities throughout Cloud Peak. Backcountry permits are not required, but you should fill out the registration cards at trailheads. Be sure to camp at least 100 feet from water sources and trails, and hang all food out of reach of black bears. Use existing campsites whenever possible to lessen your impact. The Forest Service produces a free map/guide to the wilderness area that lists additional precautions. For complete trail and historical info on the wilderness, request a copy of Kenneth Melius' book, *Cloud Peak Wilderness Area* ($11.95 to Tensleep Publications, Box 925, Aberdeen, SD 57401). Be sure to get topographic maps before heading out. Check with the Forest Service office in Sheridan for a list of local outfitters. For something different, **Cloud Peak Llama Treks** in Story, tel. 683-2732, offers llama trips for $80/day.

Access into Cloud Peak Wilderness is via several entry roads along U.S. 16 on the southern border, and from the north (U.S. 14) at Cross Creek and Ranger Creek campgrounds and Twin Lakes Picnic Ground. Other entrancepoints surround Cloud Peak, but many require long hikes up 4WD roads to get to the wilderness boundary.

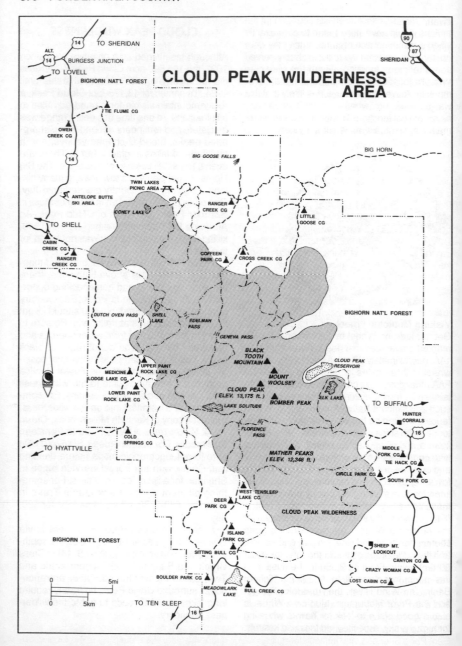

CLOUD PEAK WILDERNESS AREA

Trails
The **Stull Lakes-Coney Lake Trail** is one of the shortest and most popular hikes into the lake country of Cloud Peak. It climbs three miles from the Twin Lakes Picnic Ground, passing Stull Lake and ending in the alpine country surrounding Coney Lake. Watch for elk and deer in late summer.

An excellent 21-mile loop hike begins at **Lower Paintrock Lake Trailhead** on the west side of the wilderness. This route provides a wide variety of country, from dense timber to rocky mountain passes and small glaciers. The path climbs to a trail junction 1 1/2 miles west of Cliff Lake. From here, turn left and follow the trail to Geneva Pass (10,300 feet). The trail drops down to Lake Geneva and then follows East Fork Creek to the junction with the Edelman Trail. This trail leads over Edelman Pass, around Emerald Lake, and then back down to the Edelman Trailhead, just 1 1/2 miles by road from your starting point. There are all sorts of other hikes and side trips in this area.

Another long loop trip takes you to **Lake Solitude.** Begin at the Paint Rock Trailhead, located approximately 10 miles north of Meadowlark Lake. Take the road to Tyrell Ranger Station and turn left after a mile, continuing up the rough gravel road to the trailhead. The trail climbs to Lily Lake which is filled with water lilies, and then up a steep valley to Mistymoon Lake. A mile north of here is an undeveloped route to **Cloud Peak** (4 1/2 miles away) and some of the most desolate country imaginable. See Melius' book for specifics on climbing the peak. It is not a technical climb but you should be prepared for sudden weather changes. The main trail drops down Paint Rock Creek to Lake Solitude. Beyond this, it passes Grace Lake, and splits at Long Park where a trail takes you back to Lily Lake and the trailhead. The loop is approximately 16 miles roundtrip.

The **Elk Lake Loop** (19 miles RT) begins at Hunter Corrals Trailhead on the southeast side of the wilderness. Follow the old jeep trail to Soldier Park, a scenic grassy meadow. Turn north at the trail junction and follow the path to Elk Lake. Along the way are some outstanding views across the alpine to Cloud Peak. Turn left at Elk Lake, up over a pass, then down the other side to Soldier Park and back to the trailhead.

SHERIDAN

Sheridan (pop. 15,000) is an attractive town, with plenty to see, good restaurants, the nearby Big Horn Mountains, and a genuine sense of history. At just 3,745 feet above sea level, Sheridan has the lowest elevation of any Wyoming town, making for hot summers. The country around Sheridan was settled by a broad mixture of Europeans, including everyone from British lords to Polish coal miners. Their heritage carries on in such events as weekly polo matches at the oldest polo field in the nation (see p. 379) and an annual polka festival.

History
Sheridan, like other towns in the Powder River Basin, was built on coal, cattle, farming, and the railroad. In 1882, John D. Loucks, took a liking to the country here and decided to establish a town, drawing up a plat on a piece of brown wrapping paper. He named the new place for his commanding officer during the Civil War, Gen. Philip Sheridan, and immediately set about getting others to come. For several years Sheridan competed with nearby Big Horn City for the county seat, a title that ensured survival. Finally in 1885, Sheridan promoters offered cowboys at the fall roundup free lots in the town. When most accepted, Sheridan finally had enough folks to incorporate. Almost overnight (literally in some cases) businesses in Big Horn City moved to Sheridan, sometimes bringing buildings along too.

When the Burlington and Missouri Railroad reached Sheridan in 1892, the town suddenly changed. Now ranchers could get their cattle to market more easily and visitors could stay in the sumptuous new Sheridan Inn. Dryland farming became more profitable as investors built large grain mills and a beet sugar-processing plant. The first underground coal mines opened in 1883, but it was not until 1903 that the Burlington Railroad began using the coal in their engines. For the next several decades these "black diamonds" were the mainstay of the local econ-

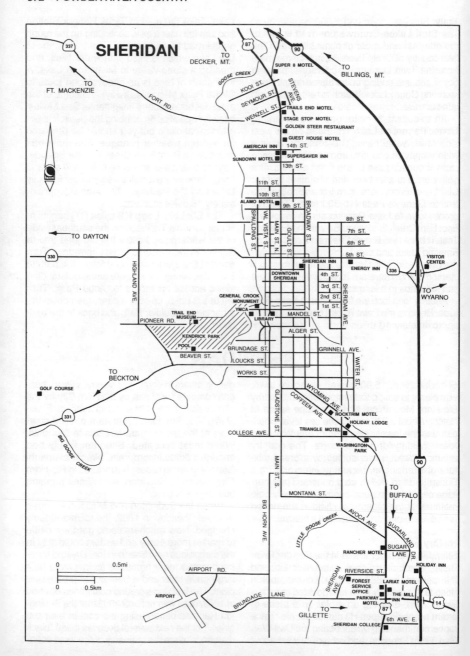

omy. Sheridan soon had 1,500 people, 30 saloons, six churches, two opera houses, and wooden sidewalks. Small mining towns—Dietz, Acme, Kooi, Model, Riverside, and Carneyville—opened in the surrounding countryside, worked by thousands of European emigrants. Newspapers often featured ads in both Polish and English. Electric street cars were added in 1911, with frequent interurban service to the surrounding coal mines.

World War II brought prosperity, as local mines operated at full tilt and new technology allowed construction of the first open-pit mine. After the war, however, trains shifted to diesel and homes began burning the less-polluting natural gas, so that by 1953 the last of the old coal towns had died. With increasing demand for western coal in the 1970s, Sheridan's population again boomed. Recent years have seen the closing of some nearby strip mines, with many workers now crossing the Montana border to work in the Decker and Spring Creek strip mines there, although a long strike in the Decker mine has split the community. Sheridan now depends upon a mixture of mining, ranching, government jobs, and tourism.

SIGHTS

Trail End Historic Center

Trail End Historic Center, 400 E. Clarendon Ave., tel. 674-4589, is Sheridan's best-known attraction. Managed by the state, it's open daily 9-5 (Wednesday till 9 p.m.) during summer and daily 2-5 in winter, no charge. This was the home of John B. Kendrick, a wealthy rancher and powerful Democratic politician. Born in Texas in 1857, Kendrick was raised as an orphan. He became a ranchhand by age 15, and after trailing cattle north to Wyoming, fell in love with the country, and took a job as a ranch foreman.

Over the years Kendrick acquired more than 200,000 acres of land in Wyoming and Montana, grazed by tens of thousands of his cattle. He personally financed local homesteaders, friends, former employees, and relatives. Once firmly established as a rancher and businessman, politics beckoned, and he served first as governor, then as a U.S. senator until his death in 1933. One paper called him "The craftiest

politician the state has ever produced." Kendrick helped expose the Teapot Dome Scandal and gained funding for the massive Kendrick Project, a series of dams and irrigation canals on the North Platte River. Shortly before entering politics, Kendrick selected the site for his end-of-the-trail mansion, high atop a hill overlooking Sheridan.

Begun in 1908, Trail End took five years to complete and served primarily as a summer home since politics kept Kendrick away the rest of the year. The mansion is in the Flemish style, with curvilinear gables on the third-floor windows, a red-tile roof, hardwood floors, mahogany walls, and exposed-beam ceilings. Many of the sumptuous original furnishings (including a 25-foot-long Kurdistan rug) are inside. Look for photos of several of Kendrick's ranches upstairs.

The house cost $165,000 in an era when typical homes went for less than $1,000. Its 18 rooms include a third floor ballroom with a loft where musicians could play without interfering with the dancers below. Heating Trail End sometimes required up to a ton of coal each day! Out back is a sod-roofed **log cabin** that was reconstructed and moved onto the grounds in recent years. Built in 1878, this historic structure served at various times as Sheridan's first post office, school, store, law office, and bank!

Sheridan Inn

Built in 1892-93, Sheridan Inn was considered the finest hotel between Chicago and San Francisco. Its visitors included presidents Theodore Roosevelt, Taft, and Hoover. Architect Thomas Kimball modeled the inn after a Scottish hunting lodge, with dormer windows on all 62 rooms; *Ripley's Believe it or Not* called it "The House of 69 Gables," a name that has stuck through the years. Inside, carpenters added hand-hewn ponderosa pine beams, three large cobblestone fireplaces, the "Buffalo Bill Bar" (imported from England), elegant oak furnishings, and the first electric lights in Sheridan. Col. William F. Cody (Buffalo Bill) led the grand march for the first dance on opening night. Later, Cody briefly owned the hotel and used the veranda to audition performers for his Wild West Show. Although currently closed, it is on the National Register of Historic Places. It would make a marvelously luxurious bed and breakfast. Tall cottonwoods guard the front, and the huge porch wraps around the sides. Try counting the gables to see if you can figure out where they hid enough to make a total of 69.

Fort Mackenzie

Built in 1902, Fort Mackenzie never really served much of a military function. Pushed through Congress by Wyoming's powerful Senator Francis E. Warren, the fort was ostensibly built as a base to put down any Indian uprising on nearby reservations. (The last major Indian battles had been 20 years earlier.) It was named for Gen. Ranald S. Mackenzie, a veteran of the Civil War and various Indian battles. Over the decades, the size of the fort shrank from 6,280 acres to 342 acres, and the last troops departed during WW I. In 1922, it became a 339-bed hospital for mentally ill vets. You're welcome to walk around the grounds and admire the old brick buildings, but be sure to check in at the administration building first.

King's Saddlery

Well worth a stop is King's Saddlery, 184 N. Main, tel. 672-2702, a Sheridan-area fixture for almost 50 years. The shop has handmade saddles, leatherwork, ropes, spurs, chaps, belt buckles, cowboy hats, and various other tack for horses. Be sure to take a look at the miles of rope in the back room; many top rodeo cowboys drop by for their lariats. A free museum in the back has dozens of gorgeous saddles—some from before the Civil War—along with rifles, spurs, chaps, and a sheep wagon. King's Saddlery is fittingly named: both Queen Elizabeth and the king of Saudi Arabia have visited, and ex-Prez Reagan has one of their leather belts.

Sheridan County Library

Sheridan's excellent library at 320 N. Brooks, tel. 674-8585, is open Mon.-Thurs. 9-9 and Fri.-Sat. 9-6. One section encloses a small collection of Indian artifacts and items from early settlers. The Wyoming Room has an extensive collection of old books, maps, and paintings, including a mural of the Wagon Box Fight (see p. 383); upstairs are more historical exhibits and current artwork, plus a model of the Medicine Wheel. Also on the walls of the library are 11 paintings by Bill Gollings (1878-1932), a self-taught, but accomplished cowboy artist.

Other Sights

Directly across from the Sheridan Inn is the old red Sheridan **train depot**, built in 1892. Nearby is a huge Chicago, Burlington, & Quincy Railroad **locomotive**. Downtown on 1st and Gould streets is one of Sheridan's **streetcars** from the early 1900s. A historic marker on the corner of Dow and Val Vista streets commemorates **Gen. Crook's campsite** at the junction of Big and Little Goose creeks. In 1876 he camped here with 1,325 men and 1,900 pack animals after being forced to a stalemate by Sioux and Crow warriors on the Rosebud River, eight days before Custer would die at nearby Little Big Horn. History and architectural buffs should pick up a copy of the guide to Sheridan's **Main Street Historic District** at the visitor center. One of the buildings included is the **Mint Bar**, 151 N. Main, tel. 674-9696, filled with stuffed critters, rodeo photos, and gnarled wood benches. A real taste of the West.

PRACTICALITIES

Motels And Dude Ranches

Most of Sheridan's 19 motels lie along Coffeen Ave. and Main Street. See the chart for specific rates. The **Mill Inn Motel** is unique in being within a historic flour mill. (Sort of adds a new meaning to the term "hitting the sack.") A warn-

ing on two places in town: the Super 8 is next to a very smelly stockyard, and the Holiday Inn is not only overpriced, but can be unfriendly.

Sheridan is surrounded by several fine dude ranches. The first in the area was run by the Hilman family who took in their first paying dudes in 1889. It operated until the 1930s. The famous **Eaton's Guest Ranch**, 18 miles west of Sheridan, tel. 655-9285, is one of the oldest and best-known dude ranches in America. The three Eaton brothers—Howard, Alden, and Willis—began ranching in North Dakota in the late 1800s, but soon found themselves overwhelmed by visiting friends from the East. Eventually one

SHERIDAN ACCOMMODATIONS

Motel	Address	Telephone	Rates	Features
Triangle Motel	540 Coffeen Ave.	674-8031	$15 s or d	kitchenettes
Super Saver Inn	1789 W. Main	672-0471	$16+ s, $25 d	
Alamo Motel	1326 N. Main	672-2455	$18 s, $25 d	
Stage Stop Motel	2167 N. Main	672-3459	$18 s, $22 d	
Parkway Motel	2112 Coffeen Ave.	672-7259	$18 s, $23 d	
Lariat Motel	2068 Coffeen Ave.	672-6475	$20 s, $24 d	
Sundown Motel	1704 N. Main	672-2439	$22 s, $24 d	
Energy Inn	580 E. 5th St.	672-9757	$23 s, $28 d	jacuzzi
Triangle Motel	540 Coffeen Ave.	674-8031	$24 s, $27 d	
X-L Motel	402 N. Main	674-6458	$24 s, $27 d	
Motel Holiday Lodge	625 Coffeen Ave.	672-2407	$24 s, $28 d	pool
Rocktrim Motel	449 Coffeen Ave.	672-2464	$24+ s or d	AAA approved
Rancher Motel	1552 Coffeen Ave.	672-2428	$25 s, $32 d	jacuzzi, sauna
Kilbourne Kastle B&B	320 S. Main	674-8716	$25+ s or d	
Guest House Motel	2007 N. Main	674-7496 (800) 341-8000	$26 s, $28+ d	AAA approved, pool
Mill Inn Motel	2161 Coffeen Ave.	672-6401	$30 s, $33 d	AAA approved
Super 8 Motel	2435 N. Main	672-9725	$36 s, $40 d	
Trails End Motel	2125 N. Main	672-2477	$38+ s or d	AAA approved, pool
Sheridan Center Motor Inn (Best Western)	609 N. Main	674-7421 (800) 528-1234	$42+ s, $46+ d	pool, sauna, jacuzzi, continental breakfast,
Holiday Inn	1809 Sugarland Dr.	672-8931 (800) 465-4329	$46+ s, $52+ d	AAA approved, pool, sauna, jacuzzi, exercise facility

offered to pay, and thus was born the dude ranch. At first these "dudes" (a term that both Buffalo Bill and Howard Eaton took credit for first using in this context) stayed wherever they could find space, eating the cowboy's grub and joining in on chores. In 1904, the brothers bought a ranch along Wyoming's Wolf Creek that would eventually grow to 7,000 acres. Today the ranch accommodates 125 dudes in modernized guest cabins. Two other fine local dude ranches are **Spear-O-Wigwam Dude Ranch**, tel. 674-4496, begun in 1923 by Virginia and Willis Spear, and **Masters Ranches** in Ranchester, tel. 655-2386.

Camping

Camp for free in town at **Washington Park**, close to Little Goose Creek but also along the busy main drag. One night only—water sprinklers enforce this every afternoon. Get your tent down in time! Many more campgrounds ($5) on nearby Bighorn National Forest; see above for details. **Bighorn Mountain KOA**, 63 Decker Rd., tel. 674-8766, has quiet tent sites for $11 and RV sites for $14. Non-campers may shower for $3.25 (before 4 p.m. only). Open May-early October.

Food

Sheridan has a broad choice of eateries, from two-bit greasy spoons to gourmet restaurants. The exterior of the **Silver Spur**, 832 N. Main, tel. 672-2749, is low-budget, and it only serves breakfast and lunch, but it has the best down-home cowboy food in town. Reasonable prices, too. **Carolyn's** in the X-L Bar, 400 N. Main, tel. 672-4472, dishes up homemade soups, salads, and sandwiches for lunch, while **Spotted Horse Cafe**, 120 N. Main, tel. 672-2838, has gourmet vegetarian lunches, homemade ice cream, and good coffee. For something completely different, don't miss **Bazels Restaurant**, 748 N. Main, tel. 672-7183. Great fries and shakes, fresh ground beef burgers, friendly waitresses, and an infectiously fun '50s diner atmosphere.

Try **Pablo's Restaurant**, 1274 N. Main, tel. 672-0737, for Mexican dishes and margaritas. One of the nicest dinner spots in town is the elegant **Cady House Ristorante**, 5 E. Alger, tel. 672-7744, which specializes in "melt-in-your-mouth steaks." Another favorite with locals and visitors alike is **Golden Steer Restaurant**, 2071 N. Main, tel. 674-9334. **Little Big Men Pizza**,

1424 Coffeen Ave., tel. 672-9877, serves reasonable pizza, burger, and salad meal deals, but **Ole's Pizza**, in the mall next to the Holiday Inn, tel. 672-3636, is usually a better bet. Fill up on rabbit food at the gigantic salad bar in **Golden Corral**, 927 Coffeen Ave., tel. 674-9249, or on barbecued buffalo at **Bighorn Mountain KOA**, 63 Decker Rd., tel. 674-8766. All-you-can-eat BBQ rib dinners are just $8. In addition to the standard mega-marts (Safeway and Buttery) in Sheridan, you'll find holistic groceries at **Nanci's Natural Foods**, 38 S. Main, tel. 674-8344.

Entertainment

Enjoy live rock 'n' roll on weekends at **LBM Pizza**, 1424 Coffeen Ave., tel. 672-9877, or watch sports on their big-screen TV. **Golden Steer**, 2071 N. Main, tel. 674-9334, often has golden oldies from the '50s, while the **Brass Banjo** at the Holiday Inn, 1809 Sugarland Dr., tel. 672-8931, has recorded dance tunes most nights and rock on weekends.

Events

The **Sheridan Wyo Rodeo** comes around in mid-July each year, bringing with it not just professional rodeo cowboys, but also a parade down Main St., a pancake breakfast, bed races, and street dances. The **Wyoming State Chili Cook-off**, also in mid-July, attracts participants from all over the country. In early August, visit the **Sheridan County Fair**, followed by the **Sheridan County Rodeo** later in the month. **Big Horn Mountain Polka Days** is a fun annual event held in early September, attracting several thousand polka enthusiasts. Oom-pa-pa! During the winter, **"Chariot Races"** are held at the Soldier Creek Complex on 5th Street.

Recreation

Kendrick City Park has a small game preserve with various native critters such as bison and elk. Swim at the outdoor **pool** in the park (summer only) or at the **YMCA**, 417 N. Jefferson, tel. 674-7488, for $3 ($1 for kids). Feel like a kid again on the 90-foot-long waterslide here. Also at the Y are racquetball and tennis courts, and weight machines. **Big Horn Mountain Sports**, 334 N. Main St., tel. 672-6866, has a good choice of camping, backpacking, skiing, and windsurfing equipment, both for sale and for rent. They also teach classes in skiing, kayaking, windsurfing, and climbing. **Fly Shop of the Big Horns**, 377 Coffeen Ave., tel. 672-5866, has classes in fly casting and flytying, and offers guided fishing trips on the Big Horn and Platte rivers. Rent float tubes and fins here. Golfers will want to try out the 18-hole **Kendrick Golf Course**, three miles west of town, tel. 674-8148.

Shopping

You'll find a good selection of Wyoming titles in **Sheridan Stationary Books**, 206 N. Main, tel. 672-8080, and **The Book Shop**, 122 N. Main, tel. 672-6505. See **Deb Mayer**, 757 Brundage Lane, tel. 672-8569, for the biggest local selection of made-in-Wyoming gifts. Several Sheridan art galleries are worth a peek: **Side Street Gallery**, 111 W. Brundage, tel. 672-6561, **Golden Crown Art Gallery**, 50 N. Main, tel. 674-7676, and **Gallery 348**, 348 N. Main St., tel. 672-6120.

Information And Services

The **Sheridan Visitor Center/State Information Center**, tel. 672-2485, is located in the rest area at the 5th St. exit of I-90. Inside is a bronze statue of a bear and cub by Dayton artist Mike Flanagan and a number of historical displays. It's open daily 8-8 in summer, and Mon.-Fri. 8-5 in winter. A small kiosk visitor center in Washington Park opens for the summer. The **Bighorn National Forest Supervisors Office** is at 1969 S. Sheridan Ave., tel. 672-0751. **Sheridan College**, tel. 674-6446, a 2,000-student, two-year school just south of Sheridan, is one of the largest in the state. Founded in 1948, it offers degrees in both academic and technical fields. The **Special Collections** room of the college library (tel. 674-6446) has a variety of Indian artifacts, including vests, moccasins, pipes, and weapons.

Transportation

The Sheridan airport is just southwest of town. Both **Rocky Mountain Air (Continental)**, tel. (800) 525-0280, and **United Express**, tel. (800) 631-1500, have daily flights to Denver and Gillette. **Powder River Transportation**, 1552 Coffeen Ave., tel. (800) 442-3682, has daily bus service to Billings, Montana, and most towns in northern Wyoming. Rent cars from **Avis**, tel. (800) 331-1212, at the airport or **Sheridan Motor**, 1766 Coffeen Ave., tel. 672-3411. Rates start around $36 a day. Two local taxi companies provide service: **Sheridan City Cab**, tel. 674-9459, and **Checker Cab**, tel. 674-6814.

SHERIDAN VICINITY

NORTH OF SHERIDAN

Ranchester

The little village of Ranchester (pop. 650) calls itself "The town where the handshake's stronger and the smile lasts longer." Seems true enough. Stay at the clean and friendly **Ranchester Motel**, tel. 655-2212 or (800) 341-8000, for $24 s or $26 d. Head to **BJ Pizza** for genuine homemade pizzas. Other good places are **Ranch House Restaurant**, tel. 655-9527, for family fare and **Magnum Restaurant**, tel. 655-9634, for steaks. **DD's Bar & Lounge**, tel. 655-9818, has live music on weekends. Kids will enjoy the kid-designed wooden playground of forts and slides at the elementary school. Ranchester's **Celebration Days**, held in early August, includes a horseshoe tournament, street dance, and picnic.

Connor Battlefield is right in Ranchester city park. It's a very pleasant place with picnic tables, free camping, and tall cottonwood trees along the Tongue River (so named because of a tongue-like rock along a tributary). Good fishing for brown trout. A cable footbridge leads across the river. Despite the bucolic setting, the park has a gruesome history, representing the worst massacre in the Powder River Basin by either side. It was the year 1865, a time of hit-and-run battles throughout the plains set off by the massacre of Cheyennes at Sand Creek in Colorado, but continued by dozens of Indian attacks upon settlers and emigrants. Red Cloud had just struck against Platte Bridge Station (see "Casper," p. 158) a few weeks before, killing 28 men, and the Army was anxious to avenge the raid and attacks on others along the Bozeman Trail.

Gen. Patrick E. Connor—a proponent of the shoot-first, ask-questions-later school of military diplomacy—attacked Indian villages throughout the West, killing 200 Shoshone in a Utah attack in 1863, and then rampaging through Nevada and Idaho. Connor's 1865 expedition to the Powder River included nearly a thousand soldiers, plus 179 Pawnee and Winnebago scouts. Most of the effort was a failure, as Indians kept ahead of the ponderous military wagons, but on August 29 they came upon Chief Black Bear's Arapaho village along the Tongue River. Connor ordered his men, "You will not receive overtures of peace or submission from the Indians, but will attack and kill every male Indian over 12 years of age." In a pell-mell rush, Connor's men slaughtered 63 men, women, and children, destroyed 250 lodges along with much of their winter supplies, and captured more than 1,100 ponies. Eight troopers died. It never was ascertained whether the Arapahos they encountered were the same ones who had been attacking along the Bozeman Trail. The expedition ended when the government realized the expedition was costing over a million dollars a month for transportation alone. A chastened Connor stashed his supplies at Fort Connor (later renamed Fort Reno; see p.381), and returned to Fort Laramie.

Four miles west of here on U.S. 14, another monument marks the **Sawyer Fight**. Here, two days after Connor attacked the Arapaho along the Tongue River, they retaliated against a 100-man road-building expedition led by Col. James Sawyer. Three of his men were killed, and the rest were pinned down for nearly two weeks before finally being rescued by Gen. Connor's troops.

Dayton

The little settlement of Dayton (pop. 700) has a number of attractions. Of note is **Dayton Mercantile**, tel. 655-2214, built in 1898 and now run by the exuberantly friendly owner, Isabel Le Beau. Inside are works by various local artisans and a fine pantry with homemade sandwiches, soups, breads, and pies. Try a sarsaparilla float. Wyoming's oldest dance hall is upstairs, while out back is a small gallery of Western art in the old icehouse. The town's old bell tower, built in 1910 to warn of fires, is now in the city park. Dayton also has a public swimming pool.

Humphrey's Blacksmithing, tel. 655-9744, has various hand-forged ironware for sale. **Big Horn Motel**, tel. 655-2242, charges just $15 s or $20 d, but be ready for black-and-white TVs. Much nicer is the **Foothills Campground and Motel**, tel. 655-2547, where cabins cost $17 s or d (kitchenettes $2 more). Camp along the river here for $7 (showers 25¢ extra) or park RVs for $10. Non-campers can shower up for $1.25. The campground is open mid-April through December.

Summerhouse Books, tel. 655-2367 (summers only or by appointment), has both new and used books for sale. At the **Packstring Gallery**, tel. 655-2350, Mike Flanagan creates traditional Western bronze works. His sculptures are in the governor's mansion and at the Sheridan Visitor Center. The studio of water colorist **Hans Kleiber** (1887-1966), "Artist of the Big Horns," is also in Dayton; call 655-2223 for permission to visit. **Dayton Days**, held the last weekend in July, has the usual country favorites, including a parade and street dance. Fishermen will find "blue ribbon" trout fishing along the Tongue River.

EAST OF SHERIDAN

Some of the prettiest plains country in Wyoming lies along U.S. 14, a quiet, scenic road that curls through mile after mile of ranch land and winter wheat. The road heads southeast from Sheridan, gradually narrowing as it climbs through rugged hills and down a long green valley filled with fine ranches and modern homes.

Ucross

At the crossroads called Ucross, a huge red barn (Big Red) dominates the view. The ranch is headquarters for the nonprofit Ucross Foundation, tel. 737-2291, an artist retreat, conference center, and restaurant. The **art gallery** here is open Sun. 12:30-5:30 and Mon.-Fri. 8:30-4:30, and contains exhibits of regional pieces. Big Red was headquarters for the enormous Pratt and Ferris Cattle Co., a spread that extended 35 miles along Clear Creek. At one time, more than 35,000 calves were branded each fall, and the huge barn could hold 30 teams of horses. The "U Cross" was their brand. Ucross also is home to a luxurious (and pricey) resort, **Ucross Guest**

Ranch, tel. 737-2281. Make reservations for a gourmet meal here. If you're in the area around July 4, stick around for a spectacular fireworks display.

The 20 miles east of Ucross are some of the prettiest in Wyoming. The road follows the cottonwood-bordered Clear Creek, winding its way down the grassy hillsides. The Big Horn Mountains form a dramatic western backdrop, while large ranches dot the countryside with stone buildings and spreading old trees. It's easy to see why the Sioux fought so hard to keep this country out of white hands! The highway crosses the Powder River at the little settlement called Arvada, and then heads east to Spotted Horse.

Spotted Horse

At Spotted Horse—named for a minor Cheyenne chief—the combination country store/gas station/saloon/cafe is worth a stop, if only to hang out with locals in the five-stool bar. Hard times show in the faces of local ranchers. During the 1930s, tourists en route to Yellowstone posed on a stuffed bucking bronc in the back paddock, but once I-90 was completed, business plummeted. The area's economy has suffered a long decline, and other tiny burgs nearby—Recluse, Arvada, Clearmont, and Leiter—appear on their way to extinction.

Beyond Spotted Horse, the highway curves southeast toward the coal mines of Gillette. The red scoria rock of the highway points through summer-green grass. (Also called clinker, this rock was created when coal burned underground, baking adjacent shale and sandstone to a bright red. Similar red roads exist all over Powder River Basin.) Old windmills pump water for cattle and sheep. From atop the hills a landscape of fences, phone lines, plowed fields, bales of hay, and horses spread out in all directions. The sun darts between the cottonball clouds as a lone cyclist pumps up the road, swerving around the smashed jackrabbits and passed by pickup trucks with gun racks and tipped-back cowboy hats. This is the true West, not the cutesified West for the tourists. Red-sided buttes rise above the rolling plains. The new ranch houses—trailer homes—stand next to aging farmsteads and collapsed log cabins; imported pickups in the driveway and satellite dishes out front. If you like grass and sky, brilliant starry nights, antelope, haystacks, and oil wells,

you'll love this place. Stop for a while and listen to the silence, broken only by the meadowlarks and the wind. God's country.

SOUTH OF SHERIDAN

Although I-90 cuts south of Sheridan toward Buffalo, U.S. 87 offers a much more interesting route, taking you through rolling ranch country and past cottonwood-lined draws. Along the way are the little settlements of Big Horn and Story, and the historically rich country around old Fort Phil Kearny and the Bozeman Trail.

Big Horn

Tiny Big Horn was founded in 1879 by O. P. Hanna (local Indians called him "Big Spit," because of his tobacco chewing), a ceaseless promoter who sent glowing accounts of "Big Horn City" to various newspapers. Unfortunately, a reporter decided to investigate and found the town consisted primarily of a few outlaws such as "Big Nose" George Parrott and Frank James (of the James Gang). A few homesteaders and settlers did come, so that by 1884 Big Horn City had a hotel, three stores, two blacksmith shops, three saloons, a newspaper, a school, a church, and even a college. Over the years, most of the businesses moved to Sheridan, but still here is the **Big Horn Store**, built in 1882, considered the oldest business in northern Wyoming. Take a look inside for the photo of Queen Elizabeth, who visited here in 1984. (The area has a prominent British heritage.) **Bozeman Trail Museum** is housed in an old blacksmith shop dating from 1881. Open Sat. and Sun. 9:30-5 during the summer, it has various local memorabilia and old photos of the town. No charge. The town park next door makes a pleasant picnic spot. Stay at **Spahn's Bed & Breakfast**, tel. 674-8150, for $45 s or d, a modern log house with solar-powered electricity. The **State Bird Farm**, tel. 674-7701, on Bird Farm Rd. raises pheasants and has show birds.

Certainly the last thing one might expect to find in Big Horn is a polo field, but the English tradition lives on at **Big Horn Equestrian Center**, south of town on Bird Farm Road. Polo games are held on Sundays at 11:30 a.m. and 2 p.m. during the summer. These are informal events with changing teams and players of varying abilities. The ranch is owned by Malcolm Wallop, one of Wyoming's U.S. senators, and the grandson of Sir Oliver H. Wallop, seventh earl of Portsmouth (who served in the Wyoming Legislature before returning to England to sit in the British House of Lords). Oliver Wallop and the two Moncrieffe brothers (see below) bought Western horses for the British Army during the Boer War, shipping 20,000 of them overseas. To test the ponies, the British purchasing officer would ride them the length of a polo field. Malcolm Moncrieffe trained a team on this field, later competing with them in England. Thus began what is believed to be the oldest polo field in America.

Bradford Brinton Memorial Museum

In 1893, two Scottish brothers, William and Malcolm Moncrieffe, built a spacious two-story ranch house along Little Goose Creek, headquarters for their Quarter Circle A Ranch. A businessman and lover of the West, Bradford Brinton bought the ranch in 1923 and enlarged the home to 20 rooms, furnishing it with his art collection. After his death in 1936, the house was owned by his sister. Her will established it as a museum in honor of Bradford Brinton, which it has been since her death in 1960. The museum, tel. 672-3173, is open daily 9:30-5 in summer (closed winters) with free guided tours. Step inside to taste the genteel life and to view works by some of the West's best-known artists, many of whom were friends of Bradford Brinton. The collection includes over 600 works by such artists as John James Audubon, Hans Kleiber, Charles M. Russell, Frederic Remington, and Will Gollings. Also here are various Indian handicrafts, books, and historic documents. Horses are still raised on the 600-acre ranch, and the rural setting is most enjoyable: mountains rise on two sides, and big old cottonwoods line the drive. Get here by heading five miles west on State 335 from the junction with U.S. 87. Follow the signs.

Story

The town of Story (pop. 650) is surprisingly different from nearby Sheridan and Buffalo. The road winds more than a thousand feet above the valley floor to the pine-covered slopes of the Big Horns. Locals and visitors come up to escape the hot summer air, enjoy the restaurants, and look for deer, elk, moose, and wild turkeys.

Because of the summertime popularity of the Story area, it's a good idea to reserve motel rooms ahead of time. Story is the site of "Piney Island," a stand of timber used to build nearby Fort Phil Kearny in 1866. It was named for Nelson Story, the first man to trail cattle north across Powder River Basin. **Story Fish Hatchery,** established in 1907, raises trout for Wyoming lakes and streams. Open daily 7 a.m. till dark; tel. 683-2234.

Lodore Supper Club and Lounge, tel. 683-2355, first opened in 1919, is a very popular steak and seafood restaurant with live country music on summer weekends. For good fish and chips ($3.50), and a menu that covers the spectrum from frog legs to enchiladas, head to **Tunnel Inn,** tel. 683-9921. **Wagon Box Inn,** tel. 683-2444, has cozy creekside cabins for $35 and bunkhouse accommodations for $25 pp, including a sauna and jacuzzi. On weekend nights, folks come here for live music and good meals. **Story Pines Motel,** tel. 683-2550, charges $25 s or $30 d. Ed and Sali Smyth's **Line Camp Gallery** on Rosebud Lane, tel. 683-2213, exhibits fine Western artwork. **Piney Creek Pottery,** across from Tunnel Inn, tel. 683-2181, sells pottery and other artwork. Check with **North Piney Horse Corral,** tel. 683-2838, for trail rides and pack trips.

THE BLOODY BOZEMAN

The discovery of gold in Montana during the 1860s started an avalanche of miners and businessmen. The fastest route to the Virginia City gold fields headed northwest from Bridger's Ferry (near present-day Douglas, Wyoming), through the Powder River Basin, and then west across Montana. One of the pioneers who scouted and constantly promoted the "Montana Road" was John M. Bozeman (as in Bozeman, Montana). Before being killed by Indians on the Yellowstone River in 1857, he led several groups up the "Bozeman Trail," as the route became known. Hundreds of others would die along Bozeman's route to the gold fields. Guide Jim Bridger knew that the Sioux would never stand for whites in their Powder River country—a place they had recently wrested from the Crows, Shoshone, and Arapaho. Instead, he recommended a different route that would cut west of the Big

Horn Mountains. Unfortunately, Bridger's advice went unheeded, and as attacks on emigrant wagon trains increased in 1864, so did pressure to protect them from the Sioux. Appeals to Washington brought military assistance in the form of forts filled with soldiers and cavalry. Parallels between the events that followed and America's experience in Vietnam—from the guerilla warfare to the hurried exit of U.S. troops at the end of the conflict—are disconcertingly similar.

Red Cloud's War

The first salvo by the Army came in Gen. Connor's savage wanderings through the Powder River in 1865 (see p. 377). The following year, while treaty negotiations were being held at Fort Laramie, Col. Henry B. Carrington and a battalion of infantry marched in, heading to the Bozeman Trail where they planned to construct new forts. Red Cloud, a fiery military leader of the Oglala Sioux, grew more and more angry, shouting, "Great Father sends us presents and wants new road, but White Chief goes with soldiers, to steal road before Indian says yes or no." The treaty was signed by older chiefs and the "Laramie Loafers," who hung around the fort, but not by Red Cloud. He and his warriors stormed out, arriving at Powder River ahead of Col. Carrington.

Carrington was a strange man to direct this massive undertaking. A political appointee with no battlefield experience—let alone experience with guerilla warfare—he approached the task of building forts and protecting travelers along the Bozeman Trail with a take-no-chances attitude that rankled his trigger-happy men. (The troupe left Nebraska with a 30-piece brass band, carriages, and comfortable furnishings, gaining the name "Carrington's Overland Circus.")

Once finally in the Powder River country, Carrington split his men into three groups, stationing some at Fort Reno near present-day Buffalo (begun the previous year by Gen. Connor), and sending others to build Fort C. F. Smith in Montana. These way stations were to provide military escorts for travelers and a haven from Indian attacks. Instead, they themselves came under attack, and Carrington's men nearly became prisoners inside them.

Fort Phil Kearny

In the heart of the Powder River country, Carrington found what seemed a perfect site for a fort along Little Piney Creek: good water, grass so thick that horses could barely walk through it, and timber close at hand. His guide, Jim Bridger, pushed instead for a site farther north, and away from the center of Sioux country. To Bridger, these "damn paper collar soldiers" seemed bound and determined to get killed. The new garrison—named Fort Phil Kearny for a Civil War general—measured 600 by 800 feet, entirely enclosed by a heavy log stockade. It was big enough for 1,000 men, though it never housed nearly that many. Both Indian attackers and its white defenders came to view this as the West's most hated fort. From the very first day, Carrington found himself harassed by the Sioux; by mid-December, more than 50 raids on the troops and civilians had left 17 military men and 58 civilians dead. Many of the horses and mules were stolen in the raids, and more than 700 cattle were lost when the Indians created a stampede by driving a herd of buffalo into them. With winter setting in, food and ammunition shortages made conditions worse, and even the nightly band concerts could not maintain morale. Jim Bridger revealed something of even greater concern after one of his scouting trips: "Crow chiefs report that it took a half a day's

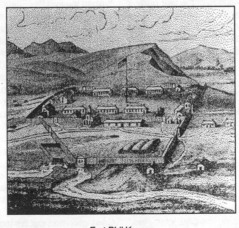

Fort Phil Kearny

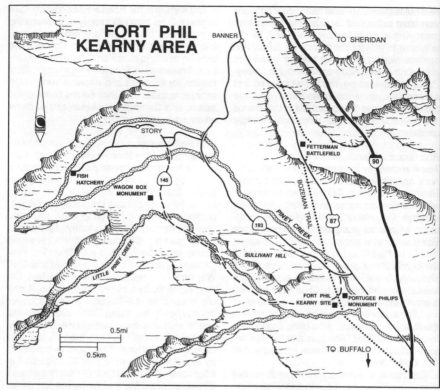

FORT PHIL KEARNY AREA

BANNER

TO SHERIDAN

STORY

FISH HATCHERY

WAGON BOX MONUMENT

145

FETTERMAN BATTLEFIELD

90

BOZEMAN TRAIL

PINEY CREEK

193

87

SULLIVANT HILL

LITTLE PINEY CREEK

FORT PHIL KEARNY SITE

PORTUGEE PHILIPS MONUMENT

TO BUFFALO

0   0.5mi

0   0.5km

ride to go through the villages of the war parties on Tongue River. The Sioux chiefs said they would not touch the new fort on Powder River [Fort Reno] but would destroy the two new forts, in their hunting grounds, meaning Phil Kearny and C. F. Smith."

Fetterman Fight

Again and again, the Sioux tempted soldiers into traps, drawing them away with attacks on the vital wood wagons (more than 12,000 logs were used to build the fort) and those cutting hay, or by stealing stock and then attacking the pursuers. Carrington's caution caused dissention in the ranks, and when a new company of cavalry arrived, led by Capt. William J. Fetterman, the dissention edged on open revolt. Fetterman, like Gen. George A. Custer, had achieved fame for his bravery during the Civil War. And, like Custer, he would meet an early death. Fet-

terman viewed the Sioux with reckless disdain, claiming, "I can take 80 men and go to Tongue River through all the Sioux forces." Jim Bridger responded to this boast with, "Your men who fought down South are crazy! They don't know anything about fighting Indians."

On the morning of December 21, 1866, Indians attacked a wood train, and a force of cavalry and infantrymen under Capt. Fetterman was sent out. Disobeying orders from Col. Carrington, Fetterman responded to taunts by Sioux decoys (including young Crazy Horse) by following them into an ambush. Perhaps 2,000 warriors of Red Cloud, High Back Bone, Red Leaf, and Little Wolf suddenly appeared in the tall grass. Within a half-hour, all 81 soldiers had been killed. It was, until Custer's last stand a decade later, the worst annihilation of any American force. Carrington had lost his most experienced fighters. Perhaps 30 Sioux died in the raid. Troops sent out to investigate what had happened found the frozen bodies horribly mutilated. They buried the men in a mass grave.

After the Fetterman Fight, just 119 soldiers remained to guard against several thousand Sioux. Fearing further attacks (which never came), Carrington put the fort on full alert and sent messengers to Fort Laramie in a desperate bid for help. John "Portugee" Phillips made the 236-mile ride in four nights of hard riding, struggling through sub-zero temperatures and blinding blizzards, and traveling at night to avoid Indian attacks. In a scene straight out of a Hollywood movie, Phillips staggered into a gala Christmas night ball with the stunning news. His horse collapsed and died. Because of bad weather, help did not reach Fort Phil Kearny for another two weeks. Col. Carrington was sent in humiliation to Nebraska, and it took many years to clear his name.

Wagon Box Fight

The tables were turned in the Wagon Box Fight. Wood cutters took the running gear off their wagons to haul logs back to the fort, and arranged the wagon boxes in a makeshift fortress filled with ammunition and supplies in case of attack. The attack came on August 2, 1867, when Red Cloud's 3,000 warriors suddenly surrounded 32 wood choppers and soldiers led by Capt. James Powell. Unbeknownst to Red Cloud, they were armed with new Springfield rifles that could fire up to 20 rounds per minute. Expecting the soldiers to take time to reload, Red Cloud sent waves of men, only to meet a withering gunfire each time. Finally, after six hours of this, soldiers from Fort Phil Kearny arrived with their howitzer, sending the Sioux fleeing. Four soldiers died in the Wagon Box Fight, while estimates of Indian casualties range from six to over a thousand. (Sioux warriors removed their dead after a battle, making it impossible to know how many had been killed.)

The Fighting Ends

By late 1867, public sentiment had moved against the Army's invasion of Sioux country, and the Bozeman Trail had become an anachronism, with miners heading to Montana via steamboat up the Missouri River. Besides, the Union Pacific Railroad was well on its way across Wyoming and the diversion was no longer needed. (Some historians believe this was the primary reason for the forts being built in the first place.) In 1868, the three Bozeman Trail forts were all abandoned. As the soldiers left Fort Phil Kearny, they turned back to see smoke on the horizon. The Sioux were burning it to the ground. Thus ended, at least temporarily, one of the most senseless conflicts in American history. Red Cloud finally returned to Fort Laramie to sign the treaty, having (he thought) forced the government to leave Powder River to the Sioux. Actually the treaty was ambiguous and contradictory, giving them rights to hunt buffalo on the Powder River, but saying they would have to live on reservations in Dakota Territory. Six years later, the country would again boil over when another gold rush—this time in the Black Hills—brought Gen. Custer north to fight the Sioux.

The Bozeman Trail Today

Ruts from the Bozeman Trail are still visible along much of its path, and the battle sites are all marked with monuments of various sorts. Get to the site of the **Wagon Box Fight** by heading a mile south from Story on a rutted dirt road. The **Fetterman Fight** is marked by a stone obelisk on the hilltop where the final stand was made. **Fort Phil Kearny** is now simply an open field with various signs marking building locations, the cemetery, and the Bozeman Trail. It is 17 miles north of Buffalo and 21 miles south of Sheridan off I-90, and is managed by the Wyoming State Archives Department. A small free **museum** (tel. 684-7629) is open daily 8-6 from mid-May through Sept., and Wed.-Sun. noon-4 the rest of the year. Inside, find a model of the fort, videos about the Bozeman Trail and the fort, and displays on Indian life. Portugee Phillips' ride is noted by a pyramid-shaped monument not far away. In mid-August each year, **Bozeman Trail Days** at Fort Phil Kearny brings living history demonstrations, battlesite tours, Indian art, concerts, historical talks, and speeches.

BUFFALO

Buffalo (pop. 3,800) is one of those wonderful small towns that seem to define rural America. The "Buffalo bench sitters" hang out each morning where Main St. crosses Clear Creek, and pickup trucks park out front of the local donut shop. Buffalo is primarily a ranching, tourism, and oil center. Johnson County is at the center of sheep raising in Wyoming; more than 100,000 sheep roam across the sageland here. Although many of the herders now arrive from Mexico, hundreds of Basque shepherds have come over the years, giving Buffalo a prominent Basque heritage. There is even a Basque radio program on Sunday nights. (Despite the fact that Buffalo's Main St. curves along an old bison trail, the town got its name from Buffalo, New York. The name was picked out of a hat.)

HISTORY

In 1876, during one of Gen. George Crook's campaigns against the Sioux, he had Capt. Edwin Pollock build a supply center along the Powder River, calling it Cantonment Reno. It was later renamed **Fort McKinney**, after Lt. John A. McKinney who had been killed in the Dull Knife Battle. In 1878, Fort McKinney was moved 40 miles north to where the Bozeman Trail crossed Clear Creek. Gradually the new fort took shape, not as the stockade-walled structures generally thought of, but as a collection of barracks, mess halls, and two-story houses with board and batten exteriors. Soldiers marched from here to South Dakota's Pine Ridge Reservation to put down the Ghost Dance uprising in 1890. More than 150 Sioux and 25 soldiers died at Wounded Knee, the last major battle between Indians and whites in North America.

The establishment of Fort McKinney created an immediate market for all sorts of businesses. Carpenters, blacksmiths, farmers, loggers, merchants, bartenders, and prostitutes arrived, quickly establishing the town of Buffalo two miles downstream. By 1883, a Cheyenne newspaper noted a dozen saloons and no churches. "Houses of dissipation" seemed more numerous than any other establishment. Much of the barley harvested locally went to supply two breweries. Buffalo had become the largest town in the northern part of Wyoming. This boom suddenly ended in 1894 when the Army declared Fort McKinney excess property and aban-

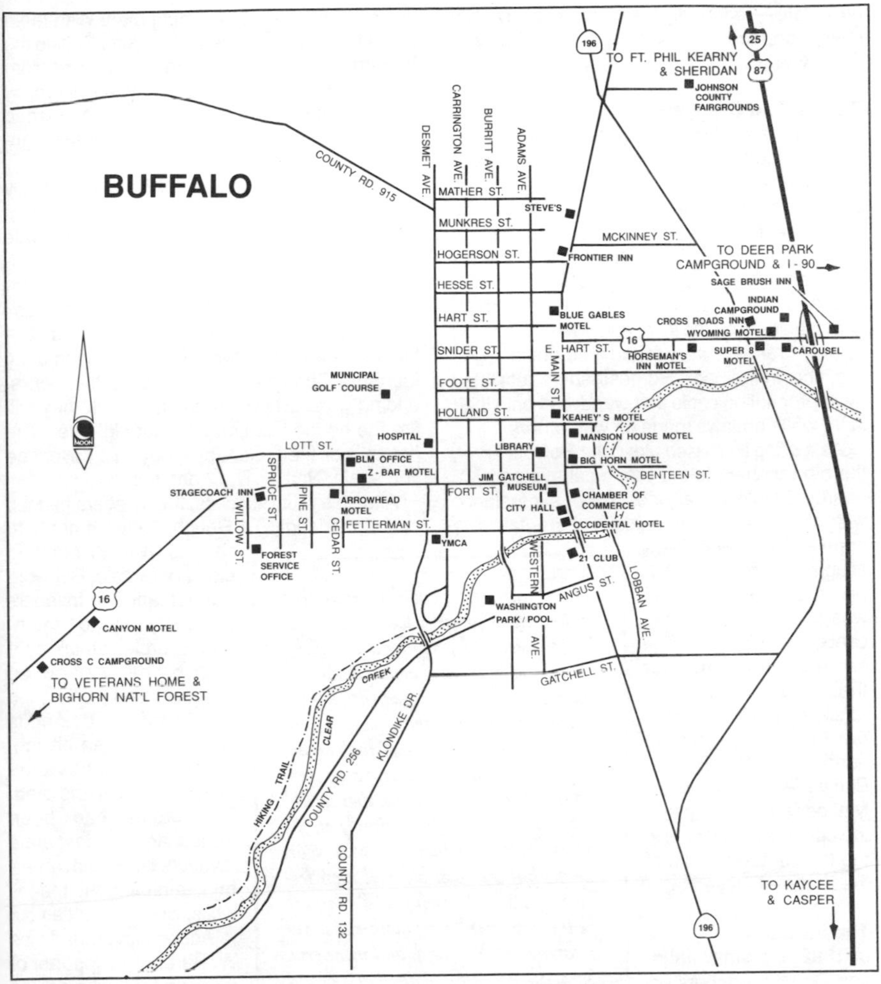

doned it. The buildings became the Wyoming Soldiers' and Sailors' Home in 1903 (now the Veterans Home of Wyoming). It is still one of the county's largest employers. After WW II, oil and gas explorations and development of the region's vast coal deposits turned Buffalo into an energy center. Today the coal resources of Johnson County remain essentially undeveloped, but substantial amounts of oil and gas are produced.

THE JOHNSON COUNTY WAR

Wyoming's history is one of constant conflict between white emigrants and Indians, between Chinese and white miners, between big ranchers and homesteaders, and between sheepherders and cattlemen. The Powder River had more than its share of confrontation; one of the most notorious was the so-called Johnson County War of 1892. (The 1980 box office flop *Heav-*

en's Gate—reportedly the most expensive film ever produced—was based on the Johnson County War.)

Barons And Grangers

The first white settlers in the Powder River Basin were the "cattle barons," men who owned enormous herds of cattle, but who generally resided on the land only part of the year. During the 1880s, more and more homesteaders ("grangers") began to settle here, fencing their spreads and gradually forcing the large cow outfits onto less and less land. The barons tried to force homesteaders off the land, and several Johnson County grangers were found face down in gullies, shot in the back. Homesteaders retaliated by appropriating cattle that wandered onto their land, while outlaws made off with others.

As rustling increased along the Powder River, the big ranchers found little local sympathy in nearby Buffalo. Local juries, either sympathetic with or intimidated by cattle rustlers, failed to convict men who were caught, and even the Buffalo sheriff, "Red" Angus, was accused of being in cahoots with rustlers. The cattle barons feared for their lives. The small ranchers and homesteaders in the largest town north of the Platte River—Buffalo—were soon openly at odds with the absentee cattle barons based in the largest town south of the Platte—Cheyenne.

The Invasion

In 1892, the small Johnson County ranchers organized their own roundup, an action that proved too much for the powerful Wyoming Stock Growers Association. In a secret meeting, they proposed a military coups d'état. On April 6, two days after the association's annual meeting in Cheyenne, a train headed for Douglas with 25 hired Texas gunmen (mostly ex-sheriffs and ex-U.S. marshals) along with

Three years ago a guileless tenderfoot came into Wyoming, leading a single Texas steer and carrying a branding iron; now he is the opulent possessor of six hundred head of fine cattle—the ostensible progeny of that one steer. . . A poor boy can in a few years, with an ordinary Texas steer and a branding iron, get together a band of cattle that would surprise those who figure simply on the ordinary rate of increase. Men soon learn that it is possible and even frequent for a cow wearing a 'Z' brand to be the fond and loving mother of a calf wearing the 'X' brand, and vice versa. Sometimes a calf will develop a brand that has never been in the family before.

—19th-century humorist Bill Nye

an equal number of Wyoming men. With them was a hit list of 70 suspected rustlers. Cutting the telegraph lines to keep advance word from reaching folks in Johnson County, and traveling in darkened railway cars, the "Invaders" headed north, stopping the train near Casper and continuing on by horseback.

They first came to the KC Ranch—actually just a couple of cabins—and discovered two of the most notorious rustlers holed up inside, Nate Champion and Nick Ray. In the day-long shootout that followed, Ray died quickly, but Champion managed to hold off the Invaders until dusk when they finally torched the cabin and shot him as he ran for safety. A blood-stained diary found on Champion described his last hours, ending with: "Shooting again. I think they will fire the house this time. It's not night yet. The house is all fired. Goodbye, boys, if I never see you again. Nathan D. Champion."

After this initial success, the Invaders headed on to the friendly TA Ranch, 30 miles north, to rest up for their planned siege of Buffalo. But word got out, and the Invaders suddenly found themselves under attack by a mob of 200 well-armed grangers and rustlers led by Sheriff Red Angus (who was on the hit list). In the shoot-out that followed, two Texans died. The tables had been turned, and the desperate Invaders faced almost certain annihilation. Meanwhile, word had gotten out to Acting Governor Amos W. Barber (a supporter of the Invaders) who cabled President Harrison for help. Troops from nearby Fort McKinney arrived before the "Defenders" could attack with their tank-like wagon and dynamite bombs. Newspapers around the nation castigated the cattle barons for their effrontery, the *Laramie Sentinel* noting, "of all the fool things the stock association ever did this takes the cake."

Justice Denied

The events that followed made a mockery of the legal system. After being rescued by Army troops, the Invaders were taken to Cheyenne to stand trial. Not surprisingly, two trappers who had happened upon the raid at the KC Ranch mysteriously disappeared until the trial was over, leaving no witnesses for the prosecution. Everyone pleaded not guilty, but when the judge discovered that Johnson County was unable to pay for room and board of the prisoners, he ordered everyone released on their own recognizance. After each being paid, the hired Texas gunmen immediately skipped town, never to be seen again. The Wyoming men involved in the raid were released when Johnson County had no more money to prosecute. Many of Wyoming's most prominent citizens—including Acting Governor Barber and senators Carey and Warren—would later be implicated as supporters of the raid. Johnson County would take years to settle down after the battles of 1892, and for a while the large cattlemen lived in fear for their lives.

SIGHTS

Jim Gatchell Memorial Museum

Historic artifacts gathered by druggist Theodore James Gatchell now comprise the core of a collection of over 10,000 artifacts, making Buffalo's museum one of the finest in Wyoming. The museum occupies two downtown buildings. Out front are several wagons, including the *de rigueur* sheepherder wagon, while the front building contains historic photos and other items. Inside the main building are two floors; downstairs is the standard collection of old junk, but upstairs is a treasure trove of unusual artifacts. Included are dioramas and displays of items found at various local battle sites: the Wagon Box Fight, the Johnson County War, and the Fetterman Fight. Most touching is the flattened horn of bugler Adolph Metzger who was the last to die at the Fetterman Fight. The note here says that his body was the only one the Indians did not mutilate after the massacre; instead covering it with a buffalo robe out of respect for his valor. Other stories say that after trying to fight off the warriors with his hands and bugle, he was taken captive and tortured to death at the Sioux camp.

Scattered around the room are other surprises: a pair of Cheyenne medicine rattles used in the Dance of Victory after Custer's defeat at Little Big Horn, an arrowhead that belonged to Red Cloud, a cartridge belt made by mountain man Jim Bridger, and the outlaw Tom Horn's spurs and a bridle he braided while awaiting execution. Ask the folks at the museum to point out a rifle probably used by the cavalry at Little Big Horn and a shell from Custer's handgun. Look around, and you'll find even more surprises at this most-impressive small museum. Midsummer hours for this free museum, 100 Fort St., tel. 684-9331, are 9-8 daily. The schedule seems to change every other week through the rest of the year, and between Nov. and mid-May it's only open by appointment. If they are closed, see the chamber of commerce.

Petrified Forest

One of the more unusual local sights is a petrified forest on BLM land, seven miles south of Buffalo. Take the Red Hills exit from I-90 and follow the road another seven miles to the Dry Creek Petrified Forest. An easy three-quarter-mile trail loops through the hot sagebrush country, with markers along the way describing the geologic history. Some 60 million years ago, this was a swampy plain, dominated by towering metasequoia trees. You can still count the growth rings on the petrified stumps, some of which are over four feet in diameter.

Other Sights

Injured or aged veterans live on the grounds of **Veterans' Home** (old Fort McKinney), two miles west of Buffalo on U.S. 16. Of the original fort, only an old cavalry stable and the post hospital building are still standing. Check in at the office (tel. 684-5511) before doing any sightseeing. Children (and those who never really grew up) will love the antique **Carousel Park**, tel. 684-7033, on the east end of town behind Col. Bozeman's Restaurant. This is the only carousel in Wyoming, and is open daily in the summer and on winter holidays. Just $1 a ride. Included are a dozen custom-carved Wyoming bucking horses. The **Occidental Hotel**, 10 N. Main St., was the place where Owen Wister's Virginian "got his man." The hotel is now closed. The chamber of commerce has a walking tour of Buffalo's other historic buildings. **Big Horn Wildlife Mu-**

seum, a half mile east of town on I-25, may or may not be open. Inside are stuffed critters from around Wyoming.

The Johnson County War helped dissuade the Chicago, Burlington, and Quincy Railroad from coming through Buffalo, and for many years Buffalo remained America's largest inland city without a railway. Eventually a spur line was built, connecting Buffalo to Clearmont. Locals called it BC & BM (Buffalo-Clearmont and Back, Maybe). Even it was abandoned in 1946 due to competition from trucking companies. Wyoming Railroad's **Engine 105** now rusts in the city park.

PRACTICALITIES

Accommodations
Plenty of motels to choose from in Buffalo, but it's a good idea to reserve ahead during midsummer when tourists flood the area. See the chart for rates. Free camping at **Lake DeSmet**, eight miles north of town, but the sites can get steaming hot. Mostly for the RV crowd. Other nearby public campgrounds ($5) are in Bighorn National Forest, approximately 15 miles west of Buffalo on U.S. 16. **Cross C Campground**, two miles west on U.S. 16, tel. 684-2307, has tent spaces for $10, RV sites for $13. Showers for non-campers cost $3; open year-round. The friendly folks at **Indian Campground**, on U.S. 16 east of town, tel. 684-9601, charge $10-14 for shady spots. Showers for non-campers run $3. Open mid-April through October. Farther out on U.S. 16 is **Deer Park Campground**, tel. 684-5722, where sites run $11 for tents or $13 for RVs. They also serve meals and have a small pool. Open May to mid-Oct., this is a quiet out-of-town place to stay.

Restaurants
For breakfast, head to **Kozy Korner** in the Cenex truckstop on west U.S. 16, tel. 684-7397,

BUFFALO ACCOMMODATIONS

Motel	Address	Telephone	Rates	Features
Bear Track Lodge	U.S. 16 West	684-2528	$18 s or d	
Stagecoach Inn	845 Fort St.	684-2507	$20 s or d	
Big Horn Motel	209 N. Main St.	684-7611	$21 s, $24 d	kitchenettes
Blue Gables Motel	662 N. Main St.	684-2574	$23 s, $25 d	pool, cabins
Arrowhead Motel	749 Fort St.	684-9453	$23 s, $25 d	AAA approved, kitchenettes
Frontier Inn	800 N. Main St.	684-7453	$25 s or d	
Canyon Motel	997 Fort St.	684-2957	$25 s, $28 d	AAA approved, kitchenettes
Keahey's Motel	350 N. Main St.	684-2225	$26 s or d	
Z-Bar Motel	626 Fort St.	684-5535 (800) 341-8000	$26 s, $28 d	AAA approved, kitchenettes
Mansion House Motel	313 N. Main St.	684-2218	$29 s, $34 d	AAA approved, historic building
Wyoming Motel	U.S. 16 at I-25	685-5505 (800) 666-5505	$32+ s or d	AAA approved, pool, jacuzzi, kitchenettes
Cross Roads Inn (Best Western)	U.S. 16 West	684-2256 (800) 528-1234	$34+ s, $40+ d	AAA approved, pool,
Horseman's Inn Motel	U.S. 16 East	684-2219	$35 s, $39 d	
Super 8 Motel	U.S. 16 at I-25	684-2531	$39 s, $44 d	AAA approved

or to **Busy Bee**, 2 N. Main, tel. 684-7544. **The Breadboard**, 57 S. Main, tel. 684-2318, has decent sub sandwiches and soups for lunch. **Andy's Deli**, 215 N. Main, tel. 684-9057, also makes fresh sandwiches, soups, and salads. **Seney's Rexall Drug**, 38 S. Main, tel. 684-7182, contains an old-fashioned soda fountain. Two popular family dining places with good salad bars and daily buffets are **Cross Roads Inn**, on U.S. 16 east, tel. 684-2256, and **Col. Bozeman's**, 610 E. Hart, tel. 684-5555. Check out the historic photos around Bozeman's dining room. Also try **Stagecoach Inn**, 845 Fort St., tel. 684-2507, for dinners.

Don't miss Buffalo's claim to gastronomic fame, **Steve's Restaurant**, 820 N. Main St., tel. 684-5111. Gourmet dinners (at gourmet prices), fresh homemade bread, and a pleasant decor make this a favorite of locals and travelers. Desserts are a specialty. For lunch, try the over-stuffed sandwiches (around $5) and the fresh soups. For all-American dinner fare, head to **Sage Brush Inn**, east of Buffalo on U.S. 16, tel. 684-2222. When folks are looking for an enjoyable evening away from town, they drive to **Lodge in the Pines**, 14 miles west, tel. 686-4620, or **South Fork Inn**, 17 miles west of Buffalo, tel. 684-9609. Both places have a bar and lounge, along with a standard supper club menu.

Entertainment And Events

There are three places to go for live C&W tunes most weekends: **Sage Brush Inn**, east of Buffalo on U.S. 16, tel. 684-2222; **Cross Roads Inn**, closer to town on U.S. 16, tel. 684-2256; and **21 Club**, 4 S. Main, tel. 684-7332. The big event each year is the **Johnson County Fair and Rodeo**, held the third weekend of August. Other night rodeos are also held through the summer months. In February, the **Pole Creek Cross-Country Ski Challenge** attracts racers from near and far. Other events include a **Horse-shoe Tournament** in late June, and a big **Christmas Parade**, on the first Saturday in December.

Recreation

The impressive outdoor **pool** (free) in Washington Park is Wyoming's largest. It has swimming lanes, two diving boards, and a shallow end for tots; open summers only. Inside the modern **YMCA**, 101 Klondike Dr., tel. 684-9558, is a pool, jacuzzi, weight room, and racquetball and handball courts for just $3. Buffalo has two **walking paths** that make for a pleasant afternoon stroll or bike ride. One heads up Clear Creek and the other follows U.S. 16 near the Veterans Home. Buffalo's 18-hole **municipal golf course**, northwest of town, tel. 684-5266, is one of the finest in Wyoming. One hole features a 90-foot vertical drop over 140 yards. Greens fees are $10 for 18 holes.

Information And Services

The **Buffalo Chamber of Commerce** office, 55 N. Main St., tel. 684-5544, is open 8-6 daily in summer, and Mon.-Fri. 8-5 at other times. The new **Johnson County Public Library**, at the intersection of Adams and Lott streets, tel. 684-7888, is open Tues.-Thurs. 10-8 and Fri.-Sat. 10-5. Head to **The Office**, 33 N. Main, tel. 684-2215, to buy guidebooks and volumes of Western history. The **Bighorn National Forest District Office** is at 300 Spruce, tel. 684-7981, while the **Bureau of Land Management Office** is located at 189 N. Cedar, tel. 684-5586.

The **Sports Lure**, 66 S. Main, tel. 684-7682, sells sporting goods. If you think you're starting to see spots, you may be at **Alabam's Polka Dot Spot**, 421 Fort St., tel. 684-7452, a shop geared to hunters and anglers. Pretty strange. The factory outlet for **Powder River Gear**, 1040 Fort St., tel. 684-5684, sells packs and bags of all sorts, from soft luggage to snowboard covers. **Cowboy Town Saddlery**, U.S. 16 east, tel. 684-2759, has custom-made tack and saddles.

Transportation

Powder River Bus Lines, tel. (800) 442-3682, connects Buffalo with most of northern Wyoming. Rent bikes from **Indian Campground**, on U.S. 16 east of town, tel. 684-9601. Get rental cars at **Northside Car Sales**, north of Buffalo, tel. 684-5136. The airport in Buffalo does not have scheduled service. Therefore, it was quite a surprise one day in 1979 when a Western Airlines 737, carrying 94 passengers, mistakenly landed in Buffalo instead of Sheridan. The pilot has since been "honored" by the celebration of Buffalo's Lowell Ferguson Day (July 31).

BUFFALO VICINITY

LAKE DESMET

Eight miles north of Buffalo, and just east of I-90 is Lake DeSmet. Named for Father Pierre Jean DeSmet (1801-1873), this deep natural lake is surrounded by open range country. A stone **monument** to this important historical figure stands along the western shore. A Belgium-born Jesuit missionary, DeSmet was one of the few men who remained a lifelong friend of both the Indians and whites. Indians called him "Black Robe," and trusted him with various peace-making roles at Fort Laramie. The Indians viewed the lake named for DeSmet with suspicion, as did early settlers who told of sea monsters and mermaids that came out at night from a seemingly bottomless body of water. When first found by DeSmet in 1851, it was a salton lake—the second largest in the West (after Great Salt Lake)—but dams and dikes have increased its size and decreased its salinity. Today, it's a popular place for local boaters. Try your luck at catching one of the mermaids, but you're more likely to pull in a big rainbow trout. Also here are brown trout, crappie, yellow perch, and rock bass. **Lake DeSmet Fishing Derby** is held each Memorial Day weekend. There is free **camping** just south of the Father DeSmet monument. Volleyball nets, picnic tables, and outhouses, but no shade or water. **Lake Stop Resort**, tel. 684-9051, rents boats, and has a cafe, bait shop, and cabins ($20 and up). Also here—so the sign claims—is the "world's smallest bar." Just north of the lake is a bed of coal that, in some places, is more than 200 feet thick—second only to one in Manchuria. No wonder Texaco owns most of the land around Lake DeSmet!

KAYCEE

The town of Kaycee (pop. 270) is named for the nearby KC Ranch, and serves as a bentonite-hauling, oilfield, and ranching center. Get on the side roads in spring or fall and you're likely to find yourself behind huge flocks of sheep being herded to or from the Big Horn Moun-

tains. Events in Kaycee include a **Sheepherders Rodeo and Parade** in July, and a **professional rodeo** and **cowboy poetry gathering** in September. If you're around in mid-June, ask about the annual wagon-train trip through Hole-in-the-Wall country. Free **camping** in the town park. There are two friendly motels where you can stay in Kaycee: **Siesta Motel**, tel. 738-2291, for $15 s or $20 d, and **Cassidy Inn Motel**, tel. 738-2250, for $20 s or $25 d. The former gives tours to area sights (such as Hole-in-the-Wall), or can provide directions if you want to try it yourself. Call 684-5433 for Johnson County "Invasion" tours of the TA Ranch and Crazy Woman Canyon. Both the **Feed Rack Restaurant** and **Country Inn** offer good all-American food.

Frewen Castle

When the Powder River country was opened to white settlers in the late 1870s, it quickly attracted ranchers and farmers of all types, from homesteaders trying to prove up their 160 acres to wealthy international investors. Two of the most interesting were the English brothers Moreton and Richard Frewen, nephews of Sir Winston Churchill. Coming originally to hunt buffalo, the two saw the lush Powder River area and decided to invest in cattle. Near present-day Kaycee, they erected an elaborate two-story log house, filling it with furniture and fixtures from England, and even adding an incredible luxury, a telephone. Frewen Castle, as it was soon called, became the center of a huge spread with at least 60,000 cattle.

Their kingdom attracted English hunting parties, and became something of an unofficial dude ranch. (To keep their ladies in the proper spirit, the Frewens set up relay stations so that hothouse flowers could be brought up on galloping horses from Denver.) The Frewens' Powder River Cattle Company, Ltd. attracted investments from the British royal family and various lords before reality struck. The cattle did not do as well as expected, competition from surrounding ranchers and rustlers cut into profits, and the disastrous winter of 1886-87 forced the company to the brink of bankruptcy. The

Frewens and many other "cattle barons" never really recovered. Today almost nothing remains of Frewen Castle.

Sights

Just south of Kaycee, a marker describes the killing of rustlers Nate Champion and Nick Ray in the Johnson County War of 1892 (see p. 386). The old **KC Ranch house**, where the two were killed by the Invaders, stood here. The **TA Ranch** (now the Gammon Ranch), where the Invaders holed up after raiding the KC Ranch, is approximately 30 miles north of here along State 87. Bullet holes are still visible in many of the ranch buildings.

In 1876, Gen. Crook's soldiers surprised Dull Knife's band of Northern Cheyennes in a remote valley 20 miles west of present-day Kaycee. The attack killed at least 40 Cheyenne, and ended what was viewed by whites as a campaign of terror on settlers. (Indians viewed it as retaliation for invading their last stronghold.) **Dull Knife Battlefield** lies on property owned by Kenny Graves who generally charges a $5 pp access fee. The Graves family (tel. 738-2319) also runs a **bed and breakfast** ranch here and offers a choice of local tours.

THE WILD BUNCH

Glorified in the 1969 Oscar-winning film *Butch Cassidy and the Sundance Kid,* the Wild Bunch is one of the most famous of all Western outlaw gangs. The Wild Bunch consisted of a constantly changing membership, held together by two friends, Robert Parker (Butch Cassidy) and Harry Longabaugh (the Sundance Kid). In 1884, Parker, then a teenager, met up with a local ranchhand and part-time cattle rustler named Mike Cassidy. Rebelling against a strict Mormon upbringing, Parker picked up a few of the master's tricks before getting caught and told to move on. But when he left Utah for Colorado and Wyoming, he took with him his mentor's name, Cassidy. (The "Butch" came when he later worked in a Rock Springs butcher shop.) Linking up with other outlaws, Cassidy held up the San Miguel Valley Bank of Telluride and then drifted back to horse-stealing in Wyoming. Several years later, those horses landed him in the Wyoming State Prison in Laramie. Cassidy was pardoned by the governor after 18 months, reportedly after agreeing not to pursue that line of work in Wyoming anymore. (Other places were fair game, however.)

The Gang

If anything, prison made Cassidy more determined than ever to outwit the lawmen. Joining up with Harry Longabaugh (who picked up his Sundance Kid sobriquet while spending time in jail in Sundance, Wyoming for horse thievery), and Harvey Logan (Kid Curry)—a deadly and fearless Montana fugitive—the three assembled a rogues' gallery of other rustlers, drifters, killers, and wanted men soon known as the Wild Bunch. They operated from remote hidden canyons in the West, especially Brown's Park in western Colorado, Bighorn Canyon in Montana, and the famous Hole-in-the-Wall southwest of Buffalo, Wyoming, places where entire herds of stolen cattle could be hidden, and where the finest horses could be trained for quick getaways.

The Wild Bunch achieved a measure of respect from local ranchers who bought horses and cattle at low prices and found ready workers when the outlaws needed to rest up awhile. For many, Cassidy seemed a modern-day Robin Hood, taking from the rich railroads, banks, mines, and cattle barons, while leaving the small folks alone. To this day, locals in Kaycee, Wyoming still talk fondly of the affable Butch Cassidy.

The gang's activities reached a peak in the late 1890s, with bank robberies in Utah, South Dakota, and Idaho (the latter to pay for a lawyer to clear a gang member in a murder charge). Cassidy—breaking his promise to Wyoming's governor—also led a train robbery in Wilcox, Wyoming that netted $50,000, but only after he'd blown up the safe with 10 pounds of dynamite, sending money and banknotes in all directions. Within hours, a sheriff's posse was in hot pursuit, and in a gun battle near Casper the sheriff was killed. Somehow, the Wild Bunch managed to slip through the posse's lines for a clean getaway.

In 1900, they struck another Union Pacific train near Tipton, Wyoming. Amazingly, the same express messenger was present for both robberies; the first time he had refused to open the railcar door, and was literally blown out with explosives.

continued on next page

The second time the conductor persuaded him to open the door. Perhaps he knew that the safe only held $54; the train carrying $100,000 worth of gold had passed just a few hours before. Then it was off to Nevada for the Wild Bunch, where a bank holdup netted them a cool $32,000. After a fling at Fanny Porter's Sporting House in San Antonio, the gang members bought some new hats at a Fort Worth haberdasher and, dressed as dudes, posed for the famous group portrait later used by Pinkerton detectives. Cassidy and two other gang members tried their hands once again at train robbery in 1901, taking at least $40,000 from the dynamited safe in Montana. The law was closing in, however. Of the gang members who stayed behind, all but one died a violent death. For Butch Cassidy and the Sundance Kid, the future lay in South America.

Gringos

In 1901, a trio headed for Argentina: Butch Cassidy, the Sundance Kid, and Etta Place—a strikingly beautiful woman whom Sundance apparently met in Fanny Porter's Sporting House. (Butch later called her "a fine housekeeper, but a whore at heart.") There they settled with their ill-gotten wealth to a quiet life of ranching, traveling occasionally to Buenos Aires, where they stayed in the finest hotels and dressed in formal clothes, befitting their new role as bourgeois American settlers. But even in South America, Pinkerton detectives managed to pick up their trail, and sensing this, the three decided to try their skills in virgin territory. They robbed three banks in Argentina and a train in Bolivia before Etta Place came down with acute appendicitis. A hurried trip took the trio back to the States, but in Denver, where the operation was performed, the Sundance Kid got in trouble for getting drunk and shooting up his hotel room. Rather than face the law, he fled to New York, where he and Cassidy again boarded a steamer bound for Argentina. Etta remained behind.

The two outlaws now worked part-time at a Peruvian gold mine, using the work as a cover for their periodic forays into banks, trains, and stores in search of money. For many years it was believed that Butch Cassidy and the Sundance Kid died in a blaze of gunfire at a remote village on the Bolivian-Argentine border in 1909. Today, however, it appears that Cassidy escaped (and perhaps the Kid as well), using his reported death as a convenient opportunity to change his ways. According to Larry Pointer's *In Search of Butch Cassidy,* Cassidy later fought with Pancho Villa in the Mexican Revolution, met Wyatt Earp in Alaska, and settled down to running a Spokane machine shop, living under the name of William T. Phillips until his death from cancer in 1937. Several Wyoming residents, old friends of the famous outlaw, met him in Lander on a number of occasions before his death. Cassidy reportedly spent considerable time in a fruitless effort to recover buried loot that he had stashed near Mary's Lake in the Wind River Mountains.

The Wild Bunch: Harry Longabaugh (Sundance Kid), Bill Carver, Ben Kilpatrick, Harvey Logan (Kid Curry), and George Parker (Butch Cassidy).

Hole-in-the-Wall

The remote Hole-in-the-Wall country lies some 30 miles west from Kaycee. The wealthy Frewen brothers who ranched in this country named it after a tavern in London of the same name. Take State 190 west to where the pavement ends. (The map says Barnum, but there is no town here.) Gorgeous red-walled canyons rise above the Middle Fork of the Powder River, while the waters provide a fine place to fish for rainbow, brook, and brown trout. At the end of the pavement, head left on the very rough dirt road (it turns to slick mud when it rains) and go four miles to the Bar C Ranch. Ranchers still guard their privacy here, and don't want folks stopping on their property, although they do allow access to the BLM-owned land that includes the old caves and rustler hideouts. Stop at the Bar C to ask about permission and road conditions.

Outlaw Cave—once owned by Butch Cassidy—is approximately four miles southwest of the ranch on a 4WD dirt road. The corral used by rustlers is still here. Also nearby is a cave containing some of the most unusual Indian rock art in Wyoming, including a large warrior figure, bear claws, and stenciled handprints. A major buffalo jump site (where Indians drove bison over a cliff) is nearby, along with many tipi rings. **Hole-in-the-Wall** itself is approximately five miles south of the Bar C Ranch, accessible by foot, mountain bike, or 4WD. Most folks find Hole-in-the-Wall a disappointment, since it is really just a notch in a steep butte. The BLM office in Buffalo (tel. 684-5586) can provide a xeroxed map of the Hole-in-the-Wall country. They also maintain a campground approximately 1 1/2 miles north of Outlaw Cave.

GILLETTE

Campbell County proclaims itself "Energy Capital of the United States," a title gained by producing more coal and oil than any other county in Wyoming. There are more than 188 oil fields, yielding over 25 million barrels per year, while 14 giant strip mines shovel up an eighth of total U.S. production of coal. At the center of all this is the modern-day boomtown of Gillette (pop. 18,000). Gillette isn't known as a tourist destination, and its neighborhoods and shopping malls are indistinguishable from a thousand other pleasantly homogenized American cities. This could just as well be Des Moines or San Antonio. Gillette is a young town; the median age in 1980 was less than 27 years. Interpret this your own way: Gillette actually has an E-Z Street! (By the way, despite the lack of any connection to the shaving company, Gillette is jokingly called "Razor City.")

The Past

When you drive into Gillette, the sense of history that permeates much of Wyoming quickly gives way to the raucous present. History is decidedly not Gillette's strong suit, even though the town is nearly a century old. When the Burlington and Missouri route to Sheridan was being planned, it was originally set to go south of the present location, but an astute surveyor, Edward Gillette, discovered a route farther north that saved construction of 30 bridges. The new company-platted town of Gillette was named in his honor. (Edward E. Gillette later served a term in Washington as a congressman from Wyoming, but preferred to live in the more scenic town of Sheridan than in his namesake.) The railroad reached Gillette in 1891 and the town was incorporated the following year. It became a shipping point for local ranchers and homesteaders, growing slowly over the decades.

The Present

Since the late 1960s, Gillette has ridden an enormous growth rocket, powered first by oil, then by coal. Gillette's oil boom really began in the fall of 1967 when a drilling company hit an oil gusher that ignited an enormous fire. Firefighter Red Adair was called in to extinguish the flames, attracting worldwide attention. Not surprisingly, Hollywood soon followed—John Wayne's *Hell Fighters* was based on the events. Other oil companies flooded the area with exploratory rigs, and almost overnight, Gillette grew from a sleepy cow town to a major energy center. A frantic scramble for the almighty dollar ensued, with real estate values quadrupling between

1966 and 1970. Longtime residents complained of the "oilfield trash" who took over the town and crowded the bars, demanding services and housing, but voting down bond measures to pay for them.

Unlike the rest of Wyoming, where the oil boom of the '70s was quickly followed by the bust of the '80s, Gillette caught the coal wave just as the oil tide was heading back out to sea. With enormous reserves of low-sulfur coal throughout the surrounding countryside, Campbell County became a major player on the energy scene, and stands to gain by recent clean air legislation that limits sulphur emissions. (East-ern coal has a higher sulfur content.) During the peak of growth in the early 1980s, the "Gillette Syndrome" reached the national media, and the city was put up as an example of what goes wrong when a city grows too fast. Things calmed down considerably in the late 1980s, giving residents a respite.

Sights

The fine **Rockpile Museum**, on U.S. 14-16, tel. 682-5723, is open Tues.-Sun. 10-8, May 15-Oct. 15. Winter hours are by appointment only. Out front is a minor local landmark that gives the museum its name. This is a fairly large, free

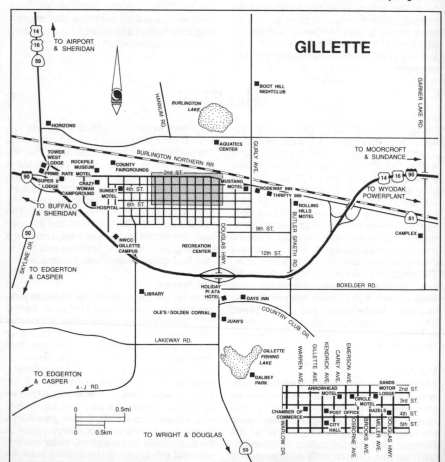

GILLETTE

museum with sheep wagons, a horse-drawn hearse (originally from Montana, its first eight customers died from gunshots), and other wagons, along with a blacksmith shop, an impressive arrowhead collection, and dozens of elaborate spurs and old rifles. A big board contains a directory of several hundred brands. Be sure to see the floating rocks from Lake DeSmet. Out front is a tiny one-room schoolhouse that could have served double duty as a dog house.

The new **Campbell County Public Library**, 2101 Four J Rd., tel. 682-3223, is one of the finest in the state. Besides a large collection of books about Wyoming, it houses a remarkable collection of art, including paintings by Hans Kleiber, Gene Kloss, and Conrad Schwiering. Library hours are Mon.-Thurs. 9-9 and Fri.-Sat. 9-5. Between Sept. and May, it's also open Sun. 1-5. The **planetarium**, 1000 W. Lakeview Rd., has a variety of free public events throughout the school year; call 682-2225 for details.

Accommodations

See the chart for lodging at any of a dozen different motels and hotels. Campers and RVers will enjoy **Crazy Woman Campground**, 1001 W. 2nd St., tel. 682-3665. It's a pleasant, friendly place with genuine shade trees, a rarity in Wyoming's private campgrounds. Rates are $5-10 for tents, $14 for RVs. Showers for non-campers cost $3.

Food

Gillette has a number of interesting eateries. For breakfast, head to **Bazels Restaurant**, 408 S. Douglas Hwy., tel. 686-5149. The decor is retro-'50s diner style, and the portions are huge. Recommended. Also try **Granny's Kitchen**, 413 S. Douglas Hwy., tel. 682-4181, or 1414 W. U.S. 14-16, tel. 687-1200, for breakfast or lunch. **Bailey's Bar & Grill**, 301 S. Gillette Ave., tel. 686-7667, is a fine place for homemade lunches and dinner specialties such as chicken-

GILLETTE ACCOMMODATIONS

Motel	Address	Telephone	Rates	Features
Goings Hotel	111 Gillette Ave.	682-4727	$11 s, $13 d	tawdry
Sunset Motel	300 Rohan	682-4047	$20 s, $24 d	
Circle L Motel	410 E. 2nd St.	682-9375	$22 s, $25 d	
Arrowhead Motel	202 Emerson Ave.	686-0909 (800) 227-8483	$26 s, $29 d	kitchenettes
Mustang Motel	922 E. 3rd St.	682-4784	$26 s, $29 d	
Rolling Hills Motel	409 Butler Spaeth Rd.	682-4757	$27 s, $31 d	
Prime Rate Motel	2105 Rodgers Dr.	686-8600	$29 s, $33 d	AAA approved, jacuzzi, sauna, continental breakfast
Super 8 Lodge	208 S. Decker Ct.	682-8078 (800) 843-1991	$33 s, $36 d	
Thrifty Inn	1002 E. 2nd St.	682-2616	$34 s, $36 d	
Days Inn	910 E. Boxelder Rd.	682-3999 (800) 325-2525	$34 s, $38 d	AAA approved, continental breakfast
Rodeway Inn	1020 E. U.S. 14-16 (800) 221-2222	682-5111	$36+ s, $42+ d	AAA approved, pool, sauna
Holiday Plaza Hotel	2009 S. Douglas Hwy.	686-3000	$39 s, $44 d	pool, sauna
Sands Motor Lodge (Best Western)	608 E. 2nd St.	682-9341 (800) 528-1234	$39 s, $45 d	AAA approved, pool,
Tower West Lodge (Best Western)	109 N. U.S. 14-16	686-2210 (800) 528-1234	$44+ s, $50+ d	AAA approved, pool, jacuzzi, sauna, exercise facility

fried steak, burgers, or Mexican fare. Great finger food, too. **Simply: Subs**, 1201 S. Douglas Hwy., tel. 686-9221, makes good sandwiches.

Great pizza and pasta at **Ole's Pizza Parlor**, 114 N. U.S. 14-16, tel. 682-8484. **Juan's**, 2702 Douglas Hwy., tel. 682-9110, has decent Mexican food, along with **Casa Del Rey**, 409 W. 2nd St., tel. 682-4738. Try **Hong Kong Restaurant**, 115 S. Gillette Ave., tel. 682-5829, for American-style Chinese cooking. The big salad bar at **Golden Corral**, 2700 S. Douglas Hwy., tel. 682-9130, makes for a bargain meal. Last, but not least, **Boot Hill Nightclub**, 910 N. Gurley Ave., tel. 682-1600, is the place to go for prime rib, steak, or seafood.

Entertainment And Events
The state's largest dancehall is **Boot Hill Nightclub**, at 910 N. Gurley Ave., tel. 682-1600. It's a popular place to dance the night away to country music. **Horizons**, 1400 N. U.S. 14-16, tel. 686-7624, has C&W or rock tunes nightly. **Fillys Lounge**, in the Holiday Plaza Hotel, 2009 S. Douglas Hwy., tel. 686-3000, is the place to go for rock and pop tunes. The **Campbell County Fair** is held each August at the fairgrounds. Two rodeos attract locals and visitors alike: the **Old Timers Rodeo** in late July, and the **PRCA Rodeo** on Labor Day weekend. **Camplex**, a multi-events center on U.S. 14-16, frequently has concerts, cattle shows, rodeos, conventions, and other events.

Recreation
Gillette has outstanding recreation facilities. The **Campbell County Recreation Center**,1000 S. Douglas Hwy., tel. 682-5470, houses an indoor pool with a diving well, a huge waterslide (summer only), plus all sorts of other facilities. The cost is just $1.50 per swim (75¢ for kids), or $3 for access to all the facilities ($2.50 for kids). There is also a brand new **Aquatic Center** at S. Gillette and 10th, tel. 682-1962. Golfers head to **Bell Nob Golf Links**, 1316 Overdale Dr., tel. 686-7069.

Information And Services
The **Gillette Chamber of Commerce**, 314 S. Gillette Ave., tel. 682-3673, is open Mon.-Fri. 8-5. Get books at **Your Book Store**, 320 S. Gillette Ave., tel. 682-8266, or **Books-N-Things**,

Holiday Plaza, tel. 682-1155. Booming Gillette has the state's fastest-growing junior college (900+ students), the **Gillette Campus** of Northern Wyoming Community College. Located at 720 W. 8th St., tel. 686-0254, the campus offers a range of classes and degree programs, from business to mining.

Transportation
Powder River Transportation, 1700 E. U.S. 14-16, tel. (800) 442-3682, has daily bus service to most other northern Wyoming towns. The airport is five miles north of Gillette. Both **United Express**, tel. (800) 631-1500, and **Rocky Mountain Air (Continental)**, tel. (800) 525-0280, have daily commuter service to Denver and Sheridan. Rent cars from **Gillette Auto Brokers**, 501 S. Butler Spaeth Rd., tel. 686-8250, for $15/day plus 12¢/mile. More expensive are two companies at the airport: **Avis Rent-A-Car**, tel. 682-8588, and **Hertz Rent A Car**, tel. 686-0550. **Yellow Checker Cab**, tel. 686-4090, is the local taxi company.

HEADING SOUTH

Two roads point south from Gillette; State 50 is the more remote and would make a fine bike route. The distinctive red road was built from scoria. The drive south from Gillette along State 59 takes you into the heart of the mixed-grass prairie, with oil pumpjacks, windmills, enormous bales of hay, and thousands of cattle and sheep. Tumbleweeds are plastered against the barbed-wire fences and abandoned farm equipment rusts on hilltops. Amax's Belle Ayr mine stands on the eastern horizon a dozen miles south of town, with flat-topped mesas and nipple-shaped buttes adding a little spice to the scenery. Far to the west, the Big Horn Mountains rise from the plains. Be sure to pause for a look at the grasses—blue grama is especially pretty when seen up close. Approximately 30 miles south of Gillette is **Durham Buffalo Ranch**, the largest private buffalo herd in existence. Watch for some of the 2,500 head of buffalo along the highway. Herds more than 1,000 times this size once roamed across this land; this is a rare opportunity to see bison today in a relatively natural setting.

Wright

Wyoming's newest town is Wright, right in the center of America's largest low-sulphur coal deposit. Established in 1976, Wright quickly grew to some 1,600 residents. Modern schools, a small shopping mall, and five churches popped up, along with trailer courts and suburban split-level homes on curving streets. Funded partly by Atlantic Richfield Company (ARCO), Wright was built to house workers for nearby coal mines. Pretty weird place. Imagine an enclave of middle-class America plunked down in a setting straight out of *High Plains Drifter*. The town has a fine recreation center with an indoor heated pool and gym.

The annual event here is **Wright Days,** held each August with the standard games, parades, and the obligatory rodeo. Gigantic coal strip mines surround Wright; all of them using Paul Bunyon-scale equipment and a skeleton crew of employees. Much of this is public land belonging to Thunder Basin National Grassland, meaning enormous revenues for the federal government, along with severance taxes for the state of Wyoming. The coal trains seem to never end. Stop on the railroad overpass near the dot of a settlement called Bill, and you'll see a hundred cars of coal pass every couple of minutes, with empty trains waiting on the sidings. Most of this coal is on its way to electric generating plants in Texas and the Midwest.

STRIP MINING

Coal mining has been an important part of the Campbell County economy for many years. The first mines were underground, but once the technology developed to remove the overlying soil, strip mining became feasible. Today, 14 Campbell County strip mines are scattered along an enormous coal seam that is five miles wide, over 50 miles long, and up to 100 feet thick, enough to last hundreds of years. Most of the mines are owned by giant multinational energy companies such as Exxon, Amax, Kerr-McGee, and ARCO. All of these mines are quite new, the oldest (Belle Ayr) opened in 1973. Cranking out over 30 million tons per year, the Black Thunder Mine just east of Wright is the largest coal mine in America.

Powder River Basin mines are heavily mechanized operations with relatively few employees; despite massive increases in production, the number of employees continues to drop. Mining coal here is a relatively simple process, made easier by the use of machinery and blasting equipment that are something beyond gargantuan; all the vehicles seem to be on steroids. Imagine a truck that carries 240 tons of coal (that's 2½ railroad coal cars worth), and is powered by a 2,200-horsepower engine. Then try changing a flat when the tire stands 11 feet tall and weighs four tons! Even this behemoth is dwarfed by the dragline used at the Black Thunder Coal Mine. Its 300-foot boom pulls in a 90-cubic-yard bucket (a typical dump truck holds 12 cubic yards). Powered by electricity, the 3,600-ton machine wad-

dles along like a duck, dragging its powerline behind. After blasting loosens the overburden, it is stripped away and dumped into waiting trucks. (Topsoil is stored for later reclamation.) Below this overburden lies the deep black coal seam that must be drilled and blasted. Electric shovels scoop up the loosened coal and dump it into the trucks for delivery to crushing and storage facilities. The entire scale of the operation comes into focus by watching as mile-long, 100-car trains move constantly through the loading facility. Up to 12 trains can be loaded in a day—over 130,000 tons.

The strip mining of coal has always been a controversial subject, with environmentalists concerned over the impacts from burning coal in an era of acid rain, global warming, and escalating atmospheric carbon dioxide. They also question whether reclamation will really work on Wyoming's arid lands. The other impacts from mining are equally important: access roads divide up antelope and deer habitat, subdivisions for the workers spread out over the countryside, and wells draw down the water table. Mining companies, however, point with pride to herds of antelope grazing near the coal mines, and believe that the land can be restored after the coal is gone.

A visit to the coal mines is an eye-opening odyssey into the Super Bowl of mining. Free summertime tours of several local mines are available; the Gillette Chamber of Commerce has an up-to-date listing.

THE BLACK HILLS

Northeast Wyoming feels quite unlike any other part of the state. The scenic South Dakota Black Hills roll across an arbitrary state line into Wyoming, while the Belle Fourche River (pronounced bell-FOORSH; the word is French for "Beautiful Fork" of the Missouri River) drifts through the hills, heading northeast and then cutting a sudden right angle to the southeast and across the South Dakota line. Cattle graze in rich pastures along the river. Nearby, one of the most stunning of all sights—Devils Tower—seems almost alive in its abrupt rise from the land. South of the Black Hills in Weston County, the country rapidly opens into the mixed-grass prairie of the plains. This out-of-the-way part of Wyoming is truly a special place. It is no wonder that the Sioux considered the Black Hills home for the Great Spirit.

Only 13,000 people live in Crook and Weston counties, scattered on rural ranches or in the small settlements of Sundance and Hulett in the midst of Wyoming's Black Hills, plus Newcastle, Moorcroft, and Upton along the southern edge. Cattle grazing, bentonite mining, oil wells, and logging provide the jobs.

The Land

The Black Hills stretch in a long ellipse, 125 miles north to south, and 65 miles across, rising 3,000 to 4,000 feet above the surrounding plains. South Dakota's Harney Peak, at 7,242 feet, is the tallest mountain in the Black Hills; in fact, it's the tallest peak between the South Dakota/Wyoming line and the Atlantic Ocean. The most famous attraction in this part of Wyoming is Devils Tower, but the Black Hills north of Sundance are captivating, especially in the spring and fall. Most visitors who come to northeast Wyoming do so as part of a trip that includes Yellowstone and various South Dakota sights, including Mt. Rushmore and Deadwood.

From a distance, the dark green carpet of ponderosa pine makes the hills appear black; hence the Sioux name Paha Sapa, meaning "Hills That Are Black." The land is a blend of open meadows, rocky hills crowded with forests of pine and aspen, and valleys lined with bur oak. This is one of the few places you're likely to see native oak trees in Wyoming.

White-tailed deer are abundant throughout the Black Hills, while herds of elk are found southeast of Sundance. Merriam's turkeys are another common sight all through this country. Introduced from New Mexico in 1948, they are now the most widespread game bird in northeast Wyoming.

NEWCASTLE

Newcastle (pop. 3,700) sits at the junction of several major roads, acting as a gateway to the Black Hills. Like much of northeast Wyoming, the town's economy is a mixture of energy, ranching, and logging. Every half-hour, day and night, traffic backs up on the railroad tracks across Main St., waiting as one hundred soot-black coal cars rumble past, bound for Midwestern power plants. A Newcastle refinery produces jet fuel for South Dakota's giant Ellsworth Air Force Base, and a natural gas processing plant sits 25 miles south of town in the midst of the Finn-Shurley fields. Large ranches encompass the town, dotted with oil pumpjacks, windmills, and Herefords. Piles of fresh-cut ponderosa pine surround Newcastle's sawmill.

THE BLACK HILLS

HISTORY

The first white settlement of the Newcastle area came in 1875, when Professor Walter P. Jenney and Lt. Col. R.I. Dodge led 432 soldiers and an army of mining engineers, scientists, and mapmakers to a base camp along Beaver Creek. They built the "Jenny Stockade" which became a stage station and distribution point along the Cheyenne-Deadwood Trail. Many of the West's most famous characters stopped en route to Deadwood, including Wild Bill Hickok, Calamity Jane, and Wyatt Earp.

Tubb Town
In 1888, the Chicago, Burlington & Quincy Railroad announced plans to construct tracks across northeast Wyoming and into Montana. Speculators established Tubb Town, a ramshackle collection of saloons and hotels along the proposed railroad route. (All visitors were required to pay a toll upon entrance: "set 'em up for the bunch.") The party didn't last long; when the Burlington Railroad decided instead to build a town at present-day Newcastle, Tubb Town faded into history. At Whoopup Canyon (so named because the spring floods came "a'whoopin' through"), a railroad worker attempted to pry the cap off a 25-pound can of black powder. After struggling without success, he decided to try a more forceful approach—using a pick axe to punch a hole in the lid. His co-workers found little left to bury.

The Cambria Mines

Coal was discovered in Cambria Canyon in the 1880s, and the coal-mining town of Cambria popped up almost overnight. It became a model community, with a water system, modern homes, three churches, electric lights, and some of the safest underground mines in the nation. Alcohol was banned, along with bawdy entertainment. At its peak more than 1,500 people lived in Cambria, but when the coal ran out in 1928, the mines were forced to close.

The discovery of coal at Cambria led the Burlington Railroad to establish a townsite as near the mouth of Cambria Canyon as possible, with a spur to the four mines. It was called Newcastle, after the English coal port of Newcastle-upon-Tyne. At first, the wide-open frontier town of Newcastle contrasted sharply with quiet, sedate Cambria. When the new mayor, Frank Mondell (who had established the Cambria mines), decided to get rid of 20 of the Newcastle's undesirables, a local hotel owner—fearing that he would lose most of his business—shot the mayor. Mondell (who later served for 26 years as Wyoming's lone congressional representative) carried the bullet in his spine the rest of his life.

After the Cambria mines closed, the town of Newcastle faded, but with the discovery of huge oil deposits nearby in the 1950s, it again boomed. By the mid-'50s more than 25,000 people crowded the surrounding countryside. A bust soon followed, only to be repeated by a similar cycle in the 1970s. Now Newcastle perks along on an economy of equal parts oil, coal, logging, and ranching. Folks from Nebraska or Kansas would feel right at home among the quiet streets, staid older homes, pickup trucks, and freight trains. The local movie rental outlet is appropriately named: Our Town Video.

SIGHTS

Anna Miller Museum

The Newcastle museum at Delaware St. and U.S. 16, tel. 746-4188, is open Mon.-Fri. 9-5. It's housed in the old National Guard Cavalry Barn, a stone structure built in the 1930s by the WPA. Inside is the typical collection of local paraphernalia: items from the Cambria mines, a horse-drawn hearse, a noose (not, however, the one that vigilantes used to hang murderer Diamond Slim Clifton from the Newcastle railroad trestle), a model of the giant KB&C ranch, and even a six-legged lamb and a two-headed Hereford calf as a sideshow. Be sure to try a couple of cranks on the old carnival noisemaker. (Trivia tip: Anna Miller, for whom the museum was named, was a local school superintendent whose husband, Sheriff Billy Miller was the last white man to die in a battle with the Indians. He was killed in 1903.) Outside the museum is a furnished one-room schoolhouse built in 1890, along with the **Jenney Stockade cabin** (built in 1875), the oldest building in the Black Hills. Ask

The coal-mining town of Cambria was considered a model community in its time.

ANNA MILLER MUSEUM

at the museum for directions to the Cheyenne-Deadwood Trail ruts and an Indian petroglyph site in Whoopup Canyon.

Accidental Oil Company

Certainly the most amusing sight around Newcastle is the kitschy Accidental Oil Company. In 1966 (around the time Jed Clampett of television's "Beverly Hillbillies" was "shooting at some food and up from the ground came a bubbling crude—oil that is, black gold, Texas tea . . ."), Newcastle rancher Al Smith decided to dig a hole to see how far down it was to oil. Using a pick and shovel, and later dynamite, he reached oil at 21 feet. The "world's only hand-dug oil well" is now a small run-down tourist trap along the U.S. 16, four miles east of Newcastle. An old oil storage tank encloses a gift shop, and you can walk down to view the oil-bearing rock under black light. Pure Americana.

PRACTICALITIES

Accommodations

There are nearly a dozen different places to stay in Newcastle (see chart), but of particular note is the historic **Flying V Cambria Inn**, a place filled with antique furnishings. You can pitch a tent for free anywhere on nearby public lands within both Thunder Basin National Grassland (see p. 152) and Black Hills National Forest

(see p. 407). The closest public campground ($7) is across the South Dakota border at **Jewel Cave National Monument**, 25 miles east of Newcastle. Back in Newcastle, **Corral Rest RV Camp**, 2206 W. Main, tel. 746-2007, has tent sites for $7 and RV sites for $12; open mid-April to mid-November. **Crystal Park Campground**, 3 Seminoe Ave., tel. 746-4426, is open year-round, with tent sites for $7, and RVs for $11. Showers for non-campers are $2. Neither of these places is particularly appealing.

Food

For excellent breakfasts, head to **Old Mill Inn**, 500 W. Main, tel. 746-4608, housed in the old Toomey's Flour Mill. They also have a salad bar and all-American dinners. The **Slatewood Inn**, 66 Old U.S. 85, tel. 746-4686, is one of the best steak and prime rib establishments in this part of Wyoming. On Wednesday nights, they offer a reasonable BBQ rib all-you-can-eat special. Next door is **Pizza Barn**, tel. 746-9464, with homemade pizza, but most locals prefer **Pizza Hut**, E. U.S. 16, tel. 746-3507. For surprisingly good fast food and sit-down meals, head to **Hi-16 Drive In**, 2951 W. Main, tel. 746-4055. Try the shrimp basket for dinner. Good breakfasts and lunch bargains too. Historic **Flying V Cambria Inn**, eight miles north of town on U.S. 85, tel. 746-2096, offers a special Italian night on Thursdays; huge two-pound steaks and fish at other times. Big portions and great

NEWCASTLE ACCOMMODATIONS

Motel	Address	Telephone	Rates	Features
Stardust Motel	833 S. Summit	746-4719	$18 s or d	
Roadside Motel	1605 W. Main St.	746-9640	$18 s, $20 d	kitchenettes
Supreme Motel	2503 W. Main St.	746-2734	$18 s, $20 d	
Pines Motel	248 E. Wentworth	746-4334	$23 s, $26 d	quiet location
Sage Motel	1227 S. Summit	746-2724	$26 s or d	AAA approved
Sundowner Inn Motel	451 W. Main St.	746-2796	$26 s, $28 d	kitchenettes
Hilltop Motel	1121 S. Summit	746-4494	$26 s, $28 d	kitchenettes
Morgan's Motel	205 S. Spokane	746-2715	$30 s, $35 d	
Flying V Cambria Inn	8 miles north	746-2096	$39 s, $49 d	B&B, historic place
Fountain Motor Inn	3 Seminoe Ave.	746-4426	$49 s, $53 d	AAA approved, pool

food in a nostalgic setting. Get groceries at **Decker's Food Center**, 709 W. Main, tel. 746-2779, or **Safeway**, 622 W. Main, tel. 746-3511. Decker's has a good bakery.

Entertainment And Events

Head to the **Gay Nineties Lamplighter** for C&W or rock tunes. The **Buckhorn Bar and Grill**, tel. 746-3675, 25 miles north of Newcastle on U.S. 85, is a favorite spot for both travelers and locals. Good food and live C&W music. The big local event is the **Weston County Fair**, held in early August each year. You're likely to find a **rodeo** going on at the fairgrounds most summer weekends.

Information And Services

The **Newcastle Chamber of Commerce** at the intersection of U.S. 16 and 85, tel. 746-2739, is open Mon.-Sat. 9-5. **Weston County Library**, 23 W. Main, tel. 746-2206, is open Mon.-Wed. and Fri. noon-5, Thurs. noon-8, and Sat. 9-1. **Swim** at the high school pool, 15 Stampede, tel. 746-2713. Try your fishing skills at **LAK Lake** east of town (named for the Lake, Allenton, and King ranch here), or play a few rounds of golf at **Newcastle Country Club**, 2302 W. Main, tel. 746-2639. There is no bus or plane service into Newcastle.

NEWCASTLE VICINITY

Heading North

North of Newcastle, U.S. 85 climbs quickly into the pine-covered Black Hills, providing wide vistas over the town and the open plains to the south. The road continues up through this scenic country, with pullouts along the way. Eight miles north of Newcastle is **Flying V Cambria Inn**, constructed in 1928 as a memorial to the Cambria miners and completed just months before the mines closed down for good. It is listed on the National Register of Historic Places. The ghost town of Cambria is on private land nearby.

Another nine miles north is **Red Butte**, a steep-sided sandstone peak rising right along the road like a miniature Devils Tower. A local landmark, it was used by both Indians and early whites as a lookout. Beyond this, the land begins to open up into an undulating grassy terrain with rich red-black soil. Just a couple more miles

up the road is **Four Corners**, a little country store with old fixtures and gas pumps. Not far away is the site of the 1878 Canyon Springs robbery on the old Cheyenne-Deadwood Stage Route. In the shoot-out a passenger and an outlaw died, and at least $20,000 (some accounts claim up to $140,000) in gold was taken and buried nearby. Many years later, a local farmer digging potatoes near Red Butte apparently found some of the loot. Packing up his family, he split town without a word. The gravelled Mallo Rd. heads east from Four Corners, offering a colorful fall drive as the aspens turn a brilliant yellow.

Heading South

South of Newcastle, U.S. 85 is an arrow aimed at the horizon, pointing across the almost-flat landscape of grass, wind, and antelope. A few bottomland trees line the creeks and the Cheyenne River etches a narrow line through the land, nearly dry in the late-summer heat. This is the heart of the great mixed-grass prairie that borders eastern Wyoming, reaching into adjacent Nebraska and south into Colorado.

Upton

On the edge of Upton (pop. 1,200) a sign makes no bones about where you are: the "Best Town on Earth!" Who am I to argue? Like its neighbors—Osage and Newcastle—Upton lies right along the edge of the Black Hills, with ponderosa pines topping the ridge to the north (appropriately named Pine Ridge), and open range spreading across the country to the south. The Chicago, Burlington & Quincy Railroad established a depot here in 1892, and railroad tracks now form Upton's southern border. Beyond this, State 116 climbs over gentle grassy hills through the heart of Thunder Basin National Grassland. It's a high plains landscape filled with windmills and scattered ranches with sheep, cattle, antelope, and mule deer. The sky completely dominates the landscape, sending giant white thunderheads over the plains. Upton's limited economy is dependent upon American Colloid's bentonite mine, local ranchers, oil pumping, and coal mining in nearby Campbell County.

If you don't mind in-town, no-shade camping, pitch a tent next to the **Country Market Conoco**, tel. 468-2551, for $3.50 a night, $10 for RVs. Stay at **Upton Motel**, tel. 468-9282, for

$16 s or $19 d, or the somewhat nicer **Weston Inn Motel**, tel. 468-2401 or (800) 341-8000, for $24 s or $26 d. **Western Bar & Cafe**, tel. 468-9257, offers the best restaurant meals, or get groceries at **Joe's Super Valu**. The **library**, tel. 468-2324, Pine and 4th streets, is open Mon.-Fri. 1-5, and Wed. 6-9.

Osage

Located halfway between Newcastle and Upton, tiny Osage (pop. 350) has a bar, gas station, and general store, but not much else to show for having once been the center of the oil industry in northeast Wyoming. In 1920, a huge oil gusher turned the surrounding country into a madhouse of oil prospectors, and Osage into a tent city of 1,500 people. When the boom inevitably turned to bust, only a core of folks remained in what is now a railroad way station.

MOORCROFT

Moorcroft (pop. 1,000) is a nondescript ranching and oil field town perched within a few miles of popular Keyhole Reservoir. It isn't particularly attractive, but will do as a stop on the way to somewhere else. Because the famed Texas Trail passed through Moorcroft, it became an important cattle town. Until the end of WW II, it served as the largest cattle shipping point along the entire Chicago, Burlington & Quincy Railroad.

Practicalities

Lodging is available at **Cozy Motel**, 219 W. Converse, tel. 756-3486, for $25 s or $28 d, or **Wyoming Motel**, 111 W. Converse, tel. 756-3452, for $26 s or $30 d. The nicest place in town is **Moorcroft Motel**, 214 Yellowstone Ave., tel. 756-3411, with rooms for $30 s or $35 d. Good breakfasts and all-American dinners at **Sonny's Cafe**, 102 S. Bighorn, tel. 756-9738. The **Yellow Rose**, 116 S. Bighorn, tel. 756-3727, is also a good place for breakfasts. Try their fresh homemade rolls. Families like **Donna's Diner**, 203 W. Converse, tel. 756-3422. The **library**, 105 E. Converse, tel. 756-3232, is open Mon.-Fri. 10-5. Check at the **Town Hall**, 104 N. Big Horn, tel. 756-3526, for more about the moors and mores of Moorcroft.

KEYHOLE STATE PARK

Keyhole State Park, tel. 756-3596, surrounds Keyhole Reservoir, a 14,720-acre warm-water lake that backs up water from the Belle Fourche River. (The name comes from the keyhole brand, used by a local ranch.) The dam was built in 1952 by the Bureau of Reclamation, and supplies irrigation water for South Dakota farmers. Recent drought years have left a bathtubring effect, particularly in late fall. Most of the visitors are locals, but it's an okay place to camp. Pine trees crowd hills to the east, while grass and sage grow around the reservoir's western shore. Anglers angle for the biggest walleye and northern pike in the state; birdwatchers watch for Merriam's turkeys and white pelicans; and snowmobilers 'bile around in winter. **Camping** costs $4 at seven different state campgrounds along the lake's east and south shores. Nicest are Pats Point and Pronghorn campgrounds. Get to Keyhole State Park from I-90 by taking the Pine Ridge exit and continuing eight miles north. A swimming beach is here plus a motel, cafe, and marina (tel. 756-9529), with supplies and boat rentals.

SUNDANCE

The quiet country town of Sundance (pop. 1,100) nestles at the foot of Sundance Mountain. The mountain—"Temple of the Sioux"—rises a thousand feet above the town, and was an important sacred spot to the various tribes who claimed this land. Sun dances were performed at its base each year. Sundance got its start in 1879, when rancher Albert Hoge set up a trading post. The town grew slowly until the 1950s, when Sundance Air Base arrived. A nuclear reactor (the only one in Wyoming) was built on the base, but was torn down when the base closed in 1968. The pipes, valves, and other fittings were buried on the site in cylindrical tanks filled with concrete and then covered with a thick layer of dirt. A plaque—meant to be a permanent marker of the danger from this radioactive waste—was stolen. Today, the old base is used by a local religious group and home for troubled kids. (Who needs a halo when you can glow by just attending classes?) The town of Sundance has settled into middle age, with the old standbys of ranching and logging as economic mainstays, though tourism is increasingly important.

SIGHTS

Museum
Crook County Museum, tel. 283-3666, is open Mon.-Fri. 9-5, and is located in the basement of the Crook County Courthouse on Cleveland Street. Inside is the usual collection of local

---

SUN DANCES

The most spectacular of all Plains Indians religious ceremonies was the sun dance. An annual event, it frequently attracted hundreds or even thousands of tribal onlookers, serving not simply as an important religious service, but also as a social and political rally. Indian legends say that it originated centuries ago when a hunter was approached by a buffalo who suddenly spoke to him, offering a cure for sickness. Much later, an eagle came to another young man in a dream, proscribing the complete ceremony. The name sun dance is something of a misnomer, since it was not a worship of the sun, but a highly involved ceremony representing the creation of life and the triumph of good over evil. The specifics varied somewhat between the tribes. A common Indian term for it is "Thirsting Dance," referring to the long periods of dancing without water.

Sun dances were always held in late spring and early summer, and were led by a young man who spent considerable time learning the complex ceremonial steps from a priest. If he passed the test, the pledger gained immense status in the village as a fearless leader. The festivities lasted up to two weeks, with the main ceremony an intense four-day event. Central to the sun dance were an eagle representation (air), a buffalo head (earth), and a pole connecting the two, signifying the sacred Tree of Life. The ceremony took place in a lodge, generally built around a central pole that was forked at the top. After the sacred cottonwood tree had been selected by a scouting party, warriors attacked the tree in a furious charge. If it withstood this symbolic battle, the tree was cut down by a respected tribal woman and carried to the sun dance site where it was carefully erected. A bundle of brush (to represent an eagle or thunderbird nest) and a buffalo head were placed in the fork of the pole. Twelve other poles (the number varied with different tribes) were erected around the central one, with crossbeams to the center. (Missionaries would later claim these represented Jesus and the 12 apostles.) Brush was then laced around the outside to provide partial shade, and a buffalo skull altar was erected at the center of the structure.

Supplicants spent four days without food or water, dancing, praying, blowing on eagle bone whistles,

paraphernalia such as arrowheads, "period" rooms, wooden wheelchairs, bison skulls, and cowboy gear. There is also a model of Devils Tower. More interesting are the momentos from Harry Longabough's visit to the town. Better known as the **"Sundance Kid"** (see "Powder River Country," p. 391), Longabough spent 18 months in Sundance's Crook County Jail for horse stealing before being pardoned by the governor in 1889. The museum has the criminal bar docket signed by Longabough during his trial, and furnishings from the original courthouse. A replica (built in 1983) of the jail that once housed the Sundance Kid stands beside the old stone high school.

Around Sundance

Access to 5,829-foot **Sundance Mountain** is via a dirt road that heads east from State 116, about a half mile south of town. An enjoyable trail leads to the top, gaining 800 feet in elevation along the way. From the top, you're treated with

staring at the buffalo head, at the sun, or at a sacred doll, as they waited for a vision of power. In most tribes, the sun dance also involved self-mutilation. Assistants commonly cut small pieces of skin from the candidates' arms and shoulders as a blood sacrifice to the Great Spirit. (Before the battle at Little Big Horn, Sitting Bull sacrificed one hundred pieces of flesh in a sun dance ceremony, after which a vision told him of the coming destruction of Gen. Custer and his men.) Torture commonly went even further, as assistants cut slices into the back or chest of the dancers and slid bone skewers into the muscle. Thongs would be attached between the skewers and the central pole, while other skewers held heavy buffalo skulls to be dragged behind. The candidates would lean back until the ropes were taunt, jerking as they danced. Eventually the skin and muscle ripped loose and the dancers collapsed on the ground. In some tribes, the dancers were actually lifted off the ground by these tethers.

Whites found the sun dance's torture difficult to understand, and thought even less of the various sexual aspects of the ceremony. When the Indians were forced to reservations, the sun dance was outlawed, but some tribes continued to practice it secretly. Finally, in the late 1920s, the government relented, and a more sedate version of the sun dance was resurrected. The traditional blood sacrifice still exists among some tribes, but not in Wyoming. Today, the sun dance is performed in separate ceremonies by both the Shoshone and the Arapaho on the Wind River Reservation. Visitors may watch, but cannot take photos or recordings.

The sun dance is now performed primarily as a thanksgiving ceremony, to cure disease, and to pray for the coming year. After several days of preparation, the main ceremony lasts for four long days. Without food or water, the dancers move into a trance state that brings visions and power. One authority describes dancers seeing the buffalo head shaking and steam coming out of its nostrils as the power is imparted. On the fourth day, a bucket of water is passed around to signal the end of the sun dance, and that evening more dancing and feasting complete the ceremony.

BOB RACE

views of the nearby Black Hills and, on clear days, even the Big Horn Mountains, 180 miles west. Ask at the visitor center for directions. Near the small settlement of Beulah (on the South Dakota border, 18 miles east of Sundance) is the **Vore Buffalo Jump** where Indians drove hundreds of bison into a pit between A.D. 800 and 1600.

Eleven miles south of Sundance on State 116 is **Inyan Kara Mountain** (an Indian name meaning "Stone-made Peak"), a 6,368-foot summit that dominates the surrounding country. In 1874, Gen. George A. Custer led a large scientific expedition through this region en route to the Black Hills. Custer and others climbed the mountain, carving "G. Custer '74" on a rock near the summit. The inscribed rock is still here, though access to the mountain may be restricted by surrounding ranchers. Ask at the information center for access info.

PRACTICALITIES

Accommodations

Visitors will find four places to stay in Sundance. Least expensive, but very nice, is **Bear Lodge Motel**, 218 Cleveland, tel. 283-1611 or (800) 341-8000, with rooms for $32 s or d. **Arrowhead Motel**, right next door at 214 Cleveland, tel. 283-3307 or (800) 456-6016, charges $34 s or d, and **Deane's Pine View Motel**, 117 N. 8th St., tel. 283-2262, has cabins for $35 s or d, with kitchenettes for $3 extra. The town's fanciest lodging is **Apache Motel (Best Western)**, 121 S. 6th, tel. 283-2173 or (800) 528-1234. Rates are $48 s or $51 d. Located between Sundance and Keyhole Reservoir, **Hawken Guest Ranch**, tel. 756-9319 or (800) 544-4309, offers a variety of lodging options, from bed and breakfast to tipi camping. Rates start at $40 pp.

Camping

The Forest Service's fine **Reuter Campground** ($5) is just four miles northwest of Sundance. (See "Black Hills National Forest" and "Devils Tower National Forest" for other public campgrounds.) The private **Mountain View Campground**, tel. 283-2270, 1 1/2 miles east of town, has sites for $8 and up.

Food

Good burgers and other American food at **Higbee's Cafe**, 101 N. 3rd, tel. 283-2165. Mexican or Italian specials some nights. For breakfast, head to **Sundance Cafe**, 1620 Cleveland, tel. 283-2722. **Aro Restaurant**, 307 Cleveland, tel. 283-2000, has homemade soups and a salad bar. Get fast food at **Mountain View Drive-In** west of town, tel. 283-2205, or groceries from **Decker's Food Center**, 106 N. 7th, tel. 283-3155.

Information And Services

The **Sundance Information Center** at Exit 186 off I-90, tel. 283-3307, is open daily 7-7 from mid-May through October. **Crook County Library**, 122 N. 4th, tel. 283-1006, is open Mon.-Fri. 10-5. It has several big pieces of petrified wood out front. Swim or take a shower at the grade school **pool**, tel. 283-2133, for $1.50. Open June-Sept. only. **Powder River Transportation**, tel. (800) 442-3682, has daily service to Gillette, as well as Deadwood and Rapid City, South Dakota. They do not offer tours of the Black Hills.

BLACK HILLS NATIONAL FOREST

Black Hills National Forest lies primarily within South Dakota, reaching across the state line around Sundance. It was established in 1897 by President Grover Cleveland, after a series of large forest fires had focused attention on the need to protect the timber resource. The Forest Service's very first commercial timber sale was held within the Black Hills, and the area is still a supplier for lumber mills in Hulett and Newcastle. Nearby, South Dakota's Black Hills maintain a wide range of justifiably famous sites: the Homestake Gold Mine at Lead, historic Deadwood (now a gambler's mecca), Jewel and Wind caves, Mt. Rushmore, and an enormous bison herd in Custer State Park. Black Hills National Forest offices are in Sundance, tel. 283-1361, and Newcastle, tel. 746-2783. Pick up a forest map ($2), along with information on camping and sights in the area.

Camping

Three campgrounds lie within the Wyoming portion of the forest. **Reuter Campground** ($6) is five miles northwest of Sundance, while **Cook Lake Campground** ($4-6) is 16 miles north of Sundance on a tiny forest pond. Free camping at **Bearlodge Campground**, seven miles west of Aladdin on State 24. You can also camp for free on Forest Service land throughout the Black Hills. Over on the South Dakota side of the line, you'll find more than two dozen additional Forest Service campgrounds; call (800) 283-2267 for reservations (extra charge).

Scenic Drives

Many gravel roads wind up through the forested hills, and fall colors are brilliant along the aspen-lined stretches of the road just south of Cook Lake. A considerable amount of logging is going on within the ponderosa pine forests here, but it is selective logging, not clearcutting, and hence not as visible. Be sure to stop at **Warren Peak Lookout**, eight miles north of Sundance. The road is paved to this point, and you can climb the tower for a magnificent vista and a chance to visit folks at one of the few active fire lookouts remaining in Wyoming. **Grand Canyon Creek**, located southwest of Sundance along County Rd. 141, offers a long, scenic route into the hills of South Dakota, but be ready for 25 miles of gravel road. There are no hiking trails in the Wyoming portion of Black Hills National Forest.

ALADDIN AND VICINITY

Aladdin was established in the 1870s to supply coal for gold smelters in Lead and Deadwood, South Dakota. At 3,740 feet, it's the lowest settlement in Wyoming. Don't blink or you'll miss it, but if you do blink, turn around and stop for a visit. Aladdin is dominated by the fluorescent red **Aladdin Store** built in 1890 and operated continuously ever since. Out front is a "liars bench" for local storytellers; inside is a pot-belly stove and an ancient post office with the original boxes. Worth a visit for a taste of unspoiled Americana. The small **Aladdin Hotel**, tel. 896-4317, has rooms for $20 s or d, plus a cafe that serves up all-American grub.

Ten miles northeast of Aladdin is the **lowest point in Wyoming**. From here, the Belle Fourche River drops only another 3,125 feet on its several-thousand-mile descent to the sea via the Missouri and Mississippi rivers. Approximately two miles east of Aladdin is a historical marker noting the still-visible tracks left by the party of 110 wagons, 2,000 animals, and 1,000 men led by Gen. George A. Custer in the summer of 1874. Despite the Treaty of 1868 that reaffirmed this as Sioux Indian land, Custer's geologists, scouts, miners, and engineers had come to explore the Black Hills, and to investigate the rumors of gold. Gold was indeed found by Custer's miners, and when word got out, the rush was on. Custer's own rush to judgment at Montana's Little Big Horn had also begun. He and all 268 of his men would die there just two years later.

On the other side of Aladdin, State 24 follows Beaver Creek past 150-foot-tall sandstone cliffs, ridge-top pines, and valley-bottom oaks. Old farmsteads appear, surrounded by fields filled with huge pyramid-like hay piles. The dot of a place called **Alva** (pop. 50) has a few old homes in the midst of the Bear Lodge Mountains, but nothing in the way of services. West of Alva the road climbs up into rolling grassy hills with trees in the draws, and cattle grazing along the Belle Fourche River.

HULETT AND VICINITY

The tiny logging and ranching town of Hulett (pop. 300) lies right along the Belle Fourche River. Two lumber mills saw up timber from the adjacent Black Hills National Forest. It's hard to miss **The Stockman**, tel. 467-5315; the huge signboard on top of the building dwarfs the enterprise within. Actually, Carson Thomas who runs the place, is a master leather craftsman, making handcrafted saddles, belts, and other items for everyone from rodeo cowboys to Grade-B movie stars like Ronald Reagan. This place is a must-see. For another taste of the Wild West, check alongside **Hulett National Bank** for the burned-in brands from local cattle ranchers.

For food in Hulett, try **Hulett Cafe, Ponderosa Cafe**, or **Little Wrangler Cafe**. Two places to stay in town are: **Pioneer Motel**, tel. 467-5656, $24 s or $28 d, and **Hulett Motel**, tel. 467-5220, $24 s or $26 d. Park RVs at **S-A RV Camp** for $10. The library is in the high school. For entertainment, most evenings you'll find folks at the horseshoe pit next to the hardware store, or head to **Rodeo Saloon** or **Ponderosa Bar** for a beer with the locals. The big annual event is **Loggers and Ranchers Play Days**, held each September. Horse shows, cookouts, and old farm machinery are on display, along with downhome neighborliness. A couple of miles west of Hulett, you'll see bison grazing at a private ranch, while magnificent Devils Tower looms on the horizon.

West and then south from Hulett is the tiny town of **Oshoto** (an Indian word meaning "Bad Weather"), accessible only via gravel roads. The Brislawn Cayuse Ranch near Oshoto is one of the last places in America to have pure-blooded Spanish Mustangs, a tough, small horse that was the pride of the Wild West. The nearly extinct mule-footed Spanish pigs (say what?) are also here.

Alzada And Colony

North from Hulett, State 112 heads to the Montana border settlement of Alzada, cutting across land not unlike the foothills of California's Sierra Nevada. Cottonwoods and oaks fill the draws, and grassy meadows alternate with tree-topped hills. Very scenic and with an abundance of whitetailed deer all the way. The road doesn't really go anywhere most tourists are heading, but because of this, it is perfect for cyclists and anyone with a streak of exploration. From Alzada, U.S. 212 cuts southeast across Wyoming and to the South Dakota town of Belle Fourche. Along the way it passes a couple of bentonite mines in the grass and sage country around the nothing settlement called Colony. Antelope and cattle abound. Talk about confusion: since there is no post office in Colony, Wyoming, locals have South Dakota addresses on a Montana delivery route!

DEVILS TOWER NATIONAL MONUMENT

Devils Tower is a strange other-worldly apparition that rises some 1,267 feet above the surrounding plains. It is fitting that such a place should be used as the contact place for aliens and earthlings in the 1977 film, *Close Encounters of the Third Kind*. The flat-topped tower of rock seems to push out of the earth like an enormous sawed-off stump from Paul Bunyan's forest. From a distance the tower looks as if it had been scratched by some giant beast, with parallel gouges running up the sides. Up closer, the gouges turn into enormous columns of rock molded into four-, five-, and six-sided shapes. In the setting sun, Devils Tower glows a golden red long after the surrounding hills no longer reflect the sun's rays, and as night comes on, the stars and moon outline its bold shape against the horizon. The tower is surrounded by ponderosa pine and bur oak forests, while the winding Belle Fourche River flows less than a mile away. A large colony of **black-tailed prairie dogs** exists along the river just inside the park, and you're likely to also see white-tailed deer feeding in the meadows. On top, the tower is a relatively flat oval that reaches approximately 300 by 180 feet.

Geology

Geologists argue over two similar theories for the creation of Devils Tower; most accepted is that it formed as the core of an ancient volcano. Some 60 million years ago, a mass of molten magma was forced up through the overlying sedimentary rocks. As it cooled and contracted, vertical fractures formed in the magma, creating long columnar joints—the "scratches" up the side of Devils Tower today. (Some of these columns are as much as 14 feet in diameter!) Eventually, the nearby Belle Fourche River eroded away the surrounding sedimentary rock, leaving the ancient volcanic neck exposed to the elements. Surrounding the 1,000-foot-wide base of Devils Tower is a mass of talus from fallen pieces of columns, but erosion of this very hard igneous rock is almost imperceptible. The four prominent peaks of the **Missouri Buttes**, located four miles northwest of Devils Tower, were formed in the same manner. At 500 to 800 feet in height, they are not as dramatic and lie outside the national monument boundaries.

HISTORY

Devils Tower was known to Indian tribes by a variety of names, most commonly as Bear Lodge, Tree Lodge, or Bear's Tipi. Fur trappers and early explorers certainly knew of the existence of Bear Lodge, but it wasn't until 1857 that any note of it was made—an exploration party led by Lt. G.K. Warren saw the rock from a distance. In 1875, Col. Richard I. Dodge, finally led a U.S. Geological Survey party to the formation. Dodge somehow came up with the name Devils Tower, claiming that the Indians called it "Bad God's Tower." Despite protests that "Bear Lodge" had long been the aboriginal name, the label Devils Tower stuck.

Creating The Monument

After the Indians had been driven from their traditional homeland in the 1870s, northeast Wyoming opened to settlement by whites. Most lands were available to the homesteaders, but the General Land Office prevented developers from

---

THE LEGEND OF BEAR LODGE

The place we call Devils Tower was known to the Kiowa Indians as Mato Tipila, meaning "Bear Lodge." Many tales are told about the origins of this mystical place, but the best-known is that of the Kiowa. Once upon a time, the people camped along a stream that had many bears. Seven sisters and their brother were playing nearby when the boy suddenly turned into a ferocious bear and began chasing the girls. In desperation, the girls climbed on a small rock and prayed, "Rock, take pity on us—rock, save us!" The rock started to grow, pushing them higher and higher as the bear clawed at the sides, trying to get them. Eventually the seven girls were pushed upward into the sky, forming the points of the Big Dipper. The gouges from the bear remain today on the sides of Bear Lodge.

gaining this freak of geology. Wyoming already had America's first national park in Yellowstone, and soon support grew to make the tower a park. After years of effort, President Theodore Roosevelt proclaimed Devils Tower the country's first national monument in 1906. Unfortunately, the final monument was only 1,153 acres in size, excluding the Missouri Buttes.

The First Climb
In the early years of Devils Tower National Monument the area served as a popular spot for picnics and camping, especially on the 4th of July, when Independence Day celebrations attracted settlers from the entire region. The most famous of all these came in 1893. Handbills announced that the previously unclimbable tower would be scaled, and "On July 4th, 1893, Old Glory will be flung to the breeze from the top of the Tower, 800 feet from the ground by Wm. Rogers." The stunt was well planned. Several days before, two local ranchers, William Rogers and Willard Ripley drove wooden pegs into a long crack that led to the top, tying the pegs together with strips of wood to make a ladder. They hauled a 12-foot flagpole to the top and returned on July 4 to scale the ladder in front of 800 people. Once on top (it took an hour to climb), Rogers unfurled a flag, but a gust of wind blew it off. Wives of the promoters tore it up and sold the pieces as souvenirs (stripes cost 25¢, while stars went for 50¢). The climb had

DEVILS TOWER

been a smashing success.

On July 4, 1895, Mrs. Rogers became the first woman to climb the ladder to the top of Devils Tower, and many other adventurous folks followed over the next several decades. The ladder was last climbed in 1927, but pieces of it are still visible today along the southeast side of the Tower. (An iron stairway to the top, proposed by Wyoming's Congressman Mondell as a tourist attraction, was never built.)

Developing The Tower
For many years, Devils Tower remained undeveloped, and it was not until 1928 that a bridge was built across the Belle Fourche River to the site. During the Depression era, the CCC constructed a log visitor center, new roads, trails, picnic areas, and a campground. Visitation increased as access became easier and more families gained automobiles. One of the strangest events came in 1941, when George Hopkins—one of the top skydivers in the world—parachuted out of a plane to the top of Devils Tower as a publicity stunt. He had planned to descend on a 1,000 foot rope, but the rope landed on the side of the tower, leaving him stranded on top. Newspapers all over the country headlined his plight. Food and blankets were dropped to him, and for the next six days he spent a lonely vigil on top, waiting to be rescued. Finally, Jack Durrance, a mountain climber who had scaled Devils Tower three years before, arrived to lead seven other climbers to the top and to help Hopkins down. Many years later, in 1976, *Close Encounters of the Third Kind* was filmed here. Several hundred locals appeared in the crowd scenes. When the movie was released the following year, tourism suddenly hit the stars.

Climbing The Tower
Although Devils Tower was first climbed in 1893 on a wooden ladder, the first ascent using modern rock-climbing techniques was not until 1937. Led by Fritz Wiessner, three New York City climbers made it to the top in a little under five hours. Over the years, as climbing technology has improved and as more people were attracted to the sport, Devils Tower has become one of the favorite climbing spots in the nation. During the summer you're bound to meet several dozen climbers heading for the base of the tower each morning. More than 25,000 people

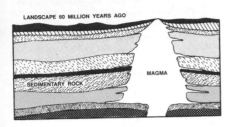

LANDSCAPE 60 MILLION YEARS AGO

MAGMA

SEDIMENTARY ROCK

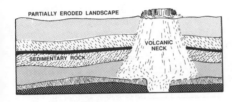

PARTIALLY ERODED LANDSCAPE

VOLCANIC NECK

SEDIMENTARY ROCK

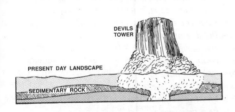

DEVILS TOWER

PRESENT DAY LANDSCAPE

SEDIMENTARY ROCK

have reached the top, and the figure grows by at least 2,000 each year. For information on the various routes (at least 120 have been climbed), pick up one of the small technical guides in the visitor center, or get *Devils Tower National Monument—A Climber's Guide,* by Steve Gardiner and Dick Guilmette (The Mountaineers, Seattle). Displays in the visitor center and at a kiosk out front describe climbing routes and techniques. Climbing demonstrations are given here at 9:30 a.m., 1 p.m., and 4:30 p.m. each day during the summer. If you're planning to climb Devils Tower, be sure to register at the visitor center. **Devils Tower Trading Post,** tel. 467-5555, right next to the entrance station, has a limited amount of climbing gear for sale.

Hiking Trails
Four different trails loop through this small na-

tional monument, providing fine views of the tower and surrounding country. Most popular is the 1¹/₄-mile **Tower Trail** that circles the tower. It is an easy, paved path with periodic openings offering impressive views of the tower, along with side paths to see the nearby Missouri Buttes and Belle Fourche River. Be sure to look through the peep sight to find the old wooden ladder that once went all the way to the top of Devils Tower.

Red Beds/South Side Trail is a three-mile dirt path that also takes off near the visitor center, but makes a longer (and less crowded) loop around the tower. Along the way you get nice views of the Belle Fourche River and the Red Beds, iron-stained bluffs near the river. A 30-minute side loop, **Valley View Trail,** takes you to the prairie dog town and the Belle Fourche River. The finest views of Devils Tower can be had from the **Joyner Ridge Trail,** a 1¹/₂-mile path. Views from this hilltop trail are unforgettable, especially at sunrise or sunset.

PRACTICALITIES

Camping And Food
The Park Service maintains a fine **campground** ($6; open May-Oct.) a half mile inside the entrance. In midsummer, get a space at the campground in the morning to be sure of having a spot. Just outside the monument are two private campgrounds. The friendlier of the two is **Devils Tower KOA,** tel. 467-5395, where sites cost $12 for tents or $16 for RVs. Showers are $3 for non-campers. Open May-September. Most folks stock up with food in nearby towns, but if you want a meal out, **Mateo Village,** tel. 756-3201, also at the park entrance gate, has meals, including prime rib and seafood.

Access And Information
Devils Tower is 33 miles northeast of Moorcroft. You enter the park from State 24, seven miles north of its junction with U.S. 14. Entrance fees are $3 for vehicles or $1 for hikers or cyclists; the passes are good for seven days. Annual passes to the monument cost $10, or purchase the Golden Eagle Pass ($25) that lets you in all national parks and monuments. Seniors get in free with a Golden Age pass. The monument is open year-round, although most

of the over 300,000 annual visitors arrive during the summer. Beyond the entrance station, it is approximately three miles along a paved road to the base of the tower, where you'll find a pleasant old log **visitor center** (tel. 467-5501), and a parking lot that overflows on sunny summer days with rock climbers and gawkers. The center is open daily 8-7:45 from mid-June to Labor Day, and daily 8-4:45 the rest of the year. Inside you can watch a six-minute film on the history of Devils Tower, look at ecological displays and photos showing the dozens of climbing routes, or buy books on local lore. Nightly **campfire programs** are held at the amphitheater in the campground during the summer, with the standard Park Service fare of talks, tunes, and transparencies. Ask at the visitor center for tonight's activities.

> *If the reader thinks he is done, now, and that this book has no moral to it, he is in error. The moral of it is this: If you are of any account, stay at home and make your way by faithful diligence; if you are "no account," go away from home, and then you will have to work, whether you want to or not. Thus you become a blessing to your friends by ceasing to be a nuisance to them—if the people you go among suffer by the operation.*
>
> —Mark Twain in Roughing It

BOOKLIST

DESCRIPTION AND TRAVEL

Anderson, Susan. *Living in Wyoming: Settling for More.* Oakland, CA: Rockridge Press, 1990. A witty and insightful book about the people of Wyoming. Outstanding photos by Zbigniew Bzdak.

Burt, Nathaniel. *Wyoming.* Oakland, CA: Compass American Guides, 1990. Provides a tour of Wyoming and its historical attractions. Photography by Don Pitcher.

Ehrlich, Gretel. *The Solace of Open Spaces.* New York: Viking Penguin Inc., 1985. A stunningly beautiful collection of observations and stories about ranch life in Wyoming from one of America's finest writers.

Hanesworth, Robert D. *Daddy of 'em All; The Story of Cheyenne Frontier Days.* Cheyenne: Flintlock Publishing CO., 1967. Stories and photos from the early days of Cheyenne's Frontier Days celebration.

Kelsey, Joe. *Wyoming's Wind River Range.* Helena, MT: American Geographic Publishing, 1988. A profusely illustrated and well-written book about Wyoming's finest hiking country.

Pence, Mary Lou, and Lola M. Homsher. *The Ghost Towns of Wyoming.* New York: Hastings House, 1956. Describes the state's many historic towns that are slowly fading into the landscape.

Perry, John, and Jane Greverus Perry. *The Sierra Club Guide to the Natural Areas of Idaho, Montana, and Wyoming.* San Francisco: Sierra Club Books, 1988. Information on national parks, national forests, wilderness areas, state parks, wildlife refuges, and other natural areas. Of limited usefulness except as a general description.

Roberts, Philip J., David L. Roberts, and Steven L. Roberts. *Wyoming Almanac.* Laramie: Skyline West Press, 1989. Packed with 376 pages of Wyoming trivia, including such things as the Wyoming man who invented a cattle guard for use on railroad tracks and Wyoming news stories on CBS Evening News between 1977 and 1988. Hard to plow through it all (no index), but there are some real gems buried in this avalanche of facts.

Skinner, Holly L. *Only the River Runs Easy: A Historical Portrait of the Upper Green River Valley.* Boulder, CO: Pruett Publishing Co., 1985. An attractive and lovingly written history of the Upper Green River. Excellent.

Stienstra, Tom. *Rocky Mountain Camping.* San Francisco, Foghorn Press, 1989. Describes over 1,200 public and private campgrounds in Wyoming, Colorado, and Montana.

Urbanek, Mae. *Wyoming Place Names.* Missoula: Mountain Press Publishing Co., 1988. An excellent sourcebook for the names of everything from Abiathar Peak to the town of Zenith.

Williamson, Chilton, Jr. *Roughnecking It.* New York: Simon and Schuster, 1982. A funny, insightful, and disturbing portrait of Wyoming during the oil boom years of the the early 1980s. Gonzo journalism at its best.

Works Projects Administration. *Wyoming: A Guide to its History, Highways, and People.* Lincoln: University of Nebraska Press, 1981. Reprint of a depression-era guide to Wyoming (originally printed in 1940), this classic guide still makes fascinating reading.

Wyoming Department of Administration and Fiscal Control. *Wyoming Data Handbook.* Cheyenne: Wyoming Department of Administration and Fiscal Control. A free annual publication jammed with all sorts of technical information about Wyoming. Helpful for folks writing guides to Wyoming.

Wyoming Recreation Commission. *Wyoming: A Guide to Historic Sites.* Basin, WO: Big Horn Publishers, 1988. An excellent collection of descriptions of more than 300 historic sites in Wyoming.

GEOLOGY, GEOGRAPHY, AND WEATHER

Blackstone, D. L., Jr. *Traveler's Guide to the Geology of Wyoming.* Laramie: Geological Survey of Wyoming, 1988. An excellent overview of Wyoming's geological history and how to see it through today's landscapes.

Brown, Robert Harold. *Wyoming: A Geography.* Boulder, CO: Westview Press, 1980. All sorts of interesting info about Wyoming, from political party affiliations to Indian handicrafts.

Largeson, David R., and Darwin R. Spearing. *Roadside Geology of Wyoming.* Missoula: Mountain Press Publishing Company, 1988. Wyoming is perhaps the most geologically interesting of any state. This is an invaluable road guide for anyone wanting to know more geology without resorting to dense textbooks.

McPhee, John. *Rising from the Plains.* New York: The Noonday Press, 1986. A delightful intertwining of the story of Wyoming's complex geology and the life of its preeminent geologist, David Love.

FICTION

Ehrlich, Gretel. *Heart Mountain.* New York: Viking Penguin Inc., 1988. A touching novel about life in the Heart Mountain Relocation Camp near Cody, forced home for hundreds of Japanese Americans during WW II.

Nye, Bill. *Bill Nye's Western Humor.* Lincoln: University of Nebraska Press, 1968. A collection of delightfully wry essays by one of America's best-known 19th-century humorists.

Wister, Owen. *The Virginian.* Originally published in 1902 and now available from various publishers. The classic Western novel that established the cowboy hero and the lure of Wyoming.

BIOGRAPHY

Alter, J. Cecil. *Jim Bridger.* Norman: University of Oklahoma Press, 1962. The incredible story of the most famous of all mountain men.

Olsen, Jack. *Doc: The Rape of the Town of Lovell.* New York: Atheneum, 1989. The true, but hard-to-believe story of a respected physician who raped dozens of women in this small religious town.

Pointer, Larry. *In Search of Butch Cassidy.* Norman: University of Oklahoma Press, 1977. A thoroughly researched book that seems to show that Butch Cassidy's death in South America was a ruse, and that he died much later in Seattle.

Sell, Henry Blackman, and Victor Weybright. *Buffalo Bill and the Wild West.* Basin, WY: Big Horn Books, 1979. The authors attempt to sort the incredible true story of William Cody from the legends created by decades of tall tales. Nicely illustrated.

Woods, L. Milton. *Moreton Frewen's Western Adventures.* Boulder, CO: Roberts Rinehart, Inc., 1986. The strange tale of a wealthy British adventurer who made and lost his (and other folks') fortunes in Wyoming.

HIKING AND CLIMBING

Note: See also Grand Teton and Yellowstone national parks (below).

Bach, Orville E., Jr. *Hiking the Yellowstone Backcountry.* San Francisco: Sierra Club Books, 1979. A pocket-sized volume with descriptions of the park's trails.

Gardiner, Steve, and Dick Guilmette. *Devils Tower National Monument—A Climber's Guide.* Seattle: The Mountaineers, 1986. A detailed guide to one of the most varied and enjoyable rock faces in Wyoming.

Kelsey, Joe. *Climbing and Hiking in the Wind River Mountains.* San Francisco: Sierra Club Books, 1980. The definitive guide to climbing and hiking in the Winds.

Mitchell, Finis. *Wind River Trails.* Salt Lake City: Wasatch Publications, 1975. A folksy, inexpensive guide by a man who has hiked this country since 1909.

Melius, Kenneth W., ed. *Cloud Peak Primitive Area: Trail Guide, History, and Photo Odyssey.* Aberdeen, SD: Melius Petterson Publications, 1984. A fine, complete guide to trails, history, and the environment of the Big Horn's dramatic wilderness country.

HISTORY

Baber, D. F. *The Longest Rope*. Caldwell, ID: The Caxton Printers, Ltd., 1953. The fascinating story of the Johnson County War as told by William Walker, only surviving "rustler" witness of the siege at KC Ranch.

Bille, Ed. *Early Days at Salt Creek and Teapot Dome*. Casper, WY: Mountain States Lithographing Co., 1978. The story of oil boomtimes in Wyoming's most famous oil fields. Many fine old photos.

Burt, Struthers. *Powder River: Let 'er Buck*. New York: Rinehart, 1938. A classic book on this famous part of Wyoming, by one of the finest writers to come out of the state.

Cheyenne Centennial Committee. *The Magic City on the Plains: Cheyenne 1867-1967*. Cheyenne: Cheyenne Centennial Committee, 1967. A comprehensive history of Cheyenne.

Combs, Barry B. *Westward to Promontory: Building the Union Pacific Across the Plains and Mountains*. New York: Crown Publishers, 1986. How the West was really won. Includes a wonderful collection of historic photos by Andrew J. Russell.

DeVoto, Bernard. *Across the Wide Missouri*. New York: Houghton Mifflin Co., 1947. The Rocky Mountain fur trade and how it shaped American culture. A classic.

Gowans, Fred R., and Eugene E. Campbell. *Fort Bridger, Island in the Wilderness*. Provo, UT: Brigham Young University Press, 1975. An excellent book about the first way station specifically built to serve immigrants on the Oregon Trail.

Gowans, Fred R. *Rocky Mountain Rendezvous: A History of the Fur Trade Rendezvous 1825-1840*. Layton, UT: Peregrine Smith Books, 1985. Describes each of the rendezvous in detail.

Gunderson, Mary Alice. *Devils Tower: Stories in Stone*. Glendo, WY: High Plains Press, 1988. A small book on the history of Devils Tower National Monument.

Haines, Aubrey L. *Journal of a Trapper: Osborne Russell*. Lincoln: University of Nebraska Press, 1955. The fascinating first-person account of a fur trapper from 1834-43. A classic and surprisingly well-written book.

Hedgpeth, Don. *Spurs Were A-Jinglin'*. Cody: Northland Press, 1975. Brief text follows the excellent photos by Charles J. Belden of cowboys and ranching in the early parts of this century.

Homsher, Lola M., editor. *South Pass, 1868; James Chisholm's Journal of the Wyoming Gold Rush*. Lincoln: University of Nebraska Press, 1960. Tales of life in the gold-mining town of South Pass shortly after the first wave of boomers had left. Very interesting.

Junge, Mark. *Wyoming: A Pictorial History*. Norfolk: The Donning Company, 1989. A gorgeous coffee table book filled with historic black and white photos from throughout Wyoming.

Kahin, Sharon, and Laurie Rufe. *In the Shadows of the Rockies: A Photographic History of the Pioneer Experience in Wyoming's Big Horn Basin*. Powell, WY: Northwest Community College, 1983. Outstanding photos and interesting historical quotes on the Big Horn Basin.

Larson, T. A. *History of Wyoming*. 2nd edition. Lincoln: University of Nebraska Press, 1978. The definitive tome (663 pages worth) on Wyoming's history, with an emphasis on politics and development rather than on outlaws and Indian wars.

Lavender, David. *Fort Laramie and the Changing Frontier*. Washington, D.C.: U.S. Department of the Interior, National Park Service, 1983. An interesting little book filled with history of the people who made Fort Laramie a primary center of trade and war in the west. Excellent illustrations too.

Mead, Jean. *Casper Country*. Boulder, CO: Pruett Publishing Co., 1987. A profusely illustrated history of Casper.

Mercer, Asa Shinn. *Banditti of the Plains; or, The Cattlemen's Invasion of Wyoming in 1892: the Crowning Infamy of the Ages*. Norman: University of Oklahoma Press, 1954. A reprint of a classic book about the Johnson County Invasion.

Mothershead, Harmon Ross. *The Swan Land and Cattle Company, Ltd*. Norman: University of Oklahoma Press, 1971. The story of the most famous of all Wyoming ranches, the million-acre spread begun by Alexander Swan in 1883.

Murray, Robert A. *The Bozeman Trail; Highway of History.* Boulder, CO: Pruett Publishing Company, 1988. An attractively illustrated history of the West's most violent trail.

Osgood, Ernest Staples. *The Day of the Cattleman.* Chicago: University of Chicago Press, 1929. An authoritative history of the 50 years when cowboys and cattle barons ruled Wyoming and Montana.

Parkman, Francis. *The Oregon Trail.* Boston: Little, Brown and Co., 1886. A classic first-person account of the great westward migration.

Pinkerton, Joan Tregs. *Knights of the Broadax.* Caldwell, ID: The Caxton Printers, Inc., 1981. An account of the life of the tie hacks in the upper Wind River country.

Rhode, Robert B. *Booms & Busts on Bitter Creek: A History of Rock Springs, Wyoming.* Boulder, CO: Pruett Publishing Company, 1987. A fine history of one of Wyoming's most turbulent cities.

Spring, Agnes Wright. *The Cheyenne and Black Hills Stage and Express Routes.* Lincoln: University of Nebraska Press, 1948. Tales from the early days of eastern Wyoming.

Thybony, Scott, Robert G. Rosenberg, and Elizabeth Mullett Rosenberg. *The Medicine Bows: Wyoming's Mountain Country.* Caldwell, ID: The Caxton Printers, Ltd., 1985. An outstanding historical account of the Indians, explorers, miners, and tie hacks who called this scenic part of Wyoming home.

Twain, Mark. *Roughing It.* First published in 1872, this is one of the classics in American literature. Samuel Clemens' witty descriptions of the Old West seem ageless.

NATIVE AMERICANS

Clark, Ella E., and Margot Edmonds. *Sacagawea of the Lewis and Clark Expedition.* Berkeley: University of California Press, 1979. A fascinating investigation into the truth behind one of the best known women in Wyoming history. Bursts a few bubbles.

Frison, George C. *Prehistoric Hunters of the High Plains.* New York: Academic Press, 1978. The authoritative source on the earliest inhabitants of Wyoming.

Hendry, Mary Helen. *Indian Rock Art in Wyoming.* Lincoln, NE: Augstams Printing, 1983. Descriptions of rock art sites in the state. Her ages for the rock art are too recent, and she intentionally omits locations.

Lowie, Robert. *Indians of the Plains.* New York: The Natural History Press, 1954. Famed anthropologist Robert Lowie presents a detailed picture of life on the plains before the arrival of whites.

Nadeau, Remi. *Fort Laramie and the Sioux Indians.* Englewood Cliffs, NJ: Prentice-Hall Inc., 1967. A thorough historical account of the impact of Fort Laramie on the high plains Indians.

Trenholm, Virginia Cole, and Maurine Carley. *The Shoshonis: Sentinels of the Rockies.* Norman: University of Oklahoma Press, 1964. The history of Chief Washakie and the Shoshone tribe.

Trenholm, Virginia Cole. *The Arapahoes, Our People.* Norman: University of Oklahoma Press, 1970. The history of this important Wyoming tribe, from prehistory to their forced relocation to the Wind River Reservation.

Urbanek, Mae. *Chief Washakie.* Boulder, CO: Johnson Publishing Co., 1971. The fascinating story of the chief who led the Shoshone people for 60 years, always remaining a friend of whites.

Utley, Robert M. *The Indian Frontier of the American West 1846-1890.* Albuquerque: University of New Mexico Press, 1984. An even-handed portrayal of a half-century of conflict between Indians and whites.

NATURAL HISTORY

Note: See also Grand Teton and Yellowstone national parks (below).

Blair, Neal. *The History of Wildlife Management in Wyoming.* Cheyenne: Wyoming Game and

Fish, 1987. A large, detailed book covering the time from when the bison blackened the plains to the present.

Clark, Tim W., and Mark R. Stromberg. *Mammals in Wyoming*. Lawrence, KS: University of Kansas Museum of Natural History, 1987. The definitive guide to 117 native or naturalized Wyoming mammals: their identification, distribution, biology, and ecology.

Craighead, Frank J. *Track of the Grizzly*. San Francisco: Sierra Club Books, 1979. The life of grizzlies in Yellowstone by one of the most famous bear researchers.

Crowe, Douglas M. *Furbearers of Wyoming*. Cheyenne: Wyoming Department of Game and Fish, 1986. A small book describing the state's fur-coated critters, with distribution maps.

Dorn, Robert D. *Vascular Plants of Wyoming*. Cheyenne: Mountain West Publishing Company, 1988. The authoritative key to Wyoming plants; a dense book with few illustrations. For botanists.

Petersen, David. *Among the Elk*. Flagstaff: Northland Publishing, 1988. The story of wapiti, with outstanding photos by Alan D. Carey.

JACKSON HOLE AND GRAND TETON NATIONAL PARK

Betts, Robert B. *Along the Ramparts of the Tetons; the Saga of Jackson Hole,* Wyoming. Boulder: Colorado Associated University Press, 1978. A substantial, detailed, and beautifully written book about Jackson Hole's fascinating history.

Burt, Nathaniel. *Jackson Hole Journal*. Norman: University of Oklahoma Press, 1983. Tales of growing up as a dude in Jackson Hole. Contains some very amusing stories.

Carrighar, Sally. *One Day at Teton Marsh*. Lincoln: University of Nebraska Press, 1979. A classic natural history of life in a Jackson Hole marsh. Made into a movie by Walt Disney.

Clark, Tim W. *Ecology of Jackson Hole, Wyoming: A Primer*. Salt Lake City: Paragon Press, 1981. An excellent scientific introduction to ecological interrelationships within Jackson Hole.

Harry, Bryan. *Teton Trails*. Moose, WY: Grand Teton Natural History Association, 1987. An inexpensive small guide to the hiking trails of Grand Teton National Park.

Hayden, Elizabeth Wied, and Cynthis Nielsen. *Origins, A Guide to the Place Names of Grand Teton National Park and the Surrounding Area.* Moose, WY: Grand Teton Natural History Association, 1988. A guide to the obscure sources for place names in Grand Teton.

Huidekoper, Virginia. *The Early Days in Jackson Hole*. Boulder: Colorado Associated University Press, 1978. Filled with over 100 photos from old time Jackson Hole.

Johnsgard, Paul A. *Teton Wildlife*. Boulder: Colorado Associated University Press, 1982. A descriptive book by a noted naturalist from the University of Nebraska.

Lawrence, Paul. *Hiking the Teton Backcountry*. San Francisco: Sierra Club Books, 1979. Outdated, but still useful guide to trails in Grand Teton National Park.

Love, J.D., and John C. Reed, Jr. *Creation of the Teton Landscape: the Geologic Story of Grand Teton National Park*. Moose, WY: Grand Teton Natural History Association, 1971. A small but authoritatively detailed guide to the geology of Jackson Hole and the Tetons.

Murie, Margaret, and Olaus Murie. *Wapiti Wilderness*. Boulder: Colorado Associated University Press, 1985. The lives of two of America's most-loved conservationists in Jackson Hole, and their work with elk.

Ortenburger, Leigh N., and Reynold G. Jackson. *A Complete Guide to the Teton Range*. Palo Alto, CA: self-published, 1990. A very thorough two-volume climbing guide.

Petzoldt, Paul. *Petzoldt's Teton Trails*. Salt Lake City: Wasatch Publishers, Inc., 1976. An enjoyable small hiking guide by one of the grand old men of mountain climbing.

Raynes, Bert. *Birds of Grand Teton National Park and the Surrounding Area*. Moose, Wyoming: Grand Teton Natural History Association, 1984. A guide to local birds.

Righter, Robert W. *Crucible for Conservation: The Creation of Grand Teton National Park*. Boulder: Colorado Associated University Press, 1982. The story of how the Tetons were spared through a half-century battle.

Thompson, Edith M., and William Leigh Thompson. *Beaver Dick: The Honor and the Heartbreak.* Laramie: Jelm Mountain Press, 1982. A touching historical biography of Beaver Dick Leigh, one of the first white men to settle in Jackson Hole.

U.S. Department of the Interior, National Park Service. *Grand Teton: Official National Park Handbook.* Washington, D.C.: National Park Service, 1984. An attractive small book about the park and its history.

YELLOWSTONE NATIONAL PARK

Back, Orville E. *Hiking the Yellowstone Back Country.* San Francisco: Sierra Club Books, 1979. A pocket-sized guide to hikes in the park.

Balthis, Frank, Steve Bogen, and Fred Hirschmann. *Winter at Old Faithful.* Yellowstone: Firehole Press, 1980. A thin guide to the natural history of Yellowstone and how to see it on cross-country skis.

Bartlett, Richard A. *Yellowstone: A Wilderness Besieged.* Tuscon: University of Arizona Press, 1985. The history of Yellowstone and the fight to prevent its destruction by railroad magnates, concessionaires, and others.

Bryan, T. Scott. *The Geysers of Yellowstone.* Boulder: Colorado Associated University Press, 1979. A complete and detailed guide to more than 400 geysers and other geothermal features in Yellowstone.

Charlton, Robert E. *Yellowstone Fishing Guide: A Comprehensive Guide to Fishing the Lakes and Streams Located in Yellowstone National Park.* Portland, OR: Flying Pencil Publications, 1990. A detailed guide to fishing in the park. Leaves no trickle unfished.

Chase, Alston. *Playing God in Yellowstone: The Destruction of America's First National Park.* Boston: Atlantic Monthly Press, 1986. A long tirade against everything the Park Service has ever done in Yellowstone. Disturbing to read and with many valid criticisms, but so one-sided that it is difficult to sort truth from opinion. Read both this and *Wildlife in Transition* for two sides of the issues.

Colling, Gene. *The Bicyclist's Guide to Yellowstone National Park.* Helena, MT: Falcon Press Publishing Co., 1984. Includes maps and all you need to know about cycling in America's oldest park.

Fritz, William J. *Roadside Geology of the Yellowstone Country.* Missoula: Mountain Press Publishing Co., 1985. All the park roads are covered in this easy-to-follow Yellowstone geology primer.

Haines, Aubrey L. *The Yellowstone Story: A History of Our First National Park.* Yellowstone Library and Museum Association, 1977. A definitive two-volume history of the park. Volume one (history up to the park's establishment) is the most interesting.

Hirschmann, Fred. *Yellowstone.* Portland, OR: Graphic Arts Center Publishing, 1982. Exceptional photography.

Janetski, Joel C. *Indians of Yellowstone Park.* Salt Lake City: University of Utah Press, 1987. A general overview of the earliest settlers in Yellowstone and later conflicts with incoming whites.

Krakell, Dean, II. *Downriver: A Yellowstone Journey.* San Francisco: Sierra Club Books, 1987. A extraordinarily moving journey down the magnificent Yellowstone River.

Marschall, Mark C. *Yellowstone Trails: A Hiking Guide.* Yellowstone National Park: The Yellowstone Association, 1990. An excellent, up-to-date and detailed guidebook to the park's 1000 miles of hiking trails.

McEneaney, Terry. *Birds of Yellowstone.* Boulder: Roberts Rinehart, 1988. A guide to Yellowstone birds and where to find them.

McNulty, Tim (text), and Pat O'Hara (photos). *Yellowstone National Park: Land of Fire and Falling Water.* San Rafael, CA: Woodlands Press, 1986. A coffee-table book of luscious pictures from the park.

Reese, Rick. *Greater Yellowstone: The National Park and Adjacent Wildlands.* Helena: Montana Magazine, 1984. An attractive book with considerable information on ecological conditions in one of the lower 48's largest intact ecosystems.

Schmidt, Jeremy, and Steven Fuller. *Yellowstone Grand Teton Road Guide.* Jackson:

Free Wheeling Travel Guides, 1990. A nicely done pocket-sized guide to the roads of the two parks with accurate, up-to-date information. Easily the best road guide available.

Schreier, Carl, editor. *Yellowstone: Selected Photographs 1870-1960.* Moose, WY: Homestead Publishing, 1989. An outstanding collection of historic photographs from the park.

Schreier, Carl. *Yellowstone's Geysers, Hot Springs and Fumaroles.* Moose, WY: Homestead Publishing, 1987. An attractive small book filled with color photos and brief descriptions.

Scott, M. Douglas, and Suvi A. Scott. *Wildlife of Yellowstone and Grand Teton National Parks.* Salt Lake City: Wheelwright Press, Ltd., 1988. A brief descriptive guide to Yellowstone and Grand Teton critters.

Shaw, Richard J. *Plants of Yellowstone and Grand Teton National Parks.* Salt Lake City: Wheelwright Press, 1981. Photos and descriptions of the most commonly found plants in the park.

Varley, John D. *Freshwater Wilderness: Yellowstone Fishes and Their World.* Yellowstone Library and Museum Association, 1983. A lovely book for anglers and those interested in fish.

Whittlesey, Lee H. *Yellowstone Place Names.* Helena: Montana Historical Society Press, 1988. For the trivial pursuit enthusiast; detailed descriptions of every possible name from every possible obscure corner of Yellowstone.

Wuerthner, George. *Yellowstone and the Fires of Change.* Salt Lake City: Haggis House Publications, 1988. Good photos and an ecological look at the fires make this perhaps the best book about the fires of '88.

INDEX

Page numbers in **boldface** indicate the primary reference; page numbers in *italics* indicate information found in maps, charts, illustrations, callouts, or captions.

THE METRIC SYSTEM

1 inch = 2.54 centimeters (cm)
1 foot = .304 meters (m)
1 mile = 1.6093 kilometers (km)
1 km = .6214 miles
1 fathom = 1.8288 m
1 chain = 20.1168 m
1 furlong = 201.168 m
1 acre = .4047 hectares (ha)
1 sq km = 100 ha
1 sq mile = 2.59 sq km
1 ounce = 28.35 grams
1 pound = .4536 kilograms (kg)
1 short ton = .90718 metric ton
1 short ton = 2000 pounds
1 long ton = 1.016 metric tons
1 long ton = 2240 pounds
1 metric ton = 1000 kg
1 quart = .94635 liters
1 US gallon = 3.7854 liters
1 Imperial gallon = 4.5459 liters
1 nautical mile = 1.852 km

To compute centigrade temperatures, subtract 32 from Fahrenheit and divide by 1.8. To go the other way, multiply centigrade by 1.8 and add 32.

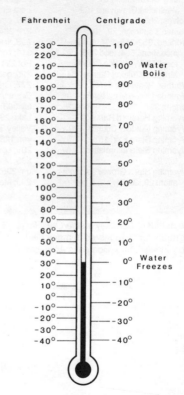

ABOUT THE AUTHOR

Born in Atlanta, Georgia, Don Pitcher grew up on the East Coast, but moved west to attend college. He immediately fell in love with the wide-open American West. Don holds a B.S. in Biology from Pacific Union College (1976) and an M.S. in Wildland Resource Science from U.C. Berkeley (1981). Once out of school, he traveled north to Alaska to work on a fire research project, and in subsequent years as a trail crew foreman and wilderness ranger. In 1989, he headed to Wyoming's Teton Wilderness to take part in a grizzly bear habitat study. Don remained in Wyoming to research and write this guidebook, living in a tiny Wilson cabin within Jackson Hole.

Trained as an ecologist, Don Pitcher's love of travel has led him to work on various guidebooks as both a writer and photographer. While employed by the Park Service in Alaska, in 1983, he picked up a copy of the *Alaska-Yukon Handbook* (Moon Publications) and his long letter of feedback to the author led to his writing the Southeast Chapter in later editions. He is also the author of *Berkeley Inside/Out* (Heyday Books, 1989), a guide to Berkeley, California. His photographs have appeared in many books, calendars, magazines, and other publications, most notably in *Wyoming* (Compass American Guides, 1991).

MOON HANDBOOKS
The Ideal Traveling Companions

Open a Moon Handbook and you're opening your eyes and heart to the world. Thoughtful, sensitive, provocative, and highly informative, Moon Handbooks encourage an intimate understanding of a region, from its culture and history to essential practicalities. Fun to read and packed with valuable information on accommodations, dining, recreation, plus indispensable travel tips, detailed maps, charts, illustrations, photos, glossaries, and indexes, Moon Handbooks are ideal traveling companions.

TO ORDER BY PHONE: (800) 345-5473 Monday-Friday 9 a.m.-5 p.m. PST

The Americas Series

NORTHERN CALIFORNIA HANDBOOK   by Kim Weir
An outstanding companion for imaginative travel in the territory north of the Tehachapis. Color and b/w photos, 69 maps, illustrations, booklist, index. 760 pages.   **$16.95**

NEVADA HANDBOOK   by Deke Castleman
Nevada Handbook puts the Silver State into perspective and makes it manageable and affordable. 34 b/w photos, 43 illustrations, 37 maps, 17 charts, booklist, index. 302 pages. **$12.95**

NEW MEXICO HANDBOOK   by Stephen Metzger
A close-up and complete look at every aspect of this wondrous state. 8 color pages, 85 b/w photos, 63 illustrations, 50 maps, 10 charts, booklist, index. 350 pages.   **$11.95**

TEXAS HANDBOOK   by Joe Cummings
Seasoned travel writer Joe Cummings brings an insider's perspective to his home state. 12 color pages, b/w photos, maps, illustrations, charts, booklist, index. 482 pages.   **$11.95**

ARIZONA TRAVELER'S HANDBOOK by Bill Weir
This meticulously researched guide contains everything necessary to make Arizona accessible and enjoyable. 8 color pages, 194 b/w photos, 74 illustrations, 53 maps, 6 charts, booklist, index. 505 pages. **$13.95**

UTAH HANDBOOK by Bill Weir
Weir gives you all the carefully researched facts and background to make your visit a success. 8 color pages, 102 b/w photos, 61 illustrations, 30 maps, 9 charts, booklist, index. 452 pages. **$12.95**

WYOMING HANDBOOK   by Don Pitcher
All you need to know to open the doors to this wide and wild state. Color and b/w photos, illustrations, 66 maps, charts, booklist, index. 428 pages. **$12.95**

ALASKA-YUKON HANDBOOK   by Deke Castleman, Don Pitcher, and David Stanley
Get the inside story, with plenty of well-seasoned advice to help you cover more miles on less money. 8 color pages, 26 b/w photos, 92 illustrations, 90 maps, 6 charts, booklist, glossary, index. 384 pages. **$11.95**

WASHINGTON HANDBOOK   by Dianne J. Boulerice Lyons
Covers sights, shopping, services, transportation, and outdoor recreation, and has complete listings for restaurants and accommodations. 8 color pages, 92 b/w photos, 24 illustrations, 81 maps, 8 charts, booklist, index. 425 pages. **$12.95**

OREGON HANDBOOK   by Ted Long Ishikawa and Stuart Warren
Brimming with travel practicalities and insider views on Oregon's history, culture, arts, and activities. Color and b/w photos, illustrations, 28 maps, charts, booklist, index. 422 pages. **$12.95**

BRITISH COLUMBIA HANDBOOK   by Jane King
With an emphasis on outdoor adventures, this guide covers mainland British Columbia, Vancouver Island, the Queen Charlotte Islands, and the Canadian Rockies. 8 color pages, 56 b/w photos, 45 illustrations, 66 maps, 4 charts, booklist, index. 396 pages.   **$11.95**

GUIDE TO CATALINA AND CALIFORNIA'S CHANNEL ISLANDS   by Chicki Mallan
A complete guide to these remarkable islands, from the windy solitude of the Channel Islands National Marine Sanctuary to bustling Avalon. 8 color pages, 105 b/w photos, 65 illustrations, 40 maps, 32 charts, booklist, index. 262 pages.   **$9.95**

YUCATAN HANDBOOK   by Chicki Mallan
All the information you'll need to guide you into every corner of this exotic land. 8 color pages, 154 b/w photos, 55 illustrations, 57 maps, 70 charts, appendix, booklist, Mayan and Spanish glossaries, index. 391 pages. **$12.95**

CANCUN HANDBOOK AND MEXICO'S CARIBBEAN COAST by Chicki Mallan
Covers the city's luxury scene as well as more modest attractions, plus many side trips to unspoiled beaches and Mayan ruins. Color and b/w photos, illustrations, over 30 maps, Spanish glossary, booklist, index. 257 pages. **$9.95**

BELIZE HANDBOOK   by Chicki Mallan
Complete with detailed maps, practical information, and an overview of the area's flamboyant history, culture, and geographical features. *Belize Handbook* is the only comprehensive guide of its kind to this spectacular region. Color and b/w photos, illustrations, maps, booklist, index. 201 pages.   **$11.95**

The Pacific/Asia Series

BALI HANDBOOK by Bill Dalton
Detailed travel information on the most famous island in the world. 12 color pages, 29 b/w photos, 68 illustrations, 42 maps, 7 charts, glossary, booklist, index. 428 pages. **$12.95**

INDONESIA HANDBOOK by Bill Dalton
This one-volume encyclopedia explores island by island the many facets of this sprawling, kaleidoscopic island nation. 30 b/w photos, 143 illustrations, 250 maps, 17 charts, booklist, extensive Indonesian vocabulary, index. 1,050 pages. **$17.95**

PHILIPPINES HANDBOOK by Peter Harper and Evelyn Peplow
Crammed with detailed information, *Philippines Handbook* equips the escapist, hedonist, or business traveler with a thorough introduction to the Philippines's colorful history, landscapes, and culture. Color and b/w photos, illustrations, maps, charts, index.
550 pages. **$12.95**

SOUTH KOREA HANDBOOK by Robert Nilsen
Whether you're visiting on business or searching for adventure, *South Korea Handbook* is an invaluable companion. 8 color pages, 78 b/w photos, 93 illustrations, 109 maps, 10 charts, Korean glossary with useful notes on speaking and reading the language, booklist, index. 548 pages. **$14.95**

SOUTHEAST ASIA HANDBOOK by Carl Parkes
Helps the enlightened traveler to discover the real Southeast Asia. 16 Color pages, 75 b/w photos, 11 illustrations, 169 maps, 140 charts, vocabulary lists and suggested readings, index. 874 pages. **$16.95**

HAWAII HANDBOOK by J.D. Bisignani
Winner of the 1989 Hawaii Visitors Bureau's Best Guide Book Award and the Grand Award for Excellence in Travel Journalism, this guide takes you beyond the glitz and high-priced hype and leads you to a genuine Hawaiian experience. 12 color pages, 318 b/w photos, 132 illustrations, 74 maps, 43 graphs and charts, Hawaiian and pidgin glossaries, appendix, booklist, index. Approx. 870 pages. **$15.95**

KAUAI HANDBOOK by J.D. Bisignani
Kauai Handbook is the perfect antidote to the workaday world. 8 color pages, 36 b/w photos, 48 illustrations, 19 maps, 10 tables and charts, Hawaiian and pidgin glossaries, booklist, index. 236 pages. **$9.95**

MAUI HANDBOOK: Including Molokai and Lanai by J.D. Bisignani
"No fool-'round" advice on accommodations, eateries, and recreation, plus a comprehensive introduction to island ways, geography, and history. 4 color pages, 60 b/w photos, 72 illustrations, 34 maps, 19 charts, booklist, glossary, index. 350 pages. **$11.95**

OAHU HANDBOOK by J.D. Bisignani
A handy guide to Honolulu, renowned surfing beaches, and Oahu's countless other diversions. Color and b/w photos, illustrations, 18 maps, charts, booklist, glossary, index.
354 pages. **$11.95**

BIG ISLAND OF HAWAII HANDBOOK by J.D. Bisignani
An entertaining, yet informative text, packed with insider tips on accommodations, dining, sports and outdoor activities, natural attractions, and must-see sights. Color and b/w photos, illustrations, 20 maps, charts, booklist, glossary, index. 347 pages. **$11.95**

SOUTH PACIFIC HANDBOOK by David Stanley
The original comprehensive guide to the 16 territories in the South Pacific. 20 color pages, 195 b/w photos, 121 illustrations, 35 charts, 138 maps, booklist, glossary, index. 740 pages. **$15.95**

MICRONESIA HANDBOOK:
Guide to the Caroline, Gilbert, Mariana, and Marshall Islands by David Stanley
Micronesia Handbook guides you on a real Pacific adventure all your own. 8 color pages, 77 b/w photos, 68 illustrations, 69 maps, 18 tables and charts, index. 288 pages. **$9.95**

FIJI ISLANDS HANDBOOK by David Stanley
The first and still the best source of information on travel around this 322-island archipelago. 8 color pages, 35 b/w photos, 78 illustrations, 26 maps, 3 charts, Fijian glossary, booklist, index. 198 pages. **$8.95**

TAHITI-POLYNESIA HANDBOOK by David Stanley
All five French-Polynesian archipelagoes are covered in this comprehensive guide by Oceania's best-known travel writer. 12 color pages, 45 b/w photos, 64 illustrations, 33 maps, 7 charts, booklist, glossary, index. 225 pages. **$9.95**

NEW ZEALAND HANDBOOK by Jane King
Introduces you to the people, places, history, and culture of this extraordinary land. 8 color pages, 99 b/w photos, 146 illustrations, 82 maps, booklist, index. 546 pages. **$14.95**

BLUEPRINT FOR PARADISE: How to Live on a Tropic Island by Ross Norgrove
This one-of-a-kind guide has everything you need to know about moving to and living comfortably on a tropical island. 8 color pages, 40 b/w photos, 3 maps, 14 charts, appendices, index. 212 pages. **$14.95**

The International Series

EGYPT HANDBOOK by Kathy Hansen
An invaluable resource for intelligent travel in Egypt. 8 color pages, 20 b/w photos, 150 illustrations, 80 detailed maps and plans to museums and archaeological sites, Arabic glossary, booklist, index. 510 pages. **$14.95**

PAKISTAN HANDBOOK by Isobel Shaw
For armchair travelers and trekkers alike, the most detailed and authoritative guide to Pakistan ever published. 28 color pages, 86 maps, appendices, Urdu glossary, booklist, index. 478 pages. **$15.95**

MOSCOW-LENINGRAD HANDBOOK by Masha Nordbye
Provides the visitor with an extensive introduction to the history, culture, and people of these two great cities, as well as practical information on where to stay, eat, and shop. Color and b/w photos, illustrations, maps, charts, booklist, index. Approx 250 pages.
$15.95

IMPORTANT ORDERING INFORMATION

TO ORDER BY PHONE: (800) 345-5473 Monday-Friday 9 a.m.-5 p.m. PST

PRICES: All prices are subject to change. We always ship the most current edition. We will let you know if there is a price increase on the book you ordered.

SHIPPING & HANDLING OPTIONS:
1) Domestic UPS or USPS 1st class (allow 10 working days for delivery): $3.50 for the 1st item, 50 cents for each additional item.

Exceptions:
Moonbelt shipping is $1.50 for one, 50 cents for each additional belt.
Add $2.00 for same-day handling.
2) UPS 2nd Day Air or Printed Airmail requires a special quote.
3) International Surface Bookrate (8-12 weeks delivery): $3.00 for the 1st item, $1.00 for each additional item.

FOREIGN ORDERS: All orders which originate outside the U.S.A. must be paid for with either an International Money Order or a check in U.S. currency drawn on a major U.S. bank based in the U.S.A.

TELEPHONE ORDERS: We accept Visa or MasterCard payments. Minimum order is US$15.00. Call in your order: (800) 345-5473. 9 a.m.-5 p.m. Pacific Standard Time.

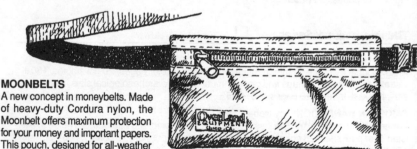

MOONBELTS
A new concept in moneybelts. Made of heavy-duty Cordura nylon, the Moonbelt offers maximum protection for your money and important papers. This pouch, designed for all-weather comfort, slips under your shirt or waistband, rendering it virtually undetectable and inaccessible to pickpockets. Many thoughtful features: one-inch-wide nylon webbing, heavy-duty zipper, and a one-inch high-test quick-release buckle. No more fumbling around for the strap or repeated adjustments, this handy plastic buckle opens and closes with a touch, but won't come undone until you want it to. Accommodates traveler's checks, passport, cash, photos. Size 5 x 9 inches. Available in black only. **$8.95**

ORDER FORM

Name:_____ Date:_____

Street:_____

City:_____

State or Country:_____ Zip Code:_____

Daytime Phone:_____

Quantity	Title	Price

Taxable Total _____

Sales Tax (6%) for California Residents _____

Shipping & Handling _____

TOTAL _____

Ship to: ☐ address above ☐ other (fill in below)

_____

_____

_____

Make checks payable to:
Moon Publications, Inc., 722 Wall Street, Chico, California, 95928, USA
We Accept Visa and MasterCard
To order: Call in your Visa or MasterCard number, or send a written order with your Visa or MasterCard number and expiration date clearly written.

Card Number: ☐ Visa ☐ MasterCard

☐☐☐☐ ☐☐☐☐ ☐☐☐☐ ☐☐☐☐

expiration date:_____

Exact Name on Card: ☐ same as above ☐ other (fill in below)

_____

signature_____

WHERE TO BUY THIS BOOK

Bookstores and Libraries:
Moon Publications guides are sold worldwide.
Please write our sales manager for a list of whole-
salers and distributors in your area that stock our
travel handbooks.

Travelers:
We would like to have Moon Publications guides
available throughout the world. Please ask your
bookstore to write or call us for ordering information.
If your bookstore will not order our guides for you,
please write or call for a free catalog.

**MOON PUBLICATIONS, INC.
722 WALL STREET
CHICO, CA 95928 USA
tel: (800) 345-5473
fax: (916) 345-6751**